FIELDING'S
LOS ANGELES
AGENDA

Fielding Titles

Fielding's Alaska Cruises/Inside Passage
Fielding's Amazon
Fielding's Australia
Fielding's Bahamas
Fielding's Belgium
Fielding's Bermuda
Fielding's Borneo
Fielding's Brazil
Fielding's Britain
Fielding's Budget Europe
Fielding's Caribbean
Fielding's Caribbean Cruises
Fielding's Caribbean East
Fielding's Caribbean West
Fielding's Europe
Fielding's European Cruises
Fielding's Far East
Fielding's France
Fielding's Freewheelin' USA
Fielding's Guide to the World's Most Dangerous Places
Fielding's Guide to Kenya's Best Hotels, Lodges & Homestays
Fielding's Guide to the World's Great Voyages
Fielding's Hawaii
Fielding's Holland
Fielding's Italy
Fielding's Las Vegas Agenda
Fielding's London Agenda
Fielding's Los Angeles Agenda
Fielding's Malaysia and Singapore
Fielding's Mexico
Fielding's New York Agenda
Fielding's New Zealand
Fielding's Paris Agenda
Fielding's Portugal
Fielding's Rome Agenda
Fielding's San Diego Agenda
Fielding's Scandinavia
Fielding's Southeast Asia
Fielding's Southern Vietnam on Two Wheels
Fielding's Spain
Fielding's Thailand Including Cambodia, Laos, Myanmar
Fielding's Vacation Places Rated
Fielding's Vietnam
Fielding's Worldwide Cruises
The Indiana Jones Survival Guide

FIELDING'S LOS ANGELES AGENDA

The most informative and irreverent guide to the many faces of LaLa Land

Robert Young Pelton

Fielding Worldwide, Inc.
308 South Catalina Avenue
Redondo Beach, California 90277 U.S.A.

Fielding's Los Angeles Agenda

Published by Fielding Worldwide, Inc.

Text Copyright ©1995 Robert Young Pelton

Icons & Illustrations Copyright ©1995 FWI

Photo Copyrights ©1995 to Individual Photographers

Fielding's Los Angeles Agenda uses copyrighted material from WAB, Inc. Databases.

FIELDING WORLDWIDE INC.

PUBLISHER AND CEO	**Robert Young Pelton**
PUBLISHING DIRECTOR	**Paul T. Snapp**
ELEC. PUBLISHING DIRECTOR	**Larry E. Hart**
PUBLIC RELATIONS DIRECTOR	**Beverly Riess**
ACCOUNT SERVICES MANAGER	**Christy Harp**
DATABASE PUBLISHING MGR.	**John Guillebeaux**

EDITORS

Linda Charlton   **Kathy Knoles**

PRODUCTION

Gini Sardo-Martin   **Chris Snyder**
Craig South   **Diane Vogel**
                Janice Whitby

COVER DESIGNED BY	**Digital Artists, Inc.**
COVER PHOTOGRAPHERS	**Andrea Pistolesi/Image Bank, Chad Slattery & Bob Torrez/Tony Stone Images**
INSIDE PHOTOS	**Robert Young Peloton, L.A. Convention & Visitors Bureau, Orange County Convention & Visitors Bureau, Palm Springs Convention & Visitors Bureau**

Inquiries should be addressed to: Fielding Worldwide, Inc., 308 South Catalina Ave., Redondo Beach, California 90277 U.S.A., Telephone (310) 372-4474, Facsimile (310) 376-8064, 8:30 a.m.–5:30 p.m. Pacific Standard Time.

ISBN 1-56952-040-2

Library of Congress Catalog Card Number
94-068336

Printed in the United States of America

TABLE OF CONTENTS

LIST OF MAPS

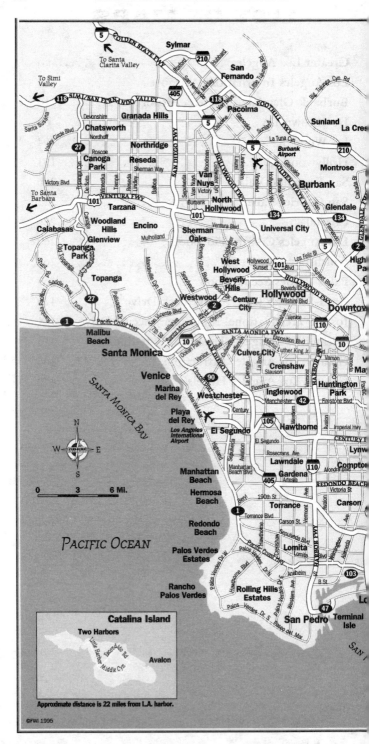

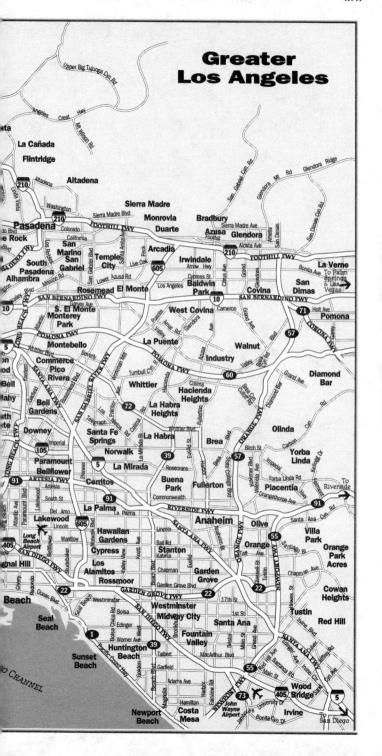

Greater Los Angeles

PREFACE

Detective novelist Raymond Chandler once described Los Angeles as "a big, hard-boiled city with no more personality than a paper cup." Today, that statement seems more ludicrous than ever, for whatever else L.A. may be lacking, it has personality in abundance. Where else can you start the day with a three-figure haircut at a Beverly Hills salon, follow it up with a thermal seaweed body wrap, do brunch while overlooking the blue Pacific, take in a passel of notorious celebrity crime scenes, and show up for a session of the Gay Men's Shyness Therapy Group before "night crawling" till dawn through a maze of underground clubs in the warehouse district?

L.A. has personality all right. Scads of it. Hip, fun, irreverent, and downright sassy, L.A. appeals to an upscale crowd on the lookout for a good time.

Even die-hard fans, however, have to admit that there's a down side to L.A.'s "fun-in-the-sun" image. A growing number of detractors, fed up with earthquakes, fires, smog, clogged freeways, gangs, riots, drive-by shootings, carjackings, and a lousy California economy, insist that the City of the Angels is going to Hell in a handbasket.

In an obvious defensive move to bolster the city's lagging reputation, *Los Angeles* magazine recently countered a spate of L.A.-bashing by producing an issue listing "300 Reasons Not to Pack Up and Leave L.A." which included, in addition to a nod to L.A.'s cultural treasures, such "total L.A." experiences as buying condoms at Condomania and getting to know Helen, the beer lady at the Forum's Coors beer stand. One reader was apparently not impressed, wryly commenting on the city's economic realities by submitting a nomination for number 301: even if you want to move, you can't sell your house.

Despairing and hapless homeowners trapped like sewer rats in the bowels of a dark and ever-spreading metropolis? Hardly. It seems that the same people who are constantly bitching about L.A. are also its staunchest defenders, local trendites who could afford to move if they wanted to, but never do. Why? Because L.A. is one of the most "happening" places on the planet.

It's a haven for art lovers, museum-goers, club-hoppers and sun-worshippers, with opportunities for general hanging out with an eclectic crowd that runs the gamut from Melrose Avenue hipsters to staid Pasadena matrons to Mickey Mouse.

L.A. is the proverbial "Alice's Restaurant" of West Coast cities, where the star-struck can do the Hollywood/celebrity thing, the cultured can do the high-brow entertainment thing, and the laid back can bag the whole thing and wallow on the beach.

If trendy eateries are your passion, L.A. offers some of the best restaurants in the country, with more superstar chefs and celebrity restaurateurs than you can shake a spatula at.

The weather is (mostly) fabulous, the pro sports teams are (mostly) hot, and there are enough personal trainers, luxury car dealers, avant garde clothing stores, tanning salons and beauty spas to keep everyone in town looking like a star whether they are one or not.

Last, but not least, L.A. is—plain and simple—a hangout for the Beautiful People. An unbelievable number of movie stars, rock legends, and mega-hit producers and directors call L.A. home, along with their entourages of agents and fitness gurus and a truckload of requisite attorneys. The fact that you can drive around L.A. all day and half the night and never see a celebrity doesn't detract the least bit from the mystique. The rich and the famous are out there, and you—yes, even you—may at any time find yourself standing in the shadow of some Hollywood luminary such as Michelle Pfeiffer or Arnold Schwarzenegger.

So, there you are. Sure, not all the karma coming out of L.A. is good karma, but if you know where to hang out, it doesn't get much better than this.

Which brings us to the point of this book.

Since "hanging out" in L.A. is one of our specialties, we feel pretty confident about giving you the inside scoop on the L.A. scene: how to get around, where to stay, where to dine, what to see and do, and how to otherwise get the most out of your stay in the proverbial "LA LA Land." Sure, we love L.A., but we'll give you the down side as well as the up, and we aren't above bashing the places that deserve it.

So read on, and get the coolest tips yet on what's happening in one of the hottest travel destinations west of the Big Apple!

GETTING AROUND L.A.

Beverly Hills, the classic "L.A." fantasy

You're Not In Kansas Anymore

Los Angeles is, well, quite frankly HUGE. L.A. County takes in more than 4000 square miles, 88 incorporated cities and scores of smaller neighborhoods, nearly all of which are criss-crossed by a maze of freeways and surface streets that can leave the uninitiated confused, exasperated, or literally quaking with fear. Of course, those amazingly savvy L.A. residents are used to breezing merrily (okay, sometimes begrudgingly) from one end of L.A. to the other, but if you don't know your way around, and don't take the time to find out, you're going to get lost. (Just ask the two Dutch tourists who checked into an L.A. motel on a Friday, went to the beach on Saturday, and then—with their sense of direction hopelessly out of whack—required the services of LAPD to refind their place of lodging, which they could only remember was green and had security bars on the window.)

Because people in L.A. are used to doing their own "thing," and because doing it almost always requires a lot of driving (the average commuting distance for driving to work in L.A. is a 30-mile round trip), nearly everyone is fiercely protective of his or her one-person, one-car mode of transportation. This insistence on driving themselves seems a bit out of character for Southern Californians, who, as a rule, are always on the environmental bandwagon, but—politically correct or not—being able to come and go wherever and whenever they please is a freedom few in L.A. are willing to give up. According to a recent survey, 81 percent of L.A. drivers drive to work alone.

The battle to get some clean, safe, reliable public transportation in the L.A. Basin continues with mixed results, but the reality is that you're going to need a car unless you plan on doing nothing but lazing on a beach strategically located just across the street from your hotel.

But first things first.

The Airports

Greater Los Angeles is served by three major airports: Los Angeles International (LAX), Burbank-Glendale-Pasadena, and John Wayne. LAX, located approximately 17 miles from downtown L.A., is by far the busiest of them all, a giant facility serving nearly 48 million passengers annually. The place is pretty much a madhouse every day, but it's negotiable, and there are always at least a few people around to direct you if you get lost (although you may get some serious attitude along with the advice). Look for the Travelers Aid sign (a circle with a question mark in the middle) on the lower level of your terminal, or go to the central information center at Tom Bradley International Terminal if you need help.

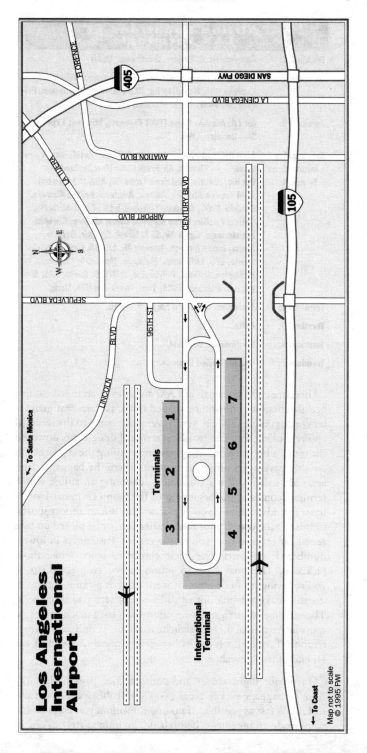

Los Angeles International Airport

Terminals 1 2 3 4 5 6 7

International Terminal

To Santa Monica

To Coast

Map not to scale
© 1995 FWI

LINCOLN BLVD
96TH ST
SEPULVEDA BLVD
AIRPORT BLVD
CENTURY BLVD
AVIATION BLVD
LA CIENEGA BLVD
SAN DIEGO FWY
FLORENCE
LA TIJERA

405

105

Airline Locations In LAX Terminals

Terminal 1:	America West, Empire, Southwest, USAir
Terminal 2:	Air BC; Air Canada, Air Mobility Command, Avianca, Express One, Hawaiian Air, KLM, Markair, Northwest, Private Jet, VASP, Virgin Atlantic, World.
Terminal 3:	Air LA, Alaska, Alpha (TWA Express), Midwest Express, Sun Country, TWA.
Tom Bradley International Terminal:	Aero California, Aero Cancun, Aeroflot, Aerolineas Argentinas, Aero Mexico, Air France, Air New Zealand, Air Pacific, Alitalia, American Trans Air, ANA (All Nippon), AOM French Airlines, Asiana, Aviateca, British Airways, Canada 3000, Canadian Airlines Int'l., Carnival/Iberia, Cathay Pacific, China Airlines, China Eastern, CorsAir, Ecuatoriana, Egypt Air, El Al Israel, EVA Air, Garuda, Iberia, Japan Airlines, Korean Air, LACSA, Lan Chile, Lauda, LTU, Lufthansa, Malaysia, Martinair, Mexicana, Philippine Airlines, Polynesian, QANTAS, Saeta, SAS, Singapore, Swissair, TACA, Thai, Tower Air, UTA, Varig.
Terminal 4:	American, American Eagle, Reno Air.
Terminal 5:	Delta.
Terminal 6:	Continental, Skywest.
Terminal 7:	United, United Express.

There are eight terminals at LAX, and they're arranged along a heavily congested horseshoe-shaped traffic pattern that guarantees once you get inside it, you'll eventually come to the terminal you're looking for. The two-level terminal design cuts down on the traffic a bit, with departing passengers using the top level and arriving passengers using the bottom, where the baggage claim areas are located. If it's convenient, choosing an airline whose terminal comes at the beginning of the loop (Terminal 1 or 2) has a few advantages if you're planning to use an airport shuttle or bus to take you to your final destination, or be picked up by a rental car tram to take you to the car lot. Passengers in lower-numbered terminals have their choice of seats, while those picked up later may have to squish in—or even stand up. If you're taking a cab or limo, or if someone is picking you up, it doesn't make a whole lot of difference where you disembark. Those flying on foreign airlines often don't have much choice, as most international flights originate from the Tom Bradley International Terminal, which sits between terminals 3 and 4 at the far end of the horseshoe.

Once your flight arrives and you get your bags (follow the signs to baggage pickup areas), you'll probably want to get out of LAX as fast as possible. If no one is meeting you and you haven't made arrangements beforehand, go immediately to one of the ground transportation booths located outside the baggage claim area of each terminal, where you can find out about transportation options, schedules and fees.

Where in the World?

Living near LAX has always made the short cab ride home a pleasant experience for me but usually results in a stream of foreign invective when I announce my destination. The fare is about half the $25-30 downtown fare. Curious to understand why the location of my domicile is so repugnant to cab drivers and why so few know where it is, I was surprised to learn that the average wait for an airport fare is 45 minutes to two hours and that more than 2400 trips originate in LAX. There are 5000 licensed cab drivers, eight licensed taxi companies, and excluding limos there are only about 1500 cabs. The L.A. Department of Transportation figured out that according to license registrations, drivers come from more than 100 countries. Most hail from the former Soviet Union (864), Iran (684) and Ethiopia (288), Mexico (288) and Nigeria (210)

More than 2400 trips start at LAX. The DOT wants to add another 600 licensed cabs this year.

Source: April 2, 1995 LA Times

Cabs are found parked along the curb on the lower level of each terminal, and typically charge between $25 and $30 for a trip downtown. Ask for a flat fee to avoid the high cost of cabbies that take unnecessary "alternate routes." If you're taking another form of transportation, you'll have to wait on the ground transportation island under the sign that designates your particular mode of transport: Bus Stop/Van (shuttles that provide door-to-door services; $10-15 to downtown); Courtesy Tram (such as those that take you to hotels, car rental lots or private parking lots); or the LAX Shuttle, which transports passengers from one terminal to another within the airport, or to airport parking lots.

Standing on a ground transportation island at LAX is one of the most daunting experiences on the planet, although—thankfully—you usually don't have to stand there very long. Imagine you and your luggage being crammed with dozens of other people (and their luggage) onto a thin strip of pavement with cars, limos and cabs whizzing by on one side, buses, trams and vans jockeying for position on the other. You're surrounded by honking horns, deadly carbon monoxide fumes and roaring engines, all the while staring anxiously through the haze for the bus or van that will deliver you (both literally and figuratively) from the clutches of one of the largest airports in the world. Even if you're a cheapskate, there's something to be said for spending the extra fifteen or twenty bucks to hire a cab and get the heck out of there. You can arrange for your rental car later, from your hotel.

Those departing LAX and looking for short- or long-term parking options have their choice of several locations. Generally, parking spaces within the airport complex fill up fast, and unless you're willing to make a time-is-no-object, row-by-row search of the parking structure, your best bet may be one of the off-site parking lots. (Parking is also considerably more expensive in the Central Lot, at $16 per day).

Rental Car Companies			
Name	Local Phone Number	National (800) Number	LAX Courtesy Phone Number
Able Rent-A-Car	(310) 672-0225	(800) 225-3768	56857
Aegis Car Rental	(310) 672-6920	(800) 222-3447	56712
All International	(310) 216-0000	(800) 400-0080	56899
Avis	(310) 517-9994	(800) 331-1212	56852
Budget	(800) 527-0700	(800) 221-1203	56854
Dollar	(310) 645-9333	(800) 800-4000	56855
Enterprise	(310) 820-1030	(800) 325-8007	56856
Fox Rent-A-Car	(310) 641-3838	(800) 225-4369	55228
Hertz Rent-A-Car	(310) 306-0221	(800) 654-3131	56851
Midway Rent-A-Car	(310) 330-4600	(800) 643-9294	56862
National	(310) 417-8240	(800) 227-7368	56863
Rocket Rent-A-Car	(213) 678-2629	N/A	56866
Stopless Rent-A-Car	(310) 673-9899	N/A	55239
Thrifty	(310) 823-3327	(800) 367-2277	56869
U-Save Auto Rental	(310) 649-5806	(800) 272-8728	55093

Lots B (at 111th Street and La Cienega) and C (96th Street and Sepulveda) offer frequent, free shuttle service to all LAX terminals and cost approximately $5 (lot B) to $7 (lot C) for each 24-hour period that your car is parked there. Parking in these lots can be surprisingly hassle-free, but allow plenty of extra time to catch your flight, especially during peak travel periods when shuttle buses are crowded and making stops at every terminal along the loop.

Another parking option is **Airport Valet** (☎ *800-32-VALET*), which, although more expensive than the airport lots, is guaranteed to lessen parking hassles. Simply pick up a valet driver near the airport, drive to your terminal, then turn the keys over to the valet, who takes the car from there to Airport Valet's facilities. When you return, simply call the company, who sends a valet to pick you up in your car. Rates range from about $8 to just over $13 per day, depending on the number of days you are away.

LAX: The New Power Scene?

No matter how much trepidation surrounds your coming in and/or going out of LAX, take a little time to sit down and marvel at the whole picture. Sure, this isn't exactly an island of tranquility, but the people-watching here is about as good as it gets, and it will definitely give you a good idea of the cultural, racial and ethnic mix that characterizes Los Angeles. If you're lucky, you might even see a real Hollywood star (or at least a whole lot of people who look like one), usually hiding behind a hat and shades.

If you plan on grabbing a bite while checking out the LAX scene, be aware that all the food sold in the airport is frightfully expensive and you seldom get what you pay for. (One local comic quipped that when his girlfriend complained that he never took her anyplace expensive for dinner, he took her to LAX on their next date.) The airport is in the process of expanding consumer choices by bringing in fast-food restaurants such as McDonald's, Burger King, and Kentucky Fried Chicken, plus a couple of upscale restaurants, one of which will occupy the airport's high-profile "Theme Restaurant," the dominant structure on the LAX skyline that looks rather like some space-age assemblage. Disney is rumored to be in on plans for the latter, which may be turned into a high-tech restaurant with a space theme.

The **Burbank/Glendale/Pasadena Airport**, located in the San Fernando Valley, is served by a handful of airlines (Alaska, American, America West, Reno Air, SkyWest, Southwest and United) that depart out of two terminals, but compared to LAX in terms of hassles, Burbank is nirvana. The facility's 4.3 million passenger load—even though it's growing each year—is 10 times less than LAX's, and direct flights are available in and out of many major U.S. cities, including Oakland, Sacramento, San Diego, San Francisco, San Jose, Las Vegas, Reno, Portland, Seattle, Salt Lake, Dallas/Fort Worth, Denver and Phoenix. If you don't mind a few stops, there are connections to almost anywhere in the United States.

Burbank continuously promotes itself as a logical alternative to LAX, claiming faster trips to downtown (28 minutes versus 41 minutes during rush hour), and a location closer to Pasadena (12 miles versus 28 miles), Hollywood (seven miles versus 20 miles), and Universal Studios (five miles versus 23 miles). On-airport rental cars (Alamo, Avis, Budget, Hertz and National) are a mere 75 feet away from the terminal at Burbank (versus 2.6 miles at LAX), and economy parking is a quarter-mile away, with free shuttle service offered to all parking lots.

To make traveling out of Burbank even more attractive, the airport is only one block away from the AMTRAK station at the intersection of Empire Avenue and Hollywood Way, and a free airport shuttle meets each of the six daily trains that run between San Diego and Santa Barbara. Metrolink trains are also met at

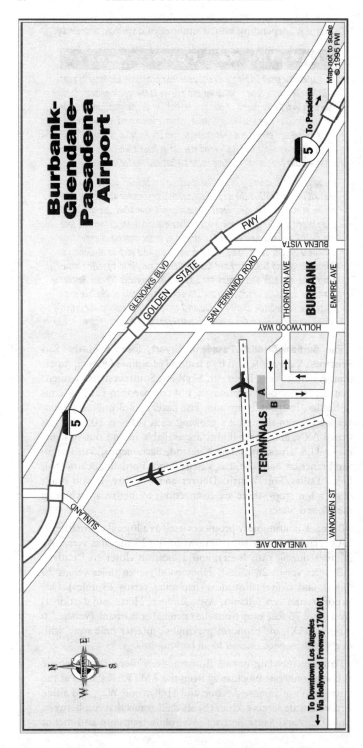

the downtown Burbank station for transportation to the airport, with plans to include a Metrolink stop at the airport AMTRAK station now under discussion.

There are several parking options at Burbank, including short-term, long-term and economy lots, as well as private parking and valet parking, which are both very close to the airport. (Note that the airport's Economy Lot B is closed from midnight to 8 a.m. each day, and you have to contact an attendant at one of the other lots to admit you if your flight arrives between those hours.) Daily parking rates are $24 if you park in an hourly lot (don't), $16 for valet parking, $14 for daily parking, and $8 for economy parking, which is obviously the best deal. Recorded parking information is available by calling ☎ *(818) 840-8837.*

Orange County's **John Wayne/Orange County Airport**, located in Costa Mesa, is a great alternative if your destination is Disneyland, and while there's only a distance of 15 miles' difference between LAX and Disneyland (31 miles) and John Wayne and Disneyland (16 miles), in L.A. traffic this represents a considerable amount of time saved. Enough of the large airlines serve John Wayne (Alaska, American, America West, Continental, Delta, Northwest, Southwest, TWA, United and USAir) that you should be able to make connections to or from just about anywhere, and shuttles can whisk you to Anaheim for about $12. More than 6 million passengers are currently served by John Wayne every year.

Like Burbank, John Wayne is much easier to negotiate than LAX, and it has only one main terminal, the sleek, strikingly high-tech, two-level Thomas F. Riley Terminal, which opened in 1990. Arriving passengers pick up baggage and leave the airport from the lower level, while departures are from the upper level, both of which are directly accessible from the Costa Mesa Freeway (SR 55), Campus Drive, and Michelson Drive.

The Trains

AMTRAK serves Los Angeles from downtown's Union Station, offering both cross-country trips and service to destinations within California. Its "Coast Starlight" superliner, which runs along the scenic Pacific coastline north to Seattle is especially appealing. AMTRAK also has a station in Orange County, at Anaheim Stadium. Call ☎ *(800) 872-7245* for information on AMTRAK schedules and fares.

Union Station

Fielding's Best Restaurant for Train Buffs

Pacific Dining Car (1310 West Sixth Street, L.A., ☎ (213) 483-6000). This plush, polished restaurant is situated in a restored 1921 rail car. While you're enjoying the decor, munch on steaks to die for, or go for breakfast, which is a terrific bargain. There's another branch in Santa Monica, at 2700 Wilshire Boulevard.

The Metro System

Hard to believe, but LA finally has a subway system.

For the past several years (and no doubt for many years to come) Los Angeles County has been in the throes of trying to expand transportation options by establishing reliable subway and light rail systems. The result of all this planning is the city's Metro System, which will eventually become a fully coordinated network of light rail, subway, bus, freeway, bikeway and dial-a-ride services.

When it comes to getting all of these services on-line, success has been mixed, mostly due to serious (and costly) construction snafus and budget problems, but the following are up and running:

Metrolink, a regional rail network that operates Monday through Friday, provides service between Los Angeles and Riverside, San Bernardino, the Antelope Valley, Ventura County, and Oceanside, with more than 40 stops along the way. When the line celebrated its second birthday in October of 1994, it was already the eighth-largest commuter railway service in the country, serving 16,000 riders with 75 daily trains. Several more connections (San Bernardino-Redlands, Riverside-Hemet, and Riverside-Fullerton) are scheduled to be completed in 1995 or 1996, and Metrolink is expected to handle more than half a million passengers each day by the year 2010.

The system, whose hub is at Union Station in downtown L.A., uses low-emission diesel locomotives propelling bi-level cars, each of which carries 160 passengers and is capable of going up to 80 miles per hour. All of the information you need about Metrolink is available by calling ☎ *1-800-371-LINK*, an interactive phone system that covers destinations, schedules, stops and fares.

(Commuter parents take note: Metrolink recently opened a child care center at the Montclair station in San Bernardino County, and two more child care centers are on the drawing board for Metrolink stations in the San Fernando Valley.)

The **Metro Blue Line**, a light rail service, offers commuter transport between Los Angeles and Long Beach daily from 5 a.m. to 11 p.m., with 22 stops along the main route. The $877 million Long Beach Blue Line, which opened in 1990, was the first completed line in the Metro Rail System, and in less than a year was getting more than 30,000 commuters off L.A. freeways every day.

Trains run every six to 10 minutes during weekday rush hours (6 to 9 a.m. and 3–6 p.m.), and every 15 minutes during non-rush hours, on holidays, and on weekends. Commute time from downtown L.A. to Long Beach is approximately 45 minutes, and tickets are available from computerized, self-service ticket machines located in each station. The fare runs just over $1 for the 22-mile trip from downtown L.A. to Long Beach, but was expected to increase to $2.35 when (and if) a recent cap on MTA fares was lifted. Connections to buses or Red Line subways are also available and combined fares can be accommodated at the time you purchase your ticket.

Scheduled to start service in 1998 is the **Pasadena Blue Line**, which will link downtown Los Angeles with Pasadena, alleviating traffic congestion on the Pasadena and Foothill freeways. The 13.6-mile line will run from Union Station to the Sierra

Madre Villa Station in East Pasadena, and will connect with both the Metro Red Line subway system and Metrolink at Union Station and (eventually) the Long Beach Blue Line.

The **Metro Green Line**, scheduled to be completed in 1995, will begin in Norwalk and run 16.5 miles west in the center of the I-105 (Glenn Anderson Freeway), then curve south at Aviation Boulevard and Imperial Highway for the 3.5-mile El Segundo branch, ending up at Freeman and Marine avenues in Redondo Beach. A north branch continues from Aviation Boulevard and Imperial Highway into Westchester.

The initial Metro Green Line stations will be located at Studebaker Road and the 605 Freeway (where there will be a park-and-ride lot with more than 1500 spaces); Lakewood Boulevard and Imperial Highway (433 park-and-ride spaces); Long Beach Boulevard and Imperial Highway (575 spaces); Imperial Highway and Wilmington Avenue (492 spaces; transfer to Long Beach-Los Angeles Metro Blue Line available here); Avalon Boulevard and 117th Street (159 spaces); the Harbor Freeway and 117th Street (220 spaces); Vermont Boulevard and 117th Street (249 spaces); Crenshaw Boulevard and 119th Street (521 spaces); Hawthorne Boulevard and 111th Street (758 spaces); and Aviation Boulevard and Imperial Highway (575 spaces and shuttle service to LAX). Currently, the line branches in two directions, with the southern branch to El Segundo stopping at Mariposa Avenue and Nash Street, El Segundo Boulevard and Nash Street, Douglas Street, and Marine Avenue (350 park-and-ride spaces). The north coast branch stops at Westchester Parkway and Sepulveda Boulevard.

Eventually, plans call for the Green Line to be linked with an LAX People Mover and an airport ground transportation center, and with a proposed LAX/Palmdale rail line, with the north branch continuing to Culver Boulevard in Marina del Rey. Buses will serve all Green Line stations, and passengers can transfer from the Green Line to the Long Beach-downtown L.A. Blue Line, which will run from the shared Wilmington Avenue/Imperial Highway station to downtown.

Then there's the city's troubled **Metro Red Line**, an underground subway system intended to be the backbone of the Los Angeles Metro System. Everyone thought L.A. had entered a new era in public transportation when, on Jan. 30, 1993, the Red Line's first shiny red cars whisked passengers between the system's hub at Union Station and MacArthur Park, just over four miles away. City officials gloated over this first link in "one of the world's newest and most modern subways," but if they'd known how soon the whole project would dissolve into a monumental pain in the backside, perhaps they wouldn't have been so glib.

The Red Line was scheduled to be expanded into Hollywood by 1998, but problems with project management, collapsing tunnels (and the streets above them), water main breaks and financial fiascoes brought the underground rail project's construction to a complete halt in the late summer of 1994. While city fathers argued over who was to blame for what and ordered designers back to the drawing board, the completion date was set back significantly.

In the meantime, the San Fernando Valley is closely—and anxiously—watching the subway's progress. The Red Line is scheduled to be up and running between Universal City and Canoga Park starting in the year 2000, despite the many who recommended an elevated monorail as a better solution to the valley's transportation problems.

Meanwhile, the hapless road warriors of L.A. doggedly continue their commute while public officials wrangle over alternative transportation methods. Some promising steps have been taken, but at least until the Red Line gets back on line, the problem is far from solved.

The Bus

Yes, there is bus service all over L.A. provided by the Metropolitan Transit Authority, the third-largest bus system in the country, but—face it—taking the bus is a terribly inefficient (albeit cheap) way to get around. Exceptions worth considering are DASH (Downtown Area Short Hop), a minibus that takes you around downtown L.A. with a stop every couple of blocks; Santa Monica's Big Blue Buses, which are generally less crowded and faster than MTA buses; the Sunset Shuttle, which covers West Hollywood; Long Beach's free Runabout Shuttle; and Pasadena's ARTS buses, whose themes make riding the bus imaginative, informative and fun.

Oh, Those Freeways

Surprisingly, in a recent survey 31 percent of local drivers said that commuting in greater Los Angeles is getting easier, with 24 percent calling the daily drive to and from work "always good." "HA!" said the critics, citing the distinct probability that commuting in L.A. is as bad as ever, and that self-deluded residents have simply made some sort of strange psychological adjustment, not unlike hamsters forever running around and around on a wheel. (One study suggested that, on a "bad car day," commuters suffered negative mood swings, higher blood pressure and even an increased incidence of chest pains.) For the record,

39 percent of those who participated in the 1994 survey said commuting is getting worse.

The Harbor Freeway

The fact is (whether you believe the rose-colored-glasses crowd or not), if you haven't spent the past three decades (and it takes about that long) learning how to negotiate L.A.'s freeway systems, you're in for a big shock. Sure, there are other freeway systems in the world, but nothing quite compares with L.A. drivers, who generally drive like the proverbial bat out of hell and artfully whip unexpectedly from lane to lane, all the while talking on the car phone and popping New Age music CDs in and out of their CD players.

When they're not zipping along at a pace 10–20 miles faster than the posted speed limit (55), they're used to either crawling or standing still. This is when the car phone comes in really handy, because chatting it up with a hot client is the perfect way to pass the time while sitting around in your Beemer waiting for things to get moving again.

Even if you don't have a Beemer (or a cellular phone), here are a few tips to make your freeway time a little less unnerving:

Fielding Freeway Survival Tips

Get a map.

No matter how smart you think you are, L.A. freeways are going to throw you. Get a good freeway and street map (Thomas Brothers maps are about the best you can find), and don't wait until you're on the road to try to read it and map out your route. Note that every freeway in L.A. has both a name and a number. Learn which freeways have which names (and numbers), and which direction they run (the Ventura Freeway, for example, is the 134, and runs east/west). As a reinforcement (or just to see if you're on track), call the place you're headed to and ask for directions. Most major attractions in the L.A. area have an information line that gives recorded directions on how to get there, including reference to freeways and which off-ramps to take.

Allow More Time Than You Think You Need.

Although the distance from point A to point B looks manageable in 20 minutes, it may take you 45 if the traffic is backed up. L.A. rush hour officially runs from 6:30–9:30 a.m. and from 3–6:30 p.m., which means that at any time during these periods, you can end up in a stupendous traffic jam. Planning an alternate route over surface streets may seem like a wise move, but most L.A. drivers will tell you that getting off the freeway virtually never saves you time, as surface streets are equally clogged with other drivers also trying to save time, plus you have to contend with traffic signals. The exception may be when the freeway is completely closed because of an accident or other mishap, in which case alternate routes are often broadcast on local radio traffic reports (see below), or you may be directed by Highway Patrol officers at the scene.

Don't Drive Too Slowly.

You may think you're just being careful—and driving safer—but drivers who travel under the speed limit can be a hazard to normally flowing traffic, and you can get a ticket for going too slow on the freeway. Even if you're going 55, stay in the right lane if faster traffic is continuously passing you (which it will be).

AM RADIO IN LOS ANGELES

Adult Contemporary			Spanish Language		
KRLA	1110		KKHJ	930	
Asian			XEGM	950	
KORG	1190		XPRS	1090	
KAZN	1300		KTNQ	1020	(213) 465-3171
Big Band			KWKW	1330	(213) 466-8111
KGRB	900	(213) 686-0300	KALI	1430	(213) 466-6161
Children			KWIZ	1480	(714) 554-5000
KPLS	830		KNSE	1510	(714) 981-8893
Financial			KXED	1540	
KMNY	1600		**Sports**		
Korean Language			KWNK	670	
KBLA	1580	(310) 788-1580	XTRA	690	
News			KMPC	710	(213) 460-5672
KFWB	980	(213) 462-5392	**Talk Shows**		
KNX	1070	(213) 460-5672	KOGO	600	
Nostalgia			KABC	790	(310) 839-4636
KOJY	540		KIEV	870	(213) 245-2388
KLAC	570		**Top 40**		
KGFJ	1230	(213) 462-3007	KFI	640	(213) 385-0101
KJQI	1260		KIIS	1150	
KWRM	1370				
Religion					
KBRT	740				
KFRN	1200				
KPPC	1240				
KGER	1390	(213) 636-4774			
KTYM	1460	(213) 678-3731			

Pay Attention.

When you're on the freeway, there are a ton of things to pay attention to, including—but not limited to—the speed of traffic and freeway signs that direct you to upcoming interchanges and offramps. If you miss (or are about to miss) your offramp, continue to the next offramp, then exit the freeway and get back on to circle back if necessary. Never suddenly cut across several lanes of traffic to get to an offramp, and don't even think about stopping your car in a freeway lane while you figure out where you're going. If you get confused, get off the freeway and get your bearings, then get back on.

FM RADIO IN LOS ANGELES

Adult Contemporary			Religion		
KBIG	104.3	(213) 874-7700	KFSG	96.3	(213) 484-1100
Alternative			KKLA	99.5	(818) 762-5552
KSPC	88.7		KYMS	106.3	
KUCI	88.9		KMAX	107.1	(213) 681-2486
KXLU	88.9		KWVE	107.9	
KLOS	95.5	(310) 840-4861	**Rock**		
KSCA	101.9		KNHS	89.7	
KROQ	106.7	(800) 520-1067	KLSX	97.1	
Asian			KNAC	105.5	
KFOX	93.5		**Soft Rock**		
KWIZ	96.7		KQLH	92.7	
Classical			KXEZ	100.3	
KUSC	91.5		KOST	103.5	
KKGO	105.1	(310) 478-5540	**Spanish Language**		
Contemporary			KLAX	97.9	
KYSR	98.7		KLVE	107.5	(213) 465-3171
Country			**Top 40**		
KZLA	93.9		KBPK	90.1	
KIKF	94.3		KEZY	95.9	(213) 625-7018
KFRG	95.1		KGGI	99.1	
Jazz			KIIS	102.7	(213) 466-8381
KLON	88.1		**Urban**		
KSBR	88.5		KHTZ	90.3	
KCRW	89.9	(310) 450-5183	KKBT	92.3	(213) 466-8381
KACD	103.1		KJLH	102.3	(213) 299-5960
New Age			KACE	103.9	
KTWV	94.7		KPWR	105.9	
News			**Variety**		
KPFK	90.7		KCSN	88.5	(818) 885-3089
Nostalgia					
KPCC	89.3				
Oldies					
KCBS	93.1				
KOLA	99.9				
KRTH	101.1				

Listen to the Radio.

Sometimes (but not always—see "Allow More Time Than You Think You Need," above), one of the best ways to avoid getting into a traffic jam is to anticipate it and get off the freeway before you come to it.

Several local radio stations, including KNX 1070 AM (which gives traffic reports every six minutes), KFWB 980 AM, KFI 640 AM and KCRW 89.9 FM keep freeway drivers informed of the latest road conditions, accidents and other snafus that will impede your progress. Really perk up your ears if you hear the word "SigAlert" associated with any location along your route: SigAlerts mean BIG TROUBLE on the road ahead.

Don't Drive in the Carpool Lane If You're Alone.

Many L.A. freeways have a carpool lane—or "diamond" lane—on the far left, designated by white diamond shapes painted onto the roadway. To be eligible to drive in these lanes, you must have at least two people in your car. If you're by yourself and succumb to temptation (these lanes usually move faster than other traffic lanes), you may be fined up to $300.

Wear Your Seatbelt.

It's the law in California, and the Highway Patrol can (although officers seldom do) pull you over and give you a ticket solely because you're not wearing your belt. If you get pulled over for another violation and are not wearing a seatbelt, you'll get a second fine for the seatbelt violation. You can also be fined if other passengers (including small children, who must be secured in car seats) are not properly belted in, so buckle up!

Use Your Cellular Phone.

If you have one, a cellular phone can be your best friend on the L.A. freeways. Several local companies, including Air-Touch Cellular (☎ *800 851-9815),* Roadirector (☎ *310 641-8868),* and L.A. Cellular (☎ *213 625-0405),* offer up-to-the-minute traffic information to subscribers that includes advice on how to get around or otherwise reroute to avoid a jam. Many will also provide maps and/or pre-trip planning that includes the fastest way to get where you're going and an estimate of how long the trip will take.

Help is Available.

If you have car trouble, immediately get off the freeway, or, if that's not possible, pull off onto the right shoulder and stop, then turn on your blinking emergency lights. Call boxes (4200 of 'em) located at intervals along all L.A. freeways, usually within walking distance from wherever you are. Lock your car, then find the nearest box and call for help, which is available in several languages. The Freeway Service Patrol, a fleet of 144 tow trucks that patrol the most congested corridors of local freeways in search of stranded motorists, can also be of help if they happen to show up when you need them—and the service is free. (Although this may seem like a generous act of benevolence, the main reason for the Freeway Service Patrol's existence is to get you and your car off the highway so traffic can proceed unimpeded.) Use extreme caution if you have to exit your car on the freeway; freeway pedestrians are hit by passing cars more often than you would care to think about.

If you take all these hints to heart, your freeway driving experience should definitely be bearable, and maybe you can relax enough to watch the world go by and take some interest in the sightseeing opportunities offered on L.A. freeways.

Vanity Plates

Personalized, or "vanity," license plates are so clever that it takes you awhile to puzzle them out, which—if you're not careful—may distract you and greatly enhance the odds that you'll plow into the vehicle in front of you. "SKIUTAW" may be pretty obvious, but how about "10SNE1" (think of it as a question from a sports enthusiast), or "ND2THDK," the plate on a Southern California professional's late-model Volvo (hint: he's a dentist)? There probably isn't an L.A. driver on the road who hasn't felt like an idiot after trying to sound out a vanity plate only to find that it made no sense whatsoever and probably wasn't a vanity plate after all. It's all part of the fun of driving L.A. freeways.

Murals

Many artists have contributed to the city's store of "public art" by using as a canvas the walls connected to—or visible from— L.A. freeways. You never know when you'll come across some painting of a larger-than-life movie star staring down at you from a perch several stories high. (For a complete guide to L.A.'s public art scene, pick up a copy of Robin Dunitz' "Street Gallery: A Guide to 1000 L.A. Murals," RJD Enterprises, 1993.)

Tagging

That other kind of "art," generally known as graffiti but more precisely known (in L.A. at least) as "tagging," can also be seen along many freeways in spite of efforts to squelch the clandestine activities of the young artists. Tagging has become a huge problem in Los Angeles, and it is often associated with gang activity, which has city officials well aware that an area riddled with tagging is an area perceived not to be safe. In certain neighborhoods, you'll see coils of barbed wire placed on freeway signs to discourage taggers.

Speaking of signs, you may also see posted warnings along some freeways about carrying backyard fruit from one place to another in L.A. These warnings have to do with the Mediterranean fruit fly which, if spread by people moving contaminated fruit from one neighborhood to another, could cause catastrophic damage to local crops. Note that the warning does not apply to fruit bought at a grocery store or produce market, as it is inspected before being sold.

A SURVIVOR'S GUIDE TO L.A.

I DROVE THE ALASKA HIGHWAY

I DROVE THE COQUIHALLA HIGHWAY

I DROVE THE CALIFORNIA HIGHWAYS

Rollerblading through the Apocalypse

"Welcome to L.A." "There is no parking in the white zone." "Have a nice day." "Life is a beach." "Welcome to fantasy land." "Welcome to California, now go home."

What is the real L.A.? What can a visitor hope to understand from a brief sojourn to one of the world's largest and most diverse metropolises. Not much. But that's OK since L.A. does not ask that anyone understand or even try to analyze our tangled existence. All we ask is that you carry on the Southern California myth. Blondes, sunshine, happiness, glamour and eternal fun.

You can choose to stay within the warm blurry amniotic sac of amusement parks, shopping malls, theme restaurants and beach-going or you could explore the multicultural kaleidoscope of black, yellow, brown, gay, straight, bi, kinky in a non-stop day and night orgy of sensory intake. Better yet you could skirt the maelstrom and spend your time in the cold clear air of the mountains, contemplate the arid solitude of the desert or our rustic backcountry. You can even flash a cardboard sign at a freeway exit, sell oranges at a stop light or hustle your drug-wracked body in Hollywood. All we ask is that you remember that you are in L.A., the land of dreams, sunshine and eternal hope. So remember to have a nice day.

This is the real Los Angeles, a city of hope, despair, fear and whatever-else-you-want-it-to-be-at-the-moment.

Los Angeles is unique in American history as the city that can reinvent itself whenever it feels like it. Iowa with palm trees? Not quite. How about Mexico with health insurance or Vietnam with freeways or Bladerunner without the rain? Depending on which offramp you take, L.A. can be heaven or hell.

There is perhaps no better place to be discriminating in your travels and time than Los Angeles. Just for fun, the next time you arrive at LAX, drive due east on Century Boulevard without taking the left turn on Sepulveda (Sa-pull-va-duh, not sepul-vee-da) and you will find yourself in the heart of the third world. A taco shop, liquor store, motel and church on every corner. This is not the L.A. you came for but it is more L.A. than Beverly Hills. L.A. is a grey-brown patchwork of poverty, wealth, life, death and birth.

To many, L.A. is a faded, deluded, old harlot dreaming of better days. Once attracted by its siren song, today white-collar workers are leaving paradise in droves for the wet Pacific Northwest and the arid Southwest. Studios now prefer to make movies in Florida, movie stars live in Montana and Aspen, the rich and glamorous prefer Vancouver, Canada. Freeway entrances are populated with cardboard sign-toting beggars and the skies are smoggy all day. No other city perpetuates so many conflicting images than L.A.: Land of Millionaires, Land of Riots, Land of Earthquakes, Land of Fires, Land of Palm Trees, Land of Babes, Land of the Cop Show, Land of the Sitcom, Land of the Famous, Land of the Dispossessed, Land of Opportunity. In short, L.A. is The Land of Whatever-Else-You-Want-It-To-Be-At-The-Moment. But gentle visitor, do not be afraid to enjoy the hard edge, the frantic pace and roar: the desperate sound of a country-sized city reinventing itself.

L.A. is just contemplating its next move. What is undeniably hip about L.A. is its hipness. No other city tries so hard to be so different, so new, so...L.A. If New York is the city of power, then L.A. is the city of fame. L.A.'s hard edge will either strop you razor sharp or cut you to ribbons. If you make it here, you are somebody. But even if you don't you can still act like somebody even if you are "nobody." This is L.A. Remember The Land of Whatever-Else-You-Want-It-To-Be-At-The-Moment.

So remember, plan your visit like Angelenos runs their lives. You must write your own script, prop it, direct it and act it. Successful or not, you must hype it and promote it.

So rent that fantasy car, wear those crazy clothes you bought on Melrose, slip on those $120 shades and crank up the boom box. It's show time, folks! L.A. does something to all of us. Don't forget that big ending when you take off your shoes and take a walk at sunset in the surf. That's a wrap and everyone goes off to resume their normal lives.

L.A. is not all dark and evil. L.A. is everything and anything you want it to be. L.A. is clear blue skies and 75 degrees on New Year's Day. L.A. is serendipity. Fairy tales do come true here. Waitresses do become movie stars. Movie stars become presidents. You can find yourself standing next to your favorite celebrity at the checkout stand at the supermarket. I once spent a curious few hours with a very well known television star who was locked out of his hotel room and came barging into my room naked. L.A. is showbiz incarnate. Why would Steven Spielberg open a multi-million dollar restaurant just to sell submarine sandwiches? Because tourists love it. Why would people pay money to experience an earthquake? Because folks from out of town love it.

L.A. makes dreams come true. But L.A. needs an agenda. If you think you will just stroll around and snap pictures, make sure you hire a bodyguard. If you think you will just drive aimlessly, you will soon think you are watching an endless loop of burger joints, franchises and faded pastel commercial buildings. So, how do you do L.A. right? How do you get right down to avoiding the tourists, the obvious and the pedantic? Grab your Fielding Agenda Guide, your shades, jump in your 5.0 and let's do L.A.

If your trip to L.A. is limited to the usual tourist stuff such as visiting Disneyland and taking a bus tour of stars' homes, you're going to miss out on a lot. The smart visitor is always armed with a list of phone numbers and other information sources that allow him or her to get a very hot itinerary together—sometimes without even leaving the hotel room! The following sources are designed to put you in touch with everything that's happening in L.A.

Audiences Unlimited
☎ *(818) 506-0043*

There are more famous people in Los Angeles than there should be. The best way to see celebs is to find out where they are shooting movies and hang around. Next best is to get tickets to the show tapings. Try eating at Morton's, Le Dome, Hampton's, Patrick's Roadhouse or other favorite celebrity dining spots. Next best is to hang out at the supermarkets in Trancas and Malibu where even the famous have to buy there own groceries. Worst way is take a studio tour or hope they are watering their lawns when your bus tour rolls by.

Business Services

A variety of information and business services are available through the *Los Angeles Times*, including an on-demand research service, faxed copies of the day's verified loan rates from top Southern California banks, stock quotes by phone, Times marketing research reports and maps, a daily fax of your personal investment portfolio with same-day closing prices, and profiles of Southern California houses or condos for sale. Most of these services are not free. See the Directory of Business Services in the Times' Business Section for complete information.

Cultural Affairs Resource Directory
☎ *(213) 688-ARTS.*

Sponsored by the City of Los Angeles Cultural Affairs Department, this recorded hotline highlights the cultural arts, including music, dance, theatre, museums, special events, and information on discount tickets.

Emergency Response 911

Unlike New York, which has legions of muggers, bad Angelenos have to be more creative. Carjacking, car theft and car vandalism are real threats. Stay out of bad neighborhoods after dark. Park in a supervised garage and don't leave any valuables in your car.

Ethnic Directories
☎ *(213) 624-7300.*

Ethnic directories were developed by the L.A. Convention & Visitors Bureau as part of its Cultural Kaleidoscope series aimed at visitors of various ethnic backgrounds. Each booklet covers ethnic sights, attractions, shopping, dining, nightlife, and special events, plus information on local services, businesses, and outreach programs. Currently available are Asian and Pacific Islander, African-American, and Latino editions. The free booklets, which are printed in English, are updated annually and are available from the C&VB at both of its visitors centers or by mail.

Guidebooks

There are a ton of guidebooks about L.A., and nearly every one of them contains a list recommending more guidebooks. If you decided to buy everything ever written about Los Angeles, you'd fill your bookshelves to overflowing, and would have to contend with so many opinionated views of the "real" L.A. that you'd end up having to figure it out for yourself, which is probably the best way to approach it anyway.

Buying a guide to L.A. is a lot like picking a restaurant: what you choose depends a lot on your individual taste. The standard guides include Fodor's, the AAA guide (which is free to AAA members), and the Mobil Travel Guide (which covers all of California and the West), all updated every year.

Those with more eclectic tastes might appreciate *The Los Angeles Times'* "Inside Track" (1994), which is packed with lots of insider tips and presents a hip, straightforward format. Pluses include the fact that it's relatively inexpensive ($12), and is published in both English and Spanish. Major weaknesses are that it doesn't cover L.A. or its major attractions in any sort of depth and that its size (8 1/2 x 11") doesn't lend itself to being tucked into a pocket or purse.

Also worth considering are Gil Reavill's *Los Angeles* (1992), offering lots of information on the individual geographical areas of L.A., along with their attendant history and gossip in an easy-reading narrative style; or Peter Theroux's *Translating L.A.: A Tour of the Rainbow City* (1994), a wonderful literary exploration of Los Angeles and all of her colorful neighborhoods and residents.

Highway Conditions
☎ *(213) 628-7628*

Rent a fun car, preferably a convertible. The best prices are found by working the phone book, not booking at the airport. If renting a convertibel or exotic, remember to ask how much insurance is, it can be equal to the price of the car. Get a good map. Try to confine your driving between 9 a.m. and 3:30 p.m., and 6 p.m. onwards. Traffic is a bitch like any other city but since you will probably be covering great distances make sure you don't waste precious time in stop-and-go traffic. You can turn right on a red light. Cops love to give speeding tickets here despite the fact that most cars will be traveling at least 70 mph. The speed limit is 55 but CHiPs (California Highway Patrol) must give you a ticket if you are clocked over 65. CHiPs officers do not use radar since they are considered by the courts to be experts in determining speed.

Los Angeles Convention & Visitors Bureau (L.A. C&VB)
☎ *(213) 689-8822.*

Stop by one of the bureau's two visitor information centers (downtown, at *685 South Figueroa Street between Wilshire and Seventh Street*, or in Hollywood at the Janes House, *6541 Hollywood Boulevard*) for a broad range of brochures on what to see and do in L.A. Assistance is available in several languages, and, if you're planning a future trip to L.A., the C&VB will send you a trip planning packet in advance.

L.A. County Disaster Services
☎ *(213) 974-1120*

Stand with your arms straight out, palms upwards. Now press the sides of your hands together as hard as you can. When they slip, voila, an earthquake. L.A. is on one plate heading north while the rest of the U.S. is heading south. The normal pressure caused by this pressure is OK if it weren't for the little spur L.A. creates. This extra resistance releases once in a long while and we get a humdinger. Earthquakes are measured using the Richter scale, but the severity of the earthquake depends on how close you are to the epicenter and what type of ground you are on. A mild earthquake feels like somebody bumped into your house. A more violent earthquake is like being in a paint shaker in slow motion. It is preceded by a low roar like an oncoming freight train. You will hear windows rattle, car alarms go off and then you will find it very difficult to walk as you watch even solid objects such as sidewalks undulate like the ocean. See Earthquake tips for what to do.

L.A. Fire Department
(Main number ☎ *384-3131*)

When it gets dry in L.A. the natural brush is very flammable. The hillsides in Malibu, Laguna and to the east contain brush that is explosive when ignited. Once the fire begins the fire and sparks travel quickly. Fires are first spotted by the yellow-gray smoke they give off. If you are in a rural area, try to get to a developed area where you will not be trapped in a canyon road.

The fire department will close off most areas affected by fires. The steep undeveloped canyon areas in September are most affected.

L.A. Flood Control
☎ *(213) 458-5100*

When it rains in Southern California, it pours. Our rains tend to come in short, violent downpours. The water quickly rolls down the hills and gathers on streets and canyons. The water carries with it dirt and debris that can knock people down. In areas where there have been fires the downpours usually create mudslides. The Pacific Coast Highway north of Santa Monica is especially vunerable to mudslides. The heavy rains are usually between December and March.

Meeting People
☎ *(900) 993-3339*

Nearly every L.A. newspaper (including the tabloids) has a classified section where people, both gay and straight, advertise to meet other people with various purposes in mind. A more upscale version of back-page classifieds is DateNet, sponsored by the slick new L.A.-based magazine, *Eligible*, which promises that you can "connect with professional, sincere and well-respected men and women just like you!" The system, which works via a 900 number costing $1.99 per minute, allows you to set up a personal phone "mailbox" with a description of yourself and the man/woman of your dreams. Browsing through the system can result in a "match" that will generate an automatic callback linking the two people together, and you are soon swapping messages with a possible Mr. or Ms. Right. Or, you can peruse the classified ads in the back of the magazine, then call and leave a message in the mailbox of someone who sounds interesting. (Recent ad-placers included "Prince Charming," "Attorney with Heart," "Sensuous Writer," and "Handsome, Roguish Computer Animator," to give you an idea of what to expect.) Eligible also showcases a pack of rich and/or successful L.A. singles in each issue who are anxiously awaiting a message from you in their personal voice mailbox.

The *L.A. Times* also has a 900 number voice mailbox dating service called Dateline, with information listed in the classified section of the Friday and Sunday papers.

If dating services aren't your thing, and you're uneasy about answering classified ads, you might want to go looking in person at one of the prime locations where successful singles are likely to hang out. Try strolling the Universal CityWalk, going shopping at Pavilion's market, frequenting the law libraries at USC or UCLA, or showing up at trade shows that attract the wealthy, young and single, such as "Ski Dazzle," the city's annual (November) trade show highlighting winter sports. If none of the above produces the results you're looking for, perhaps it's time to get into one of L.A.'s plethora of support groups, such as "Images of Psyche," an "archetypal approach" that uses dreams, mythology, astrology, the arts, and the works of a spate of psychologists to solve the problems plaguing your everyday life; or "Abandon Your Co-Dependency," designed to help you stop your obsessional thinking about "him/her." Look in the classified section of any L.A. paper (including the tabloids), and you'll find a workshop or support group to help you cope with almost anything. (Note: the above does not constitute an endorsement of the groups mentioned.)

Movies
☎ *(213)* or *(310) 777-FILM.*

If you simply can't find anything else to do in L.A. except go to a movie, by all means put in a call to MovieFone, a free, interactive phone service. Enter the title of the movie you want to see and the service will give you the name of the theater nearest you where it is showing, and the showtimes, or you can opt for a list of all movies playing at local theatres. You can also buy your tickets in advance by phone, or parents can take advantage of the "Parents' Guide," which gives an explanation of why certain movies have received their (usually PG-13 or R) rating.

Online Services

If you travel with a computer and a modem you might want to try the L.A. specific online data sources.

L.A. ONLINE
☎ *(213) 936-1160*

L.A. Online, in operation since 1985, provides free, text-only, 24-hour computer access to various community newspapers (such as *L.A. Reader*), world news (updated hourly), a local calendar of events (updated weekly), shopping, movie showtimes, classified ads, business news, etc. You don't need any special software to access the text, but if you buy the company's graphical software (a one-time purchase of about $30), the graphics are a kick. ☎ *(213) 936-1160* for computer access; ☎ *(310) 372-9364* for customer service/voice support. In the fall of 1994, the *Los Angeles Times* also launched an interactive on-line service called TimesLink, which is available on Prodigy. Through TimesLink, you can get information about hundreds of things to see and do in greater L.A., including dining, recreation, and shopping.

NewsLine
☎ *(818) 883-6397*

The *Daily News* sponsors a similar service called NewsLine, also available 24 hours a day.

TimesLine
☎ *(213) 808-8463*

This 24-hour service, sponsored by the *Los Angeles Times*, dispenses recorded information on such diverse subjects as stocks and bonds, business news, mortgage rates, real estate, sports, surf and beach reports, health issues, lottery results, soap opera updates, domestic and international weather, TV and movies, and gardening. Dial the main number, then select your choice from the menu.

The Press

Options for reading material in Greater Los Angeles run the gamut from the well-respected *Los Angeles Times, Orange County Register* and the *Daily News* (which focuses on the San Fernando Valley) to a plethora of community newspapers and funky tabloids such as the *Los Angeles Reader, L.A. Weekly;* (which was recently purchased by *The Village Voice* of New York City, who says no journalistic changes are in the works), the *LA Village View*, and the new *School* (published from September through June and distributed on local college campuses and at selected other locations). There's also a ton of fringe stuff such as *URB*, a tabloid providing a hard-edged look at the music and underground club scene, and *BAM* (Beat, Attitudes, and Music), which bills itself as "THE music lifestyle magazine for California."

Foreign-language newspapers include the *Chinese Daily News* and *Sing Tao* (Chinese); *California Staats-Zeitung* (German); *Rafu Shimpo* (Japanese); *Korea Times* (Korean); and *La Opinion, Mi Casa, Nuestro Tiempo,* and *Vencinos de Valley* (Spanish).

Don't overlook the monthly *Los Angeles Magazine,* or *Orange Coast* magazine, which fill you in on everything going on in L.A. and Orange counties and provide a listing of area restaurants and events, or opt for the Generation X focus and sassy attitude of *Buzz.* There are also several ethnic magazines such as *YOLK* (targeted for hip English-speaking Asian-Americans), *Image* (whose stated mission is to "empower the man of color"), and *Que Linda!* (a magazine for young Latino women). All of the above are available at newsstands in various locations, such as World Book and News, which is open 24 hours *(1652 North Cahuenga Boulevard in Hollywood).*

Rent Line
☎ 789-*RENT.*

Looking for a place to rent? You can't beat the services offered by Rent Line, a computerized, interactive telephone system designed to help you find a perfect housing match for your taste and your budget. Updated every day, the system asks you to key in the area code of the location where you most want to live (310 = Beverly Hills, Santa Monica, Long Beach and West L.A.; 213 = downtown L.A. and Hollywood; 818 = the San Fernando and San Gabriel valleys; 714 = Orange County and parts of East L.A.; 909 = Riverside and San Bernardino counties), then the first three letters of the desired city, the number of bedrooms you need, and the maximum amount of rent you want to pay. Voila! You then hear a listing of properties matching your specifications. Information is available in both English and Spanish.

Smog Report
☎ (800) 242-4022

Smog is a fact of life in cities from Denver to Bombay. It is the effect of poor air circulation and too many cars. Los Angeles sits in a basin that is capped by cold ocean air bottling in hot, polluted air. Smog is at its worst when it is very hot and Santa Ana conditions prevail. Do not confuse smog with "early morning low cloud," the maritime fog that burns off by about 10 a.m.

Traffic Number

L.A.'s 700 miles of freeways are not that scary. If you screw up just go to the next exit, do a horizontal loop–de–loo and get back on the freeway going the other direction. Since most streets in L.A. are on a grid system you can use common sense in finding your way to a freeway entrance. There are free emergency phones every half mile on most of the major freeways. You will soon get used to high speed close formation driving. Keep your distance (drivers eat breakfast, do their makeup and talk on the phone simultaneously here), look over your shoulder when you change lanes (people here like to sneak into your spot when you put your signals on) and don't give people the finger or get into a shouting match. (We like to shoot people who disagree with our driving style.)

Underground Clubs

Many of the L.A. tabloids list hotline numbers you can call to find out what's happening on the alternative music scene. These include Underground Source (☎ *310 289-3171*), which gives information on underground events and showcases interviews with alternative artists, and Hip-Hop One Network (☎ *818 782-2400*), featuring news about the hip-hop genre.

Visitor Events Hotline
☎ *(213) 689-8822*

A must for visitors, this hotline operated by the L.A. Convention & Visitors Bureau gives you an up-to-date listing of local events, including music, dance, theatre, sports, museum exhibits, studio tapings, and festivals. Information is available in English, Spanish, French, German and Japanese.

Weather Reports
☎ *(213) 554-1212*

Normally the wind blows from the Pacific Ocean to the desert. Somedays the wind reverses, bringing hot dry conditions. Dust, smog and a sense of hating L.A. are the results. Just for fun drive up into the mountains to see the razor-sharp distinction between the clean desert air and the filthy L.A. air trapped below.

The Welcome Channel

Available in more than 30,000 hotel rooms citywide, The Welcome Channel provides a 30-minute video introduction to the city, including spotlights on major attractions, restaurants, shopping, and a quarterly calendar of events and major museum exhibits. The television channel number for The Welcome Channel varies between hotels. Ask when you check in.

Shake and Bake: Earthquakes, Fires and Other Natural Disasters

Don't rely on the Los Angeles Convention and Visitors Bureau to enlighten you on the subject of earthquakes. No way. Touting "fabulous and fun" L.A. is their job, and they're not about to tell you that at any moment the parking garage in which your luxury car is currently parked could collapse like a house of cards, compressing $50,000 worth of steel and rubber (but hopefully not you) into a tangled mass a mere six inches high.

This cavalier attitude toward earthquakes seemingly ran rampant among most Angelenos until the early morning of January 17, 1994, when a magnitude 6.8 quake, centered in the San Fernando Valley community of Northridge, shook everyone awake in more ways than one.

Thirty seconds of violent quaking killed 55 people (16 of whom were peacefully sleeping in a three-story apartment house when it collapsed on top of them), caused more than $9 billion in structural damage (making it the country's most costly earthquake since 1906), and scared the hell out of everyone; even those in the most serious throes of earthquake denial were forced to sit up and take notice.

While most Southern Californians had previously considered earthquakes just another "little inconvenience"—a small price to pay for living in Paradise—it was not encouraging to learn from scientists that the Northridge quake was not the dreaded "Big One," a mega-sized earthquake of magnitude at least 8 that is predicted for sometime within the next 50 years "somewhere" in California. Nor was the revelation by state Senator Tom Hayden two weeks after the Northridge quake that, in the previous three years, the state of California had spent more money on landscaping its freeways than on retrofitting to make them earthquake-safe. (Or at least safer. Most experts agree that in a magnitude 8 earthquake—125 times more powerful than the Northridge quake—a heck of a lot of stuff would fall down, retrofitted or not.)

These findings were the proverbial last straw for some local companies, such as the heretofore Riverside-based Alcor Life Extension Foundation, whose livelihood involves the business of freezing the heads and bodies of its (temporarily, it believes) dead clients until scientists come up with a way to thaw them out and revive them. Faced with the possibility of a larger quake toppling its liquid nitrogen-, head-, and body-filled freezing containers, the company picked up and moved to Scottsdale.

In addition, six of the state's largest homeowners' insurers (such as 20th Century Industries, which posted a $256 million loss wiping out more than half of its capital after $475 million in claims were filed following the Jan. 17 quake) began declining new business altogether, with several more reducing their business and/or raising deductibles on earthquake policies up to 35 percent.

Dallas-based Republic Insurance Company actually withdrew entirely from California, and homeowners throughout the L.A. area are finding that a policy costing $1000 before the quake now costs up to three times that amount, and offers less coverage. Many observers who predicted a crash and burn of the housing market following these developments are surprised that people are still actually moving to L.A. and buying houses.

That there was not an immediate mass exodus from the city after the Northridge quake is just another testament to pure L.A. "attitude," which falls somewhere between "hey, babe, this is, like, real life" and "my understanding and enlightenment concerning the cosmos protects me from the violent and evil forces of nature." One reporter wryly remarked that, in the end, only the "most desperate," the "most damaged" or the "most convinced"—of impending doom, one assumes—would actually leave earthquake-ravaged L.A. because, well, this is California, and frankly, where else is there?

Fielding's Earthquake Survival Guide

If the Big One hits while you're in town (or even just a Small One–aftershocks of the January 1994 quake are still jolting Southern California every once in awhile, and will continue to do so for years), here are some basic safety tips on how to survive a quake (more information is listed in the front matter of your local phone book, which has a section on earthquake survival):

1.   *Don't panic. Okay, okay, go ahead and panic. Everyone else does. (Except those icy-cool seismologists from Caltech who show up on TV to assure the world that all of this horrendous shaking is "perfectly normal.");*

Fielding's Earthquake Survival Guide

2. *If you're indoors, stay there, and get under a sturdy table or desk. Even though the ground isn't likely to swallow you up if you run outside (you've been watching too many earthquake movies), you could get hurt by all kinds of dangerous stuff out there. Stay away from windows, bookcases, mirrors, fireplaces, or other objects that can fall on you, and if there's one of those huge fish aquariums in the room, prepare to swim. Earthquake veterans advise that it's always good to keep some solid footwear by your bedside at night, because many post-earthquake injuries involve panicked people running across a floor littered with broken glass. Having a flashlight at hand is also a good idea; if the quake knocks out the power, it will be dark as a tomb inside and out. Don't light candles until you're sure there are no gas leaks that—with just a little encouragement from a lighted match—could blow what's left of you and your surroundings to smithereens;*

3. *If you're outside when the quake hits, get into the open, away from buildings (which usually fall outward), trees, walls, and especially power lines, which can turn you to toast in about five seconds if they fall on you;*

4. *If you're in your car, resist the temptation to come to a complete stop under—or on top of, for that matter—an overpass or bridge or beneath the aforementioned power lines. Stay in the car and turn on the radio for emergency instructions from civil defense frequencies, which will remain up and running even if other stations are knocked off the air;*

5. *After the shaking stops, catch your breath, assess your situation, and then get ready for aftershocks, some of which can be nearly as powerful as the original quake.*

And, hey, WELCOME TO CALIFORNIA!

While we're on the subject of natural disasters, we might as well address the other half of Southern California's "Shake and Bake" reputation: fires. Brush fires have been happening in Los Angeles for years, and they seem to have a penchant for breaking out (or being set) in the city's most upscale neighborhoods. The fact is that seclusion and exclusivity usually involve lots of foliage (not to mention lots of money), and foliage—especially in fall, when everything is dried out from the summer heat—makes great fuel for wind-whipped infernos. Which means that lots of rich people and Hollywood types tend to lose their homes when a big fire rages out of control for any length of time. In the Malibu fire of November 1993, 350 structures were lost, including the homes of actress Ali McGraw and several other celebrities, with damages estimated at $215 million. The arson-caused Laguna fire a month earlier resulted in the loss of 486 homes and caused more than $528 million in damage.

To add insult to injury, wildfires are nearly always followed by mudslides if the next rainy season is particularly wet, and the bare hillsides are unable to stem the resulting rush of rainwater. Mudslides aren't apt to be a problem for the visitor, but stay away from Pacific Coast Highway during and just after periods of heavy rain—it's the mudslide capital of L.A., and a few large boulders always get swept along in the muck.

"Everyone talks of the hazards of living in L.A., but the last
earthquake caused a mudslide, which extinquished a wild brush fire
that would have consumed our house, so I can't complain."

Fielding's What Next? Award

*As if Los Angeles' disasters don't get enough bad press, scientists report that
killer bees are making a beeline for Los Angeles County, with an expected
arrival date of summer, 1995. Since most people have seen one movie too
many about bees running amok, the Los Angeles Convention & Visitors
Bureau is doing its best to keep this one under wraps. Fact is, the so-called
killer bees aren't killers at all unless you get stung about 2000 times, which
you won't if you steer clear of bees and/or their hives (which you're probably in the habit of doing already). See? Not to worry.*

L.A.'s Famous (and Infamous):
Sex, Crimes and Videotapes

Knock knock.

Who's there?

O.J.

O.J. who?

Oh, good! You're on the jury!

This joke, which made the rounds shortly after the media got hold of the
O.J. Simpson murder case, illustrates as well as anything else the sort of
morbid fascination that Los Angeles has with celebrity criminal suspects, or
at least with celebrated crimes and other nefarious acts. By the time most of
these cases come to trial—if they ever come to trial—the local media have
put so many spins on the alleged evidence that everyone in town has a head
full of preconceived notions disqualifying them completely from using any
sort of rational judgment if called upon to do so.

In the circuslike case of local resident Simpson—heretofore known as the quintessential Mr. Nice Guy— hijinks outside of the courtroom included the establishment of a special 900 phone number where—for $2.95 per minute—callers could speculate on whether or not O.J. had been framed, comment on different aspects of his trial and/or send a "personalized up-lifting message to O.J." In addition, a TV movie was in the works before the case ever came to trial, causing O.J. supporters to hopefully suggest—to no avail—that the former football star be "sprung" to appear as himself in the starring role. So taken were Californians with the whole sordid case that the state Registrar of Voters respectfully submitted that the trial be sus-pended during the November 1994 election so that the compelling tele-vised courtroom drama wouldn't tempt voters to stay at home and neglect their civic duty.

And let's not forget the case of Lyle and Eric Menendez, spoiled rich kids from Beverly Hills who admittedly blasted their parents to kingdom come, celebrated with a buying spree of stupendous (even for L.A.) propor-tions, then used their ill-begotten inheritance to hire a big-time L.A. attor-ney who convinced at least one of 12 perfectly intelligent people that "the boys" were merely reacting to a tortuous past and weren't to blame for all that nasty business with the gun. The first trials of both brothers resulted in a hung jury, but retrials were expected to follow. In the meantime—in true Hollywood style—one of the jurors from the first trial was in the process of suing another juror who allegedly made slanderous comments about her on the Maury Povich talk show.

The nation was also privileged to watch (ad nauseam) the notorious vid-eotape depicting several LAPD officers' beating of the now-famous Rodney King, followed by a trial where the officers were acquitted, causing South–Central L.A. to erupt in riots that effectively destroyed the participants' own neighborhoods.

And then there was that strange molestation non-case against pop star Michael Jackson, dropped by district attorneys in two counties after exten-sive investigations turned up no solid evidence that the King of Pop had sexually abused a young boy who was a "close" friend of the superstar. The whole affair seemed to suggest that if you know someone rich and famous, it pays (big) to make scandalous charges against him and then shut up after receiving a couple of million dollars.

There have also been, of course, enough intriguing celebrity deaths in L.A. over the years to inspire a heap of books, and most of them have al-ready been written. The debate is still raging over the circumstances sur-rounding the death of Marilyn Monroe, whose nude body was found in her Brentwood bungalow in 1962; young presidential candidate Robert Kennedy was shot to death at the Ambassador Hotel during his 1968 pres-idential campaign and actress Sharon Tate and her unborn child were bru-tally stabbed to death by members of the Charles Manson "family" at her Benedict Canyon home in August of 1969.

Not that you have to be rich and/or famous to end up embroiled in L.A.'s crime scene. In a poll conducted by the *Los Angeles Times* in 1994, 34 percent of the 1239 adult residents of L.A. County who were inter-viewed said crime was their community's biggest problem, followed by the related problems of gangs (31 percent), and drugs (12 percent). It is estimated that Los Angeles residents become crime victims approximately 40 times during each hour of every day, and carjackings, ATM robberies and drive-by shootings have become so commonplace that they no longer command front-page headlines.

As if all of this violence wasn't bad enough, the city has recently been plagued by a new kind of crime: parking meter theft. More than half a million dollars' worth of meters were vandalized or stolen between early 1993 and mid-1994, mostly by transients or druggies looking for easy money.

Crime frankly has the most jaded of L.A. residents worried. (But not all. A top-flight forensic anthropologist who moved to L.A. to advance her career enthusiastically told the *L.A. Times* that "there's more crime and more bodies just thrown away in remote areas here than anywhere in the world." Oh boy.) A 20 percent jump in the purchase of weapons was recorded statewide between 1992 and 1993, with more than 650,000 Californians packing guns in 1993, most for "personal protection."

There were more than 47,000 gunshot victims in California in 1993 (5000 of them died), with a 32 percent increase in firearm murders between 1989 and 1993, prompting the chairman of the Assembly Committee on Gun Violence to speculate that firearm homicide would soon overtake automobile accidents as the leading cause of death by injury in California. Between 1989 and 1993, tourism to the state dropped 45 percent among Japanese visitors, who are reportedly under the mistaken (?) impression that all Californians have guns, which they use with some regularity on people who don't speak English.

Meanwhile, in an effort to stem the tide of violence among the city's young people, Governor Pete Wilson signed a bill in mid-1994 authorizing $1 million in federal money to be spent for metal detectors in L.A. schools in an effort to keep guns off high school campuses. Is it any wonder that the rest of the country is wondering what in the heck is going on out there in California?

How Not to Become a Statistic

So, how bad is it—really?

Somewhat surprisingly, not so bad. There are 8.6 million residents of the county of Los Angeles—plus a whole lot of visitors on any given day—and the vast majority of them do business, run errands, hang out, have fun, and party late into the night without ever being held up, shot at, sexually assaulted, or even having their neighborhood parking meters stolen. Sixty-seven percent of L.A. County residents say they feel safe in their communities, which means your chances of becoming a crime victim are a lot less than you might have thought after having read the newspaper or watching virtually any local station's spin on the news.

In a recent study, the FBI reported that "serious" crime in Los Angeles was down 13 percent for the first half of 1994 (as compared with the first half of 1993), and that 1994 might be hailed as the first year L.A.'s homicide rate had dropped below 1000 since 1989. While authorities were quick to point out that these new statistics were not enough to predict a trend, and that local police had no intention of slacking off in the crime fighting department, it was at least a little good news.

Where your car is concerned, a national study by the Highway Loss Data Institute in 1994 indicated that Los Angeles has one of the lowest car theft rates in the country, lower than those in Houston, Philadelphia, Denver, and Portland, Oregon—to name a few. Luxury automobiles are the most likely to be stolen, but improved security systems often thwart would-be thieves, and studies show that, if you take precautions, you're not likely to lose your car.

The statistics truly do indicate that the odds are in your favor, but L.A. is still a high-crime city, so a bit of caution is certainly warranted during your visit. Here are a few tips on how to avoid becoming a major player on the L.A. crime scene:

It's a jungle out there: the L.A. Basin

L.A. Survival Guide

Know Where You're Going.

L.A. encompasses a vast system of freeways whose exits lead into a countless number of neighborhoods. If you don't know where you're going, you run the risk of ending up lost in one of the seedier parts of town (such as Watts, Compton, South–Central and East L.A.), which significantly increases your chances of becoming a crime victim—especially at night. Plan your route ahead of time. If you should have car trouble along the freeway, stay with your vehicle and wait for help.

Lock Your Car.

If you've driven in from Small Town, U.S.A., where no one locks any-thing, wake up and smell the coffee! You're in the city now, and you should never leave your car unlocked. Roll the windows up, too, and don't leave anything valuable—such as your purse, shopping pur-chases, or your portable CD player—in open view on the front or back seat. (Thieves won't think twice about breaking a window if the potential booty is worth it.) Lock valuables in the trunk before you walk away.

Don't Resist Carjackers.

If you are assailed by a carjacker (this shouldn't be a problem if you drive a VW van left over from the original Woodstock), get out and hand him the keys. All he really wants is to steal your car, but if you resist, the consequences could be considerably more dire. Your car is replaceable. You're not.

Be Cautious When Using ATMs.

Even though banks are making a concerted effort to upgrade the safety features of automated teller machines, withdrawing cash from ATMs may be hazardous to your health—especially at night, when most ATM crimes occur. Beware of ATMs in isolated locations, and watch for anyone who looks suspicious. Get in your car and drive away without using the ATM if you feel uneasy. Don't stand around fumbling with large wads of cash while you search for your keys or balance your checkbook; in other words, take the money, put it in your pocket or purse quickly, and leave. If you're held up in spite of all precautions, hand over the money.

Watch Who is Watching You.

Watch out also for so-called "shoulder surfers" who stand behind you and watch you punch in your personal identification number (PIN), which allows them access to your account. Cover the keypad with your free hand when punching in your numbers, and always take your receipt—which also gives valuable information to a would-be thief—with you.

(Note that shoulder surfers can also set their sights on your long-distance calling card number, which they later sell on the street, so keep your card hidden from possible observers when making calls in public places.)

If you're truly freaked out by the idea of using an ATM at night, be aware that many L.A. police stations have installed ATMs in their lobbies as part of a pilot program to discourage thieves and offer ATM users more security than they might find at the average bank. The program was expected to expand throughout the city in 1995. Call your nearest LAPD station for more information.

Watch Out for Pickpockets.

Travelers in airports or other bustling locations (such as hotel lobbies) run the risk of being victimized by pickpockets who use a variety of ruses to distract them while lifting their wallet, purse or baggage. Watch out for seemingly innocent distractions (such as someone spilling a large amount of change on the ground, then soliciting your help in picking it up), hang onto everything you're carrying that is valuable, and don't accept help from strangers who may offer to help carry your luggage.

Use Common Sense.

Just as you would in any other city, you should use common-sense measures for avoiding crime in L.A., such as locking your car doors when you're on the road, staying out of high-crime neighborhoods, and not wandering the streets at night with large pocketfuls of cash and undue amounts of expensive jewelry hanging around your neck. Call 911 for assistance if you need help.

Summer and Smog:
A Look at L.A. Weather

When *Los Angeles* magazine published its "300 Reasons Not to Pack Up and Leave L.A." in April of 1994, the number one reason was this: No blizzards. Not that anyone needed reminding. Good weather has been luring people to California since the first time Midwesterners and East Coast dwellers realized that the sun was shining in California while they were buried in snow.

Smog

Late-night talk show host David Letterman, shooting a week of shows in L.A., once remarked in his opening monologue that the local weatherman had predicted an air quality rating of "good" for the following day. "What that means," Dave quipped, "is that every healthy adult in L.A. can set their respirator on 'LOW.'"

While this little jest drew wails of laughter from the appreciative audience, there are a lot of people that don't see anything funny about L.A.'s smog problem.

Smog, of course, is that nasty mixture of god-knows-what that contaminates the air above L.A., then stoops low enough to invade the respiratory system of every living creature and leaves a dingy deposit on everything else, from shrubbery to billboards to freeway signs. The term is derived from the words "smoke" and "fog," but the fact is that fog is often an innocent bystander in the smog situation.

The brownish haze over L.A. is in fact mostly made up of all sorts of emissions of potentially poisonous fumes and other chemicals such as carbon monoxide, hydrocarbons, ozone, benzene, nitric acid, and a whole lot of other stuff that you don't want to know about.

Smog forms when high pressure over the city effectively puts a cap on the air above L.A., keeping air-born impurities from escaping into the upper atmosphere. This so-called "inversion layer" has the same effect as putting a lid on a bowl, and, unfortunately, the "bowl" is the Los Angeles Basin.

As bad as the smog problem is in L.A., in 1990 the air was estimated to be 60 percent cleaner than it was during the 1950s, when the Firestone Tire plant and other heavy smog contributors were in full operation in the city. The 1993 smog season (yes, there really is a smog season in L.A. - it runs from May-October) recorded the fewest "smog alert" days in 40 years, and 1994 was just as good (relatively speaking), prompting city officials to point to the downturn as a sign that things are improving.

This may be small consolation to those who spend the summer in L.A. feeling like their lungs are being ripped out, but clean air advocates say it's at least a start in the long-term process of making the sky blue again in the L.A. Basin. (And it will be a long-term process. In 1994, the EPA estimated that it will be the year 2010 before the city is able to meet federally approved pollution standards.)

Smog

Trouble is, although everyone suffers when smog levels are high, not many are willing to make personal sacrifices to do anything about it. Cutting down on the number of cars on the road doesn't have much appeal to most L.A. residents, who have a love affair with their cars and can't fathom the idea of being in a carpool or taking public transportation. There has been all sorts of wrangling between local, state and federal officials trying to implement Congress' 1977 Clean Air Act, but a solution does not seem near at hand.

In a stunning announcement made in August of 1994, the South Coast Air Quality Management District (AQMD) revealed that more than 6000 local restaurants would have to do their part in reducing smog by controlling smoke from griddles, grills and fryers, a move that might cost each offending establishment anywhere from $5000 to $30,000. Needless to say, local fast-food chains went ballistic, claiming that they couldn't possibly comply without jeopardizing their businesses, or—at the very least—passing the cost on to consumers with significant price increases.

The AQMD is also working on special smog sensors on L.A. freeways that will measure the emission level of cars as they pass by. If the pollution level is high, the sensor will record the vehicle's license number, and the owner will be notified to bring the offending car in for service. Failure to comply would mean a stiff fine.

In the meantime, motorists who spot a vehicle that is obviously a polluter can report the license number to 1-800-CUT-SMOG, which receives more than 100,000 calls a year from anonymous "smog police."

While baby steps are being taken to solve the smog problem, it doesn't appear that anything is going to change anytime soon, so smog is a force you will have to reckon with when visiting L.A. Be aware that smog is worse in summer than winter, and that you can almost always find a respite from air pollution along the coast, which—because of the cooler air and sea breezes—is one of the few places where you can escape polluted air.

If your lungs are especially sensitive, watch the weather report on any local network, which always includes information on the next day's expected smog levels. If there is a first-stage alert (smog levels of 100 or higher), you should consider curtailing active sports activities such as jogging, cycling or tennis, especially if you have asthma or other respiratory problems.

Although you can't do much about the outside air you breathe in L.A. County, the Board of Supervisors has tried to make life easier on the respiratory system by passing some of the toughest anti-smoking laws in the country. Currently, smoking is banned in all city-owned buildings, as well as in workplaces and enclosed restaurants (bars are exempt), a great relief to those concerned about drawing a clean breath of fresh air. (Chain-smoking actor Liam Neeson, perhaps best known for his role in Shindler's List, was reportedly so disgusted with the severity of L.A.'s anti-smoking laws that he decided to settle in New York to avoid the "insidiousness" of the West Coast's "anti-smoking brigade.")

(It's only fair to note, however, that some—generally East Coast snobbish types—see this weather business as highly overrated. Playwright Neil

Simon is reputed to have said the following on the subject: "When it's 20 below in New York, it's 78 in L.A. When it's 110 in New York, it's 78 in L.A. Of course, there are 8 million interesting people in New York, and only 78 in L.A.")

AVG. TEMPERATURES IN L.A.

	Jan.	Feb.	Mar.	Apr.	May	June	July	Aug.	Sept.	Oct.	Nov.	Dec.
Lows	46°	48°	50°	52°	55°	58°	61°	60°	58°	54°	50°	47°
Highs	65°	66°	67°	70°	72°	76°	81°	82°	81°	76°	73°	67°
Days With No Rain	25	22	25	26	29	29	31	31	29	29	27	25

Average low and high temperatures by month (in Farenheit)

Generally, the weather in L.A. is fabulous, as anyone who has ever looked out over the crystal-clear, windswept skyline will tell you. (Wind-sweeping is generally required in L.A. to ensure crystal-clearness). Statistically, the city offers approximately 142 clear days, 115 partly cloudy days, and 107 cloudy days a year, which means it's totally, unalterably sunny a little more than a third of the time. The humidity ranges between 65 and 77 percent, except on extremely foggy days or when southerly winds push tropical influences north and the city feels more like Mexico than L.A. The annual rainfall average is about 12 inches, but, like the rest of Southern California, L.A. has recently experienced both serious drought and exceptionally rainy years. The latter are often influenced by the presence of "El Nino," a current that waxes and wanes from year to year, warming the Pacific Ocean and increasing both the number and severity of California storms when it lingers.

Sea Breezes and Devil Winds

The chain of greater L.A. cities that runs along the Pacific coastline is almost literally L.A.'s salvation. Even in summer and early fall–the warmest times of the year–cool breezes blow in from the west, making the beaches a respite from hot temperatures and stifling air farther inland.

Although they are also subject to the "marine layer" that drapes them in dense fog, especially in the spring and early summer, L.A.'s beaches are arguably the most consistently gorgeous places (weather-wise, anyway) in greater L.A. Ah, yes. Those swaying palm trees, bikini-clad beauties, surfer dudes, and aquamarine waters dotted with sailboats.

Sea Breezes and Devil Winds

So-called Santa Ana (or "devil") winds are another matter altogether. These hot, dry gusts—which typically blow from 15 to 40 miles an hour but sometimes reach hurricane-level velocities of up to 100 miles an hour—slam into Southern California from the north/northeast when high air pressure builds up in the deserts of California, Arizona, Nevada, and Utah and the warmed air makes a rush for the sea. This phenomenon can drive temperatures well into the hundreds, and is nearly always a factor in pushing brush fires (many of which are arson-set) beyond the limits of firefighters to control. Santa Anas usually happen in summer or fall, and have been blamed for a variety of strange happenings over the years, including an alleged five-hour, high-temperature reading of 133 degrees near Santa Barbara in 1859, a phenomenon that reportedly caused birds to fall from the sky and cattle to drop dead in the fields.

Finally, it is inevitable that at least one high pressure system will park itself over Southern California during the summer, blocking cool ocean breezes and driving air high in the atmosphere downward, where it heats up and can be unrelenting. In this case, even beach temperatures can soar into the 100s, and basically everyone in the city is hot and cranky—except the owners of local ice and air conditioning companies, who invariably sell out everything they've got.

You almost never need a heavy coat in L.A., which is a good thing because most local trendites would find it absolutely unbearable if they had to go traipsing around town with their designer wardrobe hidden under a ton of insulation. Not to mention the problems that a severe winter would cause L.A.'s luxury convertible owners, who are used to speeding down the freeway, hair flying in the wind as they make big movie deals on their cellular phones.

LA KULTURE

"Good evening. I'm Tim, your waiter, and this is Andy, who'll be putting pepper on everything."

L.A. is a big city. Although L.A. proper is hard to define to the tourist, L.A. is that massive sprawl of development on the Pacific Ocean that bumps up against the San Gabriel Mountains in the North and the San Bernardinos, the San Jacintos to the east. If it weren't for the artificial barrier of Camp Pendleton Marine Base south of San Clemente, the sprawl would continue all the way to Tijuana.

Although there are officially only 3.5 million people here, if you add in all the surrounding 'burbs, towns and tote up all the illegal immigrants and commuters, Los Angeles is the largest urban center in the United States with 13.5 million people. Southern California is the largest single business marketplace in America. The entire metropolitan area covers 34,000 sq. miles. Inside L.A. County's seamless patchwork are 88 incorporated cities that represent the pinnacle of American success and the depths, from Beverly Hills to Wilmington. Inside this vast basin is a melting pot of the new ethnic mix. No longer Iowa with palms L.A. The formerly waspy look of the California Girl or the Surfer Boy is more likely to be Latino, Black or Asian. Caucasians are about 40 percent of the population here. Latino (36 percent), African-American (11.2 percent) and Asian (10.4 percent) are the new mix. Many new ethnic groups can be found in Koreatown, Little Saigon, Chinatown, Little Tokyo or the Latino stronghold of East Los Angeles and the black centers of South–Central L.A.

This new mix is appropriate considering our central position in the Pacific Rim, the new trading center that straddles the Pacific along with Canada and Mexico. The Pacific Rim has long replaced Europe as the U.S.' largest trading region.

The visitor to L.A. should not try to bite off too much on any one visit. Better to put together a mix of eclectic and mainstream activities.

The visitor must learn to separate the scores of smaller cities, towns and neighborhoods that are contained within L.A.'s boundaries.

Travel writer Stephen Brook perhaps hit it on the head when he called L.A. an "urban omelette;" if you're new to the city, however, it's going to look a whole lot more like scrambled eggs.

Residents of greater L.A, whose cumulative miles of driving on any given day total about 150 million, don't seem to mind zooming from one end of town to the other in search of the perfect beach, steak or late-night scene—but you might. For this reason, we have divided Los Angeles into five specific areas that we think will help you in sorting out the options in order to make sure that where you stay is reasonably close to what you want to see and do. Each section includes an introduction followed by listings of local sightseeing and entertainment options, hotels and restaurants, putting everything you need to know about L.A.'s various enclaves at your fingertips.

What Makes L.A. Different?

1) Nobody walks in L.A.

Imagine this town without cars. Nah, the imagery doesn't work. Hey that sounds like a great idea for a screenplay. Half of the mass of L.A. is cars and the roads required to move them around. Nobody motors here, we hit the freeways. Do the drive. Make the commute. Here distances are measured in time and time has no meaning, unless it involves a parking meter. Everybody is late and the freeways are slower than a side street and a SIG Alert is not a Swedish manhunt.

The 405 turns into the 5. The 405 is actually called the San Diego Freeway. Unless of course you want to go to Sacramento, then it is still called the San Diego Northbound. Stay off the freeways between 4:30 and 7 p.m. Always be 15 minutes late. Carpooling requires two or three people.

Cars below $10,000 are never washed, cars above are detailed and valet parked. A car is as necessary to life in L.A. as cabs are to New York City. In any case, here are the few places you can actually walk in L.A.:

Hollywood Boulevard

Under the gum and spray paint is the only solid proof that many of these celebrities actually existed. The trouble is you buy your way to immortality here. Ahh! Hollywood. Call the Hollywood Information Line ☎ *(213) 469-8311* to find out who will be the next minor celebrity whose publicist has plunked down the dough for his or her 15 minutes of fame.

Universal Citywalk:

Take Hollywood Freeway (101) to Lankershim, Cahuenga or Barham Boulevard exit. 11 a.m.–11 p.m. daily. ☎ *(818) 622-4455.*
A make-believe street with genetic mutant replicas of other streets. Bring your industrial strength credit card. Who says shopping isn't entertainment? The Main Street USA for the '90's.

El Pueblo de Los Angeles & Olvera Street

You won't have too far to walk since most of historic L.A. was razed in the '50s. But squint real hard and you can pretend you are in Tijuana.

Venice Beach

You can walk but it would be more appropriate if you rented Rollerblades.Venice Beach is the most overworked cliché for Los Angeles. Ideal for first–time visitors, a bit tedious for locals.

South Bay Strand

The best place to walk in L.A. Covering three piers from Manhattan Beach to Palos Verdes. It can feel like an expressway on Sundays, complete with flashing yellow lights and speed limits.

Santa Monica's 3rd Street Promenade

L.A.'s best (and only) attempt at a pedestrian-friendly street that finally gives up at the south end and turns itself into a shopping mall.

2) L.A. is an attitude.

Nothing is "in" or "hot" but it is "happening," "righteous" or "way bitchin'." Everything in L.A. is cool or scary. Close friends are referred to as dudes, homeys or significant others. People here have relationships, then get married and move away. People from back home visit and wonder why everybody doesn't live here. Riots, earthquakes, fires, mass murders and floods are PR stories designed to keep Iowa from being emptied out the day after the Rose Bowl. Those leather–clad guys on Harleys are accountants and lawyers. Lunch, meetings and drugs are "done," not eaten, attended or taken. "Let's do lunch" really means I like you but you're a flake. "I'll call you" means get lost and "Let's do sushi" means the beginning of serious commitment. Now you are a homey. Never take your sunglasses off and a 38 is a bullet calibre, not a bra size. If you want to get past the veneer and hang with the real Angelenos, head to:

Grand Central Public Market

317 South Broadway
Los Angeles
☎ *(213) 624-2378*

3) You can die in L.A.

A "G" thing is not a monetary denomination or a religion, but it is a gangster thing. L.A. can be a bad place. If you want to live and die in L.A., here are two of our most dangerous places.

South Bureau

Mayhem anyone? Along a tiny industrial, poor housing strip that runs beside the Harbor freeway lies L.A.'s most dangerous place. How about 429 murders, 502 rapes, 9650 robberies and a whopping 12,914 aggravated assaults per year? The area bounded by 79th, Hoover, Broadway and Florence is the nexus of the violent vortex.

Central Bureau

The parched, bleached area east of downtown has its own daunting statistics: 342 murders, 408 rapes, 11,898 robberies and 11,975 aggravated assaults. Anyone with a calculator can figure out that you need plenty of fodder to keep those stats up. The tiny triangle where the Pasadena Freeway is bordered by the 101 and Alameda is "Allstate hell" with 221 robberies last year.

4) You can be famous in L.A.

Millionaires are the ones dressed like surfers, surfers are the ones who dress like homeless people (but with more tattoos), suburban kids dress like Compton gang bangers and the people with the cardboard signs at freeway entrances and airports are actually the people who used to design Star War systems and B2 bombers.

Television writers make around $350,000 a year thinking up gags for ex-stand-up comics. Stand-up comics become talk show interviewers. Talk show interviewers become television pitchmen. Television pitchmen become producers who hire young stand-up comics to host game shows. The wheel turns.

If you want to see the comics who become the writers, who become the stars, who become the interviewers, who become the moguls try:

The Comedy & Magic Club

1018 Hermosa Avenue, Hermosa Beach, ☎ *(310) 372-1193*
Hours: Tues.–Fri. 8–10 p.m.; Sat. 8–10:30 p.m.;
Sun. 12:30 p.m.—Kids' Matinee;
and a 7 p.m. evening show.
Reservations required.
Jay Leno actually performs here on a regular basis (usually a Sunday night) to keep in touch with the real America.

5) L.A. has bad vibes.

When someone says they had a 6.7 last night, it is neither his or her boy-friend, the alcoholic content of his or her drink nor the displacement of his or her car. Earthquakes help everyone remember exactly where they were the last time it happened. The "big one" is coming. People discuss their most recent burglaries as being cool or uncool depending upon the conduct of the robber. We invented carjacking because too damned few people walk around anymore. We invented drive-by shootings because the bus service sucks. And we invented freeway shootings because all Angelenos are entitled to express themselves.

Fires are God's way of selling tile roofs. Earthquakes keep the flatlanders away. Riots are society's way of redistributing luxury goods and poverty just makes the middle class work harder. Best place to feel the earth move:

The Salton Trough
Take the 5 freeway south to Highway 78, go inland to Highway 86.
The Coachello and Imperial Valley areas around the Salton Sea are the real home of rock and roll. The Salton Trough is the most seismically active area in the U.S. There are 11,000 measurable tremors per year in this remote desert area (that's about one earthquake every 48 minutes). Faults in this area have caused over 20 magnitude 6.0 quakes since 1989.

6) L.A. is a nice place to live.

The sun always shines in L.A., you just can't see it for the smog, marine layer, rain or buildings. Nobody talks about the weather here. It's always perfect. Angelenos go to the desert for sun, San Francisco for culture and San Diego for vacations. Los Angeles is the baddest, greatest, fastest, hardest, rockin'est town in the Western Hemisphere. If you can't take the heat, step aside. There's a thousand more who'll take your place. God, I love L.A.

Angelenos tell their friends they wouldn't live anyplace else. They can't. The houses they bought for $500,000 are now only worth $350,000.

7) L.A. is a great place to escape from.

Head for the Pacific Ocean. Head for the desert, head for the mountains, head for Mexico, head for anyplace that lets you get your head together.

8) Conspicuous consumption is still in fashion.

USC grads still drive red BMWs with USC GRAD license plate frames. Silver haired producers still drive around in Rolls Royce convertibles with the top down, and the newly rich still shop in Beverly Hills. It's more than a ZIP code, more than a great TV show title. More than a diet, it's the last bastion of the nouveau riche. The most spectacular example of conspicuous consumption since Camille met Armand.

Insiders adopt the defenses of the truly rich and famous. Shop hard but never buy. Make 'em grovel. Ask them what color Julia or Arnold bought. Never take your sunglasses off. Best place to not buy anything but try everything on:

Fred Hayman
273 North Rodeo Drive, ☎ *(310) 271-3000*
Mon.–Fri. 10 a.m.–6:30 p.m.; Sat. 10 a.m.–6 p.m.; Sun. 12 noon–6 p.m.
Forget Gucci. Forget Bijan. Chanel who? Move on down Rodeo to the only store we know that serves complimentary wine at an oak bar

and has a pool table for idling away the split seconds between bodware of the hottest, newest, youngest designers in town. There's even a fireplace to keep your credit cards warm.

9) Where fashion is conspicuous.

I hope you don't think you can just pack shorts and a T-shirt and fit in in L.A. On any 90 degree day you will find the well dressed Angeleno outfitted in basic black complete with Levis, leather and tattoos. Preferred mode of transport is via V-Twin or '60s era convertible. Here in the capital of sun and fun real fashion hurts. More pierced flesh than a Malaysian *sate* vendor, more tattoos than a Grade A butcher shop, more army boots than a Russian division and more Harleys than Milwaukee. Here trash costs dearly, used cowboy boots go for $200, and ripped and faded jeans will set you back about $60. Hamburgers in faux '50s diners are the choice of sustenance and Ray Bans rule. Melrose Avenue is the place where "trendy" became a verb. Unlike the glitz of Rodeo Drive, Melrose is boutique *noire*. Shops are the most compelling in town. Best place to buy trendy gear:

Retail Slut

> 7308 Melrose Avenue, ☎ (213) 934-1339
> Mon.–Thurs. 11 a.m.–7 p.m.; Fri.–Sat. 11 a.m.–9 p.m.; Sun. 1 p.m–7 p.m.
> Camp à la mode. Madonna's drop-in shop when she's overwhelmed by the urge to put something on—other than the world. This is where the slings and arrows of outrageous fashion come out of the closet and Kitchy embraces Tacky as if they had been separated at birth.

Best place to buy a strange souvenir:

Off the Wall

> 7325 Melrose, ☎ (213) 930-1185
> My favorite collection of wacky signs and homespun American icons. Can be considered a museum to American cultural fans.

10) Where everybody is famous.

L.A. is great. You've been stalking celebs at Spago, prowling Trancas Market, scoping out the Polo Lounge and even tried to scam "Tonight Show" tickets. But alas no celebs, no autographs. Dejected you wander into a nondescript greasy spoon for a bite, and whammo *Omygod* you are in the actual restaurant owned by Steven Spielberg's actual mother. Best undiscovered place to brag about discovering to your friends back home:

The Milky Way Restaurant

> 9108 West Pico Boulevard Los Angeles (west of Doheny); ☎ (310) 859-0009.
> Yes, this is the restaurant owned by Stephen Spielberg's mother. When we spoke to Mrs. Spielberg, she defined the place as "an upscale dairy restaurant." Splattered with posters of Spielberg movies. Park your tush, put on a pair of 3-D glasses and welcome to E.T.'s bar-mitzvah dinner: plate after plate of previously living life forms that actually resemble Chinese, Italian and American dishes.

Best Places to Hang Out and Feel the Vibes

1. Sunset Strip at Night

Sunset Boulevard from Doheny to Laurel Canyon Boulevard
Still strutting its stuff after all these years. Wall-to-wall paparazzi, comedy clubs, rock stars and more wanna-be's than in

a sperm bank. L.A.'s other classic cruise (besides PCH). Rock stars, movie stars, everything that's nighttime hip about the City of Angels. The best places to die of a cocaine overdose. Check out The Rainbow and The Roxy. Skip the Whisky, The Comedy Store, Club Lingerie— old, cold and closed, respectively.

2. Old L.A.: Union Station and Olvera Street

Union Station/800 North Alameda Street, Los Angeles.
Olvera Street/one block away in El Pueblo de los Angeles Historic Park, Los Angeles. For information: ☎ *(213) 628-1274.*
A time capsule of old Los Angeles. Union Station is a dark, moody, mission-style temple that conjures up the *Day of the Locust* rather than *The Player*. It's the closest thing Angelenos have to the Statue of Liberty. Up the street is the last trace of old Hispanic L.A. Stroll through this mini-Tijuana, buy a souvenir, have a Turista-Mex snack and wear your heartburn proudly.

3. Mann's Chinese Theater

6925 Hollywood Boulevard, Hollywood; ☎ *(213) 464-8111.*
Footprints, handprints of the stars. If you have time for a movie, this is the place to see it. Don't for a moment think it's too corny. Just go.

4. The View from Mulholland Drive

Go north from corner of Sunset and Crescent Heights Blvds. and don't come down until you reach Beachwood Canyon.
Find a designated driver so nothing interrupts you from staring out the window.

5. Huntington Library and Art Gallery

1151 Oxford Road, San Marino; ☎ *(818) 405-2141.*
A shrine to bookdom in San Marino (near Pasadena). Cappuccino bars, a Gutenberg Bible, bookstores with classical music, here a Blue Boy, there a Dead Sea Scroll, a couple of hundred acres blooming with botany and thousands of gray-haired intellectuals.

6. Beach L.A.—Venice

Coming from L.A., turn left at the water.
No Californians here, only people from Wisconsin who are discovering themselves. They juggle chainsaws, play Jimi Hendrix while rollerblading, have heads smaller than their necks and desperately search for a pair of cheap sunglasses. They've gone as far as they can go, there's no more America from which to escape. And, of course, there are tourists staring at tourists staring at tourists staring at tourists.

7. The Beit Hashoah Museum of Tolerance

9786 West Pico Boulevard, Los Angeles; ☎ *(310) 553-9036.*
Mon.–Thurs. 10 a.m.–5 p.m.; Fri. 10 a.m.–3 p.m.; Sun. 10:30 a.m.–5 p.m.
$7.50/advance purchase recommended.
Eastern Germany in L.A. Housed in the Simon Weisenthal Center, no prisoners are taken in this required course in Bigotry and Racism 101. A devastating personal confrontation with the Holocaust via photographs of Auschwitz that make Diane Arbus about as dark as Norman Rockwell.

8. J. Paul Getty Museum

17985 Pacific Coast Highway, Santa Monica; ☎ *(310) 458-2003.*
Tue.–Sun. 10 a.m.–5 p.m.; free; call for reservations.

Ancient Rome in L.A. A Pompeiian villa reproduced on a hill over-looking Malibu, the symbolism of which is equally hard to overlook. Harry Truman was wrong: the buck stops here with more Greek and Roman stuff than an outdoor furniture catalog. A Van Gogh-for-broke collection. Pure L.A. Admissions are arranged as per available parking.

9. Watts Towers/Towers of Simon Rodia

1765 East 107th Street, Watts.

The only tourist attraction in the "real L.A." This "Heaven's Gate" of folk art took 33 years to finish and had no discernible plan other than a dream. Hundred-foot tall mosaics of shells, mirrors, broken dishes—the flotsam of Watts that serves as an optimistic vision for the jetsam of Watts that "they" are worth salvaging.

10. Max Factor Beauty Museum and Cosmetic Outlet

1666 North Highland Avenue; ☎ *(213) 463-6668.*
Mon.–Sat. 10 a.m.–4 p.m.; free

Located in the landmark Max Factor Building, this is where superstars since the '30s have been led into transformation. Our favorite exhibit: headblocks of the rich and famous that were used to create wigs and toupees. But best of all, you can buy MF cosmetics at up to 70 percent off retail.

11. Doing Pacific Coast Highway (PCH)

Not a drug, but close. Rent a convertible at Rent-a-Wreck (☎ *(800) 622-9090; 4111 Redondo Beach Boulevard; Lawndale*—about a 15–minute cab ride from LAX; Chrysler LeBaron convertible at $49.95 a day), Hertz Rent A Car at LAX (☎ *(310) 568-3400, 9000 Airport Boulevard*; Ford Mustang convertibles—they won't commit to specific rates for publication. A reservation clerk stated that rates go up as availability goes down and it would be $50 a day or more, if available at all.), or at any major car rental spot. Head west and then north. Drive slow, wave a lot. Cruise through Santa Monica, Malibu, Trancas, Point Dume, on up to Santa Barbara. Or head south through the South Bay. Do not pass GO. Take the scenic drive around Palos Verdes Peninsula to Long Beach and then hit the Harbor Freeway, then 405 back to L.A.

12. Behind doors L.A.—The Club Scene—wild and mild

From gay to just very happy there's no one list of L.A.'s happening clubs, Mexican transvestite bars, cowboy gay bars, leather, line dancing, biker bars, country & western, Latin dancing, Royal Order of Moose, retro disco, techno, Latvian, funk, techno-funk, hard rock, rap, jazz, comedy and more. Just hang, react and go for it. Here are a few places to start your quest:

Best Art Bar:

Al's Bar

305 South Hewitt Street, Los Angeles, ☎ *(213) 687-3558.*
For more than 10 years, the best bar for artists. Dirty, noisy, covered with graffiti. The literature found written on the bathroom walls is worth the trip. Our staff prefer the women's approach to self-expression.

Best '70s Retro:

The Crush Bar

1743 Cahuenga Boulevard, Los Angeles, ☎ *(213) 463-7685.*
The seventies never went away for some folks, but did we really look that stupid?

Best Low Culture, Mainstream Joint:

The Palace

1735 North Vine, Hollywood, ☎ *(213) 462-3000.*
Wanna groove with the working folks? Get married, settle down and plan our future. Great for bottom feeders and snaggers.

Best Cowboy Bars:

Cowboy Palace Saloon

21635 Devonshire Street, Chatsworth, ☎ *(818) 341-0166.*
A long way out from downtown, but if you are into country and western, this is the place. Live country seven nights a week.

Longhorn Saloon

21211 Sherman Way, Canoga Park, ☎ *(818) 340-4788.*
One of the two last real cowboy bars in L.A. The other one is listed above.

Best Original Unplugged Venue:

McCabe's

3101 Pico Boulevard, Santa Monica, ☎ *(310) 828-4497.*
Store hours: Mon.-Thurs. 10 a.m. to 10 p.m.
Fri.–Sat. 10 a.m.–6 p.m., Sun. 1 p.m. to 5 p.m.
For the best in unplugged guitar music, whether it be folk, rock, bluegrass, try McCabe's. McCabe's is a music store with a back room for intimate concerts. While you're waiting, you can hang out in the store with local musicians. Also an excellent place for that authentic guitar transcription you may have looked for everyplace else.

Concerts are usually Fridays and Saturdays after the shop closes. Prices range from $15 to $20.

Best Gay Club:

Rage

8911 Santa Monica Boulevard, West Hollywood, ☎ *(310) 652-7055.*
Hours: 1 p.m. till 2 a.m.
The premier, flashy, high profile gay men's bar. Check for cover.

Best Ex-Lesbian Bar:

Jewel's Catch One

4067 West Pico, Los Angeles, ☎ *(213) 734-8849.*
Hours: 3 p.m.-2 a.m. (Wed. until 3 a.m., 4 a.m. on weekends)
Predominantly gay, some lesbian, some mixed, with three dance floors, four bars, 20 video screens, pool tables, video arcade, karaoke, drag shows. Check for cover charge.

Best Lesbian Bar:

The Palms

8572 Santa Monica Boulevard, West Hollywood, ☎ *(310) 652-6188.*
Hours: 12 noon–2 a.m., Sun.–Sat.
Lesbian bar/all welcome; dancing, Top 40, dancing.

Best Place To See "What Ever Happened To?" Musicians:

The Normandie Casino

1045 West Rosecrans Avenue, Gardena, ☎ *(310) 352-3400.*
Just about every one-hit wonder and late-night TV album artists can
be found here on weekends. Shows start at 8 & 10:30 p.m. $20 a pop,
plus two-drink minimum. Gamble Southern Cal style until the show
starts.

13. Breakfast and biking in the South Bay

Sunday morning, hung over, crunching Anacin. Time to eat at Joe's
or Martha's or Good Stuff. Pecs, glutes, buns, boobs, babes, dudes
and rays all come together in the original land of the Beach Boys. No
ectomorphs allowed. Carb up, work out, hydrate and groove on the
endorphins. Bring your brand-name exercise wear, eyeglasses, your
latest T-shirt with the correct political cause and you are in like flint.
Breakfast is never eaten before 11 and never without a two-hour wait.
Afterward, hit the Rollerblades or strand cruisers (no mountain bikes
please) and cause retinal tears with your fish-belly white skin. (Caution: They give out speeding tickets for bicyclists.)

Best Place To Eat Breakfast Outdoors On Sunday Morning:

Martha's

2203 Hermosa Avenue, Hermosa Beach, ☎ *(310) 379-0070.*

14. Tourist L.A.—Disneyland/Knotts Berry Farm/Universal Studios/Magic Mountain/Southwest Museum

Need a little '50s entho-wasp culture? See the mouse, be attacked by
the giant ape, have an earthquake, be attacked by pirates, watch Roy
Rogers videos, see Michael Jackson touch himself in 3-D (Oops!
Sorry, he's canceled.), movies, magic and your grandparent's version
of California. We locals are coerced into visiting these money vacuums
when our relatives arrive from out of town. The least we can do is
have a little fun not going to them.

Best Rides For Ex-hippies:

Pirates of the Caribbean (on acid)

Space Mountain (on uppers)

Universal Studios (on television)

Best Museum For Rednecks:

Gene Autry Western Museum

4700 Zoo Drive in Griffith Park, Los Angeles, ☎ *(213) 667-2000.*
Hours: Tues.–Sun. 10 a.m.–5 p.m. $6 admission.
Cowboys, guns, Indians, lunch boxes and more guns.

Best Theater

Actor's Gang Theater

6209 Santa Monica Boulevard, Hollywood, ☎ *(213) 466-1767.*
Hours: Thurs.–Sun. 8 p.m. Prices range from $12 to $15. Call for reserva-
tions.
The Actor's Gang is a top-notch troupe under the direction of Tim
Robbins. They do original productions and repertory pieces with a
twist (Cassandra with her own psychic hotline). The performances are
stellar, the price is cheap and sometimes you can see Susan Sarandon
in the audience.

Best Tours

Warner Brothers Studio Tour

4000 Warner Boulevard, Burbank, ☎ (818) 954-1744.
Open Mon.–Fri. Tours are two hours, call for times. Phone one hour before tour to make reservations.

Forget about the NBC tour and Spago. If you want to see real movie-making and actors, try the Warner Brothers Studio Tour. This is a real working studio. Tours are restricted to 12 people (children under 10 are not admitted). In addition to backlots, craft production studios and soundstages, you may see actors such as Candice Bergen, Kevin Costner and Robert Wagner hard at work and you may receive a copy of the script they're shooting that day.

Los Angeles Conservancy

Roosevelt Building, 727 West Seventh Street, Suite 955, Los Angeles, ☎ (213) 623-2489.
Cost: $5. Call ahead for reservations.

Would you like to see the theater where Bette Midler filmed *Gypsy* or where Kenneth Branagh filmed *Dead Again?* Maybe you'd like to see the real L.A. Law building or Union Station, one of the last great American railway stations. The Los Angeles Conservancy sponsors walking tours of downtown L.A. Members of the conservancy are experts on architecture and the history of Los Angeles. You never knew that L.A. could be so safe or have so much culture, did you?

15. Most Overrated L.A. Experiences.

L.A. has a bad habit of being not only rude to its guests but charging them a lot of money while doing so. The '80s are over, so strike a blow for the cause and spend your money where they appreciate it. Attitude shouldn't sell by the pound here.

Disneyland/Knott's Berry Farm/Universal Studios

"The '50s are over, can I have my money back?" The best and newest ride at the mouse house is Indiana Jones and the Temple of Cashflow. Cliché lovers take note: There is no such thing as an "E" ticket ride.

Hollywood:

The dark, aging side of tinseltown. Hanging around Hollywood and Vine means you're lost.

Spago:

"Oh we'll just split a pizza. Whoa! *How* much for a pizza?!"

The Comedy Store:

"Ha Ha, whoa, *how much* for those beers?"

Fielding Guide to L.A. Restaurants

First, it was The Brown Derby and Romanoff's. Then, Chasen's, Scandia and Ma Maison. Enter Wolfgang Puck and restaurants graduated from venues for star-gazing to star-grazing. L.A. discovered it had the one thing everyone said it lacked—taste. Today, in the very same town (can you hear Robin Leach's voice?) that buys paintings by Elke Sommer and books by Joan Collins, you can eat at least as well, and often better, than anywhere else. If you want to conserve calories (and your wallet), make sure you make a short list of L.A.'s best restaurants:.

Grown-Up Meals

Patina
> (best L.A. French)

Chinois on Main
> (best L.A. Far Out)

Bel-Air Hotel
> (best L.A. Old Money)

Ca'Brea
> (best L.A. Cal-Ital)

Rockenwagner
> (best of the Young Turks)

Best Breakfasts

Gladstone's

Hugo's

Duke's

Roscoe's Chicken and Waffles

John O'Groats
> and (Sigh)

The Bel-Air Hotel

Best Ethnics

(Restaurants that generally don't have chefs—they have cooks. And only the I.N.S. knows their names.)

El Cholo
> (Mex-Mex)

Canter's
> (Deli)

Georgia
> (Movie Star Soul)

Yujean Kang's
> (Pasadena Chinese)

Mon Kee's
> (Downtown L.A. Chinese)

Matsuhisa
> (Japanese—breaks all the rules: has a great chef, costs a fortune and is worth it.)

Best Fast Food/Snacks

Apple Pan
> (Burgers)

Pink's
> (Hot dogs)

Jody Maroni's
> (Sausages)

Benita's Frites

(Fries)

Farfalla On La Brea

(Pizza)

Stan's

in Westwood (Buttermilk Donuts)

Kokomo

in the Farmer's Market (Sandwiches)

Memorabilia Hollywoodiana

The Official Recipe for the Coconut Grove Cocktail

2 oz. dry gin

1/2 oz. maraschino liqueur

dash of lime juice

dash of grenadine

Pour over cracked ice, shake, strain and serve

Fielding's Top Authentic L.A. Eats

OK. We confess, we don't travel with a tuxedo or our own mother-of-pearl caviar spoon. We also know that most of these high-brow culinary meccas are full of New Yorkers and agents. Like all serious travelers we tire quickly of the cold precision of culinary perfection. In order to understand the real gustatory standards of a city you have to rub elbows with the locals, pass the sugar, tip a quarter or even do a "drive thru" once in a while.

So let's get authentic. We're not talking retro here (faux '50s) or trying to be cute (sawdust on the floor) or even overly upscale (scrawny models fronting bizarre decor) or even pandering to the hip (eco-ethno-new age-veggie-southwest-tofu bars). We want to get real. Real food, like the kind your mama would make if you grew up in a sand-blown trailer park in Azusa.

You already know where to find the expensive tourist places found in every other guidebook and you probably dropped enough of your expense account money in Beverly Hills to pay off the national debt. So when it comes to your time we're also watching your pocketbook. Where do you get guaranteed heartburn and sit in amazement at the real L.A.? Here are some of my favorite picks:

1) The Old Place

29983 Mulholland Drive, Agoura Hills, ☎ (818) 706-9001.
Hours: Open Thurs., Fri., Sat.

They don't come like this anymore. Steamed clams, steak over an open fire. Prices around $14. Building is more than 100 years old and it looks it.

2) The Rock Store

30354 West Mulholland, Agoura Hills, ☎ (818) 889-1311.
Hours: Fri.–Sat. 10 a.m.–6 p.m., Sun. 7 a.m.–7 p.m.
Weekend motorcycle hot spot. Jay Leno can be seen here. Outdoor barbecue pit. The oak tree sports a beer opener, but they've clamped down on the drinking.

3) The Lawdogs

114 Sherman Way, Van Nuys, ☎ (818) 989-2220.
Hours: Open everyday: 10 a.m.–9 p.m.
Hot dog stand owned by a lawyer who drops by Wednesday nights at 7 p.m. to give free legal advice. Most popular item, a $1.68 chili dog named "The Judge."

4) Sunset Ranch/Viva's

3400 No. Beachwood Drive, Hollywood, ☎ (213) 464-9612.
A dusty old stable with gentle old plugs. On Fridays, take the ride at sunset to Viva's, a funky Mexican restaurant. The rate for the sunset ride is $30, not including your meal and drinks. After a few margaritas, you'll be glad the horses know their way back to the stables!

5) Father's Office

1018 Montana Avenue, Santa Monica, ☎ (310) 393-2337.
Hours: Mon.–Thurs. 3 p.m.–1:30 a.m., Fri.–Sun. 12 noon–1:30 a.m.
For those who think beer is a food group. Exclusively microbeers, 31 on tap. Largest display in Southern California. Too many yuppies now. Ask for Lou.

6) Formosa Cafe

7156 Santa Monica Boulevard, Hollywood, ☎ (213) 850-9050.
Call for hours.
Our favorite restaurant where we don't recommend the food. A dark creaking old diner with wall-to-wall celebrity glossies—Liz Taylor, Elvis, Frank Sinatra, Gregory Peck, Charles Bronson, Ronald Reagan. Bono from U2 is a regular. Menu is American and Chinese. They also have a vegetarian menu. A complete meal goes for about $12.95. Can you think of a better place to read *Day of the Locust* while picking through an overcooked BLT? No.

7) Papadakis Taverna

301 West Sixth Street, San Pedro, ☎ (310) 548-1186.
Men dance together and then smash plates. It's OK; they're Greek. Papadakis is a once a year treat for Angelenos tired of the veneer and face-lifted smiles of chichi restaurants. Get drunk (take a limo home), eat too much and dance.

8) Tokyo Delves

5239 Lankershim, North Hollywood, ☎ (818) 766-3868.
Open 6 p.m. to midnight; Fridays till 2 a.m.
All right, all right so I stuck in one trendy spot. I figured after all that greasy food cooked by people with hairy forearms it's time for a little change. This is *the* sushi place for the terminally hip. Japanese waiters are connected by headphones and choreographed to look like ducks in a shooting gallery. There are 15 kinds of cocktails, when you order one the waiter will make your drink and your night. He'll shake the

cocktail at the table, eyes bulging out of his head, and yell "Shake! Shake! Shake!" You gotta be there to appreciate it.

Tokyo Delves was started by a jazz musician. Music, or at least dancing is part of the experience. There's dancing on the tables, dancing in a conga line, dancing on the chairs. Try playing "Lucky Lamp." You dance on a chair, and if you dance hard enough to bounce your lamp off the table, you get a prize. Sometimes the sushi chef dances, too.

9) Sagebrush Cantina

23527 Calabasas Road, Calabasas, ☎ (818) 222-6062
Mon.–Fri. 11 a.m.–8:30 p.m. or till everybody goes home. Sat.–Sun.
9 a.m.–11 p.m.
Across from the AFTRA retirement home hospital.

Imagine sitting outdoors, in an enclosed patio surrounded with water misters to keep it cool even on a typically hot, summer day on the outskirts of the Valley. An expansive and impressive corral of Harleys outside, and lots of bikers, lots of babes, and lots of dudes inside. Very California.

Now add to that, the Mother of all Brunches. The brunch consists of numerous bars filled with numerous choices of pastas, waffles, salads, deserts, hot entrees, and a seafood bar, with crab legs, shrimp, and oysters and clams on the half-shell. Champagne and orange juice are also included, plus two free watermelon, pineapple or other fruit-flavored vodka shots.

All this happens every Sunday from 9 a.m.–2 p.m., more than enough time for any mortal to fill their bellies, soak up some sun and have a good time. Also, it's reasonably priced at $19.95 per person.

Most popular items during normal dining hours: the Sagebrush Burrito and the Chicken Tostada, $7.95. They also serve steaks and ribs, appetizers and nachos.

Live entertainment at night, classic rock and lots of Eagles music. "Good place to hang out, sit outside and munch on appetizers." Five-dollar cover charge on Sundays after the Brunch.

Where to See Celebrities

Coming to Los Angeles without seeing a celebrity is a little like going to Arizona and missing the Grand Canyon. After all, it's those tantalizing tidbits about Hollywood's rich and famous that keep you buying *People* magazine and watching those boring awards shows, isn't it? Face it: if Heather Locklear and/or Brad Pitt look that good on TV, imagine running into them in the grocery store, for heaven's sake.

Not that this is likely to happen. Most celebrities don't shop like normal people, dropping by the corner market for a quart of milk. No, they're much more "get outta my face" types, opting for private rooms in nightclubs and fitness clubs, driving along in cars or limos with severely tinted windows. Of course, there are times when they're more "in your face" types, such as at the aforementioned awards shows, when they hop out of limos onto red-carpeted walkways, smiling and waving to all of the "little people." This may or may not be what you had in mind.

Frankly, there are only a few choices for getting a close-up look at the Hollywood elite, and even then, we're not talking about a soul-searching conversation over lunch. We're talking about an "Omigosh, can you believe I actually saw him/her, and I could swear he/she turned and looked right into my eyes!!," an "I can't believe I'm standing on the very place where he/she lives/ once stood/danced/got sick/fell down/died/was buried," or an "I don't care if it isn't the real thing, it looks just like him/ her."

Here you go, folks. And good luck.

Overhyped celeb joints:

> While we are on the subject of stars, let's include those celeb spots that blatantly appeal to the chronically unhip.
>
> **The Viper** (Johnny Depp's place); **The Monkey Bar** (owned by Jack Nicholson); **Carroll O'Connor's Place** (owned by Archie Bunker?); **Glam Slam** (Prince's dance joint); **72 Market Street** (owned by Tony Bill & Dudley Moore); **Planet Hollywood** (purportedly owned, but definitely hyped, by Schwarzenegger, Stallone and Willis) and **Shatzi's** (Arnold's attempt at low-key hip) and, of course, the **Bel Air Hotel** (owned by the Sultan of Brunei); **Twin Palms** (owned by Kevin Costner); **Thunder Roadhouse** (owned by Peter Fonda & Dennis Hopper); and the latest version of freeze-dried American Culture: The **House of Blues** (hyped by Dan Aykroyd) the only "authentic" blues club where poor blacks will never break into the big time.
>
> **Note:** If any restaurant listing hypes celebs or lineups, run, do not walk, to the nearest McDonald's.

Current Movie Locations/ Studio Tapings

If you find out where stars are working, you can generally get a decent look without them freaking out because there are barriers between them and you (not to mention a lot of hefty body-guards). Go to the city of Los Angeles Film and Video Permit Office *(6922 Hollywood Boulevard, Suite 602)* at 8:30 in the morning and pick up a list of locations for the day's film, commercial and video shoots in the L.A. area. Pick out the ones that sound appealing, then show up and watch.

If your interest is in TV tapings, contact the networks them-selves (tickets are always free), or call Audiences Unlimited (☎ *(818) 506-0043*) or Audience Associates (☎ *(213) 467-4697*), which handle tickets (also free) for such popular shows as "Roseanne," "Mad About You," "Home Improvement," "Mur-phy Brown," "The Wayans Brothers," and "Friends."

No matter where you get your tickets, you'll soon find out that this is a rather complicated undertaking—and the process varies from place to place. You're advised to call the numbers listed for complete information (often recorded) regarding schedules, age limits (most shows admit children over 16 only, although there are a few exceptions), where and how to obtain tickets in person and/or by mail, and whether tickets are even available to your favorite show.

Network numbers for ticket information: ABC *(☎ (213) 644-7777);* CBS *(☎ (213) 852-2624);* Fox *(☎ (213) 856-1520,* during business hours); NBC *(☎ (818) 840-3537);* Paramount *(☎ (213) 956-5575;* will take reservations over the phone five working days before the actual taping).

And then there are, of course, the various studio tours, which often give you a look at whatever (and whoever) is shooting at the time. These include the Universal Studios Tour (which is more of an amusement park than a real look at filmmaking), the Warner Brothers VIP Studio Tour (one of the best), and a plethora of less interesting tours of the smaller studios.

DOWNTOWN

L.A.'s skyscraper building boom is on hold until the economy catches up.

Most tourists, especially if they're looking for the show biz angle on L.A., tend to avoid downtown Los Angeles. It's compact, busy and congested—especially during the week—and is generally far from the Hollywood scene (except for a few buildings that have turned up on television, such as City Hall, which was depicted as both Sgt. Friday's headquarters in "Dragnet" and Clark Kent's place of employment in the "Superman" TV series). A bit bedraggled and seedy, downtown L.A. is not often perceived as the sort of place for serious hanging out.

But that is changing. Currently in the process of putting on a new face, the downtown district is "coming back," according to developers who have forked over $64 million for an ambitious renovation project expected to be completed in 1996.

In November of 1993, the Los Angeles Convention Center completed a $500 million expansion, doubling its size to 810,000 square feet and making it the largest convention facility on the West Coast and one of the 10 largest in the country. This state-of-the-art showpiece is highlighted by two striking 150-

foot glass and steel lobby pavilions, and the interior contains several interesting works of art, including a a 40,000-square-foot terrazzo mosaic floor by local artist Alexis Smith depicting the Pacific Basin as seen from outer space. The new convention center nicely complements the mix of upscale apartments, shops, and office buildings that are being constructed as part of the downtown upgrade.

Fielding's Architectural Guide to L.A.

When you've tired of looking at all those normal buildings in the city, here are a few architectural wonders that are worth finding. (Note: bring your camera. The photos will make great conversation pieces.)

1. **The Dark Room**, *5370 Wilshire Boulevard. Designed by Marcus P. Miller and built in 1938, this photo-finishing store looks like a camera from the front, with a large porthole in the glass serving as the lens. There are new tenants in the building since its debut, of course, but the camera motif remains.*

2. **Coca-Cola Bottling Plant**, *1334 South Central Avenue. This is one of L.A.'s most famous buildings. Designed by Robert V. Derrah circa 1936, it looks like a giant ocean liner, complete with portholes, a ship's bridge, and metal railings.*

3. **Fleetwood Center**, *19611 Ventura Boulevard. Although this little piece of programmatic architecture was erected in 1987, it looks more like "back to the '60s." The face of the building is the front of a bright pink Cadillac, complete with double headlights and radiator.*

4. **Capitol Records Building**, *1750 Vine Street. This 12-story Hollywood landmark appropriately looks like a stack of old 45s. A mural of Capitol's most famous recording stars is painted on the first level.*

5. **First Hebrew Christian Church**, *northeast corner of North Chicago Street and East Michigan Avenue. This interesting structure was built in 1905 in a sort of Islamic/Near Eastern style. What catches your eye is the large sign on the roof that is in the shape of a giant open scroll.*

6. **Chiat/Day Ad Agency** *(northeast side of Main Street, between Brooks and Clubhouse, Venice). This modern (1985), Frank Gehry-designed building features a three-stories-high pair of giant binoculars sitting eyepiece-down on the pavement. (We told you to bring your camera.)*

7. **La Brea Tar Pits** *(5801 Wilshire Boulevard). You'll think you've gone back to the Flintstones' era when you see this huge mastodon rising up out of the muck. Go inside to see lots more cool stuff.*

8. **Hard Rock Cafe** *(8600 Beverly Boulevard). This mecca for rock memorabilia fans has a Cadillac sticking out of the front of it. Try to make up a story about how it got there to impress the kids.*

In contrast are the several historic buildings (including Sid Grauman's 1918 Million Dollar Theater) that are in the process of being restored to their original grandeur, helping to create a funky downtown ambience approximating that of New York's Greenwich Village. Angel's Flight, a landmark funicular railway dating from 1901, will also be resurrected, and will connect the

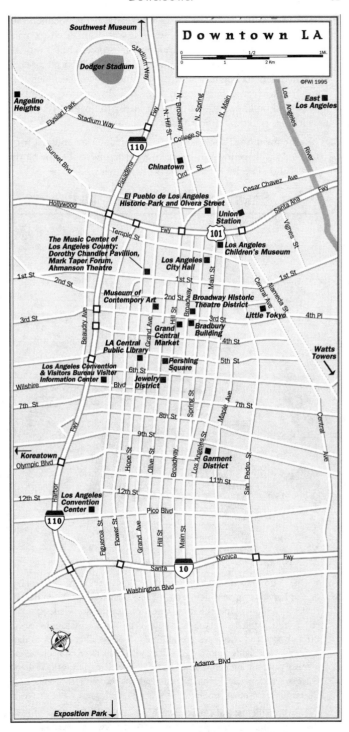

Downtown LA

©FWI 1995

Southwest Museum

Dodger Stadium

Angelino Heights

East Los Angeles

Elysian Park

Stadium Way

Sunset Blvd

College St

Chinatown

Ord St.

El Pueblo de Los Angeles Historic Park and Olvera Street

Cesar Chavez Ave

Union Station

Hollywood

Temple St

The Music Center of Los Angeles County: Dorothy Chandler Pavilion, Mark Taper Forum, Ahmanson Theatre

Los Angeles Children's Museum

Los Angeles City Hall

1st St

1st St

2nd St

Museum of Contempory Art

2nd St

Broadway Historic Theatre District

3rd St

Beaudry Ave

Hill St

Grand Ave

Grand Central Market

Bradbury Building

Little Tokyo

4th Pl

4th St

LA Central Public Library

5th St

Los Angeles Convention & Visitors Bureau Visitor Information Center

Pershing Square

Watts Towers

6th St

Jewelry District

Wilshire Blvd

7th St

8th St

Spring St

Maple Ave

7th St

9th St

Hope St

Olive St

Broadway

Los Angeles St

Garment District

Koreatown

Olympic Blvd

San Pedro St

11th St

12th St

Los Angeles Convention Center

12th St

Central Ave

Pico Blvd

Figueroa St

Flower St

Grand Ave

Hill St

Main St

Santa Monica Fwy

Washington Blvd

Exposition Park

Adams Blvd

heart of downtown to the top of Bunker Hill. The inclined railway was in service until 1969, when it was dismantled to make way for the downtown redevelopment project, but residents complained loudly about its demise. The $4 million restoration is scheduled to begin in early 1995 and will be completed in about one year. The colorful, renewed downtown neighborhood will be linked to the rest of L.A. by the Metro Red Line, which has a station at nearby Pershing Square.

In the meantime, those interested in architecture and historical sights don't have to wait to find lots of reasons for exploring the nooks and crannies of downtown Los Angeles.

Downtown: Things to See and Do

L.A. still has a few remnants of architectural glory left.

One of downtown's most boasted-about showplaces is the new and improved **Pershing Square**, fresh from a $14.5 million revitalization that includes a 125-foot purple bell tower with a striking fuchsia bell designed by architect Ricardo Legorreta. A "star walk" depicts the constellations seen in the L.A. sky, and telescopes provide "views" of Pershing Square in days gone by. There is also a lovely pool lined with black riverbed pebbles, and a grassy outdoor amphitheater and cafe. Bordered by 5th, 6th, Hill and Olive streets, five-acre Pershing Square Park has become a true refuge from the bustling downtown traffic.

Nearby is the **Central Library**, which was refurbished at a cost of more than $214 million and reopened in 1993 after two devastating arson-caused fires in 1986 and 1987 destroyed 400,000 books and closed the building, which was badly in need of renovation even before the fires.

The result is an expanded, state-of-the art facility that is now the largest public library in the western U.S. and among the three largest in the country. Included within its multi-levels are a language learning center, a public computer center, an extensive music listening department, a collection of 10,000 videotapes with viewing carrels provided, a homework and tutorial center, a genealogical center, a photographic collection of more than 2 million prints, and 2.1 million books and 10,000 magazines.

The library also boasts one of the country's largest collections of Asian language publications, and catalogue cards are now available in Chinese, Japanese and Korean. It's only a matter of time until the cards make the transition into the computerized files, making the Asian books and other materials easily accessible to L.A.'s burgeoning Asian-speaking population.

Fielding's Favorite Free Things to Do in L.A.

1. *Go to the beach. Almost any beach will do, but the happening places are Zuma, Santa Monica and Venice.*

2. *View the city from Griffith Park Observatory. This is an especially cool thing to do at night.*

3. *Spend a day at the Museum of Science and Industry. Admit it. Watching those chicks hatch is a kick.*

4. *People watch on Melrose Avenue west of La Brea, or on Rodeo Drive in Beverly Hills. See how the other half lives (and shops).*

5. *Go cemetery-hopping (especially to Forest Lawn in Hollywood and Glendale) and visit the graves of the rich and famous. Nothing macabre here, just a low-key paying of respects.*

6. *With David Gebhard's* Los Angeles: An Architectural Guide *(1994, Peregrine-Smith) as your companion, take a serious architectural tour of L.A. It might take a few days. You won't believe all the stuff there is to see.*

7. *Climb to the top of Mt. Lukens, the highest peak within L.A. city boundaries, starting from the Vogel Flats campground in Big Tujunga Canyon. This is not a hike for sissies, and should definitely not be tried on a rainy day.*

8. *Eschew the Hollywood scene and visit the International Surf Museum and Surfing Walk of Fame in Huntington Beach. Very cool, and you might even run into a famous surfer dude (or babe).*

9. *Hang out in a bookstore. Like **Book Soup** (8818 Sunset Boulevard, West Hollywood), the **New Age-oriented Bohdi Tree** (8585 Melrose, West Hollywood), or **Midnight Special** (1318 Third Street Promenade, Santa Monica).*

**Fielding's Favorite
Free Things to Do in L.A.**

10.   *Drop by the* **City of L.A. Film and Video Permit Office** *(6922 Hollywood Boulevard) for a free listing of film, TV, commercial and music video shoots going on in the area, then show up and watch the action.*

Architecturally and artistically speaking, the Lodwrick M. Cook Rotunda, with its elaborate stenciling and 2000-pound bronze chandelier representing the universe, is breathtaking, as are the library's several restored historical murals (including a ceiling mural in the first-floor lobby by contemporary artist Renee Petropoulos).

In the Tom Bradley wing, named for the city's former mayor, an eight-story atrium contains three chandeliers by local artist Therman Statom representing the natural, the technological and the ethereal worlds. Even the elevators have become whimsical works of art, lined with some 7 million obsolete catalog cards.

Several major works of art are incorporated into the 1.5-acre Robert F. Maguire III Gardens, which provide a quiet respite atop the library's 942-car parking garage. Here, you'll find Jud Fine's "Spine" (as in the spine of a book), a grotto fountain by landscape architect Lawrence Halprin, and porcelain objects by Mineo Mizuno that are the source of water for Laddie John Dill's fountain at the north entrance.

Also newly refurbished is Union Station, originally built in 1939, and just oozing with Southern California charm. Although the locals are justifiably proud of its place in Los Angeles history, movie buffs may be more likely to recognize it as the futuristic police station featured in the 1982 movie, *Blade Runner*, starring Harrison Ford.

Speaking of police stations, in the works for the downtown district is a **Los Angeles Police Department Museum** focusing on the history of the LAPD. To be housed in the old 1923 Highland Park police station (which has been vacant for a decade and requires extensive retrofitting for earthquake protection), the museum is expected to be completed by 1997 if the necessary $3.3 million is raised by the Los Angeles Police Historical Society, which has had the project on the drawing board since the late 1980s. This is expected to be a major addition to the L.A. museum scene and a step toward rebuilding the somewhat tattered relationship between the LAPD and the community.

You don't have to wait to visit the **Grand Central Public Market**, a must-see open food bazaar that has been in operation in Los Angeles since 1917. You can find all sorts of really cool stuff here, from sheep's brains to exotic produce to medicinal herbs guaranteed to cure what ails you, all hawked by an incredibly colorful array of vendors. The planned centerpiece of the downtown renovation project, the market will be refurbished and upgraded as the project continues into 1995.

 If you're a history buff, plan a stop at **Olvera Street**, which is the heart of El Pueblo de Los Angeles Historical Monument, site of the 1818 Avila Adobe, the city's oldest home. Here, you'll get a terrific taste of Mexican culture in the form of authentic food, music and lots of opportunities for shopping. The Cinco de Mayo celebration, held each year on May 5, doesn't get any better than this anywhere else in the city, and the kids will enjoy getting their picture taken while sitting on a stuffed donkey at any time of year.

Don't ignore downtown L.A.'s other ethnic neighborhoods, especially **Little Tokyo** (bounded by Los Angeles, San Pedro, 1st and 3rd streets) and **Chinatown** (approximately two blocks north of Union Station), both of which are thriving cultural centers. They are especially lively when festivals such as Nisei Week or the Chinese New Year are going on, when you can take in a variety of parades, cultural performances, and lots of authentic cuisine.

Little Tokyo

No matter how much the kids protest against things educational, drag them off to the **California Museum of Science & Industry and the Natural History Museum**, where they'll have more fun than a pack of Mighty Morphin Power Rangers, and they'll learn something, too. Even if you don't have kids in tow, put these excellent museums on your sightseeing list, along with the L.A. County Museum of Art, the fabulous new Peterson Automotive Museum, and the 1300 block of Carroll Avenue, where you'll find an impressive collection of Victorian homes.

Across from the L.A. County Museum of Art is the **Carole & Barry Kaye Museum of Miniatures**, touted as the "most humongous" miniature museum in the world. Established in 1990, the museum features the work of many famous miniaturists such as Eugene and Henry Kupjack, and includes exhibits of Victorian mansions, medieval abbeys, antique cars, an 18 kt. gold train with a cargo of diamonds, rubies, sapphires and emeralds, and even the Hollywood Bowl complete with "Satchmo" and his orchestra—all at a scale no larger than 1/12th inch.

MOCA is the West Coast answer to MOMA.

The **Museum of Contemporary Art** (MOCA) is one of the country's finest art museums, and recently put another feather in its cap with a gift of 70 works by California artists donated by Italian collectors Giuseppe and Biovanna Panza di Biumo. Included in the collection, which will not go on view until 1997, are works by Robert Therrien, Peter Shelton, Gregory Mahoney, Jeff Colson, Greg Colson, Mark Lere, Ross Rudel, Ron Griffin, Roy Thurston and Lawrence Carroll.

The well-respected Temporary Contemporary, the Museum of Contemporary Arts' annex located in Little Tokyo, has been closed since mid-1992 due to construction on the adjacent First Street North complex. Its projected reopening is currently scheduled for August of 1995, but construction hassles may delay the opening further, so call ahead if you plan to visit.

Getting around to these and other downtown locations is a snap on DASH (Downtown Area Short Hop), a shuttle service that runs six days a week until 10 p.m., circling the downtown area with stops every few blocks.

Also of note in the downtown area (although it's actually located in Highland Park, between L.A. and Pasadena) is the **Southwest Museum**, founded in 1907 and the oldest museum in Los Angeles. Its collections come from the Southwest Society, the western branch of the Archaeological Institute of America, and they are impressive. There are more than 250,000 objects in the museum's holdings, with emphasis on archaeological and ethnographic objects from the American Southwest, California, the Great Plains, the Northwest Coast and Mexico. The 11,000-piece Poole basketry collection is one of the largest in the United States, as is the 1200-piece Navajo textile collection. Unfortunately, the building itself is too small to do the collections justice, and plans for upgrading and expanding the facility have so far not been realized.

Fielding's Favorite Museum Gift Shops

Shopping 'til you drop in L.A. is a favorite pastime, but after you've done the malls, stop by one of these unique museum stores for something different. Even though museum shops are often ultra-expensive, you may be able to find something so rare that you'll be willing to cough up whatever it takes.

1. **The Richard Nixon Presidential Library** (18001 Yorba Linda Boulevard, Yorba Linda). *You won't believe the variety of stuff you can find here—everything from a birdhouse shaped like Nixon's boyhood home to a watch bearing a picture of the ex-president with Elvis Presley dubbed "The Dream Team." The holiday catalog is especially appealing.*

2. **The Museum of Miniatures** (5900 Wilshire Boulevard, Los Angeles). *After you've toured the museum, drop by the gift shop for historical fashions, furniture, paintings, dolls, silver, crystal chandeliers, porcelains and accessories—all at 1/12 scale of the real thing. Prices aren't downscaled, though. You can drop as much as $100,000 here.*

3. **The Petersen Automotive Museum** (6060 Wilshire Boulevard, Los Angeles). *Car buffs will find much to get revved up about here, from obscure books on automotive history to metal gas-station signs perfect for that college dorm.*

4. **The Southwest Museum** (234 Museum Drive, Los Angeles). *THE place to go for anything Native American, including baskets, dolls, pottery, musical instruments and jewelry. Items are arranged by tribe, and range in price from a few dollars to several hundred.*

5. **The Museum of Flying** (2772 Donald Douglas Loop North, Santa Monica). *This isn't the largest museum in L.A. by any means, but its gift shop offers lots of fun stuff for the aviation buff, from scale models of World War II planes to books and T-shirts.*

The Casa de Adobe, a re-creation of a pre-1850s Spanish California rancho located directly below the museum, houses the museum's Southwest Spanish Colonial collections, and the museum's library contains thousands of books, photographs, and manuscripts dedicated to the native and Hispanic peoples of the Americas and the history and exploration of the West. Many special performances, classes, and artisan demonstrations are also scheduled throughout the year.

New at the Southwest Museum is its Ethnobotanical Garden, dedicated to the indigenous plants of North America. Plants used for food, tools and medicinal purposes by American Indian tribes are planted in seven distinct environments, with learning stations set along the trails to make this a fun—as well as educational—experience for children.

Three miles south of downtown is the **University of Southern California** (USC), founded in 1880 and one of the most prestigious private universities in the country. (Plus, it always has a pretty good football team.) There are many things to see and do on the SC campus (the Fisher Art Gallery is excellent), and you can arrange a tour of the many facilities by calling the Alumni House at ☎ *(213) 740-2300.*

Finally, if you're interested in folk art, don't miss the **Watts Towers**, 100-foot-tall structures made of bottles, shells, pottery, tiles, pipe, rocks and whatever else Italian immigrant Simon Rodia could get his hands on. Begun in 1921 in Rodia's backyard at *1765 East 107th Street*, they're an amazing monument to 30-some years of creative genius, and are surely one of the world's greatest pieces of folk art. Now in the process of being refurbished after years of punishment by earthquakes and weather, the towers are currently surrounded by scaffolding, but tours have not been suspended.

No matter how you travel in downtown L.A., be aware of personal safety issues; although the revitalization of downtown has made it a safer place to be, caution is still advised, especially at night.

Museums and Exhibits

Afro-American Museum   ★★

600 State Drive, Los Angeles, 90037, ☎ *(213) 744-7432.*
Hours open: 10 a.m.–5 p.m.
In Exposition Park.
African-American culture, history, and art are explored in a series of changing exhibits. A biennial exhibit of emerging artists and summer programs for children are also offered, and a research library and museum store are located inside. Free escorted tours may be arranged. Free admission.

California Museum of Science & Industry   ★★★★★

700 State Drive, Los Angeles, 90037, ☎ *(213) 744-7400.*
Hours open: 10 a.m.–5 p.m.
In Exposition Park.

This participatory science and technology museum shouldn't be missed, and make sure you have the kids in tow. See the country's largest earthquake simulator, interactive computer exhibits, the miniature winery, the Hall of Health, the chick hatchery, Halls of Economics and Finance, and hands-on space, agriculture, math, and energy exhibits that are especially popular with children. The IMAX theater, which charges a fee, screens films such as "Destiny in Space," "Africa: The Serengeti," and "Hidden Hawaii." Call for showtimes. Note: there is a branch of the museum in Burbank, at *555 North Third Street.* Free admission.

Fisher Art Gallery   ★★★

University of Southern California, Los Angeles, ☎ *(213) 743-2799.*
Hours open: noon–5 p.m.
This gallery on the USC campus features important temporary exhibits, and also boasts a fine selection of 18th- and 19th-century Dutch paintings from the Armand Hammer collection.

George C. Page Museum ★★★★

5801 Wilshire Boulevard, Los Angeles, 90036, ☎ (213) 936-2230.
Hours open: 10 a.m.–5 p.m.
At La Brea and Wilshire Boulevard
This exciting archeological museum displays Ice Age fossils retrieved
from the nearby La Brea Tar Pits (which are actually not tar pits at all,
but asphalt pits). Included are preserved skeletons of extinct sabre-
toothed cats, an imperial mammoth, and the La Brea Woman,
believed to have lived more than 9000 years ago. Needless to say, this
is a VERY cool place for kids, who will get a big thrill out of watching
the animated model of a young mammoth or touching the bones of a
giant ground sloth. One can also peep over scientists' shoulders in the
Paleontological Laboratory as they work with fossils freshly wrenched
from the tar. Children's, students', and senior citizens' discounts.
Admission is free to all on second Tuesday of each month. General
admission: $5.

Homestead Museum ★★★

15415 East Don Julian Road, City of Industry, ☎ (818) 968-8492.
Hours open: 1–4 p.m.
This six-acre historical site includes the Workman House, an adobe
built in the 1840s, La Casa Nueva, a Spanish Colonial Revival mansion built in the 1920s, and a private cemetery that is one of the oldest
in Southern California. The Homestead is also an important cultural
center, and art fairs, concerts, lectures and seasonal activities are frequently scheduled. The research library is open by appointment only.
In addition to Mondays, the museum is closed the fourth weekend of
every month. Free admission.

Japanese American National Museum ★★

369 East First Street, Los Angeles, 90012, ☎ (213) 625-0414.
Hours open: 10 a.m.–5 p.m.
This Japanese cultural center focuses on the "Issei pioneers," the first
Japanese to come to America. One exhibit tells the story of World
War II encampments, and an interactive display allows relatives to find
out if their Japanese ancestors were held in camps. General admission:
$4.

Los Angeles County Museum of Art ★★★★★

5905 Wilshire Boulevard, Los Angeles, 90036, ☎ (213) 857-6111.
Hours open: 10 a.m.–5 p.m.
The LACMA houses one of the country's finest collections of American 20th-century art, European painting and sculpture, costumes and
textiles, graphic arts, decorative arts, and cultural arts from all over the
world. (The museum recently acquired Georgia O'Keeffe's painting,
"Horse Skull with Pink Rose" (1931), which is on display in the
Ahmanson Building, Plaza level.) Its temporary exhibitions are also
excellent, and many superb traveling exhibits find their way here. In
addition to works of art, the museum hosts an award-winning chamber music series and schedules a plethora of special events, such as the
1995 American Festival, which featured major exhibitions relating to
American history and culture. For those who just can't wait to get
there to find out what's going on, LACMA recently established a
World Wide Web presence on the Internet, which will tell you all you
need to know. LACMA online is located at http://www.lacma.org.

If you want to stop for a bite after seeing the museum, the Plaza Cafe opens at 10 a.m. on weekdays, 11 a.m. Saturday and Sunday. Admission for children and students under 18, $1; children 5 and under, free; students over 18 with ID and seniors over 62, $4. Admission free to all on the second Wednesday of every month. General admission: $6.

MOCA/Temporary Contemporary

152 Central Avenue, Los Angeles, 90012, ☎ (213) 626-6222.
Hours open: 11 a.m.–6 p.m.
Originally conceived as a temporary exhibition space during the construction of the Museum of Contemporary Art (MOCA), the Temporary/Contemporary has made a permanent place for itself in the Los Angeles art scene. Unfortunately, due to construction of the First Street Plaza redevelopment project, MOCA at the Temp is closed until sometime in late 1995. General admission: $4.

Museum of Contemporary Art

250 South Grand Avenue, Los Angeles, 90012, ☎ (213) 626-6222.
Hours open: 11 a.m.–5 p.m.
This beautiful red sandstone building designed by Arata Isozaki houses a permanent collection of modern and contemporary art dating from 1940. Abstract expressionism, minimalism, pop and more recent innovations are all well represented. Seniors and students' admission is $4; free admission for all on Thursdays, 5–8 p.m. General admission: $6.

Museum of Miniatures ★★★

5900 Wilshire Boulevard, Los Angeles, 90036, ☎ (213) 937-6464.
Hours open: 10 a.m.–5 p.m.
This unique museum is a delightful wonderland of tiny things. Everything here—from the collection of historical figures to the Victorian village to the golden train with its cargo of precious stones—is on a scale of 1/12 or less. A complete tea set sits on a quarter, a tobacco pipe requires a magnifying glass to see, and miniature houses are furnished down to the last detail. The gift shop is also a delight, with tiny little purchases that will set you back from $1.50 to $100,000. Admission for students 12-21, $5; children 3-12, $3; seniors (60+), $6.50. General admission: $7.50.

Natural History Museum

900 Exposition Boulevard, Los Angeles, 90007, ☎ (213) 744-3466.
Hours open: 10 a.m.–5 p.m.
In Exposition Park.
One of the largest natural history museums in the U.S., with more than 35 halls and galleries, including exhibits on paleontology, California history, minerals and metals, mammals, pre-Columbian cultures, birds, insects, marine life and plants. Don't miss the new main floor exhibit on dinosaurs. Docent tours daily at 1 p.m. The Discovery Center contains many hands-on exhibits for children. Admission for children 5-12, $2; children under 5, free; seniors and students with ID, $3.50. Admission is free to all on the first Tuesday of each month. General admission: $6.

Petersen Automotive Museum

6060 Wilshire Boulevard, Los Angeles, ☎ (213) 930-2277.
Hours open: 10 a.m.–6 p.m.

It had to happen—the city built around the automobile just had to have a site for car-culture worship. Opened in June 1994 as a new addition to the Natural History Museum, the Petersen Automotive Museum has quickly become one of the hottest tickets in L.A. Three floors of exhibits showcase more than 200 historical, fantasy, and classical vehicles, including James Bond's Aston Martin, a 1958 Edsel, a Helms bakery truck, a 1922 Leach and cars belonging to various celebrities. The whole shebang is mixed in with special effects and nostalgic backdrops, making this a true blast from the past. Don't miss it. Admission for children 5-12, $3; children under 5, free; students and seniors, $5. General admission: $7.

Wells Fargo History Museum   ★★

333 South Grand Avenue, Los Angeles, 90017, ☎ (213) 253-7166.
Hours open: 9 a.m.–5 p.m.
At the Wells Fargo Center.
The history of Wells Fargo's involvement in the opening of California to Gold Rush pioneers and settlers is told in a series of illuminating exhibits, which include a vintage stagecoach in which one traveler's journey is recounted by tape, a replica of an 1860s Wells Fargo agents' office, and gold mining artifacts. A video presentation recounts the history of Wells Fargo and shows how the bank's Old West television commercials are made. Free admission.

Historical Sites

Carroll Avenue   ★★★

1300 block, Carroll Avenue, Los Angeles, 90026.
North of downtown in Angelino Heights.
Carroll Avenue has the largest concentration of Victorian homes in Los Angeles and has been designated a historical monument. Especially notable is the Sessions House, located at 1330 Carroll. Self-guided walking tours. Free admission.

El Pueblo de Los Angeles Park   ★★★

845 North Alameda Street, Los Angeles, 90012, ☎ (213) 625-5045.
Across the street from Union Station.
This historic 44-acre park is located near the original pueblo that would become the city of Los Angeles. Located here is Olvera Street, Nuestra Senora la Reina de Los Angeles Church (1818), the Old Plaza Firehouse (1884), the Avila Adobe (1818), and a visitors center. Guided walking tours available at the Docent Office next to the Old Plaza Firehouse. ☎ *628-1274* for tour reservations. Free admission.

Los Angeles Central Library   ★★★

630 West Fifth Street, Los Angeles, 90071, ☎ (213) 612-3200.

The Central Public Library, gutted by arson fire in 1986, is once again enjoying its rightful status as a community center and one of downtown's greatest landmark buildings. The library's architectural theme is part art deco, part Egyptian and part Byzantine. The building is reached by a grand staircase overlooking a waterfall, and there are several terraces where one can relax with cappuccino and sandwiches bought from nearby kiosks. Don't forget to explore the library's interior, where several imaginative architectural touches—such as the stunning Lodwrick M. Cook Rotunda—make it worthwhile—even if you're NOT looking for a good book. Free admission.

City Hall was once the tallest building in L.A.

Los Angeles City Hall   ★★

200 North Spring Street, Los Angeles, 90012, ☎ (213) 485-4423.
Hours open: 9 a.m.–5 p.m.
Between First and Temple streets.

Erected in 1928, this jagged, 454-foot pyramidal structure was the
first skyscraper in Southern California. Panoramic views of the city
from the 27th-floor observation deck. Guided tours of City Hall are
available by appointment, 10 a.m.–noon. Free admission.

Simon Rodia Watts Towers   ★★★

1765 East 107th Street, Los Angeles, 90002, ☎ (213) 569-8181.
Italian tilesetter Simon Rodia spent more than 30 years building eight
towers made of reinforced steel and cement, covering them with bits
of tile, pottery, broken shells, and glass, creating in the process one of
the greatest folk art structures in the world. The complex containing
the Watts Towers is open to the general public 10 a.m.–2 p.m. on Saturdays. Group tours of 15 or more may be scheduled for visits during
the week. Children's admission, $1.50. General admission: $2

Tours

Downtown L.A. offers a wide variety of walking tours, many of which
center around the city's ethnic neighborhoods or historical sites. It's always
best to call ahead for a reservation, and to confirm prices and hours. Note
that tours having to do with the entertainment industry are included in the
sections on Hollywood and the San Fernando Valley.

Farmer's Market   ★★★

6333 West Third Street, Los Angeles, 90017, ☎ (213) 933-9211.
Hours open: 9 a.m.–6:30 p.m.
In the Fairfax District next to CBS Television City.

The site where local farmers used to sell their produce is now home to
more than 150 produce and food stalls, restaurants and small shops
with a large selection of fresh vegetables and imported food items.
This popular marketplace has a colorful ambience that attracts locals
as well as visitors. Free admission.

Los Angeles Conservancy   ★★★

727 West Seventh Street #955, Los Angeles, 90017, ☎ (213) 623-2489.

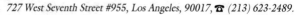

A wide variety of guided walking tours focus on Los Angeles' architectural heritage. Most tours are offered on Saturday; one is available
Sunday. Check out Little Tokyo, downtown Los Angeles, or the Art
Deco beauty of Bullock's Wilshire department store, among the many
choices offered. General admission: $5.

Los Angeles Times ★★

202 West First Street, Los Angeles, 90053, *(213) 237-5757.*
Enter at the corner of First and Spring streets.
One-hour tours of the Times complex, including newsroom, press-
room, photocomposition facilities and other areas. Children must be
over 10 years old. Free admission.

Pacific Stock Exchange ★★★

233 South Beaudry Avenue, Los Angeles, 90012, *(213) 977-4500.*
Hours open: 7:30 a.m.–1:30 p.m.
A Visitors Gallery overlooks the trading floor of the largest U.S. stock
exchange outside of New York City. You will find historical exhibits,
memorabilia, quotation machine and video presentations here. Free
admission.

University of Southern California ★★

University Park, Los Angeles, 90089.
Located just three miles south of the skyscrapers of downtown Los
Angeles, the University of Southern California offers one-hour tours
of the campus, Hancock Memorial Museum, Fisher Gallery, and the
Cinema Television Center complex, whose distinguished alumni
include George Lucas and Steven Spielberg. Tours by appointment
only.

Parks and Gardens

In addition to the splendid Robert F. Maguire III gardens atop the Central Library's parking structure and the pleasant ambience of the new Pershing Square, a new park has recently opened in the heart of downtown.
The Grand Hope Park, a $20 million, 2.5-acre facility bordered by Grand
Avenue, Hope, 9th Street and Olympic Boulevard, includes a large grassy
area for relaxing, a playground for kids, a 53-foot clock tower, and a whimsical fountain. A boon for brown-baggers who work downtown, the park is
a safe haven by day, but gates on the eight-foot wrought iron fence that en-
circles the park are locked at night in order to protect the park from vandalism.

Author's Tip

*Since every discriminating yuppie has a dog these days, it's nice that the L.A.
City Council has accommodated their needs by approving a couple of leash-
free parks where man's best friend can run around and frolic with other
doggies to his heart's content. Silver Lake Park (next to the Silver Lake Recreation Center) and Laurel Canyon Park (in the Hollywood Hills) are currently the city's only leash-free zones. When you're not letting Fido run
around at either of these locations, make sure he's reined in.*

Grand Hope Park ★★

Bounded by Grand, Hope, 9th Street and Olympic, Los Angeles.
This 2.5-acre park has been a welcome addition to downtown since it
opened in the fall of 1994. Included inside the wrought-iron fence

that borders the park (and is closed and locked at night) is a 53-foot clock tower, a fountain, a children's playground and a grassy slope. It's a great spot for unwinding at lunchtime.

Downtown for Kids

The Los Angeles Children's Museum, located near the Civic Center, attracts up to a quarter-million kids a year with its interactive exhibits that are both educational and fun. Club Eco, a new permanent exhibit offers hands-on experience related to taking care of the environment and is a big hit with kids. The museums in Exposition Park are just as much fun for the whole family. No kid who grew up in L.A. will ever forget trips to the California Museum of Science and Industry, where their favorite exhibit was inevitably the still-popular chick hatchery with its damp and exhausted chicks struggling to push their way out of the egg. There are all sorts of other hands-on exhibits that kids will love, each teaching a principle of—what else?—science or industry. The museum's IMAX theatre is always a hit, and usually offers at least one film program geared toward children.

The Natural History Museum is equally as compelling, with its Ralph M. Parsons Discovery Center devoted to teaching children about natural history, its historical dioramas and an amazing dinosaur exhibit that makes the paunchy, purple and popular "Barney" pale in comparison. (Hang onto your wallets, mom and dad! There's a great gift shop with all kinds of dinosaur-themed stuff that the kids will love.) After you've done the "dinosaur thing" there, go over to the George C. Page Museum near the L.A. County Museum of Art. Here, kids can see how real dinosaurs and sabre-toothed tigers were excavated from the pits of sticky tar that trapped them thousands of years ago. Cool!

Children who are interested in cars (and this may also include parents) will also get a tremendous kick out of the nearby Petersen Automotive Museum, where changing exhibits are so varied that they might even include Cinderella's carriage or Barbie's dream car for the women in the family. And don't leave out the **Carole & Barry Kaye Museum of Miniatures**, where kids can gaze in wonder at a tea set that sits on a quarter, or a gallery of tiny little historical figures.

Finally, L.A. is rich in cultural arts for children, so be sure to contact the **L.A. Music Center** for news of upcoming family-oriented performances. The Central Library, also offering many programs for children, is the site of radio station KLOS' Story Theatre, the centerpiece of the Children's Literature Department. Puppet shows and other entertainment are always going on here, flanked by stacks of tempting books and magazines guaranteed to keep kids busy on a rainy day.

Author's Tip

If you've got the kids in tow and are looking for truly "kid-friendly" accom-
modations, write to Kids Welcome (3924 East 14th Street, Long Beach 90804)
for a list of B&Bs, inns, ranches and guest houses in California that not only
accept kids, but go out of their way to make them feel as welcome as the
adults. Really.

Children's Activities

Bob Baker Marionette Theater   ★ ★ ★

1345 West First Street, Los Angeles, 2363, ☎ *(213) 250-9995.*
Every child should have the memory of at least one good puppet
show. This well-established marionette theater offers a magical experience for your child's pleasure and store of memories with a variety of
puppet shows and holiday programs. General admission: $10.

Los Angeles Children's Museum   ★ ★ ★ ★

310 North Main Street, Los Angeles, 90012, ☎ *(213) 687-8800.*
Between Temple and Aliso streets.
Hands-on exhibits for children include a TV and recording studio
where real equipment allows kids to make up their own shows; a hospital for young doctors and nurses; city streets where children can
drive a bus or policeman's motorcycle; a huge room for pillow fights;
and many other exhibits that invite play and creativity. New at the
museum is Club Eco, a major, permanent hands-on exhibit designed
to teach kids about taking care of the environment. It's great fun, and
educational, too! All children must be accompanied by an adult; children under 3 are admitted free. General admission: $5.

Ralph M. Parsons Discovery Center   ★ ★ ★ ★

900 Exposition Boulevard, Los Angeles, 90007, ☎ *(213) 744-3466.*
Hours open: 10 a.m.–3 p.m.
In the Natural History Museum.
This children's center within the Natural History Museum contains
excellent science-related participatory exhibits. Children will also
enjoy the Dinosaur Shop, which sells books, toys and other dinosaur-
related goods. Center admission free with museum admission.

Events

Most of the events held in downtown L.A. revolve around the city's ethnic neighborhoods and their cultural festivals, and they are always lively and
colorful (plus, you can usually get a lot of really good food). Olvera Street
celebrates Cinco de Mayo in style, and on Nov. 1, Dia de Los Muertos
(Day of the Dead), there are holiday-related arts and crafts for sale, workshops for kids, and a spooky procession.

Chinatown is a great place to celebrate the Chinese New Year in January,
while Little Toyko features a variety of festivities during Nisei Week, held in
August.

The annual Harvest Festival and Christmas Crafts Market, held at the
Convention Center each November, is an L.A. tradition that features more
than 350 craftspeople, entertainment and plenty of food and drink. And
speaking of the Convention Center, the Greater Los Angeles Auto Show,
held in January, is one of the biggest around, and features more than 1000

vehicles, including classic, specialty, and "concept" cars and a ton of accessories for cars and trucks.

Also watch for the fall Downtown Lives!, which celebrates its third anniversary in 1995. Billed as the largest exhibition of downtown art and performance in the city, it features the visual and performance art of more than 500 artists at several downtown venues.

The more athletically inclined can take to the streets in the grueling Los Angeles Marathon, one of the most popular marathons in the country, held each March beginning at the Coliseum.

African Marketplace & Cultural Faire ★★
Rancho Cienega Park, Baldwin Hills, ☎ *(213) 734-1164.*
This two-week event, held in late August, is a celebration featuring arts, crafts, gifts, clothing, entertainment and foods from more than 22 African cultures.

Art Expo ★★★
L.A. Convention Center, Los Angeles, ☎ *(310) 271-3200.*
This International Contemporary Art Fair has offered museum-quality artworks for sale for nearly a decade. More than 100 international contemporary galleries participate in this December event.

Chinese New Year ★★★
978 North Broadway, #206, Los Angeles, 90012, ☎ *(213) 617-0396.*
Between Hill Street and North Broadway.
A three-day February celebration in Chinatown featuring fireworks, music, dance, a Miss Chinatown beauty pageant, a carnival and the traditional Golden Dragon parade down North Broadway. Free admission.

Cinco de Mayo Celebration ★★★★

622 North Main Street, Los Angeles, 90012, ☎ *(213) 625-5045.*
Off US-110, next to Union Station.
Mariachi music, dancing, food and game booths fill the Plaza of El Pueblo de Los Angeles State Historic Park during citywide celebrations in May that commemorate Mexico's victory over the French. Free admission.

Downtown Lives! ★★★
Various locations, Los Angeles, ☎ *(213) 625-3232.*
Downtown Lives! was born in L.A. in 1993 as an affirmation that the arts are thriving in the downtown area. It's a grass-roots extravaganza nurtured by the Downtown Arts Development Association and dedicated to promoting the downtown arts scene. More than 500 visual and performing artists participate in the festival, which runs for three weeks in October and November. For a nominal fee ($2 at the 1994 festival), you can wander through large warehouses that contain paintings, sculpture, photographs, graphic arts, multimedia installations and performance artists doing their "thing." Hours vary.

Greater Los Angeles Auto Show ★★★

Los Angeles Convention Center, Los Angeles.
Hours open: 11 a.m.–10:30 p.m.
Watch for this premiere event each January at the Convention Center. Whether you're shopping for a new car or are just a car buff with no particular focus, you'll find lots to like about this nine-day show, which features more than 1000 new domestic and imported cars and

DOWNTOWN   77

trucks, "concept" vehicles, and a very cool exhibit of cars from the Petersen Automotive Museum. Children under 12 are admitted free when accompanied by an adult; senior admission, $4. There is an extra charge for parking. General admission: $6.

Harvest Festival ★★

Los Angeles Convention Center, Los Angeles, ☎ *(213) 741-1151.*
This annual weekend festival happens around Thanksgiving, and features more than 300 costumed craftspeople, entertainment and demonstrations of crafts such as wheat weaving, drum making, woodcarving, quilting, and candy making. It's a great place to do some Christmas shopping.

Nisei Week Festival ★★★

Little Tokyo, Los Angeles, 90012, ☎ *(213) 687-7193.*
Between Main and San Pedro streets.
August celebration featuring music, dance, a carnival and a parade. Other attractions in Little Tokyo include the Japanese-American Cultural and Community Center, scores of sushi bars and restaurants, import shops and presentations by the Japan America Theatre. Free admission.

Shakespeare Festival—Los Angeles ★★

411 West Fifth Street, Los Angeles, 90013, ☎ *(213) 489-1211.*
This free summer festival offers professional productions of Shakespeare's plays. In addition, a celebrity fund-raiser is scheduled for January.

Southern California Boat Show ★★

L.A. Convention Center, Los Angeles, ☎ *(714) 633-7581.*
Hours open: 1–9 p.m.
If you're into boats, fishing or any sport having to do with water, you won't want to miss this, the largest boat show in the West. A fixture in L.A. for more than 65 years, the show—held for a week in early February—includes new boats and other products on display, seminars, and other activities. Children under 12 are admitted free. General admission: $8.

Sports and Recreation

The Dodgers were imported from Brooklyn.

Los Angeles seems to have a love/hate relationship with its sports teams, and the AFC's vagabond Raiders are no exception. Currently based at the Coliseum in Exposition Park, the Raiders found a good excuse to go "stadium shopping" after the 1994 Northridge quake heavily damaged the historic sports venue. After more than $90 million in repairs, the Coliseum was rendered safe for another season, but the Raiders still didn't get everything they wanted (including a bunch of luxury suites and/or—even better—a whole new stadium) and fans continued to complain about the stadium's lack of comfort and amenities. The county supervisors put the kabosh on the new stadium idea, and the Raiders' old stomping grounds—Oakland—wooed them back. There's more than enough evidence that lots of people in L.A. are happy to see them go, especially after a lackluster performance in 1994. Stay tuned, and be comforted in the knowledge that as the Raiders leave L.A., you can still watch USC play home games at the Coliseum.

More well respected are L.A.'s baseball (Dodgers), basketball (Lakers and Clippers), and hockey (Kings) teams, although the Clippers haven't turned many heads in recent seasons.

Although L.A. has the potential to become a major player in soccer, the debate continues to simmer over whether high-spirited L.A. residents would support a sport that isn't fast-moving, high-scoring and peppered with modern-day sports legends. (Okay, okay. By this definition the Raiders probably had no business being in town either.) There was a brief-but-glorious focus on soccer during the 1994 World Cup matches played in Pasadena, but since then enthusiasm has largely fizzled. Still, soccer devotees have not given up their efforts to bring serious soccer to L.A., so far with mixed results.

The news is better for cyclists, who will soon have a bicycle path that will take them from the Sepulveda Dam Recreation Area in the San Fernando Valley to downtown L.A. The three-mile path from Griffith Park to downtown—was expected to be completed by early 1996. It is hoped that, in addition to providing more recreational bike trails in the city, the improved bike paths would encourage commuting by bicycle, thereby taking another cut out of L.A.'s traffic problems.

Fitness buffs have a wide variety of choices in L.A., from the many branches of the Family Fitness Center to The Spectrum Club, to L.A. Fitness clubs, all at several locations throughout L.A. and Orange counties.

Want to find yourself one of those rich, athletic, outdoor types? The following aren't bad places to do some hunting.

Beverly Hot Springs

308 North Oxford Avenue, Los Angeles, ☎ *(213) 734-7000.*
"Relax, Rejuvenate, Refresh, and Rejoice" is the motto of this exclusive health club, where L.A.'s Beautiful People come for mineral baths, shiatsu massage, body scrubs, and other treatments-of-the-moment. If you can afford it, it's the ultimate in pampering.

Forum Boxing

3900 West Manchester Boulevard, Inglewood, 90305, ☎ *(310) 673-1773.*
Championship boxing featuring world title fights is fought in a major sports arena, with 22 matches each year.

Holiday Spa Health Club

1607 Gower Street, Los Angeles, 90028, ☎ *(213) 461-0227.*
Those in search of a workout will find everything they need at this
club, which provides weight and aerobics rooms for men and women,
pools, an indoor track, racquetball courts and a juice bar.

Hollywood Park Racetrack

1050 South Prairie Avenue, Inglewood, 90301, ☎ *(310) 419-1500.*
Between Manchester and Century Blvds.
Thoroughbred racing April through mid-July, and mid-November
through December.

Industry Hills & Sheraton Resort

One Industry Hills Parkway, City of Industry, 91744, ☎ *(818) 965-*
0861.
The Eisenhower Course here is among the nation's top public golf
courses. Also on the premises is another 18-hole course, tennis courts,
riding trails, swimming pools and restaurants. Reservations can be
made up to three days in advance.

Los Angeles Clippers

3939 South Figueroa Street, Los Angeles, 90037, ☎ *(213) 748-8000.*
At Exposition Park.
Catch all the excitement of live NBA action during the October
through May season.

Los Angeles Dodgers

1000 Elysian Park Avenue, Los Angeles, 90012, ☎ *(213) 224-1400.*
Excluding the plethora of management/player squabbles that have
plagued Major League Baseball in the recent past, the Dodgers play
home games April through October at Dodger Stadium.

Los Angeles Kings

3900 West Manchester Boulevard, Inglewood, 90306, ☎ *(310) 419-*
3100.
The National Hockey League season runs October through April,
and all the Kings' home games are played at the Forum.

Los Angeles Lakers

3900 West Manchester Boulevard, Inglewood, 90306, ☎ *(310) 419-*
3100.
Catch the former World Champion Lakers in NBA regular season
play at The Forum October through May.

Los Angeles Marathon   ★ ★ ★

11110 West Ohio Avenue #100, Los Angeles, 90025, ☎ *(213) 444-*
5544.
The annual City of Los Angeles Marathon is one of L.A.'s most pub-
licized sporting events. Held each March, it attracts up to 20,000
competitors from around the world. The race starts and ends at the
Los Angeles Memorial Coliseum and winds through a variety of communities along the 26-mile course.

Rancho Cienega Sports Center

5001 Rodeo Road, Los Angeles, 90016, ☎ *(213) 294-6788.*
Twelve lighted tennis courts, an indoor pool, an all-weather track and
open basketball and volleyball keep sports enthusiasts hopping at this
center.

Rancho Park Golf Course

10460 West Pico Boulevard, Los Angeles, 90064, ☎ *(310) 838-7373.*

A two-story driving range and nine-hole pitch-and-put complement this lovely, pine-lined course, one of the most heavily played in the country.

Ski Dazzle

Los Angeles Convention Center, Los Angeles.

Everything having to do with skiing and snowboarding is happening at Ski Dazzle, L.A.'s annual ski show. Hundreds of exhibitors show their wares, there are experts on hand to answer questions, and ski resorts from all over the U.S. are represented. In addition, there are vacation giveaway contests, discounts on lift tickets, and a ski sale and swap. Beginners can even take lessons on a ski ramp. This is THE place for skiers to hang out on a weekend in mid-November, and local singles swear it's a great place to meet people.

The Merchant of Tennis

1118 South La Cienega Boulevard, Los Angeles, 90035, ☎ (310) 855-1946.

The draw to this small facility with only two courts is that it is open 24 hours a day. Lessons, pros and a ball machine are available.

The Tennis Place

5880 West Third Street, Los Angeles, 90036, ☎ (213) 931-1715.

Twelve pros, private and group lessons, a two-hour aerobic-tennis workout and 15 lighted courts are featured at this facility.

Downtown: Music, Dance and Theater

The major performing arts center in Los Angeles, the **Music Center of Los Angeles**, with its **Dorothy Chandler Pavilion**, **Mark Taper Forum** and **Ahmanson Theater**, is located downtown, and should inspire a pilgrimage for those seeking the cultural arts. The Dorothy Chandler Pavilion is home to the world-class Los Angeles Philharmonic Orchestra (which celebrated its 75th anniversary in 1994 by inviting maestro Zubin Mehta to its classy birthday party), the Los Angeles Music Center Opera, and the Joffrey Ballet when it makes an L.A. appearance.

In January of 1995, the Ahmanson completed a $17 million renovation that turned it into a state-of-the-art performance venue, and the center is anxiously awaiting the construction of the fourth jewel in its crown, the **Walt Disney Concert Hall**.

A generous gift of $50 million from Disney's widow, Lillian, provided a base of funds for the 2380-seat, Frank Gehry-designed hall, and the county donated the land, but the project—originally scheduled to be finished in 1997 at a cost of $210 million—almost immediately found itself $50 million over budget, and in late 1994 a study was instigated in order to find ways to trim the cost. Construction was expected to be delayed a year or more, but when it's completed, the state-of-the-art hall will serve as home to the Los Angeles Philharmonic Orchestra.

Downtown L.A. is still the cultural center.

On a much smaller scale—but an important addition to the neighborhood—is the new **Center for Performing Arts** scheduled to open in 1995 in South-Central L.A. The $3 million center, to be housed in a refurbished Presbyterian church building at 53rd and Vermont, has been funded by generous donations from Motown mogul Barry Gordy—among others—and will seat 450 people and serve as a venue for both live performances and first-run films.

Music

L.A. Classic Jazz Festival ★★★★

Various locations, Los Angeles, ☎ (310) 521-6893.
The musicians are cool and the jazz is hot at this annual September festival that generally includes performances at large L.A. hotels. More than 200 musicians perform everything from ragtime and Dixieland to blues, swing and Big Band sounds during the four-day event that draws artists from throughout the U.S., London and Paris. Tickets are available for individual events, or you can purchase an "all-event" pass. If you are a jazz fan, this is Nirvana.

Los Angeles Bach Festival ★★★

540 South Commonwealth Avenue, Los Angeles, ☎ (213) 385-1345. At First Congregational Church.
This week-long homage to Johann Sebastian Bach and his contemporaries has been a tradition in Los Angeles for more than 60 years. A variety of concerts takes place throughout the week with free noon performances at the church. Held mid- to late October.

Los Angeles Chamber Orchestra ★★★

315 West Ninth Street, Suite 300, Los Angeles, 90015, ☎ (213) 622-7001.
This fine 40-member orchestra presents programs of Baroque, classical, and contemporary works at various locations in the greater Los Angeles area. As part of the UCLA Center for the Performing Arts' season, the orchestra performs monthly on campus at Royce Hall.

Los Angeles Music Center Opera ★★★★★

135 North Grand Avenue, Los Angeles, 90012, ☎ (213) 972-7211.
Marking its ninth season in 1995-96, the renowned Music Center Opera presents a full season of superb productions such as "Don Gio-

vanni," "Xerxes," and "Porgy and Bess." All performances take place at the Dorothy Chandler Pavilion. Tickets are available at the Music Center Box Office and through Ticketmaster outlets.

Los Angeles Philharmonic Orchestra ★ ★ ★ ★ ★

135 North Grand Avenue, Los Angeles, 90012, ☎ (213) 850-2020.
Conducted by Esa-Pekka Salonen, this outstanding orchestra presents chamber and contemporary music in addition to full orchestral works performed at the Dorothy Chandler Pavilion.

Music Center of Los Angeles ★ ★ ★ ★

135 North Grand Avenue, Los Angeles, 90012, ☎ (213) 972-7211.
At First Street and Grand Avenue.
Completed in 1969, the Music Center includes the Dorothy Chandler Pavilion, Mark Taper Forum and Ahmanson Theater. It is the city's main venue for concerts, plays and dance. Free guided tours. (See individual theater listings which are located in this guide).

Outdoor Courts at California Plaza ★ ★ ★

300 South Grand Avenue, Los Angeles, 90071, ☎ (213) 687-2020.
The Plaza is Los Angeles' largest mixed-use project, best known for housing the Museum of Contemporary Art. Now, it's becoming well-known for free, ongoing music, arts and entertainment events held at the Water Court, the Spiral Court and other unique outdoor sites. Call for a schedule of events. Free admission.

Dance

Joffrey Ballet ★ ★ ★ ★ ★

3674 Wilshire Boulevard , Los Angeles, 90010, ☎ (818) 902-3721.
At the Music Center of Los Angeles.
This outstanding ballet company with bicoastal residence in New York and Los Angeles performs the works of choreographers such as Balanchine, Nijinsky, Joffrey and Jooss. Call for production information.

Lewitzky Dance Company ★ ★ ★

700 South Flower Street, Los Angeles, 90017, ☎ (213) 580-6338.
Known for its innovative style and exploration of space, this company founded by L.A. native Bella Lewitzky has been performing for more than 25 years. When not on tour, the group performs at several local venues, including UCLA.

Theatre

Ahmanson Theatre ★ ★ ★ ★

135 North Grand Avenue, Los Angeles, 90012, ☎ (800) 762-7666.
The Ahmanson reopened in January 1995 after a stunning renovation that improved sightlines, enhanced acoustics and added new side boxes. Some of the top Broadway shows in the country are always on the boards here, such as the mega-hit "Miss Saigon," which is scheduled to run through the fall of 1995.

Colony Studio Theatre ★ ★

1944 Riverside Drive, Silver Lake, 90039, ☎ (213) 665-3011.
This distinguished membership company mounts original and well-established dramas, comedies and musicals in a 99-seat theater near Griffith Park. Currently, plans are in the works for the troupe to move to a new location in Glendale, hopefully by the opening of the 1996 season.

East-West Players

4424 Santa Monica Boulevard, Silver Lake, 90029.
A resident theatre of mostly Japanese-American and Asian-American actors, playwrights and directors who produce their own original shows. East-West was founded by the distinguished stage and screen actor Mako. Under the artistic direction of veteran actress Nobu McCarthy, the group puts on four mainstage productions a year—a musical and three experimental works-in-progress.

Japan America Theatre

244 South San Pedro Street, Los Angeles, ☎ (213) 628-2725.
In Little Tokyo.
The theatre space in the Japanese Cultural and Community Center is a showcase for regular performances of Grand Kabuki, Noh and Bugaku drama, thrilling KODO drum masters, Bunraku Puppet Theatre and other traditional arts of Japan. Western dance and chamber music are also featured.

Mark Taper Forum

135 North Grand Avenue, Los Angeles, 90012, ☎ (213) 972-7211.
The Mark Taper Forum features performances of classic, modern and experimental plays in a 752-seat theater-in-the-round at the Music Center.

Ticket Agencies

CBS Tickets

7800 Beverly Boulevard, Los Angeles, 90036, ☎ (213) 852-2624.
Hours open: 9 a.m.–5 p.m.
Free tickets to taping of "The Price Is Right" and other CBS shows.

Ticketmaster

3701 Wilshire Boulevard, Suite 700, Los Angeles, 90010, ☎ (213) 381-2000.
Call for outlet locations or to charge by phone with major credit cards.

Ticketron/Teletron

6060 West Manchester Boulevard, Los Angeles, 90045, ☎ (310) 410-1062.
Tickets for professional and collegiate sports, concerts, theater and other events.

Downtown: Nightlife

Jazz lovers should plan an evening at the newly restored 5-4 Ballroom and Supper Club, a downtown cultural landmark that opened in 1922 to the sounds of big band music. The scene is very cool here, but the neighborhood (South-Central L.A.) is one of the city's most crime-ridden, so caution is advised.

And speaking of South-Central, much of L.A.'s underground after-hours **rave** scene happens in the industrial area that runs from downtown L.A. to Long Beach—and not always in the best neighborhoods. Most ravers say that since the 1992 riots, it's a little too dangerous out there and, harassed by cops, partiers packing weapons, and malevolent types from local gangs, kids have gotten tired of the hassles, the bad drugs, and even the techno music that sustained them through the "good" years. Not that you can't still find rave clubs in L.A. There are several still around, including Abyss, a dingy club inside a run-down hotel in the downtown Ramparts District that is periodically closed down by police for one reason or another. Check the alternative music tabloids such as URB for what's happening in underground L.A., but be warned that there are dangers associated with making the late-night/early morning party scene.

For something a great deal more subdued, try THE place of the moment in downtown L.A.—the **County Museum of Art**. On Fridays, there's free live jazz, classic films, poetry readings and one-act plays, and the central court is transformed into a trendy food and drink emporium. The whole thing starts at 5 p.m., which means you can make the scene here and still get home in time for "The X Files."

There are, of course, dozens of clubs in L.A. that offer everything from blues to country to pop to techno entertainment. No matter what you're looking for, you're sure to find it. Pick up a free copy of *BAM*, The *L.A. Reader* or any number of new magazines for what's on at the clubs.

Author's Tip

Lots of very hip people will tell you that drugs are out, alcohol is out, and the club scene is very passe. (Of course, lots of other very hip people will tell you otherwise.) In any case, if your idea of a cool scene is a hot cup of cappuccino or espresso, some quiet conversation, jazz playing quietly in the background, maybe a poetry reading, or just sitting in the corner with a good book, pick up a copy of Louis Nicolaides' Caffe L.A., a new guide to the city's coffee-houses. Pick one, then sit back and be glad you're not one of the celebrity wannabes lined up outside the House of Blues.

5-4 Ballroom and Supper Club

308 West 54th Street, Los Angeles, ☎ *(213) 752-4933.*
This jazz club, which first opened in 1922, was recently reopened after 25 years of being closed. Its reputation earned it the title "the Apollo of L.A.," and it currently showcases jazz on weekends only. (Note: this is one of L.A.'s toughest neighborhoods.)

Checkers Lounge

535 South Grand Avenue, Los Angeles, ☎ *(213) 624-0000.*
The martinis are reportedly "silky smooth" at this perfectly civilized downtown spot where you can listen to live piano music and munch hors d'oeuvres while getting ever-so-comfy on a plush velvet couch. If you are tired of hot L.A. "scenes," this is the place for you.

Club Phil

Los Angeles Music Center, Los Angeles, ☎ *(213) 850-2050.*
Club Phil—as in Philharmonic—is a great new concept whereby you attend a concert by the L.A. Philharmonic, then move to the Pavilion Restaurant atop the Music Center for a post-concert party where you can dance the rest of the night away. Club Phil is only open after orchestra concerts—which are generally once a month during the Philharmonic's season. Cover is $10; reservations are required.

Crush Bar

1743 North Cahuenga Boulevard, Los Angeles, ☎ *(213) 463-7685.*
Come casual and dance to the best of the '60s and '70s, with lots of Motown and soul, Fridays and Saturdays. On Wednesdays, move to the best in dance hall reggae and lovers rock; Thursday features

dancehall reggae and hip-hop. Three full bars insure plenty of liquid refreshment between dances.

Derby, The

4500 Los Feliz Boulevard, Los Feliz, ☎ *(213) 663-8979.*
The Derby has been an L.A. institution since it was built by Cecil B. DeMille in 1929. It has had several names over the years, but has now been restored to its former art deco elegance, and offers a mix of jazz, swing, R&B, and rockabilly. On Wednesday nights, when the house band plays, the club is always packed. Free dance lessons are offered Wednesdays and Thursdays at 8 p.m. $5 cover; over 21.

Epicentre

200 South Hill Street, Los Angeles, ☎ *(213) 625-0000.*
Traditional and swing jazz and sophisticated vocalists charge up the night here; observe it all from tiered dining levels. On Thursday nights at 8:30, stand-up comedy is featured. Music from 9 p.m. nightly. Free parking at Second and Hill streets.

Gate, The

643 North La Cienega Boulevard, Los Angeles, ☎ *(310) 859-5568.*
A dressy disco set in an English manor-style nightclub with a dance floor, rooms for conversation, three fireplaces and two outdoor patios. Musical styles run from disco to techno to hip-hop to industrial. Four full bars and dining are also available. Cover charge ranges from $10–$15.

Glam Slam

333 South Boylston Street, Los Angeles, ☎ *(213) 482-6626.*
Owned by "the rock star formerly known as Prince," (his original club is in his hometown of Minneapolis), Glam Slam offers dancing, concerts and special events. Almost every night of the week a different performance can be seen, featuring acts that run the gamut from R&B, funk and hip-hop to professional dancers, performance artists and choreographers. "Fashionable" nightlife attire is requested and there's a full restaurant. Cover varies. Over 21 only.

Grand Avenue Bar

506 South Grand Avenue, Los Angeles, 90071, ☎ *(213) 624-1011.*
In the Biltmore Hotel.
You can catch live music from 5–9 p.m., fortify yourself at the pasta bar, and enjoy a bit of the high life downtown. No cover charge.

Jabberjaw

3711 West Pico Boulevard, Los Angeles, ☎ *(213) 732-3463.*
In the Crenshaw District.
All ages are welcome at this hard-to-find, hole-in-the-wall java house that features underground rock. Recent performers have included Flood Gate and Go Cart.

Jack's Sugar Shack

8751 West Pico, Los Angeles, ☎ *(310) 271-7887.*
Live rock and blues nightly along with dining and a full bar including 32 kinds of beer on tap. For other entertainment, there are two pool tables and a juke box. The James Armstrong Band, Jamie James and the Kingbees, the Red Devils, and others play here; call for current bookings.

Kibitz Room

419 North Fairfax Avenue, Los Angeles, ☎ *(213) 651-2030.*
At Canter's Deli.

This Fairfax landmark is the hip new spot for jam sessions most nights of the week by off-duty rockers, along with regular daily presentations of rock, blues, jazz and cabaret/pop stylists such as Joe Simon, Johnny and Donny Salami and Tina Steven. A near-ideal setting for an evening of toe-tapping fun that includes dining, a full bar and no cover charge. 21 and over.

L.A. County Museum of Art

5909 Wilshire Boulevard, Los Angeles, 90036, ☎ *(213) 857-6111.*

You probably aren't thinking of the art museum as a happening night-spot, but on Fridays at 5 p.m., it's an extremely popular place to hang out, sip a glass of wine, see a classic film, tour the galleries, or listen to free live jazz. The price is right, the place is always packed, and even parking is free. Such a bargain!

Mint, The

6010 West Pico Boulevard, Los Angeles, 90035, ☎ *(213) 937-9630.*

You'll hear some of the city's best blues played at The Mint, which has been in business for more than five decades. It isn't in the best neighborhood, but the music compensates, and regulars pack the place nearly every night.

Shark Club

1024 Grand Street, Los Angeles, 90015, ☎ *(213) 747-0999.*
Hours open: 5 p.m.–3 a.m.
At Olympic and Grand streets.

This eclectic dance club offers a different theme each night, a relaxed (for L.A.) dress code, and witty shark-tooth decor.

The Improvisation

8162 Melrose Avenue, Los Angeles, 90046, ☎ *(213) 651-2583.*

"The Improv" was America's original comedy showcase where such greats as Robin Williams and Bette Midler got their start. Rising stars of today are showcased. Another branch is located in Santa Monica, at *321 Santa Monica Boulevard.* Open 6 p.m. to 2 a.m.

Chinatown

Downtown: Shopping

Upscale shoppers will enjoy a stop at Citicorp Plaza's **Seventh Market Place** *(735 South Figueroa, Los Angeles)*, where more than 50 stores including Robinsons-May, Bullock's, Ann Taylor and Godiva Chocolates are located, along with a plethora of international cafes. Also in the plaza are Gallery 777, displaying a collection of original Ansel Adams prints, and Poet's Walk, a collection of seven installations featuring original verse and sculpture.

Arco Plaza, a subterranean complex at Fifth and Flower streets, has more than 55 shops and restaurants, and Broadway Plaza at Seventh and Flower near the Hyatt Regency, features an international food court in addition to more than 30 upscale shops.

If high-priced retail puts too much of a strain on your bank account, head over to the downtown **Garment District**, where even designer clothes are available at a big discount. It can be a madhouse in some of these places, and shops are far from fancy, but if you have the patience to look through the merchandise, you'll come away with some real bargains. Lots of people swear by the **Cooper Building** on South Los Angeles at 9th, where seven floors of shops include factory outlets and discount stores selling everything from clothing and accessories to cosmetics and home furnishings. **Santee Alley**, located between Santee Street, Maple Avenue, Olympic Boulevard and 12th Street, is another place to find good bargains in clothing. It's a sort of outdoor marketplace where local wholesalers sell retail.

The downtown **California Jewelry Mart** *(Sixth Street and Hill, south of Pershing Square)* will save you big bucks on quality jewelry, and stores are often willing to dicker over the price, so you have the opportunity for some real bargains. Skiers will appreciate the **H & H Jobbing Co**. *(840 South Los Angeles Street)*, an outlet for famous-maker ski wear that can save you up to 70 percent on clothing for adults and children.

The old **Uniroyal Tire Factory** site *(5675 East Telegraph Road)* in the City of Commerce now houses The Citadel, a collection of factory outlet shops that include Eddie Bauer, Ann Taylor, Benetton, Capezio, Gap, Corning/Revere, and the Book Warehouse, to name a few. Other outlet malls located a fair distance from L.A.—but close enough for a day's shopping—can be found in Oxnard, Ontario, Barstow, Lake Elsinore and Cabazon.

Author's Tip

Outlet malls do not always deliver the great deals you expect (unless getting a pair of $300 shoes for $200 is the kind of bargain you're looking for). When outlets have a sale, however, you can really save money. Call ahead to find out when sales will be happening, then get ready to fight the crowds.

Don't overlook the ethnic areas of downtown, including Koreatown, Chinatown, Little Saigon and Little Tokyo, where you'll find interesting places to shop and a variety of international culinary delights. Little Tokyo also boasts a duty-free shop, located on Third Street.

And for another of those "only in L.A." experiences, head over to **Skeletons in the Closet**, a "unique" (and slightly morbid) gift shop run by the L.A. County Coroner's office in the county administrative building. Here you'll find lots of murder-oriented souvenirs of L.A., including body toe tags (personalized with your name!), chalk outline beach towels, and stuff emblazoned with the department's official mascot—Sherlock Bones. Proceeds from the shop go to the Youthful Drunk Driving Program, designed to keep troubled kids out of Sherlock's domain.

Equally quirky is the "**city store**" set to open in the Los Angeles Mall sometime in 1995. Available for purchase will be a ton of salvaged authentic city memorabilia, including old street signs, parking meters, and other city-related discards with potential to be a hit with collectors and add money to city coffers at the same time. (There are already several "salvage-oriented" stores in L.A. County, including **Scavenger's Paradise** in North Hollywood.)

Downtown: Where to Stay

Downtown has a variety of first-class hotels to choose from, including the recently renovated Biltmore, the luxurious Checkers Hotel Kempinski, and the new, $100 million Inter-Continental. Several other hotels have undergone recent renovations, including the Sheraton Grande, the Holiday Inn at the L.A. Convention Center, and the dramatic Hyatt Regency on South Hope Street.

The long-established L.A. Hilton and Towers recently changed hands and is now under new management as the Omni Los Angeles, but changes in accommodations and services are not expected.

Although several new hotels have been announced for downtown L.A., including the Evergreen Laurel Hotel at Alameda and First streets, the Grand Avenue Plaza on 7th Street, and the Halekulani Hotel on Figueroa, postponements have pushed most of their completion dates into 1997 and beyond.

Hotels and Resorts

Best Western Mayfair   **$80–$130**   ★★

1256 West Seventh Street
☎ *(800) 528-1234, (213) 484-9789, FAX: 213-484-2769.*
Single: $80–$115. Double: $90–$130.
Good service and upscale accommodations define this Best Western hotel that offers in-room movies, valet/laundry service, currency exchange, a multilingual staff, a free downtown shuttle, newspaper, coffee, and hors d'oeurves to its guests. A restaurant, a lounge, a gift shop and a car rental desk are also on-site. Amenities: exercise room, conference facilities, business services. 295 rooms. Credit Cards: V, MC, A.

Biltmore   **$185–$275**   ★★★★

506 South Grand Avenue
☎ *(800) 245-8673, (213) 624-1011, FAX: 213-612-1545.*
Single: $185–$275. Double: $215–$275.
Grand, old-style brick hotel that recently underwent a $40 million renovation. It includes modern guest rooms decorated in pastel colors, an elegant health and fitness club, and a beautiful lobby ceiling painted by Giovanni Smeraldi. The hotel's spa, with its steam room

and Roman pool, served as a backdrop for scenes in the film *Bugsy*. Accommodations are graded Gold, Silver and Bronze. Gold rooms offer such amenities as robes, complimentary continental breakfast, health club privileges, and newspapers. All rooms have French furniture and armoires. Ranked restaurant: **Bernard's**. Amenities: pool, health club, Jacuzzi, sauna, conference facilities. 704 rooms. Credit Cards: CB, V, MC, DC, A.

Holiday Inn City Center $105–$140 ★★★

1020 South Figueroa Street
☎ *(800) 465-4329, (213) 748-1291, FAX: 213-748-6028.*
Single: $105–$120. Double: $105–$140.

In-room movies, valet/laundry, non-smoking rooms, multilingual staff, fax and transportation to area attractions are some of the amenities offered at this hotel. Recent renovations have kept the hotel spiffy, if less than exciting. Its handy location and reasonable rates make it popular with budget-conscious business and leisure travelers. Amenities: pool, exercise room, balcony or patio, conference facilities, business services. 195 rooms. Credit Cards: CB, V, MC, DC, A.

Hotel Inter-Continental $160–$200 ★★★★

251 South Olive Street
☎ *(800) 327-0200, (213) 617-3300, FAX: 213-617-3399.*
Single: $160–$180. Double: $180–$200.

This new $100 million hotel located near Bunker Hill is part of the 11.2-acre California Plaza, which includes office towers, condominiums, gardens and an art museum. All rooms come equipped with three telephones—two have ports for fax and computer—and half the rooms are non-smoking. Phone messages for absent guests are left on the guest's voice mail. A wonderful art collection graces the public spaces. Amenities: pool, health club, exercise room, sauna, conference facilities, club floor, business services. 439 rooms. Credit Cards: CB, V, MC, DC, A.

Hyatt Regency $100–$200 ★★★

711 South Hope Street
☎ *(800) 233-1234, (213) 683-1234, FAX: 213-629-3230.*
Single: $100–$200. Double: $100–$200.

This recently renovated high-rise hotel with a dramatic 26-story atrium connecting it with the Broadway Plaza complex has city views from all rooms. Besides the convenience of being close to entertainment and shopping, the hotel also offers in-room movies, marble bathrooms, non-smoking rooms, a multilingual staff, currency exchange, fax, complimentary newspaper and the Camp Hyatt program for children. Amenities: health club, hair salon, conference facilities, club floor, business services. 485 rooms. Credit Cards: CB, V, MC, DC, A.

Metro Plaza Hotel $60–$75 ★★

711 North Main Street
☎ *(800) 223-2223, (213) 680-0200, FAX: 213-620-0200.*
Single: $60–$75. Double: $69–$75.

This motel is in the heart of Chinatown. Rooms have refrigerators, and all guests receive a complimentary morning newspaper and evening beverage. Amenities: Jacuzzi, sauna, private spas, conference facilities, business services. 80 rooms. Credit Cards: CB, V, MC, DC, A.

Miyako Inn $89–$99   ★★

328 East First Street
☎ *(800) 228-6595, (213) 617-2000, FAX: 213-617-2700.*
Single: $89. Double: $99.
Located in the heart of Little Tokyo and adjacent to the Civic Center, this hotel offers in-room movies, refrigerators, non-smoking rooms, a multilingual staff, fax, a coffee shop and a restaurant. Amenities: health club, Jacuzzi, sauna, conference facilities. 174 rooms. Credit Cards: V, MC, DC, A.

New Otani Hotel & Garden $155–$230   ★★★

120 South Los Angeles Street
☎ *(800) 421-8795, (213) 629-1200, FAX: 213-622-0980.*
Single: $155–$205. Double: $180–$230.

Japanese-oriented, -owned and -managed with great efficiency—and close to the Japanese Cultural Center—this hotel offers guests a choice between a king-size bed or futon, European or shiatsu massage, and sushi or steamed Maine lobster. A "Japanese Experience" weekend is available, and includes a Japanese-style suite, a Japanese dinner with sake, shiatsu massage, and yakata robes. A beguiling aura of East meets West. Rates include breakfast. Ranked restaurant: **A Thousand Cranes**. Amenities: health club, Jacuzzi, sauna, hair salon, conference facilities, business services. 434 rooms. Credit Cards: CB, V, MC, DC, A.

Omni Los Angeles $130–$150   ★★★

930 Wilshire Boulevard
☎ *(800) 843-6664, (213) 629-4321, FAX: 213-612-3989.*
Single: $130. Double: $150.
This long-established convention and group hotel has bright and comfortable guest rooms with city views. Four restaurants, in-room movies, minibars, multiline phones, a multilingual staff, child care, currency exchange and a business center are other features. Ranked restaurant: **Cardini**. Amenities: pool, exercise room, hair salon, family plan, conference facilities, club floor, complimentary airport pickup service. 900 rooms. Credit Cards: V, MC, A.

Radisson Wilshire Plaza $110–$140   ★★

3515 Wilshire Boulevard
☎ *(800) 333-3333, (213) 381-7411, FAX: 213-386-7379.*
Single: $110–$130. Double: $120–$140.
Formerly the Hyatt Wilshire and the Wilshire Koreana, this hotel is set in the heart of the Wilshire financial district—not the greatest neighborhood in town. Recently renovated, it has a decided Asian influence with a Japanese restaurant and sushi bar. Request a rear room to escape Wilshire street sounds. Amenities: pool, health club, balcony or patio, hair salon, conference facilities. 396 rooms. Credit Cards: CB, V, MC, DC, A.

Sheraton Grande $180–$450   ★★★★

333 South Figueroa Street
☎ *(800) 325-3535, (213) 617-1133, FAX: 213-613-0291.*
Single: $180–$450. Double: $180–$450.

Architecturally striking 14-story hotel with glassed atrium lobby and lounge. Marble baths with phones, butler service on every floor, and limo service to Beverly Hills are special amenities offered. The guest rooms are large with executive work areas, designer fabrics, cherry wood and king or double beds. Twenty-four hour room service is available. A welcome addition to the downtown renaissance. Ranked restaurant: **Scarlatti**. Amenities: pool, health club, conference facilities, business services. 469 rooms. Credit Cards: V, MC, DC, A.

Westin Bonaventure $157–$175 ★ ★ ★

404 South Figueroa Street

☎ *(800) 228-3000, (213) 624-1000, FAX: 213-612-4800.*

Single: $157. Double: $175.

This futuristic L.A. landmark boasts five gleaming glass towers and a six-story atrium lobby with a one-acre lake, 20 retail stores, 20 restaurants, five lounges and a nightclub. The structure is mazelike, so to keep guests from becoming too bewildered, the round towers have been color-coded. Beware of this hotel if you are color-blind; you may become lost and never be seen again! If you can find your way to your room in one of the glass-paned elevators, the views can be spectacular. The rooms are small, decently furnished—except those on floors 30-35—and have the usual amenities. Recently, an all-suite tower was added, and the $195 standard suite rate includes continental breakfast. Amenities: pool, family plan, conference facilities, club floor. 1400 rooms. Credit Cards: CB, V, MC, DC, A.

Wyndham Checkers Hotel $209–$229 ★ ★ ★ ★

535 South Grand Avenue

☎ *(800) 996-3426, (213) 624-0000, FAX: 213-626-9906.*

Single: $209. Double: $229.

This small but luxurious hotel is the essence of peace and comfort, and may be the best place to stay in downtown Los Angeles if you don't mind paying for the parking. An excellent restaurant, elegantly decorated rooms, service with a personal touch, and a fine art collection throughout are worth the price. Do yourself a favor and splurge on afternoon tea, held from 3–5 p.m. daily. Ranked restaurant: **Checkers**. Amenities: pool, exercise room, Jacuzzi, sauna, family plan, conference facilities, business services. 188 rooms. Credit Cards: CB, V, MC, DC, A.

Downtown: Where to Dine

Although certainly not thought of as the city's culinary center, downtown L.A. has its share of good restaurants, including such venerable institutions as Rex Il Ristorante, Bernard's (at the Biltmore), and Checkers (at the Checkers Kempinski), plus the hot new Ca'Brea, which attracts a varied menu of show biz types, and Ginza Sushi Ko, reputedly the most expensive restaurant in L.A., but worth it for fresh sushi to die for.

The Seattle-based McCormick's & Schmick's, which has been rapidly expanding into California markets, and the Water Grill are currently battling it out for the title of the best seafood restaurant in downtown L.A., with the Water Grill getting a slight edge in our estimation.

THE ☆☆☆☆ MIRACLE OF THE LOAVES AND FISHES

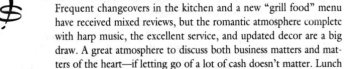

Author's Tip

It is generally acknowledged that the Kachina Grill (330 South Hope Street) has one of the best selections of tequila in town. You'll find all kinds of hard-to-find brands among its more than 40 varieties, and knockin' 'em back has evolved into one of downtown's favorite forms of TGIF recreation.

Ethnic eateries abound downtown, but our recommendation is to try Al Amir, which offers authentic, four-star Lebanese food, an exotic atmosphere, and warm service. It's one of the best places for adventurous eating in L.A.

Los Angeles

American

Bernard's   **$$$**   ★★★★

506 South Grand Avenue, ☎ (213) 612-1580.
Specialties: fresh seafood; wild game.
Lunch: 11:30 a.m.–2 p.m., entrees $17–$30.
Dinner: 6–10 p.m., entrees $30–$45.
Associated Hotel: Biltmore Hotel.

Frequent changeovers in the kitchen and a new "grill food" menu have received mixed reviews, but the romantic atmosphere complete with harp music, the excellent service, and updated decor are a big draw. A great atmosphere to discuss both business matters and matters of the heart—if letting go of a lot of cash doesn't matter. Lunch served Monday through Friday. Closed: Sun. Features: own baking, full bar, rated wine cellar, late dining. Jacket requested. Reservations recommended. Credit Cards: D, CB, V, MC, DC, A.

Campanile $$$ ★★★

624 South La Brea Avenue, ☎ (213) 938-1447.
Specialties: rosemary charred baby lamb; toasted walnut bread salad.
Lunch: 11:30 a.m.–2:30 p.m., entrees $10–$15.
Dinner: 6–10 p.m., entrees $18–$28.
This charming Mediterranean-style restaurant is set in a landmark 1920s building. The dining room can be a bit crowded, and the lighting in the tower at night is a bit unpleasant, but the food and the service are wonderful. Soups, breads, flavorful meats and fowl—all are prepared with flair and lots of tasty herbs. Both the wine list, which offers a variety of fine vintages from around the world, and the desserts are to die for. One of L.A.'s best. Closed for lunch on Saturday, and open only for breakfast on Sundays, from 8 a.m.–1:30 p.m. Features: outside dining, own baking, full bar, rated wine cellar, late dining. Jacket requested. Reservations required. Credit Cards: V, MC, A.

Checkers $$$ ★★★★

535 South Grand Avenue, ☎ (213) 624-0000.
Specialties: roasted rack of Colorado lamb; grilled salmon.
Lunch: 11:30 a.m.–2 p.m., entrees $15–$25.
Dinner: 5:30–9 p.m., entrees $17–$35.
Associated Hotel: Wyndham Checkers.
The restaurant's new chef, William Valentine, was formerly at the Windsor Hotel in New Orleans. He has apparently hit his stride, for early lukewarm reviews of his cooking have warmed up considerably. His presentation also earns raves, and the homemade breads are wonderful. An elegant respite from the downtown hustle and bustle. Features: Sunday brunch, full bar, rated wine cellar. Reservations recommended. Credit Cards: CB, V, MC, DC, A.

Engine Company No. 28 $$ ★★★

644 South Figueroa Street, ☎ (213) 624-6996.
Specialties: Grilled Seafood and Steak.
Lunch: from 11:15 a.m., entrees $10–$19.
Dinner: to 9 p.m., entrees $10–$19.
A former firehouse is home to this bistro, which serves up generous portions of meatloaf, mashed potatoes, and other true-blue goodies—just the way mom made 'em. Business folks hang out at the bar. Lunch served Monday through Friday. Features: own baking, full bar. Reservations required. Credit Cards: V, MC, A.

Epicentre $$ ★★

200 South Hill Street, ☎ (213) 625-0000.
Lunch: from 11 a.m., entrees $9–$14.
Dinner: to 10 p.m., entrees $10–$18.
Situated below the Kawada Hotel at Second and Hill, this hot new eclectic restaurant has a menu that lists "epitizers," "seismic entrees" and "aftershocks" (desserts). L.A. residents may not see the humor in this theme after the recent earthquake, but they're packing the place nonetheless. Live music Friday and Saturday nights. Closed: Sun. Features: own baking, full bar, late dining. Reservations recommended. Credit Cards: CB, V, MC, DC, A.

Muse $$ ★★★

7360 Beverly Boulevard, ☎ (213) 934-4400.

Dinner: 6–10:30 p.m., entrees $10–$20.

The ambience is stark but classy, and the food is always good at this understated restaurant in a nondescript location. The new, lower-priced menu shows the trend towards lighter, healthier eating, always a plus for Californians. Closed: Mon, Sun. Features: full bar, late dining. Reservations required. Credit Cards: V, MC, A.

Nicola $$$ ★ ★ ★

601 South Figueroa Street, ☎ (213) 485-927 .
Specialties: Nicola oysters; pan-fried rice noodles with roast duck.
Lunch: 11:30 a.m.–2 p.m., entrees $8–$17.
Dinner: 5–9 p.m., entrees $14–$23.

Larry Nicola, who owned the now-shuttered L.A. Nicola in Silver Lake, has opened this modern—even futuristic—dining room in the Sanwa Bank Plaza downtown. The interior is by Michael Rotondi, and Nicola himself mans the kitchen, turning out an eclectic menu of cuisine with California, Asian and Mediterranean influences. While some are muttering that the food is TOO far out, others are finding everything to their liking. The wine list is short, but well-rounded, and the desserts first-rate. One of the country's best new restaurants, according to *Bon Appetit* magazine. Closed: Sun. Features: own baking, full bar, rated wine cellar. Reservations recommended. Credit Cards: V, MC, A.

Pavilion $$$ ★ ★

135 North Grand Avenue, ☎ (213) 972-7333.
Specialties: rack of lamb; fresh fish.
Lunch: 11:30 a.m.–2:30 p.m., entrees $9–$16.
Dinner: 5:30–8 p.m., entrees $19–$29.

Most everyone who eats here is in a hurry to get to the Music Center, so everything is just a little too hurried, but the food is usually pretty good and sometimes excellent. Lunch is served only when there is a matinee performance and on Saturdays. Features: Sunday brunch, full bar. Jacket requested. Reservations recommended. Credit Cards: CB, V, MC, DC, A.

Chinese

Empress Pavilion $$ ★ ★ ★

988 North Hill Street, ☎ (213) 617-9898.
Specialties: Hong Kong style seafood; dim sum.
Lunch: from 11 a.m., entrees $8–$15.
Dinner: to 10 p.m., entrees $8–$15.

Dim sum is a treat at this Hong Kong-style cafe, which also specializes in seafood. A welcome addition to the Chinese District. Lunch served Monday through Friday. Features: own baking, late dining. Reservations recommended. Credit Cards: V, MC.

Mon Kee $$ ★ ★ ★

679 North Spring Street, ☎ (213) 628-6717.
Specialties: crab with garlic pepper and onion; crispy shrimp.
Lunch: 11:30 a.m.–3 p.m., entrees $5 $22.
Dinner: 3–9:45 p.m., entrees $5–$22.

The decor isn't much, there's always a wait, and the service is often abrupt, but the seemingly endless variety of seafood, prepared with a seemingly endless variety of sauces, never fails to please. The lunch special, which starts at $3.95, is a good buy. Another location in Santa

Monica. Features: wine and beer only. Reservations recommended.
Credit Cards: CB, V, MC, DC, A.

French

Grill Lyon $$$ ★ ★

424 East 2nd Street, ☎ (213) 620-1223.
Lunch: 11:30 a.m.–2 p.m., entrees $5–$10.
Dinner: 5:30–9 p.m., entrees $13–$19.

Grill Lyon is known for being efficient when you're trying to catch a quick bite on your way to the Music Center, and its French-influenced Japanese food is very good in spite of what the low-brow mini-mall location would indicate. Lunch served Monday through Friday. Closed: Sun. Features: own baking, wine and beer only. Reservations recommended. Credit Cards: V, MC.

Maison Magnolia $$$ ★ ★ ★ ★

2903 South Hoover Street, ☎ (213) 746-1314.
Lunch: from 12:30 p.m., prix fixe $0.
Dinner: to 8 p.m., prix fixe $50.

This little-known restaurant is situated in a beautifully restored post-Victorian home near USC. Every meal has a set price, and reservations are absolutely required for the one lunch sitting and one dinner sitting each night. There are only 30 seats in the gorgeous dining room, which features gilded mirrors, antique furniture, thick carpets and tables adorned with crisp linens, heavy silver and the finest crystal. And the food is as sumptuous as the ambience. Two wines and champagne are included with the five-course dinner, which can take up to three hours to savor and enjoy. A dining experience you won't soon forget. Sunday brunch seating at 12:30 p.m.; $25. Closed: Mon. Features: outside dining, own baking, Sunday brunch, rated wine cellar. Reservations required. Credit Cards: A.

Tower, The $$$ ★ ★ ★

1150 South Olive Street, ☎ (213) 746-1554.
Specialties: fresh seafood; roast duckling; veal.
Lunch: 11:30 a.m.–2 p.m., entrees $15–$26.
Dinner: 5:30–10 p.m., entrees $17–$26.

The Tower is located on the 32nd floor of the TransAmerica Building, where the view is to die for and some guests are willing to pay for the privilege of being received via helicopter on the roof. Classic French cuisine (don't miss the house-smoked salmon) shines in a sophisticated environment. Lunch served on weekdays only. Closed: Sun. Features: splendid view, own baking, full bar, rated wine cellar, late dining. Jacket requested. Reservations recommended. Credit Cards: CB, V, MC, DC, A.

Italian

Ca'Brea $$$ ★ ★ ★

346 South La Brea Avenue, ☎ (213) 938-2863.
Specialties: grilled eggplant; osso buco.
Lunch: 11:30 a.m.–2:30 p.m., entrees $10–$20.
Dinner: to 10:30 p.m., entrees $10–$25.

One of THE hottest new restaurants in town was opened in 1991 by Jean Louis De Mori and Antonio Tommasi of Locanda Veneta fame. The three-level, upscale eatery is noisy, crowded, and it's hard to get a seat, but everything shines. Popular with a variety of entertainment types, from stars to civilians. Lunch served Monday through Friday. Closed: Sun. Features: own baking, full bar, rated wine cellar, late dining, private dining rooms. Reservations required. Credit Cards: CB, V, MC, DC, A.

Cardini $$$ ★★★

930 Wilshire Boulevard, ☎ *(213) 227-3464.*
Specialties: pasta; veal; fish.
Lunch: 11:30 a.m.–2 p.m., entrees $12–$19.
Dinner: 5:30–10 p.m., entrees $13–$24.
Associated hotel: Omni Los Angeles.

Elegant Italian decor featuring marble floors and columns, and a dramatic piazza around the pool. Excellent pasta and fish. Lunch served Monday through Friday. Closed: Sun. Features: outside dining, own baking, full bar, rated wine cellar, late dining. Jacket requested. Reservations recommended. Credit Cards: D, V, MC, A.

Farfalla $$ ★★

143 North La Brea Avenue, ☎ *(213) 938-2504.*
Lunch: 11:30 a.m.–2:30 p.m., entrees $7–$18.
Dinner: 6–11 p.m., entrees $7–$18.

The people-watching here is just as much fun as the grazing, and the noise level is high enough to put a damper on dinner conversation. Lots of trendy pizzas and pastas, but the service is sometimes lacking. Lunch served Monday through Friday. Features: own baking, full bar, late dining. Reservations recommended. Credit Cards: CB, V, MC, DC, A.

Locanda Veneta $$$ ★★★★

8638 West Third Street, ☎ *(310) 274-1893.*
Lunch: 11:30 a.m.–2:30 p.m., entrees $10–$25.
Dinner: 5:30–10:30 p.m., entrees $10–$25.

Simple, fresh ingredients are combined here to produce hearty Italian dishes that may surprise you with their sophistication. A small but pleasant dining room and warm service add to the appeal. Ask for the Linguini with Rock Shrimp, Asparagus and Tomatoes, an insiders' specialty that isn't on the menu. Lunch served Monday through Friday. Closed: Sun. Features: wine and beer only, late dining. Reservations required. Credit Cards: V, MC, A.

Orso $$ ★★★

8706 West Third Street, ☎ *(310) 274-7144.*
Lunch: from 11:45 a.m., entrees $10–$19.
Dinner: to 11 p.m., entrees $10–$19.

The food is trendy, the clientele glamorous (and often famous), and the waiters hip at this sophisticated eatery where the menu changes daily and the wine list is heavy with Italian vintages. Dining on the patio is a quintessentially L.A. experience. Features: full bar, rated wine cellar, late dining. Reservations recommended. Credit Cards: V, MC.

Pane e Vino $$ ★★★

8265 Beverly Boulevard, ☎ *(213) 651-4600.*
Lunch: from 11:30 a.m., entrees $8–$20.
Dinner: to 11 p.m., entrees $8–$20.

Pane e Vino (whose other branch is in Santa Barbara) is a lively cafe where you'll be assailed by the aroma of fresh-baked bread, garlic, and classic Italian dishes. The owners are from Prego, and they really know what they're doing. Great food, fair prices. Features: outside dining, wine and beer only, rated wine cellar, late dining. Reservations recommended. Credit Cards: V, MC.

Rex II Ristorante $$$ ★★★★

617 South Olive Street, ☎ *(213) 627-2300.*
Lunch: noon–2 p.m., entrees $18–$28.
Dinner: 6–10 p.m., entrees $18–$28.

Rex Il Ristorante, opened in the art deco Oviatt Building in 1981, is currently turning out some of the best Italian food in L.A., and it's doing it in an incredibly classy setting. With black marble tables, elegant oak columns, and well-orchestrated service by tuxedoed waiters, the Rex harks back to the kind of dining experience associated with days gone by. The whole experience is a first-class exercise in indulgence, especially if you end your evening with dancing in the classy lounge upstairs. Rex was one of only two Italian restaurants in L.A. (the other was Valentino) to receive the highest rating in Luigi Veronelli's new book, The Best Italian Restaurants in America. Lunch is served only on Thursday and Friday. Rex's owner, Mauro Vincenti, is one of the partners in the new Alto Palato, which is also getting rave reviews Closed: Sun. Features: full bar, rated wine cellar, late dining. Jacket and tie requested. Reservations required. Credit Cards: CB, V, MC, DC, A.

Scarlatti $$ ★★

333 South Figueroa Street, ☎ *(213) 617-6045.*
Dinner: 5:30–10 p.m., entrees $10–$18.
Associated hotel: Sheraton Grande.

The former Ravel offers a pre-theater menu and free limo service to and from the Music Center. Trey Foshee, formerly of Rockenwagner and John Sedlar's stylish Abiquiu, is currently turning out California-style cuisine here, and the imaginative pastas and homemade breads are excellent. Closed: Mon, Sun. Features: own baking, full bar, rated wine cellar, late dining. Reservations recommended. Credit Cards: CB, V, MC, DC, A.

Japanese

A Thousand Cranes $$$ ★★★

120 South Los Angeles Street, ☎ *(213) 629-1200.*
Specialties: shabu-shabu; tempura & sushi bars.
Lunch: 11:30 a.m.–2 p.m., entrees $14–$20.
Dinner: 6–9:30 p.m., entrees $22–$30.
Associated hotel: New Otani Hotel & Garden.

This beautiful, serene restaurant atop the New Otani offers authentic (and expensive) Japanese fare in a lovely setting, with excellent service. You can order a la carte, or opt for the Kaiseki dinners, which run from $22 to $85. The Sunday brunch (served 11 a.m.–2 p.m.) is a good value. Features: splendid view, own baking, Sunday brunch, full bar, private dining rooms. Reservations recommended. Credit Cards: CB, V, MC, DC, A.

Garden Grill $$$ ★★★

120 South Los Angeles Street, ☎ *(213) 629-1200.*
Lunch: 11:30 a.m.–2 p.m., entrees $15–$100.
Dinner: 6–9:30 p.m., entrees $25–$150.
Associated hotel: New Otani Hotel.

If you're going to spend a fortune here, you might as well go for the prix fixe menu, which costs $16.50 at lunch and ranges from $38 to

$48 per person at dinner. You'll get fabulous Wagyu beef (or Black Angus if you can't afford Wagyu, which, at about $12 an ounce, will eat up your expense account in no time), and other delicacies served teppan-yaki style, but in a much more sophisticated manner than you'll find at Benihana. There's no doubt that—if you can afford it— this place delivers Japanese-style luxury to die for. Features: splendid view, own baking, full bar, rated wine cellar. Reservations required. Credit Cards: CB, V, MC, DC, A.

Katsu 3rd $$ ★★★
8636 West Third Street, ☎ *(310) 273-3605.*
Specialties: bento box; seafood.
Lunch: 11:30 a.m.–2 p.m., entrees $8–$12.
Dinner: 6–10 p.m., entrees $10–$15.
Called everything from "weird" to "whimsical," this branch of Katsu has offered everything from pot roast in a bento box to sashimi to wienerschnitzel. Now, it focuses more precisely on the cuisine of Japan, which is as good as ever, but not quite so quirky. Lunch served Monday through Friday. Closed: Sun. Features: wine and beer only, late dining. Reservations recommended. Credit Cards: V, MC, A.

O'toto $ ★★
7119 Melrose Avenue, ☎ *(213) 937-5435.*
Lunch: noon–3 p.m., entrees $5–$10.
Dinner: 6–10:30 p.m., entrees $5–$10.
When O'toto opened, it was the restaurant of the moment. Now, Melrose's formerly "hip-sophisto" meeting place is a family-style Japanese restaurant. Talk about the rapid comings and goings of L.A. restaurants! Pity. Lunch served Monday through Friday. Features: wine and beer only, late dining. Reservations recommended. Credit Cards: CB, V, MC, DC, A.

Mediterranean

Al Amir $$ ★★★★
5750 Wilshire Boulevard, ☎ *(213) 931-8740.*
Specialties: hoomos; tabouli; falafel; kibbe.
Lunch: 11:30 a.m.–3 p.m., entrees $7–$11.
Dinner: 3–9:30 p.m., entrees $11–$16.
Excellent (and authentic) Lebanese fare draws crowds from the nearby County Art Museum, and there's an especially nice selection of coffees to accompany your dessert. Considered by many to be the best restaurant of its kind in the city. Lunch Monday through Friday. Closed: Sun. Features: outside dining, own baking, full bar. Reservations recommended. Credit Cards: D, CB, V, MC, DC, A.

Atlas $$$ ★★★
3760 Wilshire Boulevard, ☎ *(213) 380-8400.*
Specialties: oyster loaf; grilled fish and meats.
Lunch: 11:30 a.m.–3 p.m., entrees $9–$16.
Dinner: 6–11 p.m., entrees $9–$25.

One of those places to see and be seen in L.A., the Atlas Bar & Grill (the locals just call it "the Atlas") delivers an eclectic menu that is a grazer's delight. The food isn't all that great, but the startling art deco decor and live jazz in the evenings draw an extremely hip crowd from the adjacent Wiltern Theatre. Lunch served Monday through Friday. Features: Sunday brunch, full bar, late dining. Reservations recommended. Credit Cards: CB, V, MC, DC, A.

Patinette at MOCA $$ ★★

250 South Grand Avenue, ☎ *(213) 626-1178.*
Specialties: salads; soups; sandwiches; pasta.
Lunch: 10:30 a.m.–4 p.m., entrees $7–$12.

Chef Joachim Splichal (Patina) has provided a boon for museum-
goers in this upscale lunch-only cafeteria located at the Museum of
Contemporary Art. Having to stand in line isn't fun, but the soups,
salads and sandwiches are good and the desserts are yummy. This isn't
as good as Patina, of course, but it's the best place around these parts,
and the price is right. Open until 8 p.m. on Thursdays. Closed: Mon.
Features: outside dining, own baking, wine and beer only. Credit Cards:
V, MC, A.

Sofi $$ ★★★

8030 3/4 West Third Street, ☎ *(213) 651-346 .*
Specialties: moussaka; gallactoboureko.
Lunch: noon–2:30 p.m., entrees $7–$10.
Dinner: 5:30–11 p.m., entrees $8–$15.

Sofi draws rave reviews for fabulous homemade Greek food. Restaurant critic Paul Wallach called the cuisine at Sofi's "eons above" that
of most other Greek restaurants. Takeout food is also available. Features: outside dining, own baking, wine and beer only, late dining.
Reservations recommended. Credit Cards: V, MC, A.

Seafood

McCormick's & Schmick's $$ ★★★

633 West Fifth Street, ☎ *(213) 629-1929.*
Lunch: from 11:30 a.m., entrees $10–$20.
Dinner: to 10 p.m., entrees $10–$20.

Located on the fourth level of the First Interstate World Center, this
outpost of the Pacific Northwest seafood chain offers nearly 30 vari-
eties of fresh fish, large portions, reasonable prices, a variety of good
beers and wines, and a view of the city. Critics complain that you can't
always count on what comes out of the kitchen. Free shuttle to the
Music Center, and a late night menu for post-theatre grazing that fea-
tures a selection of items for $1.95. Lunch served Monday through
Friday. Features: splendid view, outside dining, full bar, rated wine
cellar, late dining. Reservations recommended. Credit Cards: CB, V, MC,
DC, A.

Water Grill $$$ ★★★★

544 South Grand Avenue, ☎ *(213) 891-900 .*
Specialties: fruits of the sea platter; oyster bar; scampi.
Lunch: from 11:30 a.m., entrees $9–$20.
Dinner: to 10 p.m., entrees $12–$30.

Fresh seafood is flown in daily to this downtown newcomer in the
Pacific Mutual Building. High points are crab cakes, which are some
of the best on the West Coast, fabulous homemade desserts, and a
staff said to be one of the best-trained in L.A. Water Grill may just be
the best seafood restaurant in the city. Lunch served Monday through
Friday. Features: own baking, full bar, rated wine cellar, late dining.
Jacket requested. Reservations recommended. Credit Cards: CB, V, MC,
DC, A.

Southwestern

Kachina Grill $$ ★★

330 South Hope Street, ☎ *(213) 625-956 .*
Specialties: tostadas; salads.
Lunch: 11:30 a.m.–3 p.m., entrees $7–$10.
Dinner: 5–9 p.m., entrees $9–$15.

Good reviews for this new restaurant at Wells Fargo Center, which
many say offers something new, even if Southwestern is becoming a
bit passe. The food is fresh, tasty, and served in generous portions,
and it's a great spot for after-work grazing. This is definitely the place
to be when Friday night happy hour rolls around and everyone stands
around the bar throwing back shots of tequila. The Kachina Grill has
one of the best selections in L.A., with more than 40 varieties on
hand—many of them hard to find in other bars around town. Down-
ing a few is guaranteed to loosen you up for the weekend! Closed:
Sun. Features: outside dining, own baking, full bar, late dining. Credit
Cards: CB, V, MC, DC, A.

Sonora Cafe $$$ ★★★

180 South La Brea, ☎ *(213) 857-1800.*
Specialties: duck tamales; crab and wild mushroom enchiladas.
Lunch: 11:30 a.m.–3 p.m., entrees $10–$20.
Dinner: 5:30–9 p.m., entrees $15–$25.

A Southwestern-Mexican mix famous for (among other things) its
potent, individually shaken margaritas with Cuervo 1800 Tequila and
Cointreau. The restaurant moved to the City Restaurant's former
location in midtown L.A. in 1994, and celebrated the move with a
complete renovation at the new address. The management spared no
expense, and the result is a sort of Southwestern theme room with a
big fireplace and other accoutrements of the genre. Great food.
Brunch served on Saturday. Closed: Sun. Features: splendid view,
outside dining, full bar. Jacket requested. Reservations recommended. Credit Cards: CB, V, MC, DC, A.

Los Feliz

Chinese

Chi Dynasty $$ ★★★

2112 Hillhurst Avenue, ☎ *(213) 667-3388.*
Specialties: orange-flavor beef; veal mandarin; fresh seafood.
Lunch: from 11:30 a.m., entrees $6–$9.
Dinner: to 10 p.m., entrees $9–$12.

There's much to offer at the Chi Dynasty, starting with impeccable
service and really good food. The ten-course degustation dinner, at
about $30, is a great way to sample the excellent preparations that
come out of the kitchen, and you are certain to find wines that nicely
complement the meal. You must reserve ahead. Features: own baking,
full bar, rated wine cellar, late dining. Jacket requested. Reservations
recommended. Credit Cards: CB, V, MC, A.

International

Vida $$$ ★★★

1930 Hillhurst Avenue, ☎ *(213) 660-4445.*
Specialties: beef babcock; shrimp x 3.
Dinner: 6–11:30 p.m., entrees $12–$29.

You'll have to squeeze your way past a passel of Generation Xers to get into Vida, currently THE hot topic on the L.A. dining scene. Chef Fred Eric (The Olive, the Lipp) turns out exceedingly eclectic cuisine (a gumbo called Okra Winfrey and a Cobb salad dubbed Ty Cobb), incongruously trendy and "down home" at the same time, and the Beautiful People are eating it up (pun intended). Lunch served Tuesday through Friday. Closed: Mon. Features: Sunday brunch, late dining, private dining rooms. Credit Cards: V, MC, A.

Italian

Louise's Trattoria **$** ★★

4500 Los Feliz Boulevard, ☎ *(213) 667-0777.*
Specialties: pizza; pasta; grilled meats.
Lunch: from 11:30 a.m., entrees $5–$10.
Dinner: to 11 p.m., entrees $7–$10.

There's a slew of Louise's Trattorias all over L.A. and beyond, and fans insist that the food—most of it homemade—is fabulous for the price. Not everyone agrees with this assessment: one critic, referring to Louise's as a "chain threatening to devour L.A.," found nothing much to cheer about. Still, improvements have been in the works since last year, and Louise's may finally be getting some respect. Features: own baking, wine and beer only, late dining. Credit Cards: V, MC, A.

Japanese

Katsu **$$** ★★★

1972 Hillhurst Avenue, ☎ *(213) 665-1891.*
Specialties: sushi; kaiseki.
Lunch: noon–2 p.m., entrees $7–$9.
Dinner: 6–10 p.m., entrees $11–$15.

For an adventurous dining experience you won't soon forget, sit at the counter and devour the fresh sushi and sashimi being turned out by chefs with a magical touch. Fabulous food served in a minimalist room. Lunch served Monday through Saturday. Features: own baking, full bar, wine and beer only, late dining. Reservations recommended. Credit Cards: V, MC, A.

Latin American

Cha Cha Cha **$$** ★★★

656 North Virgil Avenue, ☎ *(213) 664-7723.*
Specialties: cha cha chicken; pizza latina; empanadas.
Lunch: entrees $9–$18.
Dinner: to 10:30 p.m., entrees $11–$17.

Spicy Latin American cuisine draws crowds, which means that the noise level is just a tad below unbearable, but the food is terrific and the atmosphere fun. Opens for breakfast at 8 a.m. and stays open all day. Features: wine and beer only, late dining. Reservations required. Credit Cards: V, MC, A.

Monterey Park

Asian

Ocean Star **$$** ★★★

145 North Atlantic Boulevard, ☎ *(818) 308-2128.*
Specialties: dim sum; fresh, live seafood.
Lunch: 10 a.m.–3 p.m., entrees $8–$15.
Dinner: 5–10 p.m., entrees $9–$20.

More than 800 diners at a time can be accommodated, and on weekends the place is often packed to capacity. Literally hundreds of varieties of dim sum, and live crabs, lobsters, prawns and other seafood wriggling in saltwater tanks are the main attractions. Another location at *112 North Chandler*, where the restaurant is smaller and a little more cozy, but the seafood is just as fresh. Buy your shrimp by the pound at both locations, and eat 'til you're stuffed. Features: full bar, late dining. Credit Cards: V, MC, A.

Chinese

Dragon Regency   **$$$**   ★★

120 South Atlantic, ☎ *(818) 282-1089.*
Specialties: dim sum; eastern sole & crab with garlic & black bean sauce.
Lunch: 11 a.m.–3 p.m., entrees $4–$50.
Dinner: 3–10 p.m., entrees $6–$50.
The food is the thing at this casual Cantonese restaurant specializing in seafood—especially shellfish. Tables full of Chinese patrons testify to the authenticity and quality of its dishes. Features: non-smoking area, late dining. Reservations recommended. Credit Cards: V, MC.

Harbor Village   **$$**   ★★★

111 North Atlantic, ☎ *(818) 300-8833.*
Specialties: live seafood; Peking duck; dim sum.
Lunch: 10 a.m.–2:30 p.m., entrees $7–$12.
Dinner: 5:30–10 p.m., entrees $10–$20.
If you know your way around a Chinese menu, there are lots of nice surprises at Harbor Village, one of the best Chinese restaurants in L.A. Unfortunately, the cooking can be inconsistent, so you never know whether your inevitable wait will be worth it when your meal arrives. Features: Sunday brunch, full bar, late dining, private dining rooms. Reservations recommended. Credit Cards: V, MC, A.

Lake Spring   **$$**   ★★

219 East Garvey Avenue, ☎ *(818) 280-3571.*
Specialties: noisette of pork pump.
Lunch: 11 a.m.–3 p.m., entrees $5–$10.
Dinner: 5–9:30 p.m., entrees $7–$15.
If you like well-prepared Chinese pork dishes, you aren't going to do much better than Lake Spring. If your dining companions aren't as crazy about pork as you are, there's much more to choose from on the interesting Shanghai menu. Features: no bar. Credit Cards: V, MC.

THE WESTSIDE

If you slice greater Los Angeles up like so many pieces of pie, you'll find that the Westside is a rather small piece, but it takes in some of the city's most exclusive (and most expensive) neighborhoods. Although they may be thrown into the same pie (to extend the metaphor), not all of the cities on the Westside have a whole lot in common. The hoity-toity city of Beverly Hills, for example, seems far removed from the hip goings-on in West Hollywood, even though there's not much in terms of distance to separate the two.

Because of this diversity within Westside neighborhoods, and because we doubt you will want to make a mistake in this regard (read: if you're low on money, stay away from Beverly Hills), below is a summary of each Westside area, its personality, and our list of the best stuff to see and do there.

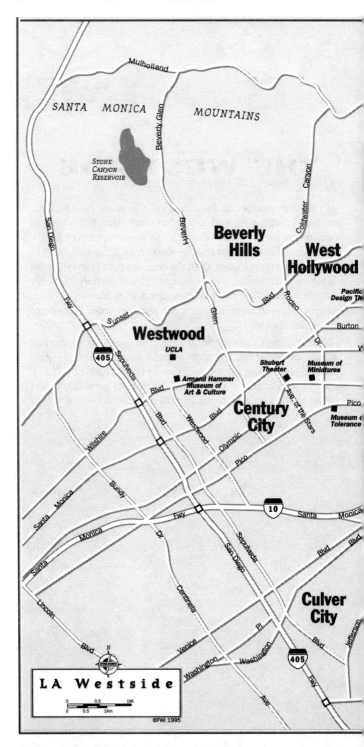

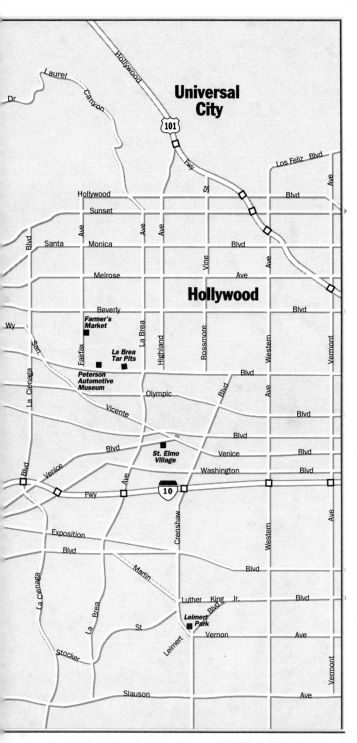

BEVERLY HILLS

Winged Victory, the classic symbol of Beverly Hills

As much as the City of Beverly Hills would like to deny it, there's a lot of truth to the "rich people's playground" image portrayed on the otherwise forgettable Fox TV series, "Beverly Hills 90210." There are lots of spoiled kids tooling around in outrageously expensive cars, there are mega-buck mansions set back from secluded, tree-lined streets, and the shopping is world-class. To give you an idea of how precious real estate is in Beverly Hills, in 1994, actor John Travolta and wife Kelly Preston rented a neat little place here for $25,000 a month, a tony little four-bedroom, seven-bath affair that completes the Travolta family's trio of homes—they have another on an island off the coast of Maine, and one in Carmel.

In Beverly Hills, you'll find the largest "day spa" in California, the 12,000 square-foot Umberto, whose clients include Madonna, Cher and "90210's" former bad girl, Shannen Doherty. Beverly Hot Springs, featuring L.A.'s only natural springs, offers hot mineral baths, massage, skin and body care, not to mention all that frolicking in the 105 degree springs (males and females have separate grottos, so "going natural" is encouraged), and attracts the Hollywood set like a magnet. Clients include Jodie Foster, Brooke Shields, Cindy Crawford, Keanu Reeves and Magic Johnson, to name a few.

Belgian-born hairdresser-to-the-stars Cristophe also has his salon in Beverly Hills, but it's unlikely you can get an appointment with the master, who counts among his customers Sally Field, Bill and Hilary Clinton and Kate Capshaw (aka Mrs. Spielberg).

At the Beverly Hilton Hotel, the concierge will accommodate your every whim, from filling your bathtub full of rose petals to satisfying your craving for expensive, imported chocolate at three in the morning; and at the Regent Beverly Wilshire, you can dine in one of L.A.'s most elegant restaurants, simply called The Dining Room.

The epitome of Beverly Hills attitude may have been reflected in a fund-raiser held at the city's exclusive All Saints' School. Eschewing the usual student-involved bake sale or door-to-door candy pedaling, school officials sponsored a Spring Fling Silent Auction, where items on the block included a registered Paso Fino mare with an estimated value of $10,000, a non-speaking, walk-on part in a feature film, a private screening for 200 at Paramount, and a crew jacket from the "Melrose Place" TV series.

Fielding's Star Hangouts

Nearly everyone who comes to L.A. is dying to see a movie star, but only insiders know where to find them. In most of the trendy clubs, stars hibernate in private rooms, so waiting in line for an hour at the House of Blues is no guarantee that you'll see someone famous once you get inside. Your chances are much greater at one of these places:

Tea Garden Herbal Emporiums in West Hollywood (9001 Beverly Boulevard) and Santa Monica (1609 Montana Avenue). *Healthful New Age libations for the Beautiful People. Closes early—at 7 p.m. on weekdays and Saturdays, 6 p.m. on Sundays.*

Beverly Hot Springs Spa (308 North Oxford Drive, L.A.). *Sure, you might not be able to afford to "Relax, Rejuvenate, Refresh, and Rejoice" (as the ad promises), but a massage or mineral bath may not be out of the question. Some of THE hippest people in Hollywood regularly show up here for the total body treatment.*

American Rag (La Brea between Wilshire and Beverly, West L.A.). *This way-cool empire of style has everything from vintage apparel to designer jeans to housewares to espresso. Give yourself plenty of time to browse and keep one eye on the door; stars come in all the time.*

These and all of the above-mentioned luxuries come at a horrific cost, of course, and the city of Beverly Hills wears its snootiness on its sleeve as if warning the "unworthy" to stay away. According to an advertisement for the "new" Beverly Hills, "[the city] wears its glamour rather shamelessly, tantalizing the visitor with potential." Right. The only sort of "potential" available in Beverly Hills costs a whole lot of money.

There isn't much crime in Beverly Hills, and what does occur is usually a big-time heist such as the holding up of a jewelry store or Brinks truck, or a messy family matter such as the Menendez murders. There was also, of course, that high-profile case of Zsa Zsa Gabor slapping a cop, who arrested her at the corner of Olympic and La Cienega and put her in jail. This incident, minor by most standards, got the fading Zsa Zsa more publicity than she'd had in ages, plus a few appearances on TV, a payoff no doubt worth all the alleged trauma she suffered at the hands of police.

The biggest crisis to hit Beverly Hills in years came in the unseasonably hot summer of 1994, when—while the rest of L.A. sweltered—the massive turn-on of air conditioners in the city caused a local power shortage and a cooling unit burn-out for unhappy residents who aren't at all used to being inconvenienced. They got over it.

Everything is so utterly immaculate, so perfectly groomed, and so highly maintained in Beverly Hills that city streets sometimes seem devoid of any personality at all, which is just the way residents like it. Nearly everyone in Beverly Hills is perfectly content to exist anonymously in their exclusive bastion of Westside superiority.

Beverly Hills: Things to See and Do

You won't find many opportunities for sightseeing in Beverly Hills proper, but a trip aboard the Beverly Hills Trolley will take you past the city's historical and architectural highlights. If you love exotic gardens, don't miss the beautiful 6.2-acre Virginia Robinson Gardens, one of the city's best-kept secrets. You must reserve by phone a week ahead, but the tour is well worth waiting for.

Stars at Home

Last—and certainly least—you can spring for a map of stars' homes (they are hawked on street corners all over the place), which will entitle you to park near the outside gate of a huge mansion that may or may not be occupied by the person you hope to see, and stare at virtually nothing until you get tired of it. Trust us; Heather Locklear is not going to come out of the house in her bathrobe to pick up the morning paper. If you're really into seeing stars' homes, take one of the tours. That way, you don't have to worry about parking and you'll get all the inside scoop from guides in the know.

Movie stars—although many live there—are not much easier to spot in Beverly Hills than are the rest of the city's publicity-shy residents. The best places for stargazing may be at the Beverly Hills Farmer's Market, held on Sundays on Canon Drive; along Rodeo Drive (where Richard Gere spent a fortune on Julia Roberts in *Pretty Woman*); on Wilshire Boulevard; and at some of the city's most popular restaurants such as the Bistro Garden, Maple Drive or Tatou (which also hosts a very hot late-night club scene).

Fans of the aforementioned "Beverly Hills 90210" will want to make a pilgrimage to the city's soon-to-be built reproduction of the series' "Peach Pit" restaurant in Beverly Center. (Rich kid Brandon Walsh inexplicably made enough money slinging burgers at this formerly fictional Beverly Hills diner to buy a way-cool BVH wardrobe and other necessities of life in the fast lane.) Don't expect to find cast members hanging out here, but you'll be able to order namesake dishes from the cutesy menu. (The restaurant has already missed its scheduled opening date, and "negotiations are continuing," so you may or may not see a Peach Pit in Beverly Hills in 1995 or 1996.)

Far more impressive than the Peach Pit will be the city's 23,000-square-foot **Museum of Television and Radio**, which is scheduled for a late-1995 opening on the corner of North Beverly Drive and Little Santa Monica Boulevard. This West Coast branch of the New York original will be designed by Richard Meier and is expected to cost $10 million. High-tech wizardry will link the entire collection of the East Coast museum to L.A., including more than 60,000 TV and radio shows that will be available to the visiting public.

Fielding's Choice: Best Reference for Cyclists

Robert Winning's "Short Bike Rides In and Around Los Angeles" (1993) is the perfect resource for both residents and visitors who want to see the local sights on a bike. Many of the rides included in the book are unique—such as the "Marilyn Monroe Memorial Tour" that takes you to the ill-fated actress' former haunts. (Note: Not all of these rides are "short" unless you're in good shape and used to biking. The Monroe tour, for example, covers 22 miles, takes two hours, and includes a "couple of hairy intersections!")

Beverly Hills certainly has its share of fancy events, but a new one may turn out to be the most popular with tourists. **Happy Harley Days**/Rejoice on Rodeo, a parade and bike show held in December, features more than 1000 Harleys, many with celebrity riders (Grand Marshal Cher led the 1994 parade) who roar down Rodeo Drive to make money for charity. Even though there are nearly as many Hell's Angels in the crowd as there are celebs, the event is for a good cause (it raises money for the Ronald McDonald camp for children with cancer) and the more affluent among the participants and spectators wander into the shops on Rodeo Drive and spend money, which keeps the local merchants happy. (Winners in the several categories at the bike show get gift certificates to chic Rodeo Drive shops as prizes.) The first annual parade was held in December of 1994, but the event is expected to become a tradition, so check the Beverly Hills calendar of events if you're in town in December.

Author's Tip

Happy Harley Days/Rejoice on Rodeo is just one of the places where the unbearably hip hang out with their Harleys in L.A. Others include the Rock Store (a casual cafe/tavern which has been around for more than two decades just east of Kanan Dume Road on Mulholland), where dozens of pricey bikes and their owners can be found on Sunday afternoons; and Westbrook Originals (13434 Saticoy in North Hollywood), where RUBs (Rich Urban Bikers) and celebrity clients go to have their Harleys turned into classic works of art by "Motorcycle Michelangelo" Billy Westbrook, who redesigns, rebuilds, paints and customizes bikes into cutting-edge pieces of machinery.

Parks and Gardens

Virginia Robinson Gardens   ★★★★

1008 Elden Drive, Beverly Hills, 90210, ☎ (310) 276-5367.
Until recently, the address of this exquisite 6.2-acre garden estate of Mr. and Mrs. Harry Robinson was never published, part of an effort to preserve its status as L.A.'s "Secret Garden." Tours are by appointment only, and reservations should be made a week in advance. Once you find the place, you will see what has been called "a botanical feast for the fortunate visitor": rare tropical trees and plants, flowers, a palm forest, and some striking landscaping, all offset by statuary, ponds and fountains. Tours are at 10 a.m. and 1 p.m. Tuesday through Thursday; 10 a.m. Friday. Free admission. General admission: $5.

Sports and Recreation

Aida Thibiant Day Spa

449 North Canon Drive, Beverly Hills, 90210.
Another of those expensive, hoity-toity day spas, this one admonishes you to "surrender to our expert and soothing pampering," which includes European facials, hydrotherapy, panthermal baths, body contouring, detoxifying seaweed cocooning (huh?), Swiss aromatherapy showers, aromatherapy, phytotherapy and marinetherapy. Face it: ya gotta have it!

Theater

Canon Theatre   ★★★

205 North Canon Drive, Beverly Hills, ☎ (310) 859-2830.
There's always something interesting on the boards at this small, local theater, such as "Shakespeare For My Father," a recent production. Call for the latest.

Theatre 40   ★★★

241 Moreno Drive, Beverly Hills, 90210, ☎ (213) 466-1767.
There's generally lots of good stuff coming out of this small local theater, which presents a mix of classic, contemporary, and premiere works. Its annual One-Act Festival, held in January, is generally regarded as one of the most eclectic—and superb—mixes in town. Tickets must be reserved through Theatix ☎ *(213) 466-1767).*

Ticket Agencies

Al Brooks Ticket Agency

900 Wilshire Boulevard, Suite #104, Los Angeles, 90017, ☎ (213) 626-5863.

Tickets for sporting events, concerts, theater, and other entertainment events for L.A., San Francisco and New York.

Tours

Beverly Hills Trolley   ★★
455 North Rexford Drive, Beverly Hills, 90210, ☎ *(310) 285-2551.*
Hours open: 10 a.m.–5 p.m.
Fans of the popular TV series will love this 40-minute trolley tour of the REAL "Beverly Hills 90210," with jaunts past some of the world's most exclusive Rodeo Drive shops and other star-studded locations. Trolleys depart every hour on the half-hour from the corner of Dayton Way and North Rodeo Drive, in front of the Chanel Boutique. No tours when it rains. General admission: $2.

Beverly Hills: Nightlife

While Beverly Hills doesn't offer much in the way of performing arts (all those rich people can take limos to the Music Center downtown whenever they're in the mood), it has a few trendy nightspots that range from the ultra-sophisticated (The Polo Lounge at the Beverly Hills Hotel) to the exceedingly hip (China Club at Tatou). The Hana Lounge at the Hotel Nikko has a popular bar area where the atmosphere is casual and you can even sit on the floor. The Paul Turner Trio plays swing music on weekends.

The newest "in" place in town is Sanctuary, partially owned by that "Baywatch" babe, Pamela Anderson. There's not a lot of ear-splitting music (although jazz and blues are on the menu Tuesday-Thursday), but there's oodles of atmosphere and lots of nooks and crannies for being inconspicuous. Don't miss the larger-than-life drawing of a nude by Renoir that takes up nearly an entire wall in the back room.

Of course, if you REALLY want some action, you may have to go to Hollywood, which is where most of L.A.'s trendier clubs are.

Regent Beverly Wilshire
9500 Wilshire Boulevard, Beverly Hills, 90212, ☎ *(310) 275-5200.*
South end of Rodeo Drive at Wilshire.
Established in 1928, this renovated and expanded hotel rates highly for its hosting of celebrities, its classy bar, and the afternoon high tea served in the nearby lounge. Piano is played nightly beginning at 5 p.m.

Sanctuary
180 North Robertson Boulevard, Beverly Hills, ☎ *(310) 358-0303.*
Sanctuary, one of whose backers is "Baywatch's" Pamela Anderson, is another of those hotbeds of celebrity activity, where actresses in tiny black dresses and buff actors eye each other or ogle the huge—and some say offensive—drawing of a nude by Renoir that takes up an entire wall. This is an ULTRA-cool place to spend an evening, with unique decor and live music.

Tatou

235 North Beverly Drive, Beverly Hills, ☎ *(310) 274-9955.*
One of "The Best" places to be in Los Angeles on Monday nights is Tatou, where what amounts to an all-star jam session is the scene of the moment, often attended by enough of the "Beautiful People" to

take your breath away. Stephen Stills, David Crosby and other rock legends have jammed here recently and the scene is always as hot as the music. (Note: although the owners of Tatou are reportedly about to move the restaurant/club to Century City and give it a new name, the original Tatou is expected to remain open as a dance club in its current location.)

Beverly Hills: Shopping

"No. 319. A long silk–organza halter dress with arabesque crystal beading. With it Clarisse carries an unobtrusive .38 revolver with a handle of cloisonné enamel."

The stretch of **Rodeo Drive** between Santa Monica Boulevard and Wilshire has a long-standing reputation as one of the most exclusive shopping areas in the world. Such designer names as Giorgio Armani, Gucci, Yves St. Laurent, Christian Dior and Chanel are only a few represented on Rodeo Drive, where you can pick up a cute little jacket for $2000, or drop several times that on a piece of jewelry at Cartier, Tiffany, Fred Joaillier, or Van Cleef & Arpels. One of the most exclusive addresses on the street is 2 Rodeo, boasting a European-style complex of fine shops and restaurants located at the corner of Rodeo Drive and Wilshire.

Although the outward appearance of the stores is architecturally underwhelming, the classy boutiques do attract the rich and famous—many of whom shop by appointment and don't often stroll in and out of stores along the boulevard or leisurely window-shop. If you're not part of the "in" crowd, you may not be able to get an appointment, or are likely to be thrown the kind of snooty attitude Julia Roberts got as the unclassy strumpet shopping off the rack in *Pretty Woman*.

A recent arrival on Wilshire Boulevard (at 9570) is the exclusive **Barneys New York**, a dramatic $50-million, five-story neo-Spanish structure whose opening has reportedly given local trendites a new place to see and be seen away from Rodeo Drive, which—in spite of its worldwide reputation—no longer has a complete lock on Beverly Hills glamour.

Rumors are also afoot that Bloomingdale's has its eye on Beverly Drive for a West Coast flagship store to be completed in 1996.

Designer Georges Marciano, who recently purchased the Bank of America building across the street, is expected to turn the structure into a first-rate fashion showroom emporium by spring of 1997. Also expected to make an appearance in Beverly Hills in the near future are a 10,000-square-foot Williams-Sonoma flagship store and a new Sotheby's, located on Bedford at Wilshire.

Beverly Hills: Where to Stay

For such a small hunk of real estate, Beverly Hills boasts more than its share of first-rate hotels. Unfortunately (but predictably), most of them cost a small fortune, but you can usually count on getting what you pay for. We say usually, because even the hotels that don't measure up to the quality of the Four Seasons, the Peninsula, the Regent Beverly Wilshire, or the Hotel Nikko are pretty pricey because of the neighborhood.

The Four Seasons remains one of the top choices in Beverly Hills, and was just awarded its fifth diamond by the American Automobile Association (AAA). The Regent Beverly Wilshire, one of the city's other top-rated hotels, recently completed a $5 million renovation of its spacious ballroom, which is now dripping with pricey chandeliers and other objets d'art. The Beverly Prescott has also been in the news with the transformation of its Rox restaurant into Sylvie, owned by Sylvie Darr, formerly of San Francisco's Zuni Cafe.

If all of the above (and most of those below) are out of your price range, try the Beverly House, a very nice but reasonably priced bed and breakfast in the heart of Beverly Hills. It reportedly has many celebrity clients, who come and go quietly to avoid detection. (It's nice to know that even the rich and famous sometimes watch their expenses.)

Hotels and Resorts

Beverly Hilton   **$170–$220**   ★ ★ ★

9876 Wilshire Boulevard
☎ *(800) 922-5432, (310) 274-7777, FAX: 310-285-1313.*
Single: $170–$245. Double: $145–$220.
Located half a mile from famed Rodeo Drive, the Beverly Hilton is quite popular with foreign visitors and has an unmistakable cachet. Its amenities include a Rolls-Royce that shuttles guests in style, both a beauty salon and barber shop, a business center with a notary public and secretarial services, currency exchange, and several restaurants and bars. Ranked restaurant: **Trader Vic's**. Amenities: pool, exercise room, balcony or patio, family plan, conference facilities, business services. 581 rooms. Credit Cards: V, MC, A.

Beverly Plaza   **$139–$179**   ★ ★ ★

8384 West Third Street
☎ *(800) 624-6835, (213) 658-6600, FAX: 213-653-3464.*
Single: $139–$179. Double: $139–$179.

This modern, five-story property is near the Pacific Design Center and Farmers Market. The rooms are pleasant and large. Restaurants and shopping are easily accessed. Ranked restaurant: **Cava**. Amenities: pool, health club, Jacuzzi, sauna, family plan, conference facilities. 97 rooms. Credit Cards: CB, V, MC, DC, A.

Beverly Prescott Hotel $185   ★ ★ ★
1224 Beverwil Drive
☎ *(800) 421-3212, (310) 277-2800, FAX: 310-203-9537.*
Single: $185. Double: $185.
A sibling of the well-regarded Prescott Hotel in San Francisco, the Beverly Prescott is a newer luxury hotel featuring palm-lined gardens, canopied walkways and a lobby that brings back a vision of the 1930s. Guest rooms are well-appointed, plush, and comfortable, and many have views of the Hollywood Hills or Pacific Ocean. Rock stars may appreciate a stay in the new Jerry Garcia Suite, honoring the lead guitarist of the Grateful Dead. Ranked restaurant: **Sylvie**. Amenities: pool, health club, balcony or patio, conference facilities. 150 rooms. Credit Cards: V, MC, DC, A.

Beverly Rodeo $145–$185   ★ ★
360 North Rodeo Drive
☎ *(800) 356-7575, (310) 273-0300, FAX: 310-859-8730.*
Single: $145–$165. Double: $165–$185.
This small and unpretentious haven is the only hotel located on exclusive Rodeo Drive, but when you get tired of shopping you'll appreciate the lovely contemporary French Renaissance accents and luxurious guest rooms available here. Accommodations include coffee makers, bathrobes, hair dryers, and makeup mirrors, and extras include same-day laundry service. There's also a jogging track for working off whatever you eat at those nearby Beverly Hills restaurants. Some critics contend that the hotel is too basic for Beverly Hills, but others appreciate its friendly charm. Request one of the back rooms (which have balconies overlooking the restaurant) to escape street noise, or pamper yourself and splurge for a penthouse suite. Amenities: balcony or patio, family plan, club floor. 86 rooms. Credit Cards: CB, V, MC, DC, A.

Four Seasons $295–$510   ★ ★ ★ ★ ★
300 South Doheny Drive
☎ *(800) 332-3442, (310) 273-2222, FAX: 310-859-3824.*
Single: $295–$480. Double: $325–$510.
Elegant 15-story hotel decorated in formal European style amid gardens and flowing fountains. Sumptuous decorations, two excellent restaurants, a 12th-floor outdoor pool with snack bar and lounge area and first-rate service throughout combine to make this luxury hotel a first choice for Los Angeles visitors. Accommodations are done in shades of peach and sea-foam green and have hardwood furniture, minibars and French doors that open onto balconies. All is bright and efficient. Ranked restaurant: **Gardens**. Amenities: pool, exercise room, Jacuzzi, balcony or patio, conference facilities, business services. 285 rooms. Credit Cards: V, MC, A.

Hotel Nikko Beverly Hills $250–$450   ★ ★ ★ ★
465 La Cienega Boulevard
☎ *(800) 645-5687, (310) 247-0400, FAX: 310-247-0315.*

Single: $250–$450. Double: $275–$450.
Newer seven-story luxury class hotel that combines a striking contemporary exterior design with exquisite Japanese interior features. The hotel's central location is just minutes away from the downtown Wilshire business corridor, Pacific Design Center, Rodeo Drive, and the Los Angeles County Museum of Art. Its features include a multilingual staff, complimentary local limousine service, and a technologically advanced business center. Rooms are well-furnished with such extras as CD players and coffee makers. Amenities: pool, health club, sauna, balcony or patio, conference facilities, club floor, business services. 304 rooms. Credit Cards: V, MC, DC, A.

Peninsula Beverly Hills   **$300–$330**   ★★★★★

9882 Little Santa Monica Boulevard
☎ *(800) 462-7899, (310) 273-4888, FAX: 310-788-2309.*
Single: $300–$330. Double: $300–$330.
Newer, luxurious French Renaissance-style hotel located in the heart of Beverly Hills. Includes a rooftop garden with lap pool, whirlpool, and cabanas with private phones; gourmet restaurant with indoor and patio dining; and guest rooms attractively furnished with antiques, marble floors, rich fabrics, and mini-bars. (Suites and detached villas are even more luxurious.) Emphasis is on first-rate service at all hours of the day and night, and amenities include 24-hour butler service, valet, dry cleaning and laundry service, and a Rolls limousine to chauffeur guests. There are also extensive business services, including photographic and overnight printing services, portable cellular phones, and two-line phone service in each room that includes fax and modem connections. Complimentary newspapers are offered in several languages. Ranked restaurant: **Belvedere**. Amenities: pool, golf, exercise room, Jacuzzi, sauna, houses, cottages or bungalows, balcony or patio, conference facilities, business services. 200 rooms. Credit Cards: CB, V, MC, DC, A.

Radisson Beverly Pavilion   **$155–$200**   ★★★

9360 Wilshire Boulevard
☎ *(800) 441-5050, (310) 273-1400, FAX: 310-859-8551.*
Single: $155–$180. Double: $175–$200.
A European-style hotel with a rooftop pool in a garden setting, located two blocks from fashionable Rodeo Drive. Most rooms have refrigerators. There are limited extra amenities (including meeting space), but free limo service is provided throughout Beverly Hills, and guests looking for fitness opportunities can use the adjacent Santa Monica Boulevard jogging trail. Ranked restaurant: **Colette**. Amenities: pool, balcony or patio, conference facilities, business services. 110 rooms. Credit Cards: CB, V, MC, DC, A.

Ramada Beverly Hills   **$110–$145**   ★★★

1150 South Beverly Drive
☎ *(800) 666-2295, (310) 553-6561, FAX: 310-277-4469.*
Single: $110–$130. Double: $125–$145.
Some consider it sophisticated, others bland. Though the address is in Beverly Hills, the locale is rather plain and generic. Still, the hotel is professionally run and guests can patronize a nearby health club. Amenities: pool, exercise room, family plan, conference facilities, business services. 260 rooms. Credit Cards: V, MC, A.

Regent Beverly Wilshire $260–$4000 ★★★★

9500 Wilshire Boulevard
☎ *(800) 421-4354, (310) 275-5200, FAX: 310-274-2851.*
Single: $260–$4000. Double: $275–$4000.

Renovated to become one of the most outstanding hotels in Los Angeles, the Regent Beverly Wilshire features old-fashioned, European-style service on every floor. The decor is stunning, the management savvy, and the spa and fitness center superb, with a state-of-the-art health club, facials, massage and manicures available. Other services include currency exchange, the help of a multilingual staff, same-day laundry service, and a complete business center. If you have the chance, peek in at the newly-renovated ballroom, which, at a cost of about $5 million, now boasts stunning Venetian-glass chandeliers and gorgeous carpets and upholstery. Ranked restaurant: **The Dining Room**. Amenities: pool, health club, Jacuzzi, sauna, balcony or patio, hair salon, family plan, conference facilities, business services. 300 rooms. Credit Cards: V, MC, A.

Sofitel Los Angeles $195–$450 ★★★

8555 Beverly Boulevard
☎ *(800) 521-7772, (310) 278-5444, FAX: 310-657-2816.*
Single: $195–$250. Double: $195–$450.

New, luxurious country French-style hotel offering intimate lodging and dining, a multilingual staff, and access to downtown and Beverly Hills shopping. Soundproofed rooms and two-line phones with voice mail are standard. Amenities: pool, health club, sauna, balcony or patio, hair salon, family plan, conference facilities. 311 rooms. Credit Cards: CB, V, MC, DC, A.

Inns

Carlyle Inn $95–$105 ★★★

1119 South Robertson Boulevard
☎ *(800) 322-7595, (310) 275-4445, FAX: 310-859-0496.*
Single: $95. Double: $105.

Small motor inn featuring complimentary full breakfast and evening beverages. Rooms are located on four levels of circular terraces overlooking a lush courtyard and spa. Amenities: Jacuzzi, club floor. 32 rooms. Credit Cards: CB, V, MC, DC, A.

Beverly Hills: Where to Dine

Everyone's talking about Sylvie, the new restaurant adjacent to the Beverly Prescott Hotel that took the place of Rox. Sylvie Darr, formerly of the Zuni Cafe in San Francisco, owns the restaurant, which features an innovative menu of Mediterranean-inspired dishes.

L'Escoffier, located in the Beverly Hilton Hotel, was one of Beverly Hills' most prestigious special-occasion restaurants until its closure in the fall of 1994. There's a slight chance that it may be resurrected in 1995, but most feel a nod to more modern culinary trends would be necessary for L'Escoffier to succeed.

Celestino, a well-known Italian eatery on South Beverly Drive, recently changed its name to Cent'Anni after a dispute between feuding co-owner and former chef Celestino Drago and investor Art Vella. Drago, who left in

1991, wanted his name disassociated with the restaurant, but the name is all that has changed according to Vella, who retains ownership.

Although Beverly Hills sometimes seems as if it can't decide whether sophistication or trendiness is best, trendy is the by-word in many of its most popular restaurants. These include Bo Kaos, the Emporio Armani Express, Maple Drive, Piazza Rodeo, Tatou and Trilussa, all of which are loaded with Beautiful People.

Then there's Mezzaluna, which, in spite of criticisms about service, vaulted into prominence after Nicole Brown Simpson had her last meal there before being murdered. Reportedly anxious to cash in on the notoriety, the restaurant contacted at least one local restaurant critic soon after the murder, suggesting that it might be a good time to review the restaurant again in print. The critic declined. You have to give Mezzaluna credit, though; the restaurant business is pretty cutthroat in L.A., and cashing in on any gimmick possible may get you a leg up on the competition.

American

Barney Greengrass $$$ ★★★

9570 Wilshire Boulevard, ☎ (310) 777-5877.
Specialties: smoked sturgeon.
Lunch: from 11 a.m., entrees $6–$33.
Dinner: to 7 p.m., entrees $6–$33.

Smoked fish reigns supreme at Barney Greengrass, located above Barney's New York, and this West Coast version of the New York deli is making a big splash with the Beverly Hills set. Smoked sturgeon is a Barney's classic, but the smoked Nova Scotia salmon is also wonderful, and there are more than 100 other items to choose from. This is no corned beef sandwich place; Barney's offers high-class cuisine at high prices to chic patrons who shop at Armani next door and then come to fill up on fabulous deli food. Famous faces seen here since opening include Roseanne, Jerry Seinfeld, Ellen DeGeneres and Winona Ryder, to name a few. Features: outside dining, own baking, wine and beer only. Credit Cards: V, MC, DC, A.

Belvedere $$$ ★★★★

9882 Little Santa Monica Boulevard, ☎ (310) 273-4888.
Lunch: 11:30 a.m.–2:30 p.m., entrees $11–$18.
Dinner: 6–10:30 p.m., entrees $18–$26.
Associated hotel: Peninsula Beverly Hills.

This fancy dining room in the Peninsula Beverly Hills Hotel is known for its power breakfasts, afternoon tea and pricey New Wave cuisine. The food is generally quite good, but at these prices you have a right to expect stellar service, and you sometimes don't get it. Unless you're a hotel guest looking for a convenient place to dine, your money may be better spent elsewhere. Features: outside dining, own baking, Sunday brunch, late dining. Jacket requested. Reservations required. Credit Cards: CB, V, MC, DC, A.

Bistro Garden $$$ ★★★

176 North Canon Drive, ☎ (310) 550-3900.
Specialties: chicken burger; choucroute garni aisacienne; canellone.
Lunch: 11:30 a.m.–3 p.m., entrees $15–$25.
Dinner: 5:30–11 p.m., entrees $18–$30.

Since the demise of the nearby Bistro, this spinoff has really taken up the slack. The ambience is the real attraction, but the food is good, too, and the highly charged atmosphere is typical Beverly Hills. Plan to have dinner early if you want to avoid the irreverent buzz of the L.A. "scene." Another branch in Studio City. Features: outside dining, full bar, late dining. Jacket requested. Reservations recommended. Credit Cards: CB, V, MC, DC, A.

David Slay's La Veranda $$$ ★ ★ ★

225 South Beverly Drive, ☎ (310) 274-7246.
Lunch: 11:30 a.m.–2:30 p.m., entrees $7–$14.
Dinner: 5:30–10:30 p.m., entrees $15–$25.
David Slay's takes hearty Italian comfort food upscale with eclectic touches utilizing lots of garlic and fresh seafood. Most of what comes out of the kitchen is very good, but you'll have to judge whether or not the exorbitant prices are worth it. Lunch served Monday through Friday; three-course prix fixe lunch, $15; early bird prix fixe dinners weekdays, 5:30–7 p.m., $20. Sunday and Monday nights feature a "grazing" menu, where dishes run from $2 to $7 and provide an opportunity to taste David Slay's fare without spending a fortune. Features: full bar, rated wine cellar, late dining. Reservations recommended. Credit Cards: V, MC, A.

Dining Room, The $$$ ★ ★ ★ ★

9500 Wilshire Boulevard, ☎ (310) 274-8179.
Specialties: grilled seafood; foie gras; veal chops.
Lunch: 11:30 a.m.–2:30 p.m., entrees $15–$30.
Dinner: 6–10:30 p.m., entrees $15–$30.
Associated hotel: Regent Beverly Wilshire.
One of L.A.'s most elegant restaurants, The Dining Room will cost you plenty, but the American/Continental cuisine lives up to the surroundings, and the service is impeccable, making this a very special dining experience. You'll be surrounded by stunning flower arrangements, polished wood, crystal, linen and silver, and choose from a seasonal menu with specials that change daily. Don't miss the mashed potatoes. If you can't afford to dine here in the evening, go for breakfast or lunch, or try the Lobby for afternoon tea. Features: own baking, Sunday brunch, full bar, late dining, private dining rooms. Jacket requested. Reservations required. Credit Cards: V, MC, DC, A.

Grill, The $$$ ★ ★ ★

9560 Dayton Way, ☎ (310) 276-615 .
Specialties: prime steak; chops; fresh seafood; liver and onions; corned beef hash.
Lunch: from 11:30 a.m., entrees $15–$25.
Dinner: to 11 p.m., entrees $20–$35.
Everything from pot pie to rice pudding graces the menu at The Grill, an unpretentious spot where power dining goes on under the watchful eyes of friendly waiters. It's a clear break from trendy nouveau California cuisine, and all your comforting favorites are served in a masculine, clublike atmosphere. Large portions are a plus, and the martinis are terrific. Closed: Sun. Features: own baking, full bar, rated wine cellar, late dining. Reservations required. Credit Cards: CB, V, MC, DC, A.

Lawry's The Prime Rib $$$ ★ ★ ★

100 North La Cienega Boulevard, ☎ (310) 652-2827.
Specialties: prime rib; Yorkshire pudding.
Dinner: 5–10 p.m., entrees $19–$26.

Lawry's has been serving prime rib tableside from silver carts since 1938, and it shows no sign of slowing down. The restaurant recently moved into dramatic new quarters, and even though the menu now gives you a few more choices, such as seafood, the prime rib is still the star. According to *Los Angeles* magazine, this is the best prime rib in L.A.—and don't miss the creamed spinach. Features: own baking, full bar, late dining. Jacket requested. Reservations recommended. Credit Cards: D, CB, V, MC, DC, A.

Maple Drive Restaurant $$$ ★ ★ ★
345 North Maple Drive, ☎ *(310) 274-9800.*
Specialties: charred rare tuna; grilled chicken with garlic; oyster bar.
Lunch: 11:30 a.m.–2:30 p.m., entrees $12–$18.
Dinner: 6–10 p.m., entrees $15–$29.
Rave reviews for the food at Maple Drive, which may be surprising given that the restaurant is known as a local hangout for the show-biz crowd (stars come in the back entrance to hopefully escape notice by the "regular" people). It's nice to find a restaurant where the food is as hot as the scene (ask for the Veal Chop Milanese—it's not on the menu). Dine on the terrace for a pleasant diversion, or hang around and listen to live jazz late into the night with the rest of the Beautiful People. Lunch served Monday through Friday. Closed: Sun. Features: outside dining, own baking, full bar, late dining, private dining rooms. Jacket requested. Reservations required. Credit Cards: V, MC, A.

RJ's The Rib Joint $$$ ★ ★
252 North Beverly Drive, ☎ *(310) 274-7427.*
Specialties: Barbecued Ribs; Mile High Cakes; Salad Bar.
Lunch: 11:30 a.m.–3 p.m., entrees $7–$11.
Dinner: 3–10 p.m., entrees $8–$25.
R.J.'s is a sort of old-fashioned steakhouse with sawdust on the floor, a huge salad bar, and large portions of ribs, steak and chicken. Guests almost always say they get plenty for the moderate prices. Don't miss the chocolate cake. Features: own baking, Sunday brunch, full bar, late dining. Reservations recommended. Credit Cards: CB, V, MC, DC, A.

Ruth's Chris Steak House $$$ ★ ★ ★
224 South Beverly Drive, ☎ *(310) 859-8744.*
Specialties: Steak; Fresh Seafood.
Dinner: 5–10 p.m., entrees $17–$30.
Rebuilt after a fire in the spring of 1991, the restaurant is thriving in the same location. The new look is stylish, the steaks are terrific (if you like them swimming in sizzling butter), and the side dishes (including the breaded onion rings) are good, too. It's not The Palm or Arnie Morton's, but if you're a meat-lover, you'll find most everything to your satisfaction. Features: full bar, late dining, private dining rooms. Jacket requested. Reservations recommended. Credit Cards: V, MC, A.

Tatou $$$ ★ ★ ★
235 North Beverly Drive, ☎ *(310) 274-9955.*
Dinner: 6:30–11 p.m., entrees $17–$30.
Tatou, which has other branches in New York and Aspen, has all the trappings of a New York-style 1930s supper club—including a cigarette girl. The scene is the thing here, with live entertainment nightly,

a dance floor upstairs, and a dense mix of celebrities and cigarette smoke. The food? Average by most accounts, but no one comes here just to eat, anyway. Plan ahead: tables at Tatou are hard to get. Closed: Tue, Sun. Features: full bar, rated wine cellar, late dining. Reservations required. Credit Cards: V, MC, A.

Tribeca $$ ★★★

242 *North Beverly Drive,* ☎ *(310) 271-1595.*
Specialties: Maryland crabcakes; Montoak stew.
Lunch: 11:30 a.m.–4 p.m., entrees $7–$15.
Dinner: 6–midnight, entrees $9–$20.

There's a little slice of New York, New York in this clublike cafe where singles congregate downstairs at the happening bar. Some say Tribeca can't decide if it's a bar hangout or a restaurant, but most agree it does a good job of being both. If you have a weakness for fresh bread dipped in olive oil, this is your place. Lunch served Monday through Friday. Features: full bar, late dining. Reservations recommended. Credit Cards: D, CB, V, MC, DC, A.

Asian

Pangaea $$$ ★★★

465 *La Cienega Boulevard,* ☎ *(310) 246-2100.*
Specialties: hibachi style Chilean sea bass; rack of lamb with oriental ratatouille.
Lunch: 11:30 a.m.–2:30 p.m., entrees $6–$22.
Dinner: 6–10:30 p.m., entrees $7–$29.
Associated hotel: Hotel Nikko.

Esquire magazine named Pangaea L.A.'s best new restaurant in 1994, and it's showing all the signs of turning into a classic. Chef William Bertouzos flew in from the Grand Hyatt Wailea to take over the kitchen here, and he's turning out an eclectic menu of Pacific New Wave cuisine that is mostly excellent (there are a few dishes that just don't make it, though). You can order portions to suit your appetite, and most dishes come in small-, medium-, or large-plate portions (with small-, medium- or large-plate prices). The classy dining room makes this the perfect special occasion restaurant, and one of the best "special occasions" is the Big Band Sunday brunch (11:30 a.m.–3:30 p.m., $32), where you'll sip champagne, partake of the scrumptious buffet, and hear the tunes of Tommy Dorsey and Benny Goodman. This is nirvana. Features: own baking, Sunday brunch, rated wine cellar, late dining. Reservations recommended. Credit Cards: V, MC, A.

Woo Lae Oak $$ ★★★

170 *North La Cienega,* ☎ *(310) 652-4187.*
Specialties: neng myon.
Lunch: 11:30 a.m.–2:30 p.m., entrees $7–$12.
Dinner: to 10:30 p.m., entrees $7–$12.

Nouvelle Korean cooking goes uptown and upscale at this smart branch of the Seoul-based chain. The sophisticated crowd—much of it Asian—has clearly taken to Woo Lae Oak, which has L.A. trendites finally talking about something other than designer pizza. Another location in Koreatown. Features: own baking, full bar, rated wine cellar, late dining, private dining rooms. Credit Cards: V, MC, DC, A.

Chinese

Mr. Chow   **$$$**   ★★

344 North Camden Drive, ☎ *(310) 278-9911.*
Specialties: Peking duck; lobster; seafood.
Lunch: 10 a.m.–2:30 p.m., entrees $8–$10.
Dinner: 6–11:30 p.m., entrees $33–$38.

Critics say the food doesn't always measure up to the stylish setting, the upscale appointments, and the high prices. That doesn't stop Mr. Chow from being somewhat of a celebrity hangout, however, so you can watch the Beautiful People come and go while you wait for your food. Lunch served Monday through Friday. Features: full bar, late dining, private dining rooms. Jacket requested. Reservations required.
Credit Cards: V, MC, DC, A.

East European

Players, The   **$$**   ★★★

9513 Little Santa Monica, ☎ *(310) 278-6669.*
Specialties: braised short ribs; veal; borscht.
Lunch: from 11:30 a.m., entrees $7–$15.
Dinner: to 10:30 p.m., entrees $10–$17.

People still remember when Mama Weiss operated her Hungarian restaurant in Beverly Hills back in the '30s and '40s, and the same family owns this warm restaurant, which also gives a nod to nouvelle American cuisine. A charming and relaxing atmosphere and lots of good food at reasonable prices. On Monday nights, a violin-accordian duo adds to the atmosphere with a variety of music that runs from gypsy melodies to songs requested by the audience. Lunch served Monday through Saturday. Features: own baking, Sunday brunch, full bar, late dining. Credit Cards: CB, V, MC, DC, A.

French

Chez Helene   **$$$**   ★★★

267 South Beverly Drive, ☎ *(310) 276-1558.*
Specialties: bouillabaisse; rosemary chicken; chocolate cheesecake.
Lunch: 11:30 a.m.–3 p.m., entrees $9–$14.
Dinner: 5:30–10:30 p.m., entrees $13–$24.

Some wonderful French-Canadian dishes often show up here, but cooking is occasionally uneven, which is a big disappointment. Still, fans say this is a real treasure, and you certainly can't go wrong with the bouillabaisse, which is always exceptional. The service is warm and friendly, and the setting is charming, too: a delightful country cottage with a garden patio. The prices are pure Beverly Hills (yikes!), but you can opt for the prix fixe dinner ($27), which is a good value. Lunch served Monday through Saturday. Features: outside dining, own baking, wine and beer only, late dining. Reservations recommended.
Credit Cards: CB, V, MC, A.

Gardens   **$$$**   ★★★

300 South Doheny Drive, ☎ *(310) 273-2222.*
Specialties: grilled Norwegian salmon; rack of lamb.
Lunch: 11:30 a.m.–2:30 p.m., entrees $9–$20.
Dinner: 6–10:30 p.m., entrees $21–$32.
Associated hotel: Four Seasons.

Ratings for Gardens have fluctuated with the changing of its chefs, which has happened frequently in the past few years. Most recently departed is Rene Bajeux, who was replaced by the chef from Santa

Barbara's Biltmore Hotel in early 1995. Menu changes are reportedly in the works. The restaurant is pretty pricey, but if you can afford it, Gardens offers luxury in both ambience and cuisine that's worth a pretty penny. Sunday brunch is exceptional. Be sure to dress the part at this gorgeous hotel dining room. Lunch served Monday through Saturday. Features: outside dining, own baking, Sunday brunch, full bar, rated wine cellar, late dining, private dining rooms. Jacket and tie requested. Reservations required. Credit Cards: CB, V, MC, DC, A.

Jimmy's $$$ ★★★★
201 Moreno Drive, ☎ *(213) 879-2394.*
Specialties: warm duck salad; peppered salmon on a bed of spinach.
Lunch: 11:30 a.m.–3 p.m., entrees $13–$20.
Dinner: 5:30–midnight, entrees $15–$30.
"Hip" is not a word that you would associate with Jimmy's, which usually hosts an older crowd that is impressed with the excellent service, the classic French/Continental cuisine, and the elegant, country-club-like atmosphere. There's nothing really trendy on the menu, but Jimmy's never has based its success on the faddish food of the moment. People come because the food is always good and the atmosphere is just what they're looking for. Lunch served Monday through Friday. Closed: Sun. Features: outside dining, own baking, full bar, rated wine cellar, late dining, private dining rooms. Jacket and tie requested. Reservations recommended. Credit Cards: D, CB, V, MC, DC, A.

Nouveau Cafe Blanc $$$ ★★★
9777 Little Santa Monica Boulevard, ☎ *(310) 888-0108.*
Lunch: 11:30 a.m.–2:30 p.m., entrees $7–$12.
Dinner: 6–9 p.m., prix fixe $32–$38.
Cafe Blanc has moved lock, stock and barrel from its former location in midtown L.A. to Beverly Hills (hence the addition of the word "nouveau" to the name). The French-Asian cuisine is the thing here, and it's fabulous and artfully presented. The only option that makes sense at dinner is the five-course prix fixe menu, which is really a steal. (You can order specific dishes off the prix fixe menu, but portions are extremely small.) Lunch served Wednesday through Saturday only; no reservations taken for lunch. Closed: Mon, Sun. Features: own baking, wine and beer only.

Indian

Bombay Palace $$ ★★★
8690 Wilshire Boulevard, ☎ *(310) 659-9944.*
Specialties: Tandoori chicken; skewered lamb.
Lunch: 11:30 a.m.–2:30 p.m., entrees $7–$16.
Dinner: 5:30–10:30 p.m., entrees $7–$16.
Part of a wide-ranging chain, the Bombay Palace is beautifully decorated and appointed, and offers excellent Indian cuisine (although some complain that it needs to be spiced up a little). If you can't afford dinner, go for the excellent brunch. Features: Sunday brunch, full bar, rated wine cellar, late dining. Jacket requested. Reservations recommended. Credit Cards: CB, V, MC, DC, A.

Gaylord India Restaurant $$ ★★★
50 North La Cienega, ☎ *(310) 652-3838.*
Specialties: Tandoori dishes.
Lunch: 11:30 a.m.–2:30 p.m., entrees $8–$14.

Dinner: 5:30–10:30 p.m., entrees $8–$14.
A lovely dining room filled with the smell of fresh-baked bread from clay ovens and mesquite-fired meat and seafood. Lunch buffet, $6.95. Features: own baking, Sunday brunch, full bar, private dining rooms. Reservations recommended. Credit Cards: CB, V, MC, DC, A.

International

Bo Kaos   **$$$**   ★★
8689 Wilshire Boulevard, ☎ *(310) 659-1200.*
Dinner: 7:30–midnight, entrees $15–$20.
You have to try this place to believe it: the bar has, in addition to traditional cocktails, Chinese elixirs (including aphrodisiacs), and the food ranges from chicken chili to Yemenite bread to shrimp satay to vegetarian lasagna to French fries with melted brie. The whole scene is slightly bizarre, but it's great for grazing and it's hot, hot, hot! Features: own baking, full bar, late dining. Reservations recommended. Credit Cards: CB, V, MC, DC, A.

Italian

California Pizza Kitchen   **$$**   ★★
207 South Beverly Drive, ☎ *(310) 272-7878.*
Specialties: barbecued chicken pizza; chicken tequila fettuccine.
Lunch: from 11:30 a.m., entrees $5–$15.
Dinner: to 11 p.m., entrees $12–$15.
The Beverly Hills outpost of the California Pizza Kitchen chain offers the latest in designer pizza and pastas served in the familiar bright white and yellow dining room at the usual slightly-higher-than-reasonable prices (the pizzas are worth it, though). The food is definitely the thing here, but it's always crowded and noisy, so don't plan on having an intimate conversation. Features: wine and beer only, late dining. Reservations not accepted. Credit Cards: CB, V, MC, DC, A.

Cent' Anni   **$$$**   ★★★★
236 South Beverly Drive, ☎ *(310) 859-8601.*
Specialties: veal carpaccio; spaghetti al cartoccio.
Lunch: 11:30 a.m.–3 p.m., entrees $5–$15.
Dinner: 5:30–11 p.m., entrees $8–$25.
The former Celestino has had a name change since partners Celestino Drago (who was the chef) and Art Vella went their separate ways, settling their differences in court. Drago took his name with him, but Vella claims the name is the only thing that's changed. The art- and flower-filled room is not the fanciest in Beverly Hills, but the creative cuisine continues to be the real star. The menu changes often and always reflects the bounty of the season. A great choice for lunch or dinner. Features: wine and beer only, rated wine cellar, late dining. Reservations required. Credit Cards: V, MC, A.

Da Pasquale   **$$**   ★★
9749 Little Santa Monica, ☎ *(310) 859-3884.*
Lunch: 11:30 a.m.–3 p.m., entrees $7–$12.
Dinner: 5–11 p.m., entrees $10–$15.
Da Pasquale may be the best Italian restaurant in the neighborhood, and its real, down-home Italian dishes—derived from old family recipes—keep its fans coming back for more. Another branch of the restaurant is located in West Hollywood, at *8782 Sunset Boulevard.* Lunch served Monday through Friday. Closed: Sun. Features: own

baking, wine and beer only, late dining. Reservations recommended.
Credit Cards: V, MC, A.

Da Vinci Ristorante $$$ ★★
9737 Santa Monica Boulevard, ☎ *(310) 273-0960.*
Specialties: homemade pasta; veal; fresh fish.
Lunch: 11:30 a.m.–2:30 p.m., entrees $15–$20.
Dinner: 5:30–11 p.m., entrees $30–$40.
Sink into one of Da Vinci's large, cozy booths and relax with a double
martini while you wait for your meal of wine-sauced specialties and
old favorites that don't stray very far into new territory. Service is
attentive and always makes you feel like a regular, whether you are one
or not. Lunch served Monday through Friday. Features: own baking,
late dining. Jacket requested. Reservations recommended. Credit Cards:
CB, V, MC, DC, A.

Emporio Armani Express $$$ ★★★
9533 Brighton Way, ☎ *(310) 271-9940.*
Specialties: carpaccio.
Lunch: from 11:30 a.m., entrees $11–$18.
Dinner: to 11 p.m., entrees $15–$20.
The truth about Emporio Armani Express is that we're ambivalent
about its merits. There's no denying that the setting is divine and the
service near-perfect; it's the food that's in question. Some dishes both
look and taste stunning, while others fall far short of what you'd
expect. No matter what you think of the food, though, it's a great
spot for watching some of L.A.'s most gorgeous people. The bar
offers a variety of flavored vodkas. Features: splendid view, own baking, full bar, rated wine cellar, late dining. Credit Cards: CB, V, MC, DC, A.

Il Cielo $$$ ★★★
9018 Burton Way, ☎ *(310) 276-9990.*
Specialties: fresh seafood; veal.
Lunch: 11:30 a.m.–3 p.m., entrees $10–$15.
Dinner: 6–10:30 p.m., entrees $15–$25.
The setting is romantic, the service is relaxed but efficient, and the
food is consistently both authentic and hearty. Nearly everything—
from pastas to desserts—is homemade. You can't go wrong at Il
Cielo. Closed: Sun. Features: outside dining, own baking, wine and
beer only, late dining, private dining rooms. Jacket requested. Reservations recommended. Credit Cards: V, MC, A.

La Dolce Vita $$$ ★★
9785 Santa Monica, ☎ *(310) 278-1845.*
Dinner: 5–11 p.m., entrees $14–$20.
This small dining room is almost always full of patrons who come for
excellent homemade pastas and osso buco (served only one day a
week). Closed: Sun. Features: own baking, full bar, rated wine cellar,
late dining. Jacket requested. Reservations required. Credit Cards: CB, V,
MC, DC, A.

La Scala $$$ ★★★
410 North Canon Drive, ☎ *(310) 275-0579.*
Specialties: linguine genovese; veal; fettuccine leon.
Lunch: from 11:30 a.m., entrees $9–$19.
Dinner: to 10:30 p.m., entrees $15–$29.
La Scala, which has been in business for years, sadly toppled off its
pedestal as one of L.A.'s best Italian restaurants a few years ago, but it

still has a loyal following of locals. The restaurant's chopped salad is one of the best in L.A., there's a decent wine list, and everyone aims to please. Closed: Sun. Features: own baking, full bar, rated wine cellar, late dining, private dining rooms. Jacket requested. Reservations required. Credit Cards: CB, V, MC, DC, A.

Piazza Rodeo　　　　　　**$$**　　　　　　★★

208 Via Rodeo Drive, ☎ *(310) 275-2428.*
Lunch: from 11 a.m., entrees $8–$15.
Dinner: 5–9 p.m., entrees $10–$16.

A trendy new people-watching spot frequented by those who want to see and be seen, Piazza Rodeo offers a moderately priced menu of mostly salads and sandwiches. There aren't many entrees to choose from, but most people just come for the scene anyway. Brunch served Saturday and Sunday. Features: outside dining, Sunday brunch, wine and beer only. Reservations not accepted. Credit Cards: V, MC.

Prego　　　　　　**$$**　　　　　　★★★

362 North Camden Drive, ☎ *(310) 277-7346.*
Specialties: risotto con funghi porcini; salsiccia luganega; bresaola.
Lunch: from 11:30 a.m., entrees $9–$19.
Dinner: 5–11:30 p.m., entrees $9–$19.

Homemade pasta and pizza and charcoal-grilled meats turned out of wood-fired ovens star at this popular Northern Italian restaurant, which proves that there really are some restaurants in Beverly Hills that don't deliver a plateful of attitude along with your food. Lunch served Monday through Saturday. Features: own baking, full bar, late dining, private dining rooms. Reservations recommended. Credit Cards: CB, V, MC, DC, A.

Trilussa　　　　　　**$$**　　　　　　★★

9601 Brighton Way, ☎ *(310) 859-67 .*
Specialties: fettuccine al funghi porcini; bruschetta; pizza.
Lunch: from 11:30 a.m., entrees $7–$15.
Dinner: to 10:30 p.m., entrees $7–$15.

There are lots of Beautiful People here toting bulging shopping bags from tony Rodeo Drive shops. The cafe's sister restaurant in Italy insures that its roots are firmly planted in the real thing. Features: outside dining, own baking, full bar. Credit Cards: CB, V, MC, DC, A.

Japanese

Ginza Sushi Ko　　　　　　**$$$**　　　　　　★★★★

218 North Rodeo Drive (at Two Rodeo), ☎ *(310) 247-8939.*
Lunch: noon–2 p.m., entrees $110–$130.
Dinner: 6–10 p.m., entrees $150–$200.

This unpretentious mini-mall sushi bar, reputed to have the best sushi in L.A., made an uptown move to Beverly Hills' exclusive Two Rodeo last year. With a reputation for exquisitely fresh fish flown in twice weekly from Japan, the restaurant is often overrun with wealthy Japanese businessmen, who may be the only ones who can afford it (there is no menu; you simply put yourself in the hands of the chef). This is reportedly the most expensive restaurant in all of Los Angeles, and, frankly, unless you are thoroughly acquainted with and adore small portions of Japanese specialties, it may be extremely overrated. Blow this much money at Patina, and you'll really have a night to remember! Closed: Sun. Features: own baking, full bar, wine and beer only, late dining. Reservations required. Credit Cards: V, MC, A.

Matsuhisa $$$ ★★★★★

129 North La Cienega, ☎ (310) 659-9639.
Specialties: sushi: black cod with miso sauce.
Lunch: 11:45 a.m.–2:15 p.m., entrees $15–$25.
Dinner: 5:45–10:15 p.m., entrees $40–$60.

The setting is nothing special, but the food has been described as fabulous enough to "inspire a pilgrimage." You may not get out of here without spending a fortune, but Matsuhisa is turning out what is probably the best Japanese seafood in the country. Plan to arrive before six to avoid a LONG wait. Sushi simply doesn't get any better than this. Lunch served Monday through Friday. Features: own baking, wine and beer only, rated wine cellar, late dining, private dining rooms. Jacket requested. Reservations required. Credit Cards: V, MC, A.

Mediterranean

Rustica $$$ ★★★

435 North Beverly Drive, ☎ (310) 247-9331.
Specialties: designer pizzas; pasta; grilled meats and seafood.
Lunch: 11:30 a.m.–2:30 p.m., entrees $17–$27.
Dinner: 6–10:30 p.m., entrees $17–$27.

Although this new spot is located where restaurants have failed before, it may have a chance to make a go of it based on the good food that's turned out by chef John Beriker, who was once associated with Wolfgang Puck. The ambience is also charming, with a patio that opens out of the back. An up-and-comer. Lunch served Monday through Friday. Closed: Sun. Features: outside dining, late dining. Credit Cards: V, MC, DC, A.

Sylvie $$ ★★★

1224 South Beverwil Drive, ☎ (310) 772-2999.
Lunch: 11:30 a.m.–2:30 p.m., entrees $10–$15.
Dinner: 6–10 p.m., entrees $11–$17.
Associated Hotel: Beverly Prescott.

Rox restaurant has become Sylvie, with a bold, tropical ambience and the solid influence of Sylvie Laly Darr, formerly of the Zuni Cafe in San Francisco. Not everything works perfectly yet, but the food is quite exciting, with Mediterranean touches throughout, and a nice wine list to match. An up-and-comer. Features: outside dining, own baking, rated wine cellar, late dining. Reservations recommended. Credit Cards: V, MC, DC, A.

Polynesian

Trader Vic's $$$ ★★★

9876 Wilshire Boulevard, ☎ (310) 276-6345.
Specialties: Indonesian lamb roast; mahi mahi; shellfish.
Dinner: 5–1 a.m., entrees $14–$29.
Associated hotel: Beverly Hilton.

The Hawaiian atmosphere may be hokey, but Trader Vic's still can't be beat for its caring service, and the food is sometimes better than you'd think. Sometimes. Features: full bar, late dining. Jacket and tie requested. Reservations required. Credit Cards: CB, V, MC, DC, A.

Seafood

Fish House   **$$**   ★ ★ ★

206 North Rodeo Drive, ☎ *(310) 859-0434.*
Lunch: from 11:30 a.m., entrees $10–$20.
Dinner: to 11 p.m., entrees $10–$20.

This classic restaurant at the exclusive Two Rodeo complex is from
McCormick and Schmick, and you can expect the same upscale sea-
food found at the other restaurants. There are a half-dozen varieties
of oysters, and lots of fresh fish that is sometimes served in compli-
cated sauces that do little to enhance the seafood. The food could be
better, but the Fish House shows promise. Features: outside dining,
own baking, late dining. Reservations recommended. Credit Cards: V,
MC, DC, A.

Southwestern

El Torito Grill   **$$**   ★ ★ ★

9595 Wilshire Boulevard, ☎ *(310) 550-1599.*
Specialties: fresh seafood; chicken.
Lunch: 11:30 a.m.–3 p.m., entrees $6–$14.
Dinner: 3–10 p.m., entrees $7–$17.

Lots of fun, noisy and crowded, El Torito Grill offers a huge assort-
ment of Mexican, Tex-Mex, and Southwestern cuisine, killer margaritas and an interesting selection of tequilas. Note that the El Torito
Grill is not the same as the ubiquitous El Torito restaurant chain, and
you can expect better food. Other locations in Newport Beach and
Torrance. Features: own baking, Sunday brunch, full bar, late dining.
Reservations recommended. Credit Cards: D, CB, V, MC, DC, A.

Spanish

Cava   **$$$**   ★ ★ ★

8384 West Third Street, ☎ *(213) 658-8898.*
Specialties: paella; tapas; gazpacho.
Lunch: from 11:30 a.m., entrees $14–$19.
Dinner: to 10 p.m., entrees $16–$21.
Associated hotel: Beverly Plaza.

Cava, opened in late 1993 by Toribio Prado of Prado, Cha Cha Cha
and El Mocambo, is a serious Spanish restaurant that advances far
beyond the trendy tapas craze—and does so admirably. Good and
hearty food, nice Spanish wines, and—yes—there ARE enough tapas
on the menu for serious grazing. Features: full bar, rated wine cellar,
late dining. Reservations recommended. Credit Cards: CB, V, MC, DC, A.

HOLLYWOOD

The Hollywood sign is undergoing another facelift to keep it youthful and beautiful.

Hollywood, wedged into Los Angeles between downtown and Beverly Hills, has been drawing an eclectic star-struck crowd since Cecil B. DeMille made his first picture there in 1913. In fact, most of the major Southern California movie studios moved to the San Fernando Valley years ago (Paramount is the only movie studio still based in Hollywood), but the glitz and glitter associated with Hollywood remain in the minds of those who come to the city to overdose on the remnants of days gone by, when the intersection of Hollywood and Vine was considered the very heart of LA LA land, the place where agents who held court in the nearby Taft Building might at any moment come down and snatch you off a stool at the corner drugstore to make you a star.

Not only does that Hollywood no longer exist, but the city has declined in recent years into a veritable sleaze pit for druggies and prostitutes (both male and female), an area full of dilapidated, graffiti-marred storefronts, army surplus stores and seedy characters. Lovers of the Hollywood of yesteryear recently decided to do something about their favorite (if fading) dowager, and have begun a 30-year redevelopment plan calling for a clean-up of city streets and vacant lots, the planting of trees and other greenery, and the construction of a $150 million Hollywood Promenade, a Hollywood Galaxy entertainment complex, and the Hollywood Entertainment Museum, a major new, $60 million facility dedicated to the entertainment industry. The entire project is expected to be completed somewhere around the year 2020, with the museum scheduled for a late-1995 opening.

"You heard me. This is it. We had a three-picture deal."

Not that tourists will be avoiding Hollywood for the next 25 years or so. It's still a major stop on the out-of-towner's itinerary, and a recent flap illustrating the city's dependence on tourist dollars occurred when, in the summer of 1994, underground tunneling for an MTA subway caused a four-block section of the star-studded Hollywood Walk of Fame to begin buckling and sinking. This led to all sorts of puns in the local press ("Hollywood stars buckle under pressure"), and a massive star rescue ensued after John Forsythe (this would be the concrete-and-brass John Forsythe and not the actor, himself) was seriously damaged. Nearly 30 of the stars had to be jackhammered and removed for safekeeping, including Carol Burnett, Melissa Gilbert, and Fred MacMurray.

Tourists who had made a pilgrimage only to find their favorite star missing were furious, local vendors along Hollywood Boulevard lost a ton of money, and at least one Hollywood resident wrote to President Clinton to ask that the area be declared a federal disaster area. (Such a declaration would have put the star debacle on the same level as Hurricane Andrew or the Northridge earthquake in terms of damage done to people and property. The petition was denied.)

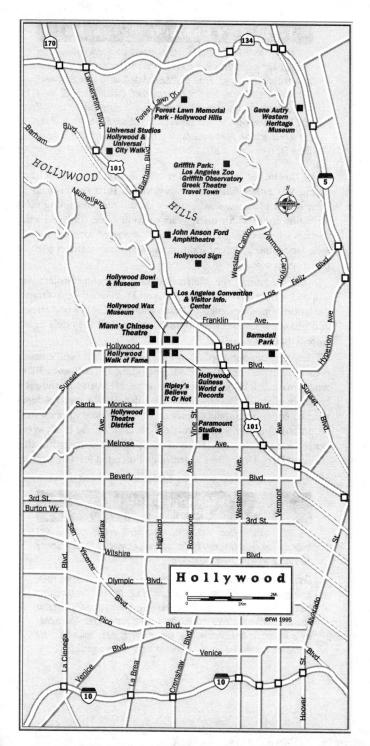

Fielding's Choicest Margaritas

In a massive southwestern region such as greater Los Angeles, you can bet there are a lot of margarita lovers, and debates are always raging about who delivers the best in town. Some candidates: Rubi Rosa in West Hollywood, which offers more than 30 flavors, including the El Diablo (The Devil), made with Jagermeister; downtown's Kachina Grill, with more than 40 kinds of tequila; and the Riviera Mexican Bar & Grill in Redondo Beach, where, if you can take it, you can down a margarita that includes Cuervo 1800 and Bols Triple Sec (with a shot of Grand Marnier as a chaser).

The threatened stars were to remain in storage until the tunneling was either finished or abandoned, then be replaced in their original locations, where they should remain shining (and attracting tourists) for many years to come. The Walk of Fame, itself, is scheduled to be extended and improved with California-style landscaping, accent lighting, and showbiz touches such as filmstrip crosswalks.

In the meantime, the Metro Red Line tunneling project was stopped while everyone regrouped, and Hollywood's mass transportation hopes, designed to lessen traffic on Hollywood streets and provide a fast, efficient option for travel to the city's heart, were temporarily dashed.

There are, of course, parts of Hollywood that are still considered "exclusive" neighborhoods, including the **Hollywood Hills**, where many celebrities have their homes. Here, the attitude is a bit more hip and "Beverly Hills" than downtown, and residents tend to covet both their privacy and their opulent little estates. (A posted sign on the immaculate front lawn of one Hollywood home warned the careless and irresponsible away with this threat: "Dog Droppings Cheerfully Force-fed to Dog Owners").

Fielding's Choice: Best Tours

L.A. offers walking tours, cycling tours, bus tours, helicopter tours, boat tours and just about any other kind of tour you can imagine. Frankly, among the dozens, we think these two stand out:

Grave Line Tours *(☎ 213 469-4149). This is truly one of the coolest ways possible to see a unique (if slightly morbid) side of L.A. Your tour bus is a classic Cadillac hearse, and your tour guide delivers a running monologue that is both informative and laced with an abundance of black humor. The emphasis is on murder and intrigue here, with a look at many infamous crime scenes and gravesites. Sure, $40 is steep for a tour, but it's worth it.*

Fielding's Choice: Best Tours

The Warner Brothers Studio VIP Tour (☎ 818 840-3537). *If your idea of seeing how Hollywood really works involves standing in line for an hour, loading onto a tram with as many other people as can squeeze in, and being attacked by phony apes and sharks, by all means do the Universal Studios thing. If you're REALLY interested in filmmaking and in a behind-the-scenes look at the process, take the Warner Brothers Studios VIP Tour. You will be with a SMALL group of mature people (kids under 10 are not allowed), and you will learn about the history and mechanics of moviemaking (the tour was originally designed by a film historian) by watching the goings-on in a WORKING studio. This has TONS more class than the Universal Studios Tour. Make a reservation ahead, or you may be disappointed.*

Between Hollywood and Beverly Hills is the two-miles-square city of **West Hollywood**, which is by no means Hollywood's orphaned child. West Hollywood has a strong identity of its own, and is packed with excruciatingly trendy small hotels, restaurants, shops, art galleries, and nightclubs, including those that line the famous Sunset Strip.

Much of L.A.'s gay population calls West Hollywood home (more than 25 percent of the city's inhabitants are gay), attracted by the city's many creative opportunities. Here you'll find The **Pacific Design Center** (which is normally not open to the public) and interior design district, whose showrooms stretch along Melrose, Beverly and Robertson, forming what has been called the interior design capital of the Pacific Rim. While most find West Hollywood a fairly safe haven, there are occasional incidents of so-called "gay-bashing," usually instigated by people who live outside the area.

West Hollywood has often been described as more "Hollywood" than Hollywood, itself, and has a long history of insider intrigue and nefarious goings-on. The Chateau Marmont hotel has enough stories about it to write a book (which someone did), and has counted among its guests director Billy Wilder, Marilyn Monroe, Jean Harlow, Greta Garbo, Boris Karloff, Errol Flynn, Dustin Hoffman and John Belushi, who died of a drug overdose in Bungalow No. 2 in March of 1982.

Halloween is always a really big bash in West Hollywood, and Santa Monica Boulevard is closed between Robertson and La Cienega to accommodate all the goings-on that accompany "Halloween Carnival," an annual fete that features food booths, street performers, live bands, and thousands of celebrants, most of whom are attired in outrageous costumes. Even if you don't feel like dressing up, it's great fun to watch everyone else. These festivities sometimes do get out of hand, though, and police may be on hand to break up pockets of rowdy activity and vandalism.

Interestingly, it is in West Hollywood (at a condominium complex located at *1320 North Harper*) where you'll find the Reina de los Angeles (Queen of the Angels), a stunning nine-foot bronze statue of an angel recently created as a tribute to Los Angeles by artist Sally Marr. Marr plans to erect more angel statues around the city, but her first effort seems at home in a city that definitely leans toward the creative.

Famous Has-Been Locations

L.A. is full of historic movie- and TV-making sites, as well as locations where monumental things happened to monumental stars. Here are just a few spots—some historic, some sordid—that may be of interest to the hard-core entertainment buff:

1.   *One of the earliest movies filmed in the L.A. area was 1907's "The Count of Monte Cristo," which shot some scenes downtown, at* 751 South Olive Street. *This little bit of local history is now a parking lot.*

2.   *The house where Dolly Parton, Jane Fonda and Lily Tomlin kept Dabney Coleman prisoner in the movie* 9 to 5 *is located at* 10431 Bellago Road *in West L.A.*

3.   *The Santa Monica pier, its famous carousel and former ballroom have been featured in a number of movies, including* They Shoot Horses, Don't They?, The Sting, *and* The Glenn Miller Story.

4.   *Marilyn Monroe died in early August of 1962 at her bungalow located at* 12305 Fifth Helena Drive, *in Brentwood. The structure was recently sold, but may be made into a Monroe memorial.*

5.   *The original* Beach Blanket Bingo *and its recent sequel,* Back to the Beach, *both starring Frankie Avalon and Annette Funicello, were filmed at Zuma Beach.*

6.   *The* Poseidon Adventure *did not actually feature the U.S.S. Poseidon. The Queen Mary played the part.*

7.   *Michael Jackson's hair was accidentally set on fire while he was filming a Pepsi commercial at the Shrine Auditorium,* 665 West Jefferson Boulevard.

8.   *The Bonaventure Hotel has appeared (in a wide variety of manifestations) in* Buck Rogers in the 25th Century, This Is Spinal Tap, Breathless, *and* Blade Runner.

9.   *Los Angeles' City Hall was featured in the "Dragnet" and "Superman" TV shows, and in the movies* Mildred Pierce *and* D.O.A.

10. *The Arden Villa near CalTech appeared as the Carrington mansion on the "Dynasty" TV series.*

If these tidbits whet your appetite, take the tours, buy the books, call the historical societies! This is just the tip of the proverbial iceberg, and chasing down famous places associated with famous names can keep you busy for a long time in greater L.A.

Waxing Poetic

At first, it's kind of hard to imagine what the big deal is about wax museums. The experience is several notches below seeing real stars, yet there is a certain amount of mystery and charm about these places, almost as if the cold, waxy representations were the real thing. Maybe it's those glass eyes, staring right through you. If you want, you can even get your picture taken with a wax movie star; it might fool the folks back home, but you'll look at it later and inevitably feel creepy.

There are only two major wax museums in greater L.A., the 30-year-old **Hollywood Wax Museum** *(6767 Hollywood Boulevard, Hollywood)* and the **Movieland Wax Museum** *(7711 Beach Boulevard, Buena Park)*. The Hollywood version has the most history, and it's an odd mix of old and new. (The "Baywatch" set is the latest addition, scheduled for a prime spot near the museum's entrance. Pamela Anderson in wax? Ya gotta see it.) Once-popular stars who have faded from public view have their heads removed and put in storage, but bodies are often recycled (museum officials have admitted, for example, that Arnold Schwarzenegger used to be Rex Harrison).

The Hollywood museum is spookier than usual around Halloween, when a special "museum of monsters" and a lot of special effects will scare the pants off you. Museum hours are extended to midnight or later in celebration of the holiday. (Watch out! Some of those wax-faced monsters are alive!)

There's other stuff to do at wax museums besides gaze at wax people. They do their best to make it a big tourist attraction with chambers of horrors and movie scenes and all that. Actually, both the Hollywood and Buena Park museums are pretty cool—if you're into wax museums.

If you're into museum versions of your favorite celebrities, we think the **Museum of Miniatures** provides a much more, shall we say, upbeat experience. You get to see all kinds of teensy, tiny famous people sitting in teensy, tiny chairs or playing teensy, tiny pianos. And, by the way, the Museum of Miniatures is keeping up with current events. A scale model of the O.J. Simpson courtroom is now on display with a teensy, tiny O.J., a teensy, tiny Judge Ito, and a teensy, tiny doggie witness—Kato, the Akita—on the teensy, tiny stand.

Hollywood: Things to See and Do

If you enjoy wandering around looking at concrete, stone, wax or metal substitutes for real movie stars (as lots of people obviously do), Hollywood is the place. You can walk for a mile along the Walk of Fame and be rewarded by staring at a brass star with a famous person's (or a famous animal's—Rin Tin Tin has a star) name on it, or poke around in the courtyard of Mann's Chinese Theater trying like Cinderella's stepsisters to cram your foot (or other body part—none of them X-rated) into the concrete impressions left by stars of bygone eras. It may be a thrill to find that you have the same shoe size as Marilyn Monroe or Clark Gable, but there's a whole lot more to do in Hollywood than walk in the footsteps of the dearly departed.

Hollywood Walk of Fame

Hollywood Myth or Mythtake?

Despite an exodus of film production to other locales, California is still the number one spot for film production. In fact last year, California produced 56 percent of all made-for-theatre movies in the country, up from 46 percent in 1993. California produces only 40 percent of made-for-TV movies and that amount is shrinking. For now Hollywood is still the mythical and real capital of show business and the Golden State's $16.3 billion dollar movie and television industry easily beat out its top four competitors combined. Folks interested can call the California Film Commission, 6922 Hollywood Boulevard, Hollywood, CA 90028 or call ☎ (800) 858-4-PIX.

The number of films:

California	*338*
New York	*73*
Texas	*18*
Florida	*17*
Nevada	*16*

Source California Film Commission

It's inevitable that you'll want to at least take a look at the famous 50-foot "Hollywood" sign that's perched above the city atop Mt. Lee. It was originally erected in 1923 to attract business to a real estate subdivision called "Hollywoodland," but the extraneous "land" was removed when it was deeded to the Hollywood Chamber of Commerce in the late 1940s. The sign was completely renovated in 1978 at a cost of $27,000 per letter (many celebrities, always anxious to get in on a good cause, "adopted" a letter and paid the fee for its refurbishment) and is undergoing another facelift in 1995. In truth, the sign isn't all that much to look at, and you can't get to it without a hike that (trust us) you don't really want to make, but it's a LA LA land classic and a definite must for shutterbugs who want to wow the folks back home. Best views are from Beachwood Canyon.

Fielding's Choice: Best View

If you don't have the time (or the inclination) to drive to some of the higher peaks around L.A., the Griffith Park Observatory atop Mt. Hollywood at Griffith Park offers a supreme view of Los Angeles. Day or night, you can look through one of the outdoor telescopes and study the cityscape below, or, on clear nights, wander into the observatory and peruse the heavens. (Although you're not likely to see any whales from Griffith Park, you CAN from Point Dume, accessible from Zuma Beach. Whale-watching season runs from late December to mid-March, when California gray whales migrate.)

Also of interest may be several homes (some of which extend into the San Fernando Valley) whose exterior shots are familiar to fans of popular TV shows and movies. These include the Cunningham's house from "Happy Days" *(565 North Cahuenga Boulevard)*, the home where the Nelson family of "Ozzie and Harriet" resided *(1822 Camino Palmero Drive)*, the adobe house from *Lethal Weapon 2 (7436 Mulholland in the Hollywood Hills)*, and the house pictured in the 1962 thriller, *Whatever Happened to Baby Jane? (172 South McCadden Place)*.

Hollywood has some of the most imaginative public art in the L.A., including Susan Stinsmuehlen-Amend's "Ivar Intermission" that joins the New Ivar and Doolittle theatres to a kiosk designed by artist Kenny Schneider; Alfredo de Batuc's "A Tribute to Dolores del Rio" on Hudson; Richard Wyatt's "Hollywood Jazz 1945–1971" on the Capitol Records Building; Roberto Delgado's stunning mural in the lobby of the Eastman Kodak Company on Las Palmas; "Il Duomo Celeste," an artistic structure by artist Michelle Griffoul and architect Michael Mekeel on Hollywood Boulevard; and the artistic (or exceedingly tacky by some estimations) "gateways" set at both ends of Hollywood Boulevard.

One of the city's most famous murals, Eloy Torrez's "Legends of Hollywood," was a legend in and of itself until the wall it was painted on collapsed in the 1994 Northridge earthquake. Efforts are underway to restore the mural—picturing larger-than-life versions of some of Hollywood's brightest stars—at its original location south of Hollywood Boulevard at Hudson. In the meantime, concrete shards—all that's left from the original mural—are being sold as a moneymaker to fund the restoration.

On the gallery scene, **L.A.C.E.** (Los Angeles Contemporary Exhibitions) at *6522 Hollywood Boulevard* is one of the most important galleries in the new Hollywood arts district, while the **L.A. Art Association Gallery** at *825 North La Cienega* showcases Southern California artists. Other notable Hollywood galleries include **Animation Plus** *(7977 Melrose Avenue)*, dedicated to the art of animation; **Newspace Gallery** *(5241 Melrose Avenue)*, which concentrates on 20th century art; **Re:Solution**, the L.A. Center for Photographic Studies building at *6518 Hollywood Boulevard*; and the **Space Gallery** *(6015 Santa Monica Boulevard)*, featuring contemporary painting and sculpture.

For a comprehensive look at what's going on in the Hollywood area, pick up a copy of "Discover Hollywood," a quarterly publication of Hollywood Arts Council.

Museums and Exhibits

Gene Autry

Gene Autry Western Heritage Museum   ★ ★ ★ ★

4700 Western Heritage Way, Los Angeles, 90027, ☎ (213) 667-2000.
Hours open: 10 a.m.–5 p.m.
In Griffith Park, across from the L.A. Zoo.

The seven galleries of this small and entertaining museum are dedicated to the history of the American West. Videos, artifacts and "Imagineering" by Disney Studios are used to explore the roles played by the Spanish, Native Americans, cowboys and pioneers in shaping the West. Displays include an 1873 fire engine, ranch equipment, a Colt gun collection, film clips of old Westerns, as well as significant changing exhibits. A museum store and cafe are on the premises. Guided tours are available with reservations. Seniors' and students' admission, $5; children, $3. General admission: $7.

The Griffith Observatory, the location for the fight scene in Rebel Without a Cause.

Griffith Observatory ★★★

2800 East Observatory Road, Los Angeles, 90027, ☎ *(213) 664-1191.*
Hours open: 2–10 p.m.

View the stars through the large 12-inch telescope on clear nights
from dark until 9:45 p.m., free of charge. At the planetarium, a multi-
media show, "Comet Crash" is playing along with "Voyage to the
Planets," a children's show that follows an alien around the solar system from the scorched plains of Mercury to the icefields of Pluto.
Laser shows are featured nightly at the Laserium (extra charge). General admission to the planetarium is $4, $3 for seniors, and $2 for chil-
dren 5–12.

Hollywood Studio Museum ★★★

2100 North Highland Avenue, Hollywood, 90068, ☎ *(213) 874-2276.*
Hours open: 11 a.m.–4 p.m.
Across from the Hollywood Bowl parking lot.

Film buffs will enjoy this museum, housed in the Cecil B. De Mille
Barn, where Hollywood's first full-length motion picture was filmed
in 1913. You can watch film clips of silent movies, check out the replica of Cecil De Mille's office, and enjoy exhibits of vintage costumes
and old movie-making equipment. Children's and senior citizens' discounts. General admission: $2.

Hollywood Walk of Fame ★★★★

Hollywood Boulevard, Hollywood, 90028.
Between Gower Street and Sycamore Avenue

The sidewalks of downtown Hollywood are inlaid with brass stars that
immortalize the names of past and present movie, TV, radio, theater,
and popular music figures. More than 1800 notable celebrities have
stars on the Walk of Fame, including Clark Gable, Marlon Brando,
Charlie Chaplin, Marilyn Monroe, John Wayne, Rudolph Valentino,
Tom Cruise and Elvis Presley. Free admission.

Hollywood Wax Museum ★★★

6767 Hollywood Boulevard, Hollywood, 90028, ☎ *(213) 462-8860.*
A somewhat creepy collection of more than 180 wax figures of celebrities set in realistic scenes from their most famous movies. A Movie
Awards Theatre also screens scenes from Acadamy Award-winning
films. The museum is creepier than usual around Halloween, when its
monsters (some of which will surprise you by being alive) participate
in a chamber of horrors and museum hours are extended to midnight
and beyond. Admission for children 6–12, $6.95; under 6 free;
seniors, $7.50. General admission: $8.95.

Historical Sites

Hollyhock House ★★★

4800 Hollywood Boulevard, Hollywood, 90027, ☎ *(213) 662-7272.*
Hours open: 10 a.m.–2 p.m.
Just west of Vermont Avenue

The first home in Los Angeles designed by Frank Lloyd Wright was
commissioned by oil heiress Aline Barnsdall and built in 1921. The
hollyhock motif is reproduced in stained glass, wall decorations and
furniture design. Hourly tours. General admission: $1.50.

Mann's Chinese Theatre

Mann's Chinese Theatre ★★★

6925 Hollywood Boulevard, Hollywood, 90028, ☎ (213) 464-8111.
Between Highland and La Brea avenues.
This colorful, ornate Chinese-style theatre first opened in 1927 and
has become famous for its elaborate opening nights and the handprints and footprints of the stars that are immortalized in cement in
the theater's courtyard. Movies are still shown inside, and you must
have a ticket in order to view the interior. Self-guided and escorted
tours available. The first show of the day is discounted (tickets $4)
before 6 p.m.; senior and children's discounts. Call for daily movie
updates. General admission: $7.50.

Tours

If you want the inside info on "movieland morbidity," don't miss Grave
Line Tours, which chauffeurs you around in a restored Cadillac hearse to
visit 80 of the most notorious sites of Hollywood "death, sin and scandals."
This is, hands-down, one of the best tours in L.A., so call ahead and don't
quibble over the high cost. It's a heck of a lot more fun than looking at
bronze stars all morning.

Grave Line will also provide you with a map of where stars are buried in
local cemeteries, so, if you're still in a morbid mood, head over to Hollywood Memorial Cemetery *(6000 Santa Monica Boulevard)* for a look at the
tombs of such luminaries as Cecil B. DeMille (whose feet reportedly point
toward Paramount Studios), Jayne Mansfield, Charlie Chaplin, Rudolph
Valentino, Peter Finch and John Huston. Forest Lawn Cemetery *(6300
Forest Lawn Drive)* in the Hollywood Hills is the final resting place of Buster Keaton, Stan Laurel, Freddie Prinze and Liberace.

There are plenty of other tours with a less morbid Hollywood slant (note that the popular Star Line company went out of business in late 1994), but if you elect to strike out on your own you can get a map of celebrities' homes from vendors who hawk them on local streetcorners. For a price, natch.

Casablanca Tours ★★★

6362 Hollywood Boulevard, Hollywood, 90028, ☎ (213) 461-0156.
Mini-bus tours include the Stars Home Tour, a four-hour excursion that takes in homes of the stars, the Hollywood Bowl, Chinese Theater, Sunset Strip, Rodeo Drive, Farmer's Market; the L.A. City Tour, a four-hour tour covering downtown, Beverly Hills, and Hollywood; the Universal Studios Tour, five to six hours; the Night Tour, covering West Los Angeles and the coast; and the Disneyland Tour, an all-day excursion to the Magic Kingdom. Pick up at most area hotels.

Grave Line Tours ★★★★

P.O. Box 931694, Hollywood, 90093, ☎ (213) 469-4149.
"Life in the past lane" is the theme of this Hollywood tour of stars' former homes, gravesites and other ghoulish sites. Tour departs daily at 9:30 a.m. from the east wall of Mann's Chinese Theatre, at Hollywood and Orchid Avenue, with overflow tours at noon. The two-hour pun-laced tour is conducted in a classic Cadillac hearse. Cost is "per body" and advance reservations are suggested. One of THE best tours in L.A. General admission: $40.

Hollywood Fantasy Tours ★★★

1651 North Highland Avenue, Hollywood, 90028, ☎ (213) 469-8184.
Two- to five-hour guided tours of Hollywood and Beverly Hills include views of movie stars' homes, movie studios, Rodeo Drive, and other popular sights. Prices vary according to the type of tour. All tours by mini-van. Children's discount.

Parks and Gardens

Griffith Park, the largest city park in the country (yes, it's even bigger than New York's Central Park) occupies more than 4000 acres near the edge of Hollywood, and is the home of the L.A. Zoo, which, in addition to being a fun place to spend the day, is well-known for its efforts to breed animals as part of worldwide conservation efforts. (The captive breeding program of the California condor comes to mind.) Take the Safari Shuttle for an initial look at what's there, then explore on your own. (Currently in the L.A. city coffers is a zoo improvement fund of $23 million, which is expected to be used to improve the quality of life for the zoo's animals. No date has been set for the commencement of the project.)

Also in the works at Griffith Park is a $25 million underground exhibition hall and education center set to open at the Griffith Observatory by the year 2000. With construction expected to get under way in 1997, the project will close the popular observatory and Laserium for up to a year while the subterranean complex is under construction. The finished product will include a complete redesign of the planetarium and a new, $3 million planetarium projector.

In addition to several other major attractions such as the Gene Autry Western Heritage Museum, the Greek Theatre and Griffith Observatory, Griffith Park boasts four golf courses, miles of hiking, biking and riding trails (stables are on hand for renting horses), tennis courts, pony rides, a carousel, plenty of picnic sites, and wide expanses of lawn for playing on.

Griffith Park   ★★★

Santa Monica Mountains, Hollywood, ☎ *(213) 665-5188.*
Hours open: 6 a.m.–10 p.m.

Griffith Park, nestled at the east end of the Santa Monica Mountains, contains more than 4000 acres of recreational possibilities. Within its boundaries are the L.A. Zoo, the Griffith Observatory and Planetarium, a carousel, pony rides, the Travel Town museum, the Gene Autry Western Heritage Museum, and myriad opportunities for hiking, picnicking, horseback riding, and much more. The visitor center is located at *4730 Crystal Springs Drive;* stop there on your way in for information on the park's facilities. Free admission.

Los Angeles Zoo   ★★★

5333 Zoo Drive, Los Angeles, 90027, ☎ *(213) 666-4090.*
Hours open: 10 a.m.–5 p.m.
In Griffith Park.

More than 2000 animals, including rare, white tigers, are housed in natural settings in this 80-acre zoo park. Animals are grouped according to their normal geographical habitats in Africa, Asia, Australia, and North or South America. The walk-through aviary, koala bears, gorillas and animal nursery are popular exhibits, along with the new Tiger Falls, where three Bengal tigers frolic alongside an eight-foot waterfall. Kids love Adventure Island, with its many hands-on technical exhibits and petting zoo. Animal rides, picnic grounds, a gift shop and bookstore are included. Admission for children 2–12, $3.25; children under 2, free; seniors over 60, $5.25. General admission: $8.25.

Hollywood for Kids

Traveltown in Griffith Park

The L.A. Zoo is a very cool place for kids to hang out. Not only are there more than 2000 animals to see, but there's also the zoo's Adventure Island, where interactive computer programs, live animals and exhibits teach about animals of the Southwest. Kids will also enjoy the live performances featuring zoo animals, watching the baby animals in the zoo nursery, and the holiday activities such as "Boo at the Zoo!" (Halloween), "Beastly Feast"

(Thanksgiving), and "Presents for Primates" (Christmas). Call for information on these activities, as well as other special classes and programs for kids.

Also in Griffith Park is Travel Town, where kids can climb to their heart's content on all kinds of old vehicles, from fire engines to trolleys to trains; and the observatory, where the mysteries of the skies come alive in special children's planetarium shows and telescope viewings after dark.

Hollywood offers many more activities for children, and not all of them revolve around show business. There is, of course, the Hollywood Christmas Parade, a tradition that has always been a must for kids, but many opportunities with a more cultural bent are also appealing. For example, Open House at the Hollywood Bowl, a series of events held each summer, presents a wonderful opportunity for kids 3–12 to participate in workshops and view performances designed to expand their cultural horizons. The fare runs from ballet to storytelling to puppet shows.

If they're in a museum mode, take them to the Gene Autry Western Heritage Museum, where there's a Children's Discovery Gallery offering hands-on exhibits, classes, and cultural workshops relating to the American West, many of them held in conjunction with various holidays.

Other activities for children include the monthly family matinees at the Directors Guild Theater (there are always free activities for kids before the movie); the John Anson Ford Amphitheater's family Summer Nights at the Ford series featuring music, dance, and theatre especially geared toward children; and a host of youth theatre productions around town.

The annual **Children's Festival of the Arts**, held in August at Barnsdall Art Park, is a wonderful creative adventure where kids learn and do a variety of things relating to that year's theme. (In 1994, the theme was "MAKE*A*CIRCUS," and the little tykes were soon clowning, juggling, tumbling and stiltwalking up a storm. No lion taming, though.)

The Hollywood Visitors Information Center at *6541 Hollywood Boulevard* offers a free children's coloring and activity book about the city that will be a hit with any kid, so stop by and pick up a copy if you're in the neighborhood.

Junior Arts Center   ★★★
4800 Hollywood Boulevard, Hollywood, 90027, ☎ *(213) 485-4474.*
Hours open: 10 a.m.–5 p.m.
At Barnsdall Park.
Open Sunday workshops are one highlight of this arts center, where parents and children can engage in art projects together from 2–4 p.m., at no cost. No registration is necessary, and the facility provides materials. An art gallery for children and ongoing art classes, particularly plentiful during the summer, are also offered.

Open House at the Hollywood Bowl   ★★★
2301 North Highland Avenue, Hollywood, 90068, ☎ *(213) 850-2000.*
This annual summer series by the Los Angeles Philharmonic features music, dance and theatre performances, arts and crafts workshops, and open orchestra rehearsals for children ages 3–12. An excellent opportunity to expose kids to the cultural arts.

Travel Town   ★★★
5200 Zoo Drive, Los Angeles, 90027, ☎ *(213) 662-5874.*
In Griffith Park.

All aboard at this museum of vintage railway engines, plush passenger cars, and little red cabooses! Kids can scurry around on these and other outdoor displays, and everyone can take a ride on the Melody Ranch Special, a miniature train which, for a nomimal fee, chugs around the edge of the grounds. Indoors, an extensive display of model trains comes to life on the weekends. Open 10 a.m.–4 p.m. Weekends, 10 a.m.–5 p.m. Free admission.

Events

The Hollywood Christmas Parade is one of the biggest events of the year in Hollywood, and every year it seems to attract a larger audience than the year before. The 1994 parade, which was the city's 63rd, was headed by Grand Marshal Louis Gossett Jr., and drew more than 750,000 paradego-ers. Of course, Santa makes an appearance, as do more celebrities than you'll see in any other parade.

With its inaugural event taking place in April of 1995, the Los Angeles Independent Film Festival became a new player on the Hollywood scene, offering a wide range of films, documentaries and shorts at the Raleigh Studios. Expected to become an annual tradition, the festival will appeal to independent filmmakers from around the world.

Tattoo aficionados won't want to miss the annual Inkslingers Ball, a fall weekend celebration of body art that includes on-the-spot tattooing by world-reknown tattooists, body piercing, tattoo contests, and other related activities.

Halloween Carnaval

Santa Monica Boulevard, West Hollywood, ☎ *(310) 659-4744.*
They close Santa Monica Boulevard between La Cienega and Robertson on Halloween night to make way for a huge—and generally outrageous—costume parade, followed by people milling around the food booths, listening to live bands and having their fortunes told by resident psychics. This wild celebration can sometimes get out of hand—especially if Halloween falls on a weekend. Free admission.

Hollywood Christmas Parade   ★★★★

Sunset Boulevard and Van Ness, Hollywood, 90028, ☎ *(213) 462-2394.*
This annual Christmas extravaganza—usually held in late November—features more than 100 celebrities, floats, equestrian units and classic antique convertibles—and a visit from Mr. Claus. The parade begins its 3.2-mile route at Sunset Boulevard and Van Ness Avenue and winds its way to Highland Avenue, then north to Hollywood Boulevard and east to Bronson Avenue. No admission fee, but reserved grandstand seats are available for $15–$20. Parade begins at 6 p.m. and finishes at 8 p.m.

Inkslingers Ball   ★★

6215 Sunset Boulevard, Hollywood, ☎ *(800) 824-8046.*
At the Hollywood Palladium.
If you're into body piercing, tattooing or otherwise decorating your body (they sell jewelry, too), don't miss this annual weekend event, held in mid-September in—where else?—Hollywood. Some of the best tattooists in the world are on hand to make your body into a work of art, or you can just show off what you already have. General admission: $12.50.

Sports

Hollywood is concentrated too much on the entertainment industry to spend much energy on its sports facilities, but there are a few golf courses, and several stables for riding in the Hollywood Hills. The old Hollywood YMCA, a famous workout spot and celeb hangout since 1921 (Johnny Weissmuller trained for his role as Tarzan, the Ape Man here) is currently undergoing a $9 million renovation and will reopen as a state-of-the-art fitness facility in late 1995. In the meantime, Gold's Gym on Cole Avenue is open for business.

Harding Golf Course

4730 Crystal Springs Drive, Los Angeles, 90027, ☎ *(213) 663-2555.*
Located in Griffith Park, this attractive course overlooks the San Gabriel Mountains and is ringed by the park's equestrian trails.

Wilson Golf Course

Crystal Springs Drive, Los Angeles, 90027, ☎ *(213) 663-2555.*
Griffith Park's bridle trails surround this 18-hole course, with the San Gabriel Mountains in the background.

Hollywood: Music, Dance and Theatre

Hollywood contains some of greater Los Angeles' largest theater venues, including the Pantages, but—as in many other areas of L.A.—some were hit hard by a combination of the January 1994 Northridge earthquake and the Red Line subway construction as it snaked its way into Hollywood. The Pantages remained opened in spite of more than $1 million in earthquake damage (emergency repairs rendered the building completely safe), but its artistic embellishments, including the opulent art deco-style ceiling, have yet to be restored. Across the way, the Henry Fonda Theatre reopened after $600,000 in repairs.

The **Groundling Theatre**, a comedy/improv troupe that celebrated its 20th anniversary in 1994, is a major fixture in Hollywood, and has as its alumni such comedic luminaries as Phil Hartman, Jon Lovitz, Paul Reubens (aka Peewee Herman), Laraine Newman and horror-movie hostess Elvira. The troupe presents limited-run shows that change every few months or so, and they are generally hilarious.

Celebration Theatre, one of the city's most well-respected—and oldest—gay and lesbian theatre companies, performs at various venues throughout the Hollywood area.

Then, of course, there's the **Hollywood Bowl**, a natural outdoor amphitheatre and L.A. landmark designed by Frank Lloyd Wright. The bowl serves as the summer home to the Los Angeles Philharmonic Orchestra, as well as the venue for many local events, including the Playboy Jazz Festival, held in June. Holiday programs are also popular here, with the Fourth of July spectacular and traditional Easter sunrise service being among the standouts. Originally built in 1923, the bowl is in the midst of a much-needed renovation.

Audiences Unlimited (☎ *818-506-0043*) and the studios themselves are the best source for free tickets to tapings of your favorite TV shows (Audiences Unlimited handles tickets for "Roseanne," "Blossom," "Dave's World," "Step by Step," "Family Matters" and "Coach," to name a few), but be prepared to spend the better part of the day (or night) either waiting in line or sitting in the audience for hours while scenes are shot and re-shot. (It may be hard to imagine, but those little half-hour sitcoms you're so fond of watching take hours to tape.)

If you prefer watching stars at work in the great outdoors, your best bet is to find a location where filming is going on and show up as a spectator. **The City of Los Angeles Film and Video Permit Office** (*6922 Hollywood Boulevard, Suite 602*) will give you a free listing of all on-location film, commercial and video shoots in the L.A. area each day; you must come to the office between 8:30 a.m. and 5 p.m. to pick it up.

Music

Greek Theater   ★★★

2700 North Vermont Avenue, Los Angeles, 90027, ☎ (213) 665-1927. In Griffith Park.
This outdoor amphitheater is an extremely popular venue for pop, rock and jazz artists in a May through October season.

Hollywood Bowl   ★★★★

2301 North Highland Avenue, Hollywood, 90068, ☎ (213) 850-2000.
Surrounded by 116 acres of parkland, the acoustically perfect bowl designed by Frank Lloyd Wright is the home of the summer Symphony Under the Stars series played by the Los Angeles Philharmonic Orchestra and other popular summer series. The Hollywood Bowl Museum (*☎ 850–2059*) offers tours and a video presentation on the history of the bowl.

Playboy Jazz Festival   ★★★★

2301 North Highland Avenue, Hollywood, 90068, ☎ (310) 246-4000.
This annual weekend festival held in June at the Hollywood Bowl features some of the top names in jazz. Performers who have appeared recently include Herbie Hancock, Ray Charles and Wynton Marsalis. This is an event that ALWAYS sells out, so you are advised to purchase tickets ahead by mail or through Ticketmaster. If you are unable to get tickets, there are lots of free, pre-festival events going on all over town.

Dance

Dance at the Fountain   ★★

5060 Fountain Avenue, Hollywood, ☎ (213) 663-1525.
At the Fountain Theatre.
Dance at the Fountain continues its phenomenally successful series of events that showcase a broad range of L.A. dance companies. Dance events are held on the third Sunday of each month at 3 p.m.

Theater

Actors' Gang   ★★★

6209 Santa Monica Boulevard, Hollywood, ☎ (213) 465-0566.
This enduring theatre ensemble has been providing Los Angeles with a steady diet of entertainment for more than 10 years. The Gang has been honored with numerous awards and has toured productions to San Francisco, New York and Scotland. In addition to its season of plays, on occasion it also features late-night shows or "off-night presentations." Tickets are available through Theatix (*☎ (213) 466-1767*).

Doolittle Theatre   ★★

1615 North Vine Street, Hollywood, 90028, ☎ (213) 972-0700.
This 1038-seat theater located in the heart of Hollywood presents a year-round program of comedy, drama, musicals and original plays. Tickets are available at the box office, which is open from noon to 8 p.m. Tuesday through Sunday, or from Ticketmaster outlets.

Fountain Theatre   ★★

5060 Fountain Avenue, Hollywood, ☎ (213) 663-1525.
This local theatre presents plays on a wide variety of subjects throughout the year.

Groundling Theatre   ★★★

7307 Melrose Avenue, West Hollywood, 90046, ☎ *(213) 934-9700.*
Now in its second decade, this improvisational comedy group is one
of the city's most professional, and served as a training ground for
such comedic luminaries as Saturday Night Live cast members, Pee
Wee Herman, and Elvira. New improv groups are featured each
Thursday and the show changes every few months. Now running
indefinitely is the zany "Green Eggs and Groundlings." No liquor is
served, and reservations are recommended. Call for performance
times and ticket prices.

Odyssey Theatre   ★★★

2055 South Sepulveda Boulevard, Los Angeles, 90025, ☎ *(310) 477-2055.*
This talented theater ensemble offers its own productions, co-produc-
tions and guest productions.

Pantages Theatre   ★★★★

6233 Hollywood Boulevard, Hollywood, ☎ *(213) 468-1770.*
The Pantages is known for its steady lineup of top entertainment and
broadway shows, including performances by the Civic Light Opera.

Theatre/Theater   ★★

1713 Cahuenga Boulevard, Hollywood, 90028, ☎ *(213) 850-6941.*
A variety of entertainment is offered here, including offbeat productions such as "The Dysfunctional Show" and "Paparazzi!," a Gib
Johnson play. THEATRESPORTS ☎ *(213-469-9689)*, presenting
comedy/improv as a sporting event, also performs at the theatre. Call
for performance times and ticket prices.

Zephyr Theatre   ★★★

7456 Melrose Avenue, West Hollywood, 90046, ☎ *(213) 951-9545.*
An eclectic lineup of plays is always on the menu at the Zephyr.

Ticket Agencies

ABC Tickets

4151 Prospect Avenue, Hollywood, 90027, ☎ *(310) 557-4396.*
Hours open: 9 a.m.–5 p.m.
Free tickets to taping of ABC shows.

Audiences Unlimited

5746 Sunset Boulevard, Hollywood, 90028, ☎ *(818) 506-0043.*
Hours open: 8:30 a.m.–6 p.m.
At the Sunset exit from U.S. 101.
Free tickets to TV shows produced by Fox, Lorimar, Universal and
other studios. Tickets for the following week become available each
Wednesday, and are given out on a first-come, first-served basis.

Paramount Tickets

860 North Gower Avenue, Hollywood, 90038, ☎ *(213) 468-5575.*
Hours open: 10 a.m.–4 p.m.
Free tickets to tapings of Paramount shows.

Hollywood: Nightlife

Hands down, the Hollywood and West Hollywood areas have the hottest nightlife scene in Southern California, and currently one of the hottest
places to see and be seen is Sunset Strip's House of Blues. A combination
restaurant/art gallery/nightclub/bar, the **House of Blues** was conceived by
Isaac Tigrett, one of the founders of the Hard Rock Cafe chain, and in

many ways, H.O.B. is faithful to the genre, although the theme is down-scale Southern rather than cutting-edge rock.

The Strip

A sampling of H.O.B. habitues containing Lisa Minnelli, Jerry Seinfeld and Richard Pryor recently flushed out onto Sunset Boulevard when a nearby water main burst and temporarily closed the club, which goes to show that there are always celebrities lurking inside, and there may not be much room for plain old people such as yourself.

"Hey, dude, it's like a subsection of Disneyland—Bluesland!" effused one wannabe member of the "in" crowd who waited two hours and 45 minutes to get inside for dinner. "Nobodies," he conceded, can pretty much count on standing outside on the sidewalk.

If you do manage a coveted spot inside, you can choose from a menu of Southern favorites such as catfish, dirty rice or jambalaya, and hear some incredible (and authentic) music in what looks amazingly like a transplanted Delta hangout (even though the occupants look nothing like transplanted Delta residents). Just hope that the H.O.B. isn't taping its show the night you're there, or you might end up with lights endlessly shining in your face, an experience that detracts considerably from your enjoyment of whatever's happening onstage.

Other cutting-edge rock clubs in the area include Club Lingerie (rumored to be closing soon), where true hipsters show up on Monday nights for free shows by alternative bands; the **Viper Room**, which has gained in popularity since River Phoenix died of a drug overdose on the sidewalk just outside the front door; Coconut Teaszer, where several hard rock bands perform nightly; and Whisky, the modern interpretation of Whisky-a-Go-Go, which has been a nightclub fixture on Sunset for decades.

The **Burgundy Room** on Cahuenga is a happening place nearly every night, but it changes pace on the first and third Saturday of each month to become the Love Club, where lovers can snuggle while listening to love songs from the past 20 years or so, with an emphasis on the sexy soul music of the '60s and '70s. In sharp contrast to the Love Club is the Love Lounge in West Hollywood, which transforms itself into the Cherry Club on Friday nights and spins the hottest sounds in glam rock.

If you're too tired to make the scene at one of Hollywood's mega-trendy clubs, mosey on over to **The Room**, a very laid-back bar on Cahuenga where lots of writers hang out and the main attractions are the draft beer and the conversation. If you're a Frank Sinatra fan, you won't want to miss The Room's tribute to Ol' Blue Eyes, held every year on his birthday, Dec. 12 (the guest of honor has yet to make an appearance).

The opulent 1920s **Hollywood Athletic Club** is a huge star hangout that's best described as a tribute to the glory days of Hollywood. In addition to the bar and the live blues played upstairs every Monday, there are pool tables and private rooms (which is where most of the celebs go to avoid the crowds).

The best-known comedy club on the Hollywood circuit is the **Improvisation** (informally known as "the Improv"), which was the spawning ground for Robin Williams, Bette Midler, Richard Pryor and Liza Minelli, to name a few. It's still a very hot comedy venue, and you never know when one of the old "alums" might show up to spice up the show.

Anti-Club

4658 Melrose Avenue, Hollywood, ☎ *(213) 661-3913.*
Over the past 15 years, underground comers such as Henry Rollins, Primus, Soundgarden, Red Hot Chili Peppers and Dwight Yoakam have performed in this bastion for real Hollywood music. The Anti has full bar service, admits minors and has a varying cover charge. For show information after 7:30 p.m., ☎ *667-9762.*

Bar One

9229 Sunset Boulevard, West Hollywood, ☎ *(310) 271-8355.*
The "bad" and the "beautiful" gather here for dancing and dining in a charged '80s-style atmosphere.

Catalina Bar & Grill

1640 North Cahuenga Boulevard, Hollywood, 90028, ☎ *(213) 466-2210.*
Famous jazz entertainers, continental cuisine and a cozy atmosphere combine to make this a popular spot. Cover varies.

Cinegrill

7000 Hollywood Boulevard, Hollywood, 90028, ☎ *(213) 466-7000.*
In the Radisson Hollywood Roosevelt Hotel.
A small cabaret featuring top name performers, an art deco interior, and an historic Hollywood setting that makes it a great choice for a relaxing and entertaining evening. The entertainment menu is quite eclectic, and you might find anything from live radio theater to stand-up comedy to live jazz to slightly risque revues. Call ahead to see what's happening.

Club Lingerie

6507 Sunset Boulevard, Hollywood, ☎ *(213) 466-8557.*
A pleasant, comfortable Hollywood club with a wide variety of local and national alternative rockers such as Stonewheat, Gnome, Penny Dreadfuls, Backlash and Neverland. Currently, Monday night offers one of L.A.'s hottest scenes, with FREE performances by the city's best alternative bands. ALWAYS arrive early, as sellouts are frequent any day of the week.

Club Love

1621 Cahuenga Boulevard, Hollywood, ☎ *(213) 465-7530.*
The Burgundy Room turns into Club Love on the first and third Saturday of each month, and lovers are invited to snuggle up and listen to songs about love. No cutting edge stuff here; just lots of good music designed to fan the flames of romance.

Coconut Teaszer

8117 Sunset Boulevard, West Hollywood, ☎ *(213) 654-4773.*
They say this is hard rock heaven—usually offering five or more glam, metal or alternative bands each night, up to 10 p.m. on Sundays. Stikkitty, Pepper Soup, God Squad, Dogs of Pleasure, Smithouse Rag and Ring of Myth have all been recent performers. Call for current bookings of your favorite bands and for information about the cover charge, which varies. Two full bars offer drink specials.

Comedy Store

8433 Sunset Boulevard, West Hollywood, ☎ *(213) 656-6225.*
Some of the biggest names in comedy often drop in to perform here, and three separate rooms feature comedy acts. Cover charge varies, so call ahead for information.

Gardenia

7066 Santa Monica Boulevard, Hollywood, 90038, ☎ *(213) 467-7444.*
Elegance is the theme at this supper club that also features jazz and cabaret entertainment. Open 7 p.m. to midnight, except Sunday.

Hollywood Athletic Club

6525 Sunset Boulevard, Hollywood, ☎ *(213) 962-6600.*
The Hollywood Athletic Club is a HUGE star hangout, but most of the celebrities hide out in the upstairs private rooms. "Regular" people can play pool, have a few drinks at one of the three bars, or listen to music (live blues happens every Monday). The 1920s atmosphere is a true tribute to the glory days of Hollywood. Cover varies.

House of Blues

8430 Sunset Boulevard, West Hollywood, ☎ *(213) 650-0476.*
A tin-shack decor characterizes the House of Blues, which is the hottest club in L.A. at this moment. A plethora of famous headliners perform, a ton of celebrities hang out, and hoards of "regular people" stand out on the sidewalk wondering what all the fuss is about. The Sunday Gospel Brunch is a kick, with music from a gospel choir and a down-home southern buffet. Call the 24-hour concert hotline (☎ *(213) 650-1451)* for the latest on what's happening.

Laugh Factory

8001 Sunset Boulevard, West Hollywood, ☎ *(213) 656-1336.*
Things can get wild at this popular comedy venue, which has seen the likes of Robin Williams, Jay Leno and Eddie Murphy over the years. Monday is Latino Night, Tuesday and Thursday feature the "Comic Strip Live Showcase," and on Saturday, "Comic Strip Live" is taped.

LunaPark

665 North Robertson Boulevard, West Hollywood, ☎ *(310) 652-0611.*
This two-level cabaret with two stages offers an eclectic mix of music and performers running from the bizarre to the sublime. Three bars and a dinner menu with French, Italian and soul food should provide

something for just about everybody, although the food isn't all that hot. The scene is, though. 21 and over. Cover charge varies.

Natural Fudge Company

5224 Fountain Avenue, Hollywood, ☎ *(213) 669-8003.*
This small, really different place features natural foods, great desserts, and beer and wine in a laid-back atmosphere. Live music from rock and pop to R&B, plus comedy acts, add to the attraction of the Fudge.

Nucleus

7267 Melrose Avenue, West Hollywood, 90046, ☎ *(213) 939-8666.*
Come to this spot to hear and dance to blues and jazz in a casual atmosphere. Shows 9:30 and 11 p.m. and 12:30 a.m. nightly. Open 6 p.m. to 2 a.m.; Sunday, 7 p.m. to 2 a.m.

Palace, The

1735 North Vine Street, Hollywood, 90068, ☎ *(213) 462-3000.*
Top rock, rhythm & blues, pop, and jazz acts are consistently featured at The Palace, where the dancing is just as hot as the acts. This is a popular local hangout with teenagers because you only have to be 16 to get in. Cover varies, depending on the act.

Roxbury

8225 Sunset Boulevard, West Hollywood, 90046, ☎ *(213) 656-1750.*
Two clubs and a dining room with bar make up this happening spot, where you're likely to see a celebrity or two, and crowds of perfectly dressed beautiful people.

Roxy, The

9009 Sunset Boulevard, West Hollywood, ☎ *(310) 276-2222.*
This Sunset Strip club has showcased some of the hottest recording talent for more than two decades. Bonnie Raitt, Maria Muldaur and Keith Carradine have all appeared here. A great sound system and tables full of record-company bigwigs add to the excitement, and a casual menu offers appetizers and sandwiches. Expect to be hot and crammed in when there's a national act onstage. Call the box office for current booking. Cover varies, no age limit.

Royal, The

7321 Santa Monica Boulevard, West Hollywood, ☎ *(213) 850-7471.*
Acoustic jazz is the specialty at this bistro/supper club where there is live music every night. No cover charge.

St. Germain Cafe

8454 Melrose Avenue, West Hollywood, ☎ *(213) 852-1420.*
Live jazz, classical, Brazilian and other types of music are featured at this French bistro. It offers dining and a full bar, with no cover charge for the entertainment.

Viper Room

8852 Sunset Boulevard, West Hollywood, ☎ *(310) 358-1880.*
The Viper Club was propelled into the annals of infamy when young River Phoenix died outside the front door of a drug overdose. That, combined with the fact that the club is owned by Johnny Depp, has made for lots of business. It's a pretty cool place to hang out, and you may even get a glimpse of Depp and some of his famous friends if there's a particularly appealing headliner. Dancing on Saturday nights. Over 21 only. Cover varies.

Whisky

8901 Sunset Boulevard, West Hollywood, ☎ (310) 652-4202.
This spacious, two-level dark venerable club that "made" the Sunset Strip still offers hot music, now running the gamut from hard rock to alternative with performers such as Acid Rain, Johnny Socko, Sugartooth and The Buck Pets; call for the current schedule. Two full bars, and no age limit make this a wide-open fun forum. Monday nights, there's no cover and local alternative bands take the stage.

Author's Tip

The coffee/latte/cappuccino/espresso fad is alive and well in L.A., and there are probably more coffee houses here than there are lawyers (a difficult concept to grasp). Here are some funky ones with lots of atmosphere that stand out:

Bourgeois Pig (5931 Franklin Avenue, Hollywood). *Sink down into a comfy velvet couch, peruse the oft-changing art exhibit, or play pool in the back room. It's Paris-cum-Hollywood.*

Macondo Espacio Cultural (4319 Melrose, also in Hollywood). *If you're looking for something a little different, this coffee house with a Latin flavor might be just the thing. You never know what's going to be served along with the cappuccino here, but the possibilities range from art exhibit openings to music that runs the gamut from Salsa to punk.*

The Espresso Bar (1039 Green Street, Pasadena), *locally known as the E-Bar, is a hip (in a downscale sort of way) hangout that has been in Pasadena since the late '70s. Once located in an out-of-the-way alley, it's recently moved to a new address. Devotees hope its funky ambience will remain intact.*

Hollywood: Shopping

There are some stores in Hollywood that are uniquely L.A. and shouldn't be missed. In this category is the original **Frederick's of Hollywood** *(6608 Hollywood Boulevard)*, that mecca of trashy lingerie whose ads you've seen in the back of movie magazines for decades. (The sexy stiletto heels are a bargain at about $30) The store shows off the unmentionables of a generation of stars in its lingerie museum, although some of the items on display—such as a dress worn on television by Milton Berle—aren't all that unmentionable and scarcely reflect the essence of femininity one tends to associate with the Frederick's name. Frederick's reported a net loss of more than $900,000 in the 12 months between mid-1993 and mid-1994, but no one is saying if the chain is in danger of closing. (Yes, Virginia, there really was a Frederick: Frederick Mellinger, who founded his see-through bra-and-panty empire in 1947.) If you can't make it to the original, there are branches of Frederick's throughout greater Los Angeles and Orange County.

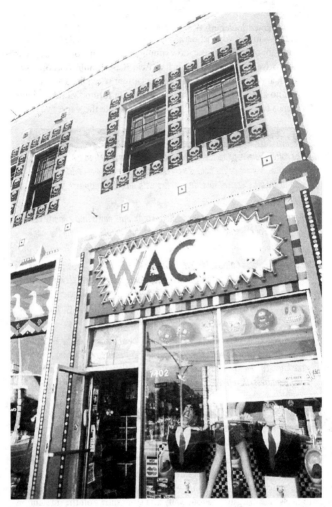

Melrose Avenue

Author's Tip

"Browse or just be" is the motto at Playmates (6438 Hollywood Boulevard), a self-proclaimed Zen and lingerie shop that's a sort of Frederick's of Hollywood clone with incense. If your search for the perfect sexy little teddy proves fruitless, sign up for one of Playmates' meditation classes to relieve your frustration. Quintessentially L.A.

A more recent addition to the Hollywood scene is Condomania *(7306 Melrose)*. No, this does not have anything to do with condominiums. Here, safe-sex advocates can choose from more than 200 varieties of condoms, including the hot new Pleasure Plus brand, the self-proclaimed "dynamic action" condom for the discriminating user. Other sex-oriented products and novelties are also sold here.

Fielding's Choice: Shopping Funky

We're talking about REALLY funky stuff here, and some of the shops that are known for filling the bill:

American Rag (West L.A.). *Funky clothes, funky shoes, funky housewares, funky people. American Rag is THE thrift shop/cool stuff emporium of the moment, often frequented by the Hollywood elite.*

Marz (Montrose). *Where the San Gabriel and San Fernando valleys converge, you'll find Marz. There's all sorts of really cool stuff here, from hand-painted kids' clothes to hats to chi chi fashions.*

Scavenger's Paradise (North Hollywood). *You won't believe all the funky stuff in this place. The 3500-square-foot store caters to customers intent on accumulating "architectural salvage," the collection of which is one of L.A.'s hottest new trends. You'll find everything here from antique knobs and drawer pulls to wrought iron light fixtures that once belonged to Charlie Chaplin ($275) to a pair of four-foot Art Deco lamps ($10,000). Make sure you have lots of time to browse.*

Trot on over to **Cinema Collectors** *(1507 Wilcox Avenue)* for one of the country's best selections of movie posters, star photos, autographs, books and magazines, or to **Collectors Bookstore** *(1708 North Vine Street)*, which has for sale everything from movie posters to photos, movie stills, scripts, magazines and other souvenirs. Larry Edmunds Book Shop *(6644 Hollywood Boulevard)* is another classic if you're looking for books about Hollywood as well as for posters, movie stills, and other good stuff.

Searching for an obscure record album that you've always wanted to own? Drop by **A-1 Record Finders** *(5639 Melrose)*, where the shelves are crammed with old 45s and albums, some costing up to $10,000. Music industry collectors often come to browse here, and they usually find what they're looking for. Or try **Counter Point Records** *(5911 Franklin Avenue)* in the Hollywood Hills, which also sells used books. Magicians both up-and-coming and well-established will find everything they need at **Hollywood Magic** *(6614 Hollywood Boulevard)*, a 50-year-old Hollywood institution, and fans of Spike Lee will think they've died and gone to heaven at **Spike's Joint West** *(7263 Melrose)*, which features merchandise from Lee's movies, including clothing, caps, mugs, and postcards.

West Hollywood's eclectic mix of shops includes everything from upscale Sunset Plaza designer stores to funky little Melrose places such as **Wacko** *(7416 Melrose)*, **The Soap Plant** *(7400 Melrose)*, the **Wound and Wound Toy Company** *(7374 Melrose)*, and **Aardvark** *(7579 Melrose)*, where vintage fashions sell for a pretty penny. Also here is **The Wizard** *(7513 Melrose)*, a T-shirt shop extraordinaire where you can get just about anything you can imagine expertly printed on the T-shirt of your choice. No mere touristy souvenir shop, The Wizard prints stuff for clientele as varied as members of the American Mt. Everest Expedition (who had 3000 shirts picturing the daunting mountain landscape printed up to be sold as a fundraiser for the team) to Hollywood types and "regular" people who enjoy wearing such whimsical slogans as "My Parents Went Looting in L.A. and All I Got Was This Lousy T-Shirt."

If your interest runs to rare books and manuscripts, stop in at the **Heritage Book Shop** *(8540 Melrose, West Hollywood)*, where you'll find a splendid collection of mostly first-edition literary jewels in what *The New York Times* has called the best rare-book store in the country (hint: bring lots of money). Then there's **Book Soup** on the Strip *(8818 Sunset Boulevard)*, where you can often find celebrities browsing among the huge selection of books and foreign and domestic magazines and newspapers. Book Soup is open until midnight every night.

On the gallery scene, **Name That Toon** *(8483 Melrose, West Hollywood)* features cel, clay and computer animation art from Disney, Warner Brothers, Hanna-Barbera, Dr. Seuss and Walter Lantz, including original art from current favorites "The Simpsons" and "Ren and Stimpy." The **Louis Stern Gallery** *(9002 Melrose, West Hollywood)*, which specializes in 19th- and 20th-century American and European paintings, recently relocated to West Hollywood from Beverly Hills, and now shares space with the Jan Abrams Gallery, whose focus is more contemporary, on Melrose. For a listing of other distinguished West Hollywood galleries, contact the West Hollywood Convention & Visitors Bureau.

Sunset Boulevard between Bronson and Van Ness has recently turned into the "Little Indonesia" of L.A., and a stop at the outdoor plaza around the Metropolitan Hotel allows you to sample both the culture and cuisine of this interesting archipelagic nation at a variety of Indonesian-owned shops and a gourmet Indonesian restaurant.

Hollywood: Where to Stay

Some of the biggest news on the Hollywood hotel scene is the changing hands of the very exclusive St. James Club & Hotel, now owned by the Lancaster Group of Houston, which also manages The Jefferson in Washington, D.C., The Tremont in Chicago, and The Lancaster in New York. The hotel's name has changed to The Argyle, and it's had a $40 million restoration and renovation. The art deco ambience has been played to the hilt, and all the furnishings—commissioned from Italy—are exact replicas of museum pieces. Prices have remained about the same, although you can still expect to put out more than $1000 a night for the one-bedroom townhouse. The old hotel's gorgeous St. James Club restaurant is now the Fenix (see listing in the Hollywood Restaurants section).

Changes have also been made at the swanky Bel Age, which was recently acquired by Wyndham Hotels.

If you're interested in Hollywood hotels with a past, try the Chateau Marmont in West Hollywood, which has hosted a who's who of Hollywood over the years, including Greta Garbo, Errol Flynn, Jean Harlow, Marilyn Monroe, Boris Karloff and John Belushi, who died in one of the hotel's bungalows of a drug overdose in March of 1982. Stars still come here, but mostly to find a little peace and quiet, so don't expect any flashy entrances by Hollywood types.

The ghost of Marilyn Monroe has reportedly appeared in a mirror at the Hollywood Roosevelt, which in its heyday also hosted its share of stars. (For a complete look at Hollywood's famous ghosts, pick up a copy of Laurie Jacobson's "Hollywood Haunted".)

Hollywood

Hotels and Resorts

Best Western Hollywood Plaza $70–$90 ★★

2011 North Highland Avenue
☎ *(800) 232-4353, (213) 851-1800, FAX: 213-851-1836.*
Single: $70–$85. Double: $75–$90.
This hotel is right in the heart of Hollywood, within walking distance of the Hollywood Bowl and Mann's Chinese Theater. Universal Studios (ask about special packages) is five minutes away. All rooms have refrigerators, and there's a restaurant on-site. Amenities: pool, private spas. 82 rooms. Credit Cards: CB, V, MC, DC, A.

Chateau Marmont $170–$1200 ★★

8221 Sunset Boulevard
☎ *(800) 242-8328, (213) 656-1010, FAX: 213-655-5311.*
Single: $170–$1200. Double: $170–$1200.
This isn't exactly the Ritz-Carlton, but if you have a fascination with Hollywood history, you'll find it intriguing to wander the grounds where Jean Harlow, Greta Garbo, Marilyn Monroe, Jim Morrison and other entertainment figures once walked. The drug-related death of actor John Belushi vaulted the hotel into the annals of infamy, but this Normandy-style castle is still a favorite with those who don't want to be seen. A recent restoration included the addition of new TVs, telephones and air conditioning. Guest amenities include cellular phones, pagers, a multilingual staff and child care. You have your choice of rooms or cottages here; the $170 rooms do not include kitchenettes. Amenities: secluded garden atmosphere, pool, houses, cottages or bungalows, balcony or patio. 62 rooms. Credit Cards: CB, V, MC, DC, A.

Holiday Inn Hollywood $80–$125 ★★★

1755 North Highland Avenue
☎ *(800) 465-4329, (213) 462-7181.*
Single: $80–$115. Double: $80–$125.
This hotel offers first-class service for the vacationer with a family. In-room movies, non-smoking rooms, multilingual staff, child care and currency exchange are some of the amenities. An added plus is its location in the heart of Hollywood. Amenities: pool, family plan, conference facilities. 470 rooms. Credit Cards: CB, V, MC, DC, A.

Radisson Hollywood Roosevelt $80–$110 ★★★

7000 Hollywood Boulevard
☎ *(213) 466-7000, FAX: 213-462-8056.*
Single: $80–$110. Double: $80–$110.
Beautifully refurbished old Hollywood hotel with Spanish Colonial architecture, Spanish tile floors and arched windows. The guest rooms are simple and small, but the pool is literally a work of art—the walls and floor are original David Hockney. Its location near the Hollywood Bowl makes it convenient for concert-goers. If you're a Montgomery Clift fan, reserve on the ninth floor, where the actor's ghost is said to wander the hallway, reciting lines or playing his trumpet. Other haunting tales involving the hotel include a mirror in the manager's office that sometimes reflects the face of Marilyn Monroe (the mirror once hung in Suite 1200, often used by the actress), the ghost of a crying child that wanders the halls looking for her mother,

and a ghostly man in white who hangs out in the ballroom, where the first Academy Awards ceremony was held in 1929. Even if you don't see a ghost, there's lots of movie memorabilia on display in the lobby to acquaint you with the goings-on of Old Hollywood. For nightlife, you can't beat the hotel's CineGrill, one of the hottest spots in town. Amenities: pool, exercise room, Jacuzzi, balcony or patio, family plan, conference facilities, club floor. 330 rooms. Credit Cards: V, MC, A.

West Hollywood

Hotels and Resorts

Argyle, The   **$170–$1200**   ★★★★

8358 Sunset Boulevard
☎ *(800) 225-2637, (213) 654-7100, FAX: 213-654-9287.*
Single: $170–$1200. Double: $225–$1200.

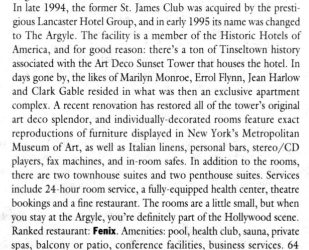

In late 1994, the former St. James Club was acquired by the prestigious Lancaster Hotel Group, and in early 1995 its name was changed to The Argyle. The facility is a member of the Historic Hotels of America, and for good reason: there's a ton of Tinseltown history associated with the Art Deco Sunset Tower that houses the hotel. In days gone by, the likes of Marilyn Monroe, Errol Flynn, Jean Harlow and Clark Gable resided in what was then an exclusive apartment complex. A recent renovation has restored all of the tower's original art deco splendor, and individually-decorated rooms feature exact reproductions of furniture displayed in New York's Metropolitan Museum of Art, as well as Italian linens, personal bars, stereo/CD players, fax machines, and in-room safes. In addition to the rooms, there are two townhouse suites and two penthouse suites. Services include 24-hour room service, a fully-equipped health center, theatre bookings and a fine restaurant. The rooms are a little small, but when you stay at the Argyle, you're definitely part of the Hollywood scene. Ranked restaurant: **Fenix**. Amenities: pool, health club, sauna, private spas, balcony or patio, conference facilities, business services. 64 rooms. Credit Cards: V, MC, DC, A.

Best Western Sunset Plaza   **$72–$190**   ★★★

8400 Sunset Boulevard
☎ *(800) 421-3652, (213) 654-0750, FAX: 213-650-6146.*
Single: $72–$190. Double: $77–$190.

The Best Western Sunset Plaza's location on Sunset Strip makes it convenient to both Hollywood and Beverly Hills, and it's a good bargain for the neighborhood. Guests receive a complimentary buffet breakfast served in a charming bistro-style dining room, complimentary coffee and tea, morning newpapers and the services of a multilingual staff. Rooms and suites include VCR (movies are available for rental), fax and refrigerators—or kitchenettes. Several Hollywood tour groups pick up in the hotel lobby. Amenities: pool, private spas, balcony or patio, conference facilities. 85 rooms. Credit Cards: V, MC, A.

Hyatt on Sunset   **$135–$185**   ★★★

8401 Sunset Boulevard
☎ *(213) 656-1234, FAX: 213-650-7024.*
Single: $135–$185. Double: $160–$185.

In-room movies, valet/laundry, non-smoking rooms, multilingual staff, currency exchange, fax, a restaurant, a lounge and a gift shop are some of the amenities offered here. There are special packages for the business traveler, and the club floor offers extra security. The hotel's location on the Sunset Strip is perfect for guests who want to be near the stars, and the famous Comedy Store nightclub is right next door. (Hollywood history buffs will be interested in the fact that the Doors' Jim Morrison once lived here, but was evicted for hanging out the window by his fingernails, a pastime that Morrison reportedly engaged in at more than one L.A. hotel.) Amenities: pool, balcony or patio, conference facilities. 262 rooms. Credit Cards: CB, V, MC, DC, A.

Le Montrose de Gran Luxe $145–$350 ★★★

900 Hammond Street
☎ *(800) 776-0999, (310) 855-1115, FAX: 310-657-9192.*
Single: $145–$350. Double: $145–$350.
Formerly Valadon, this all-suite hotel in a quiet residental neighborhood features a rooftop terrace with a pool and tennis court and outstanding views. Other amenities include a small library and free use of bicycles. The suites are deluxe, with step-down living areas, modern art on the walls and gas fireplaces—perfect for long-term stays. Its proximity to Beverly Hills—one block from the city limits—makes the hotel convenient for shopping and fine dining. Amenities: pool, tennis, exercise room, Jacuzzi, balcony or patio, family plan, conference facilities. 110 rooms. Credit Cards: CB, V, MC, DC, A.

Le Parc $170–$230 ★★★

733 North West Knoll Drive
☎ *(800) 578-4837, (310) 855-8888, FAX: 310-659-7812.*
Single: $170–$230. Double: $170–$230.
This all-suite hotel located in a quiet neighborhood has always been popular with touring and recording musicians, but it now attracts many foreign visitors. Suites have sunken living rooms, mirrored walls, real wood furniture, kitchenettes, plants, fireplaces and wet bars. There's a rooftop pool and Jacuzzi, a lighted tennis court, and a health club featuring Stairmasters and weight machines. An added feature is a fashionable cafe with an adjoining bar that's closed to the general public. Amenities: pool, tennis, exercise room, Jacuzzi, sauna, balcony or patio, conference facilities, business services. 154 rooms. Credit Cards: V, MC, A.

Le Reve $115–$175 ★★★

8822 Cynthia Street
☎ *(800) 835-7997, (310) 854-1114, FAX: 310-657-2623.*
Single: $115–$175. Double: $115–$175.
This all-suite (the smallest suites don't offer much more space than a hotel room, though) hotel is located near the Los Angeles Design Center. The decor is French country-style, and rooms feature high-quality furnishings, gas fireplaces, mirrored walls, bathroom phones and TVs with VCRs. The pool and spa are on the roof. There is no restaurant, but a kitchen provides a room-service menu. Amenities: pool, Jacuzzi, balcony or patio. 77 rooms. Credit Cards: CB, V, MC, DC, A.

Mondrian $125–$250 ★★★

8440 Sunset Boulevard
☎ *(800) 525-8029, (213) 650-8999, FAX: 213-650-5215.*
Single: $125–$250. Double: $155–$250.

The Mondrian has been a fixture in West Hollywood for ages. Industry types often choose to stay here, and it's the site of one of the largest parties in town after the annual Academy Awards presentations. The view from the terrace is said to be one of the best in L.A. The exterior of the hilltop hotel is painted to resemble a Mondrian painting, and the public rooms of the all-suites hotel are decorated with more than 2000 original works of art. The hotel was purchased in early 1995 by New York hotelier Ian Schrager for $17.4 million. A $15 million renovation, which is expected to continue into 1996, will completely revamp the property and add a new restaurant and club. Amenities: pool, health club, Jacuzzi, sauna, private spas, balcony or patio, hair salon, family plan, conference facilities. 219 rooms. Credit Cards: CB, V, MC, DC, A.

Park Sunset $80–$160   ★★

8462 Sunset Boulevard
☎ *(800) 821-3660, (213) 654-6470, FAX: 213-654-5918.*
Single: $80–$160. Double: $80–$160.

The Park Sunset, located in the heart of the Sunset Strip, is due for a renovation, but is expected to stay open during the project. All rooms include Georgian-influenced furnishings, safes, hair dryers and VCRs; some have fully equipped kitchens. Ask for a corner room if you want a view. Guests are attended by a multilingual staff, and there's a skin spa for when you feel like pampering yourself. Amenities: pool, hair salon, family plan, conference facilities. 84 rooms. Credit Cards: CB, V, MC, DC, A.

Ramada West Hollywood $90–$115   ★★★

8585 Santa Monica Boulevard
☎ *(800) 272-6232, (310) 652-6400, FAX: 310-652-2135.*
Single: $90–$115. Double: $100–$115.

This postmodern hotel, recently renovated, is located in the heart of the Design Center district and attracts many Hollywood types and fashion people. Guest rooms are decorated with vibrant colors, rock-star posters, and modern furnishings in black and chrome. All accommodations, including 22 loft suites, have wet bars and white combination baths. Guests have health club privileges nearby (you still have to pay, but there's a discount for hotel guests), and you can walk to clubs on the Strip. Amenities: sauna, balcony or patio, hair salon, family plan. 176 rooms. Credit Cards: CB, V, MC, DC, A.

Summerfield Suites $100–$180   ★★★

1000 Westmount Drive
☎ *(800) 833-4353, (310) 657-7400, FAX: 310-854-6744.*
Single: $100–$180. Double: $150–$180.

This small all-suite hotel is tucked away on a quiet tree-lined street just minutes from shops, theaters and restaurants. A favorite with movie and record producers and artists, it features fine art in the public areas and gas fireplaces in executive suites, mirrors over the beds in junior suites. Complimentary newspaper, shoeshine, cocktails in the hospitality room and local limo service. Formerly named Le Dufy. Amenities: pool, Jacuzzi, sauna, balcony or patio, conference facilities. 103 rooms. Credit Cards: CB, V, MC, DC, A.

Sunset Marquis Hotel   **$215–$275**   ★★★★

1200 North Alta Loma Road
☎ *(800) 858-9758, (310) 657-1333, FAX: 310-652-5300.*
Single: $215–$275. Double: $215–$275.

This all-suite Mediterranean-style hotel with its lush gardens, fish ponds and terrific fitness facilities is the place to go to be pampered, which explains why its clientele usually consists of well-heeled guests in the advertising, fashion and music business (for the latter, there's a full recording studio available). It was extensively renovated in 1990, and amenities include two heated swimming pools, a health club (fitness trainers and masseurs are available 24 hours a day), and complimentary limo service to nearby areas. If you really feel like living it up, stay in one of the hotel's villas ($450–$1200 per night), each of which contains a baby grand piano, a fireplace, a private jacuzzi, and has its own private butler. Even if you can't afford to stay here, hang around the popular Whiskey bar, and you may see one of the hotel's famous guests hobnobbing over cocktails. Amenities: secluded garden atmosphere, pool, exercise room, Jacuzzi, sauna, private spas, houses, cottages or bungalows, balcony or patio, hair salon, conference facilities. 118 rooms. Credit Cards: CB, V, MC, DC, A.

Wyndham Bel Age   **$250–$500**   ★★★★

1020 North San Vicente Boulevard
☎ *(800) 424-4443, (310) 854-1111, FAX: 310-854-0926.*
Single: $250–$500. Double: $250–$500.

The Bel Age (which was recently purchase by Wyndham) has been consistently recognized as one of the top hotels in Los Angeles in just about every category, from service to decor to its very fine restaurant. It is a European-style all-suite hotel that offers a long list of amenities to its guests, including plush robes, daily newspapers, 24-hour room service, and complimentary limo service. The view is stunning from the deck of the rooftop swimming pool (and from some rooms), the decor includes a plethora of original artworks, and all suites are decorated with pastel fabrics and rosewood and pecan furniture. A perfect spot to hide away from the world and be pampered (if you can afford it). Ranked restaurant: **Diaghilev**. Amenities: pool, Jacuzzi, balcony or patio, hair salon, family plan, conference facilities, business services. 189 rooms. Credit Cards: CB, V, MC, DC, A.

Hollywood: Where to Dine

Esquire magazine named Pangaea, new at the Hotel Nikko, L.A.'s best new restaurant of 1994, but write-ups by L.A. reviewers have been mixed. While some say it's the most exciting new restaurant in Hollywood, others say that chef William Dertouzos' cuisine is a little too complicated for its own good. Across-the-board kudos for the Big Band Sunday Brunch, though.

Another promising newcomer is Alto Palato, a fairly casual and moderately priced Italian restaurant owned by Mauro Vicenti of Rex Il Ristorante and Danilo Terribili, former manager of Rex. Pizzas are the standout here, and the homemade gelato is superb.

Wolfgang Puck's Spago, the first restaurant in his empire and the veritable birthplace of California cuisine, remains a strong fixture in Hollywood, even if it has suffered a bit from Puck's having spread himself too thin to personally oversee everything that comes out of the kitchen. The restaurant still hosts one of the hottest post-Oscar bashes in the city, with everyone who is anyone appearing prominently on the coveted "A" list. Those in the know order the Jewish pizza (smoked salmon, caviar, creme fraiche), which does not appear on the menu.

Tourists looking for the venerable Chasen's, which hosted some of Hollywood's biggest stars for more than 50 years and was a bastion of old-fashioned class, will be disappointed to know that the restaurant closed in the spring 1995. Chasen's famous chili and hobo steak were as legendary as its glamorous clientele, but as most other "old guard" Hollywood hangouts, the restaurant succumbed to the trends of the less formal '90s. Nonetheless, rumors are afoot that a smaller version of the original may open on the same spot in late 1996, and that Wolfgang Puck may have something to do with the restaurant's future. Stay tuned.

Another long-time West Hollywood fixture is Morton's, which recently relocated to the old Trump's restaurant site across the street from its old location and made some changes in the menu that have longtime patrons complaining in droves. "If it ain't broke, why fix it?" is the overwhelming sentiment among Morton's regulars, who generally complain that they want their old restaurant back, but still come to the new place to see and be seen.

In the old Morton's spot on Melrose (and drawing the same sort of celebrity crowd) is the upscale new Eclipse, a venture of a couple of Spago alumni that has received mixed reviews since its opening, most centering around the fact that it's too trendy for its own good, and doesn't concentrate enough on the food. Time will tell.

Fielding's Choice: Buildings that Look Like Food

If you've temporarily lost the hankering for REAL food, you might get your appetite back after observing these L.A. originals:

Randy's Doughnuts (805 West Manchester, Inglewood). *Randy's has been around since the '50s, when it was called something else. It's a tiny little building with a giant doughnut on top. Look at it long enough, and you'll be tempted to go inside for the real thing.*

The Burger that Ate L.A. (Melrose and Stanley Avenue, Hollywood). *This is pretty weird, even for L.A. The restaurant looks like a giant hamburger that has just taken a bite out of city hall. If you feel like eating after seeing this, go inside for a burger, or stay out on the patio, which is just slightly out of reach of the monstrous bun.*

Tail o' the Pup (329 San Vicente, West Hollywood). *This one's a hot dog, complete with painted-on mustard oozing from its bun and a cheery, awning-covered window through which the real thing is dispensed—to go.*

Also new in Hollywood is Georgia, which opened last year backed by the likes of Denzel Washington and Eddie Murphy, and dedicated to the serving of up- as well as downscale Southern cooking in a chic atmosphere. You can get everything from cornmeal mush to crispy fried catfish (reportedly the favorite dish of local basketball legend Kareem Abdul Jabbar). Although many critics have called the restaurant exceedingly overrated, it remains a popular new celeb hangout.

And speaking of down-home southern cooking, although the House of Blues has largely made its impact on L.A. because of its nightlife scene, the food is pretty good, too. Sample a variety of artery-clogging (but fabulous) food such as chicken-fried steak with mashed potatoes and gravy, spicy ribs, or an old fashioned New Orleans po' boy. The Sunday Gospel Brunch is an experience you won't soon forget.

Author's Tip

The Urth Caffe (8565 Melrose, West Hollywood; open 6:30 a.m. to 10 p.m.) *is a very cool place to hang out and sip organic coffee or tea chosen from the dozens of varieties on hand. Organic soups, sandwiches and other light items are also on the menu, and the cafe is open for breakfast and tea daily.*

If your tastes are more downscale and you're not on a fat-free diet, head on over to Pink's hotdog stand on La Brea and Melrose. In business for more than 50 years, Pink's sells more than 1500 dogs a day from its eclectic menu, which includes hot dogs in endless varieties. You'll occasionally see a movie star hanging around (rumor has it that Bruce Willis—what a romantic!—proposed to Demi Moore over one of Pink's famous hot dogs), and owner Paul Pink has a photo gallery of famous guests who have frequented his establishment. There's some talk of franchising Pink's, but nothing can hold a candle to the original.

Finally, rumors are afoot that Yujean Kang, who already has an extraordinarily successful Chinese restaurant in Pasadena, will soon open a new restaurant at La Toque's old location in West Hollywood. If the deal goes through, it will be a major new player on the Hollywood restaurant scene.

Hollywood
African

Dar Maghreb   **$$$**   ★★

7651 Sunset Boulevard, ☎ (213) 876-7651.
Specialties: couscous; bistilla; chicken with lemons.
Lunch: 11:30 a.m.–3 p.m., entrees $8–$15.
Dinner: 6–11 p.m., entrees $25–$29.
There's no a la carte menu for dinner here. For one price, you get a complete feast and floor show featuring whirling belly dancers set in the ambience of a Moroccan palace. Lunch served Thursday and Friday only. Features: full bar, late dining. Reservations recommended.
Credit Cards: V, MC, DC.

American

Citrus   **$$$**   ★★★★★

6703 Melrose Avenue, ☎ (213) 857-0034.
Lunch: noon–2:30 p.m., entrees $9–$16.
Dinner: 6:30–10 p.m., entrees $23–$29.
This trendy California-French bistro is the first restaurant opened by Michel Richard, and where he gained his fame before he went galavanting off to open more restaurants around the country. The tradi-

tional open kitchen surrounded by a sunny indoor patio sets the scene for food that is extremely creative and nearly flawless, and pastries that are divine. Some will tell you that since Richard can't be here all the time, the quality may slip when he's not around. But Citrus is clearly the best California-style restaurant in L.A., and certainly one of the five best restaurants in the city. You will not be disappointed. Lunch served Monday through Friday. Closed: Sun. Features: outside dining, own baking, full bar, rated wine cellar, late dining. Jacket requested. Reservations required. Credit Cards: V, MC, A.

Georgia $$$ ★★★

7250 Melrose Avenue, ☎ *(213) 933-8420.*
Lunch: noon–3 p.m., entrees $8–$13.
Dinner: 6:30–10 p.m., entrees $14–$19.

Another of those much-anticipated ventures from the celebrity crowd (Denzel Washington, Eddie Murphy, et al), this "down-home" Southern-style restaurant has turned out to be (in the words of one critic) "just another noisy, crowded—if pleasant—dining room full of more celebrities that serves so-so food and wines at inflated prices." Some needed changes in the kitchen have been made, so perhaps all is not lost at this star-studded venture that was at least partially eclipsed by the House of Blues. All of your southern favorites are on the menu at this slightly elegant supper club, including fried chicken, macaroni and cheese, and good ol' fried catfish. Lunch served Monday through Friday. Features: own baking, full bar, rated wine cellar, late dining. Reservations required. Credit Cards: V, MC, A.

Hollywood Canteen $$ ★★

1006 North Seward Street, ☎ *(213) 465-0961.*
Specialties: chili; canteen chicken.
Lunch: from 11:30 a.m., entrees $9–$15.
Dinner: 5:30–9 p.m., entrees $10–$20.

A new menu was recently introduced, along with a new chef. Both are so-so, but the Canteen gets points for its congenial atmosphere and hassle-free accessibility. Lunch served Monday through Friday. Closed: Sun. Features: outside dining, own baking, wine and beer only, non-smoking area. Credit Cards: CB, V, MC, DC, A.

Musso & Frank Grill $$$ ★★

6667 Hollywood Boulevard, ☎ *(213) 467-7788.*
Specialties: homemade chicken pot pie; grilled chops; sauerbraten.
Lunch: from 11 a.m., entrees $7–$33.
Dinner: to 11 p.m., entrees $7–$33.

A virtual Hollywood institution, the Musso & Frank Grill has been around for seven decades and it's still packing 'em in with old-style Continental/American food that may not be good for the heart, but warms the soul. Check your cholesterol level at the door and down a couple of great martinis (some say they're the best in L.A.) and you'll forget how bad this food is for you. While you're eating, don't forget to absorb all that Old Hollywood atmosphere—the place is dripping with it. Closed: Mon, Sun. Features: full bar, late dining. Reservations recommended. Credit Cards: CB, V, MC, DC, A.

Pink's Famous Chili Dogs $ ★★

711 North La Brea, ☎ *(213) 931-4223.*
Specialties: chili dogs.

Lunch: from 10 a.m., entrees $3–$5.
Dinner: to 2:30 p.m., entrees $3–$5.

Pink's has been serving its famous chili dogs for more than 55 years, and it's become a Hollywood institution. Paul Pink, 86, is still the owner, and he comes around regularly to schmooze with the customers while they down Pink's famous chili dogs and a bunch of other VERY BAD FOR YOU food. You might even see some celebrities hanging out at Pink's (Bruce Willis supposedly proposed to Demi Moore while both were eating Pink's dogs). No one hangs around long, though—Pink's is just a hot dog stand, after all. But where else can you satisfy a craving for chili dogs at two in the morning? Don't miss the foot-long jalapeno dog, which *Los Angeles* magazine listed as one of the "300 Reasons Not to Leave L.A." Features: outside dining, late dining. Reservations not accepted.

Tam-O-Shanter Inn   **$$$**   ★ ★

2980 Los Feliz Boulevard, ☎ (213) 664-228 .
Specialties: prime rib; Yorkshire pudding; duckling; lamb.
Lunch: 11 a.m.–3 p.m., entrees $8–$12.
Dinner: 5–10 p.m., entrees $10–$23.

A Hollywood institution for over 60 years, the Tam-O-Shanter still offers good Scottish-leaning American food to a well-established clientele. Nothing hip or trendy here, but the regulars say everything is first-rate. Holidays such as Robert Burns' birthday are always punctuated with bagpipes, and the rest of the time the piano bar is an Old Guard hangout. Features: Sunday brunch, full bar, late dining. Reservations recommended. Credit Cards: CB, V, MC, DC, A.

Asian

Mandalay   **$$**   ★ ★

611 North La Brea Avenue, ☎ (213) 933-0717.
Specialties: grilled catfish.
Dinner: 6–11:30 p.m., entrees $9–$16.

You'll find all your favorite Vietnamese dishes here, making Mandalay a good stop for spicy Asian fare. Features: full bar, late dining. Reservations recommended. Credit Cards: CB, V, MC, DC, A.

French

Patina   **$$$**   ★ ★ ★ ★ ★

5955 Melrose Avenue, ☎ (213) 467-1108.
Lunch: 11:30 a.m.–2 p.m., entrees $14–$18.
Dinner: 6–10 p.m., entrees $22–$26.

Chef Joachim Splichal was given the James Beard Award as best chef in California in 1991, and since then Patina has been difficult to de- throne from the highest echelons of the L.A. dining scene (the Zagat Survey of L.A. restaurants has named Patina's cuisine the best in L.A. for four years running). The atmosphere is California laid-back, but what's coming out of the kitchen is sophisticated, creative, and near-flawless enough to put Patina in the running for one of the top restaurants in the country. You can easily drop a small fortune here, but it doesn't get much better than this. One critic suggested that mortgaging the house ought to at least be considered in order to round up the cash to eat at Patina. Reserve ahead or forget it. Lunch served Tuesday through Friday. Ask for the two-course spa cuisine lunch, at about $20. Features: outside dining, own baking, full bar, rated wine cellar, late dining. Jacket requested. Reservations required. Credit Cards: V, MC, A.

International

Authentic Cafe   **$$**   ★★★

7605 Beverly Boulevard, ☎ (213) 939-4626.
Specialties: potstickers; Santa Fe chicken salad; tortilla soup.
Lunch: from 11:30 a.m., entrees $6–$10.
Dinner: to 10 p.m., entrees $7–$15.

Very popular downtown cafe where you are advised to eat at an odd hour to avoid the crowds. Bring your own bottle. Features: own baking, no bar, late dining. Reservations not accepted. Credit Cards: V, MC.

Italian

Caioti   **$$**   ★★

2100 Laurel Canyon Boulevard, ☎ (213) 650-2988.
Specialties: gourmet pizza.
Dinner: 4:30–10:30 p.m., entrees $9–$16.

This rustic spot in Laurel Canyon was in the news recently when one of its salads was rumored to start labor in impatient pregnant women whose delivery date was drawing near. Pretty soon, the place was bulging (pun intended) with moms-to-be eating salad. Whatever the magical effects of the salad, the fact is that Caioti has REALLY good pizzas, probably because the chef learned how to make them from Wolfgang Puck at Spago. Best bet: mild Italian sausage, sauteed oyster and shiitake mushrooms, fresh basil, pine nuts and Gorgonzola—yes, all on one pizza. Yum! Features: own baking, non-smoking area. Reservations recommended. Credit Cards: D, V, MC, DC, A.

Chianti & Chianti Cucina   **$$$**   ★★★

7383 Melrose Avenue, ☎ (213) 653-8333.
Specialties: pasta; fish; veal.
Lunch: from 11:30 a.m., entrees $5–$10.
Dinner: to 11:30 p.m., entrees $15–$20.

Chianti, the restaurant, is dark, fairly subdued and open for dinner only, 5:30 to 11:30 p.m. The Cucina, which shares the kitchen with Chianti, is hip, oh-so-noisy, and open for both lunch and dinner, seven days a week. Pick your kind of atmosphere and dig in: the food and the wines are superb. Features: own baking, full bar, late dining, private dining rooms. Jacket requested. Reservations recommended. Credit Cards: CB, V, MC, DC, A.

Emilio's   **$$$**   ★★★

6602 Melrose Avenue, ☎ (213) 935-4922.
Specialties: panzerotti con ricotta; agnolotti alla panna e spinaci; osso buco.
Lunch: 11:30 a.m.–2:30 p.m., entrees $8–$15.
Dinner: 5–midnight, entrees $11–$20.

Wonderful, Abruzzi-style food stars at chef Emilio Baglioni's restaurant. Don't miss the Sunday Italian feast where for just over $20 you can eat like a king. Save room for desserts, which are homemade by Baglioni's sister. Emilio, himself, provides the entertainment—on the accordian. Mama mia! What a place! Lunch served Thursday and Friday only. Features: own baking, full bar, rated wine cellar, late dining, private dining rooms. Jacket and tie requested. Reservations recommended. Credit Cards: CB, V, MC, DC, A.

Marino   **$$**   ★★★

6001 Melrose Avenue, ☎ *(213) 466-8812.*
Specialties: seafood; pasta.
Lunch: 11:30 a.m.–3 p.m., entrees $9–$15.
Dinner: 5–10 p.m., entrees $9–$15.
This neighborhood place with a clubby atmosphere has garnered
excellent reviews for consistently good food and a caring staff. Lunch
served Monday through Friday. Closed: Sun. Features: own baking,
full bar, rated wine cellar, late dining. Reservations recommended.
Credit Cards: CB, V, MC, DC, A.

Japanese

Yamashiro   **$$$**   ★★

1999 North Sycamore, ☎ *(213) 466-5125.*
Specialties: Japanese Feast; Tornedos Imperial; Sushi.
Dinner: 5:30–10 p.m., entrees $16–$30.
Set on what was once a private estate, this delightful restaurant offers
an expansive view of the city and a recently improved selection of Jap-
anese/American cuisine. Features: splendid view, outside dining, full
bar, late dining, private dining rooms. Reservations recommended.
Credit Cards: CB, V, MC, DC, A.

Mexican

Antonio's   **$$**   ★★

7472 Melrose Avenue, ☎ *(213) 655-0480.*
Specialties: chicken in chipotle; mole.
Lunch: 11 a.m.–4 p.m., entrees $5–$14.
Dinner: 5–11 p.m., entrees $9–$17.
Light, Mexico City-style cuisine and a good wine list. Closed: Mon.
Features: full bar, rated wine cellar, late dining, private dining rooms.
Reservations recommended. Credit Cards: V, MC, A.

Russian

Uzbekistan   **$$**   ★★★

7077 Sunset Boulevard, ☎ *(213) 464-3663.*
Specialties: Plov.
Lunch: from 11:30 a.m., entrees $8–$13.
Dinner: to 10 p.m., entrees $8–$13.
The numbers of Russian diners here are a testament to the authentic-
ity of the food (if you don't understand Russian, you may have a
problem figuring out the menu). Uzbekistan is an offshoot of the
original restaurant located in the Russian republic of the same name,
and it has carried on here with flair. Music adds to the ambience on
weekends. Same menu for lunch and dinner. Features: own baking,
late dining. Reservations recommended.

Thai

Chan Dara   **$**   ★★

1511 North Cahuenga Boulevard, ☎ *(213) 464-8585.*
Specialties: curries; satay.
Lunch: 11 a.m.–4 p.m., entrees $6–$8.
Dinner: 4–11 p.m., entrees $6–$8.
Good Thai cuisine served in a hip, noisy environment punctuated
with loud rock music. Lunch served Monday through Friday.
Another location at Larchmont Village. Features: own baking, wine
and beer only, late dining. Reservations recommended. Credit Cards: V,
MC, A.

West Hollywood
American

Basix Cafe   **$$$**   ★★★

8333 Santa Monica Boulevard, ☎ (213) 848-2460.
Specialties: pizzas; pastas; grilled meats and fish.
Lunch: from 11:30 a.m., entrees $8–$12.
Dinner: to 11 p.m., entrees $12–$20.

You'll bypass this little cafe if you aren't looking for it, but inside you'll find a comfortable ambience and some really good food. Eat breakfast and lunch at the counter, or enjoy a table for the evening's repast. Luscious baked goods and pastas are a hallmark, and simple grilled dishes are tasty and reasonably priced. Desserts are fabulous, service warm and friendly. Features: own baking, wine and beer only, late dining. Credit Cards: V, MC, A.

Clinton Street   **$$**   ★★★

8490 Melrose Avenue, ☎ (310) 652-8030.
Specialties: Turkey Meatloaf; Spicy Chickenburger; Turkey Chili.
Lunch: from 11 a.m., entrees $7–$12.
Dinner: to 10 p.m., entrees $7–$12.

Clinton Street is a new manifestation of a restaurant that has been around for years, and it delivers a heap of "down home" American food in an upbeat atmosphere. It has a host of regulars who come for the good food and the eclectic scene. Features: outside dining, Sunday brunch, late dining, private dining rooms. Reservations recommended. Credit Cards: D, V, MC, DC, A.

Fenix   **$$$**   ★★★

8358 Sunset Boulevard, ☎ (213) 654-7100.
Lunch: noon–3 p.m., entrees $8–$15.
Dinner: 6–11 p.m., entrees $15–$30.
Associated Hotel: The Argyle.

The exclusive private dining room at the former St. James Club has been transformed into Fenix, and it's now open to the public. The gorgeous art deco room, sprinkled with photographic images of Hollywood's most famous stars and featuring linen-clad tables laden with silver, forms an elegant backdrop for inspired California-French cuisine. At the helm is Ken Frank of the now-shuttered La Toque, and he's cooking up many of his favored specialties, such as truffled eggs and rosti potatoes with caviar. In addition to breakfast, lunch and dinner, the restaurant serves a late night supper from 11 p.m. to 1 a.m., Sunday brunch from 11:30 a.m. to 3 p.m., and afternoon tea Mondy through Saturday from 3:30–5 p.m. Features: splendid view, outside dining, own baking, Sunday brunch, full bar, rated wine cellar, late dining. Jacket requested. Reservations recommended. Credit Cards: CB, V, MC, DC, A.

House of Blues   **$$**   ★★

8430 Sunset Boulevard, ☎ (213) 650-0247.
Specialties: fried catfish; fried chicken; New Orleans Po' Boy.
Lunch: from 11:30 a.m., entrees $5–$15.
Dinner: to midnight, entrees $5–$20.

First of all, the House of Blues is primarily a nightclub and not a restaurant, and you can't have anything to eat here without being in the midst of the whole scene (unless, that is, you are a "member," eligible to dine in the private room designed to insulate celebrities from the masses). Although the menu covers lots of ground, it is "down home" Southern cooking that is the House of Blues' trademark, and the food is generally pretty good. The Sunday gospel brunch is a not-to-be-missed experience. You'll think you're on the bayou. Features: own baking, Sunday brunch, late dining, private dining rooms. Reservations not accepted. Credit Cards: V, MC, A.

Ivy $$$ ★★★

113 North Robertson, ☎ *(310) 274-8303.*
Specialties: crabcakes; barbecue fresh vegetables and lime chicken salad.
Lunch: from 11:30 a.m., entrees $15–$23.
Dinner: to 11 p.m., entrees $22–$35.

One of 50 restaurants nationwide to receive *Conde Nast Traveler's* 1993 Distinguished Restaurant Award, Ivy may be the quintessential California restaurant, with a laid-back style reflected in both the homey ambience and the excellent New American-style food, which seldom misses. Features: outside dining, own baking, full bar, late dining. Reservations recommended. Credit Cards: CB, V, MC, DC, A.

Jackson's $$$ ★★★

8908 Beverly Boulevard, ☎ *(310) 550-8142.*
Lunch: 11:30 a.m.–2 p.m., entrees $10–$15.
Dinner: 6–10 p.m., entrees $18–$23.

The American West motif combines with solidly executed California-style cuisine handily whipped up by two experienced L.A. chefs at Jackson's, owned by the son of talk show host Michael Jackson (no, not THAT Michael Jackson). Everyone's brimming over with compliments about this stylish new venture, which may well be on the way to four-star notoriety. Don't miss the baby vegetable salad or the banana-cream pie. Features: outside dining, own baking, full bar, wine and beer only, rated wine cellar, late dining. Reservations required. Credit Cards: D, CB, V, MC, DC, A.

Morton's $$$ ★★★

8764 Melrose Avenue, ☎ *(310) 276-5205.*
Specialties: spicy tuna sashimi salad; grilled marinated lamb.
Lunch: noon–2:30 p.m., entrees $9–$13.
Dinner: 6–11 p.m., entrees $17–$27.

When Morton's moved to new digs (located in the former Trumps Restaurant), a new chef was hired and the menu was revamped to include a lot of "updated" concepts. While the new room is very chi chi, virtually EVERYONE in L.A. is complaining that both the move and the new concept were a BIG mistake. Everyone wants the "old" Morton's back (although they concede that the comfort and modern ambience of the dining room are an improvement). There have been some changes in the kitchen since the move, and the menu allows you to request that your food be prepared in the "old" Morton's style, but the new Morton's still leaves a lot to be desired. If you're star-struck, though, come here on a Monday night, and you'll find all sorts of Beautiful People dropping by to schmooze. Lunch served Monday through Friday. Closed: Sun. Features: outside dining, own baking, full bar, rated wine cellar, late dining. Jacket requested. Reservations required. Credit Cards: V, MC, A.

Palm, The　　　$$$　　　★★★

9001 Santa Monica, ☎ *(310) 550-8811.*
Specialties: steaks; Nova Scotia lobster; fresh seafood.
Lunch: noon–3 p.m., entrees $15–$30.
Dinner: to 10:30 p.m., entrees $35–$50.

West Hollywood outpost of the national chain, known for its Continental-style menu of steak and seafood and its rude waitstaff. Steak and lobster star here, and trimmings include hearty mashed potatoes, creamed spinach, and cheesecake to die for. There are plenty of people who think this is the best steakhouse in L.A., but they're probably from New York, where they're used to waiters with an attitude. Virtually no one quibbles about the food, though—even at these exorbitant prices. Lunch served weekdays only. Features: full bar, late dining. Reservations recommended. Credit Cards: CB, V, MC, DC, A.

Spago　　　$$$　　　★★★★

1114 Horn Avenue, ☎ *(310) 652-4025.*
Specialties: gourmet pizza; fresh seafood.
Dinner: 6–11:30 p.m., entrees $18–$26.

If you can even get into Spago, you'll be so busy watching celebrities that you may not appreciate what's on your plate. Too bad, because Wolfgang Puck (who now has so many restaurants all over the place that it's not likely he'll be in the kitchen on any given night) has his chefs well-trained to turn out his famous cutting-edge California cuisine. In fact, Spago may not shine as brightly as it once did, but virtually no one in L.A. is willing to admit it. Ask for the Jewish Pizza, which has become legendary in L.A., even though it's not on the menu. Features: splendid view, own baking, full bar, rated wine cellar, late dining. Reservations required. Credit Cards: D, CB, V, MC, DC, A.

Thunder Roadhouse　　　$$　　　★★

8371 Sunset Boulevard, ☎ *(213) 650-6011.*
Specialties: chili; burgers; sweet potato pie.
Lunch: from 11 a.m., entrees $6–$15.
Dinner: 6–midnight, entrees $6–$15.

This ain't the Ritz-Carlton, but if you're looking for a cool place to hang out with your Harley, this is it. The decor of this bike shop/restaurant is pure biker heaven, with antique bikes, biker memorabilia and a sort of Old West theme. It's unique for Sunset Boulevard, and the price is right, so put on your black leather and make the scene. Unlike most biker hangouts, this one has valet parking and will take reservations. Breakfast served on weekends. Features: own baking, late dining. Reservations recommended. Credit Cards: V, MC.

Ziggy G's　　　$$$

8730 Sunset Boulevard, ☎ *(310) 659-1225.*
Specialties: eight-decker Zellagabetsky sandwich.
Lunch: entrees $5–$15.
Dinner: entrees $8–$25.

If you have a terrible craving for pickled herring at three in the morning, go to Ziggy G's. The place is open 24 hours and has more than 400 items on the menu, including all the deli classics. You get a ton of food for the money, and Ziggy G's will deliver if you can't make it in person. Features: countryside locations, late dining. Credit Cards: V, MC, A.

French

Drai's $$$ ★★★

730 North La Cienega, ☎ *(310) 358-8585.*
Dinner: 6–10:30 p.m., entrees $18–$27.

The site of the old L'Ermitage is now teeming with L.A.'s Beautiful People, who come as much to schmooze as to partake of chef Claude Segal's (Ma Maison, Bistango, Picnic, etc.) rather simple-but-elegant bistro food. Don't even THINK of showing up without a reservation, and hope that on the night you come everything is working in the kitchen, because sometimes it isn't. Fans of the old L'Ermitage think Drai's is a ghastly replacement for the former culinary shrine, but life goes on and no one ever said that being "trendy" means having high-class cuisine. Lunch served on Fridays. (Gossip indicates that Victor Drai may be opening a classy music lounge soon—possibly in the spot formerly occupied by Olive on Fairfax. Stay tuned.) Features: own baking, full bar, rated wine cellar, late dining. Reservations required. Credit Cards: CB, V, MC, DC, A.

L'Orangerie $$$ ★★★★

903 North La Cienega, ☎ *(310) 652-9770.*
Specialties: baby vegetable stew.
Dinner: 6:30–11 p.m., entrees $27–$35.

This classic restaurant has just undergone a $300,000 renovation that included the addition of an outside terrace and redecoration of the interior. By all accounts, the results are stunning. Service is now as elegant as the surroundings, and the food is first-rate, although sometimes a little too predictable. L'Orangerie has little competition for the title of best French restaurant in the state. Prix fixe dinner, $60, with a two-person minimum order. Closed: Mon. Features: outside dining, own baking, full bar, rated wine cellar, late dining. Jacket requested. Reservations required. Credit Cards: V, MC, A.

Le Dome $$$ ★★★

8720 Sunset Boulevard, ☎ *(310) 659-6919.*
Specialties: osso buco; fish soup with rouille and garlic croutons.
Lunch: from noon, entrees $11–$18.
Dinner: to 11:45 p.m., entrees $15–$25.

Several dining rooms make up this popular restaurant, where the menu leans toward the French—with Belgian touches. The food strives to be all things to all people, including rustic, heavy dishes along with a nice selection of salads and other choices for light eating. Uneven service can sometimes be a problem, but the food is consistently excellent, and Le Dome is another of those L.A. restaurants where celebrities and other trendites come to see and be seen, especially at lunch. Lunch served Monday through Friday. Closed: Sun. Features: splendid view, outside dining, own baking, full bar, rated wine cellar, late dining. Jacket requested. Reservations required. Credit Cards: V, MC, DC, A.

Le Petit Bistro $$ ★★★

631 North La Cienega, ☎ *(310) 289-9797.*
Specialties: mussels petit bistro; braised lamb shank.
Lunch: 11:30 a.m.–3 p.m., entrees $7–$13.
Dinner: 5:30–midnight, entrees $7–$13.

Dreams DO come true for those seeking wonderful French/Mediterranean cuisine at affordable prices. Le Petit Bistro fills the bill perfectly, and makes you feel just like you're in Paris. Features: outside dining, own baking, full bar, rated wine cellar, late dining. Reservations required. Credit Cards: CB, V, MC, DC, A.

International

Cafe La Boheme   **$$$**   ★★★

8400 Santa Monica Boulevard, ☎ (213) 848-2360.
Specialties: panfried duck cake; grilled salmon.
Lunch: 11:30 a.m.–2:30 p.m., entrees $9–$13.
Dinner: 5:30- p.m.10:30 p.m., entrees $15–$23.

Cafe La Boheme is Hollywood personified. The imaginative, dark and slightly outlandish homage-to-Hollywood decor raises expectations of an equally special meal, but, unfortunately, that is rarely the case. The food—a sort of quirky Pacific New Wave combination of eclectic flavors—is sometimes very good (especially if you go with something simple such as grilled chicken), but it often misses. If you want atmosphere, though, it's here in abundance, from the heavy draperies and tapestries to the warm fireplace to the overhead balcony. Features: outside dining, own baking, Sunday brunch, full bar, late dining. Reservations recommended. Credit Cards: V, A.

Italian

Alto Palato   **$$$**   ★★★

755 North La Cienega Boulevard, ☎ (310) 657-9271.
Specialties: pizzas; grilled meats; gelato.
Lunch: noon–2:30 p.m., entrees $13–$19.
Dinner: 6–11 p.m., entrees $13–$19.

Alto Palato is a new, two-room (the cafe and the trattoria) restaurant opened on busy La Cienega by Mauro Vicenti, the owner of the fancy Rex Il Ristorante downtown. Vicenti's upscale cuisine has made the transfer mostly intact, although the ambience is less formal and the prices lower—which suits the patrons of Alto Palato just fine. The fabulous thin-crusted pizzas from the wood-burning ovens, soups, grilled meats and homemade gelato shine, and the service is efficient. The bar is open until 1:30 a.m., serving a light bar menu, and it draws a hip crowd from off the street. Lunch served Monday through Saturday. Features: outside dining, own baking, late dining. Reservations recommended. Credit Cards: CB, V, MC, DC, A.

Dan Tana's   **$$$**   ★★

9071 Santa Monica, ☎ (310) 275-9444.
Specialties: fettucini; linguini with clams; cioppino; eastern veal.
Dinner: 5–1 a.m., entrees $13–$39.

Known for its solid commitment to red meat (including steaks "the size of paperback bestsellers"), well-sauced pastas and a classic Caesar salad, Dan Tana's has been a favorite local hangout of moguls, agents and other entertainment types since its opening in 1947. Rocker Bruce Springsteen reportedly still comes here on a regular basis, probably because it reminds him of his East Coast roots. The bar is reminiscent of the sort of bars that were around when drinking was still socially acceptable—and they can make any drink you've ever heard of. Features: full bar, late dining. Reservations recommended. Credit Cards: V, MC, A.

Madeo   **$$$**   ★★★

8897 Beverly Boulevard, ☎ (310) 859-4903.

Specialties: *osso buco; risotto; roasted leg of veal.*
Lunch: *noon–3 p.m., entrees $12–$14.*
Dinner: *6–11 p.m., entrees $16–$19.*

The cuisine of Tuscany is the main focus at this busy (and pricey) restaurant often frequented by Italians hungry for the taste of home. The smell of herbs and olive branches sizzling in the wood-burning ovens pervades the chic atmosphere, the food is authentically hearty, and the service shines. Lunch served Monday through Friday (the antipasto lunch buffet is a favorite). A pianist plays most nights. Features: own baking, rated wine cellar, late dining. Reservations recommended.

Mediterranean

Chaya Brasserie $$$ ★★★
8741 Alden Drive, ☎ (310) 859-8833.
Specialties: *spaghetti with Japanese eggplant; pasta; grilled salmon.*
Lunch: *11:30 a.m.–2:30 p.m., entrees $8–$16.*
Dinner: *6–10:30 p.m., entrees $12–$25.*

It's noisy and stark, but that doesn't stop movie stars and just plain folks from enjoying the interesting fare, which includes French, Italian and Asian dishes that range from superb grilled seafood to seaweed salad to roast rack of veal. Chaya Brasserie is practically an L.A. institution. Lunch served Monday through Friday. Late night supper menu Tuesday through Saturday. Features: full bar, rated wine cellar, late dining. Reservations recommended. Credit Cards: CB, V, MC, DC, A.

Cicada $$$ ★★★
8478 Melrose Avenue, ☎ (213) 655-5559.
Specialties: *Norwegian smoked salmon; lobster-leek ravioli.*
Lunch: *noon–2:30 p.m., entrees $11–$15.*
Dinner: *6–10 p.m., entrees $12–$25.*

One of THE places for the entertainment industry's movers and shakers, now featuring a more Italian menu presided over by the former chef at Il Giardino. Perhaps the persistent rumors of inconsistent cooking are finally on the way out. The celebrity crowd indicates as much, and Cicada has become a hot reservation. Lunch served Monday through Friday. Closed: Sun. Features: own baking, rated wine cellar, late dining. Reservations recommended. Credit Cards: V, MC, A.

Eclipse $$$ ★★★
8800 Melrose Avenue, ☎ (310) 724-5959.
Specialties: *whole baked fish.*
Dinner: *6–10 p.m., entrees $20–$30.*

Eclipse (housed at the revamped location of the old Morton's) is one of the hottest new restaurants to open in L.A. in ages. At the helm is Bernard Erpicum, formerly the maitre d' and sommelier at Spago, who has engaged chef Serge Falesitch (also from Spago) to cook up a fantastic array of "cuisine of the sun." The restaurant has plenty of celebrity backing (Steven Seagal), and plenty of celebrity customers, which means that getting a reservation is nigh on to impossible unless you're SOMEONE. This is a very classy place, with a fancy velvet and brocade interior designed by the grandson of Claude Monet, the Impressionist painter. And the food? Not always great, but who cares? Closed: Sun. Features: outside dining, own baking, rated wine cellar, late dining. Credit Cards: V, MC, A.

Jones   **$$$**   ★★

7205 Santa Monica Boulevard, ☎ *(213) 850-1727.*
Specialties: pizza; pasta.
Lunch: noon–2 p.m., entrees $7–$15.
Dinner: 5 p.m.–2 a.m., entrees $9–$25.

There are two words usually used to describe Jones Hollywood: retro,
and hip. the "retro" has to do with the decor, and "hip" has to do
with the patrons of this little cafe, who often arrive on Harleys and/
or have parts of their bodies pierced other than ears. Owned by res-
taurateur/clubster Sean MacPherson (Swingers, Good Luck Bar,
Olive), this is a place to see and be seen, with a ton of models and
Generation X types hanging around all the time. Oh, and the food is
decent, too. Lunch served Monday through Friday. Features: own
baking, late dining. Reservations required. Credit Cards: V, MC, DC, A.

Le Chardonnay   **$$$**   ★★★★

8284 Melrose Avenue, ☎ *(213) 655-8880.*
Lunch: noon–2 p.m., entrees $14–$15.
Dinner: 6–10 p.m., entrees $18–$24.

One of the most quietly comfortable, charming bistros in Los Angeles, designed to be an exact replica of a cafe on Boulevard St. Ger-
maine. Specialties range from classic French to nouvelle Italian, and
the wine list is well-chosen and expensive. In spite of kudos from the
national press, some locals have dismissed Le Chardonnay as noisy
and inconsistent; others say it has all the charm of being on the Left
Bank. You be the judge. The menu changes every day, so you're sure
to find something new every time you come. Lunch served Tuesday
through Friday. Closed: Mon, Sun. Features: own baking, full bar,
rated wine cellar, late dining. Jacket requested. Reservations recommended. Credit Cards: CB, V, MC, DC, A.

Russian

Diaghilev   **$$$**   ★★★★★

1020 North San Vicente, ☎ *(310) 854-1111.*
Specialties: caviar; borscht; chicken Kiev.
Dinner: 6–10 p.m., entrees $15–$34.
Associated hotel: Wyndham Bel Age Hotel.

Silk-covered walls, heavy silver, etched glass and French paintings add
to the elegant ambience of this French-Russian restaurant formerly
known as the Bel Age. This is arguably the best hotel restaurant in
L.A., and indulgence is the byword. Your every wish is the waiters'
command (and they sometimes anticipate your wish before you have
time to think about it), the fresh caviar and Russian specialties are
superb, the flavored vodkas divine, and the balalaika music soothing.
There's no way you can afford to dine here on a regular basis, but for
a REALLY special occasion, it's worth the money. Closed: Mon, Sun.
Features: full bar, rated wine cellar, late dining. Jacket and tie
requested. Reservations required. Credit Cards: CB, V, MC, DC, A.

Thai

Talesai   **$$**   ★★★

9043 Sunset Boulevard, ☎ *(310) 275-9724.*
Specialties: Talesai duckling; tiger prawns; homok seafood.

Lunch: 11:30 a.m.–2:30 p.m., entrees $7–$15.
Dinner: 6–10:30 p.m., entrees $8–$17.

This popular restaurant features the cuisine of Thailand, simply and elegantly prepared. Great desserts and a good wine list. Unlike many Thai restaurants, the setting here is charming. Lunch served Monday through Friday. Another branch is located in Studio City, at *11744 Ventura Boulevard.* Closed: Sun. Features: own baking, rated wine cellar, late dining. Jacket requested. Reservations recommended.

Credit Cards: CB, V, MC, DC, A.

WEST
LOS ANGELES

Westwood Village

West Los Angeles encompasses a relatively small chunk of real estate west of Hollywood and south of Beverly Hills, and includes the actual western edge of L.A. proper, plus the Bel Air, Westwood, Century City and Culver City areas.

Bel Air was once a private, gated community, and—although the gate is now open—it remains a conclave of exclusivity dotted with expensive homes. Former president Ronald Reagan and wife Nancy live here, as does TV producer Aaron Spelling, who owns a six-acre estate complete with bowling alley, skating rink and other Hollywood-stye amenities at *594 Mapleton Drive.* (The Spelling mansion is so big that Mr. Spelling reportedly has difficulty getting from one room to the other to answer the phone before it stops ringing, so the staff answers, then signals Spelling on his beeper to pick up the call.) Superstar model Cindy Crawford and ex-hubby Richard Gere also have a mansion here (rumors that it went on the market in late 1994 added to speculation that the pair was about to split up). They are each expected to reap a cool $3 million or so when the house sells.

Adult entertainment magnate Hugh Hefner, who used to cavort with a hutchful of shapely bunnies, is now living happily ever after (so far at least) in his Bel Air Playboy Mansion with wife (and former Playmate) Kimberly and a couple of kids; and overlooking the whole community is the home of Zsa Zsa Gabor, who has made it known that she thinks Bel Air has loads more class than Beverly Hills (where she reportedly goes only when in the mood for shopping—or altercations with the local police force).

Westwood Village, originally a small business district intended to serve the students and faculty at UCLA, is situated adjacent to the campus' south gate, and offers a mellow, laid-back atmosphere in which to hang out, sip a cappuccino, shop, or go to the movies (the place is packed with theaters, and the theaters are always packed with people on weekends, when you may have to wait in a very long line and literally fight your way in to see a popular first-run film).

The Westwood campus of the **University of California** was completed in 1929, and continues to be a major educational and cultural influence in Southern California. It is estimated that 60,000 people come and go on the campus each day (approximately 34,000 of them are students), many to visit the university's museums, galleries, gardens, theaters and libraries. (Note that, somewhat incongruously, UCLA's home football games are played in Pasadena—at the Rose Bowl.)

On the southern end of the campus is the university's Center for Health Services, which includes the prestigious 711-bed UCLA Medical Center, the UCLA schools of Medicine, Dentistry and Nursing, the UCLA School of Public Health, the UCLA Neuropsychiatric Institute and Hospital, the Jules Stein Eye Institute, the Jonsson Comprehensive Cancer Center, and several other components of what has become a world-class center of scientific and medical research, education and patient health care facilities.

Slightly southwest of Westwood (and for the most part situated on the opposite side of the San Diego Freeway north of Santa Monica) is **Brentwood**, which lost its status as a quiet residential community when Nicole Brown Simpson and her friend Ron Goldman were murdered there in June 1994. Since then, both curiosity seekers and O.J. Simpson supporters have descended on the upscale neighborhood to view the place where the murders took place and also to see the mansion of accused murderer Simpson. The circuslike atmosphere was greatly disturbing to neighbors at both locations, but—in spite of their best efforts to discourage sightseeing—things didn't die down until the trial was well underway.

Also in Brentwood is the four-bedroom bungalow in which Marilyn Monroe lived and died, at *12305 Fifth Helena Drive.* (The 1929, hacienda-style property was bought in 1994 by film director Michael Ritchie, who pledged to "make it more accessible" to the late actress's fans, possibly by turning it into a museum. The neighbors were not amused.)

Fortunately, whatever infamy Brentwood has had to endure will be swallowed up with the completion of the new, $735-million J. Paul Getty Center, scheduled to open in 1997 on 110 acres atop the Brentwood Hills. The Getty Trust and its research, education and administration facilities will be located here, and—most important for lovers of the cultural arts—the world-renowned Getty art collections (except for the antiquities, which will remain where they are) will be moved here from their current home in Malibu.

The Getty Center is a project of magnificent proportions, and is widely recognized as a step forward in Los Angeles' effort to become a major center of the cultural arts on par with New York or Paris. The complex, designed by New York architect Richard Meier, will contain five gallery pavilions housing paintings, drawings, photographs, European sculpture, furniture and other artifacts from the Getty collection, as well as a 450-seat auditorium, a 61,000-square-foot garden courtyard, a restaurant, a Center for the History of Art and the Humanities, a Conservation Institute and other research and administrative offices. In addition, there will be acres of gardens studded with dramatic fountains, and an electric tram that will shuttle the 1.5 million expected visitors per year from the underground parking lot to the center's front door.

Not all of the fuss about the Getty Center has been positive. Residents have complained about the center's location far from downtown, the destruction of mountaintop habitat that was necessary in order to build it, and the crush of traffic that will certainly follow its completion. Although the Getty Trust is clearly moving to make the museum's treasures more accessible to the masses, some say its very presence there, high on the hill, smacks of exclusivity.

Century City, in spite of what its name would suggest, is not a city at all, but a 180-acre upscale business center situated on what used to be the back lot of 20th Century-Fox Studios south of Beverly Hills. It includes a multitude of high-rise buildings, most housing the offices of entertainment industry agents and attorneys, and boasts its own Chamber of Commerce and calendar of events (including an annual Garlic Festival). The chic Century City Shopping Center, the three-level ABC Entertainment Center, and the Shubert Theatre, one of L.A.'s foremost theatre venues, are some of Century City's highlights.

(Century City may be the epitome of chic, but it never forgets the less fortunate: every fall, the Brooks Brothers store on Santa Monica Boulevard—in conjunction with *GQ Magazine*—hands out $50 Brooks Brothers gift certificates to customers who bring in "quality" used clothing for distribution to the poor.)

Culver City, located between downtown and the coast, is the site of the old MGM studios (now occupied by Sony), and the Hal Roach Studios (torn down 30 years ago) where the "Our Gang" and Laurel and Hardy films were made. Currently in the midst of an urban redevelopment project that has led observers to liken it to New York's SoHo district, Culver City (which has frankly always had a reputation for being a bit frumpy) includes a whole bunch of quirky, neo-industrial buildings (many designed by Eric Owen Moss) that are serving as home to a variety of artistic and design firms, and run-down warehouses that are being revamped to house small companies that need lots of lofty space and like the funky art deco look. The old trolly substation and Culver Hotel are now national historic landmarks, and the old Culver Theater may also soon come into its own as a small performance venue and movie house backed by actor Danny DeVito. Reflecting the city's newfound "attitude," rumors are afoot that a CULVER CITY sign rivaling its HOLLYWOOD counterpart may be placed on a nearby hillside as testimony to Culver City's belief that it—and not Hollywood—was the fertile ground where L.A.'s movie business first took root.

West Los Angeles: Things to See and Do

Museum of Tolerance

Don't miss the Simon Wiesenthal Center's **Museum of Tolerance**, a $50 million complex which opened to the public early in 1993. Through technologically advanced exhibits, hands-on computer stations, interactive displays, video monitors and film, the museum focuses on both the Nazi Holocaust and the history of racism and prejudice in America. Designed by

James Gardner of London and Karl Katz of New York's Metropolitan Museum of Art, the 165,000-square-foot facility lets you participate in a riveting look back at the Holocaust, as well as a video timeline documenting the Los Angeles Riots and addressing various questions of social justice and responsible citizenship. Many other excellent exhibits, a 6700-square-foot Memorial Plaza dedicated to Holocaust victims, a museum shop and a cafeteria round out the museum experience, which is also enhanced by a variety of programs and special events throughout the year.

Also in West L.A. is the **UCLA/Armand Hammer Museum of Art** (UCLA took over the museum's operations in 1994), which has some impressive works in its holdings, but has also been plagued by disgruntled critics and by continuing financial problems. Occidental Petroleum magnate Armand Hammer basically created the museum as a monument to himself and his artistic taste, but he alienated the rest of the local art community by promising his collection to other museums (such as the L.A. County Museum of Art), then reneging on his promise and turning his former headquarters into a museum with his name on it. Art critics have sniffled since the beginning that the works contained therein are merely "minor," and they soundly blasted the museum in 1994 for selling off a priceless notebook belonging to Leonardo da Vinci. The $30 million garnered from the sale was to be used for acquisitions and to establish an "insurance" policy against legal hassles that might be brought against Armand Hammer's estate. All of the political (and artistic) wrangling aside, the contents of the museum are certainly worth seeing.

In Westwood proper, you can tour the **UCLA campus** (call the Visitors Center, ☎ *(213)206-8147*, for information about guided tours, which are held Monday-Friday at 1 p.m., by reservation only), or visit the notable Frederick S. Wight Gallery, the Fowler Museum of Cultural History, or one of the campus's lovely botanical or sculpture gardens. The UCLA Hannah Carter Japanese Garden, which is actually located in Bel Air, is a standout, but you must have a reservation to visit.

Across Wilshire Boulevard from Westwood Village is **Westwood Memorial Park**, the final resting place of such Hollywood luminaries as Marilyn Monroe, Natalie Wood and Peter Lawford. Monroe's crypt is worth a visit just to see what fans have left there in tribute to the legendary actress, whose death is still shrouded in mystery thirty-some years later.

If you're tired of sightseeing and ready for a good workout, you may want to consider joining Sports Club/L.A., a plush West L.A. club that offers valet parking, two restaurants, boxing facilities, a huge coed weight area, and satellite dishes that beam down your favorite programs while you exercise—just to name a few of the state-of-the-art club's facilities. The place was completely retrofitted after the Northridge quake and claims to be crush-proof, which means the only things in danger of getting crunched are your abs. All of this comes at a price of course—more than $1200 for a membership and $120 per month. If you're not sure you want to dump that kind of money on keeping fit, call for a tour and you can judge for yourself.

Museums and Exhibits

Fowler Museum of Cultural History   ★ ★ ★

405 Hilgard Avenue, West Los Angeles, 90024, ☎ *(310) 825-4361.*
Hours open: noon–5 p.m.

Following the theme of cultural history, this museum presents excellent changing exhibitions on art, textiles, figurative sculpture and other cultural arts throughout the year. In addition, various lectures, seminars and other special events open to the public are offered on a regular basis. "Reflecting Culture: The Francis E. Fowler, Jr. Collection of Silver" is on permanent display. Admission to the museum and its programs is free, but you have to pay for parking on the campus. Free admission.

Museum of Tolerance   ★ ★ ★ ★ ★

9786 West Pico Boulevard, West Los Angeles, 90035, ☎ *(310) 553-8403.*
Hours open: 10 a.m.–4 p.m.

This new, extremely high-tech, $50-million museum—also called Beit Hashoah—is dedicated to the promotion of understanding among people from all walks of life, with an emphasis on the history of prejudice and racism in America and the story of the Nazi Holocaust. If your idea of seeing a museum consists of walking around and seeing artifacts on display, you'd better toss your expectations out the window. All of your senses will be assailed here, and the journey is much more educational than entertaining—and occasionally extremely unsettling (one journalist labeled the experience "a provacative descent into a high-tech hell"). The section that conveys the history of the Holocaust is riveting, and to bring the focus of racism and bigotry into a modern context, there is section chronicling the Los Angeles riots of 1992. Tours, which begin at 12-minute intervals and last 2 1/2 hours, are mandatory, and it is suggested that you plan on spending four hours at the museum. (Note that times listed reflect tour times.) No cameras are permitted inside. Admission price for children 3–12, $3; seniors, $6; students, $5. Advance ticket purchase is recommended for Fridays, Sundays and holidays. Parking is free. General admission: $8.

Skirball Museum   ★ ★

3077 University Avenue, Los Angeles, ☎ *(213) 749-3424.*
Hours open: 11 a.m.–4 p.m.
At Hebrew Union College.

The Skirball Museum maintains a permanent collection of archaeological and biblical Judaica, including textiles, coins, ritual objects and marriage contracts. Call for information on changing exhibits.

UCLA/Armand Hammer Museum of Art   ★ ★ ★ ★

10899 Wilshire Boulevard, Los Angeles, 90024, ☎ *(310) 443-7000.*
Hours open: 11 a.m.–7 p.m.
On the northeast corner of Wilshire and Westwood.

The private collection of philanthropist and collector Armand Hammer is housed in this, the newest art museum in Los Angeles. Permanent exhibits include Leonardo da Vinci drawings, Daumier prints and sculpture, paintings by Rembrandt, Goya and the Impressionists, as well as many other works. Also exhibited are prints, photographs and drawings from the UCLA Grunwald Center for the Graphic Arts.

A bookstore and museum shop are available for browsing. General admission: $4.50.

Tours
Celebrity Tour Company
3330 Sepulveda Boulevard, West Los Angeles, ☎ (310) 575-3651.
Small vans whisk tourists past the homes of the stars, Chinatown, Mann's Chinese Theatre, Sunset Strip, and other L.A. sightseeing hotspots. They will also take you to Universal Studios, Disneyland and the beach, or on a shopping spree to that honkey-tonk border town, Tijuana.

Parks and Gardens
UCLA Hannah Carter Japanese Garden ★★★★
10619 Bellagio Road, West Los Angeles, ☎ (310) 825-4574.
This gorgeous, traditional Japanese garden was donated to UCLA in 1965 by Edward W. Carter, then Chairman of the Regents of the University of California. Major structures in the garden include the main gate, a teahouse, a five-tiered pagoda, a moon-viewing deck, a family shrine, and bridges, all of which were built in Japan and reassembled in the garden. Major symbolic rocks, water basins, and antique stone carvings were also imported. Nearly all of the plants and trees featured in the garden are native to Japan. Tours of the garden are BY RESERVATION ONLY, Tuesdays, 10 a.m.–1 p.m.; Wednesdays, noon to 3 p.m.

Children's Activities
Children's Concerts in Historic Sites ★★★
1200 Chalon Road, West Los Angeles, 90049, ☎ (310) 440-1351.
The De Camera Society presents a wide variety of Saturday afternoon family entertainment including music, science projects, storytelling, and other cultural pursuits, plus favors and treats. All events are held at museums around town, and admission to the concert includes admission to the host museum.

Odyssey Theatre ★★★
2055 South Sepulveda Boulevard, West Los Angeles, 90025, ☎ (310) 477-2055.
This talented theatrical troupe produces a season of children's theatre.

City Celebrations
Garlic Festival ★★★
Federal Building, West Los Angeles, ☎ (213) 937-4850.
Now more than a decade old, the Garlic Festival, held on a weekend in July, is an L.A. favorite. Dozens of celebrated local chefs offer such garlic delicacies as Eggplant with Garlic Creme Brule or Onion and Garlic Tart, and you get to sample everything you are willing to pay for. A great line up of music artists also perform, and all of the proceeds go to charity.

Sports and Recreation
Culver City Ice Arena
4545 Sepulveda Boulevard, Culver City, 90049, ☎ (310) 398-5718.
Owned by the L.A. Kings hockey team, this center offers ice skating lessons for all levels. Several skating clubs meet here weekly and hockey teams hold practice sessions.

Sports Club L.A.

1835 West Sepulveda Boulevard, West Los Angeles, 90025, ☎ *(310) 473-1447.*
High-tech fitness equipment and valet parking will satisfy the most discerning fitness buff at this center, which counts celebrities among its clientele. The club is private, although guests at the finer hotels can get a pass. Reopened in early September 1994, after earthquake renovations.

Volvo Tennis

UCLA, West Los Angeles, ☎ *(310) 824-1010.*
You can count on seeing some of the brightest stars in men's tennis at this decades-old tournament billed as the "biggest men's meet held between Wimbledon and the U.S. Open." There is always some fun to go along with the serious tennis, such as pro-celebrity matches with celebrity announcers. Held in early August.

West Los Angeles: Music, Dance and Theatre

Most of the performing arts events in West Los Angeles happen at the UCLA Center for the Performing Arts, which offers a staggering menu of music, dance and theatre events throughout the year—many of them featuring world-class artists and companies. It's best to call the center when you arrive in town to see what's currently playing, and hope that tickets are still available.

Music

Da Camera Society   ★★★

12001 Chalon Road, West Los Angeles, 90049, ☎ *(310) 440-1351.*
The Society, founded at Mount St. Mary's College in 1973, specializes in presenting virtuoso chamber music performances. Since 1980, the "Chamber Music in Historic Sites" series has matched musical programs with sites of architectural or historic significance, such as the Huntington Library, the Doheny Mansion, the Biltmore Hotel, the Zane Grey House, Trinity Baptist Church and the RMS Queen Mary.

UCLA Center for the Performing Arts   ★★★★

10920 Wilshire Boulevard, Westwood, 90024, ☎ *(310) 825-2101.*
UCLA is the venue for many fine music, choral and dance programs.

Theatre

Shubert Theatre   ★★

2020 Avenue of the Stars, Century City, 90067, ☎ *(310) 201-1555.*
Popular performance hall for current hit movies and Broadway productions. Andrew Lloyd Webber's new musical, "Sunset Boulevard," is currently playing indefinitely.

Westwood Playhouse   ★★★

10886 Le Conte Avenue, Los Angeles, 90024, ☎ *(310) 208-5454.*
This small neighborhood theatre offers a wide variety of plays featuring local talent.

Ticket Agencies

Front Row Center Tickets

1355 Westwood Boulevard, Los Angeles, 90024, ☎ *(310) 478-0848.*
Mail and phone orders accepted for major L.A. events.

Ticket Time

11652 West Olympic Boulevard, West Los Angeles, ☎ *(310) 473-1000.*
Handles tickets to most local concerts and other events. From Pasadena, call ☎ *(818) 440-9700;* from Encino, ☎ *(818) 783-1033;* from Tustin ☎ *(714) 852-5800.*

West Los Angeles: Nightlife

Culver City has one of L.A.'s hottest jazz venues in the Jazz Bakery, which emphasizes contemporary jazz in a concert-like setting. There's actually more attention paid to the jazz here than to the scene, and you can't just drop in—reservations are required.

A real sleeper is Petterson's Frish Rost on Venice Boulevard in Culver City, your basic downscale coffee house where open mike comedy night on Tuesday is a hoot. (Besides, you can feel very safe here: it's a popular hangout for members of the Culver City Police Department, who stop in for take-out cappuccino all the time.)

Atlas Bar & Grill

3760 Wilshire Boulevard, West Los Angeles, ☎ *(213) 380-8400.*
Eclectic entertainment and menu along with a funhouse atmosphere make this a place to socialize, dine or enjoy live jazz. On Tuesday nights, the Black/Note quintet plays what's been described as "one of the hottest swing-bebop jams in town;" music begins at 9 every night. Cover varies; over 21 only.

Igby's Comedy Cabaret

11637 Tennessee Place, West Los Angeles, ☎ *(310) 477-3553.*
Enjoy established and up-and-coming comedians along with dining and a full bar. Cover charge ranges from $7–10.

Jazz Bakery

3233 Helms Avenue, Culver City, ☎ *(310) 271-9039.*
The Jazz Bakery, adjacent to the Helms Bakery, is a VERY cool hangout if you don't care a fig about what there is to eat or drink, but just want to settle in and listen to some truly world-class jazz. Cover varies.

Lobby Court Bar

2025 Avenue of the Stars, Century City, ☎ *(310) 277-2000.*
At the Century Plaza Hotel.
Presents a live jazz pianist nightly, with no cover charge.

Lunaria

10351 Santa Monica Boulevard, West Los Angeles, 90075, ☎ *(310) 282-8870.*
Jazz, blues, and pop are the fare at this airy and gracious night spot. Recent performers here have been Johnny "Hammond" Smith and Kate McGary. Reservations recommended. Two drink minimum. Cover varies.

West Los Angeles: Shopping

West Los Angeles has plenty to offer the shop-til-you-drop addict, including the Century City Shopping Center, the Westwood Pavilion, and the off-price Shoppers World on La Brea. If you're looking for values in wine, **The Wine House** *(2311 Cotner Avenue)* has a large selection of vintages at discount prices, and provides opportunities for tasting before you buy.

One of the hippest stores in all of L.A. is **American Rag**, located on La Brea between Wilshire and Beverly. Occupying almost the entire block, American Rag sells vintage clothing (make the latest fashion statement by purchasing jeans with the knees already ripped out) at a pretty little price. These aren't just any vintage fashions, however. Eschewing the usual thrift store mishmash, American Rag offers only the trendiest born-again fashions and accessories (including a kids' section), and it draws all kinds of designers, models, and superstars who could, of course, afford to shop anywhere they want, but know that the truly hip choose their wardrobe from American Rag.

New in Westwood, at the corner of Westwood and Rochester, is **Borders Books and Music** *(1360 Westwood Boulevard)*, which stocks more than 140,000 book titles and 60,000 music selections. Dedicated to "celebrating the opening of minds to new ideas and voices," Borders offers—in addition to its impressive inventory—lectures, readings, live music and other educational goings-on.

In Brentwood is the barn-themed complex of nearly 30 shops known as the **Brentwood Country Mart** *(225 26th Street)*. Much more low-key than the bustling Farmer's Market on Fairfax, the decades-old Country Mart offers a quiet respite for those who hang out at the Coffee and Juice Bar (don't miss the espresso milkshakes) or indulge their weakness for chicken and fries at the Reddi-Chick BBQ. This may include a handful of celebrities, who are most apt to be found here kicking back on a Saturday morning.

Just south of Century City is the **Westside Pavilion** *(10800 West Pico Boulevard)*, anchored by Nordstrom and Robinsons May and containing 180 specialty shops and restaurants. The Nordstrom Concierge will shuttle you from a nearby hotel to the pavilion.

Not to be missed in West L.A. is the **Great Harvest Bread Company** *(11640 San Vicente)*. Part of a chain founded in Montana, this spot turns out a fabulous array of healthy fresh-baked breads that you can sample there or take home to secretly savor with wicked piles of creamy butter.

West Los Angeles: Where to Stay

Unlike Beverly Hills, West L.A. offers a great deal of variety in accommodations. If you want to (and can afford it), you can stay in the best (the Bel Air, the Century Plaza, or the Westwood Marquis), or, if your taste (and your budget) are more downscale, there are plenty of chain hotels to choose from.

If you're interested in visiting the normal tourist sights in Southern California, stay away from airport hotels, which are generally located in highly populated, heavily trafficked areas that are many freeway miles from downtown, Hollywood, and the San Fernando Valley. If you have business near the airport, however, there are some good buys here—and some good hotels, including the Westin L.A. Airport and the Holiday Inn Crowne Plaza. A $10 million renovation has turned the old Travel Lodge Viscount into the spiffy Continental Plaza, another mid-priced option a half-block from the airport.

Bel Air

Hotels and Resorts

Bel Air Hotel   **$285–$435**   ★★★★★

701 Stone Canyon Road
☎ *(800) 648-4097, (310) 472-1211, FAX: 310-476-5890.*
Single: $285–$435. Double: $285–$435.

Rambling, bungalow-style rooms decorated in peach and earth tones and surrounded by lush, secluded gardens make this a very exclusive haven for the rich and famous. The Bel Air has been called the finest hotel in L.A. and one of the best in the United States, and its reputation for discretion is known far and wide. The lack of a central lobby and the labyrinthine series of pathways that lead to the guest rooms make it easy for guests and visitors to slip in and out quietly and unnoticed. The fitness facilities are superb, with 24-hour access to Stairmasters, treadmills and bicycles, and service is discreet and pampering. Ranked restaurant: **Bel Air Hotel Dining Room**. Amenities: secluded garden atmosphere, pool, health club, private spas, houses, cottages or bungalows, balcony or patio, conference facilities, club floor. 92 rooms. Credit Cards: CB, V, MC, DC, A.

Radisson Bel-Air Summit   **$150**   ★★★

11461 Sunset Boulevard
☎ *(800) 333-3333, (310) 476-6571, FAX: 310-471-6310.*
Single: $150. Double: $150.

Recently acquired and renovated by the Radisson Hotel chain. Attractively furnished rooms open onto patio or balcony and feature imaginative art, VCRs, refrigerators and hair dryers. Complimentary continental breakfast accompanied by a morning newspaper is served in your room, in the lobby, or by the pool. A good choice for the money. Amenities: pool, tennis, hair salon, family plan, conference facilities, business services. 162 rooms. Credit Cards: CB, V, MC, DC, A.

Brentwood

Hotels and Resorts

Holiday Inn Brentwood/Bel Air   **$99–$129**   ★★

170 North Church Lane

☎ *(800) 465-4329, (310) 476-6411, FAX: 310-472-1157.*
Single: $99–$129. Double: $109–$129.
This recently renovated tower hotel offers free shuttle service to
UCLA and Westwood Village. Located five miles from the ocean and
10 from LAX. Amenities: pool, health club, Jacuzzi, balcony or patio,
family plan, conference facilities. 211 rooms. Credit Cards: CB, V, MC,
DC, A.

Century City

Hotels and Resorts

Beverly Hills Ritz   **$105–$295**   ★★★
10300 Wilshire Boulevard
☎ *(800) 800-1234, (310) 275-5575, FAX: 310-278-3325.*
Single: $105–$295. Double: $105–$295.
This all-suite hotel is located across from the Los Angeles Country
Club and is five minutes from Rodeo Drive or Westwood. Attractively
landscaped with lush plantings of palms, bamboo and ferns. Guest
rooms are situated off the pool area and boast fine walnut furnishings,
parlors, two or three TVs, stocked bars and modern art. Amenities:
pool, exercise room, Jacuzzi, balcony or patio, conference facilities.
116 rooms. Credit Cards: CB, V, MC, DC, A.

Century Plaza Hotel   **$165–$245**   ★★★★
2025 Avenue of the Stars
☎ *(800) 288-3000, (310) 277-2000, FAX: 310-551-3355.*
Single: $165–$220. Double: $190–$245.

Older, 20-story hotel and newer tower amid 14 acres of tropical
plants and pools. Formerly a 20th Century-Fox back lot, the grounds
include two unheated swimming pools, several restaurants and wonderful views from many of the tower rooms. The facility is geared to
the entertainment business, as it adjoins the Century City Entertainment Center—and shopping malls. Amenities in guest rooms vary
depending on location, but units in the newer tower are best, with
plush carpets, wet bars, TVs with movies and commissioned art. May
be a little too expensive for what it offers. Amenities: pool, exercise
room, Jacuzzi, sauna, balcony or patio, hair salon, family plan, conference facilities, business services. 1072 rooms. Credit Cards: V, MC, A.

Courtyard by Marriott   **$119**   ★★★
10320 West Olympic Boulevard
☎ *(800) 321-2211, (310) 556-2777, FAX: 310-203-0563.*
Single: $119. Double: $119.
Formerly The Chesterfield, this English-style hotel offers afternoon
tea and hors d'oeuvres in a lounge with a gas fireplace. Guest rooms
include minibars and hair dryers; all guests receive free limo service
within three miles. A good spot for business travelers, especially considering the recently reduced rates. Amenities: exercise room, Jacuzzi,
balcony or patio, conference facilities, business services. 134 rooms.
Credit Cards: V, MC, A.

J.W. Marriott Century City   **$205–$225**   ★★★★
2151 Avenue of the Stars
☎ *(800) 228-9290, (310) 277-2777, FAX: 310-785-9240.*
Single: $205. Double: $225.
This property features rooms decorated in soft pastels with marble
bathrooms, minibars and a scenic view. Amenities include compli-

mentary limo service to Rodeo Drive and Century City, two pools (one indoor), fitness facilities that include tanning beds and massage, 24-hour room service, valet laundry service, and afternoon tea. Some say this is the best Marriott in the world, and they may be right. It explains the high rates, anyway (junior suites range from $215–225). Amenities: pool, health club, Jacuzzi, sauna, balcony or patio, conference facilities, business services. 375 rooms. Credit Cards: CB, V, MC, DC, A.

Inns

Century City Inn $104–$165   ★★★

10330 West Olympic Boulevard
☎ *(800) 553-1005, (310) 553-1000, FAX: 310-277-1633.*
Single: $104–$145. Double: $120–$165.
A complimentary full breakfast is included in the rates here, and rooms have refrigerators stocked with free orange juice and muffins, coffee makers and microwaves; some have Jacuzzi tubs. Suites have a sitting area and sleeping loft connected via a spiral staircase. Amenities: health club, Jacuzzi. 46 rooms. Credit Cards: V, MC, DC, A.

Westwood

Hotels and Resorts

Century Wilshire $70–$90

10776 Wilshire Boulevard
☎ *(800) 421-7223, (310) 474-4506, FAX: 310-474-2535.*
Single: $70–$80. Double: $80–$90.
This older villa-style hotel has some of the area's most economical accommodations, but you can expect to get what you pay for. The nicer units are quite acceptable, with plush carpeting and modern furnishings, but other rooms are pretty tacky. Suites have kitchens with gas ovens. Complimentary breakfast provided. Amenities: pool. 99 rooms. Credit Cards: CB, V, MC, DC, A.

Holiday Inn Westwood Plaza $120   ★★

10740 Wilshire Boulevard
☎ *(800) 472-8556, (310) 475-8711, FAX: 310-475-5220.*
Single: $120. Double: $120.
This tower hotel adjacent to Century City has minibars in most rooms and a sun deck for catching an L.A. tan. Amenities: pool, exercise room, Jacuzzi, sauna, family plan, conference facilities. 294 rooms. Credit Cards: CB, V, MC, DC, A.

Hotel Del Capri $90–$105   ★★

10587 Wilshire Boulevard
☎ *(800) 444-6835, (310) 474-3511, FAX: 310-470-9999.*
Single: $90. Double: $105.
This modest hotel, in a prime location one mile from Westwood Village, offers solid value. About half the units are suites with kitchenettes and private terraces; all rooms have adjustable beds. The complimentary continental breakfast is brought to your room. Amenities: pool, Jacuzzi, private spas, conference facilities. 80 rooms. Credit Cards: V, MC, A.

Royal Palace Westwood $60–$96   ★★

1052 Tiverton Avenue
☎ *(800) 631-0100, (310) 208-6677, FAX: 310-824-3732.*
Single: $60–$90. Double: $66–$96.

This small hotel in the heart of Westwood Village, opposite the Armand Hammer Museum of Art & Cultural Center, offers free continental breakfast. Most suites have full kitchens. Amenities: exercise room, balcony or patio, conference facilities. 35 rooms. Credit Cards: CB, V, MC, DC, A.

Westwood Marquis   **$220–$475**   ★★★★

930 Hilgard Avenue

☎ *(800) 421-2317, (310) 208-8765, FAX: 310-824-0355.*

Single: $220–$475. Double: $220–$475.

This luxurious 15-floor all-suite hotel includes two pools and lovely gardens, and offers complimentary limo service to Beverly Hills and surrounding areas. Each guest room is different but all are deluxe with mirrored closets, minibars, fabric headboards and marble combination baths. Many actors and politicians stay here. Ranked restaurant: **Dynasty Room**. Amenities: pool, health club, Jacuzzi, sauna, hair salon, conference facilities. 258 rooms. Credit Cards: CB, V, MC, DC, A.

Inns

Hilgard House   **$99–$109**   ★★

927 Hilgard Avenue

☎ *(800) 826-3934, (310) 208-3945, FAX: 310-208-1972.*

Single: $99. Double: $109.

Intimate boutique-style hotel convenient to the UCLA campus and Westwood Village. Guests receive complimentary continental breakfast. Amenities: private spas, conference facilities. 47 rooms. Credit Cards: CB, V, MC, DC, A.

West Los Angeles: Where to Dine

The big news in the Century City Shopping Center is **Dive!**, an upscale submarine sandwich shop (complete with valet parking) owned by Steven Spielberg and Jeffrey Katzenberg. Spielberg, who certainly knows "what the people want" in the field of big-time entertainment, has used similar genius here, and, hands-down, Dive! has some of the best sandwiches and burgers (not to mention the fries) in L.A. Sure, it's a tourist trap, but, like the Hard Rock Cafe and Planet Hollywood, Dive!'s success may soon put it on the map in several other locations.

Fielding's Choice
Unique Restaurants

There are scads of restaurants in L.A., some of them trendy, some of them drop-dead gorgeous, and some of them small and funky. Among the masses, these are a few of the standouts:

1. **Uzbekistan** *(7077 Sunset Boulevard, Hollywood, ☎ (213) 464-3663). This is the sister restaurant to the original that is located in the Russian republic of the same name. The food is absolutely authentic, and if you have any doubt, listen to the delighted murmurs of Russian patrons who are sitting all around you and loving every bite.*

2. **Musso & Frank Grill** (6667 Hollywood Boulevard, Hollywood, ☎ (213) 467-7788).
   This place virtually is Hollywood, and has been for more than 70 years. It's where
   everyone who's anyone comes (or has come) to eat old-time Continental cuisine,
   have a good martini, and schmooze. Classic Old Hollywood ambience.

3. **Pink's Famous Chili Dogs** (711 North La Brea, Hollywood, ☎ (213) 931-4223). A hot
   dog stand with a history, Pink's dispenses fabulous dogs with all the trimmings.
   The foot-long jalapeno dog is legendary, and one of Pink's chili dogs supposedly
   inspired Bruce Willis to propose to Demi Moore on the spot. Have a couple of dogs
   with everything and a big order of fries–you can hit the spa next week to work it
   off.

4. **Joe's** (1023 Abbott Kinney Boulevard, Venice, ☎ (310) 399-5811). Joe's started out
   as a tiny little cafe where chef-owner Joe Miller turned out a fabulous seasonal
   menu accompanied by lots of personal service. Now, Joe has enlarged his space,
   so more of you can appreciate his handiwork. The set-price meals are an unbelievable bargain.

5. **Al Amir** (5750 Wilshire Boulevard, L.A., ☎ (213) 931-8740). Some of the best Lebanese food you'll find anywhere, plus a very lively scene at night. Radio personality Casey Kasem is reportedly a regular.

6. **Cava** (8384 West Third Street, Beverly Hills, ☎ (213) 658-8898). Serious Spanish
   food served in an unusual dining room in the Beverly Plaza Hotel. Local trendites
   come here in droves for superb tapas and wonderful Spanish wines.

7. **Chez Melange** (1716 Pacific Coast Highway, Redondo Beach, ☎ (310) 540-1222).
   This trendy spot is characterized by its efforts to be all things to all people. The
   menu is huge (and eclectic), and draws from every continent on the globe. Sometimes this works and sometimes it doesn't, but Chez Melange (in the Palos Verdes
   Inn) is definitely a local hot spot and one of the best restaurants in the South Bay.

8. **DC3** (2800 Donald Douglas Loop North, at the Santa Monica Airport, ☎ (310) 399-
   2323). The ambience is the thing here, and you can dine or listen to live jazz while
   watching the air traffic come and go at the airport. The set price dinner specials
   can't be beat, and even though the food sometimes falters, this is a great place to
   spend an evening.

9. **Gordon Biersch Brewery** (41 Hugus Alley, Pasadena, ☎ (818) 449-0052). The
   brewpub craze comes to L.A. in style at Gordon Biersch, which is the best of the
   lot. Many of the microbrewed beers are made in-house, and the room is always
   full of artists, students, and yuppie types bending their elbows and chatting up a
   storm.

10. **Papadakis Taverna** (310 West Center Street, San Pedro, ☎ (310) 548-1186). Greek
    food just like mama used to make it, plus a nightly floor show with singing and
    dancing waiters. Great for a lively night on the town.

La Cachette, owned by Jean Francois Meteigner, formerly of L'Orangerie, recently opened on the site of the long-troubled and now shuttered
Champagne Bis in West L.A. The menu focuses on French bistro food prepared with natural ingredients, and the chef's reputation and moderate
prices are expected to keep the place busy.

Some of the best (or some of the worst, depending on who you talk to) souffles in the city are available at BG Souffle, which is located at the Bistro Garden restaurant in the Century City Marketplace. The same yummy souffles that are served in the restaurant are available here for half the price, and you can even buy them uncooked and take them home to savor later, hot from your oven.

West L.A. hipsters hang at Lunaria, Primi, and the aforementioned La Cachette, which seems destined to become a neighborhood favorite.

Bel Air

French

Bel Air Hotel Dining Room $$$ ★★★★

701 Stone Canyon Road, ☎ *(310) 472-1211.*
Specialties: roast Canadian duck breast; warm sweetbread; wild mushroom ravioli.
Lunch: noon–2 p.m., entrees $16–$25.
Dinner: 6:30–10 p.m., entrees $25–$35.
Associated Hotel: Bel Air Hotel.

This opulent, flower-filled, Mission-style building is surrounded by gardens and a lake on a site that has been called the most beautiful setting in L.A. Of course, no one is going to pay prices like these for the setting alone, but the kitchen delivers cuisine as elegant as the surroundings. The food is mostly California-style, with lots of grilled fish, and a menu that changes with the seasons. The Saturday and Sunday brunches are particularly appealing, and tea is served Monday through Saturday. One of the most elegant restaurants in L.A., with service polished enough to please the most discriminating diner. Features: outside dining, own baking, Sunday brunch, full bar, rated wine cellar, late dining, private dining rooms. Jacket and tie requested. Reservations required. Credit Cards: CB, V, MC, DC, A.

Four Oaks Restaurant $$$ ★★★

2181 North Beverly Glen, ☎ *(310) 470-2265.*
Lunch: 11:30 a.m.–2 p.m., entrees $16–$21.
Dinner: 6–10 p.m., entrees $20–$29.

The restaurant's rustic, romantic setting in a Bel Air home is lovely, and the California-French creations of Peter Roelant, formerly of L'Orangerie, are superb. Roelant gives particular attention to vegetarian dishes, although his culinary talents are forever evolving into some new, unexplored territory. The prix-fixe Sunday champagne brunch, at about $30, is one of L.A.'s best buys. A sedate respite from city life, Four Oaks has an excellent reputation that is well-deserved. Lunch served Tuesday through Saturday. Features: splendid view, outside dining, own baking, Sunday brunch, full bar, rated wine cellar, late dining. Jacket requested. Reservations recommended. Credit Cards: V, MC, A.

Italian

Adriano's Ristorante $$$ ★★★

2930 Beverly Glen Circle, ☎ *(310) 475-9807.*
Specialties: qualglie con uva; risotto con funghi.
Lunch: 11:30 a.m.–3 p.m., entrees $10–$15.
Dinner: 6–10:30 p.m., entrees $20–$25.

You may pay dearly for the fare at Adriano's, but the food, which comes out of a kitchen headed by the same chef for over a dozen years, is always worth it. There's also a good wine list, and both the service and the ambience are pleasing. Lunch served Tuesday through Friday. Closed: Mon. Features: outside dining, own baking, Sunday brunch, full bar, rated wine cellar, late dining. Jacket requested. Reservations required. Credit Cards: V, MC, A.

Brentwood

American

Daily Grill $$ ★ ★

11677 San Vincente, ☎ (310) 442-0044.
Lunch: from 11 a.m., entrees $8–$20.
Dinner: to 11 p.m., entrees $10–$20.

This 1940s-style chain restaurant (there are other branches in West L.A., Encino, and Studio City) is crowded and noisy, but the portions are generous and the service efficient. Best bets are such American standards as steaks, chops and fried onion rings. Features: outside dining, late dining. Reservations not accepted. Credit Cards: V, MC, A.

Gratis $ ★ ★

11658 San Vicente Boulevard, ☎ (310) 571-2345.
Specialties: gourmet pizzas.
Lunch: from 11 a.m., entrees $5–$10.
Dinner: to 10 p.m., entrees $5–$10.

Gratis—"free"—doesn't have anything to do with the prices, but with the fat- and cholesterol-free nature of the cuisine. What this means is that if you're a meat and potatoes kind of person, you'll hate this place, but if you're into the fitness craze, this is nirvana. Imagine a generous piece of fabulous vanilla bean cheesecake or a slab of triple-layer chocolate cake. You can eat them fat- and guilt-free at Gratis. Features: own baking, wine and beer only. Credit Cards: V, MC, A.

Italian

Mezzaluna $$ ★ ★

11750 San Vicente Boulevard, ☎ (310) 447-8667.
Lunch: 11:30 a.m.–3 p.m., entrees $8–$20.
Dinner: 5:30–10:30 p.m., entrees $8–$20.

The sister restaurant to Mezzaluna in Beverly Hills, this branch gained a sort of morbid fame as the place where Nicole Brown Simpson last dined before her June 1994 murder at her Brentwood home. Just like the Beverly Hills restaurant, this one gets decent marks for food, but mediocre reviews for service and attitude. Reportedly, after the Simpson murder, the restaurant sought to improve business by inviting a local critic to "update" his review. He declined, but business picked up anyway; people in L.A. just can't seem to leave this kind of stuff alone. Pizzas and pastas are the best bets. Features: outside dining, own baking, late dining. Reservations recommended. Credit Cards: V, MC, A.

Peppone $$$ ★ ★ ★

11628 Barrington Court, ☎ (310) 476-7379.
Specialties: Venetian dishes.
Lunch: 11:30 a.m.–2 p.m., entrees $13–$17.
Dinner: 5:30–10:30 p.m., entrees $20–$30.

If you're dying for some old-fashioned, New York-style Italian cuisine with wines to match, Peppone may be what you're looking for. The chef will even prepare dishes at your request if you don't find what you want on the menu. Features: own baking, full bar, rated wine cellar, late dining. Reservations required. Credit Cards: CB, V, MC, DC, A.

Toscana $$$ ★★★

11633 San Vicente, ☎ *(310) 820-2448.*
Specialties: spit-roasted meats; pasta bottarga.
Lunch: 11:30 a.m.–2:30 p.m., entrees $13–$25.
Dinner: 5:30–11 p.m., entrees $13–$25.

A true neighborhood trattoria with lots of charm and, unfortunately, lots of chic fellow diners who are crammed in like sardines and generally making a lot of noise. The Tuscan cuisine is very good—and authentic—and the staff seems happy to serve you. Lunch served Monday through Saturday. Features: own baking, wine and beer only, rated wine cellar, late dining. Jacket requested. Reservations recommended. Credit Cards: V, MC, A.

Century City

American

Dive! $$ ★

10250 Santa Monica Boulevard, ☎ *(310) 788-DIVE.*
Specialties: submarine sandwiches; burgers; fries.
Lunch: from 11:30 a.m., entrees $8–$16.
Dinner: to 11 p.m., entrees $8–$16.

Dive! is the new restaurant opened by movie bigwigs Steven Spielberg and Jeffrey Katzenberg in the Century City Shopping Center. The building looks like a submarine inside and out, and the ambience includes flashing lights, video screens set behind "portholes," and an imaginary captain calling "dive! dive!" As you might imagine, Dive! has become the quintessential tourist hangout, noisy (lots of kids), crowded (if you're claustrophobic, don't go), and slightly overpriced. The food is sort of "upscale deli," with fabulous submarine sandwiches and fries (along with several options for dipping) to die for. There's nearly always a wait, and you're often shuttled into the bar to hang out and buy drinks until you are informed via a beeper (provided by the restaurant) that your table is ready. But the food really IS good here. Dive! is undoubtedly the first of a series of chain restaurants, and the principles have plenty of money, so it could be around for a long time. (Want to take home a souvenir menu? Five bucks.) Reservations accepted for parties of eight or more only. Features: non-smoking area, late dining. Credit Cards: V, MC, A.

Chinese

Jade West $$ ★★

2040 Avenue of the Stars, ☎ *(310) 556-3388.*
Specialties: kung pao chicken, lobster and crab.
Lunch: 11:30 a.m.–3 p.m., entrees $8–$20.
Dinner: 3–9 p.m., entrees $10–$19.

This stylish Chinese restaurant near the Shubert Theatre draws mixed reviews. On a good night, you can sit amid the lush Oriental ambience and eat like a king. On an off night, the food is nothing special. Lunch served Monday through Friday. Features: full bar, rated wine cellar. Reservations recommended. Credit Cards: V, MC, A.

French

La Cachette $$$ ★★★★

10506 Little Santa Monica Boulevard, ☎ *(310) 470-4992.*
Specialties: rotisserie chicken and lamb; grilled seafood.
Lunch: noon–3 p.m., entrees $9–$17.
Dinner: 6–10 p.m., entrees $12–$20.

The success of La Cachette was practically guaranteed before the restaurant opened. At the helm is Jean-Francois Meteigner, who cooked at L'Orangerie for more than ten years, and when he and partner Liza Utter took over the space formerly occupied by Champagne Bis, they had the right combination for a winning dining establishment. The ambience is sophisticated (but not stuffy), the food is superb and nearly everything is light, natural and good for you. Try the house-smoked whitefish salad with warm potatoes, lemon and capers, or the grilled swordfish with wasabe. The restaurant's upside-down caramelized apple pie was judged the best in a competition with eleven other local French chefs, making Meteigner the tarte tatin master of Los Angeles. Reserve up to two weeks ahead, or you won't get in. This place is packed. Lunch served Tuesday through Friday. Closed: Sun. Features: own baking, wine and beer only, rated wine cellar, late dining. Reservations required. Credit Cards: V, MC, DC, A.

Italian

Harry's Bar & American Grill $$ ★★★

2020 Avenue of the Stars, ☎ *(310) 277-2333.*
Specialties: fresh pasta; fresh fish; veal.
Lunch: from 11:30 a.m., entrees $10–$19.
Dinner: to 10 p.m., entrees $10–$19.

The original Harry's is in Italy, and this one carries on the tradition with solid Northern Italian cuisine served in a stylish atmosphere near the ABC Entertainment Center—which means it's a perfect after-theatre stop if you've been to the Shubert (the restaurant stays open later on show nights). Harry's also serves American grill food, so you're bound to find something you like. Lunch served Monday through Saturday. Features: full bar, rated wine cellar, late dining. Reservations required. Credit Cards: CB, V, MC, DC, A.

West Los Angeles

American

Arnie Morton's of Chicago $$$ ★★★

435 South La Cienega Boulevard, ☎ *(310) 246-1501.*
Specialties: steak; chops; seafood.
Dinner: 5:30–11 p.m., entrees $19–$30.

"Serious" meat-eaters love Arnie Morton's, where you choose from huge slabs of beef on a cart, then gaze in wonder as your choice shows up later on your plate, cooked to perfection. You will pay dearly, but many say Arnie's are the best steaks in L.A., and the portions are so big, you'll be lunching on leftovers the next day. The masculine dining room complements the meat-and-potatoes cuisine. Features: own baking, full bar, late dining. Reservations recommended. Credit Cards: V, MC, A.

T. J. Peppercorn's $$$ ★★

6225 West Century Boulevard, ☎ *(310) 337-1234.*
Specialties: five star duck.

Lunch: 11:15 a.m.–2 p.m., entrees $8–$11.
Dinner: 5:30–10:30 p.m., entrees $20–$35.
Associated hotel: Hyatt Airport.

Besides the famous Five Star Duck and the huge salad bar, the food is pretty basic at this Hyatt located near LAX. Features: full bar, late dining. Jacket requested. Reservations required. Credit Cards: CB, V, MC, DC, A.

Cajun

Orleans Restaurant **$$** ★★★

11705 National Boulevard, ☎ (310) 479-4187.
Specialties: cajun popcorn; blackened prime rib; barbecued shrimp.
Lunch: 11:30 a.m.–2 p.m., entrees $4–$13.
Dinner: 6–9:30 p.m., entrees $10–$20.

One of the best Cajun restaurants in town, with all the old favorites for savoring in a cozy dining room. Takeout food, too. Lunch served Monday through Friday. Features: full bar. Reservations recommended. Credit Cards: V, MC, A.

French

Dynasty Room **$$$** ★★★★

930 Hilgard Avenue, ☎ (310) 208-8765.
Specialties: seafood mixed grille; veal chop; rack of lamb.
Dinner: 6–10:30 p.m., entrees $18–$24.
Associated Hotel: Westwood Marquis.

One of the few elegant, old guard French/Continental restaurants still in business in L.A., the Westwood Marquis' Dynasty Room attracts a monied crowd who can afford to pay to be pampered. There is substance as well as glitter here, with excellent (and well-sauced) cuisine that always lives up to expectations, and a harpist that sets a graceful mood. Breakfast and lunch are served in the hotel's Garden Terrace. Features: own baking, Sunday brunch, full bar, late dining, private dining rooms. Jacket requested. Reservations required. Credit Cards: CB, V, MC, DC, A.

Lunaria **$$$** ★★★

10351 Santa Monica Boulevard, ☎ (310) 282-8870.
Specialties: fish; salads; pasta; oyster bar.
Lunch: 11:30 a.m.–2:30 p.m., entrees $9–$15.
Dinner: 5:30–10 p.m., entrees $11–$25.

This hot spot is a little more dressed up than the average bistro, with excellent wines and wonderful food prepared by chef Jean Pierre Bosc, who was hailed as one of the best young chefs in France before he came to America. He uses only the freshest, highest-quality ingredients, and it shows. In addition to its status as a restaurant, Lunaria is also a happening night spot, and recently received some notoriety for the development of its own "healthy" new cocktail, "Perrier de menthe," which consists of mint syrup and Perrier sparkling water over ice. The restaurant also features live jazz nightly. Ask about multi-course, prix fixe meals, most of which also have a healthy bent. A $20, three-course, early-bird dinner is served Tuesday through Saturday from 6–7 p.m. Closed: Sun. Features: own baking, full bar, rated wine cellar, late dining. Reservations recommended. Credit Cards: V, MC, A.

Italian

Barefoot $$ ★★★

8722 West Third Street, ☎ *(310) 276-6223.*
Lunch: from 11:30 a.m., entrees $8–$15.
Dinner: 6–11 p.m., entrees $10–$16.
Barefoot replaced the old MaBe restaurant, but has a decidedly less
formal air about it, with a casual crowd (including staff from the
Cedars-Sinai Medical Center across the street) to match. Opinions are
mixed on the cooking, which can be hit or miss, but most agree that
on a good day, the food can be fabulous. Features: outside dining,
Sunday brunch, full bar, late dining. Reservations recommended.
Credit Cards: CB, V, MC, DC, A.

Il Moro $$ ★★★

11400 West Olympic Boulevard, ☎ *(310) 575-3530.*
Lunch: 11:30 a.m.–3 p.m., entrees $7–$15.
Dinner: 5:30–10 p.m., entrees $7–$15.
The owners of Ca'del Sole, Ca'Brea and Locanda Veneta are behind
Il Moro, which serves all kinds of luscious Italian food in a sophisti-
cated dining room. No doubt about it: Il Moro is destined to follow
its siblings into the upper echelons (in popularity at least) of L.A. Ital-
ian restaurants. Breakfast and lunch served Monday through Friday.
Closed: Sun. Features: own baking, wine and beer only, late dining.
Reservations required. Credit Cards: D, CB, V, MC, DC, A.

La Bruschetta $$$ ★★★

1621 Westwood Boulevard, ☎ *(310) 477-1052.*
Specialties: farfalle with crab meat & asparagus; rack of lamb.
Lunch: 11:30 a.m.–2 p.m., entrees $10–$21.
Dinner: 6–10:30 p.m., entrees $10–$21.
A refreshingly unpretentious atmosphere, great food and interesting
choice of wines makes this place a winner. The service is good, too.
Closed: Sun. Features: non-smoking area, late dining. Jacket
requested. Reservations required. Credit Cards: CB, V, MC, DC, A.

Matteo's $$$ ★★★

2321 Westwood Boulevard, ☎ *(310) 475-4521.*
Specialties: zitti; veal; whitefish.
Dinner: 5–midnight, entrees $15–$24.
The food may not taste authentic to true Italians, but garlic lovers will
be happy and well-fed. Closed: Mon. Features: full bar, late dining.
Reservations required. Credit Cards: CB, V, MC, DC, A.

Osteria Romana Orsini $$ ★★★

9575 West Pico Boulevard, ☎ *(310) 277-6050.*
Specialties: roman dishes.
Lunch: noon–3 p.m., entrees $8–$20.
Dinner: 6–11 p.m., entrees $8–$20.
Really good pastas stand out here, and are reliable even when every-
thing else is a little uneven. Nice Italian wines and friendly service.
Closed: Sun. Features: outside dining, own baking, full bar, rated
wine cellar, late dining, private dining rooms. Reservations recom-
mended. Credit Cards: CB, V, MC, DC, A.

Primi $$ ★★★

10543 West Pico Boulevard, ☎ *(310) 475-9235.*
Specialties: fresh pasta.
Lunch: 11:30 a.m.–2:30 p.m., entrees $10–$20.

Appetizers star at this lovely restaurant where an upscale crowd comes to graze. The menu has now expanded to include a good selection of all courses, and the wine list shines. The food is wonderfully authentic, and you'll see many Italians here, blissfully chowing down next to entertainment executives from Century City. Closed: Sun. Features: outside dining, own baking, full bar, rated wine cellar, late dining. Jacket requested. Reservations recommended. Credit Cards: CB, V, MC, DC, A.

Japanese

Mishima $ ★★

11301 Olympic Boulevard, ☎ (310) 473-5297.
Specialties: tanuki soba.
Lunch: from 11:30 a.m., entrees $5–$10.
Dinner: to 9 p.m., entrees $5–$10.

The clientele is largely Japanese at this little restaurant located on the second floor of a mini-mall. After tasting authentic Japanese noodles here, you may never boil another pack of Top Ramen. Best of all, these aren't Tokyo prices. Closed: Mon. Features: own baking, wine and beer only. Reservations not accepted. Credit Cards: V, MC.

THE VALLEYS

Greater Los Angeles has two widely acknowledged "valleys" that, although they may not be recognizable to the first-time visitor, have distinctly different flavors. The first is the San Fernando Valley, the undisputed heart of the Southern California entertainment industry and the home of "Beautiful downtown Burbank." The mythical "Valley Girl," who made a whole new way of talking ("like, fur shure") and a toss of the hair a way of life for American teeny-boppers, was also conceived in the San Fernando Valley and immortalized in Moon Unit Zappa's pop song of the same name ("Like, gag me with a spoon").

Burbank is the home of NBC, Disney and Warner Brothers studios, and is just east of Universal City, which houses Universal Studios and Hanna-Barbera, and the CBS Studio Center in Studio City. One of Burbank's showplaces is the new $54 million Disney Animation Complex adjacent to the Ventura Freeway at *2100 Riverside Drive*. It's hard to miss, with its 14-foot-tall letters spelling out "ANIMATION" adjacent to a two-story cone hat such as the one worn by Mickey Mouse in "The Sorcerer's Apprentice" (company vice president Roy Disney has his office inside the cone). The complex is especially stunning at night, when lit up in a variety of colors.

Universal City is a comparatively small bit of real estate straddling the line between the valley and L.A.'s West Side, and it's built almost entirely around the entertainment business. Its most famous claim to fame is the Universal Studios theme park, which is far more hype and pizazz than it is a serious look at moviemaking, but tourists love the place and come in droves. Nearby is the popular new Universal CityWalk, a pedestrian promenade linking Universal Studios, the Universal Amphitheatre and the 18-screen Universal City Cinemas complex.

Fielding's Choice: Newest Architectural Marvel

Architecture buffs (not to mention Disney buffs) shouldn't miss the new, $54-million Disney Animation Complex (2100 Riverside Drive, Burbank, and highly visible from the Ventura Freeway). Of course you would expect this kind of thing from the Disney people, but they've really outdone themselves this time. Fourteen-foot-high letters spell out "ANIMATION," and a two-stories-high replica of the moon- and star-emblazoned cone hat worn by "The Sorcerer's Apprentice" sits at its main entrance. (Disney vice chairman Roy Disney's office is located at the top of the cone.) The building also has a huge striped billboard that resembles sprocketed film on a reel. The inside is just as amazing as the exterior, with a Disneyesque fantasy interior that will house the offices of more than 600 Disney animators. If you have a chance, see the building when it's lit up at night.

North Hollywood is a bit of an anomaly, part Hollywood and part San Fernando Valley, that has recently found an identity of its own as the SoHo (or NoHo, as the natives call it) of the West Coast. Now boasting its own tabloid magazine, its own arts festival, and a reviving economy based on an eclectic mix of coffee houses, retail shops and theatres, NoHo is fast becoming another of those "happening" L.A. neighborhoods.

Fielding's Choice: Best Delis

L.A. has hundreds of neighborhood delis, but the following are among the best:

Art's Deli *(Studio City). An industry hangout, Art's has been dishing out everything from matzo ball soup to corned beef for more than three decades. Eat in or take out.*

Ziggy G's *(West Hollywood). When Nicky Blair's closed last year, Ziggy G's moved in. It hasn't been here long enough to be a classic, but it's owned by the same family who turned New York City's Rialto into one.*

Jerry's Famous Deli *(Studio City). The cast of several top sitcoms often come from their respective studios to lunch here, but the food is as rewarding as the star-gazing.*

Fielding's Choice: Best Delis

Barney Greengrass (Beverly Hills). *The name may be more indicative of an Irish pub than a deli, but Barney Greengrass, new in Beverly Hills, is a clone of the New York original, only without the attitude. Got a craving for smoked fish? It doesn't get any better than Barney's smoked sturgeon. (Warning: this place is VERY classy, and has Beverly Hills prices to match.)*

The **San Gabriel Valley**, on the other hand, has a much more sedate reputation. **Pasadena**, whose name comes from a Chippewa Indian name meaning "crown of the valley," is one of L.A.'s oldest and most distinguished communities, and it wears its proverbial crown with pride. The Tournament of Roses Parade, which draws hundreds of thousands of spectators each New Year's Day (and adds approximately $100 million to the regional economy), and the Rose Bowl game, held in the city's Rose Bowl, are Pasadena's popular claims to fame, but it also has a strong cultural heritage and some excellent museums.

The Dearly Departed

Death has been elevated to theme park status in L.A., and some of the cemeteries full of rich and famous people actually consider themselves just another L.A. "attraction," complete with maps to the stars' graves. It may not be the same as seeing stars in the flesh, but at least you can pay your respects. Here are some of the most popular cemeteries known for their famous inhabitants:

1. ***Hollywood Memorial**, 6000 Santa Monica Boulevard, Hollywood. Stars buried here include Douglas Fairbanks, Rudolph Valentino, Tyrone Power, Cecil B. DeMille, Mel Blanc, Peter Finch, Marion Davies and Jayne Mansfield.*

2. ***Forest Lawn Glendale**, 1712 Glendale Avenue, Glendale. You should know right off that the Forest Lawn cemeteries make an effort to turn your visit into a pleasant excursion involving a drive around the pleasant (and expansive) grounds, some multi-media program or other, piped-in music, and lots of museum-quality stuff to look at. The idea, of course, is to make you love the place so much that you'll be willing to fork over whatever it takes to make this your final resting place. Even if you don't want to make a commitment for eternity, you'll enjoying visiting the graves of Jean Harlow, Clark Gable, W.C. Fields, Clara Bow, Errol Flynn, Spencer Tracy, and the man who may have had a soft spot in his heart for the whole "death as theme park" thing, Walt Disney.*

3. ***Forest Lawn Hollywood**, 6300 Forest Lawn Drive, L.A. Not quite as hoity-toity as the Glendale branch, this cemetery nonetheless carries on the Forest Lawn tradition. Stan Laurel, Buster Keaton and Freddie Prinze are among the celebrities buried here.*

The Dearly Departed

4. **Westwood Memorial**, *1218 Glendale Avenue, Westwood. Marilyn Monroe is perhaps the most famous resident interred here, but you can also find other tragic figures among the gravestones, including Natalie Wood and Playboy model Dorothy Stratten.*

5. **Holy Cross Cemetery**, *5835 West Slauson Avenue, Culver City. You'll find crooners Bing Crosby, Jimmy Durante and Mario Lanza buried here, along with Bela Lugosi, who was supposedly buried in his "Dracula" cape. The grave of Sharon Tate, the famous victim of the Charles Manson murders, is also here.*

6. **Hillside Memorial Park**, *6001 Centinela Avenue, L.A. This Jewish cemetery, located near Holy Cross, has a striking monument to Al Jolson in front, and contains the graves of Jack Benny, George Jessel and Vic Morrow, who was killed on the set of the "Twilight Zone" movie in 1982.*

If Pasadena seems too far away from the glamour of Hollywood for your tastes, be advised that it has been a veritable "back lot" for the entertainment industry for years. The historic Gamble House served as the home of "Doc Brown" (played by Christopher Lloyd) in the *Back to the Future* movies; *Hocus Pocus* was filmed at the First Baptist Church; scenes from *Love Affair*, starring Warren Beatty and Annette Bening, were shot at the Pasadena Civic Auditorium; and the Beverly Hills mansion in which the "The Beverly Hillbillies" lived in the 1990s remake was not in Beverly Hills at all, but on Oakland Avenue in Pasadena.

Pasadena also boasts its own share of celebrity residents, including Van Halen, Kevin Costner (who also has a hand in the trendy Twin Palms restaurant), Jessica Lange, Delta Burke, rocker Peter Sellers, a handful of famous athletes, and a bunch of Nobel Prize winners, most of whom hang out at Caltech.

In spite of its mostly well-manicured look and upper-crust reputation, Pasadena contains a diverse population and does have neighborhoods (such as South Pasadena) where crime is high and gangs are a problem. It is best to avoid these areas at night.

Best Views

Surrounded by all those hills and mountains, you'd expect L.A. to have lots of places where you can go to get a good view of the city (providing that the smog has cleared out for the day). Some views are better at night, of course, when you can look up at the stars and down at a million twinkling lights. Here are some of the best perches from which to survey L.A.:

Best Views

1. **Griffith Park Observatory** (Griffith Park). *The best place in L.A. to see the stars, planets and city lights all at once. On a clear day, you can see forever.*

2. **Yamashiro Restaurant** (1999 North Sycamore Avenue, Hollywood). *The good news is that this is probably the best view of Hollywood you could possibly get. The bad news is that you will have to drop a fairly pretty penny to dine here—or you might try skulking around the parking lot, which is free.*

3. **City Hall** (200 North Spring Street, downtown). *Again, you may have to wait for a clear day, but from the building's 27th-floor observation deck, you can see all over the place.*

4. **Mulholland Drive**. *This extremely scenic highway, which stretches across L.A.'s back country from Malibu to the San Fernando Valley, affords fabulous views of L.A., especially at night. Allow at least a couple of hours to make the trip, and PAY ATTENTION! It can be dangerous going up there!*

5. **Palisades Park** (on the Santa Monica bluffs). *This grassy stretch looks out over the ocean, and it's one of the best places in town for watching the sunset.*

6. **Pt. Dume** (above Zuma Beach). *The view is always terrific here, but in season (December-March), you may get an extra treat; California gray whales in migration are often visible off the coast.*

Glendale, also in the San Gabriel Valley, is an even more diverse community, with its share of racial tensions and (unfortunately) hate crimes. Although it's trying to upgrade its image, Glendale still doesn't have much to offer the tourist except Forest Lawn Memorial Park, which has its own museum, and the Glendale Galleria.

And then there's Glendora, nestled against the foot of the San Gabriel Mountains. Besides garnering the dubious honor of being the unofficial "smog capital of the nation," there's not much to distinguish it from any of the other L.A. suburbs.

Fielding's Choice: Best Hike

The Cold Creek Canyon Preserve in the Santa Monica Mountains is one of the area's best places to hike and observe nature. Hiking the Cold Creek Trail isn't for the faint of heart (and the most difficult incline is on the return trail), but this Nature Conservancy preserve is a perfect getaway for birders, hikers, lovers of wildflowers, and nature freaks. It also has the distinction of being one of the least-visited parks in L.A., so you'll find a little solace along with the natural wonders (and hopefully not so many beer cans and deflated potato chip bags). You'll need a permit for the five-mile hike; call the Mountains Parks Information number (☎ 800-533-PARK) for details.

SAN FERNANDO VALLEY

Citywalk in Universal City

San Fernando Valley: Things to See and Do

Universal Studios Hollywood—which is located close to, but not in Hollywood—is the valley's answer to Disneyland and the second-largest tourist attraction in Southern California. What you see today is a far cry from the original Universal Studios, which had its beginning in California in 1914, when a 130-acre chicken ranch in North Hollywood was bought

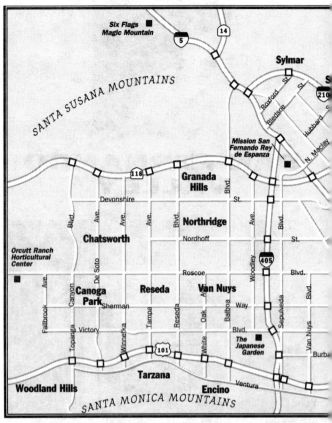

for $165,000 by the Universal Film Manufacturing Company, then based in New York City. When the state-of-the-art production facility was completed and officially opened on March 15, 1915, Thomas Edison, himself, ceremoniously started up the studio's electrical equipment.

More than 10,000 onlookers were on hand that day, and they could hardly have imagined that 50 years later, one of the West Coast's busiest studios—now owned by MCA—would become a huge, paved-over entertainment complex drawing more than 5 million visitors every year.

Even though most of **Universal Studios** is dedicated to the theme park and thrill rides based on various movies, you can get a look at some serious moviemaking or TV production if there is any going on the day you are visiting (check the posted list just inside the gate for the day's shooting schedule).

Just like its Orange County counterpart, Universal Studios can (especially during the summer and on weekends) be overrun with crowds, and you may wait in line for up to an hour for such popular attractions as the tram ride. Get to the park as early as possible, and plan to spend at least one entire day in order to see everything.

The aforementioned tram ride—which is probably the park's most famous attraction—allows you to "experience" all sorts of chilling phenome-

na such as an attack by "Jaws" and King Kong, a flash flood, an 8.3 earthquake, and the parting of the Red Sea, and takes you through the back lot where you can see old movie sets and (if you're lucky) working sets where production is currently taking place.

After the hour-long tram ride, take in the park's other attractions at the Entertainment Center and the Studio Center, then stroll along the Universal CityWalk, a sort of upscale version of funky Venice Beach where you can shop, snack or just watch the passersby, which is pretty entertaining in and of itself.

There are more than three dozen shops, restaurants and attractions on the **Universal CityWalk** promenade, including the Museum of Neon Art, the world's only institution devoted to neon, kinetic and electric fine art. Peruse the gallery here, or take the walking tour, where you'll learn about the nearly two dozen vintage signs that are placed along the CityWalk.

Wanna-be Dorothys can cavort with Toto at Out-Takes, which uses computer-generated wizardry to put you into one of hundreds of famous movie or TV scenes, or you can take the kids over to Captain Coconuts, where they can watch a ton of stuffed animals (all equipped with computer micro-chips) move to the beat of a jukebox.

Sure, the CityWalk is crowded and touristy—just like Universal Studios—and prices for everything tend to be on the high side, but it represents another of those "totally L.A." experiences, and, luckily, you can do the whole thing from morning until midnight without moving your car out of its original parking space. Now there's a novel L.A. experience.

If you're truly interested in getting a peek at goings on in the entertainment industry but aren't convinced that you want to endure another hectic day at an L.A. amusement park, opt for the Warner Brothers VIP Studio Tour, a two-hour excursion (minus the thrill rides) into the history of Warner Brothers' studios, and a tour of back lots and sound stages, where there is often filming going on.

Legends of television past and present are immortalized at the $20 million **Academy of Television Arts and Sciences** complex at Lankershim and Magnolia in North Hollywood. A huge statue of an Emmy award sits in the courtyard, surrounded by statues of TV luminaries such as Lucille Ball, Johnny Carson, Milton Berle and Mary Tyler Moore, whose MTM Enterprises was once at home in the nearby CBS Studio Center in Studio City. The Academy is not open to the public, but you're welcome to browse the plaza.

Adjacent to **Six Flags Magic Mountain**, the San Fernando Valley's largest amusement park, a new 14-acre water park opened in the summer of 1995. Called **Hurricane Harbor**, the park—which has a separate admission price from Magic Mountain's—features water slides, lagoons and other water-related experiences set around a jungle theme. The two parks together are known as Six Flags California. Also on the drawing board for the valley is a 10.5-acre lake and recreational area expected to be completed at Hansen Dam in late 1996.

 If you're in L.A. in the fall, take the kids to the October Theatre Arts Festival for Youth (or TAFFY, as it's more commonly known), an annual weekend multicultural celebration of theatre, music, dance, storytelling, puppet shows and other activities that's arguably one of L.A.'s best things to do with children.

Museums and Exhibits

Ronald Reagan Presidential Library ★★★

40 Presidential Drive, Simi Valley, 93065, ☎ *(805) 522-8444.*
Hours open: 10 a.m.–5 p.m.

Opened in November 1991, the Reagan Library contains some 50 million papers relating to Ronald Reagan's presidency, as well as a public museum devoted to the former actor's political career and recent world history. A reconstruction of the Oval Office as it was in President Reagan's day, displays of gifts from heads of state, a gallery devoted to Nancy Reagan, interactive videos, and exhibits detailing Reagan's political ideas are found in the museum. Guided tours are available 9 a.m.–noon, Monday–Friday. Reduced admission for seniors; children under age 15 admitted free. General admission: $4.

Tours

NBC Studio Tour ★★★

3000 West Alameda, Burbank, ☎ *(818) 840-3537.*
Hours open: 9 a.m.–3 p.m.

The NBC studio tours allows you to walk through the NBC newsroom and watch the "Tonight Show With Jay Leno" crew rehearsing for the evening's performance. There's also a "You Can Fly" special effects demonstration, and a look at the studio's wardrobe and make-up departments. 1-1/4-hour tours depart on the hour. Admission for children 5–12, $3.75. General admission: $6.

Oskar J's Sightseeing Tours ★★
4334 Woodman Avenue, Sherman Oaks, 91423, ☎ *(818) 501-2217.*
Oscar J's offers a variety of L.A.-area tours, with scheduled pickup service at most major hotels in Los Angeles and Anaheim. Options include tours of movie stars' homes, harbor cruises, a "Los Angeles by Night" tour, "Los Angeles by Helicopter," a three-day "California Coastal Tour," and tours to popular attractions and destinations as farflung as Tijuana and San Francisco.

Warner Brothers VIP Studio Tour ★★★★
4000 Warner Boulevard, Burbank, 91522, ☎ *(818) 954-1744.*

If you're REALLY interested in the craft of moviemaking (as opposed to being crammed into a tram and chased by a phony shark), this is the best tour in town. Small groups (12 people each) take a two-hour escorted walking/driving tour through Warner Brothers and Columbia Pictures facilities. The emphasis is on the technical and educational aspects of filmmaking, and the tour includes a look at backlot sets, a sound studio, a set construction area, and the site of a film shooting when possible. Reservations should be made two weeks in advance. Children under age ten are not admitted. Tours 10 a.m. and 2 p.m. General admission: $27.

Theme/Amusement Parks

Six Flags Hurricane Harbor ★★★★
26101 Magic Mountain Parkway, Valencia, 91385, ☎ *(805) 255-4111.*
Next to Magic Mountain.
The sister park to Magic Mountain, Hurricane Harbor is adjacent to the larger park. Here, the emphasis is almost completely on water-related fun, with a huge water play area for younger children, a 1300-foot-long river that floats guests on a raft past a variety of scenic (and some mysterious!) areas, and water slides that range from the 45-degree drop of the Daredevil Plunge to the (somewhat) tamer Lightning Falls. Rafts are provided free to guests at rides where they are necessary, or you can rent one for the day for $5 at Captain Buoy Raft Rentals in Buccaneer Village. Changing rooms with lockers and showers are located in the entrance plaza, and you can pretty much plan on wandering around all day in your bathing suit (bring sunscreen!). In 1995, the park is open daily from June to September, weekends only through Oct. 1. Opening is always at 10 a.m., but closing time varies. Children under four feet tall and seniors over 55 are admitted for $10; children under 2 are free. A combination ticket to both parks is available for $42. General admission: $16.

Six Flags Magic Mountain ★★★★
26101 Magic Mountain Parkway, Valencia, 91355, ☎ *(818) 367-5965.*
I-5 North from Los Angeles, Magic Mountain exit.

This 260-acre park is known for its thrill rides, including the Viper, Ninja, Revolution and Colossus roller coasters, and the new Flash-back, with six 180-degree vertical dives. Another popular attraction is Tidal Wave, which includes a plunge over a 50-foot waterfall. The High Sierra Territory, with the Yosemite Sam Sierra Falls water ride, the General Animal Star Theatre, Bugs Bunny World and the Discovery Trail, represents the park's nod to families with younger children, but the park is usually inhabited mostly by teenagers looking for a thrill. The newest attraction is Gotham City: The Backlot, a themed "land" based on the Batman movies. "Batman: The Ride" is the big attraction here, and if you enjoy flying through the air with feet dangling, reaching speeds of 50 miles per hour and zipping through loops and a double corkscrew, don't miss it. If you're still standing after that, take a look at the Batmobile replica or the eerie underground tunnels beneath Gotham City. Open daily in the summer; weekends and school holidays only, September–May. Opening time is always 10 a.m., but closing times vary with the season, so call ahead. Children under four feet tall, $15; children under 2 free; seniors $18 with ID. A combination ticket to Magic Mountain and Hurricane Harbor is $42. General admission: $29.

Universal Studios

100 Universal City Plaza, Universal City, 91608, ☎ (818) 508-9600. Exit at Universal Center Drive.

This quintessential tourist trap is one of the most popular attractions in Los Angeles. A narrated tram tour through the 400-acre Universal Studios complex provides (sort of) a behind-the-scenes look at movie and TV production, but that's not the main excitement here. You'll also take a trip "Back to the Future" on the new $70 million ride, experience an avalanche, a flash flood, a laser battle, and an 8.3 earthquake, and feel the heat of "Backdraft." A live stage spectacular based on "The Flintstones" opened in summer of 1994. Children will enjoy the new "American Tale Playland." Closing times vary, so call ahead. (Hint: if you want to get the REAL inside scoop on moviemaking, take the Warner Brothers Studio VIP Tour.) Admission for children 3–11 and seniors, $24.95; children under 3 admitted free. General admission: $31.

Children's Activities

The Farm ★★

8101 Tampa Avenue, Reseda, 91335, ☎ (818) 341-6805.
Kids can ride a pony, peer at farm animals, gawk at llamas, and poke around farming tools. Open weekends and holidays. General admission: $2.50.

Theatre Arts Festival for Youth

30000 Mulholland Highway, Agoura, ☎ (818) 998-2339. At the Peter Strauss Ranch.

The Theatre Arts Festival for Youth—TAFFY—celebrates its 10th anniversary in 1995, and it's a wonderful weekend for the whole family. Nationally known actors and artists always participate, and programs include puppetry, multicultural music, hands-on activities, storytelling, theater and dance. Best of all, the cost is barely more than you'd pay to take the family to a movie. Held in October. Advance tickets are available.

Sports and Recreation

Los Angeles Equestrian Center

480 Riverside Drive, Burbank, 91506, ☎ *(818) 840-9063.*
This facility is home of the L.A. Stars Professional Arena Polo team
and hosts 22 polo games and major U.S. and West Coast horse shows.
Visitors can dine while taking in a polo match; call for the schedule.

San Fernando Valley: Music, Dance and Theatre

The San Fernando Valley is the L.A. capital of celluloid and video entertainment, but it also has a surprising number of arts venues where you can
enjoy both popular and classical performances, and a bunch of neighborhood theaters. Among the former is the new, $64 million, state-of-the-art
Thousand Oaks Civic Arts Center, which includes the 278-seat Forum
Theatre, the 1800-seat Civic Auditorium, and lots of lofty public spaces.
The center's 1995 season is ambitious, indeed, and the facility seems destined to become a major player on the L.A. arts scene. There will be a special emphasis on children's productions, including musicals, puppet shows
and other special events.

In Universal City, the hottest entertainment is at the Universal Amphitheatre, a fully-enclosed, 6250-seat venue where famous acts are always on
the bill. Call ahead for information on current events; some sell out early.

Music

Universal Amphitheater   ★★★

100 Universal City Plaza, Universal City, 91608, ☎ *(818) 777-3931.*
This outdoor amphitheatre offers a year-round schedule of entertainment events, including rock, pop, country and jazz concerts—always
with top-name entertainers.

Theatre

Thousand Oaks Civic Arts Plaza   ★★★★

2100 East Thousand Oaks Boulevard, Thousand Oaks, ☎ *(805) 449-2787.*
This stunning new arts complex is just over border into Ventura
County, but as the quality of its events becomes known, lots of people
will be more than willing to make the drive. The state-of-the-art
venue includes an 1800-seat Civic Auditorium as well as the more
intimate Forum Theatre. With a full season of special events that
encompass theatre, music and dance, the Civic Arts Plaza represents a
major addition to the performing arts scene in Southern California.
Tickets are available through the box office and at Ticketmaster outlets.

Ticket Agencies

Barry's Ticket Service

18000 Ventura Boulevard, Suite 24, Encino, ☎ *(818) 708-8499.*
Barry's handles tickets for events at the new Thousand Oaks Civic
Arts Plaza, as well as for other local concerts, theatre, and sporting
events. Open seven days.

Murray's Tickets

19633 Ventura Boulevard, Tarzana, 91356, ☎ *(818) 881-0844.*
Tickets to all major sports events, concerts, and theater worldwide.
Specializes in Rose Bowl and Super Bowl tickets. Toll free in Califor-
nia: ☎ *(800) 245-6688*; National: ☎ *(800) 542-4466.*

NBC Tickets

3000 West Alameda Avenue, Burbank, 91523, ☎ *(818) 840-3537.*
Hours Open: 8 a.m.–5 p.m.

Free tickets to taping of NBC shows available on first-come, first-served basis on the day of the taping, or by mail in advance. Call for schedule of tapings, times, and specific information on "The Tonight Show," hosted by Jay Leno.

V.I.P. Tickets

14515 Ventura Boulevard, Sherman Oaks, ☎ *(800) 328-4253.*
This ticket agency, based in the San Fernando Valley, handles tickets to most L.A. events. Open seven days.

San Fernando Valley: Nightlife

Some of the hottest nightlife in the valley is happening at Universal City-Walk, where options include the L.A. version of B.B. King's Blues Club and Restaurant (the original is in Memphis); the massive Country Star Hollywood, where countryfied music and barbecue are only part of the fun; a branch of the famous Hollywood Athletic Club, a popular venue for billiards and just plain hanging out; Lighthouse Beach, a beach-themed club (with a real sand beach) illuminated by a state-of-the-art, stadium-sized outdoor Astrovision TV screen that's always tuned to the biggest sporting event of the moment; and Wizardz Magic Club and Dinner Theatre, where you can have dinner or sip a drink served in a beaker or test tube while magicians entertain you or psychics tell your fortune. As if all this wasn't enough to choose from, on tap here for 1995 is a flagship Hard Rock Cafe.

Obviously, there's a whole lot going on in the valley besides the fare at Universal CityWalk. Because the place is where loads of people in "the biz" live and work, you can find just about any kind of club here. One of the newest is the Legends of Hollywood Jazz Club, which opened in late 1994 in Studio City. The jazz is VERY cool here, and Sunday nights there's an All-Stars Pro-Jam Session that features bassist Ernie McDaniel. The Baked Potato, located near Universal Studios, is another cool venue for jazz.

Fielding's Secret Spot

Cruising is not dead, In fact it may be the next big "in" scene. Artist Robert Williams, comedian Jay Leno(L.A.'s most famous car nut) and other car nuts make the scene every Friday night after 6 at this Valley hangout. The cards are spotless, the pinstriping perfect and all the tech talk is washed down with the retro cuisine of Bob's Big Boy. Expect to find more than 100 candy-colored hot rods from the '20s to the '60s. The scene is half geriatric and half California Kool.

Bob's Big Boy

4211 Riverside Drive
Burbank, CA
☎ *(818) 843-9334*

B. B. King's Blues Club

Universal CityWalk, Universal City, ☎ *(818) 622-5464.*
The master of blues opened this nightspot, which has a sister club in Memphis, on the second level of the Universal CityWalk, and the place is always jumpin'. Sometimes King, himself, takes the stage. If

you can't get there at night, go for the Sunday Gospel Brunch, which is a real treat, complete with a gospel choir and an all-you-can eat buffet of down-home southern food such as hush puppies, biscuits and gravy, and fried chicken.

Baked Potato, The

3787 Cahuenga Boulevard, Studio City, 91604, ☎ *(818) 980-1615.*
Quality local jazz and fusion bands play late into the night accompanied, appropriately enough, by a menu of huge stuffed baked potatoes. Recent performers include Cecilia Noel & The Wild Clams and Don Randi & Quest. Another Baked Potato is located in North Hollywood.

Blue Saloon

4657 Lankershim Boulevard, North Hollywood, ☎ *(818) 766-4644.*
A comfortable low-key, no-frills watering hole offering a variety of country, blues, rockabilly and rock and roll, with performers like The Hooligans, Blue Watch, Neon Angels and Backlash. If the band isn't playing your song, you can shoot pool or watch the big-screen satellite TV.

Country Star Hollywood

Universal CityWalk, Universal City, 91608, ☎ *(818) 762-3939.*
Yeeeee hah! The Hard Rock Cafe goes Country, and Country goes Hollywood in this 14,000-square-foot restaurant/entertainment palace backed by big country names like Vince Gill, Wynonna, and Reba McEntire. It's the perfect place to eat barbecue, listen to country music and dance.

Legends of Hollywood Jazz Club

11720 Ventura Boulevard, Studio City, ☎ *(818) 760-6631.*
This sterling jazz club opened in Studio City in the Fall of 1994, and it's gaining a strong local following. In addition to the food (lunch and dinner are served daily), the drinks, and the (somewhat incongruous?) satellite sports broadcasts, there's live jazz on weekends—sometimes featuring extremely well-known jazz musicians. Call to see what's on the schedule.

Mancini's Club

20923 Roscoe Boulevard, Canoga Park, ☎ *(818) 341-8503.*
Mancini's bills itself as the "home of live hot rock," which means the crowd is usually young (Wednesday nights, college students with ID get discounted drinks), and the bands a bit out on the edge. Recent headliners include the Atomic Punks, Choking Ghost, Bovine Fetish, and Psychadelicatessan.

Moonlight Tango Cafe

13730 Ventura Boulevard, Sherman Oaks, 91423, ☎ *(818) 788-2000.*
Big band music, singing waiters, and a swinging dance floor make this nightspot the perfect place for—you guessed it!—a midnight, moonlight tango.

Palomino, The

6907 Lankershim Boulevard, North Hollywood, ☎ *(818) 764-4010.*
This showcase for both country music and rock and roll is where Linda Ronstadt got her start. Monday night is talent night and bookings change nightly, so call for current artists. The restaurant serves BBQ specialties.

Village Bar & Grill

> *4201 West Olive Avenue, Burbank,* ☎ *(818) 846-2342.*
> Live entertainment, blues and jazz, nightly. Cover charge $3–10.

Wizardz

> *1000 Universal Center Drive, Universal City,* ☎ *(818) 506-0066.*
> *On the Universal CityWalk.*
> If you're looking for something different in a nightclub, head for Wizardz, which features a "Magic Potionz" bar, dinner and magic (including a laser light show) tarot card readers, fortune tellers, and other magical goings-on. Sure it's touristy—and not cheap—but isn't this the sort of stuff you came to L.A. to see?

San Fernando Valley: Shopping

The **Sherman Oaks Galleria** and the newly renovated Fashion Square—also in Sherman Oaks—are two of the most popular shopping venues in the San Fernando Valley. Both have a variety of specialty shops and restaurants and are anchored by major department stores, and both are stops on the new San Fernando Valley DASH shuttle service that runs along Ventura Boulevard between Fulton and Haskell, making an additional stop at the cinema complex near Van Nuys Boulevard. The service operates Monday through Friday from 10 a.m. to 9 p.m.; Saturday from 11 a.m. to 8 p.m.; and Sunday from noon to 6 p.m. Another DASH route runs through Van Nuys and Studio City. There's a nominal cost (25 cents at press time) for riding on any of L.A.'s DASH shuttles.

Northridge Fashion Center had the dubious distinction of being near the epicenter of the January 1994 Northridge earthquake; the majority of stores are now back in business.

Don't overlook the unique shopping opportunities available along the **Universal CityWalk**. Here you'll find such intriguing shops as Adobe Road, featuring Native American art, jewelry and clothing; the internationally known bath and skin care products of Crabtree and Evelyn; DAPY, the first West Coast location for this Paris original; a branch of the Nature Company featuring an indoor replica of a rainforest and a wonderful selection of nature-oriented gifts; Things From Another World, where you can purchase the latest in alien-themed merchandise; and Wizardz Wonders, the quintessential magician's shop where real magicians show you how things work and entice you to make your money disappear.

One of the best bookstores for kids in all of L.A. is also located here: Crow's Nest, which adjoins the more grown-up-oriented Upstart Crow Bookstore and Coffeehouse.

Warner Brothers has two of its stores in the San Fernando Valley (at the Glendale Galleria and Topanga Mall), both selling "high end" merchandise relating to the studios' movies and TV shows. Warner Brothers cartoon characters are shown off in abundance, on everything from beach towels and key rings to pricey clothing.

There are also several little special interest stores in the San Fernando Valley that are pretty insignificant unless you're looking for what they've got, but if you are—they are THE place. You'll find everything for the well-dressed horseman (or -woman) at the L.A. Equestrian Center's **Dominion**

Saddlery *(480 Riverside Drive)* in Burbank, including boots, breeches, and pricey little hunting jackets, and North Hollywood's **Harmonica Shop** *(5151 Whitsette Avenue)*, L.A.'s only mouth organ specialty store, stocks more than 300 different kinds of harmonicas. Also in North Hollywood are **Junkies Collectibles** *(4386 Lankershim Boulevard)*, whose name pretty much describes what you're likely to find inside, and the **People's Democratic Republic of Iguanaland** *(10943 Camarillo Street)*, a sort of coffee house/used bookstore/CD shop known for its offbeat poetry readings and other live entertainment.

You can get an upscale wardrobe at downscale prices at the **Nordstrom Rack** *(21490 Victory Boulevard)* in Canoga Park. You have to take your time and look through everything carefully, but it's possible to save up to 75 percent on designer clothes here. Shopping for kids is a pleasure at **For Kids Only** *(18332 Ventura Boulevard)* in Tarzana, where designer clothes go for a big discount.

If you're into exotic foods and ethnic specialties, check the many stores in the neighborhood of Sherman Way and Reseda Boulevard in Reseda. Here you'll find a variety of shops selling delicacies from the Near, Middle and Far East, Russia, and Latin America; a couple of wonderful bakeries and casual ethnic eateries; and The Dish Factory, a restaurant supply store that carries everything for the discriminating cook.

Some of the best fresh fish in town is available at **Tarzana's Fish King** *(19550 Ventura Boulevard. There's also a branch in Glendale)*, where chefs from some of L.A.'s trendiest restaurants buy the seafood that you may be charged an arm and a leg for if you eat it at Citrus. Get the same stuff here at a fraction of the price and cook it yourself, or opt for something from the "hot" menu to eat there.

San Fernando Valley: Where to Stay

The San Fernando Valley has a bunch of moderately priced hotels, some of the best of which are at Universal City and Studio City, where tourists tend to stay. (Those in "the biz" usually choose Beverly Hills or Hollywood, where the accommodations are much more chi chi, and a limo can whisk them to work in the valley.)

Burbank

Hotels and Resorts

Burbank Airport Hilton   **$109–$159**   ★★★
    2500 Hollywood Way
    ☎ *(800) 486-3576, (818) 843-6000, FAX: 818-842-9720.*
    Single: $109–$149. Double: $119–$159.
    A recent renovation added 40,000 square feet of convention and meeting facilities and 220 rooms and suites to this hotel, which is located just a quarter-mile from the airport. Rates for the two-room executive suites run from $139 to $179. Amenities: pool, health club, Jacuzzi, sauna, family plan, conference facilities, business services, complimentary airport pickup service. 487 rooms. Credit Cards: V, MC, A.

Holiday Inn   **$99**   ★★
    150 East Angeleno Avenue
    ☎ *(800) 465-4329, (818) 841-4770, FAX: 818-566-7886.*

Single: $99. Double: $99.
This downtown hotel is two miles from the Burbank Airport, 10 miles from downtown Los Angeles. Some rooms have wet bars. Amenities: pool, family plan, conference facilities, complimentary airport pickup service. 500 rooms. Credit Cards: CB, V, MC, DC, A.

Ramada Inn Burbank AP   **$85–$105**   ★★
2900 North San Fernando Boulevard
☎ *(800) 272-6232, (818) 843-5955, FAX: 818-845-9030.*
Single: $85–$95. Double: $95–$105.
Nothing special here, but all rooms are larger than you might expect, and eight suites have Jacuzzis. Amenities: pool, Jacuzzi, private spas, balcony or patio, family plan, conference facilities, complimentary airport pickup service. 144 rooms. Credit Cards: CB, V, MC, DC, A.

Canoga Park
Low Cost Lodging

Best Western Canoga Park   **$49–$54**   ★★
20122 Vanowen Street
☎ *(800) 528-1234, (818) 883-1200, FAX: 818-883-1202.*
Single: $49. Double: $54.
Located 15 miles from the Burbank Airport, this moter inn has soundproofed rooms and a central courtyard. Eight units have kitchenettes with microwave ovens. A 32-lane bowling center is next door—a fact which you may or may not consider a plus. Complimentary continental breakfast. Amenities: pool, Jacuzzi, sauna, family plan, conference facilities, business services. 46 rooms. Credit Cards: CB, V, MC, DC, A.

Clarion Suites Warner Center   **$59–$99**   ★★★
20200 Sherman Way
☎ *(800) 252-7466, (818) 883-8250, FAX: 818-883-8268.*
Single: $59. Double: $99.
All suites feature fully equipped kitchenettes, and rates include a complimentary full breakfast and evening beverages. One lighted tennis court nearby. Amenities: pool, sauna, balcony or patio, family plan, conference facilities, complimentary airport pickup service. 100 rooms. Credit Cards: V, MC, A.

North Hollywood
Hotels and Resorts

Best Western Mikado   **$70–$90**   ★★
12600 Riverside Drive
☎ *(800) 528-1234, (818) 763-9141, FAX: 818-752-1045.*
Single: $70–$75. Double: $80–$90.
Located just off the Ventura Freeway, but rooms are soundproofed to block out traffic noise. Three suites have kitchenettes. Complimentary full breakfast. Amenities: pool, Jacuzzi, balcony or patio, family plan. 58 rooms. Credit Cards: V, MC, A.

Holiday Inn Beverly Garland   **$85–$115**   ★★
4222 Vineland Avenue
☎ *(800) 238-3759, (818) 980-8000, FAX: 818-766-5230.*
Single: $85–$105. Double: $95–$115.
Formerly an excellent budget alternative, especially for families, the former Beverly Garland recently became a Holiday Inn, and prices went up a bit. Perks include free limo service, free tennis on a lighted

court, putting green and playground. Located five miles west of Universal Studios. Amenities: pool, tennis, sauna, balcony or patio, family plan, conference facilities, complimentary airport pickup service. 258 rooms. Credit Cards: V, MC, DC, A.

Sherman Oaks

Hotels and Resorts

Carriage Inn   **$80–$99**   ★★★

5525 Sepulveda Boulevard
☎ *(800) 772-8527, (818) 787-2300, FAX: 818-782-9373.*
Single: $80–$99. Double: $80–$99.
It may look like the typical motel from the outside, but this property offers more than you might expect in the way of large guest rooms, a friendly staff, and comfortable furnishings. Request a room in the tower section for the best climate control. Amenities: pool, Jacuzzi, family plan. 181 rooms. Credit Cards: V, MC, A.

Radisson Valley Center   **$125–$160**   ★★

15433 Ventura Boulevard
☎ *(800) 333-3333, (818) 981-5400, FAX: 818-981-3175.*
Single: $125–$150. Double: $125–$160.
Accommodations have been newly redecorated in Art Deco style; all have a balcony or patio with a view. Two blocks from the Galleria Shopping Center, this hotel offers a complimentary full breakfast. Amenities: pool, exercise room, Jacuzzi, family plan, conference facilities. 216 rooms. Credit Cards: CB, V, MC, DC, A.

Studio City

Hotels and Resorts

Sportsmen's Lodge   **$105–$125**   ★★★

12825 Ventura Boulevard
☎ *(800) 821-8511, (818) 769-4700, FAX: 213-877-3898.*
Single: $105–$125. Double: $105–$125.
English country-style hotel with a resort atmosphere, featuring beautiful gardens, ponds and waterfalls. It's been around a long time and renovations are not always up to date, but its location near Universal Studios, Hollywood and NBC are a plus if you're interested in the movie and TV scene, and the usual amenities such as in-room movies, fax and valet/laundry service are offered. Amenities: pool, exercise room, Jacuzzi, balcony or patio, hair salon, family plan, conference facilities, complimentary airport pickup service. 193 rooms. Credit Cards: CB, V, MC, DC, A.

Universal City

Hotels and Resorts

Hilton and Towers   **$125–$175**   ★★★

555 Universal Terrace Pkwy.
☎ *(800) 445-8667, (818) 506-2500, FAX: 818-509-2058.*
Single: $125–$175. Double: $125–$175.
This 24-story contemporary hotel, formerly the Registry, reopened in August 1990, after extensive renovations. Its location next to Universal Studios and near Hollywood makes it convenient for both business travelers and families. Amenities include complimentary transportation to all local attractions, a health club that offers personal trainers, body wraps and massage in addition to its fitness equipment, and

packages that include a trip to Universal Studios. The deluxe tower rooms on the 19th and 20th floors are the best. Amenities: pool, exercise room, Jacuzzi, hair salon, family plan, conference facilities, club floor, complimentary airport pickup service. 446 rooms. Credit Cards: CB, V, MC, DC, A.

Sheraton Universal $160–$245 ★★

333 Universal Terrace Pkwy.
☎ *(800) 325-3535, (818) 980-1212, FAX: 818-985-4980.*
Single: $160–$225. Double: $180–$245.

Although the location is convenient to the San Fernando Valley, Hollywood, Burbank and Universal Studios, many think that's all this Sheraton has going for it. In spite of a multimillion dollar renovation, parking, rooms and service all leave something to be desired. Amenities include in-room movies, minibars, in-room safes, valet/laundry service, fax and child care. Amenities: pool, exercise room, Jacuzzi, sauna, balcony or patio, family plan, conference facilities. 446 rooms. Credit Cards: CB, V, MC, DC, A.

Van Nuys

Hotels and Resorts

Best Western Airtel Plaza $119–$129 ★★★

7277 Valjean Avenue
☎ *(800) 528-1234, (818) 997-7676, FAX: 818-785-8864.*
Single: $119. Double: $129.

Located at the Van Nuys Airport, with tie-down space for private aircraft, this hotel offers in-room movies, FAX, complimentary cocktails, hors d'oeuvres, newspaper and continental breakfast. There are two restaurants, a lounge and gift shop on the premises. Amenities: pool, exercise room, Jacuzzi, private spas, balcony or patio, conference facilities, complimentary airport pickup service. 268 rooms. Credit Cards: CB, V, MC, DC, A.

Woodland Hills

Hotels and Resorts

Holiday Inn Woodland Hills $94–$109 ★★

21101 Ventura Boulevard
☎ *(800) 465-4329, (818) 883-6110, FAX: 818-340-6550.*
Single: $94. Double: $109.

This motor hotel is located in the Warner Center area, which makes it handy for those doing business in the San Fernando Valley. There's not much that stands out here, but in-room movies provide a pleasant diversion. Amenities: pool, family plan, conference facilities. 127 rooms. Credit Cards: CB, V, MC, DC, A.

Marriott Warner Center $125–$175 ★★★

21850 Oxnard Street
☎ *(800) 228-9290, (818) 887-4800, FAX: 818-340-5893.*
Single: $125–$155. Double: $125–$175.

This sixteen-story Marriott hotel is located adjacent to the Woodland Hills Fashion Mall and Warner Center Business Park. It's probably the best hotel in the West Valley, with beautiful public areas and excellent rooms. In-room movies, child care and complimentary afternoon tea are just some of the extras available to guests. Amenities:

pool, health club, Jacuzzi, sauna, balcony or patio, family plan, conference facilities, club floor. 461 rooms. Credit Cards: V, MC, DC, A.

Warner Center Hilton   **$119–$129**   ★ ★ ★

6360 Canoga Avenue
☎ *(800) 922-2400, (818) 595-1000, FAX: 818-596-4578.*
Single: $119–$129. Double: $119–$129.
Art deco style defines this Hilton located in the West Valley near shopping malls, restaurants and entertainment. The concierge level has special amenities, and the pool is indoor/outdoor. Amenities: pool, tennis, health club, Jacuzzi, sauna, balcony or patio, family plan, conference facilities, club floor, business services. 327 rooms. Credit Cards: CB, V, MC, DC, A.

San Fernando Valley: Where to Eat

In the San Fernando Valley, those in search of the ultimate Chicago-style hot dog swear by Rubin's Red Hot, a casual joint where you can happily clog your arteries with Polish hot dogs, greasy fries, thick shakes and all the trimmings. And don't overlook Art's Deli, a Studio City institution that literally rose Phoenix-like from the ashes in the fall of 1994 after burning to the ground in an electrical fire caused by an aftershock of the Northridge quake. Art's has been a fixture in the San Fernando Valley for almost 40 years, and showbiz types are always hanging around—either eating in or taking out.

On the Universal CityWalk, you'll find lots to please your palate, including the upscale Wolfgang Puck's Cafe, the authentic Mexican cuisine available at Camacho's Cantina, and the Universal City branch of Malibu's Gladstones. Also here is Morisawa Sushi, featuring seafood flown in daily from Japan.

Snacking is also a treat with yummy options such as Cafe Puccino (yes, another of those ubiquitous cappuccino joints—but it's a goodie); Hollywood Freezway, an ice cream (it features Haagen-Daz) parlor with a freeway theme; the Island Nut Company, featuring all kinds of tempting (and hot) roasted nuts, gourmet nut butters made on the premises, and exotic trail mixes; and Jody Maroni's Sausage Kingdom, with its huge selection of artery-busting sausages whose ingredients run the gamut from Bombay curried lamb to orange-garlic-cumin. Those a little more health-conscious will appreciate L.A. Juice, an all-natural juice and salad bar, and Yo'Gert, a cafeteria-style yogurt shop where you can choose an "artists' palate" of toppings.

For a romantic getaway, ignore all of the valley hang-outs and head up to the Saddle Peak Lodge, where the view, the food, and the rustic ambience can't be beat.

Burbank

Seafood

Piero's Seafood House   **$$$**   ★ ★

2825 West Olive Avenue, ☎ *(818) 842-5159.*
Specialties: Neptune sea chest.
Lunch: 11:30 a.m.–3 p.m., entrees $8–$23.
Dinner: to 9:30 p.m., entrees $8–$23.

Seafood and traditional Italian dishes mix at this family-owned restaurant, where Piero's mom helps out in the kitchen. Lunch served Monday through Friday. Features: outside dining, own baking. Jacket requested. Reservations recommended. Credit Cards: CB, V, MC, DC, A.

Calabasas

American

Saddle Peak Lodge $$$ ★★★★

419 Cold Canyon Road, ☎ *(818) 222-3888.*
Specialties: wild game.
Dinner: 6 p.m.–midnight, entrees $18–$30.

This rustic, rambling hunting lodge overlooking the San Fernando Valley is known for its excellent game, romantic atmosphere and Sunday brunch (served 11 a.m.–2 p.m.) that's always worth the trip. Tres romantic! Closed: Mon, Tue. Features: countryside locations, own baking, Sunday brunch, rated wine cellar, late dining. Jacket requested. Reservations required. Credit Cards: V, MC, A.

Encino

French

Mon Grenier $$$ ★★

18040 Ventura Boulevard, ☎ *(818) 344-8060.*
Specialties: duck with wild cherry sauce; veal.
Dinner: 6–10 p.m., entrees $22–$30.

Mon Grenier is an eccentric little French restaurant that does several things very well. Owner Andre Lion offers a delightful menu of French specialties, many of which qualify for "Heart Healthy" status. A delighful dining discovery. All entrees come with vegetables. Closed: Sun. Features: own baking, late dining. Reservations required. Credit Cards: V, MC, A.

Indian

Akbar $ ★★

18003 Ventura Boulevard, ☎ *(818) 343-1838.*
Specialties: tandoori; lamb vindaloo.
Lunch: 11:30 a.m.–2:30 p.m., entrees $4–$6.
Dinner: 5–10 p.m., entrees $6–$10.

Reviews are mixed on this Indian restaurant, which also has a branch in Marina del Rey. Some say the food is excellent, while others complain that it's too Americanzied. Some dishes are quite innovative, though, and the prices are certainly right. Closed: Mon. Features: non-smoking area, late dining. Reservations recommended. Credit Cards: CB, V, MC, DC, A.

Italian

Terrazza Toscana $$ ★★★

17401 Ventura Boulevard, ☎ *(818) 905-1641.*
Lunch: 11:30 a.m.–3 p.m., entrees $8–$14.
Dinner: 5:30–10 p.m., entrees $10–$15.

This winning restaurant—related to Toscana in Brentwood—has a home on the second level of the fashionable Courtyard Shops complex. Excellent meat dishes, and good pizzas and pastas, tempered by some complaints about inconsistencies in the kitchen, especially on weekends. The atmosphere is industrial chic, the crowd upscale and noisy. Features: own baking, rated wine cellar, late dining. Reservations recommended. Credit Cards: V, A.

Latin American

Cha Cha Cha   **$$$**   ★ ★

17499 Ventura Boulevard, ☎ *(818) 789-3600.*
Specialties: sea bass Veracruz; banana boats.
Lunch: 11:30 a.m.–4 p.m., entrees $7–$15.
Dinner: 4:45–10 p.m., entrees $11–$22.

The wild ambience matches the eclectic menu at this spot that's always an entertaining venue for Caribbean food. Lots of exotic drinks, jazzy Caribbean music and yuppies mixing it up at the bar. Features: own baking, Sunday brunch, rated wine cellar, late dining. Reservations required. Credit Cards: CB, V, MC, DC, A.

North Hollywood

Italian

Ca' del Sole   **$$**   ★ ★ ★

4100 Cahuenga Boulevard, ☎ *(818) 985-4669.*
Specialties: pastas; grilled fish.
Lunch: 11:30 a.m.–2:30 p.m., entrees $8–$17.
Dinner: 5–11:30 p.m., entrees $8–$17.

This upscale trattoria is the brainchild of the Locanda Veneta and Ca' Brea set, and it's the best news to hit the Valley in ages. In other words, Ca' del Sole is HOT, and entertainment executives and wannabes come here to power lunch while shuffling scripts or making deals. The food is really good (and in great portions for grazing), but the scene is the real draw. Closed: Sun. Features: own baking, late dining. Credit Cards: V, MC, DC, A.

Mediterranean

Barsac Brasserie   **$$**   ★ ★ ★

4212 Lankershim Boulevard, ☎ *(818) 760-7081.*
Lunch: 11:30 a.m.–2:30 p.m., entrees $13–$15.
Dinner: 5:30–10:30 p.m., entrees $13–$15.

The French and Italian cuisine is good enough to draw stars from the nearby studios to this casual bistro, where reasonable prices are a plus. Lunch served Monday through Friday. Features: own baking, late dining. Reservations recommended. Credit Cards: V, MC, A.

Sherman Oaks

American

Rubin's Red Hot   **$**

15322 Ventura Boulevard, ☎ *(818) 905-6515.*
Specialties: hot dogs; chili; fries.
Lunch: from 11 a.m., entrees $2–$4.
Dinner: to 8 p.m., entrees $2–$4.

Rubin's may not be the quintessential Chicago-style hot dog stand, but it's as close as you can get in the Valley. Crunchy, greasy fries, thick milkshakes and—of course—the hot dog, in a ton of different manifestations . Drive through or eat in. Features: outside dining. Reservations not accepted.

French

Mistral   **$$$**   ★ ★

13422 Ventura Boulevard, ☎ *(818) 981-6650.*

Lunch: 11:30 a.m.–3 p.m., entrees $10–$16.
Dinner: 5:30–10:30 p.m., entrees $11–$23.

This intimate little bistro doesn't get much glory amidst the plethora of elegant L.A. French restaurants, but it offers all of your favorite bistro-brasserie dishes, usually very well executed. Some criticize the cuisine as too predictable and too heavily sauced, but many things succeed very well here. A delightful spot. Lunch served Monday through Friday. Features: own baking, rated wine cellar, late dining. Reservations recommended. Credit Cards: V, MC, DC, A.

Italian

La Pergola $$ ★★

15005 Ventura Boulevard, ☎ (818) 905-8402.
Lunch: 11:30 a.m.–2:30 p.m., entrees $8–$10.
Dinner: 5–10 p.m., entrees $10–$15.

Another of those ubiquitous industry hangouts, La Pergola serves both northern and southern Italian cuisine highlighted by produce from the restaurant's own organic garden. Terrific, rustic food and a pleasant, flower-filled ambience. Lunch served Monday through Friday. Features: wine and beer only, late dining. Credit Cards: V, MC, A.

Posto $$$ ★★★

14928 Ventura Boulevard, ☎ (818) 784-4400.
Lunch: 11:30 a.m.–2:30 p.m., entrees $10–$20.
Dinner: 5–10:30 p.m., entrees $17–$20.

The latest offering by Piero Selvaggio of Valentino and Primi is often overcrowded and noisy, but food this good is worth wading your way through the masses. You can really get your money's worth on Monday nights, when chef Luciano Pellegrini cooks up whatever he feels like making, and you pay only $25 for the privilege of eating it. The wine list is as fabulous as the food. Lunch served Monday through Friday. Features: own baking, rated wine cellar, late dining. Reservations recommended. Credit Cards: CB, V, MC, DC, A.

Studio City

African

Marrakesh $$$ ★★★

13003 Ventura Boulevard, ☎ (818) 788-6354.
Dinner: 5–10 p.m., entrees $19–$22.

Really good Moroccan food served in many courses that you eat with your hands while sitting on pillows amid whirling belly dancers. What more can we say? Features: non-smoking area, late dining. Reservations recommended. Credit Cards: CB, V, MC, DC, A.

American

Art's Delicatessen $$ ★★

12224 Ventura Boulevard, ☎ (818) 762-1221.
Specialties: corned beef; matzo-ball soup.
Lunch: entrees $8–$12.
Dinner: to 11 p.m., entrees $8–$12.

With the motto, "every sandwich is a work of Art," this valley standby had been turning out classic deli food for over 35 years when the January 1994 earthquake gave it a knockout blow. Since then, Art's has literally risen from the ashes (a fire that resulted from an aftershock destroyed the restaurant), and it's back in business in grand style, with the old regulars cramming the place. If you ask some of Art's customers, they'll set you straight: Art's IS Ventura Boulevard. Open until midnight on weekends. Features: non-smoking area. Reservations not accepted.

Bistro Garden Coldwater $$$ ★★★

12950 Ventura Boulevard, ☎ (818) 501-0202.
Lunch: 11:30 a.m.–3 p.m., entrees $16–$18.
Dinner: 5:30–11 p.m., entrees $22–$28.

The gorgeous setting of this sister restaurant to the Bistro Garden in Beverly Hills may have been rattled a bit in the L.A. earthquake, but the restaurant was back in business six weeks later, its elegant ambience intact. Some say the food doesn't always live up to the surroundings, but on most occasions it succeeds marvelously. The charming garden atmosphere is especially welcoming at lunch, which is served Monday through Friday. Closed: Sun. Features: own baking, late dining. Reservations recommended. Credit Cards: CB, V, MC, DC, A.

French

Pinot $$$ ★★★

12969 Ventura Boulevard, ☎ (818) 990-0500.
Specialties: pappa al pomodoro; socca galette; ravioli de Nice.
Lunch: 11:30 a.m.–2:30 p.m., entrees $14–$16.
Dinner: 6–10 p.m., entrees $18–$22.

Reviews were at first mixed on this newish restaurant owned by Patina's Joachim Splichal and located on the site formerly occupied by La Serre, but recent reviews show that things are definitely on the upswing. The bistro atmosphere is refreshingly authentic, with several dining areas studded with original art and celebrity photographs. The food is wonderful, and features all of your bistro favorites. Best of all, prices here are much lower than at Patina. Lunch served Monday through Friday. Features: own baking, rated wine cellar, late dining. Reservations recommended. Credit Cards: V, MC, A.

Wine Bistro $$ ★★

11915 Ventura Boulevard, ☎ (818) 766-6233.
Lunch: from 11:30 a.m., entrees $11–$15.
Dinner: to 10 p.m., entrees $12–$15.

The selection of wines isn't quite as good as you might expect, but the classic—not nouvelle—French bistro food is good and the setting warm and inviting. A special, three-course prix fixe dinner is available for $23.95. Lunch served Monday through Friday. Closed: Sun. Features: rated wine cellar, late dining. Reservations recommended. Credit Cards: CB, V, MC, DC, A.

Italian

Il Mito $$ ★★★

11801 Ventura Boulevard, ☎ (818) 762-1818.
Specialties: veal chop; bruschetta.
Lunch: 11:30 a.m.–2:30 p.m., entrees $10–$15.
Dinner: 6–10:30 p.m., entrees $10–$20.

Il Mito is a popular little trattoria that draws patrons from the nearby studios, who come to talk about "the biz" and schmooze over yummy Northern Italian food like scrumptious risotto, fresh pastas and a great veal T-bone expertly rendered by chef Michael Fekr, formerly at Locanda Veneta. The noise level is a bit bothersome, but high decibels tend to go with trendy restaurants. Lunch served Monday through Friday. Features: own baking, late dining. Reservations required. Credit Cards: V, MC, A.

La Loggia   **$$**   ★★★

11814 Ventura Boulevard, ☎ *(818) 985-9222.*
Specialties: veal chop; risotto; grilled seafood.
Lunch: 11:30 a.m.–2:30 p.m., entrees $9–$16.
Dinner: 5:30–10:30 p.m., entrees $9–$16.

An instant hit with those "in the business," this trendy, spartan spot dishes up great pizza and pasta. Lunch served Monday through Friday. Features: wine and beer only, late dining. Reservations recommended. Credit Cards: CB, V, MC, DC, A.

Japanese

Sushi Nozawa   **$**   ★★★

11288 Ventura Boulevard, ☎ *(818) 508-7017.*
Specialties: sushi.
Lunch: noon–2 p.m., entrees $3–$5.
Dinner: 5:30–10 p.m., entrees $3–$5.

This spare, tiny restaurant is thought by some to have the best sushi in L.A., and the fish is as fresh as you'll find it anywhere. Deceivingly low entree prices are for sushi by the piece, which means you could rack up quite a tab. Not much in the way of ambience, but everyone just comes for the food. Expect to wait when things are busy. Lunch served Monday through Friday. Closed: Sun. Features: wine and beer only, late dining. Reservations not accepted. Credit Cards: V, MC.

Teru Sushi   **$$**   ★★★

11940 Ventura Boulevard, ☎ *(818) 763-6201.*
Specialties: sushi.
Lunch: noon–2:30 p.m., entrees $8–$12.
Dinner: 5:30–11:30 p.m., entrees $10–$15.

You'll probably have to wait to get a seat here, but this is another testament to the fact that L.A. REALLY knows how to do sushi. Everything is absolutely fresh and impeccably prepared, and the chefs create a "dining as theatre" atmosphere, which is all part of the fun. It's easy to get carried away and spend a fortune, but at least you'll have company: the place is overrun with celebrities who are as impressed with the food as you are. Lunch served Monday through Friday. Features: outside dining, own baking, wine and beer only, late dining. Reservations recommended. Credit Cards: CB, V, MC, DC, A.

Thai

Talesai   **$$**   ★★★

11744 Ventura Boulevard, ☎ *(818) 753-1001.*
Lunch: 11:30 a.m.–2:30 p.m., entrees $5–$10.
Dinner: 6–10:30 p.m., entrees $10–$20.

This Valley outpost of the upscale Thai restaurant in West Hollywood has all the same things to recommend it: solid, authentic cooking, a pleasant ambience and warm service. These restaurants are making a name for themselves and stand out among the other Thais in L.A. Lunch served Monday through Friday. Features: late dining. Reservations recommended.

Tarzana

French

Le Sanglier $$$ ★★

5522 Crebs Avenue, ☎ (818) 345-0470.
Specialties: wild boar; fresh seafood; pasta.
Dinner: 5:30–10:30 p.m., entrees $15–$25.

In keeping with the wild game specialties, the atmosphere here is reminiscent of a French hunting lodge. Carnivores will find plenty to smile about. Closed: Mon. Features: own baking, late dining. Reservations recommended. Credit Cards: D, CB, V, MC, DC, A.

Toluca Lake

American

Val's $$$ ★★★

10130 Riverside Drive, ☎ (818) 508-6644.
Specialties: veal chop; chateaubriand.
Lunch: 11:30 a.m.–2:30 p.m., entrees $12–$19.
Dinner: 5–10:00 p.m., entrees $15–$25.

Val's is a VERY elegant restaurant that's slightly Old Guard, but most everything on the menu is very good. There are delicacies such as fresh goose liver, caviar, or rack of lamb on the menu, plus, there are always lots of special activities going on at Val's: once a month, there are Murder Mystery dinners; high tea is served (along with a fashion show) at 3:30 p.m. on the last Friday of every month. Be prepared to reach deep in your pocket when the check comes, but Val's is a great special occasion place and a hangout for power eaters from Burbank Studios. Lunch served Monday through Friday. Closed: Sun. Features: own baking, rated wine cellar, late dining. Jacket requested. Reservations recommended. Credit Cards: CB, V, MC, DC, A.

Universal City

American

Wolfgang Puck Cafe $$ ★★

1000 Universal Center Drive, ☎ (818) 985-9653.
Specialties: designer pizzas; chinois chicken salad.
Lunch: from 11 a.m., entrees $8–$12.
Dinner: to 10 p.m., entrees $8–$12.

This artsy cafe, located at Universal CityWalk, is another outpost of the celebrity chef's expanding empire touting designer food at modest prices. The masses are thoroughly enthralled, but snootier palates insist that the food has suffered in the transition, the atmosphere—though unbearably trendy—is much too casual for a first-rate dining experience, and Spago it's not. The crowds, which you'll have to wade through to get a seat, say otherwise. Features: own baking, wine and beer only, late dining. Reservations not accepted. Credit Cards: V, MC.

Chinese

Fung Lum $$ ★★

222 Universal Terrace Parkway, ☎ (818) 763-7888.
Specialties: Peking duck; fung lum lemon chicken; Szechuan prawns.
Lunch: 11:30 a.m.–2:30 p.m., entrees $8–$10.
Dinner: 5–9:30 p.m., entrees $8–$20.

This huge restaurant overlooking Universal Studios is beautifully appointed with hand-woven carpets, Asian art and custom-made furniture. The clientele is made up mostly of tourists, who eat decent

Chinese food and get hustled in and out in a hurry by a sometimes abrupt waitstaff. If this is your idea of a good time, go for it. Lunch served Monday through Saturday. Features: Sunday brunch. Reservations recommended. Credit Cards: V, MC, DC, A.

Woodland Hills

American

Monty's   **$$$**   ★ ★ ★

5371 Topanga Canyon Boulevard, ☎ (818) 716-9736.
Specialties: steak; veal chop; Australian lobster tail.
Lunch: from 11:30 a.m., entrees $10–$72.
Dinner: to 11 p.m., entrees $10–$72.

Monty's is old-fashioned dining at its best. There are big, thick steaks, giant baked potatoes, superb grilled seafood, and fabulous fried onion rings. The $72 entree? The Australian lobster tail. The wine list is one of the best around, and the bar serves a great martini. Lunch served Monday through Saturday. Other Monty's restaurant's are located in Westwood and Pasadena. Features: own baking, rated wine cellar, late dining. Credit Cards: V, MC, DC, A.

SAN GABRIEL VALLEY

San Gabriel still feels like Old California.

San Gabriel Valley: Things to See and Do

The most obvious "event" to see in the San Gabriel Valley is Pasadena's annual **Tournament of Roses Parade**, which winds its way through the city on New Year's Day (or the day after if New Year's falls on a Sunday). Self-proclaimed the "world's largest New Year's Celebration," this incredible spectacle is worth seeing in person at least once in your life just to say you've done it. (After that, just watch it on TV like most of the rest of America.)

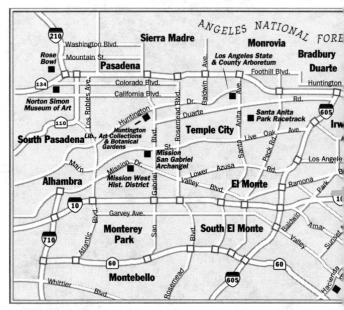

Each year, the parade has a theme which serves as the inspiration for float designers, many of whom are highly-paid professionals. There is always a lot of hubbub surrounding the selection of the Rose Queen, who is chosen from a bevy of eligible young women who live in the area on the basis of scholarship, leadership and community involvement (and looks, too, although no one will admit it). The parade also has a grand marshal, who sometimes has something to do with the theme, but often doesn't. In 1995, golfer Chi Chi Rodriguez led the festivities of the 106th Rose Parade with its theme of "Sports: Quest for Excellence." (Former grand marshals make up an interesting and eclectic list including Bob Hope, John Wayne, Hank Aaron, Shirley Temple, Edgar Bergen and Charlie McCarthy, Frank Sinatra, General Omar Bradley and Walt Disney.)

The parade route starts on South Orange Grove Boulevard at Ellis Street, proceeds north to Colorado Boulevard, where it turns east to Sierra Madre Boulevard and goes north on Sierra Madre to Paloma Street. In the "old" days, everyone just showed up and staked out a good viewing spot, but things have gotten a bit more complicated in recent years. You can still sit on the curb and watch, but the addition of bleachers and grandstands—for paying customers—has lessened the amount of open curb available, and non-paying paradegoers may find themselves in competition with a whole lot of other people for the best spots. A Pasadena city ordinance allows you to show up at noon the day before the parade to camp out and secure a space for the next day, and the Pasadena Police Department will gladly provide you with "hints" on how to successfully accomplish an all-nighter on the street in the dead of winter with thousands of other people milling around making noise and trying to muscle in on your territory.

Most of the time, the whole thing is good natured, but there can be lots of clandestine drinking and rowdyism going on, and occasionally a crime or two gets committed in the process. If it's raining (which God usually for-

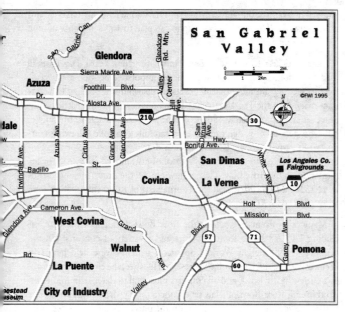

bids on such a big occasion as this), you don't want to do the all-night thing, and if you're skittish about crowds and/or traffic jams, this could be your worst nightmare.

If you don't feel like joining the all-night crowd, you may want to opt for grandstand seating, which costs anywhere from $25 to $40 per person. (And no matter how young your child is, she's a person and you have to pay for her. No exceptions!). If you don't want to walk a very long way, add on reserved car parking at $15. You can also park your RV overnight on the parade route and watch the parade from there for a cool $300, or park over-night adjacent to the parade route and set up chairs on the street ($30 for cars, more for RVs or trailers).

Buy a few souvenirs such as, say, an "official" program ($4), a T-shirt (from $9–$26), or a pin (there's a pin for each entry in the parade, sort of like that Olympic pin thing—$5 each or $450 for the set), grab a bite to eat and—mama mia!—there goes the holiday budget. You may be mumbling that all of this is a terrible rip-off, but once the parade starts, you'll perk right up.

For reserved and grandstand seating, call the Sharp Seating Company (☎ *(818) 795-4171*), which starts selling seats in February for the follow-ing year's parade. For general information on all Tournament of Roses events, call the Tournament of Roses 24-hour information line at ☎ *(818) 449-ROSE*, or call the Holiday Hotline, in operation from late December through New Year's Day, at ☎ *(818) 793-9911*.

If you can do without the bands, horses and waving float-riders, a day or two after the parade you can see all the floats on display on Sierra Madre Boulevard between Washington and Sierra Madre Villa Avenue and on Washington Boulevard between Sierra Madre Boulevard and Woodlyn Road. Post-parade float viewing is a popular pastime, and you may still find yourself in a crowd, but at least you don't have to defend any territory and it only costs $1. The park closes at 4 p.m., so plan to arrive in plenty of time to view the floats.

Getting tickets to the **Rose Bowl Game**, the New Year's Day football classic that follows the parade, is practically impossible because it's a "contractual sellout," meaning that all tickets are distributed according to a contract made with the Pac-10 and Big Ten conferences and the participating universities. Approximately 4500 end zone seats are available to the public, but who gets them is determined by a carefully-controlled drawing conducted in early October. If your name is drawn, you get the privilege of buying two tickets to the game (at a price of just under $50 each). For information on the Rose Bowl Ticket Drawing, call the Tournament of Roses at ☎ *(818) 449-4100*, or call the Tournament of Roses Information Line at ☎ *(818) 449-ROSE*.

Many other events are held at the Rose Bowl throughout the year, including UCLA's home football games and a variety of concerts. (In the summer of 1994, eight World Cup soccer matches were held here.) In keeping with Pasadena's somewhat reserved lifestyle, the city strictly enforces a curfew at the bowl, and all concerts must end no later than midnight. To this end, Rose Bowl officials synchronize their watches with promoters before the concert, then start calling on the phone to get a recorded message of the exact time as the final minutes tick away. The fine for going past midnight? $2000 a minute. (One of the more famous bands to add to Pasadena city coffers was the Rolling Stones, who had to pay $6000 in fines as a penalty for ending their concert at three minutes past the witching hour.)

In addition to the Rose Parade, Pasadena has garnered national recognition for its wacky **Doo Dah Parade**, held each year on Thanksgiving weekend. The Doo Dah started out to be a small-town spoof on the Rose Parade dreamed up by a couple of local guys hanging out at a bar one night in the late '70s. The parade quickly gained national attention for its "bad boy" image, which included parade entries that ranged from the slightly distinguished briefcase drill team (yuppies in suits performing synchronized movements with briefcases) to the bizarre (the Hibachi Grill Team, featuring soot-blackened backyard chefs carrying portable barbecues) to the decidedly off-color (marching condoms and Macho Dog, who exposed his private parts to the crowd).

As if the parade and its parody of the revered Rose Parade weren't enough to rally city fathers to call for its demise, the crowds started joining in the fun, pelting the parade entrants with marshmallows, shooting them with water guns and tossing tortillas (yes, tortillas). Downtown merchants complained about the whole mess, and the Doo Dah Parade seemed as though it was on its way out.

Having become a victim of its own wackiness, the Doo Dah Parade has been forced to make some changes in order to continue in its present mode. Currently in the process of grappling with local regulations and politics, organizers find that its exact format is in question from year to year, although recent parades came off without a hitch. Early organizers lament that the fun has gone out of putting on the parade (especially since efforts to clean up its image have been under way), but paradegoers always have a great time, so check up on the latest info if you're in town on Thanksgiving weekend.

Pasadena boasts several cultural jewels in its crown that have very little to do with parades, including the breathtaking collections to be found at the Norton Simon Museum of Art, the Huntington Library, Art Collections, and Botanical Gardens and the Pacific Asia Museum.

The **Norton Simon Museum**, formerly known as the Pasadena Art Institute, has collections that span 2500 years of art history and include works by a veritable Who's Who of renowned artists from around the world. It's a "must see" for art lovers, and, in addition to its permanent collections, mounts major temporary exhibits that cover art in all media and artists as diverse as Picasso, Kandinsky and Rembrandt. "Painting and Sculpture from Nepal, Tibet and Northwest India" is a new installation in the lower galleries featuring fifty objects of South Asian art—many of them of religious significance—dating from the eighth to the 18th centuries. Note that the museum is closed Monday, Tuesday and Wednesday. Private tours may be arranged in advance.

The **Huntington Library and Gardens in San Marino**, which celebrated its 75th anniversary in 1994 with a "Blue Boy Ball" that raised more than $750,000 for conservation of the North Vista statuary and created a fund to be used for restoration projects in the Botanical Gardens, is one of the nation's foremost centers of education and culture. The private, non-profit institution, created in 1919 by railroad and real estate magnate Henry E. Huntington, contains—in addition to a library full of rare books and manuscripts—three art galleries that house priceless paintings and other works of art, and a 130-acre botanical garden that includes one of the largest camellia collections in the country, as well as subtropical, herb, rose, and palm gardens. More than 500,000 visitors come to the Huntington Library, Art Collections and Botanical Gardens (the facility's official name) every year. If it fits into your schedule, have tea in the Rose Garden Room.

The **Pacific Asia Museum**, housed in a 1926 Chinese Imperial Palace Courtyard-style building once owned by collector and art dealer Grace Nicholson, is a true "Chinese Treasure House" of the artifacts and culture of the Pacific and Asian peoples. The building, itself, is of architectural interest, and the lovely courtyard garden is one of only two authentic Chinese gardens in the country. The museum offers classes in Japanese flower arranging, Chinese brush painting, Tai Chi Chu'an, and creative dance, yoga and movement, with special "Family Free Day" programs on the third Saturday of each month. The gift shop has an excellent collection of books on Asian and Pacific art.

Another kind of art appreciation is available on the city's ARTS buses, a fleet of six "themed" buses whose inside ambience (in the form of taped music, facts on local history and nature, poetry, and storytelling) match the murals painted on each bus's exterior. Options include the New Year's Day bus, the Historical Landmarks bus, the Multicultural bus, the Arroyo bus, the Performing Arts bus, and the Visual Arts bus, and all of them are both unique and fun to ride.

Transportation on the buses, which travel through Old Pasadena, the Playhouse District and South Lake, is free, and you can hop on or off anywhere along the way, then reboard and continue your journey later. Buses run from 11 a.m. to 8 p.m. Monday through Thursday; 11 a.m. to 9 p.m. Friday; and noon to 8 p.m. Saturday.

The 124-acre **California Institute of Technology**, better known as Caltech, is recognized throughout California for its research in the field of seismology (Caltech scientists are always featured on local newscasts whenever there's a sizeable earthquake in the Los Angeles area), but there are many things on the campus of interest to visitors. These include several buildings notable for their period architectural style (architectural tours of the campus are given on the fourth Thursday morning of each month; call ☎ *(818) 395-6327* for a reservation), displays in the Arnold O. Beckman Room (including a historical timeline of scientific discovery, a recreated chemistry lab of the 1920s, and exhibits on the life of Beckman), and the extensive Caltech libraries. There are also many public events held on campus, including first-rate lectures, concerts, films and plays. Call the Caltech ticket office ☎ *(818) 395-4652* for information on upcoming events and series.

One of the biggest biker "events" in the country is held in Glendale each November. Dubbed the **"Love Ride**," the fundraiser attracts more than 20,000 hog riders that zoom from Glendale to Castaic in order to raise money for the L.A. Chapter of the Muscular Dystrophy Association. If you think this is just small-town moped stuff, be advised that most of the participants ride Harleys, and the event always attracts a notable crowd of celebrity riders such as Jay Leno, Cher, Axl Rose and the original Easy Rider himself, Peter Fonda.

The charitable aspect aside, if you can't stand the thought of exposing the kids to all those bikers, try something a little more subdued, such as Monrovia's weekly farmer's market and street festival, held on Friday nights from 5 to 9 on Old Town's Myrtle Avenue. There are rides for the kids, food and arts and crafts vendors, and lots of wonderfully fresh produce. Where else can you take everyone out on a Friday night in L.A. and have so much fun for so little money?

Museums and Exhibits

Huntington Library, Art Collections and Gardens ★★★★

1151 Oxford Road, San Marino, 91108, ☎ (818) 405-2141.
Hours open: 1–4 p.m. Tues.–Fri.; Sat., Sun. 10:30 a.m.–4:30 p.m.

The Huntington Library, Art Collections and Botanical Gardens is a one-stop cultural treat. Here you'll see Thomas Lawrence's "Pinkie" and Gainsborough's "Blue Boy," as well as a notable collection of works by Rembrandt, Van Dyck, Watteau, Boucher and Fragonard. The Virginia Steele Scott Gallery of American Art brings together American paintings from the 1730s to the 1930s, and the Arabella Huntington Memorial Collection features Renaissance paintings and 18th-century French sculpture, tapestries, porcelain and furniture. Among the rare books in the library are the Chaucer's *Canterbury Tales*, a Gutenberg Bible, and the double-elephant folio edition of Audubon's *Birds of America*. When you've absorbed the cultural gems inside, head out to the Botanical Gardens, 130 acres containing fifteen different gardens, including a Desert Garden, a Japanese Garden, a Rose Garden, and one of the largest collections of camellias in the country. Introductory slide shows are given at regular intervals; docent-guided tours begin at 1 p.m. Tea is served in the Rose Garden

Room Tuesday–Friday from 1–3:30 p.m.; Saturday and Sunday from noon to 3:30 p.m. Admission for students, $4; seniors, $6. General admission: $7.50.

Norton Simon Museum of Art

Norton Simon Museum of Art ★★★★

411 West Colorado Boulevard, Pasadena, 91105, *(818) 449-6840.*
Hours open: noon–6 p.m.

Founded in 1924 as the Pasadena Art Institute, the internationally-known Norton Simon Museum contains a fine collection of European art from the Renaissance to the mid-20th century. Particularly celebrated are the Impressionist and Post-Impressionist paintings by Manet, Renior, Monet, Degas, Van Gogh, Toulouse-Lautrec and Cezanne, as well as 20th century works by Picasso, Matisse and the German Expressionists. Other artists with works on display here are Raphael, Rembrandt, Gauguin, Rodin, Maillol and Moore. Indian and Southeast Asian sculptures are also on exhibit, as well as a unique collection of original bronze masters by Degas. In November of 1994, a new installation of South Asian art—"Painting and Sculpture from Nepal, Tibet and Northwest India"—was opened in the museum's lower galleries. Tours by reservation. Extensive bookstore. Children under 12 admitted free; seniors and students with ID, $2. General admission: $4.

Pacific Asia Museum ★★★

46 North Los Robles Avenue, Pasadena, 91101, *(818) 449-2742.*
Hours open: noon–5 p.m.
At Colorado Boulevard.

The Chinese-style building in which this museum is housed is a State Historic Landmark. The permanent collection covers traditional and contemporary Asian art and culture, and is supplemented by imaginative changing exhibits. A Chinese garden, as well as a bookstore, gift-shop, and a research library are located on the grounds. Children are admitted free. General admission: $3.

Pasadena Historical Museum ★★

470 Walnut Street, Pasadena, **☎** *(818) 577-1660.*
Hours open: 1–4 p.m.

Housed in the 1905 Beaux Arts-style Fenyes Mansion, the Pasadena Historical Museum includes the home's original furnishings and decorative arts, as well as memorabilia chronicling the city's history. Tours begin at 1 p.m., and you are unable to see the home unless you take the tour. General admission: $4.00.

Southwest Museum

234 Museum Drive, Highland Park, 90065, ☎ (213) 221-2164.
Hours open: 11 a.m.–5 p.m.
At Marmion Way, Avenue 43 exit from Pasadena Freeway.

Four halls showcase the art and artifacts of Native Americans, with an emphasis on Indians of the Southwest, Plains, California, Northwest Coast and Northern Mexico. There is a notable collection of baskets, and a museum store and library are on the grounds. New at the museum is the Ethnobotanical Garden, which opened to the public in late-1994. Seven distinct environments focus on California's indigenous plants and how they were used by Native Americans for food, tools, medicines, basketry and in healing and agriculture. The museum also sponsors an annual film festival (January) that focuses on various Native American tribes. Admission for children 7–18, $2; children under age six are admitted free; seniors and students, $3. General admission: $5.

Historical Sites

David B. Gamble House ★★★★

4 Westmoreland Place, Pasadena, 91103, ☎ (818) 793-3334.
Hours open: noon–3 p.m.

This Craftsman-style bungalow built in 1908 by Charles and Henry Greene has been designated a National Historic Landmark, and is an internationally-recognized masterpiece of the turn-of-the-century arts and crafts movement. Noted for its Tiffany glass, handmade furniture and elegant woodwork in cedar, teak, mahogany and maple. Guided tours are available noon–3 p.m., Thursday-Sunday. Reduced admission for children, students, and seniors. General admission: $4.

El Alisal

200 East Avenue 43, Highland Park, ☎ (213) 222-0546.
Hours open: 1–4 p.m.

Charles Fletcher Lummis, founder of the Southwest Museum, built this Craftsman-style home between 1898 and 1910. It now houses the Historical Society of Southern California, which provides exhibits on local history. Free admission.

Heritage Square

3800 Homer Street, Los Angeles, 90031, ☎ (818) 796-2898.
Hours open: noon–4 p.m.
Take the Avenue 43 exit from the Pasadena Freeway.

This 10-acre collection of historic Victorian houses and buildings contains three that are listed on the National Register of Historic Places. The Hale House, built in 1885, is filled with period furniture. There is also a rare 1883 octogon house as well as other buildings in the process of being restored. Guides in period costumes conduct one-hour tours. Reduced admission for seniors; children under age 12 admitted free. General admission is $3 weekdays, $4.50 weekends.

Tournament House & Wrigley Gardens

391 South Orange Grove Boulevard, Pasadena, ☎ (818) 449-4100.

William Wrigley, Jr. (of chewing gum fame) built this mansion in 1914, and it now houses the Pasadena Tournament of Roses Association, which oversees the annual parade and Rose Bowl game. Memorabilia from the festival's past is on display inside, and tours are given on Thursday afternoons.

Tours

California Institute of Technology ★★★

315 South Hill Avenue, Pasadena, ☎ *(818) 395-6327.*
If you live in Southern California, you've become familiar with all of the Caltech seismologists, who show up on every L.A. TV station after an earthquake. Monitoring quakes is only one of the scientific activities going on at Caltech, however; take a free tour of the campus to learn much more about this prestigious university. Tours begin at the Visitors Center at 3 p.m. Monday, Thursday and Friday, and at 11 a.m. Tuesday and Wednesday. If you're at all science-oriented, this is a must. Free admission.

Jet Propulsion Laboratory ★★

4800 Oak Grove Drive, Pasadena, ☎ *(818) 354-9314.*
The Jet Propulsion Lab is operated by the California Institute of Technology (Caltech) for NASA, and is America's center for research on the unmanned exploration of the solar system. Reservations required. Free admission.

Old Pasadena Tour ★★

117 East Colorado Boulevard, Pasadena.
These two-hour walking tours of Old Pasadena are held on the second Saturday of each month and begin at the Chamber of Commerce building. The tour commences with a slide show and light refreshments, then takes you through the Old Pasadena district. Wear comfortable walking shoes. Calling ahead is appreciated. General admission: $5.

Pasadena Playhouse ★★★

39 South El Molino Avenue, Pasadena, 91101, ☎ *(818) 356-7529.*
This highly-regarded theater company presents world-class premiere productions featuring well-known stars during its Mainstage season.

Parks and Gardens

Brookside Park ★★

Adjacent to the Rose Bowl, Pasadena.
The Rose Bowl is nestled in 61.1-acre Brookside Park, but there are many other features in the park for those seeking recreational opportunities, including five lighted tennis courts, six lighted horseshoe courts, a golf course, an archery range, two handball courts, four badminton courts, a regulation baseball diamond, two lighted softball diamonds and lawn bowling facilities. And lots of space for picnics.

Descanso Gardens ★★★

1418 Descanso Drive, La Canada, 91208, ☎ *(818) 790-5571.*
Hours open: 9 a.m.–4:30 p.m.
Five miles northwest of Pasadena.
The 165 acres of Descanso Gardens boast the world's largest collection of camellias, a rose garden, live oak grove, spring azalea, rhododendron, iris and lilac displays, and blooming summer annuals. Of special note is the annual Spring Festival of Flowers featuring special

exhibits, lectures and flower shows. Also on the grounds are a Japanese tea house and garden, Hospitality House with changing art exhibits, and a gift shop. Guided tram tours are also available. Call for information on seasonal displays. Admission free on third Tuesday of each month. General admission: $3.

Huntington Gardens   ★ ★ ★ ★

1151 Oxford Road, San Marino, *(818) 405-2141.*
Hours open: 1–4:30 p.m.
At the Huntington Library.
Even if you aren't interested in the cultural treasures to be found in the library and art galleries, seeing the 130 acres of gardens that surround the estate is worth the admission price. There are 15 separate garden areas containing more than 14,000 varieties of plants and trees, and you are welcome to wander about on your own or take one of the guided tours, which begin at 1 p.m. Tuesday–Sunday. General admission: $5.

Los Angeles County Arboretum   ★ ★ ★ ★

301 North Baldwin Avenue, Arcadia, 91006, *(818) 821-3222.*
Hours open: 9 a.m.–4:30 p.m.
More than 5000 species and varieties of plants from around the world are found on 127 acres of grounds. There are aquatic, jungle, and prehistoric gardens, a tropical greenhouse, waterfalls and a restored Victorian cottage. More than 200 peacocks wander freely about. A bird sanctuary and waterfowl refuge make the arboretum a birder's, as well as a tree lover's, delight. Tram tours are available. Reduced admission for children and seniors. General admission: $3.

Pasadena Pops   ★ ★ ★

Descanso Gardens, La Canada, *(818) 792-7677.*
The Pasadena Pops presents an evening summer Picnic Concert Series in an idyllic setting at Descanso Gardens. Bring your own picnic, or order a catered meal when you reserve your tickets.

Children's Activities

Armory Center for the Arts   ★ ★

145 North Raymond Street, Pasadena, 91103, *(818) 792-5101.*
Free weekend workshops for parents and kids are offered frequently. Recent workshops have included puppetmaking and wearable art. Call for schedule.

Caltech Family Fair   ★ ★ ★ ★

Beckman Auditorium, Pasadena, 91125, *(818) 395-3847.*
This sterling series of 50- to 60-minute shows designed especially for children (ages 6 and up) and their families includes music, theatre, puppet shows, and magic shows. Performances are on Saturdays at 2 p.m.

Eaton Canyon County Park & Nature Center   ★ ★

1750 North Altadena Drive, Pasadena, 91107, *(818) 398-5420.*
Kids will enjoy the special nature trail designed for those under age five, or the Saturday morning nature walks offered for families in the spring at this 184-acre park.

Kidspace Museum   ★ ★ ★ ★

390 South El Molino Avenue, Pasadena, 91101, ☎ *(818) 449-9143.*
Hours open: 2–5 p.m.
In an elementary school gym.

Designed with preschoolers and elementary kids in mind, Kidspace attractions include interactive exhibits on anatomy, natural history, science, and technology. Kids crawl through a tunnel-like maze, dress up in football uniforms, climb aboard race cars and fire engines and are generally free to explore the museum at will. Picnic areas outside. General admission: $5.

City Celebrations

Doo Dah Parade ★★★

Pasadena, ☎ *(818) 796-2591.*
Okay, so it's not the Rose Parade, but this wacky spoof on Pasadena's biggest event has developed a life of its own and attracts hordes of spectators. From the quirky to the outlandish to the outrageous, the Doo Dah Parade will crack you up. No one seems to know the format from year to year, but if you're in town during Thanksgiving weekend, DEFINITELY check this out.

Tournament of Roses Parade ★★★★★

391 South Orange Grove Boulevard, Pasadena, 91184, ☎ *(818) 449-4100.*
Marching bands, celebrities and breathtaking floats decorated with millions of fresh flowers wind their way down Colorado Boulevard each New Year's Day. Call for information and prices on grandstand seating. Each year thousands of people line the parade route beginning the day before, and spend the night in the often freezing temperatures in order to secure a prime viewing spot. There is no admission fee to do this.

Sports and Recreation

AAF Rose Bowl Aquatics Center

360 North Arroyo Boulevard, Pasadena, ☎ *(818) 564-0330.*
The Amateur Athletics Foundation Rose Bowl Aquatics Center is an Olympic-class sports complex that hosts diving, swimming, and water polo competitions, but is also open to the public for lap swimming and other recreational activities. Call for details.

Altadena Golf Course

1456 East Mendocino, Pasadena, ☎ *(818) 797-6773.*
This nine-hole course includes a putting green, two chipping areas, a driving range, and a clubhouse with golf shop and restaurant.

Bar S Stables

1850 Riverside Drive, Glendale, 91201, ☎ *(818) 242-8443.*
In business for 30 years, this stable has 50 horses to choose from and 50 miles of equestrian trails through Griffith Park. For those who don't know how to ride or need some brushing up, lessons are offered by the stable's riding coach.

Eaton Canyon

1150 North Sierra Madre Villa Avenue, Pasadena, 91107, ☎ *(818) 794-6773.*
A nine-hole, 2900-yard course, plus pro shop, new driving range and a modern practice facility. Carts and lessons are available and the clubhouse serves breakfast and lunch.

Moonlight Rollerway Skating Center

5110 San Fernando Road, Glendale, ☎ *(818) 241-3630.*

Several theme nights, including organ music night and dance night, are slated at this popular roller skating rink. Lessons are also available.

Pasadena Ice Skating Center

300 East Green Street, Pasadena, ☎ *(818) 578-0801.*
Hours open: 1–5 p.m.
There's public skating every afternoon at this ice rink, which is sometimes also open for public skating in the evenings. Bring your own skates, or rent at the rink.

Rose Bowl Game

Rose Bowl, Pasadena, 91184, ☎ *(818) 449-7673.*
The champions of the PAC-10 and Big Ten conferences square off (often with the national championship at stake) in this annual New Year's Day bowl game. Call well ahead for tickets; it is usually sold out. During the September-November college football seaon, U.C.L.A. plays its home games here.

Santa Anita Park

285 West Huntington Drive, Arcadia, 91006, ☎ *(818) 574-7223.*
Thoroughbred racing held December to April, October, and November on a beautiful 500-acre park set in the foothills of the San Gabriel Mountains. Free tours Saturday and Sunday. The public is invited to watch morning workouts free on race days, 7:30–9:30 a.m. General admission: $3.

Theme/Amusement Parks

Raging Waters   ★ ★ ★

111 Raging Waters Drive, San Dimas, 91773, ☎ *(909) 592-6453.*
Off 210 Freeway, Raging Waters Exit.
Although it bills itself as "the world's greatest water adventure," this 44-acre park located on the outskirts of L.A. County may have some competition (such as the new Six Flags Hurricane Harbor in Valencia). It includes the usual water slides (some of them a bit daredevil-ish), pools, lagoons, sunbathing areas, food stands, and picnic areas that you'll find in any other water park—plus Kids' Kingdom, a water playground for younger children. In May 1995 the park introduced Splash Island Adventure, a four-story, Caribbean-themed "family interactive water attraction" that features 12 different levels containing water cannons, tipping buckets, web crawl tunnels, swinging bridges, and spiral cargo nets. In case you're worred about working up a sweat—don't. A 1000-gallon bucket atop a five-story tower drops its load over the whole attraction every few minutes. Bring your own towel. Dressing rooms provided. Admission for seniors and those 42–48 inches tall is $11.99; children under 42 inches are admitted free. In 1995, the park will be open 10 a.m.–6 p.m. on weekends only April 15–June 3; open weekdays from 10 a.m.–9 p.m. and weekends from 9 a.m.–10 p.m. from June 3 to Sept. 17; and 10 a.m.–6 p.m. on weekends from Sept. 23–Oct. 29. Parking is $5. General admission: $19.99.

San Gabriel Valley: Music, Dance and Theatre

The Pasadena Symphony, which performs at the Pasadena Civic Auditorium, has been around for nearly 70 years, and is an excellent choice for an evening of classical music, often including performances by well-known guests.

Don't overlook the possibilities at Caltech, which has a wonderful series of performing arts in its Caltech After Dark series, as well as other performing arts events on campus.

The well-respected Glendale Symphony celebrated its 72nd anniversary in 1994 by moving "home" to Glendale's refurbished 1925 Art Deco Alex Theatre from its former venue at the downtown Music Center. The anniversary symphony season aside, the Alex has had its share of troubles since its $6.5 million renovation was completed, and the city of Glendale filed suit against its former operators, who sold more than 10,000 tickets to a 1994-95 season of musical productions that never materialized. Once the venue's financial problems are straightened out, it will surely reign as one of the valley's top locations for all kinds of entertainment events.

Music

Coleman Chamber Music Association ★★★★

202 South Lake Avenue, Pasadena, 91101, ☎ (818) 395-4652.
The 1995 season marked the 91st anniversary of the Coleman Chamber Music Association, among the oldest organizations in the country devoted to the presentation, understanding, and enjoyment of chamber music. The annual series of concerts, held at Caltech's Beckman Auditorium, includes a nationally recognized competition for young chamber music performers.

Glendale Symphony Orchestra ★★★

401 North Brand Boulevard, Suite 520, Glendale, 91203, ☎ (818) 500-8720. Performances are at the Dorothy Chandler Pavilion.
Founded in 1924, the Glendale Symphony Orchestra celebrates its 71st anniversary season in 1995. Lalo Schifrin, music director and conductor, and ninety musicians offer classical music and other special programs, such as "Jazz Meets the Symphony", "The Classics and the Silver Screen," and "The Glorious Sounds of Christmas."

Pasadena Jazz Festival ★★★

300 West Green Street, Pasadena, ☎ (800) 266-2378. At the Ambassador Auditorium.
This weekend festival takes place each August in Pasadena and features well-known jazz artists from throughout the country. An outdoor food festival and other events coincide.

Pasadena Symphony Orchestra ★★★

300 East Green Street, Pasadena, 91101, ☎ (818) 449-7360.
This well-regarded city orchestra has been called one of the finest in California, and has been providing music to local concertgoers for more than 65 years. The main season (October–May) is comprised of a series of Saturday evening concerts that take place at the Pasadena Civic Auditorium.

Theatre

Alex Theatre ★★★

216 North Brand Boulevard, Glendale, 91203, ☎ (818) 243-2539.
This local theatre presents an array of international stars in touring productions, and also serves as home to the Gay Men's Chorus of Los Angeles.

Caltech After Dark

Beckman Auditorium, Pasadena, 91125, ☎ (818) 395-3847.
Each season, the Caltech campus sponsors a first-class performing arts
series that includes big names from the fields of music, theatre, dance
and comedy. Also available is a series of lectures and travel documen-
tary films, a chamber music series, and a series of student performances.

Knightsbridge Theatre   ★★

35 South Raymond Avenue, Pasadena, ☎ (818) 440-0821.
Pasadena's newest theatre has so far presented a fine lineup of drama.
Call for the upcoming schedule of events.

Music Theatre of Southern California   ★★★

320 South Mission Drive, San Gabriel, 91776, ☎ (818) 308-2869.
Formerly known as the San Gabriel Valley Civic Light Opera, this
musical theatre in the San Gabriel Valley presents a series of popular
shows, including Broadway musicals and celebrity entertainers.

Pasadena Civic Auditorium   ★★★

300 East Green Street, Pasadena, 91105, ☎ (818) 449-7360.
Broadway hits are often on the boards at this popular venue, which
also serves as the home of the Pasadena Symphony.

Ticket Agencies

Southern California Ticket Service

1487 East Colorado Boulevard, Pasadena, ☎ (818) 577-2557.
Hours open: 9 a.m.–6 p.m.
Handles tickets to the Rose Parade, Rose Bowl game, and events at
the Pasadena Civic Auditorium and other Pasadena and L.A. venues.

San Gabriel Valley: Nightlife

The nightlife scene in the San Gabriel Valley runs the gamut from the su-
premely sophisticated (the Ritz-Carlton Huntington) to the exceedingly
hip (Club Shelter, The Baked Potato). Probably the most famous nightspot
in town is the Ice House, a comedy club that's been a venue for upcoming
comedy stars since the '60s. Just about every famous stand-up comedian
you can think of has appeared here at least once, and alumni sometimes
come back to entertain.

Baked Potato, The

26 East Colorado Boulevard, Pasadena, ☎ (818) 564-1122.
The local hotspot for jazz, the Baked Potato has been around for
more than 20 years and always has first-rate live entertainment that
runs the gamut from jazz to jazz funk to blues. Lunch and dinner are
also served.

Club Shelter

40 South Pasadena Street, Pasadena, ☎ (818) 577-4040.
The people who own West Hollywood's popular Roxbury are behind
this 9000-square-foot "techno-industrial" dance club, where a state-
of-the-art sound system blares out the latest dance tunes. There's also
a billiards room, and you can go bar-hopping without leaving the
building—there are four full bars. 21 and over. Cover varies. General
admission: $10.

Domenico's

82 North Fair Oaks Avenue, Pasadena, ☎ *(818) 449-1948.*
There's always lots going on at Domenico's, including karaoke on Tuesdays, live jazz on Wednesdays, a male review show and live reggae on Thursdays, and rock music, blues and R&B on weekends. There's also a sports bar and decent Italian food.

Ice House, The

24 North Mentor Avenue, Pasadena, ☎ *(818) 577-1894.*
For more than 30 years, the Ice House has been bringing comedy acts to Pasadena, including such stars as David Letterman, Jay Leno, Steve Martin and Lily Tomlin, all of whom appeared here as struggling "up and comers." Call for information on current headliners and performance times. Cover varies. Tuesday is non-smoking night. The Ice House Annex, adjacent, features improv comedy sketches and other entertainment. General admission: $7.50.

In Cahoots

223 North Glendale Avenue, Glendale, ☎ *(818) 500-1665.*
Country music reigns supreme at In Cahoots, and there are occasional live acts in addition to the pre-recorded music. Also offers free line dancing, light dining and a full bar. Open to 2 a.m. nightly; over 21 only.

Jax Bar & Grill

339 North Brand Avenue, Glendale, ☎ *(818) 500-1604.*
This narrow supper club is a convivial—albeit noisy—place. Features jazz performers nightly and offers continental-style lunches and dinners along with a full bar. No cover and no minimum.

Ritz-Carlton Huntington

1401 South Oak Knoll Avenue, Pasadena, ☎ *(818) 568-3900.*
When you've tired of all the "hip" places in town, head over to this grand historical hotel, where a sophisticated ambience always prevails. It's the perfect spot for dining and dancing on weekends, or you can sample one of more than a dozen variations of the martini at the hotel's new Martini Club. Try them all and you get an engraved martini glass.

San Gabriel Valley: Shopping

The **Glendale Galleria** *(2148 Glendale Galleria)* is the quintessential Southern California indoor shopping mall. There are more than 200 shops here, anchored by major department stores such as The Broadway, Nordstrom, and Robinsons-May. If you can't afford upscale mall prices, head over to Sherman Oaks, where **Jean's Stars' Apparel** *(15136 Ventura Boulevard)*, a resale boutique featuring cut-rate designer cast-offs, is guaranteed to have something very chic that you can afford.

Old Pasadena has done much to establish itself as a prime shopping district with the opening of One Colorado, offering upscale shops such as J. Crew, Gap, a.b.s., and Banana Republic in contrast to its historical setting, galleries and antique shops.

Before you take off on that exotic vacation, check in at **Distant Lands** *(62 South Raymond)*, a distinctive traveler's bookstore with more than 7000 titles and maps, plus video travelogues and other travel literature. If you're a rose fancier, mosey on over to **Hortus** *(284 East Orange Grove Boulevard)*, a huge nursery that stocks more than 350 varieties.

San Gabriel Valley: Where to Stay

The exclusive Ritz-Carlton Huntington was recently purchased for $40 million by the Los Angeles County Employees Retirement Association from Dai-Ichi Kangyo Bank of Japan. No changes are currently anticipated, and it remains one of the most luxurious hotels in greater Los Angeles.

In comparison to the Huntington, everything else in the San Gabriel Valley looks pretty ordinary, but even if you don't have a Ritz-Carlton budget, you'll find something to fill your needs. Be aware that hotels in Pasadena often boost prices during the holiday season surrounding the Tournament of Roses parade, so accommodations will cost you more than usual.

Alhambra

Low Cost Lodging

Best Western Alhambra Inn   **$55–$100**   ★★

2451 West Main Street
☎ *(800) 528-1234, (818) 284-5522, FAX: 818-576-5937.*
Single: $55–$90. Double: $60–$100.
Rooms include refrigerators, and complimentary continental breakfast and evening cocktails are served Monday through Thursday. Amenities: pool, family plan. 58 rooms. Credit Cards: CB, V, MC, DC, A.

Quality Inn Alhambra   **$60–$68**   ★★

2221 West Commonwealth Avenue
☎ *(800) 221-2222, (818) 300-0003, FAX: 818-281-8297.*
Single: $60. Double: $68.
This motor inn has minibars in each room, plus golf and tennis nearby. Rates include complimentary continental breakfast. Amenities: pool, family plan. 73 rooms. Credit Cards: CB, V, MC, DC, A.

Arcadia

Hotels and Resorts

Embassy Suites   **$109–$170**   ★★★

211 East Huntington Drive
☎ *(800) 362-2779, (818) 445-8525, FAX: 818-445-8548.*
Single: $109–$170. Double: $109–$170.
Complimentary continental breakfast as well as evening cocktails are included in the room price at this hotel located minutes from the Rose Bowl and Santa Anita Racetrack. In-room movies, a laundry room and child care are other features. Amenities: pool, Jacuzzi, sauna, conference facilities, complimentary airport pickup service. 194 rooms. Credit Cards: CB, V, MC, DC, A.

Residence Inn By Marriott   **$85–$145**   ★★★

321 East Huntington Drive
☎ *(800) 331-3131, (818) 446-6500, FAX: 818-446-5824.*
Single: $85–$145. Double: $85–$145.
Rates include complimentary continental breakfast, evening hospitality hour, and in-room coffee. Each unit has a fully equipped kitchen. Amenities: pool, Jacuzzi, balcony or patio, conference facilities, com-

plimentary airport pickup service. 120 rooms. Credit Cards: CB, V, MC, DC, A.

Low Cost Lodging

Hampton Inn $60–$78 ★★

311 East Huntington Drive
☎ *(800) 426-7866, (818) 574-5600, FAX: 818-446-2748.*
Single: $60–$68. Double: $70–$78.
Rates include complimentary continental breakfast and in-room coffee. The grounds are well maintained. Amenities: pool, conference facilities. 132 rooms. Credit Cards: CB, V, MC, DC, A.

Glendale

Hotels and Resorts

Best Western Golden Key $81–$86 ★★

123 West Colorado Street
☎ *(800) 528-1234, (818) 247-0111, FAX: 818-545-9393.*
Single: $81. Double: $86.
This motor inn is near restaurants and shopping. Rooms include bathrobes, refrigerators, microwaves, hair dryers and VCRs, with a free movie library to help pass the time. Complimentary continental breakfast included. Amenities: pool, Jacuzzi, family plan, conference facilities, business services. 55 rooms. Credit Cards: CB, V, MC, DC, A.

Red Lion Hotel $159–$174 ★★★

100 West Glenoaks Boulevard
☎ *(800) 547-8010, (818) 956-5466, FAX: 818-956-5490.*
Single: $159. Double: $174.
This newer 19-story hotel is Glendale's first major business accommodation. Each guest room is equipped with PC and fax data ports, and a concierge takes care of all special requests. There's a spectacular view of the greater Los Angeles area from the Windows lounge on the 19th floor. The hotel's location near Universal Studios, Dodger Stadium, the L.A. Zoo and Griffith Observatory will appeal to families. Amenities: pool, health club, Jacuzzi, sauna, conference facilities, club floor, complimentary airport pickup service. 348 rooms. Credit Cards: CB, V, MC, DC, A.

Low Cost Lodging

Days Inn Glendale $64–$74 ★★

450 West Pioneer Drive
☎ *(800) 325-2525, (818) 956-0202, FAX: 818-502-0843.*
Single: $64. Double: $74.
This former Holiday Inn has 10 units with kitchenettes, but no utensils are provided. Basic lodging without frills. Amenities: pool, Jacuzzi, sauna, family plan, conference facilities. 600 rooms. Credit Cards: CB, V, MC, DC, A.

Monrovia

Hotels and Resorts

Holiday Inn Monrovia $82–$82 ★★★

924 West Huntington Drive
☎ *(800) 465-4329, (818) 357-1900, FAX: 818-357-1900.*
Single: $82. Double: $82.

This 10-story motor inn is located just off I-210, which makes it a good stop for weary travelers. Amenities: pool, Jacuzzi, conference facilities. 174 rooms. Credit Cards: V, MC, DC, A.

Wyndham Garden $65–$105   ★★

700 West Huntington Drive
☎ *(800) 996-3426, (818) 357-5211, FAX: 818-357-2786.*
Single: $65–$90. Double: $80–$105.
Formerly the Howard Johnson Plaza, this hotel became a Wyndham in early 1995. Some rooms in this nine-story property have microwaves and refrigerators; all have cable TV. Amenities: pool, exercise room, Jacuzzi. 151 rooms. Credit Cards: V, MC, DC, A.

Pasadena

Hotels and Resorts

Doubletree Pasadena $99–$205   ★★★

191 North Los Robles Avenue
☎ *(800) 222-8733, (818) 792-2727, FAX: 818-795-7669.*
Single: $99–$205. Double: $99–$205.
The Mediterranean architecture of this 12-story hotel located next to City Hall fits in nicely with the Spanish style of the city. There's a good cafe that serves California cuisine and two bar and lounge areas on the premises. The rooms—like the public areas—are done in yellow and beige and have over-sized mirrors, regional art on the walls, king, queen or two double beds and marble combination baths. The staff is efficient and friendly and room service is available 24 hours. The health club is state-of-the-art, with exercise equipment, steam rooms, and massage therapy. The lush gardens and courtyards are wonderful spots for relaxing. Amenities: pool, health club, Jacuzzi, sauna, balcony or patio, conference facilities, club floor, business services. 355 rooms. Credit Cards: V, MC, A.

Holiday Inn Pasadena $92–$104   ★★★

303 East Cordova Street
☎ *(800) 465-4329, (818) 449-4000, FAX: 818-584-1390.*
Single: $92. Double: $104.
This mid-sized hotel is adjacent to the Convention Center and one mile from the Rose Bowl. Accommodations feature fairly travel-worn cherry wood furnishings, good lighting, baths with shower massages and free in-room movies. First-floor rooms are more expensive but also nicer, with sunken bedrooms and high ceilings. There are two lighted tennis courts, and data ports and secretarial services for traveling businesspeople. Amenities: pool, tennis, balcony or patio, family plan, conference facilities. 320 rooms. Credit Cards: V, MC, A.

Pasadena Hilton $94–$139   ★★★

150 South Los Robles Avenue
☎ *(800) 445-8667, (818) 577-1000, FAX: 818-584-3148.*
Single: $94–$134. Double: $99–$139.
A recently renovated hotel in the heart of Pasadena, the Hilton is very nice, but not in the same class as the Ritz-Carlton or the Doubletree. The pool is very small and stuck off in a corner, but the guest rooms contain cherry wood furnishings, new carpets, mattresses and drapes, TVs with movies, minibars, coffee makers and phones with data ports. The health club features Stairmasters, Lifecycles and free weights, and guests can enjoy golf or tennis at the nearby La Canada/Flintridge

Country Club. One entire floor is non-smoking. Amenities: pool, golf, health club, balcony or patio, hair salon, family plan, conference facilities, club floor. 291 rooms. Credit Cards: CB, V, MC, DC, A.

Ritz-Carlton Huntington   **$165–$265**   ★ ★ ★ ★
1401 South Oak Knoll Avenue
☎ *(800) 241-3333, (818) 568-3900, FAX: 818-568-3159.*
Single: $165–$265. Double: $165–$265.

The old Huntington Hotel has been restored by Ritz-Carlton with spectacular results. Set amid 23 acres of beautiful gardens at the base of the San Gabriel mountains, the complex includes an Olympic-sized swimming pool, whirlpool with sundecks, two ballrooms and excellent dining opportunities. All the architectural charm and grace of the old (1907) hotel remain intact, combined with modern, luxurious appointments, stunning public areas and wonderful service. A popular spot for weddings. Ranked restaurant: **Ritz-Carlton Grill**. Amenities: exercise room, Jacuzzi, sauna, balcony or patio, conference facilities, business services. 383 rooms. Credit Cards: V, MC, A.

Low Cost Lodging

Best Western Colorado Inn   **$50–$55**   ★ ★
2156 East Colorado Boulevard
☎ *(800) 528-1234, (818) 793-9339, FAX: 818-568-2731.*
Single: $50. Double: $55.
All rooms in this unremarkable—but inexpensive—motel have refrigerators. Complimentary continental breakfast and in-room coffee included. Amenities: pool, Jacuzzi, balcony or patio, family plan. 77 rooms. Credit Cards: CB, V, MC, DC, A.

Best Western Royale   **$50–$55**   ★ ★
3600 East Colorado Boulevard
☎ *(800) 528-1234, (818) 793-0950, FAX: 818-568-2827.*
Single: $50. Double: $55.
Rooms have refrigerators and local calls are free. Amenities: pool, Jacuzzi, conference facilities. 61 rooms. Credit Cards: CB, V, MC, DC, A.

Comfort Inn   **$51–$56**   ★ ★
2462 East Colorado Boulevard
☎ *(800) 228-5150, (818) 405-0811, FAX: 818-796-0966.*
Single: $51. Double: $56.
All rooms have refrigerators, microwaves and VCRs. The motel is set in the foothills of the Sierra Madre Mountains. Amenities: pool, Jacuzzi, balcony or patio, conference facilities. 50 rooms. Credit Cards: CB, V, MC, DC, A.

San Gabriel Valley: Where to Eat

The San Gabriel Valley has some very good restaurants, many of which have been around a long time and have sterling reputations. Also, new restaurants are opening here all the time, indicating that this isn't one of those vast culinary wastelands that you sometimes find on the outskirts of greater L.A.

Take Yujean Kang's, for example. Named the Best New Chinese Restaurant in L.A. by *Los Angeles* magazine in 1991, it continues to rank in the top echelons of local Chinese eateries, and the rumor is that Kang is shopping for a second location in trendy West Hollywood.

One of the most exciting restaurants to open in Pasadena in ages is Twin Palms, a celebrity-backed eatery where (for once) the food is the strong suit, and not the notoriety of the owners. You can't go wrong here, especially at the reasonable prices.

Another newcomer is Les Arts, which may finally be bringing back French food for the '90s. Although the healthier trend in French cooking has been going on for years, Les Arts doesn't skimp on portions, and a sophisticated ambience and piano music add to the dining experience.

Fusion cuisine stars at the new Papashon, which now does a bustling business in the space formerly occupied by Tra Fiori. The food's about as eclectic as you can get, and it's a very happening place.

Arcadia

American

Derby, The　　　　　　　$$$　　　　　　★★
233 East Huntington Drive, ☎ (818) 447-8174.
Specialties: fresh seafood; steak; cheesecake.
Lunch: from 11 a.m., entrees $9–$12.
Dinner: to 10 p.m., entrees $13–$19.
The theme is horse racing at this pleasant restaurant near the Santa Anita Race Track. Memorabilia from the sport is on display, and the menu delivers average-to-good American/Continental fare. Lunch served Monday through Friday. Features: own baking, full bar, late dining. Jacket requested. Reservations recommended. Credit Cards: CB, V, MC, DC, A.

French

Chez Sateau　　　　　　$$　　　　　　★★★
850 South Baldwin Avenue, ☎ (818) 446-8806.
Lunch: 11:30 a.m.–2:30 p.m., entrees $8–$13.
Dinner: 5:30–10 p.m., entrees $9–$21.
A charming country French ambience and good food make this spot popular with the locals. The early evening prix fixe dinner, at about $20, is a good bargain. Closed: Mon. Features: own baking, Sunday brunch, full bar, rated wine cellar, late dining, private dining rooms. Reservations recommended. Credit Cards: CB, V, MC, DC, A.

Glendale

American

Crocodile Cafe　　　　　$　　　　　　★★
626 North Central Avenue, ☎ (818) 241-1114.
Specialties: chili; pastas; pizza.
Lunch: from 11 a.m., entrees $5–$10.
Dinner: to 10 p.m., entrees $5–$10.
This casual restaurant—a spinoff of the popular Parkway Grill—is always crowded with people wanting good food and a good time at reasonable prices. Other Crocodile Cafe locations are in Pasadena, Brea and Santa Monica. Features: own baking, full bar, late dining. Reservations not accepted. Credit Cards: CB, V, MC, DC, A.

Kix　　　　　　　　　　$$　　　　　　★★
343 North Central Avenue, ☎ (818) 956-7800.
Lunch: 11 a.m.–3 p.m., entrees $8–$13.
Dinner: 5–10 p.m., entrees $9–$13.

Occupying the former site of Phoenicia, Kix is turning out some excellent and imaginative New American cuisine at low prices. A very nice change of pace. Lunch served Tuesday through Friday. Closed: Sun. Features: own baking, wine and beer only, late dining. Reservations recommended. Credit Cards: CB, V, MC, DC, A.

International
Cinnabar $$ ★★★
933 South Brand Boulevard, ☎ *(818) 551-1155.*
Specialties: mille-feuille of yellowtail.
Lunch: 11:30 a.m.–2:30 p.m., entrees $6–$12.
Dinner: 6–9:30 p.m., entrees $10–$16.
Alvin Simon of the long-gone Cafe Jacoulet has a winner in Cinnabar, where chef Hisashi Yoshiara borrows culinary influences from several continents to create splendid cuisine with an emphasis on light eating. Nearly all dishes come in both half and full portions, so you can order as much—or as little—as your appetite and budget allow. Lunch served Tuesday through Friday. Closed: Mon. Features: own baking, full bar, rated wine cellar. Credit Cards: V, MC, A.

Italian
Far Niente $$ ★★
204 1/2 North Brand Boulevard, ☎ *(818) 242-3835.*
Specialties: carpaccio; veal scaloppini.
Lunch: 11:30 a.m.–2:30 p.m., entrees $7–$12.
Dinner: 5:30–9:30 p.m., entrees $8–$15.
Far Niente is a terrific little Italian restaurant that has great food at moderate prices. There are lots of good pastas, fresh fish, and —yes— the ubiquitous tiramisu (although this version is especially good). Lunch served Monday through Friday. Features: own baking. Reservations recommended. Credit Cards: V, MC, DC, A.

Monrovia
French
La Parisienne $$$ ★★★
1101 East Huntington, ☎ *(818) 357-3359.*
Specialties: duck a l'orange; rack of lamb; beef tenderloin.
Lunch: 11:30 a.m.–2 p.m., entrees $12–$15.
Dinner: 5:30–9:30 p.m., entrees $15–$21.
A surprisingly good French restaurant with solid, sometimes innovative, cooking, good wines and professional service. Lunch served Monday through Friday. Closed: Sun. Features: own baking, full bar, rated wine cellar. Jacket requested. Reservations required. Credit Cards: CB, V, MC, DC, A.

Pasadena
American
Beckham Place $$$ ★★
77 West Walnut Street, ☎ *(818) 796-3399.*
Specialties: prime rib; roast duckling; fresh seafood; English trifle.
Lunch: 11:30 a.m.–2:30 p.m., entrees $7–$10.
Dinner: 5:50–10 p.m., entrees $15–$20.
An antique-studded English inn decor prevails, with waitresses dressed in period costumes serving the standard Yorkshire pudding, prime rib and a good house-made English trifle. Excellent service and reasonable prices make it a popular spot for lunch and dinner. Lunch

served Monday through Friday. Features: own baking, full bar, late dining, private dining rooms. Jacket requested. Reservations recommended. Credit Cards: V, MC, A.

Chronicle, The $$$ ★★★
897 Granite Drive, ☎ *(818) 792-1179.*
Specialties: Baby Lobster Tail Appetizer; Saddle of Lamb; Chateaubriand.
Lunch: 11:30 a.m.–2:30 p.m., entrees $9–$13.
Dinner: 5–9:30 p.m., entrees $10–$22.

This popular grill emphasizes seafood, but the menu is quite far-reaching, with something for every palate. The cooking is perhaps surprisingly innovative, and the wine list is one of the best in town. Expect to wait a while if you don't have reservations, especially on weekends. Features: full bar, rated wine cellar, late dining. Jacket requested. Reservations recommended. Credit Cards: D, CB, V, MC, DC, A.

Clearwater Cafe $$$ ★★
168 West Colorado Boulevard, ☎ *(818) 356-0959.*
Specialties: dungeness crabcakes; pecan catfish.
Lunch: from 11:30 a.m., entrees $8–$25.
Dinner: 5–10 p.m., entrees $8–$25.

The Clearwater Cafe has abandoned its original concept, which was to focus completely on healthy, low-fat eating. There are still a few dishes for the terminally body-conscious (and the preparations are still fairly healthy), but the menu now approximates that at Santa Monica's Ocean Avenue Seafood, which is owned by the same people. This means that you can expect really fresh fish with lots of innovative touches (such as salsa or black muscat wine sauce), some of which is really good, and some of which isn't quite cooked to perfection. Still, the mostly sophisticated cuisine, intriguing wine list heavy with West Coast vintages, and relatively low prices make this a solid choice for health-conscious Californians. Features: own baking, rated wine cellar, late dining. Reservations recommended. Credit Cards: V, MC.

Gordon Biersch Brewery $$ ★★
41 Hugus Alley, ☎ *(818) 449-0052.*
Specialties: Pasta; Grilled Meats and Seafood.
Lunch: 11 a.m.–5 p.m., entrees $7–$13.
Dinner: 5–10 p.m., entrees $10–$15.

The food at this Colorado One complex restaurant is good, but nearly everyone comes for the intriguing variety of microbrewed beers, some of which are made in house. The scene is pretty lively, too. Depending on how many people are in the restaurant, it may close at 10 p.m. or stay open later to accommodate its customers. Features: outside dining, wine and beer only, late dining. Reservations recommended. Credit Cards: V, MC.

Parkway Grill $$$ ★★★★
510 South Arroyo Parkway, ☎ *(818) 795-1001.*
Lunch: 11:30 a.m.–2:30 p.m., entrees $7–$13.
Dinner: 5:30–10:30 p.m., entrees $16–$30.

Often dubbed "the Spago of Pasadena" because of its contemporary California cuisine, the ten-year-old Parkway Grill gets mixed reviews that range from gushing praise to plain bewilderment. Complaints mostly revolve around the food being a little too far out on the cutting edge, with pastas that are sometimes drowned in complicated sauces and crowned with other, incongruous ingredients that frankly overdo it. On the other hand, when a particular dish clicks, it can be superb eating. Pizzas are usually very good, and contain prime fresh ingredients such as the restaurant's homemade Italian sausage. Lunch served Monday through Friday. Features: own baking, Sunday brunch, full bar, rated wine cellar, late dining. Jacket requested. Reservations recommended. Credit Cards: CB, V, MC, DC, A.

Raymond, The $$$

1250 South Fair Oaks Avenue, ☎ *(818) 441-3136.*
Lunch: 11:30 a.m.–2:30 p.m., entrees $8–$14.
Dinner: 6–9:30 p.m., entrees $24–$28.
A lovely Craftsman-style cottage near the Raymond Hotel houses this restaurant, which features an excellent wine bar, classical music, and a variety of sandwiches, soups, salads and special entrees. A little out of the way, but both the food and the caring service make the Raymond worth finding. Very romantic, too! Non-smoking throughout. Prix fixe dinner, $25. Lunch served Tuesady through Friday; brunch Saturday and Sunday. Closed: Mon. Features: outside dining, own baking, Sunday brunch, wine and beer only, rated wine cellar. Reservations recommended. Credit Cards: CB, V, MC, DC, A.

Ritz-Carlton Grill $$$

1401 South Oak Knoll Road, ☎ *(818) 568-3900.*
Lunch: 11:30 a.m.–2:30 p.m., entrees $20–$50.
Dinner: 6–10 p.m., entrees $30–$60.
Associated Hotel: Ritz-Carlton Huntington.
The opulent Georgian Room has closed to all but private parties, but the handsome Grill gracefully serves some of the best dishes in Pasadena. New executive chef Denis Depoitre uses only the best ingredients, and it shows. There's less formal dining available in the Cafe, where every Friday night is a "seafood celebration" featuring a buffet of seafood bisque, seafood salads, oysters, mussels, shrimp, and six fresh fish entrees. Price is about $30 per person, and the buffet is served from 6–10 p.m. Closed: Mon. Features: own baking, full bar, rated wine cellar, late dining. Jacket and tie requested. Reservations required. Credit Cards: CB, V, MC, DC, A.

Roxxi $$$

1065 East Green Street, ☎ *(818) 449-4519.*
Specialties: pizza; pasta; grilled meats.
Lunch: 11:30 a.m.–2:30 p.m., entrees $8–$12.
Dinner: 5:30–9:30 p.m., entrees $12–$24.
Roxxi—which sounds so California-trendy—is actually named after the dog of its owner, but there's nothing low-brow about the fare here. California cuisine infused with the spices of the Orient is first-rate, with a menu of terrific pastas, pizzas and California grill food that's mostly very good and often spectacular. Don't miss the homemade bread. If you're attending an event at the Pasadena Playhouse, you might want to try Critixx, which is owned by the same people. Lunch served Monday through Friday. Features: wine and beer only, rated wine cellar. Credit Cards: V, MC, A.

Chinese

Panda Inn $$$ ★★

3488 East Foothill, ☎ *(818) 793-7300.*
Specialties: panda beef; sliced shrimp in garlic sauce.

Lunch: from 11:30 a.m., entrees $7–$25.
Dinner: to 10:30 p.m., entrees $7–$25.

You get lots for your money at this outpost of a string of chain restaurants, but the cooking is pretty standard. Features: full bar, late dining. Reservations recommended. Credit Cards: V, MC, DC, A.

Yujean Kang's   **$$**   ★★★

67 North Raymond Avenue, ☎ (818) 585-0855.
Specialties: tea-smoked duck; salmon; scallops: braised Chilean sea bass.
Lunch: 11:30 a.m.–2:30 p.m., entrees $7–$10.
Dinner: 5–9:30 p.m., entrees $10–$15.

Voted Best New Chinese Restaurant in L.A. in *Los Angeles* magazine's Best of L.A. issue, November 1991, Yujean Kang's has since made a permanent place for itself at the top of the local Chinese dining scene. The cuisine is quite innovative and the wine cellar surprisingly good for a Chinese restaurant. In spite of its reputation (and the successful Kang is rumored to be opening a second restaurant in Hollywood), there are those who think that Yujean Kang's is terribly overrated, and that you are better off going for the real thing, more downscale and much cheaper, in some of the authentic Chinese restaurants (such as the Dragon Regency, Harbor Village, Lake Spring or Ocean Star) located in Monterey Park. Features: outside dining, own baking, wine and beer only, late dining. Jacket requested. Reservations recommended. Credit Cards: CB, V, MC, DC, A.

French

Bistro 45   **$$$**   ★★★

45 South Mentor Avenue, ☎ (818) 795-2478.
Specialties: Bouillabaisse; Ravioli.
Lunch: from 11:30 a.m., entrees $7–$16.
Dinner: 6–10 p.m., entrees $15–$25.

Bistro 45 has a lot going for it; including great food, extremely attentive service, and one of the city's best wine lists. The pleasing art deco ambience adds to the dining experience, and the restaurant's location near the Pasadena Playhouse makes it perfect for pre-theatre dining. A local standout. Lunch served Tuesday through Friday. Monthly dinners with winemakers are extremely popular; reserve ahead. Closed: Mon. Features: outside dining, own baking, full bar, rated wine cellar, late dining. Reservations recommended. Credit Cards: CB, V, MC, DC, A.

Les Arts   **$$$**   ★★★

70 South Raymond, ☎ (818) 583-8275.
Lunch: 11 a.m.–2 p.m., entrees $10–$20.
Dinner: 6–11 p.m., entrees $15–$25.

In fitness-crazed L.A., Italian restaurants are all the rage, but by most accounts, this new French gem will have strong appeal. Owned by Patrick Gruest, who was the proprietor of the site's former restaurant, Fleur de Vin, Les Arts features classic French cuisine cooked with very little fat by chef Jean Marie Konnert, who came from Lyon to head the kitchen here. Desserts are divine (they haven't cut back the fat here), there's an impressive selection of cheeses, and the list of French wines is first-rate. Service still needs a little work, but it's bound to improve with time. Specials include a $45 prix fixe lobster dinner to die for. Lunch served Tuesday through Friday. Closed: Mon. Features: own baking, rated wine cellar, late dining. Reservations recommended. Credit Cards: V, MC.

Twin Palms   **$$**   ★★★

101 West Green Street, ☎ (818) 577-2567.
Specialties: Rotisserie Chicken with Roasted Garlic; Shepherd's Pie.
Lunch: 11:30 a.m.–2:30 p.m., entrees $7–$12.
Dinner: 5:30–10 p.m., entrees $7–$17.

This new, $2.5-million stunner with big-name backers like Kevin Costner and winning chef Michael Roberts (formerly of West Hollywood's now defunct Trumps) has taken Old Town by storm. The rotisserie-grill is turning out superb rustic fare at incredibly low prices, and the place is packed every noon and night. Not that the restaurant is without its critics. Those expecting something from the cutting edge (and many do, given Roberts' penchant for the eclectic at Trumps) will be disappointed, and there are a few dishes that really aren't all that hot. Judging by the crowds, though, no one is noticing the restaurant's shortcomings. There's live music every night in the garden. Lunch served Monday through Friday. Note: apparently Cindy and Kevin Costner are still "discussing" who will get custody of (or at least a nice cash settlement for) the restaurant in their recently announced divorce. Features: outside dining, own baking, Sunday brunch, full bar, rated wine cellar, late dining. Reservations recommended. Credit Cards: V, MC, A.

Xiomara   **$$$**   ★★★

69 North Raymond Avenue, ☎ (818) 796-2520.
Specialties: crispy salmon pepper steak; cassoulet; bouillabaisse.
Lunch: 11:30 a.m.–2:30 p.m., entrees $10–$15.
Dinner: 5:30–10:30 p.m., entrees $18–$25.

Chef Patrick Healy, whose most recent venture was Champagne, has taken over the kitchen here to rave reviews. The food is as refined and sophisticated as the ambience, and you'll always feel welcome and nicely cared for. Best buy is the three-course prix fixe dinner, at about $25. Don't miss the apricot souffle—or the cheeses; they're to die for. An oyster and crab bar was recently added, and the restaurant often sponsors special events such as winemaker dinners and special meals on holidays. Lunch served Monday through Friday. Features: own baking, full bar, rated wine cellar, late dining. Reservations required. Credit Cards: CB, V, MC, DC, A.

International

Papashon   **$$$**   ★★

91 North Raymond Avenue, ☎ (818) 792-6060.
Lunch: 11:30 a.m.–2:30 p.m., entrees $9–$11.
Dinner: 5:30–10 p.m., entrees $15–$20.

The old Tra Fiori has been resurrected (with a complete refurbishment) as Papashon's, a temple to fusion cuisine that may go a little too far (Pasadena Kam Pao Shrimp and Ravioli) and be a little too weird for some tastes. Still, early results are promising, and chef Sean Sheridan may just be able to deliver. Stay tuned. Papashon could well be on the way up. Lunch served Monday through Friday. Closed: Sun. Features: own baking, late dining. Credit Cards: V, MC, DC, A.

Italian

Il Fornaio   **$$**   ★★

24 West Union Street, ☎ *(818) 683-9797.*
Specialties: Spit-roasted Meat and Fowl; Pizza; Veal.
Lunch: from 11:30 a.m., entrees $9–$19.
Dinner: to 11 p.m., entrees $9–$19.

The Il Fornaio Cucina Italiana concept has been spreading all over
California, firmly grounded on the concept of an on-site bakery turn-
ing out fresh, homemade breads and a menu featuring only the best
ingredients. This branch is no different, and you can come in for an
espresso or gelato or for an entire meal. Good food, and always lots of
noise. Another branch is in Beverly Hills. Features: outside dining,
own baking, full bar, rated wine cellar, late dining, private dining
rooms. Reservations recommended. Credit Cards: V, MC, A.

Mi Piace   **$$**   ★★

25 East Colorado Boulevard, ☎ *(818) 795-3131.*
Lunch: from 11:30 a.m., entrees $6–$18.
Dinner: to 11:30 p.m., entrees $7–$18.

A Pasadena favorite, now with a cappuccino and wine bar and a popular post-theatre menu, Mi Piace caters to the local Beautiful People,
who watch each other come and go under sleek spotlights. Good
food, but the scene here is just as important as what's on your plate,
and the resulting noise level is up there. Features: own baking, wine
and beer only, rated wine cellar, late dining. Reservations recommended. Credit Cards: V, MC, A.

Japanese

Miyako   **$$**   ★★

139 South Los Robles, ☎ *(818) 795-7005.*
Specialties: sukiyaki.
Lunch: 11:30 a.m.–2 p.m., entrees $6–$13.
Dinner: 5:30–9 p.m., entrees $9–$17.

Tableside cooking and other Japanese specialties served in a garden-
like atmosphere. Lunch served Monday through Friday. Features: full
bar, private dining rooms. Reservations recommended. Credit Cards: V,
MC, A.

Mediterranean

Critixx   **$$**   ★★

39 South El Molino Avenue, ☎ *(818) 577-9944.*
Specialties: tapas.
Lunch: 11:30 a.m.–2:30 p.m., entrees $5–$9.
Dinner: 5–9 p.m., entrees $13–$17.

Critixx, from the same folks who own Roxxi, is located off the courtyard of the Pasadena Playhouse and is largely patronized by the theatre crowd. Grazing is the thing to do here, and the more than 35
kinds of tapas are mostly Mediterranean-influenced, although there
are also offerings with Asian and California-style bents. Prices are
moderate, but if you want to sample a lot of dishes, you can run up a
big bill in a hurry. Lunch served Tuesday through Friday. Closed:
Mon. Features: own baking, Sunday brunch, rated wine cellar.

Seafood

McCormick's & Schmick's   **$$**   ★★★

111 North Las Robles, ☎ *(818) 405-0064.*
Specialties: oysters.

Lunch: from 11:30 a.m., entrees $8–$20.
Dinner: to 11 p.m., entrees $8–$20.

It's hit or miss at this outpost of the Seattle-based seafood chain situated in a clubby Pasadena dining room. There's a huge menu of fresh seafood to choose from, but not everything's as good as the oysters, which, by most accounts, are fabulous. Features: outside dining, Sunday brunch, full bar, late dining. Reservations recommended. Credit Cards: V, MC, A.

South Pasadena

Japanese

Shiro   **$$$**   ★ ★ ★

1505 Mission Street, ☎ *(818) 799-4774.*
Specialties: catfish.
Dinner: 6–10 p.m., entrees $25–$35.

The location isn't the best, but the food is fabulous—and we mean fabulous by any standards in greater L.A. Pacific Rim cuisine with French accents appears in a variety of sumptuous seafood dishes created by Shiro, who was formerly the head chef at Cafe Jacoulet. The minimalist setting allows what's on the plate to shine—and it does. Closed: Mon. Features: own baking, full bar, late dining. Reservations recommended. Credit Cards: V, MC, A.

THE BEACHES

Hermosa Beach Pier during a winter storm

Los Angeles County's coastline, which stretches from Malibu south to Long Beach, is 72 miles long, and, during any given year, nearly 60 million people stake temporary claim to their own beach blanket-sized stretch of sand. Not that Southern California beaches always conform to the image of sun-blanketed strands situated along the eternally blue and pristine Pacific.

In winter, the water is chilly and—even when the weather is unseasonably warm—things don't start warming up at the beach until ten or eleven. During the summer, L.A. beaches are often shrouded in fog in early to mid-morning, a disappointment to tourists who had planned on working on their tans right after breakfast. The locals, of course, are extremely savvy about knowing when to hit the sand, which is usually around noon, when the sun breaks through. (This excludes joggers, bikers and those who enjoy the solitude of an early morning stroll, and surfers, who get "stoked" and go when the waves are "gnarly," regardless of the time of day or the weather.) If you're not familiar with Southern California's beachside weather patterns, get the latest information on beach and surf conditions by calling the

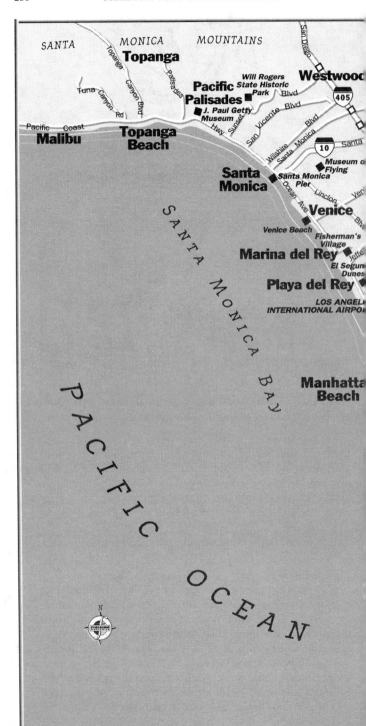

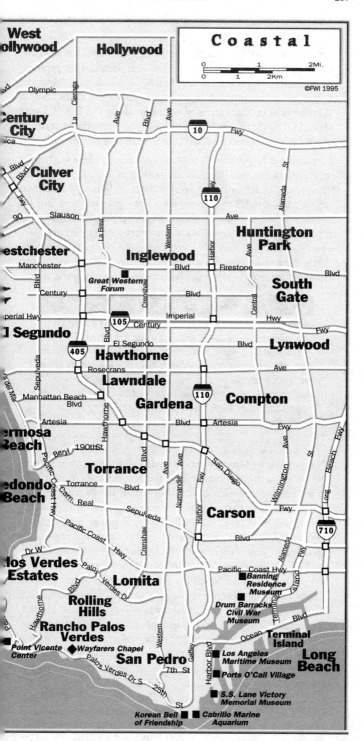

West Hollywood

Hollywood

Coastal

0   1   2Mi.

0   1   2Km

©FWI 1995

Olympic

Century City

La Cienega

Ave

Blvd

Ave

10 Fwy

St

Alameda

Culver City

Blvd

Slauson

90

Fwy

Ave

La Brea

Western

110 Hwy

Huntington Park

Westchester

Manchester

Great Western Forum

Inglewood

Harbor

Blvd

Firestone

Ave

South Gate

Blvd

Century

Crenshaw

Blvd

Central

Imperial Hwy

105

Century

Imperial

Hwy

El Segundo

405

Hawthorne

El Segundo

Blvd

Blvd

Lynwood

Fwy

Sepulveda

Rosecrans

Lawndale

Ave

Via del Mar

Manhattan Beach Blvd

Hawthorne

Gardena

110 Fwy

Compton

Artesia

Blvd

Artesia

Fwy

Hermosa Beach

Beryl

190th St

Blvd

Redondo Beach

Pacific Coast Hwy

Torrance

Ave

Ave

San Diego Fwy

Long Beach Fwy

Wilmington

St

Torrance

Cam. Real

Blvd

Normandie

Harbor Fwy

Carson

Fwy

Pacific Coast Hwy

Sepulveda

Crenshaw

Blvd

710

Alameda

Palos Verdes Estates

Dr W

Palos

Verdes Dr

Lomita

Hawthorne

Blvd

Western

Pacific Coast Hwy

Banning Residence Museum

Terminal Island

Blvd

Rolling Hills

Drum Barracks Civil War Museum

Rancho Palos Verdes

Ocean

Terminal Island

Point Vicente Center

Wayfarers Chapel

Palos Verdes Dr S

San Pedro

7th St

25th St

Gaffey

Harbor Blvd

Los Angeles Maritime Museum

Ports O'Call Village

Long Beach

S.S. Lane Victory Memorial Museum

Korean Bell of Friendship

Cabrillo Marine Aquarium

TimesLine ☎ *(213 808-8463)* and pressing *5010 (*5000 for Orange County beaches).

Pollution has also become a problem along some areas of the coast, especially in Santa Monica Bay. This situation has prompted a group of local surfers and beachgoers to found "Heal the Bay," an environmental watchdog organization dedicated to keeping tabs on the extent of pollution along the L.A. County shoreline. While things appear to be improving somewhat, there is still cause for concern when contemplating a seaside dip.

In addition to pollution problems, parking can be a nightmare at L.A. beaches, leaving you the option of paying for parking close to the beach or taking your chances on finding a place that isn't a trillion miles away from where you plan to camp out for the day. While you may be willing to pay up, be aware that parking lots can fill up just as fast as the nearby street parking spaces—especially on summer weekends—so come prepared to battle for a spot (you can get rid of all your pent-up frustration later in a game of beach volleyball or a nice jog along the coast).

Author's Tip

To be completely safe, don't go swimming or surfing after a rainstorm. All those streets in L.A. are flushed clean as a whistle by torrential downpours, and for about a day after a heavy rain, the beaches are littered with styrofoam cups, old tampon holders and other rude trash. Heal the Bay advises you to stay at least 100 feet away from flowing storm drains or piers, and to avoid swimming for at least three days after storm drains have emptied their contents into the sea. Watch also for posted signs announcing the closing of beaches due to bacteria-contaminated water.

The beach isn't just "the beach" in L.A. County. (Note that Orange County beaches are covered under the Orange County section of this book.) Nearly all of the beaches and/or beach cities are unique and each has its own special flavor. Your estimation of which is the best beach in Los Angeles will probably depend on what you plan to do there. If you're happy just to "lay out" and catch some rays on a nice, quiet and reasonably clean beach, best choices might be Zuma (very hip), Santa Monica (lots of Generation Xers showing off their hard bodies here), or Will Rogers State Beach (generally not as crowded as other L.A. beaches). Surfers prefer Malibu (Surfrider State Beach is adjacent to the Malibu Pier); swimmers will enjoy Santa Monica, Manhattan, Redondo and Bayshore Beach, located in Long Beach (no waves here—nice and calm); fishermen congregate at the Redondo Beach Pier, drop a line off Marina del Rey's 180 feet of public fishing docks or get on a charter boat out of Redondo, Marina del Rey or Long Beach (fishing from a public pier or jetty requires no fishing license; fishing from a boat or a beach does); and beach volleyball games are always going on at Zuma, Will Rogers, Santa Monica, Manhattan, Redondo and

Hermosa, which is considered one of L.A.'s prime "party beach-es" for bronzed yuppies (mostly of the single variety).

Families with children should try **Redondo's Seaside Lagoon**, a veritable sandy-bottomed heated pool on the beach (complete with diving boards), warmed by water coming out of the adjacent Southern California Edison plant; Mother's Beach in Marina del Rey, a calm, shallow-bottomed beach where kids can safely play while mom catches some rays; or Cabrillo Beach in San Pedro, where the whole family can explore the tidepools or take a guided tour offered by the Cabrillo Marine Aquarium. Will Rogers State Beach is another great place for families, with playground equipment for kids, picnic facilities and volleyball courts that always have a game going.

If you just want to "make the beach scene" somewhere in L.A. County (dressing as scantily or outlandishly as possible and having a pair of rollerblades helps), try Venice or Santa Monica, although most L.A. County beaches have boardwalks or jogging/cycling/rollerblading paths where you are welcome to cruise and show off your body and/or your athletic prowess.

Best Tidepools

Even though much of greater Los Angeles is situated along the coast, most beaches are sandy and don't offer opportunities for one-on-one encounters with sea creatures. (There's that shark at Universal Studios, of course, but we don't recommend it as a true nature experience). There are a few places, though, where tidepools offer a real glimpse of life along the California coast, and you are welcome to explore (but please don't' disturb!) this rich habitat.

1. ***Cabrillo State Beach*** (Stephen White Drive, San Pedro). *If you're not experienced at tidepooling, this is a great place to start. The Cabrillo Marine Aquarium is here, which will help you know what to look for, and even take you on a guided excursion to local tidepools. After that, you can head out on your own.*

2. ***Leo Carrillo State Beach*** (just west of Mulholland Highway on Pacific Coast Highway). *Best tidepools here are at the southeast end of the beach, where the ocean flora and fauna are especially rich and diverse. Lots of sponges.*

3. ***El Matador State Beach*** (32900 Pacific Coast Highway, Malibu). *This relatively unspoiled section of beach has impressive tidepools rich with anemones, volcano limpets, California sea hares and other flora and fauna.*

4. ***Crescent Bay*** (stairway off Cliff Drive and Circle Way, Laguna Beach). *From this spot, you can access tidepools at both Crescent Bay and Santa Ana Cove, which is slightly southeast. High marks here are for the diversity of plant and animal life and the sheer numbers of tidepools, which are impressive.*

5. ***Orange County Marine Institute*** (Dana Point). *The stairway from the institute leads to rocky beaches containing some of the richest tidepools in Orange County. To avoid walking over the rocks both coming and going, follow the path north as far as you want to go, then examine the tidepools as you work your way back.*

Any sort of privacy is practically impossible to find on L.A. beaches, especially in summer, when bodies are packed close to-

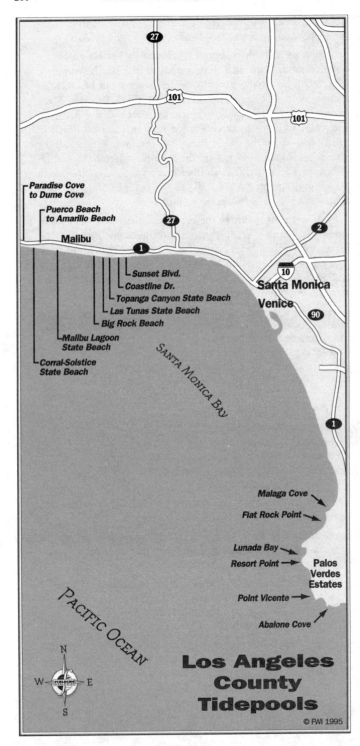

Los Angeles County Tidepools

© FWI 1995

gether, frisbees go whizzing over your head and portable stereos blast out what well may not be your style of music.

Fielding's Secret Beaches

If you want to "get away from it all," here are a few beaches that offer a bit of seclusion. Be aware that getting to these off-the-beaten path locations may require a bit of hiking.

El Pescador, La Piedra and **El Matador**, all of which are state beaches located just off Pacific Coast Highway in Malibu (their addresses are 32350, 32700 and 32900 PCH, respectively). Each has pay parking for a few dozen cars, outdoor toilets and some picnic tables. To get to the beach, you have to take a trail or stairway down the bluff, but it's worth the hike. El Matador is especially beautiful, with rock formations and more than 2000 feet of beach-front.

Lechuza Beach, a small, secluded cove where public access (available on the 31800 block of Broad Beach Road in Malibu) is limited to between 9 a.m. and sunset. There are no toilets and no picnic facilities, but it's a wonderful little spot to get away from it all.

Malaga Cove, a secluded beach on the Palos Verdes Peninsula that's accessible from Paseo del Mar and Via Arroyo in Palos Verdes. A paved path leads down to the beach, which is the only sandy beach on the peninsula.

Abalone Cove, accessible from the 5800 block of Palos Verdes Drive South in Rancho Palos Verdes. There's pay parking and a steep descent onto a narrow beach where you can bask in the sun, stare out at Catalina Island or explore the tidepools. Great for snorkeling.

Author's Tip

The handful of people who enjoy an au naturel beach experience aren't going to have much luck in L.A. The City Council recently approved a ban on nude beaches after a spate of complaints about lewd conduct and unsavory types hanging around the few spots where nudity was permitted—or at least tolerated.

And while we're on the subject of things taboo, you should know that alcohol is not permitted on any of Los Angeles County's beaches.

Fielding's Beach Finder

Whether you're looking for the ultimate beach destination, or for a pleasant seaside diversion for an afternoon, the following should help you determine which L.A. County beach is the one for you.

Malibu

Malibu has always been thought of as a mecca for surfers. Its near-perfect waves made it one of the first (and best) places ever surfed in Southern California, and it inspired trends in just about every aspect of surfing, from board design to surfing style to a whole new language (including a new '60s lingo that—to the dismay of conservative mothers all over Southern California—included the word "bitchin").

Surfing in Malibu

In true California style, art was soon imitating life, and surfing became the subject of a truckload of '60s musical hits, along with a series of "beach" movies that featured everyone from Frankie and Annette to Gidget (who, by the way, was a real person who actually lived—and surfed—in Malibu in the 1950s).

Surfers still go to Malibu, mostly because of the perfect waves, but many of those who were around in the sport's glory days think it has lost much of its appeal due to crowds, pollutants in the water and a formerly pristine coastal landscape burned black by the recent Malibu fires.

Far removed from the Malibu surfer dude of old (economically, at least) are the residents of the Malibu Colony, an exclusive enclave of the very famous and very rich whose high-security homes spill out onto the beach. (For a photographic look at some of these opulent homes, as well as others along the California coast, see Elizabeth McMillian's *Beach Houses from Malibu to Laguna*, published in 1994 by Rizzoli International. It's about as close as you're going to get to these mansions.)

And, by the way, it is in the vicinity of Malibu that "Baywatch" (or "Maliboobs," as the more cynical prefer to call it) is filmed, although location shooting can happen anywhere from Malibu to Huntington Beach. "Baywatch" is one of the most popular shows on television, syndicated in 98 percent of American markets and providing titillating entertainment for more than a billion people across the globe. It has also succeeded in giving the rest of the world the impression that simply everyone in California is either a hunk or a babe (except for those overweight, middle-aged mothers who are forever losing their kids on the beach), and perpetuates the myth that all female lifeguards are both sensitive and extremely large-breasted. Not that anyone is complaining.

Although the shooting location for "Baywatch" is moved around a lot (to avoid the inevitable gathering of large crowds, according to the production company), Will Rogers State Beach is often used, with filming taking place from May to October. It is a closed set, but Will Rogers is a public beach, so you can gawk all you want as long as you don't get too close.

Santa Monica

South of Malibu you'll find Santa Monica, an 8.3-square mile community that is one of L.A.'s most popular beach cities. Dubbed everything from "chic, funky and fun" to a "seductive city by the sea," Santa Monica has a reputation for being yet another of those California getaway spots where yuppies go to play. And it is a grand vacation destination, far enough removed from both the L.A. and the Disneyland crowds to provide a bit of solace, with palms swaying in the breeze and the sun dancing on the blue Pacific.

Although proud of its "fun in the sun" image (after all, it does bring in those tourists!), Santa Monica has been extremely serious about providing a whole lot more to boast about than its beaches. With a burgeoning commitment to the cultural arts (including some of L.A.'s most exclusive galleries and its own art museum), the opening of the pedestrian-friendly Third Street Promenade, an ongoing $45 million pier reconstruction project, and a collection of first-class hotels, restaurants and shopping areas, Santa Monica has put itself on the map as a stretch of prime beachside real estate.

Like most L.A.-area cities, Santa Monica has also been influenced by the entertainment industry, and landmarks such as the Santa Monica Pier have been showing up in Hollywood movies practically since Santa Monica was "discovered." (The city was incorporated in 1887, and by the 1920s was attracting the Hollywood elite, as well as a whole bunch of rich Easterners who came to winter there.) The pier, originally built in 1908 and situated at the end of Colorado Avenue, has appeared in several period films, but is memorable as the location where Paul Newman operated his carousel in *The Sting*, and where Jane Fonda danced 'til she dropped at the old ballroom in *They Shoot Horses, Don't They?* (The carousel, still a popular attraction, was recently refurbished.)

Currently, Santa Monica is home to several big-name entertainment companies, including producer George Lucas' LucasArts Entertainment, Steven Spielberg's Amblin Entertainment and George Harrison's Handmade Films, in addition to the business offices of a virtual galaxy of stars that includes Bill Cosby, Oliver Stone, Sylvester Stallone and Arnold Schwarzenegger.

Venice

South of Santa Monica is Venice Beach, which is a living, breathing definition of the word "funky." This circuslike ambience is not exactly what developer Abbot Kinney had in mind when he laid out a grand plan for a West Coast equivalent of Venice, Italy, complete with canals and singing gondoliers. The whole thing got off to a fine start in July of 1905, but the discovery of oil nearby, the loss of Kinney's fortune, and the fact that his canals largely became unappealing pools of stagnant water ended his dream, and Venice went into an economic and cultural tailspin.

The boardwalk, which runs along Ocean Front Walk, has been called the East Village of the West Coast, and it's packed (especially during the summer and on weekends) with street performers, scantily-clad rollerbladers, body-builders, acrobats, artists and enough other bizarre characters to entertain you for an entire afternoon. Such local talent as Barry "The Lion" Gordon, who's been playing tributes to Fats Waller on his beachside piano for more than 20 years, Bad Boyz, a group of four exceedingly buff "roller-dancers" who have all the right moves, and Harry Perry, who rollerblades and plays the electric guitar at the same time, provide the Venice boardwalk with all the fun of a three-ring circus. (For a plethora of interesting facts about Venice and its history, invest in the city's "Venice Beach Historical Calendar." Bet you didn't know that 20 years ago, L.A. County's anti-bongo ordinance was passed, a cruel and crushing blow to many of Venice Beach's most renowned "musicians.")

Author's Tip

Ready to join the New Age crowd and consult your own psychic? Why bother with expensive Hollywood types when you might be able to find what you're looking for at the Venice boardwalk, a known psychic hangout. We predict that this experience will be more than $50 cheaper than if you go the upscale psychic route.

Venice is also the world headquarters of **Gold's Gym** *(360 Hampton Drive)*, and, as the self-proclaimed "Bodybuilding Capital of the World," has several other gyms that spew out perfect bodies onto Venice's Muscle Beach (located between 18th and 19th Avenues), where weightlifters pump iron in the weight pit, and pick-up games are always happening on the basketball and handball courts. (*White Men Can't Jump* was filmed here.)

Recently, proposals have been on the table for a $10 million renovation of the Venice beachfront (rumors are afoot that Venice just may be the next "in" place for celebrities to buy a house) that would include the tearing down of the 660-seat Venice Pavilion theatre and paving the boardwalk with bricks. The locals say they like the boardwalk—along with all of its offbeat

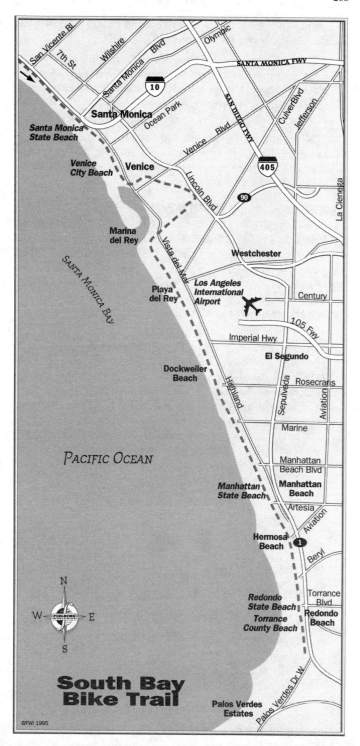

South Bay Bike Trail

charm—just the way it is, thank you, and instead propose using the money to save the theatre.

The wrangling over the future of the boardwalk is likely to continue for some time, but in the meantime, Venice is a very hip place to hang out. Wear something ultra-cool and rent a pair of skates (available from stands at beach parking lots) and you'll blend right in.

(Note: Although all this fun and frolic can be extremely entertaining, tourists are advised to avoid the area at night, when druggies and gang members sometimes resort to violence on darkened street corners.)

Marina del Rey

Down the coast from Venice is Marina del Rey, a staid (by Venice standards) 1.3-square mile waterfront community that boasts the world's largest man-made small craft harbor. With the 6000-slip marina as its centerpiece, Marina del Rey fills the rest of its small land mass with a variety of upscale hotels, condos, restaurants and shops, making a huge effort to attract both business travelers (being only 10 minutes from LAX helps) and vacationers to its "magical" shores.

In spite of objections from environmentalists, L.A. County supervisors recently okayed an ambitious redevelopment plan for Marina del Rey calling for refurbishment of the harbor and the construction of high-rise office buildings and hotels. Even though the plan has yet to be approved by the California Coastal Commission and may face challenges in court, backers hope to add more than 2500 new condos, 900 new hotel rooms, 380 new boat slips, a pedestrian walkway and a marine science museum as part of the project that one disgusted opponent predicted would result in a "Century City by the Sea."

The South Bay

The police patrol the beach on bikes.

Farther south you'll find El Segundo, Manhattan, Hermosa and Redondo, four "South Bay" beach cities that are usually not on the tourist's agenda. With only a small variety of things to do (in addition to going to the beach), and a lack of any architectural and cultural wonders, the South Bay doesn't have much to impress the out-of-towner. Each beach town has a small downtown area anchored by a pier which serves as a reminder of the days when the L.A. harbor was still a swamp and commerce was based largely around the ships that docked at the local facilities.

The entire South Bay has evolved over the years from a seaside resort for land-locked Angelenos at the turn of the century to a booming aerospace community in the 1950s to its new status as an upscale and "safe" alternative to the San Fernando Valley. Now viewed by many as a crowded white ghetto, the South Bay is slowing squeezing out the artists, surfers and bohemians that once gave it a unique and anti-establishment flavor, and is now quintessentially Southern Californian, with scantily-clad women rollerblading along the Strand and muscular "jocks" playing four-man volleyball in the sand. The beaches are massive, clean and uncrowded. You can rent a bike or in-line skates and cruise all the way to Venice Beach and back in a day if you're up for a change of scenery. Parking is a pain, and on long weekends, the place is a zoo.

El Segundo

A 1950s time-warped downtown area preserved for all time by its inaccessibility, El Segundo is pretty much disconnected from the beach by a refinery, a sewage plant, the freight side of LAX, top secret satellite office parks and an industrial zone. The view from Dockweiler State Beach includes rusting offshore oil tankers, aircraft bound for LAX zooming overhead, and smoke belching from the aforementioned refinery. Only the most hardcore RV'ers, smog-blinded inlanders and lost tourists are apt to stop here, although it has large barbecue pits on the beach that tend to attract rowdy teenagers and bonfires, especially on weekends.

Manhattan Beach

Manhattan Beach may be one of the nicest and least-known towns in all of California. A compressed collection of architecturally interesting houses, a wide Strand with bikes and pedestrians separated, a remodeled downtown (complete with infinitely enticing shops and great restaurants) make this a perfect "day at the beach" location for visitors. Shopping has a decidedly yuppie spin to it, with stores that cater to tri-athletes and offer trendy decor, beachwear and cappuccino. The north part of Manhattan (along the beach) is where the nightlife is jumping. As usual, parking is tough, prices are high and the places are packed after 8 p.m.

Hermosa Beach

A former biker haven, artists' hangout, jazzmeister stopover and now a poor stepchild to Manhattan Beach, Hermosa is still in search of itself. It lacks the polish and commercialism of Manhattan with its ramshackle collection of cheap apartments, expensive homes, car repair joints and head shops. Hermosa has a thriving brace of bars, coffeehouses and nightclubs, and every Friday and Saturday revelers can be found walking along Pier and Hermosa Avenue.

Redondo Beach

Surfing was introduced to the mainland from Hawaii by George Freeth.

Back to the fifties (the age group, not the era), Redondo is a mix of blue collar construction workers, retired or senior management and pockets of surfer dudes. North Redondo is nowhere near the beach or the mindset of South Redondo, so don't assume that if a bus drops you off at the Galleria Mall you're within walking distance of the beach. Redondo is home to Torrance Beach, the place where the Beach Boys first encountered California Kulture, and one of the first places in California to embrace surfing as a way of life.

The Redondo Pier is the only remnant of what used to be L.A.'s own Coney Island. Red trolley cars used to transport Angelenos to Redondo to wade in the ocean, bathe in the salt plunge and even stay at the sister hotel to San Diego's Del Coronado Hotel (the Redondo Hotel was unfortunately sold for scrap lumber in the '60s). The pier is crowded on weekends with inlanders looking for relief from the heat and cars backed up for hundred of yards. During the week there is plenty of parking, and a sunset dinner at *Tony's* on the pier makes for a clichéd but enjoyable outing.

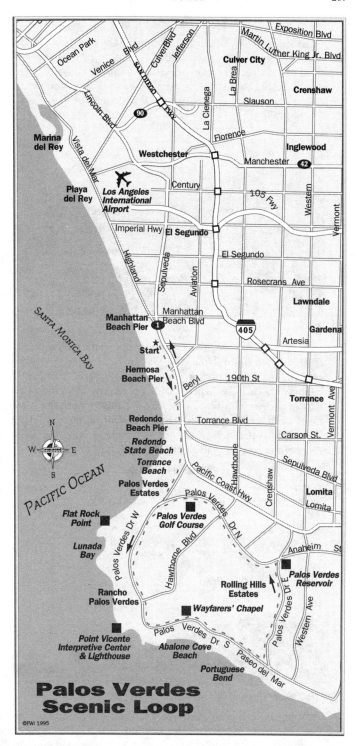

Palos Verdes
Scenic Loop

©FWI 1995

Palos Verdes

The Palos Verdes Peninsula is for those who like their beaches rugged, unspoiled and uncrowded. The only catch is that, instead of sand, beaches are covered with rounded stones, and getting there usually requires a steep walk down and back up the cliffs. Other than that, expect solitude and bliss.

The view north from Palos Verdes

The Palos Verdes Peninsula was once one of the largest private ranches in the world. Now, "PV" (as the locals call it) is considered one of those "perfect" Southern California communities (along with La Jolla, Rancho Santa Fe, Beverly Hills and Santa Barbara, to name a few), with large Spanish-style homes, tall trees, clean air, wealthy residents, abundant riding and hiking trails, spectacular cliffs, tide pools, incredible surfing spots and some of the best views in all of Los Angeles.

The Harbor

The Queen Mary

If you have ever wondered where director Ridley Scott got his inspiration for *Blade Runner*, look no further. The cities of

Wilmington, Lomita, San Pedro, Long Beach, et al., are probably the most convincing backdrop for Armageddon and nihilists
you can imagine. Refineries spewing fire and smoke, miles of
dirty, rusted pipes, buildings, oil tanks, machinery, factories,
acres of containers, acres of new new Japanese cars, old Navy
ships, train tracks and other industrial stuff provide an affront to
California environmentalists and harbor L.A.'s most lucrative industries: oil and shipping. Unless you are arriving or departing
on a cruise ship (in which case you have no choice), you aren't
apt to find many reasons to head to this part of town, and should
be advised that taking the "scenic" route south along PCH will
result in your eventually being unceremoniously dumped in the
middle of this industrial wasteland. On the other hand, if you really want to see the naked backbone of L.A., you might find it
interesting to be thrust into the black belly of the industrial
beast.

San Pedro is the home of the Port of Los Angeles (officially
known as WORLDPORT L.A.), and one of the city's busiest
centers of commerce. Fishing, shipping and cruise lines form the
base of the economy here, although there are a few historical and
cultural attractions of minor interest that reflect the city's history
and honor her past residents. Like many other L.A. cities, San
Pedro has been trying to spiff itself up of late, especially along
6th Street from Pacific Avenue to the waterfront. It's come alive
with funky little shops, restaurants and coffeehouses, and there's
a trolley to whisk you down to the World Cruise Center.

The southernmost beach in L.A. County (in fact, it's the
southwesternmost tip of North America—marked by a skytower
at Long Point) is Long Beach, a 50-square-mile former Navy
port that is—literally and figuratively—far removed from the hip
action of Malibu, Santa Monica or Venice. Although Long
Beach is California's fifth-largest city, it—like the rest of California—has suffered from economic setbacks in recent years. The
Long Beach Naval Shipyard, which employs more than 3000
workers, is in danger of being closed, a move that would leave
the city's economy reeling.

Long Beach tries hard to hide its blemishes and grab those
tourist dollars. In fact, you have to give the city an "A" for creativity in adopting Howard Hughes' giant *Spruce Goose* (which
recently flew the coop, so to speak) and the fading *Queen Mary*,
a British oceanliner that doubles as a hotel. City fathers even at-
tempted to convince Disney to build a whole new theme park in
their city, a project which never came to fruition.

The *Spruce Goose* used to be a major attraction until 1991
when the 219 ft. plane was floated by barge to McMinnville, Oregon. The **Evergreen Air Venture Museum** hopes to construct a
$20 million museum and display the giant aircraft. For now the

Spruce Goose can be seen in its plastic-wrapped glory on the ocean as you leave Portland along Highway 99.

In fact, even with all these innovations, tourists have never shown much of an interest in Long Beach, and, except for the few who have some unexplainable compulsion to see the *Queen Mary*, still don't. Even though many are convinced that Long Beach should stick to loading and unloading ships, like many other L.A. cities trying to make it in these hard economic times, Long Beach is in the midst of a redevelopment project designed to make it more tourist-friendly. The Long Beach Convention and Entertainment Center has just completed a $111 million expansion, which includes 334,000 square feet of exhibit space and two theatres—the 3141-seat Terrace Theater, and the 862-seat Center Theater. Also here is the new 14,000-seat Long Beach Arena.

Long Beach is the place to catch a boat (or helicopter) to Catalina Island, less than an hour's ride from mainland Southern California. Far from the crowded tourist attractions of L.A. (although its beaches can also get pretty crowded), Catalina, or Avalon, as it is also called, is a terrific spot to get away from it all, whether you're a nature enthusiast, a scuba diver or just want to see the famous old casino, built in 1929 by chewing gum magnate William Wrigley, Jr.

Perhaps not surprisingly, Long Beach stands shoulder to shoulder with a passel of other Southern California cities which claim they (and not Hollywood) marked the birthplace of the moviemaking industry in Southern California. Long Beach's claim to fame was Balboa Studios, where stars like Theda Bara starred in silent movies long before "talkies" made their debut. (And, decades later, Liz Taylor reportedly spent her first wedding night here with husband Nicky Hilton at—where else?— the Hilton Hotel, which is now a senior housing development.)

The Beaches: Where to Stay

Considering how much beachfront there is in Los Angeles, there is surprisingly little to choose from if you plan on staying directly on the beach. Choices range from upscale resorts like Santa Monica's Shutters on the Beach to cheesy motels like Seasprites in Hermosa Beach, a ramshackle motel right on the strand. The best bet for oceanfront vacation spots are actually south of L.A., in Laguna Beach, Oceanside, or the small beach towns between L.A. and San Diego. If you can live without the crashing surf and don't mind being inside the breakwater, your choices are much greater, and include everything from the pricey Ritz-Carlton in Marina del Rey to the Portofino in Redondo Beach.

The Beaches: Where to Eat

Author's Tip

Eating "at the beach" rarely means "on the beach" in L.A., and there are really only a handful of restaurants that give you a view of the pounding surf. The Charthouse, Tony's on the Pier in Redondo, the Sand Dollar in Malibu (of "Rockford Files" fame), and Gladstone's 4 Fish, also in Malibu, are a few true beachside eateries. Many restaurants in Redondo, at the harbor, and in Marina del Rey are inside breakwaters and overlook the harbor. Do not assume that any "oceanfront" restaurant is on the beach. Ask when you make the reservation.

SANTA MONICA

Santa Monica: Things to See and Do

Nature enthusiasts shouldn't miss an opportunity to stroll the new Solstice International Trail, a combined effort of the Southern California branch of the Pacific Asia Travel Association and the Mountains Conservancy Foundation. Found in Solstice Canyon Park in the Santa Monica Mountains above Malibu, the three-mile walk is easy going (it even accommodates wheelchairs), and showcases the flora and fauna of the mountains, with interpretive pamphlets available in six languages (English, Spanish, Korean, Japanese, Tagalog and Chinese—both Cantonese and Mandarin). Along the way you'll also see the 1865 Matthew Keller House and have plenty of opportunities to picnic.

Set back just over six miles from the beach on Malibu Canyon Road in Malibu is **Malibu Creek State** Park, a popular spot for a hike that contains both easy and moderately difficult trails. Hiking options take you past Malibu Creek, scenic vistas of the Santa Monica Mountains, Century Lake and the Las Virgines Valley; the Crag's Road trail is generally considered to be the best for a family outing, as it's easy going most of the way.

Best Hiking Trails

Once you get above (or beyond) the urban sprawl, you might be surprised to find that L.A. offers many opportunities for some truly excellent outdoor adventures. Here are some of our favorite trails–and not all of them are easy going.

1. ***Will Rogers Trail*** *to Inspiration Point (Will Rogers State Park, Santa Monica Mountains). After you tour the home and ranch, head up the Will Rogers Trail just west of park headquarters for a two-mile round trip to Inspiration Point. At the top, there are views of the city, Santa Monica Bay, the San Gabriel Mountains and–on a really clear day–Santa Catalina Island.*

2. ***Solstice International Trail*** *(Solstice Canyon Park, Santa Monica Mountains). This trail, a combined effort of the Pacific Asia Travel Association and the Mountains Conservancy Foundation, provides access to the flora and fauna of the mountains to almost everyone. The six-mile loop trail is not difficult, and will even accommodate wheelchairs. Interpretive pamphlets are available in six languages (English, Spanish, Korean, Japanese, Tagalog and Chinese–both Cantonese and Mandarin).*

Best Hiking Trails

3. **Eaton Canyon Trail** (Eaton Canyon County Park, base of Mt. Wilson, Pasadena). John Muir himself once walked the trails here, and an excursion to the park is a great activity for the whole family. Stop in at the Eaton Canyon Nature Center, then take the easy, three-mile, round-trip hike to Eaton Canyon Falls. This is a popular place for families–especially on weekends–so if you enjoy observing nature in private, this isn't for you.

4. **Point Dume** (above Zuma Beach, Malibu). Approximately a half-mile from Zuma Beach is Point Dume, which gives sweeping views of the coastline and (in season), a good chance of seeing migrating California gray whales. A mile farther on, you'll come to secluded Paradise Cove. There are lots of geological features to see along the way, not to mention the seaside flora and fauna. Trail begins at Westward Beach, at the end of Westward Beach Road.

5. **Sunset Peak** (off Glendora Ridge Road, San Gabriel Mountains). This hike is for hardy souls who are up to a five-mile (round trip) hike that gains more than 1000 feet in altitude along the way (the last 100 yards are a killer). When you get to the top, however, you'll have fabulous views of Mt. Baldy, the San Gabriel Valley, and the sunset. Best in winter, when the mountains are snow-capped.

The **Santa Monica Pier**, at the end of Colorado Avenue, was built in 1908 and is the oldest "pleasure" pier still in operation on the West Coast. It's a fun spot for strolling, or you can take the kids (and yourself) for a ride on the restored carousel or the bumper cars.

Brand new in Santa Monica is **Bergamot Station**, a complex of art galleries located in the old Red Car trolley station at *2525 Michigan Avenue*. Here you'll find everything from contemporary art and art glass to vintage photography, all arranged in a five-building complex that also includes a bookstore and a cafe. Several well-known dealers in town are moving their galleries into the new space, which is expected to give a boost to the local gallery scene. Reportedly, Yoko Ono has already been seen chatting it up with some of the artists.

Public art is on display all over Santa Monica, from "The Big Wave," a gateway of steel construction in the form of a crested wave hovering over Wilshire Boulevard at Franklin Street, to Doug Hollis' "Wind Harp Beach Chairs," a futuristic, 14-foot set of musically-tuned lifeguard chairs. (For information on walking tours to view the city's numerous outdoor murals, call ☎ *(310) 470-8864.*)

Author's Tip

Whether you're looking for some obscure book about L.A. or just want to drink tea and listen to poetry, acoustic music or jazz, L.A. (The Bookstore), at 2433 Main Street in Santa Monica may be your kind of place. There aren't many frills, but good karma abounds, especially on Free Expression Night (Mondays at 9 p.m.), when everyone gets to do their own thing.

If you're looking for a beach experience without having to get into your bathing suit and drag along towels, sunscreen and all the rest of the paraphernalia associated with the "going to the beach" thing, stop in at **Back on the Beach**, a casual spot located right on the sand north of the Santa

Monica pier. Here you can order weekend brunch or munch daily specials while watching the beach crowd stroll, jog, rollerblade or cycle by, or observe a taxing game of beach volleyball on a nearby court. **Palisades Park** is another good "beach" experience for those who don't want to get sand in their shoes. Perched atop a cliff overlooking the ocean, the 26-acre palm-studded greenbelt offers a variety of recreational opportunities that include walking, jogging, picnicking, cycling, rollerblading or just plain people-watching.

While **Venice** is associated mostly with people-watching, bodybuilding, and generally eclectic goings-on, it also has lots of public art, including Jonathan Borofsky's huge, bizarre "Ballerina Clown," a well-known—and much maligned—L.A. landmark that towers over the corner of Rose and Main Street. Now, the deal with the moving ballerina/clown, which has a dancer's body clad in a blue tutu and a huge, male clown head reminiscent of Emmett Kelly's (not to mention the red ballet shoes and oversized white gloves), is that, while some people tout it as a great piece of public art, others have decried it as everything from "a grotesque mechanized plastic joke" to "an oversized prop from *Killer Klowns from Outer Space*." So, go take a look for yourself and see what you think. Pick up a brochure at the old Art Deco police station that will give you information on a self-guided walking tour to this and other local public art, including the area's many murals.

You can contact the Venice Historical Society for information on the few interesting historical sights and structures in Venice, and, as for the Venice canals, the remnants of big plans gone awry remain along one-way Dell Avenue, where you can walk or drive over four arched bridges that cross the waterways.

Attractions

Museums and Exhibits

Angel's Attic ★★

516 Colorado Avenue, Santa Monica, ☎ (310) 394-8331.
Hours Open: 12:30–4:30 p.m.
Angel's Attic, set in a two-story, 1895 Victorian house, displays antique dollhouses, miniaturized Colonial mansions, dolls and toys. There's also a wooden version of the nursery rhyme, "The Old Woman Who Lived in a Shoe." Every little girl will love this whimsical museum. Admission for seniors 65 and over, $3. General admission: $4.

J. Paul Getty Museum ★★★★★

17985 Pacific Coast Highway, Malibu, 90265, ☎ (310) 458-2003.
Hours Open: 10 a.m.–5 p.m.
Oil magnate J. Paul Getty built this replica of a first-century Roman villa to house one of the finest collections of Greek and Roman antiquities in the U.S. Located on a bluff overlooking the Pacific Ocean, the museum boasts a sunny, peaceful setting that is as beautiful as the Greek vases and sculpture, Renaissance paintings, Old Masters' drawings, illuminated manuscripts and other vast holdings inside. The J. Paul Getty Trust is constantly purchasing new works for the museum, and recent acquisitions include "The Abduction of Europa" and "Daniel and Cyrus Before the Idol Bel" by Rembrandt. In addition to its exhibits, the museum offers a splendid lecture series featuring renowned experts on the arts and antiquities. Admission to the

museum is free, but limited parking space makes parking reservations essential. If you don't have a reservation, you can arrive by bicycle, motorcycle, taxi or bus, but walk-in traffic is not permitted. (Note that a new home for the museum is currently under construction in the Brentwood Hills. The scheduled completion date is 1997, at which time all holdings—except the antiquities—will be moved to the new facility.) Free admission.

Santa Monica Heritage Museum

2612 Main Street, Santa Monica, ☎ *(310) 392-8537.*
Hours Open: 11 a.m.–4 p.m.

Displays depict the history and culture of Southern California (yes, Virginia, Southern California really DOES have a culture). Restored period rooms show how life was from the 1890s to 1930s. Free admission.

Santa Monica Museum of Flying   ★★★

2772 Donald Douglas Loop North, Santa Monica, 90405, ☎ *(213) 392-8822.*
Hours Open: 10 a.m.–5 p.m.
At the Santa Monica Airport.

This three-story museum houses historic and antique planes and contains extensive displays on the history of flight. There's an interactive area for kids called Airventure, video kiosks showing planes in action and a model display featuring presentations on the history of flight. On weekends, curators often take some of their vintage planes out for a flight, weather permitting, and you're welcome to watch the action. General admission: $4.

Historical Sites

Historic Adamson House

23200 Pacific Coast Highway, Malibu, ☎ *(310) 456-8432.*

The Historic Adamson House, built in the 1920s (not exactly ancient, but old by California standards), is a nice example of a Moorish-Spanish Colonial-style residence adorned with colorful tile, handcrafted wood and ironwork. Tours are offered Wednesday–Saturday, 11 a.m.–3 p.m. General admission: $2.

Tours

California Wine Tours   ★★

2554 Lincoln Boulevard, #525, Marina Del Rey, 90291, ☎ *(310) 305-1475.*
All-day tours to Southern California wine country include winery tours, wine tasting, and al fresco lunch.

Heli USA

3200 Airport Avenue, Suite 6, Santa Monica, 90405, ☎ *(800) 443-5487.*
At the Santa Monica Airport.

For something different, try a romantic dinner flight or tour on a helicopter from Heli USA, the oldest helicopter touring company in California. Experience the golden coastline at sunset or the L.A. skyline at twilight. Both tours and commuter service are available. Prices range from $89 to $249, and some tours include limo service and dinner. Heli USA also flies out of Van Nuys.

Paramount Ranch

Cornell Road, off Karen Road, Malibu, ☎ *(818) 889-0781.*
Hours Open: dawn–dusk

Once owned by Paramount Studios and used as a Western movie set, the ranch can be toured and the area hiked. Rangers lead special naturalist programs; call for details.

Sunset Sail Charter Company ★★★

Marina Del Rey Channel, Marina Del Rey, 90291, ☎ *(310) 578-9248.*
Private charters on yachts from 25 to 120 feet long. A two-hour, romantic sunset cruise on a 34-foot sloop through the Marina Del Rey channel includes a candlelit dinner with wine or a bit of bubbly. A pre-dinner champagne cruise for an hour-and-a-half with your sweetheart starts at $99 and promises a perfect start to a special evening.

Parks and Gardens

Admiralty Park

Admiralty Way, Marina del Rey.
This small park is perfect for the fitness enthusiast, with an 18-station, self-guided exercise facility, a bike path and a one-mile-loop jogging path. If you don't need the exercise, sit on the lawn and watch the boats go by.

Mother's Beach ★★

Off Palawan, near Admiralty Way, Marina del Rey.
This is the perfect beach for families. The water is shallow, the beach is sandy, there are lifeguards on duty, and there are picnic tables and volleyball nets nearby. Windsurfing is also good in this vicinity, and there's a boating lagoon. Moms don't have to worry about their kids—well, not as MUCH, anyway—and can lay back and catch some rays while the kids play.

Santa Monica Beach ★★★

Pacific Coast Highway, Santa Monica, 90401, ☎ *(310) 394-3266.*
Its central location and wide expanse of sand make this one of the city's most popular beaches. Playgrounds, volleyball, the pier and the promenade all enhance the popular pastime of people watching.

Solstice Canyon Park ★★★

Santa Monica Mountains above Malibu, Malibu, ☎ *(800) 533-7275.*
This park is the site of the Solstice International Trail, dubbed the best nature trail in the Santa Monica Mountains. A round-trip hike is approximately three miles, and interpretive pamphlets are available in English, Spanish, Korean, Japanese, Tagalog, Cantonese and Mandarin. The shady, smooth trail is fairly easy-going, and will accommodate strollers or wheelchairs. Along the way, you'll learn all about the flora and fauna of the area.

Venice Municipal Beach ★★★

1531 Ocean Front Walk, Venice, 90291, ☎ *(310) 394-3266.*
This is the zany beach often viewed on television, where bodybuilders demonstrate their muscles, roller skaters perform and artists hawk their wares. Bikes and skates can be rented.

Will Rogers State Historic Park ★★★

14253 Sunset Boulevard, Pacific Palisades, 90272, ☎ *(310) 454-8212.*
Hours Open: 8 a.m.–6 p.m.
This 185-acre park includes the two-story ranch home of Will Rogers, which contains the original furniture and a collection of Western and Indian art; a museum of Rogers' memorabilia; and picnic areas, hiking

trails, and polo grounds where matches are played on the weekend. Tours available. Admission price is $3 per carload.

Zuma Beach County Park ★★★

30050 Pacific Coast Highway, Malibu, ☎ *(310) 457-9891.*
A long and sandy beach, ample parking and good waves make Zuma Beach a favorite site for a day at the beach or catching a few waves. Visitors will also find volleyball and a playground for the little ones.

Santa Monica for Kids

Kids will love riding the carousel and other rides on the Santa Monica Pier, and there's a satisfying mix of culture and fun at Kids' World, a series of live performances offered at the Santa Monica Place Mall on Friday mornings. Here, kids explore various cultures of the world through presentations of music, dance and theatre. There's also kids' fare from the Actors' Repertory Theatre, which performs children's classics and holiday offerings at the Santa Monica Playhouse. Call for a current schedule of events.

Beaches are a natural attraction for kids, and they're bound to enjoy learning about sea creatures at the Cabrillo Marine Aquarium in San Pedro, where 35 saltwater tanks contain live animals that run the gamut from anemones to sharks. Tidepool tours on the nearby beach are great fun for families.

Santa Monica Pier ★★

End of Colorado Avenue, Santa Monica, ☎ *(310) 458-8900.*
Built in 1908, the pier offers the usual fishing and ocean gazing, and kids of all sizes will enjoy the horses on the world-renowned carousel, bumper cars, a penny arcade and—coming soon—a roller coaster and an 11-story ferris wheel. There's also a children's park and play area, pitch and toss games, and lots of dining options that serve everything from seafood to hot dogs. Free admission.

Santa Monica Playhouse ★★

1211 4th Street, Santa Monica, 90401, ☎ *(310) 394-9779.*
Here, the Actors' Reperatory Theatre presents the "Best Children's Theatre in Los Angeles" according to *L.A. Parent.*

Events

Christmas Boat Parade ★★

Main Channel, Marina del Rey, ☎ *(310) 821-7614.*
This annual parade of boats adorned with Christmas lights and other holiday parpharnalia celebrated its 32nd anniversary in 1994. Each year, there is a different theme that's reflected in the vessels' decorations and music. Best viewing points are from Burton Chace Park, Mindanao Way, or from Fisherman's Village on Fiji Way. Free admission.

Sports and Recreation

Since the beach is synonymous with perfect bodies, there are lots of beach city options for sculpting yourself into a model of physical fitness. Known for its state-of-the-art equipment is Malibu Health, one of that community's tonier gyms. One of the top fitness clubs in Santa Monica (there are two locations here, plus one in Manhattan Beach) is the Spectrum Club, which supplies the requisite personal trainer in addition to everything else you need to get in shape.

Marina del Rey is one of the boating capitals of L.A. County, and a good place to rent a canoe or sailboat, take a scenic harbor cruise or whale watching excursion, or brush up on your boating skills in a variety of classes. Windsurfing is also popular here, and various boating and sailing events are on the calendar throughout the year, including the California Cup Sailing Regatta, a Marina del Rey to San Diego sailing race, and the summer Wednesday night Sunset Series of sailing races.

You'll find similar offerings in nearly every city along the coast.

Bluewater Sailing
13505 Bali Way, Santa Monica, ☎ *(310) 823-5545.*
Offers a full range of beginning and advanced sailing classes, as well as private lessons. Boats may be rented on an hourly or daily basis, or you can opt for one of Bluewater's day-sails or Catalina Island cruises.

California Sailing Academy
14025 Panay Way, Marina del Rey, ☎ *(310) 821-3433.*
This school offers classes in basic sailing, advanced sailing and racing. Group, private and semi-private courses are conducted and a fleet of craft from 14 to 40 feet is available for rental or charter.

Gold's Gym
360 Hampton Drive, Santa Monica, ☎ *(310) 392-6004.*
This self-proclaimed "mecca of bodybuilding" is the grandaddy of all Gold's Gyms, appropriately set near Muscle Beach in Venice. If you don't want to pay the fee to work out here, wander on down to Muscle Beach and see how the professionals do it. You'll either be inspired or humiliated, but it's quite a show.

Marina Tennis Association
13199 Mindanao Way, Marina del Rey, 90292, ☎ *(310) 822-2255.*
Five pros offer private and group lessons, and a round-robin service will match players up for singles or doubles every day except Tuesday and Thursday.

Nissan Open Golf Tournament
Riviera Country Club, Pacific Palisades, 90272, ☎ *(800) 752-6736.*
This golf tournament, managed by the Los Angeles Junior Chamber of Commerce, is the oldest civic-sponsored event on the PGA Tour (it celebrated its 69th anniversary in 1995). The Riviera Country Club in Pacific Palisades is the site of the February event, with proceeds going to various charitable causes. The open includes a Celebrity-Am tournament and a Pro-Am tournament.

Surfrider Beach
23200 Pacific Coast Highway, Malibu, 90263, ☎ *(818) 706-1310.*
Part of the Malibu Lagoon State Beach, this popular spot just north of the Malibu Pier is favored by surfers for longboarding. The adjacent lagoon is a sanctuary for birds and affords pleasant hiking.

Santa Monica: Music, Dance and Theatre

Music

Los Angeles Baroque Orchestra   ★ ★ ★
2554 Lincoln Boulevard, Marina Del Rey, 90291, ☎ *(310) 578-7698.*
This respected orchestra's season features seven programs, held in churches, rather than concert halls, to provide an atmosphere of inti-

macy between artist and audience. Performances are at the First Pres-
byterian Church in Santa Monica and Holliston United Methodist
Church in Pasadena; many concerts include nationally-known guest
artists.

Santa Monica Civic Light Opera

601 Pico Boulevard, Santa Monica, 90405, ☎ *(310) 458-5939.*
A light-hearted, high-spirited company presents such work as *Il Tro-
vatore* by Guiseppe Verdi.

Theatre

Cornerstone Theater Company   ★ ★ ★

1653 18th Street, Santa Monica, 90404, ☎ *(310) 449-1700.*
This highly-acclaimed theater company settled in Los Angeles in
1992, following five years of rural community-based projects and a
10,000-mile national tour.

Venice Playwright's Festival   ★ ★ ★

3116 Second Street, Santa Monica, 90405, ☎ *(310) 392-6529.*
The Powerhouse Theatre presents this December event.

Santa Monica: Nightlife

One of the most happening places to hang out in Santa Monica after
dark is the colorful Third Street Promenade, a busy complex full of street
performers, sidewalk cafes, upscale pool halls, restaurants and shops that
stay open late on weekends. Especially popular here are Gotham Hall,
which is cashing in big time on the new billiards craze; Legends, a massive
sports bar where (for some unknown reason) lots of Chicago Bulls fans
hang out; and Renaissance, with 10,000 square feet of entertainment space.

The Upfront Comedy Showcase, a popular comedy club on the promenade, was damaged in the January, 1994 earthquake and ended up moving
around the corner to *123 Broadway*, where its new state-of-the-art improv
theatre features a variety of acts such as the Amazing Onionheads and the
resident PostModernaires, the Spolin Players, the Transformers and the
Deadpan Handlers.

Author's Tip

*If you prefer take-out entertainment, stop by Vidiots (302 Pico Boulevard,
Santa Monica) for one of L.A.'s finest selections of experimental, independent
and foreign videos, plus a variety of mainstream stuff. Something for everyone here.*

Alligator Lounge

3321 Pico Boulevard, Santa Monica, ☎ *(310) 449-1844.*
If you are in a fire-engine red mood to celebrate something, the decor
here will match. Original music of every style from every corner of the
planet is the specialty, with performers like Hummingbird Tito and
Tarantula, the Blue Bonnets and the Zydeco Party Band—and there's
dancing, too! The Cajun kitchen features traditional Louisiana cuisine
and the bar serves beer and wine. For dinner reservations, ☎ *(310)
449-1843.*

Broadway Bar and Grill

1460 Third Street Promenade, Santa Monica, ☎ *(310) 393-4211.*

Hours Open: 7:30–11:30 p.m.
A comfortable spot to catch some no-cover, first-rate entertainment in the heart of Santa Monica.

Chez Jay

657 Ocean Avenue, Santa Monica, 90402, ☎ (310) 395-1741.
Los Angeles magazine calls Chez Jay the city's "Best Neighborhood Bar." Writers and artists, construction workers and Henry Kissinger are among the cross-section of people who enjoy the unpretentious, friendly surroundings of this beach area joint.

Endless Summer Sportsbar

300 Washington Boulevard, Marina del Rey, ☎ (310) 821-3577.
Billed as the place "where everyone really does know your name," this sports bar offers plenty of options for your viewing pleasure, with three satellite dishes bringing down programs to two big screens and 21 TV monitors. For the more active, there is Trivia, QB1, light pool tables and two outdoor patios for socializing. The restaurant also offers a full menu.

Gotham Hall

1431 Third Street Promenade, Santa Monica, ☎ (310) 394-8865.
Basically a billiards club, this has fast become the new hot spot for the stars. The 10,000-square-foot club includes 14 pool tables and a 50-seat restaurant, and has an eclectic green and purple interior with antler chairs, snail-shaped settees and snakelike glass rocks. Celebs get escorted in through a private entrance; you get to go through the plain front door. Open seven days a week until 2 a.m.

Harvelle's ★★

1432 Fourth Street, Santa Monica, ☎ (310) 395-1676.
The Westside's oldest blues club presents live blues shows nightly with performers such as Crossroads, The King Brothers, Earl Alexander and the Buffalo Soldiers. Dancing is also available. There is a two-drink minimum, but no cover charge on Sunday and Monday; cover varies on other nights.

Improv, The ★★

321 Santa Monica Boulevard, Santa Monica, ☎ (310) 394-8664.
The Improv, a showcase for some of the country's top comedy acts for nearly 20 years, has practically reached legendary status in L.A. Cover charge varies, so call ahead. Another location in West Hollywood, at 8162 Melrose ☎ *(213) 651-2583.*

McCabe's Guitar Shop ★★★

3101 Pico Boulevard, Santa Monica, ☎ (310) 828-4497.
First-rate folk, acoustic rock, bluegrass, rhythm and blues, and jazz is served up at McCabe's in an intimate concert-hall setting. Headliners here often include top stars such as Laura Nyro or Richie Havens, and the entertainment here is so good that concerts at McCabe's Guitar Shop were listed by *Los Angeles* magazine as one of the "300 Reasons Not to Leave L.A." There's no alcohol served, so all ages are welcome. Open from 8 p.m. Friday-Sunday.

Rebecca's

2025 Pacific Avenue, Venice, ☎ (310) 306-6266.
Singles galore (looking to be doubles?) hang out and drink margaritas at Rebecca's, which has some of the best in town. It's always a mob

scene here, but after a few drinks, everyone's swaying to the canned mariachi music and having a good ol' time.

Renaissance   ★★

1212 Third Street Promenade, Santa Monica, ☎ *(310) 587-0766.*
A spacious $1.5 million, 10,000 square-foot night club with a restaurant, bar, live performance stage and dance space, from the creators of the Spy Club in D.C. and the Surf Club in New York. Fashionable attire is requested, and there is a cover charge after 9 p.m. unless you have dinner reservations. "The hottest place to hang west of the 405," and there are always stars either schmoozing or performing. In a word, Renaissance is HOT.

St. Mark's

23 Windward Avenue, Venice, ☎ *(310) 452-2222.*
Listen to R&B, blues and jazz in a supper-club atmosphere Tuesdays through Sundays. Dining and two full bars.

Typhoon

3221 Donald Douglas Loop South, Santa Monica, 90405, ☎ *(310) 390-6565.*
This new spot at the Santa Monica airport offers great tropical drinks and a runway location that'll make you feel like you're really on vacation. Opens Monday-Friday at 11:30 a.m., Saturday at 5:30 p.m., and Sunday Brunch 11 a.m.

Upfront Comedy Showcase

123 Broadway, Santa Monica, ☎ *(310) 319-3477.*
Improv is always on the menu here, and many of the regulars are veterans of Chicago's Second City or the Groundling Theater. The house is always packed, so reservations are necessary. New groups perform on Tuesday and Wednesday nights at 8; the regulars take the stage Thursday through Saturday at 8 and 10. Cover varies.

Santa Monica: Shopping

In Santa Monica, **Montana Avenue** has loads of exclusive shops, including **Statement on Montana** *(1302 Montana)*, which carries unique gifts such as hand-painted ceramics by local artists and imported items. Other stores offer designer clothing, jewelry and accessories.

When you've shopped yourself out, take a break at **Emack & Bolio's** *(625C Montana Avenue)*, a Boston import serving natural gourmet ice creams with luscious-sounding names such as Kahlua Fudge Swirl, Coffee Heath Bar, Key Lime Pie, and Almond Madness. (The fat-conscious can opt for a power drink at the Smoothie Bar, where yogurt, sorbet, fresh fruit and protein powder are available.) Or, simply stake out a table at one of Montana Avenue's many casual cafes or coffeehouses and have a cup of latte and a pastry while you watch a host of wanna-be industry types hang out.

The three-level **Santa Monica Place Mall** *(300 Broadway)* also offers unique shopping opportunities as well as access to its two "anchor" department stores, The Broadway and Robinson's-May.

Antique-seekers should plan a visit to the **Santa Monica Antique Market** *(1607 Lincoln Boulevard)*, and if you're a lover of books on art, architecture and design, don't miss **Hennessey&Ingalls**, located along the Third Street Promenade. Another Promenade favorite is the **Puzzle Zoo**, which carries all sorts of challenges for the puzzle aficionado, including an 8000-piece jigsaw that will keep you busy for a very long time.

Chefs of some of the most popular Santa Monica restaurants frequent the Santa Monica Farmers Market, held on Wednesdays at 2nd and Arizona. Terrific produce is the main drawing card.

Marina del Rey's **Fisherman's Village**, overlooking the main channel at the end of Fiji Way, has the typical tourist-oriented gift and souvenir shops (bonuses include the free Sunday afternoon Waterside Concert series, and a schedule of holiday events), and **Waterside Center** *(4736 Admiralty Way)* offers everything from a natural foods store to a specialty tobacco shop.

And just to show that all California beaches are up with the times, any visitors' guide describing virtually any shopping area in any beach city in Southern California will point out that their shopping districts are the perfect place to "sip cappuccino and.... " (you fill in the blank).

Santa Monica: Where to Stay

Culver City

Hotels and Resorts

Ramada Airport North $70–$90   ★ ★

6333 Bristol Parkway
☎ *(800) 321-5575, (310) 670-3200, FAX: 310-641-8925.*
Single: $70–$80. Double: $80–$90.
This hotel, located two miles from LAX, has a shopping center adjacent and a jogging course nearby. Suites include a wet bar and refrigerator. Amenities: pool, exercise room, Jacuzzi, family plan, conference facilities. 260 rooms. Credit Cards: V, MC, A.

Red Lion Airport $80–$115   ★ ★ ★

6161 Centinela Avenue
☎ *(800) 547-8010, (310) 649-1776, FAX: 310-649-4411.*
Single: $80–$115. Double: $80–$115.
Formerly the Pacifica Hotel, this property is located three miles from LAX, with shuttles running to the airport every 15 minutes. The large rooms are soundproofed and rates include a breakfast buffet and morning newspaper. Amenities: pool, exercise room, Jacuzzi, sauna, family plan, conference facilities, complimentary airport pickup service. 368 rooms. Credit Cards: V, MC, DC, A.

Malibu

Bed and Breakfast

Malibu Country Inn $95–$155   ★ ★

6506 Westward Beach Road
☎ *(800) 386-6787, (310) 457-9622, FAX: 310-457-1349.*
Single: $95–$155. Double: $95–$155.
Cape Cod-style country inn located on a bluff overlooking Zuma Beach. Complimentary full breakfast included. Lots of romantic charm here; request suite 17 for its privacy and fireplace. Amenities: beach location, pool, balcony or patio. 16 rooms. Credit Cards: V, MC, DC, A.

Inns

Malibu Beach Inn   **$130–$275**   ★★★

22878 Pacific Coast Highway
☎ *(800) 462-5428, (310) 456-6444, FAX: 310-456-1499.*
Single: $130–$275. Double: $130–$275.

Snuggle up next to your fireplace, partake of wine and cheese, or
enjoy a movie in the privacy of your room at this romantic inn near
the Malibu Pier. Six rooms have private Jacuzzis set onto a deck with
sweeping ocean views. The perfect L.A. getaway spot, and situated
right on the sand for beach lovers. Full breakfast buffet included.
Amenities: beach location, pool, exercise room, sauna, private spas,
balcony or patio, family plan, conference facilities, complimentary airport pickup service. 47 rooms. Credit Cards: CB, V, MC, DC, A.

Marina del Rey

Hotels and Resorts

Best Western Jamaica Bay   **$105–$145**   ★★★

4175 Admiralty Way
☎ *(800) 528-1234, (310) 823-5333, FAX: 310-823-1325.*
Single: $105–$145. Double: $105–$145.

One of the few hotels right on the beach in the Los Angeles area, this
property attracts a younger crowd and families with kids. The atmosphere is casual; weekends are lively. Amenities: beach location, pool,
Jacuzzi, balcony or patio, conference facilities. 42 rooms. Credit Cards:
CB, V, MC, DC, A.

Doubletree Marina del Rey   **$135–$145**   ★★★

4100 Admiralty Way
☎ *(800) 528-0444, (310) 301-3000, FAX: 310-301-6890.*
Single: $135. Double: $145.

Overlooking Marina del Rey Harbor, this nine-story hotel includes
the top-floor Skyfan Lounge with spectacular views of the city. It's
especially good for business meetings, with on-site meeting planners,
teleconferencing capabilities and meeting rooms of various sizes.
Guests enjoy 24-hour room service and transportation to LAX. The
Marina City Club's athletic facilities are available to hotel guests.
Amenities: beach location, pool, sailing, balcony or patio, family plan,
conference facilities, club floor, business services, complimentary airport pickup service. 300 rooms. Credit Cards: CB, V, MC, DC, A.

Holiday Inn Marina   **$79–$99**   ★★

737 Washington Boulevard
☎ *(800) 821-8277, (310) 821-4455, FAX: 310-821-8098.*
Single: $79–$99. Double: $79–$99.

Located adjacent to the marina, this small, all-suite hotel offers the
usual amenities, including a complimentary continental breakfast and
in-room refrigerators and microwaves. It stands out from your average Holiday Inn because of its interesting "boutiquiness" and smaller
size. Amenities: pool, health club, Jacuzzi, sauna, balcony or patio,
conference facilities. 52 rooms. Credit Cards: V, MC, A.

Marina International   **$115–$295**   ★★★

4200 Admiralty Way
☎ *(800) 822-4000, (310) 301-2000, FAX: 310-301-6687.*
Single: $115–$130. Double: $155–$295.

Located near Venice Beach, shopping and water sports, this rambling property is within sight of the marina, but is actually surrounded by greenery and busy streets. The inside rooms with terraces offer the most quiet. The bungalows, some with loft areas, are exotic. Amenities: pool, Jacuzzi, houses, cottages or bungalows, balcony or patio, family plan, conference facilities, complimentary airport pickup service. 135 rooms. Credit Cards: CB, V, MC, DC, A.

Marina del Rey Hotel $130–$215 ★★★
13534 Bali Way
☎ *(800) 882-4000, (310) 301-1000, FAX: 310-301-8167.*
Single: $130–$215. Double: $130–$215.
This property is surrounded by water on three sides with great views of the main channel. Appropriately enough, the decor is nautical. The patio rooms are the nicest. Amenities: pool, balcony or patio, family plan, conference facilities, complimentary airport pickup service. 160 rooms. Credit Cards: CB, V, MC, DC, A.

Marriott Marina del Rey $99 ★★★
13480 Maxella Avenue
☎ *(800) 228-9290, (310) 822-8555, FAX: 310-823-2996.*
Single: $99. Double: $99.
Located near Fisherman's Village and Venice Beach, this hotel is the farthest from the water of all the properties in town. That's really the only quibble with this friendly, well-run hotel. Guests have complimentary privileges at a nearby health club. Amenities: beach location, pool, Jacuzzi, balcony or patio, family plan, conference facilities, complimentary airport pickup service. 283 rooms. Credit Cards: CB, V, MC, DC, A.

Ritz-Carlton Marina del Rey $225–$525 ★★★★★
4375 Admiralty Way
☎ *(800) 241-3333, (310) 823-1700, FAX: 310-823-2403.*
Single: $225–$525. Double: $225–$525.
All the rooms in this fabulous newer hotel overlook the marina and have Italian marble bathrooms, honor bars with refrigerators, TVs with free movie channels, bathrobes, hairdryers and scales. The service is befitting of the Ritz-Carlton name. The business services are especially excellent, with in-room facilities for FAX and computers, a multilingual staff, translation services, secretarial support and more than 12,000 square feet of meeting space. Recreational facilities include excellent on-site tennis facilities, a health club and a beautiful pool and lounge area. The continental breakfast, midmorning snack, afternoon tea and hors d'oeuvres, and an evening cocktail are complimentary. An absolutely lovely place, but a bit stuffy and refined for its beach location. Casual types—especially those on a budget—would probably be happier elsewhere. Ranked restaurant: **The Dining Room**. Amenities: beach location, pool, tennis, health club, Jacuzzi, sauna, private spas, balcony or patio, family plan, conference facilities, club floor, business services. 306 rooms. Credit Cards: CB, V, MC, DC, A.

Santa Monica

Bed and Breakfast
Channel Road Inn $95–$200 ★★★
219 West Channel Road
☎ *(310) 459-1920, FAX: 310-454-9920.*

Single: $95–$200. Double: $95–$200.

This bed and breakfast is housed in a 1910 mansion. Although it's located only one block from the beach, only three rooms have water views. All guest rooms are furnished with white wicker furniture, canopy beds, and down pillows. A continental breakfast, afternoon tea and wine, and hors d'oeuvres are complimentary. The atmosphere is cheery and cozy, like a trip to grandma's. Amenities: Jacuzzi, balcony or patio. 14 rooms. Credit Cards: V, MC, A.

Hotels and Resorts

Guest Quarters Suites   **$170–$210**   ★★★

1707 Fourth Street
☎ *(800) 424-2900, (310) 395-3332, FAX: 310-452-7399.*
Single: $170–$190. Double: $190–$210.
One-bedroom suites have living rooms and balconies overlooking an atrium. Some rooms have an ocean view (the beach is four blocks away); all have coffee makers. Amenities: pool, exercise room, Jacuzzi, sauna, balcony or patio, conference facilities, business services. 253 rooms. Credit Cards: V, MC, A.

Holiday Inn   **$105–$165**   ★★

120 Colorado Avenue
☎ *(800) 465-4329, (310) 451-0676, FAX: 310-393-7145.*
Single: $105–$150. Double: $120–$165.
This hotel is located near the beach and Santa Monica Pier. Amenities include complimentary continental breakfast and morning newspaper. Some rooms have fully equipped kitchens, others have microwaves and refrigerators. The hotel was recently renovated. Amenities: beach location, pool, family plan, conference facilities. 132 rooms. Credit Cards: V, MC, A.

Holiday Inn Bayview Plaza   **$110–$150**   ★★★

530 Pico Boulevard
☎ *(800) 465-4329, (310) 399-9344, FAX: 310-399-2504.*
Single: $110–$140. Double: $110–$150.
This hotel, renovated in 1992, has an attractive, four-story atrium lobby. Most rooms have a view of the ocean, four blocks away. Amenities: pool, exercise room, Jacuzzi, private spas, balcony or patio, hair salon, conference facilities. 309 rooms. Credit Cards: CB, V, MC, DC, A.

Loews Santa Monica Hotel   **$200–$355**   ★★★★

1700 Ocean Avenue
☎ *(800) 223-0888, (310) 458-6700, FAX: 310-458-6761.*
Single: $200–$355. Double: $205–$355.
Loews Santa Monica is definitely a first-class establishment, and all the accommodations here are deluxe with bleached wood armoires, art on the walls, pink or light green carpets, three phones, minibars and large baths with separate dressing areas. There are even black and white TVs in the bathrooms. The staff and service are efficient and friendly. The Victorian-style resort is highlighted by a dazzling five-story atrium, and the ocean views are magnificent. Ranked restaurant: **Riva**. Amenities: beach location, pool, health club, Jacuzzi, sauna, balcony or patio, conference facilities, business services. 352 rooms. Credit Cards: CB, V, MC, DC, A.

Miramar Sheraton   **$205–$800**   ★★★

101 Wilshire Boulevard

☎ *(800) 325-3535, (310) 576-7777, FAX: 310-458-7912.*
Single: $205–$800. Double: $205–$800.

Despite a major renovation, it's still not as splendid as Loews Santa
Monica. However, it does have tradition going for it, and the staff
treats the guests well. The nicest rooms are in the poolside bungalows, which come complete with big-screen TVs, VCRs and CD players and cost the most. Amenities: beach location, pool, houses,
cottages or bungalows, balcony or patio, family plan, conference facilities. 305 rooms. Credit Cards: CB, V, MC, DC, A.

Pacific Shore   **$110–$140**   ★★

1819 Ocean Avenue
☎ *(800) 662-8711, (310) 451-8711, FAX: 310-394-6657.*
Single: $110–$130. Double: $120–$140.

Across from the Civic Auditorium, one block from the beach, this
hotel was renovated in 1993. Rooms, which offer ocean or mountain
views, have hairdryers and safes. Complimentary local shuttle service
is included. Amenities: pool, Jacuzzi, sauna, balcony or patio, family
plan, conference facilities. 168 rooms. Credit Cards: CB, V, MC, DC, A.

Radisson Huntley Hotel   **$115–$125**   ★★★

1111 Second Street
☎ *(800) 333-3333, (310) 394-5454, FAX: 310-458-9776.*
Single: $115. Double: $125.

This modern, 18-story hotel is one block from both the beach and
Wilshire Boulevard. Amenities include a rooftop restaurant with an
ocean view, a gift shop and a coffee shop. Nothing really special here,
but it's in a good location for getting to the beach or to Santa Monica
shopping. Tours of local attractions leave daily from the hotel. Amenities: hair salon, family plan, conference facilities. 213 rooms. Credit
Cards: V, MC, A.

Shangri-La   **$110–$160**   ★★★

1301 Ocean Avenue
☎ *(800) 345-7829, (310) 394-2791, FAX: 310-451-3351.*
Single: $110–$160. Double: $110–$160.

The attractive Art Deco design and a convenient location across from
the beach and Palisades Park make this spot popular with celebrities
and show biz folk, who like its suites and studios. Unfortunately,
there is no pool. A nice alternative to the bustling atmosphere at some
of the city's larger hotels. Continental breakfast is included in the
rates. Amenities: beach location, balcony or patio. 55 rooms. Credit
Cards: CB, V, MC, DC, A.

Shutters on the Beach   **$260–$1900**   ★★★★

1 Pico Boulevard
☎ *(800) 334-9000, (310) 458-0030, FAX: 310-458-4589.*
Single: $260–$1900. Double: $260–$1900.

A newer luxury hotel, built right on the beach, which derives its name
from the New England-style shutters on all the windows. Spacious,
beautifully-decorated guest rooms feature whirlpools and classy modern furnishings, and most offer ocean views. A magnificent beach is
right in front, plus there is a great sundeck, pool and lounge area for
parties and receptions that has a splendid view. The restaurants are
also very good—especially One Pico. A true class act enhanced by little touches like the china designed by well-known California artist
Beverlye Hyman. Ranked restaurant: **One Pico**. Amenities: beach

location, pool, health club, Jacuzzi, sauna, conference facilities, business services. 198 rooms. Credit Cards: V, MC, DC, A.

Santa Monica: Where to Eat

If you want great seafood, go to **Gladstone's 4 Fish** in Malibu, which has some of the best at any beach, plus you can get a look at Spike the lobster, a sort of spiny mascot who lives in a special tank at the restaurant (they even named a drink after him). A huge controversy recently erupted around Spike when animal rights activists began to picket the restaurant and raise money to have Spike "freed" and returned to his "home" in the North Atlantic. Actress Mary Tyler Moore, citing her belief that Spike would "prefer" to be back home, donated $1000 to the cause, and United Airlines offered to fly Spike to the East Coast for free. So-called "lobster experts" predicted that Spike would never survive the trip East, and the restaurant was adamant about keeping him, but at least one patron offered his own opinion: "Cook 'im." Spike, who was probably oblivious to the whole matter, continues to bring in the customers. Only in L.A.

While the demise of John Sedlar's long-awaited Bikini, which opened in Santa Monica after Sedlar closed his popular St. Estephe in Manhattan, was a bit of a surprise, **Abiquiu**, also owned by Sedlar, is now in its place, and early reviews indicate it's off to a better start than its predecessor.

Wolfgang Puck has turned out to be the Henry Ford of trendy eating spots in L.A.. Whether it's **Spago** (the real thing), Spago, the frozen "pissa" (as Puck pronounces it), Chinese, nouvelle, or seafood, he continues to crank them out. Puck recently annexed another restaurant to his rapidly-expanding empire in the form of the new **Wolfgang Puck Cafe**, which occupies the space left vacant by Luma on Montana Avenue. It's as casual and trendy as most of Puck's other establishments, and features the requisite designer pizzas and pastas.

In funky Venice, a real sleeper is **Joe's**, a tiny little cafe offering superb California-French cuisine. With its new look and expansion, the ambience now lives up to the very fine food, and the restaurant has added more tables to its original 16.

Also in Venice is **72 Market Street**, owned by actor Dudley Moore and producer-director Tony Bill. As a sidelight to their successful restaurant, the two recently instituted a take-out service called "Just Plane Food," whereby you can stop on your way to LAX and pick up a meal to go that will be infinitely more satisfying than airline food. Recent choices included Maine lobster salad or grilled marinated chicken.

Malibu

American

Bambu	**$$$**	★★★

3835 Cross Creek Road, ☎ *(310) 456-5464.*
At the Country Mart.
Lunch: 11:30 a.m.–3 p.m., entrees $6–$10.
Dinner: 5:30–10 p.m., entrees $13–$30.
At the Country Mart.
In a day when new restaurants are a dangerous venture, Bambu seems destined to beat the odds. Enthusiastically received from the moment

it opened, the kitchen surprisingly delivers on menu items as varied as sushi, steak and mashed potatoes, and Chilean sea bass. Pleasant, warm—if a bit wobbly—service adds to the experience. Vegetarians will be pleased by some satisfying choices. Sunday brunch, 11:30 a.m.–3 p.m. Closed: Mon. Features: Sunday brunch, full bar, rated wine cellar, late dining. Reservations recommended. Credit Cards: CB, V, MC, DC, A.

Geoffrey's $$$ ★ ★ ★

27400 Pacific Coast, ☎ (310) 457-1519.
Lunch: 12 a.m.–5 p.m., entrees $10–$18.
Dinner: 5–10 p.m., entrees $12–$28.

The cuisine can be eclectic to a fault, but there are some real taste adventures on the "Tastes of the World" menu. The ambience makes the high prices worth it, even if the food sometimes misses. The $19.00, five-course sampling dinner, served from 5-6:30 p.m. on weeknights, is a great bargain. With its great view of the beach, surrounding gardens and sea breezes, Geoffrey's offers the ultra-Malibu experience—especially on a clear Sunday morning, when brunch is FABulous. Features: splendid view, outside dining, own baking, Sunday brunch, full bar, rated wine cellar, late dining. Reservations recommended. Credit Cards: V, MC, A.

Granita $$$ ★ ★ ★ ★

23725 West Malibu Road, ☎ (310) 456-0488.
Specialties: tagiatelle with sea urchin; pizza with lamb sausage.
Lunch: 11:30 a.m.–2:30 p.m., entrees $13–$20.
Dinner: 6–10:30 p.m., entrees $19–$26.

Wolfgang Puck's newest restaurant, set in the Malibu Colony Shopping Center, started out drawing rave reviews from the nationwide press, but, depending on who you talk to, things may have cooled off considerably since then. On any given day, you might get the fabulous food that made Puck famous, or you might get something substantially less exciting. Puck, himself, isn't usually at the restaurant, of course (he's got too many other projects to oversee), and even though the menu pays homage to the master, what comes out of the kitchen doesn't always hit the mark. The cynical say that in spite of the jazzy ocean-themed decor by Puck's wife Barbara Lazaroff and the superb namesake granita, the whole dining experience here can be BORing. (Insiders say the chicken soup, which is not on the menu, is always good.) Open for lunch three days a week (Wednesday-Friday) and for brunch Saturday and Sunday. Features: outside dining, own baking, Sunday brunch, full bar, rated wine cellar, late dining. Reservations required. Credit Cards: CB, V, MC, DC, A.

Italian

Beau Rivage $$$ ★ ★ ★

26025 Pacific Coast, ☎ (310) 456-5733.
Specialties: fresh seafood; game; homemade pasta.
Dinner: 5–10 p.m., entrees $12–$25.

A charming cottage setting just north of Malibu sometimes outshines the food, but the restaurant has a strong local following, and dishes span the Mediterranean with selections from Spain, Greece, Italy and France. On a clear day, you can see Catalina Island, and there's always soft music to set the mood. Features: splendid view, outside dining, own baking, Sunday brunch, full bar, rated wine cellar, late dining. Reservations required. Credit Cards: CB, V, MC, DC, A.

Tra Di Noi   **$$**   ★★

3835 Cross Creek Road, ☎ *(310) 456-0169.*
Lunch: 12 a.m.–2:30 p.m., entrees $9–$12.
Dinner: 5:30 p.m.–10 p.m., entrees $9–$19.

This pleasant, rustic little dining room offers a variety of culinary possibilities, and nearly all of them are delicious. You can graze on country-style antipasti, opt for flavorful grilled meat or fish, or mix-and-match pastas and sauces to your liking. Some complaints about lagging service, but everything else is topnotch. Features: outside dining, wine and beer only, late dining. Reservations required. Credit Cards: A.

Marina del Rey

Asian

Cafe del Rey   **$$$**   ★★★

4451 Admiralty Way, ☎ *(310) 823-6395.*
Specialties: Thai chicken pizza.
Lunch: 11:30 a.m.–2:30 p.m., entrees $5–$13.
Dinner: 5:30–10 p.m., entrees $15–$29.

The great view is only one reason this restaurant is a winner. Go for exceptional and sophisticated Japanese-French cuisine cooked up by chef Katsuo Nagasawa, and ignore the complaints about uneven service. This restaurant has been likened to what Granita is to Malibu and what Chez Melange is to the South Bay. Next to the Ritz-Carlton, this is the only really serious restaurant in Marina del Rey, and it has the wines to back it up. Non-smoking throughout. Features: splendid view, own baking, Sunday brunch, full bar, rated wine cellar, late dining. Reservations required. Credit Cards: V, MC, A.

Mediterranean

Ritz-Carlton Dining Room   **$$$**   ★★★★

4375 Admiralty Way, ☎ *(310) 823-1700.*
Specialties: rack of lamb.
Dinner: 6–10 p.m., entrees $21–$28.

This, the most formal—and priciest—of the Ritz-Carlton restaurants, offers a new menu of Mediterranean-style cuisine served in a beautiful setting overlooking the marina. The ambience slightly overshadows the food, but you can't go wrong here for a special occasion, and the new chef may soon remedy the few problems in the kitchen. The hotel's other restaurant, the Terrace, serves breakfast, lunch and dinner. Closed: Mon, Sun. Features: splendid view, own baking, full bar, rated wine cellar, late dining. Jacket requested. Reservations recommended. Credit Cards: CB, V, MC, DC, A.

Pacific Palisades

Seafood

Gladstone's 4 Fish   **$$$**   ★★

17300 Pacific Coast Highway, ☎ *(310) 454-3474.*
Specialties: cioppino; live Maine lobster; shrimp scampi.
Lunch: entrees $7–$42.
Dinner: to 11 p.m., entrees $7–$42.

The view's the thing at this restaurant frequented by tourists and locals who come for the bar scene and the live lobster. Nothing too inspired, but a great place to watch the sunset. There's a huge variety of seafood and the prices range from quite inexpensive to a small fortune. Features: splendid view, outside dining, Sunday brunch, full bar, late dining, private dining rooms. Reservations recommended. Credit Cards: CB, V, MC, DC, A.

Santa Monica
American

Carrots $$$ ★★★

2834 Santa Monica Boulevard, ☎ (310) 453-6505.
Specialties: crab cakes.
Lunch: 11:30 a.m.–2:15 p.m., entrees $5–$8.
Dinner: 6–10 p.m., entrees $14–$22.
Excellent California-Asian cuisine created by chef Takashi Iwasaki, formerly of Chinois. This popular restaurant is situated in a mini-mall, has only eight tables, and lacks in the ambience department, but the food is fantastic. The fortysomething crowd is decidedly hip. Closed: Mon. Features: wine and beer only, late dining. Credit Cards: V, MC.

Crocodile Cafe $ ★★

101 Santa Monica Boulevard, ☎ (310) 394-4783.
Specialties: designer pizzas; salads; pasta.
Lunch: from 11:30 a.m., entrees $5–$10.
Dinner: to 12 p.m., entrees $5–$10.
It's noisy, it's packed, and you can expect to wait for what seems like forever, but the menu is full of eclectic little dishes that you'll love almost as much as the trendy scene. Crocodile Cafes are sprouting up all over L.A., and they're a solid hit with the masses. Features: non-smoking area, late dining. Reservations not accepted. Credit Cards: V, MC, A.

DC-3 $$ ★★

2800 Donald Douglas Loop, ☎ (310) 399-2323.
Specialties: fresh seafood; pastas.
Lunch: 11:30 a.m.–2 p.m., entrees $8–$14.
Dinner: 6–10 p.m., entrees $10–$20.
This second-story restaurant that overlooks a real DC-3 and the runway at Clover Field got off to a poor start, but things are improving, and it's become a convivial gathering place. It has also made an effort to appeal to families by offering a special deal for kids Tuesday through Thursday evenings, when, for the price of the adults' meals, kids eat free (and supervised) at a separate table with other kids and then get taken on a tour of the adjacent Museum of Flying by a licensed child-care worker. Meanwhile, mom and dad enjoy a little peace and quiet and linger over dessert or after-dinner drinks at the restaurant. Families must reserve ahead for this service. A jazz combo plays Tuesday through Thursday nights, and there's a prix fixe dinner special for $20. Closed: Mon. Features: splendid view, outside dining, own baking, Sunday brunch, full bar, rated wine cellar, late dining, private dining rooms. Jacket requested. Reservations recommended. Credit Cards: D, CB, V, MC, DC, A.

Gilliland's $$ ★★★

2424 Main Street, ☎ (310) 392-3901.
Specialties: Irish beef stew; goat cheese chicken; grilled meats.
Lunch: 10:30 a.m.–3 p.m., entrees $8–$15.
Dinner: 5:30–10 p.m., entrees $10–$19.

A recent make-over has resulted in a dramatic new interior at Gilli-land's, whose wonderful "California-Irish" atmosphere always has a friendly feel. And the food here is often really good. Everything is homemade, and there are Irish touches in almost every dish, from the hearty soups to the fabulous mashed potatoes. There's a "healthy eating" section to the menu, too, where you can order something high in fiber and/or low in fat and salt. On Wednesday nights, there's a wine tasting and buffet served in the garden, and you can order samples of the wines in the dining room. Lunch served Monday through Friday. Features: outside dining, own baking, Sunday brunch, rated wine cellar, late dining, private dining rooms. Reservations recommended. Credit Cards: V, MC, A.

Ivy at the Shore $$$ ★★★

1541 Ocean Avenue, *(310) 393-3113.*
Specialties: fresh crab cakes; lime chicken salad.
Lunch: from 11:30 a.m., entrees $11–$20.
Dinner: to 10:30 p.m., entrees $15–$24.

This offshoot of The Ivy features large portions of tasty food served on oversized, colorful plates that are just as bright as the scene. All the good food without the attitude of the original, and at least a chance of seeing a celebrity. Don't miss the bar's collection of tropical drinks and the fried Maui onion rings. Very L.A. Features: outside dining, own baking, Sunday brunch, late dining. Jacket requested. Reservations recommended.

L.A. Farm $$ ★★★

3000 Olympic Boulevard, ☎ *(310) 829-0600.*
Lunch: 11:30 a.m.–2:30 p.m., entrees $5–$10.
Dinner: 5:30–10:30 p.m., entrees $10–$20.

L.A. Farm might sound like the name of a children's attraction, but it's actually a rather upscale eatery manned by Jean-Pierre Peiny (formerly at La Serre) and patronized by all sorts of showbiz types. The food is basically French bistro, and nearly everything is homemade. Best of all, prices are extremely reasonable. Open for lunch Monday through Friday. Features: outside dining, own baking, late dining. Reservations recommended. Credit Cards: V, MC, A.

Lincoln Bay Cafe $$$ ★★

1928 Lincoln Boulevard, ☎ *(310) 396-4039.*
Specialties: gumbo; jambalya; soft-shell crab.
Dinner: 5:30–10 p.m., entrees $16–$20.

Chef Eddie Herbert was formerly at the helm of the Ritz Cafe, and his experience shows in the New Orleans-style cooking. There are some really good dishes on the menu here, but the decor's nothing special. Although it may be deserving, the Lincoln Bay Cafe hasn't been discovered by the masses. Closed: Mon. Features: own baking, wine and beer only, late dining. Reservations recommended.

One Pico $$$ ★★★

1 Pico Boulevard, ☎ *(310) 587-1717.*
Specialties: grilled meats and fish.
Lunch: 11:30 a.m.–2:30 p.m., entrees $10–$16.
Dinner: 6–10:30 p.m., entrees $13–$20.
Associated hotel: Shutters on the Beach.

Artfully rendered American/California cuisine, a warm and relaxing atmosphere, and one of the most romantic sunset views in town warrant rave reviews, and problems in the kitchen appear to have been recently ironed out so that the whole dining experience is now first-rate. Reservations may be necessary up to a week in advance for dinner on weekends and for Sunday brunch. Features: own baking, Sunday brunch, wine and beer only, late dining. Reservations required. Credit Cards: V, MC, A.

Pacific Dining Car　　　$$$　　　★★★

2700 Wilshire Boulevard, ☎ *(310) 453-4000.*
Specialties: prime aged beef.
Lunch: 11 a.m.–4 p.m., entrees $13–$23.
Dinner: 4–11 p.m., entrees $15–$34.
The steaks are first-rate at this Santa Monica offshoot of the downtown restaurant, but this one doesn't quite measure up to the original, and prices are pretty outrageous. Open 24 hours. Features: own baking, Sunday brunch, full bar, rated wine cellar, late dining. Reservations recommended. Credit Cards: V, MC, A.

Pedals　　　$$　　　★★★

One Pico, ☎ *(310) 587-1707.*
Specialties: pizzas; pastas; salads.
Lunch: from 11:30 a.m., entrees $10–$20.
Dinner: to 11 p.m., entrees $10–$20.
Associated hotel: Shutters on the Beach.
Pedals is the more casual restaurant at the Shutters on the Beach hotel, specializing in California-style cuisine. Like One Pico, it's right on the beach, making it a pleasant spot for lunch on a sunny afternoon. Features: non-smoking area, late dining. Credit Cards: V, MC, DC, A.

Riva　　　$$$　　　★★★

1700 Ocean Avenue, ☎ *(310) 458-6700.*
Specialties: penne with spicy sausage sauce.
Dinner: 6–11:30 p.m., entrees $19–$27.
Associated hotel: Loews Santa Monica Hotel.
The ocean view is lovely and the setting charming, but there have been too many shake-ups in the kitchen lately to warrant a higher rating for Riva. Some of the food is very good, though—especially the house specials. Closed: Sun. Features: splendid view, outside dining, own baking, full bar, late dining. Reservations recommended. Credit Cards: D, CB, V, MC, DC, A.

Schatzi on Main　　　$$$　　　★★

3110 Main Street, ☎ *(310) 399-4800.*
Lunch: 11:30 a.m.–3 p.m., entrees $4–$14.
Dinner: 6–10 p.m., entrees $11–$24.
Owner Arnold Schwarzenegger must have a lot of financial muscle to keep this turkey afloat (perhaps he's looking for a tax write-off?). After a rocky start-up, Schatzi got almost unanimous rave reviews for its appealing interior and exceptional service, but the food was panned just as unanimously. Since then, it's been one chef after another, never with much improvement. Perhaps Arnold will be rewarded for his patience, but if things don't improve soon, it may be time for the Terminator to terminate Schatzi. Lunch served Monday through Friday. Features: outside dining, Sunday brunch, full bar, late dining. Reservations recommended. Credit Cards: CB, V, MC, DC, A.

Asian

Chinois on Main   **$$$**   ★★★★★

2709 Main Street, ☎ (310) 392-9025.
Specialties: Shanghai lobster; sizzling catfish.
Lunch: 11:30 a.m.–2 p.m., entrees $14–$22.
Dinner: 6–10:30 p.m., entrees $21–$30.

Chinois is another of Wolfgang Puck's Pacific New Wave (the trendy new term for California-Asian cuisine) establishments that have become legend in L.A. Here you'll find the master's touch in some of the most imaginative, delicious Chinese-cum-California dishes you'll find anywhere, and wife Barbara Lazeroff's glamorous interior design is artsy and very chic. The only drawbacks are a noise level that's almost unbearable and service that borders on just plain rude. One of the hottest tickets in town. Open for lunch Wednesday, Thursday and Friday only. Features: own baking, rated wine cellar, late dining. Jacket requested. Reservations required. Credit Cards: CB, V, MC, DC, A.

Typhoon   **$$**   ★★

3221 Donald Douglas Loop, ☎ (310) 390-6565.
At the Santa Monica Airport.
Lunch: 12 a.m.–3 p.m., entrees $8–$15.
Dinner: 5:30–10:30 p.m., entrees $12–$18.
At the Santa Monica Airport.

The menu sounds intriguing, but the pan-Asian food often doesn't exceed the mediocre. The drinks, on the other hand, range from a good selection of American and Asian beers to exotic mixed drinks to a small list of good wines. The interior is spare and modest, but also stylish and warm. Lunch served Monday through Friday. Features: splendid view, Sunday brunch, full bar, rated wine cellar, late dining. Credit Cards: CB, V, MC, DC, A.

Chinese

Madame Wu's Garden   **$$**   ★★

2201 Wilshire Boulevard, ☎ (310) 828-5656.
Specialties: shredded chicken salad; Wu's beef; Peking duck.
Lunch: 11:30 a.m.–2:30 p.m., entrees $8–$15.
Dinner: 5:30–9:30 p.m., entrees $8–$18.

Madame Sylvia Wu provides a huge menu to choose from at this popular Wilshire Boulevard restaurant emphasizing Cantonese and Szechwan dishes. Friendly service. Lunch served Monday through Friday. Features: non-smoking area. Reservations recommended. Credit Cards: D, V, MC, A.

East European

Warszawa   **$$**   ★★★

1414 Lincoln Boulevard, ☎ (310) 393-8831.
Specialties: pierogi; roast duckling.
Dinner: 5:30–10:30 p.m., entrees $9–$18.

This newcomer gets high ratings for authentic Polish food and a warm, inviting setting. The service is as good as the food, and there's a nice selection of flavored vodkas. Features: own baking, full bar, late dining. Reservations recommended. Credit Cards: CB, V, MC, DC, A.

French

Camelions   **$$$**   ★★★

246 26th Street, ☎ (310) 395-0746.
Specialties: sauteed whitefish with crispy Vidalia onions.

Lunch: 11:30 a.m.–2:30 p.m., entrees $8–$13.
Dinner: 6–10 p.m., entrees $15–$21.

The food is as charming as the surroundings at this little Spanish mission-style cottage with a warm fireplace and an ivy-covered courtyard. French-Canadian dishes are expertly prepared and artfully presented, and the flourless chocolate cake is to die for. Just right for lovers with its romantic and intimate atmosphere. Features: outside dining, Sunday brunch, rated wine cellar, late dining. Jacket requested. Reservations required. Credit Cards: CB, V, MC, DC, A.

German

Knoll's Black Forest Inn   **$$$**   ★ ★ ★

2454 Wilshire Boulevard, ☎ (310) 395-2212.
Specialties: kalbshaxe; roast goose; venison.
Lunch: 11:30 a.m.–2:30 p.m., entrees $10–$16.
Dinner: 5–10:30 p.m., entrees $13–$26.

Reliable, authentic German food served in a chalet-like dining room. This Santa Monica institution serves up some of the finest German cuisine this side of the Rockies. Lunch served Tuesday through Friday. Closed: Mon. Features: outside dining, own baking, rated wine cellar, late dining. Jacket requested. Reservations recommended. Credit Cards: CB, V, MC, DC, A.

International

Planet Earth   **$$**   ★ ★

1512 Montana Avenue, ☎ (310) 458-3096.
Lunch: from 11:30 a.m., entrees $7–$13.
Dinner: to 10 p.m., entrees $7–$13.

Alex Lombardo of Drago is at the helm here, and he's turning out a delectible variety of politically correct cuisine without the use of chemical additives, animal fat, tropical oils or refined sugars. If that doesn't sound like an appetizing proposition, consider the tortilla pizza with smoked chicken, roasted garlic and mozzarella or—can you believe it?—the three-layer chocolate cake. At Planet Earth, nothing has more than five grams of fat per serving, and the prices are just about as skimpy. A wine and beer license is in the works. Features: own baking. Credit Cards: V, MC, A.

Zenzero   **$$$**   ★ ★ ★

1535 Ocean Avenue, ☎ (310) 451-4455.
Lunch: 11:30 a.m.–2 p.m., entrees $9–$12.
Dinner: 6:30–10 p.m., entrees $18–$24.

Kazuto Matsusaka, chef and owner of Zenzero, proved his mettle at Chinois on Main, which is known for its excellent and innovative cuisine, so hopes were high for Zenzero, which opened in mid-1994. So far, reviews are mixed, with lots of negative comments about the restaurant's pretensions and uneven cooking. The wine list is first-rate, though,—and criticism notwithstanding—Zenzero is currently one of THE places to be seen in L.A. Lunch served Monday through Friday. Features: splendid view, own baking, full bar, rated wine cellar, late dining. Reservations required. Credit Cards: CB, V, MC, DC, A.

Italian

Drago   **$$$**   ★ ★ ★

2628 WIlshire Boulevard, ☎ (310) 828-1585.
Specialties: Sicilian dishes.

Lunch: 11:30 a.m.–3 p.m., entrees $9–$24.
Dinner: 5:30–11 p.m., entrees $9–$24.

New restaurant owned by Celestino Drago, formerly of his own Celestino (which is now Cent'Anni) in Beverly Hills, who was named one of *Food & Wine* magazine's "10 Best New Chefs in America" in August of 1993. The restaurant concentrates on the dishes of Sicily, which are rustic, hearty, loaded with savory garlic and extremely well rendered. Critics complain that tables are too close together and the noise level is too high, but for food like this, a few inconveniences can be ignored. Rumors are that an expansion is in the works, which may solve the problems. Lunch served Monday through Friday. Features: own baking, rated wine cellar, late dining. Reservations recommended. Credit Cards: CB, V, MC, DC, A.

Giorgio $$$ ★★

114 West Channel Road, ☎ *(310) 459-8988.*
Specialties: polenta; pasta.
Dinner: 6–10 p.m., entrees $18–$34.

Giorgio may be trendy, and the Northern Italian cuisine often superior, but critics are unanimous in panning the waiters, who are aloof, snooty and downright rude. If you're not a celebrity, don't expect anyone to be cheerfully accommodating. The grilled fish and ravioli can be quite good, but the noise level is often overwhelming. Features: own baking, wine and beer only, late dining. Reservations recommended. Credit Cards: V, MC.

Marquis West $$$ ★★

3110 Santa Monica Boulevard, ☎ *(310) 828-4567.*
Specialties: puttanesca; calamari fritti; bouillabaisse.
Lunch: 11:30 a.m.–2:30 p.m., entrees $10–$20.
Dinner: 5–10 p.m., entrees $12–$25.

Marquis West is known for its excellent Italian cuisine served in portions that nearly always call for a "doggie bag." A nice selection of pastas, and seafood dishes that are always reliable. Lunch served Monday through Friday. Features: nonsmoking area, late dining, private dining rooms. Jacket requested. Reservations recommended. Credit Cards: CB, V, MC, DC, A.

Remi $$$ ★★★★

1451 Third Street, ☎ *(310) 393-6545.*
Lunch: 11:30 a.m.–3 p.m., entrees $16–$22.
Dinner: 5:30–11 p.m., entrees $16–$28.

The offbeat menu of good Venetian food is wonderful, and the selection of grappas can't be beat, making Remi a candidate for best restaurant on the Third Street Promenade. Once a month the wine room hosts Les Amis du Cigare, an evening of food, wine and cigars for a set price. Your palate will never come away disappointed from Remi— but your wallet might feel the pinch. Features: outside dining, Sunday brunch, full bar, rated wine cellar, late dining, private dining rooms. Reservations recommended. Credit Cards: CB, V, MC, DC, A.

Valentino $$$ ★★★★

3115 Pico Boulevard, ☎ *(310) 829-4313.*
Specialties: risotto; grilled fish.
Dinner: 5:30–10:30 p.m., entrees $20–$24.

A beautiful restaurant that is consistently at the top of the list when L.A.'s best Italian restaurants are under discussion. Recently, it garnered some national fame when it was included (with the highest rating) in Luigi Veronelli's guide to "The Best Italian Restaurants in America." If you can afford such decadence, the chef will whip up a customized meal. Service is sublime. Lunch served only on Friday. Closed: Sun. Features: outside dining, own baking, full bar, rated wine cellar, late dining. Jacket requested. Reservations required. Credit Cards: V, MC, A.

Wolfgang Puck Cafe $$ ★★

1323 Montana Avenue, ☎ *(310) 393-0290.*
Specialties: gourmet pizza; chinois salad.
Lunch: from 11 a.m., entrees $8–$15.
Dinner: to 11 p.m., entrees $10–$20.

Puck shows up on chic Montana Avenue, occupying the space where Luma used to be. By now, you know the formula: bright, upscale cafes where you wait in line for up to an hour to eat trendy pizzas, salads, pastas and grilled meats and fish. It's predictably crowded and noisy, but that's because everyone LOVES these places. Features: own baking, wine and beer only, rated wine cellar, late dining. Credit Cards: V, MC.

Mediterranean

Cafe Athens $$$ ★★

1000 Wilshire Boulevard, ☎ *(310) 395-1000.*
Specialties: moussaka; dolmades.
Lunch: from 11:30 a.m., entrees $8–$15.
Dinner: to 11 p.m., entrees $12–$20.

Some say this is the best Greek restaurant in L.A. Expect solid Greek classics, performing waiters and lots of fun. The family-style dinners, at $22.00 per person, are terrific. Lunch served Tuesday through Friday. Closed: Mon. Features: nonsmoking area, late dining. Reservations recommended. Credit Cards: CB, V, MC, DC, A.

Cutters $$ ★★

2425 Colorado Avenue, ☎ *(310) 453-3588.*
Specialties: pastas; grilled meats; seafood.
Lunch: 11:15 a.m.–5 p.m., entrees $5–$13.
Dinner: 5:30–10 p.m., entrees $7–$17.

Lots of fun for grazing and people-watching, Cutters offers an eclectic menu with influences from around the world. Fare runs from meats grilled over Hawaiian Kiawe wood to barbecued ribs to Olympia oysters, and there are lots of interesting beers to match. Some say the whole scene is too crowded and too noisy, but the price is definitely right. Features: outside dining, own baking, rated wine cellar, late dining. Reservations recommended. Credit Cards: V, MC, A.

Fama $$ ★★★

1416 Fourth Street, ☎ *(310) 451-8633.*
Specialties: homemade pasta; seafood.
Lunch: 11:30 a.m.–3 p.m., entrees $6–$9.
Dinner: 6–10 p.m., entrees $11–$18.

Owned by Hans Rockenwagner and his wife, Mary, Fama early on emphasized pastas and Tuscan cuisine that often hit the mark, but not often enough to gain the restaurant a loyal following. Now, the restaurant is trying a new concept, with a seasonal menu featuring homemade pastas and other fresh ingredients. Fans hope the new trend works, as this is a wonderful little restaurant where the service is uniformly praised. Families with children are warmly welcomed, which is unusual among L.A. restaurants. Closed: Mon. Features: own baking, wine and beer only, rated wine cellar, late dining. Reservations recommended. Credit Cards: V, MC, A.

Rockenwagner $$$ ★★★

2435 Main Street, ☎ *(310) 399-6504.*
Specialties: crab souffle; loin of lamb.
Lunch: 11:30 a.m.–2:30 p.m., entrees $12–$16.
Dinner: 6–10 p.m., entrees $18–$22.
Restaurateur Hans Rockenwagner recently relocated his namesake dining room to this chic arts-complex courtyard, where the California-inspired cuisine remains as good as ever and the gorgeous presentations make it almost too pretty to eat. Breakfast on the patio, served with bread and cheese, is a truly European experience. Lunch is served Tuesday though Friday; brunch, Saturday and Sunday. Closed: Mon. Features: outside dining, own baking, Sunday brunch, full bar, rated wine cellar, late dining. Reservations required. Credit Cards: V, MC, DC, A.

Mexican

Border Grill $$ ★★

1445 4th Street, ☎ *(310) 451-1655.*
Specialties: seafood.
Dinner: 5:30–10 p.m., entrees $9–$15.
Crowded and unbelievably noisy, the Border Grill offers highly complex Mexican food that's among the best in L.A., mostly prepared without the lard often found in south-of-the-border cuisine. If you're one of those people who favors greasy, traditional Mexican fare, have a couple of killer Margaritas and you won't know the difference. Features: own baking, Sunday brunch, late dining. Reservations recommended. Credit Cards: V, MC, A.

Lula $ ★★

2027 Main Street, ☎ *(310) 392-5711.*
Specialties: botano plato; blue-corn pancakes; green-corn tamales.
Lunch: from 11:30 a.m., entrees $7–$11.
Dinner: to 10 p.m., entrees $7–$11.
An Irish chef takes a stab at authentic Mexican cooking at this upscale spot that has lots of fans and almost as many detractors. Still, Lula is a culinary adventure worth exploring if you like lots of cilantro. (Ask for the tortilla soup—it's not on the menu.) The price is certainly right, and the Margaritas are dynamite. Features: outside dining, own baking, Sunday brunch, late dining. Reservations recommended. Credit Cards: V, MC.

Michael's $$$ ★★★★

1147 Third Street, ☎ *(310) 451-0843.*
Lunch: 12 a.m.–2:30 p.m., entrees $16–$20.
Dinner: 6:30–9:45 p.m., entrees $18–$30.
Michael's, the sister (brother?) restaurant to the one in New York, was one of the most expensive restaurants in Los Angeles until Cordon Bleu graduate Michael McCarty got realistic and lowered his prices a year or so ago (not that this has resulted in "budget dining" by any means!). Michael's seems to have instilled a love/hate relationship in the locals, who either laud it as one of the best in town, or complain

that the California cuisine is too passé, and that the whole scene, while stylish and elegant, is a big yawn. Most have nothing but kudos for Michael's, however, and the setting, with its lovely garden and array of modern art, is fabulous. The Sunday brunch is also reputed to be the best in town. Lunch served Tuesday through Friday. Prix fixe lunch, $17.00; prix fixe dinner, served Tuesday, Wednesday and Thursday, $27.00. Closed: Mon, Sun. Features: outside dining, own baking, rated wine cellar, private dining rooms. Jacket requested. Reservations required. Credit Cards: V, MC, A.

Seafood

Ocean Avenue Seafood　　　　$$$　　　　★ ★ ★

1401 Ocean Avenue, ☎ *(310) 394-5669.*
Specialties: oyster bar; seafood paella; Maine lobster.
Lunch: 11:30 a.m.–3 p.m., entrees $18–$20.
Dinner: 5:30–10 p.m., entrees $18–$20.

Dine on impeccably fresh seafood while inhaling the ocean breeze coming in right off the patio at this contemporary restaurant and oyster bar. The menu changes daily to reflect the catch of the day, and the oysters are among the best in the city. Come in during "Happy Hour," and you can get lots of fresh seafood in grazing portions. The patio is perfect for lunch on a sunny Southern California day. Features: outside dining, Sunday brunch, rated wine cellar, late dining. Jacket requested. Reservations required. Credit Cards: V, MC, A.

Southwestern

Abiquiu　　　　$$　　　　★ ★ ★ ★

1413 Fifth Street, ☎ *(310) 395-8611.*
Specialties: posole; grilled chicken breast.
Lunch: 11 a.m.–2:30 p.m., entrees $5–$12.
Dinner: 5–10 p.m., entrees $12–$18.

John Sedlar is a brilliant chef who had his share of bad luck when he opened Bikini in Santa Monica. Bikini didn't last long (it closed the day after the Northridge earthquake), but now Sedlar is back, and cooking the food he loves—to perfection. Eschewing lard, saturated oils, and (thank heavens!) huge doses of that ubiquitous cilantro, he turns out a menu of inventive specials such as pumpkin-seed-crusted whitefish on jalapeno mashed potatoes, chile relleno with Thai shrimp and spicy peanut sauce, and tamale of whitefish mousse with Caspian Sea caviar and borscht garnish. If you think this sounds too weird to be believed, just go taste for yourself. And best of all, Sedlar has made the prices low enough that REAL people can afford to eat here. The only caution: when Sedlar's not in the kitchen, the food may not be up to par. Lunch served Monday through Friday. Closed: Sun. Features: outside dining, own baking, rated wine cellar, late dining. Reservations required. Credit Cards: V, MC, A.

Venice

American

72 Market Street　　　　$$$　　　　★ ★ ★

72 Market Street, ☎ *(310) 392-8720.*
Specialties: oyster bar; meatloaf; salmon.
Lunch: 11:30 a.m.–2:30 p.m., entrees $7–$12.
Dinner: 6–10 p.m., entrees $13–$26.

This friendly, cozy cafe with the high-tech decor is co-owned by Dudley Moore and Tony Bill and draws a fair amount of Beautiful People who like the attractive design and good, simple food. You can get everything from fabulous "kick ass" chili to wonderful meatloaf to fresh oysters to a steamed vegetable plate that will please any fitness fanatic. (Another suggestion: ask for the steak tartare, which is not on the menu.) The menu changes with the seasons, and music may be provided by Moore, himself, who is quite an accomplished pianist. Quintessentially L.A. Features: own baking, Sunday brunch, full bar, late dining. Reservations recommended. Credit Cards: V, MC, A.

Joe's $$ ★★★

1023 Abbott Kinney Boulevard, ☎ *(310) 399-5811.*
Lunch: 11:30 a.m.–2:30 p.m., entrees $8–$10.
Dinner: 6–11 p.m., entrees $10–$20.

The only thing that was ever wrong with Joe's was that it was too small. With only 16 tables, the restaurant didn't offer much possibility for the masses to appreciate its excellent California-French food (cooked up by chef-owner Joe Miller, himself), and terrific service—all at reasonable prices. Joe thought about moving for a while, but then decided to stay put and do a little refurbishing. There is now room for more patrons (although everything is still understated and homey), and Joe's seasonally changing menu offers two four-course prix fixe meals, at $30.00 and $38.00. When everything works, which it usually does, you really get your money's worth, and Joe is likely to stop by your table and make sure you enjoyed your meal. Sometimes there's a wait for your food, but there's plenty of homemade bread to keep you going until dinner arrives. (The desserts are just as good.) Reasonably priced California wines round out the meal. Lunch is served Tuesday through Friday. Closed: Mon. Features: outside dining, own baking, Sunday brunch, wine and beer only, rated wine cellar, late dining. Credit Cards: CB, V, MC, DC, A.

North Beach Bar & Grill $$ ★★★

111 Rose Avenue, ☎ *(310) 399-3900.*
Specialties: prime steak; garlic roasted chicken; lamb chops; chili.
Lunch: 11:30 a.m.–3 p.m., entrees $7–$12.
Dinner: 6–10 p.m., entrees $8–$20.

Good, genuine California grill food served in the shadow of the infamous "Ballerina Clown" sculpture. The inside decor is a lot more classy than the clown, and the steaks, chicken and pastas are great. You always get big portions (with enough left over for tomorrow's lunch), which may justify the high prices. Features: own baking, Sunday brunch, full bar, late dining. Reservations recommended. Credit Cards: V, MC, A.

West Beach Cafe $$$ ★★★

60 North Venice Boulevard, ☎ *(310) 823-5396.*
Lunch: 11:30 a.m.–2:30 p.m., entrees $10–$15.
Dinner: 6–10 p.m., entrees $15–$26.

This chic cafe attracts area artists—and a few celebrities—who especially like the basic grill food and leisurely breakfasts. The atmosphere is extremely laid-back, and the noise level is usually up there—as are the prices. A great stop for lunch followed by browsing the new L.A. Louver Gallery across the street. Brunch served Saturday and Sunday (don't miss the scones) Features: outside dining, own baking, Sunday brunch, full bar, rated wine cellar, late dining. Jacket requested. Reservations recommended. Credit Cards: V, MC, A.

Italian

Capri   **$$**   ★ ★ ★

1616 Abott Kinney Boulevard, ☎ *(310) 392-8777.*
Specialties: steak tartare; northern Italian dishes.
Dinner: 6–10:30 p.m., entrees $8–$17.

Although the area is somewhat overwhelmed with Italian restaurants, the food is good enough here to make Capri stand out in the crowd. It shines exceptionally bright for a restaurant so young, and attracts the local artsy crowd. Features: own baking, Sunday brunch, wine and beer only, late dining. Reservations recommended. Credit Cards: V, MC.

Mexican

Rebecca's   **$$$**   ★ ★ ★

2025 Pacific Avenue, ☎ *(310) 306-6266.*
Specialties: seafood.
Dinner: 6–10 p.m., entrees $15–$20.

Rebecca's is an extremely happening place that was made even hipper when it appeared in the pages of *People* magazine. The terrific upscale Mexican food is served up in a carnival atmosphere that seems perfect for Venice, only "regular" people may have a hard time getting a reservation. And don't think that just because this place is a bit quirky that it's some cheap dive; you pay dearly for all the owners' notoriety and for the chance to check out the aluminum crocodiles hanging from the ceiling. Have a couple of Margaritas and party on, man. Features: own baking, rated wine cellar, late dining, private dining rooms. Reservations recommended. Credit Cards: V, MC, A.

Seafood

Chaya Venice   **$$$**   ★ ★ ★

110 Navy Street, ☎ *(310) 396-1179.*
Specialties: oyster, sashimi, and sushi Bar.
Lunch: 11:30 a.m.–2:30 p.m., entrees $7–$14.
Dinner: 6–10:30 p.m., entrees $12–$33.

Imaginative cooking and a far-ranging wine list have vaulted Chaya Venice (an offshoot of Chaya Brasserie) into the local limelight, which means that trendites pack the place and make a lot of noise. Stars creative seafood with deft Asian touches. Lunch served Monday through Friday. Features: own baking, Sunday brunch, full bar, rated wine cellar, late dining. Jacket requested. Reservations required. Credit Cards: V, MC, A.

SOUTH BAY

South Bay: Things to See and Do

None of the South Bay beaches (**El Segundo**, **Manhattan**, **Hermosa** and **Redondo**) have much to offer in the way of sightseeing, but strolling (or biking or rollerblading) along the beachside bike and pedestrian walkways is a popular pastime. Also, stop by the Southern California Edison plant in Redondo to take a look at the "Whaling Wall," an astounding (and huge—over two football fields long) mural depicting—what else?—whales. The giant work of art was painted by artist Wyland in just eleven days. There's a visitor center located on the Redondo Pier if you need information on other tourist-oriented attractions.

San Pedro is hardly a tourist destination in itself, but it does offer lots of sea-oriented festivals, cruises and the notable **Cabrillo Marine Aquarium**. Visitors may enjoy meandering through The Villages at Ports O' Call, a 15-acre, "authentic" New England seaside village full of specialty shops and international restaurants, or visiting the 17-ton, copper Korean Friendship Bell—a gift from the people of South Korea purported to be the largest Oriental bell in the world—in its shelter at Angel's Gate Park. San Pedro is also the departure point for harbor and whale-watching cruises, and contains the World Cruise Center and L.A. Maritime Museum

Theme/Amusement Parks

Monsoon Lagoon Water Park ★★

2410 West Compton Boulevard, Redondo Beach, 90278, ☎ *(310) 643-6130.*

Heated pools and water slides are the attraction at this low-end water theme park that is open weekends and holidays only, except in summer, when it is open daily. $7 admission after 3, and reduced prices for parents accompanying children under 12. General admission: $10.

Sports and Recreation

Redondo Sport Fishing Company

233 North Harbor Drive, Redondo Beach, 90277, ☎ *(213) 372-2111.*

Sea bass, bonita and yellowtail await the deep-sea fishing enthusiast aboard one of this company's half or full-day charters.

South Bay: Nightlife

ONE OF THE NEW BREED OF LAID-BACK COMEDIANS.

In the South Bay, The Strand is the happening place in Redondo Beach, and in Hermosa, it's the Comedy & Magic Club, where Jay Leno keeps his "Tonight Show" act in shape on a regular basis. The club also serves as a breeding ground for punk bands such as the Circle Jerks and Black Flag. Restyle and Aardvark (both on Hermosa Avenue) are also spots where the terminally hip hang out. For pure atmosphere, you can't beat the Poop Deck, an ex-biker bar on the Strand complete with gravel-throated bartenders and worn-out pool table.

Fielding Secret Spots

Try a sunset drink in the circular bar above Tony's on the Pier in Redondo Beach. Beehive-hairdoed waitresses in Hawaiian muumuus, faded fishnets complete with glass fishing floats, and an unobstructed view of the waves make for an unforgettable experience.

Comedy and Magic Club

1018 Hermosa Avenue, Hermosa Beach, 90254, ☎ (310) 372-1193.
This club features top-name comedians and magicians, giving it an international reputation. Continental menus for cafe and show room dining. Friday and Saturday afternoons, a special kids' comedy program is offered.

Lighthouse Cafe

30 Pier Avenue, Hermosa Beach, ☎ (310) 372-6911.
With a 48-year history as an "in spot," the cafe long ago changed the formerly all-jazz policy to include an eclectic mix of music with performers like Band du Jour, The Nobodies, T.J. Parker, Mr. Ectomy and All the Others. The club offers seating for 200, assorted appetizers, burgers, pizza and a full bar.

The Strand

1700 South Pacific Coast Highway., Redondo Beach, ☎ *(310) 316-1700.*

Top name performers are almost always on tap at The Strand, which is THE happening venue in the South Bay. Recent headliners include Maynard Ferguson, B.B. King, and comedian George Wallace. For a complete listing of upcoming events, call The Strand's 24-hour concert hotline at ☎ *(310) 316-6076.* Even if there's not a major act appearing, the club's three dance floors and three bars guarantee that the action is always exceedingly hot.

Toe's Tavern

732 North Catalina Avenue, Redondo Beach, ☎ *(310) 374-4628.*

Toe's Tavern, which has a decidedly surfing-oriented decor, offers live entertainment seven days a week, beginning at 9 p.m. There is everything you can think of on the bill here, from funk to alternative, with shows often featuring local bands such as the up-and-coming Velouria. There are also a few pool tables if you're not into the music. Over 21 only; cover varies.

South Bay: Shopping

In Redondo Beach, the main shopping areas are the three-level **Galleria** at South Bay, at the corner of Hawthorne Boulevard and Artesia, the gargantuan **Del Amo Mall** (350 stores) (on Hawthorne at Carson) and the Mediterranean-style **Riviera Village**, in south Redondo. The Galleria has more than 150 stores, including anchor department stores Nordstom and Robinsons-May (as a special service to foreign visitors, flyers direct them to stores where foreign languages are spoken), while Riviera Village is more the typical California-style combination of specialty shops and those ubiquitous sit-at-an-outside-table-and-drink-cappuccino places.

South Bay: Where to Stay

Although there's not much happening beachside in the way of new hotels, a Summerfield Suites opened in El Segundo in February of 1995. While El Segundo is hardly the tourist capital of L.A., the new all-suites accommodations are handy if you need to be near the airport or have business in the South Bay.

Airport Area

Hotels and Resorts

Airport Hilton and Towers   **$99–$184**   ★ ★ ★

5711 West Century Boulevard
☎ *(800) 445-8667, (310) 410-4000, FAX: 310-410-6250.*
Single: $99–$184. Double: $119–$184.

This is one of the world's largest airport hotels, and it offers the usual Hilton amenities such as in-room movies, minibars, refrigerators, valet/laundry service, child care, currency exchange, fax, transportation to nearby shopping, two restaurants, lounge, gift shop and car rental. The hotel was recently renovated and is quite comfortable despite its massive size. Amenities: pool, health club, sauna, balcony or patio, conference facilities, club floor, business services, complimentary airport pickup service. 1279 rooms. Credit Cards: CB, V, MC, DC, A.

Airport Marina $69–$109 ★★

8601 Lincoln Boulevard
☎ *(800) 225-8126, (310) 670-8111, FAX: 310-337-1883.*
Single: $69–$109. Double: $89–$109.
This is a large property catering to business travelers, groups, air crews, a few tourists and European backpackers. The accommodations are comfortable with quality furnishings including double, queen or king beds, cable TVs, louvered closets and combination baths or large showers. While there's only a mediocre coffee shop on the premises, you can always seek solace at the nearby bowling alley or adjacent park with tennis courts. The bar is being converted to a lounge with entertainment. Amenities: pool, Jacuzzi, balcony or patio, hair salon, conference facilities. 756 rooms. Credit Cards: V, MC, A.

Best Western Royal Palace $64–$70 ★★

2528 South Sepulveda Blvd.
☎ *(800) 528-1234, (310) 477-9066, FAX: 310-478-4133.*
Single: $64. Double: $70.
Most rooms at this motel have kitchens that include coffee makers and refrigerators; some have microwaves. The pool is very small, as are the fitness facilities. Amenities: pool, Jacuzzi, sauna, balcony or patio, conference facilities. 55 rooms. Credit Cards: CB, V, MC, DC, A.

Continental Plaza LAX $65 ★★

9750 Airport Boulevard
☎ *(800) 529-4683, (310) 645-4600, FAX: 310-645-7489.*
Single: $65. Double: $65.
The new Continental Plaza (formerly a Viscount Hotel) is proof that "you've come a long way, baby" —even in the hotel business. Nearly all of the management positions at the hotel are occupied by women, and yes, we mean even the upper managment positions. And this group of well-qualified females is in the process of making the new hotel a property to be proud of. Currently in the works is a $10 million renovation of all guest rooms, meeting rooms and public areas, expected to be completed by late 1995. Currently, amenities include an Olympic-sized pool, car rental service, laundry facilities, a restaurant and a lounge where complimentary hors d'oeuvres are served in the evening. Amenities: pool, exercise room, Jacuzzi, family plan, conference facilities. 570 rooms. Credit Cards: CB, V, MC, DC, A.

Doubletree L.A. Airport $79–$154 ★★★

5400 West Century Boulevard
☎ *(800) 222-8733, (310) 216-5858, FAX: 310-670-1948.*
Single: $79–$140. Double: $79–$154.

Modern 12-story hotel with a luxurious lobby, and under the prior management (it was the Stouffer Concourse, then a Westin), it was considered to be one of the best of the airport hotels. The accommodations are elegant and include club chairs and ottomans, minibars hidden in armoires, TVs with movies, breakfast tables, desks, one king or two queen beds, two phones and large combination baths. Morning coffee or tea—brought to your room—is free. Room service is available 24 hours. This gracious hotel belies its airport designation. Amenities: pool, health club, Jacuzzi, sauna, private spas, balcony or patio, conference facilities, club floor, business services, complimentary airport pickup service. 750 rooms. Credit Cards: CB, V, MC, DC, A.

Embassy Suites LAX $230 ★★★

9801 Airport Boulevard
☎ *(800) 362-2779, (310) 215-1000, FAX: 310-215-1952.*
Single: $230. Double: $230.

This new, all-suite hotel has luxurious rooms and an atrium lobby featuring a tropical garden. All suites come equipped with two color TVs, VCR, refrigerator, microwave, coffee maker and multiline phones. FAX service, valet/laundry service and child care are available, as is a complimentary breakfast and evening cocktails. Amenities: pool, exercise room, sauna, conference facilities, complimentary airport pickup service. 215 rooms. Credit Cards: CB, V, MC, DC, A.

Holiday Inn Crowne Plaza $79–$109 ★★★

5985 West Century Boulevard
☎ *(800) 465-4329, (310) 642-7500, FAX: 310-417-3608.*
Single: $79–$109. Double: $79–$109.

This Holiday Inn caters to the business traveler and is one of the better airport hotels. There is a restaurant, a cafe serving an express breakfast and buffet, and a cocktail lounge with a dance floor. Accommodations are trendy yet subtle with wood furnishings, thick carpets, double or king beds, breakfast tables, TVs with movies and combination baths. Four floors are designated for nonsmokers. Amenities: pool, exercise room, Jacuzzi, sauna, family plan, conference facilities, club floor, complimentary airport pickup service. 615 rooms. Credit Cards: CB, V, MC, DC, A.

Holiday Inn LAX $100–$119 ★★

9901 South La Cienega Boulevard
☎ *(800) 624-0025, (310) 649-5151, FAX: 310-670-3619.*
Single: $100–$119. Double: $109–$119.

Located just a half-mile from the airport, this quite basic Holiday Inn could be greatly improved with soundproofing—airplane and traffic noise can be a distraction on the upper floors. Free parking and constant airport shuttles make this a reasonable, if uninspired, option for layovers. Amenities: pool, family plan, conference facilities, complimentary airport pickup. 402 rooms. Credit Cards: CB, V, MC, DC, A.

Hyatt Airport $89–$109 ★★

6225 West Century Boulevard
☎ *(800) 233-1234, (310) 670-9000.*
Single: $89–$109. Double: $89–$109.

This is the closest hotel to LAX and the staff is experienced at handling busy travelers. The older accommodations are adequate—if not exciting—with wood-grain formica furniture, sitting areas with club chairs and ottomans, TVs with movies, minibars, king or double beds and combination baths. Room service operates until 1:30 a.m., and guests receive a complimentary continental breakfast. Ranked restaurant: T.J. Peppercorn's. Amenities: pool, health club, sauna, hair salon, family plan, conference facilities, club floor, complimentary airport pickup service. 596 rooms. Credit Cards: CB, V, MC, DC, A.

L.A. Renaissance Hotel $79–$120 ★★★

9620 Airport Boulevard
☎ *(800) 468-3571, (310) 337-2800, FAX: 310-216-6681.*

Single: $79–$120. Double: $79–$120.
This newer 11-story hotel is of European design and features a formal lobby with textured columns, vaulted ceilings, marble floors, richly patterned carpets and mahogany details. Guest room amenities include work desks, voice mail, three telephones with call waiting and computer/fax capability, and 24-hour room service. Guests on the club level receive a complimentary continental breakfast. Amenities: pool, health club, Jacuzzi, sauna, conference facilities, club floor, business services. 505 rooms. Credit Cards: CB, V, MC, DC, A.

Marriott Airport $150–$160   ★ ★ ★
5855 West Century Boulevard
☎ *(800) 228-9290, (310) 641-5700, FAX: 310-337-5358.*
Single: $150. Double: $160.
Although geared toward large groups, conventions and the business traveler, the Marriott is more like a resort than any of the other airport hotels. Guest rooms over the heavily landscaped pool area are preferable to those facing the airport. Accommodations feature pastel colors, textured wallpaper, wood-grain furniture, sitting areas and combination baths. The staff is friendly and efficient, and serves the large number of guests cheerfully. Amenities: pool, health club, Jacuzzi, sauna, balcony or patio, hair salon, family plan, conference facilities, club floor, complimentary airport pickup service. 1012 rooms. Credit Cards: CB, V, MC, DC, A.

Sheraton L.A. Airport $140–$140   ★ ★ ★
6101 West Century Boulevard
☎ *(800) 445-7999, (310) 642-1111, FAX: 310-645-1414.*
Single: $140. Double: $140.
Business-oriented, 15-story hotel complete with executive board room and a tiered seminar room. Contemporary, oversized rooms with sitting areas, complimentary transportation to beach and shopping, two restaurants and the only sushi bar at LAX are some of the perks. The service is not always perfect; during busy periods the staff can be curt. Amenities: pool, exercise room, Jacuzzi, hair salon, family plan, conference facilities, business services, complimentary airport pickup service. 807 rooms. Credit Cards: V, MC, A.

Travelodge LAX $70–$80   ★ ★ ★
5547 West Century Blvd.
☎ *(800) 421-3939, (310) 649-4000, FAX: 310-649-0311.*
Single: $70–$75. Double: $75–$80.
Formerly known as the Airport Century Inn, this motor inn is a half-mile from LAX. When the facility changed hands, new furniture was added to all guest rooms, and the pool area was remodeled. Each room has a VCR, and movie rentals are available. Amenities: pool, balcony or patio, family plan, complimentary airport pickup service. 147 rooms. Credit Cards: CB, V, MC, DC, A.

Low Cost Lodging
Quality Hotel Airport $69–$89   ★ ★
5249 West Century Boulevard
☎ *(800) 221-2222, (310) 645-2200, FAX: 310-641-8214.*
Single: $69–$79. Double: $79–$89.
Ten-story hotel located just off I-405, one mile from the airport. Facilities include six suites, meeting space for 350, and a gym. Amen-

ities: pool, conference facilities, complimentary airport pickup service. 278 rooms. Credit Cards: CB, V, MC, DC, A.

El Segundo

Hotels and Resorts

Courtyard Airport $69–$102 ★★★

2000 East Mariposa Avenue
☎ *(800) 321-2211, (310) 322-0700, FAX: 310-322-4401.*
Single: $69–$92. Double: $79–$102.
This residential-style hotel is located one mile from LAX. The accommodations are typical Marriott, offering cable TV with movies, coffee makers, desks, and some rooms with refrigerators. It was renovated in 1991. Amenities: pool, exercise room, Jacuzzi, balcony or patio, conference facilities, complimentary airport pickup service. 146 rooms. Credit Cards: CB, V, MC, DC, A.

Crown Sterling Suites $89–$150 ★★★

1440 East Imperial Avenue
☎ *(800) 433-4600, (310) 640-3600, FAX: 310-322-0954.*
Single: $89–$140. Double: $89–$150.
This all-suite hotel located five minutes from the airport has a dining/work area and wet bar in each unit. Complimentary breakfast buffet and evening cocktails. Amenities: pool, Jacuzzi, sauna, balcony or patio, family plan, conference facilities, business services, complimentary airport pickup service. 350 rooms. Credit Cards: CB, V, MC, DC, A.

Doubletree Club $69–$112 ★★

1985 East Grand Avenue
☎ *(800) 426-6774, (310) 322-0999, FAX: 310-322-4758.*
Single: $69–$102. Double: $69–$112.
A complimentary breakfast is thrown in free at this airport hotel located one and a half miles from LAX. Guest services include valet laundry, secretarial support, and 24-hour room service. The requisite Doubletree chocolate chip cookies are supplied on arrival. Amenities: pool, exercise room, Jacuzzi, sauna, conference facilities, business services, complimentary airport pickup service. 215 rooms. Credit Cards: CB, V, MC, DC, A.

Summerfield Suites El Segundo $150–$190 ★★★

810 South Douglas Avenue
☎ *(800) 833-4353, (310) 725-0100, FAX: 310-725-0900.*
Single: $150–$160. Double: $180–$190.
This new Summerfield Suites property opened in early 1995 and includes five buildings containing one- and two-bedroom suites. Each suite contains a fully-equipped kitchen, TV, VCR and phone line with voice mail. A complimentary breakfast buffet is served daily, and there's a social hour each evening, Monday through Thursday. A 24-hour convenience store is located on-site, and there is also laundry/valet service. Amenities: pool, exercise room, Jacuzzi.

Low Cost Lodging

Hacienda $40–$76 ★★

525 North Sepulveda Blvd.
☎ *(800) 421-5900, (310) 615-0015, FAX: 310-615-0217.*
Single: $40–$76. Double: $59–$76.
Situated one mile from LAX, this hotel boasts landscaped courtyards and shuttle service to a nearby shopping mall. Accommodations are

arranged in three buildings, and the rate depends upon which building you choose, with the most expensive rooms located in the South Tower. The coffee shop is open 24 hours. Amenities: pool, Jacuzzi, balcony or patio, family plan, conference facilities, complimentary airport pickup service. 640 rooms. Credit Cards: CB, V, MC, DC, A.

Manhattan Beach
Hotels and Resorts

Barnabey's   **$98–$159**   ★★★

3501 North Sepulveda Blvd.
☎ *(800) 552-5285, (310) 545-8466, FAX: 310-545-8621.*
Single: $98–$129. Double: $98–$159.
Family-owned and loaded with European charm, this hotel is located close to beaches and minutes from LAX. Accommodations include European antiques and canopy beds, and a garden terrace with fountains provides relaxation after a round of business meetings or a hard day at Disneyland. Guests receive a complimentary breakfast, cocktails and newspaper. Amenities: pool, Jacuzzi, sauna, private spas, balcony or patio, family plan, conference facilities, complimentary airport pickup service. 128 rooms. Credit Cards: CB, V, MC, DC, A.

Radisson Plaza   **$79–$119**   ★★★

1400 Parkview Avenue
☎ *(800) 333-3333, (310) 546-7511, FAX: 310-546-7520.*
Single: $79–$119. Double: $79–$119.
Located near the South Bay's business and technological community, this hotel offers good service but small, bland rooms. Oh well, there's a golf course and beaches nearby. Ranked restaurant: Califia. Amenities: pool, golf, Jacuzzi, sauna, balcony or patio, conference facilities, club floor, complimentary airport pickup service. 380 rooms. Credit Cards: CB, V, MC, DC, A.

Residence Inn Manhattan   **$149–$185**   ★★

1700 North Sepulveda Blvd.
☎ *(800) 331-3131, (310) 546-7627, FAX: 310-545-1327.*
Single: $149. Double: $185.
This new inn is located near the Galleria Shopping Mall and beach areas. The accommodations feature in-room movies, refrigerators, valet/laundry service and a complimentary continental breakfast. Parking is free. Amenities: pool, Jacuzzi, conference facilities, complimentary airport pickup service. 176 rooms. Credit Cards: V, MC, A.

Redondo Beach
Hotels and Resorts

Best Western Galleria Inn   **$55–$70**   ★★★

2740 Artesia Boulevard
☎ *(800) 233-8059, (310) 370-4353, FAX: 310-793-7135.*
Single: $55–$70. Double: $60–$70.
Each room in this small motel has a refrigerator, and guests receive a complimentary continental breakfast. Amenities: Jacuzzi, sauna, complimentary airport pickup service. 38 rooms. Credit Cards: V, MC, DC, A.

Best Western Redondo Beach   **$85–$100**   ★★★

1850 South Pacific Coast Highway
☎ *(800) 528-1234, (310) 540-3700, FAX: 310-540-3675.*
Single: $85–$95. Double: $90–$100.

This inn is located five blocks from the beach and nine miles from LAX. Two suites feature either a Roman tub or a fireplace and Jacuzzi. Amenities: pool, Jacuzzi, sauna, private spas, conference facilities. 101 rooms. Credit Cards: CB, V, MC, DC, A.

Best Western Sunrise   **$80–$110**   ★★

400 North Harbor Drive
☎ *(800) 528-1234, (310) 376-0746, FAX: 310-376-7384.*
Single: $80–$110. Double: $80–$110.

This modern, three-story motor inn is located directly across from the King Harbor Marina, and guests are within walking distance of the beach and the pier. Rooms include refrigerators, and bicycles are available for rent. Amenities: beach location, pool, exercise room, Jacuzzi, conference facilities, complimentary airport pickup service. 111 rooms. Credit Cards: V, MC, A.

Holiday Inn Crowne Plaza   **$135–$180**   ★★★

300 North Harbor Drive
☎ *(800) 465-4329, (310) 318-8888, FAX: 310-376-1930.*
Single: $135–$180. Double: $135–$180.

Formerly the Sheraton Redondo Beach, this beachfront inn offers rooms with movies, refrigerator, minibar, hair dryer and coffee maker; valet/laundry service, a multilingual staff, child care, currency exchange, fax, transportation to local shopping malls and a complimentary newspaper are available to guests. Its large deck overlooking King Harbor is a perfect place to relax in the evening, and there are nearby opportunities for jogging, biking, sailing and other watersports. Amenities: beach location, pool, tennis, exercise room, Jacuzzi, sauna, balcony or patio, conference facilities, business services. 339 rooms. Credit Cards: V, MC, A.

Palos Verdes Inn   **$80–$115**   ★★

1700 South Pacific Coast Highway
☎ *(800) 421-9241, (310) 316-4211, FAX: 310-316-4863.*
Single: $80–$95. Double: $90–$115.

Most rooms at this motor hotel have a view of the ocean, and many have balconies. Executive suites include a bar and refrigerator. Ranked restaurant: **Chez Melange**. Amenities: beach location, pool, Jacuzzi, balcony or patio, conference facilities, business services. 110 rooms. Credit Cards: CB, V, MC, DC, A.

Portofino Inn   **$135–$193**   ★★★

260 Portofino Way
☎ *(800) 468-4292, (310) 379-8481, FAX: 310-372-7329.*
Single: $135–$193. Double: $135–$193.

Located on a private peninsula in the King Harbor Marina, this inn offers rooms with either marina or ocean views. The accommodations come fully equipped with in-room movies, multiline phones, minibars and refrigerators. Coffee, tea and evening snacks are complimentary. The sounds of the surf are a delightful enhancement to sleep. Amenities: beach location, pool, Jacuzzi, balcony or patio, conference facilities, complimentary airport pickup service. 165 rooms. Credit Cards: V, MC, A.

Torrance

Hotels and Resorts

Courtyard by Marriott   **$59–$72**   ★★★

2633 Sepulveda Boulevard
☎ *(800) 321-2582, (310) 533-8000, FAX: 310-533-0564.*
Single: $59–$72. Double: $59–$72.

Located eight miles from LAX, this residential-style hotel is situated
around a central courtyard. Rooms include clock-radios and complimentary coffee. Amenities: pool, exercise room, Jacuzzi, balcony or
patio, conference facilities. 149 rooms. Credit Cards: CB, V, MC, DC, A.

Holiday Inn Harbor Gateway   **$91**   ★★★

19800 South Vermont Avenue
☎ *(800) 465-4329, (310) 781-9100, FAX: 310-324-1695.*
Single: $91. Double: $91.

This twelve-story hotel offers amenities for business travelers such as
data ports and secretarial services. Some rooms have coffee makers
and refrigerators. Amenities: pool, exercise room, Jacuzzi, sauna, family plan, conference facilities, club floor, business services. 338 rooms.
Credit Cards: CB, V, MC, DC, A.

Holiday Inn Torrance   **$95–$105**   ★★

21333 Hawthorne Blvd.
☎ *(800) 433-5266, (310) 540-0500, FAX: 310-540-2065.*
Single: $95–$105. Double: $95–$105.

Adjacent to the Del Amo shopping and financial centers, the Holiday
Inn Torrance is seven miles from LAX. The recently renovated rooms
include coffee makers, and bicycle rentals are available. For Japanese
patrons, there is a Japanese-speaking concierge on staff, and customized Japanese breakfasts are served in the restaurant. Amenities: pool,
exercise room, Jacuzzi, sauna, conference facilities, complimentary
airport pickup service. 386 rooms. Credit Cards: CB, V, MC, DC, A.

Marriott Courtyard   **$49–$69**   ★★★

1925 West 190th Street
☎ *(800) 321-2211, (310) 532-1722, FAX: 310-532-9161.*
Single: $49–$69. Double: $49–$69.

A contemporary motor inn located near the business center and 10
miles from downtown L.A. Accommodations include TVs with movies, phones and coffee makers. A restaurant and lounge are on the premises. Amenities: pool, exercise room, conference facilities. 149
rooms. Credit Cards: V, MC, DC, A.

Marriott Torrance   **$130–$170**   ★★★

3635 Fashion Way
☎ *(800) 228-9290, (310) 316-3636, FAX: 310-543-6076.*
Single: $130–$150. Double: $150–$170.

Located adjacent to the Del Amo Shopping Center in the heart of the
business district, this hotel offers a 1 p.m. checkout, concierge, and
some bathroom phones. Rooms on the Concierge Level are more
expensive, but the rate includes use of a private lounge, honor bars
and a complimentary continental breakfast and refreshments. Amenities: pool, golf, health club, Jacuzzi, sauna, balcony or patio, family
plan, conference facilities, club floor. 487 rooms. Credit Cards: CB, V,
MC, DC, A.

Residence Inn by Marriott   **$89–$124**   ★★

3701 Torrance Blvd.
☎ *(800) 331-3131, (310) 543-4566, FAX: 310-543-3026.*
Single: $89–$124. Double: $89–$124.

This all-suite hotel is located one mile from the beach, nine miles from LAX. All units include a fully equipped kitchen, and most have fireplaces. Complimentary continental breakfast and evening hospitality hour included. Amenities: pool, Jacuzzi, balcony or patio, family plan, conference facilities. 247 rooms. Credit Cards: CB, V, MC, DC, A.

Summerfield Suites   **$95–$130**   ★★

19901 Prairie Avenue
☎ *(800) 833-4353, (310) 371-8525, FAX: 310-542-9628.*
Single: $95–$130. Double: $95–$130.

This all-suite hotel offers complimentary continental breakfast and evening beverages. Some suites have fireplaces; all have kitchens and living rooms. Amenities: pool, exercise room, Jacuzzi, conference facilities. 144 rooms. Credit Cards: V, MC, DC, A.

South Bay: Where to Eat

In the South Bay, there's lots of talk about **Descanso**, which offers a taste of the tropics just off the Hermosa Beach Pier. *Bon Appetit* magazine named Descanso one of its "Hot New Restaurants" in 1995, and it was the only restaurant in L.A. so named.

For a decidedly downscale dining experience but really good seafood, try **Tony's on the Pier** on the Redondo Pier. Try to ignore the lousy decor and the unsettling feeling of the entire restaurant moving when large waves make the whole pier shudder. If you prefer more upscale surroundings, try Tony's other location on the south side of the pier.

Papadakis Tavern is a sure bet for a good time in San Pedro, especially if you can endure the deafening bouzouki music (not to mention the sound of smashing plates). Great Greek food and rowdy entertainment make this a popular spot for the whole family, so be sure to book ahead.

Hermosa Beach

Mediterranean

Descanso   **$$**   ★★★

705 Pier Avenue, ☎ *(310) 379-7997.*
Lunch: from 11:30 a.m., entrees $6–$10.
Dinner: 5–11 p.m., entrees $8–$16.

Descanso was named one of *Bon Appetit* magazine's "Hot New Restaurants" in January of 1995, and although this honor came while David Slatkin was still whipping up an eclectic menu of Caribbean food, the restaurant is still a pretty good bet. Slatkin left after his cooking was deemed too far out, and Christine Brown, formerly at Fino, is how heading the kitchen. The menu has changed considerably, with much of the Caribbean food gone and the emphasis more on Mediterranean and Mexican dishes, but the scene is still lively and lots of fun. Familes are encouraged to graze together, and a new "bambino" menu caters to the kids. Features: outside dining, own baking, Sunday brunch, late dining. Reservations recommended. Credit Cards: V, MC, A.

Manhattan Beach

American

Cafe Pierre   **$$**   ★★

317 Manhattan Beach Blvd., ☎ (310) 545-5252.
Specialties: steak au poivre; tuna sashimi; homemade pasta.
Lunch: 11:30 a.m.–2:30 p.m., entrees $7–$19.
Dinner: 5:30–10 p.m., entrees $7–$19.
Fans say this is one of Southern California's best bistros and a great
neighborhood cafe, but detractors find the eclectic menu strange and
the service lacking. Lunch served Monday through Friday. Features:
full bar, late dining. Reservations recommended. Credit Cards: V, MC, A.

Califia   **$$$**   ★★★

1400 Parkview Avenue, ☎ (310) 546-7511.
Lunch: 11:30 a.m.–2 p.m., entrees $9–$15.
Dinner: 5:30–10 p.m., entrees $19–$30.
Associated hotel: Radisson Plaza.
Califia has the makings of a first-class restaurant, with excellent
French cuisine served in a pleasing environment, but it still needs time
to prove itself. Closed: Mon. Features: own baking, full bar, late din-
ing. Jacket and tie requested. Reservations recommended. Credit Cards:
CB, V, MC, DC, A.

French

Reed's   **$$$**   ★★★

2640 North Sepulveda Boulevard, ☎ (310) 546-3299.
Specialties: salmon in a mushroom crust.
Lunch: 11:30 a.m.–2:30 p.m., entrees $7–$11.
Dinner: 5:30–10:30 p.m., entrees $13–$18.
Reed's, backed by Joe Miller (of Joe's in Venice) and chef Brandon
Reed (formerly of L'Orangerie), occupies the space where John Sed-
lar's St. Estephe once made culinary waves. It's turning out an inter-
esting mix of inventive dishes with only a few slips in the kitchen. The
four-course prix fixe menus, at $28.00 and $33.00, are wonderful.
Portions are generous and the prices fair. Lunch served Monday
through Friday. Closed: Sun. Features: own baking, wine and beer
only, rated wine cellar, late dining. Reservations recommended. Credit
Cards: CB, V, MC, DC, A.

Palos Verdes

French

La Rive Gauche   **$$$**   ★★★

320 Tejon Place, ☎ (310) 378-0267.
Specialties: oysters Rockefeller; rack of lamb.
Lunch: 11:30 a.m.–3 p.m., entrees $7–$15.
Dinner: 5:30–10 p.m., entrees $16–$27.
Arguably one of the best restaurants in the area, La Rive Gauche
offers pricey French fare, including fresh seafood, rack of veal and
lamb, and some game dishes. Nearly everything succeeds here, and
dining on the patio is a special delight on warm days. Lunch served
Tuesday through Saturday. Features: outside dining, own baking,
Sunday brunch, full bar, late dining. Jacket requested. Reservations
recommended. Credit Cards: CB, V, MC, DC, A.

Redondo Beach
Mediterranean

Chez Melange $$ ★ ★ ★

1716 Pacific Coast Highway, ☎ *(310) 540-1222.*
Specialties: ahi burger.
Lunch: 11:30 a.m.–2:30 p.m., entrees $8–$12.
Dinner: 5–10 p.m., entrees $9–$17.
Associated hotel: Palos Verdes Inn.

In spite of the fact that Chez Melange is generally a winner, the
"melange" of food may be a little too mixed up, with a menu that
offers everything from pizza to Russian caviar. It's not easy to main-
tain the quality when the cuisine varies from one side of the globe to
the other. Good wines, though, and excellent service. A caviar and
vodka bar has recently been added. Breakfast and lunch served Mon-
day through Friday; brunch served Saturday and Sunday. Features:
own baking, Sunday brunch, full bar, rated wine cellar, late dining.
Jacket requested. Reservations recommended. Credit Cards: V, MC, A.

Torrance
American

Misto Caffe $$ ★ ★ ★

24558 Hawthrone Boulevard, ☎ *(310) 375-3608.*
Specialties: turkey chili; sloppy Joes; BLT pizza.
Lunch: from 11:30 a.m., entrees $8–$13.
Dinner: to 9:30 p.m., entrees $8–$13.

Misto is a laid-back American cafe that serves all kinds of hearty American comfort food, and offers a list of appetizers so varied and so good
that you can make a meal of them. For casual dining or evening grazing, you can't go wrong at Misto. Features: outside dining, own baking, Sunday brunch, wine and beer only. Reservations not accepted.
Credit Cards: V, MC, A.

French

Chalet de France $$$ ★ ★

23254 Robert Road, ☎ *(310) 540-4646.*
Lunch: 11:30 a.m.–2:30 p.m., entrees $5–$12.
Dinner: 4:30–10:30 p.m., entrees $12–$24.

The owner brings the tastes of Monaco to Palos Verdes at this French
restaurant. The food is generally reliable, although nothing is too
inspired. Nice wine list. Lunch served Tuesday through Friday.
Closed: Mon. Features: outside dining, own baking, full bar, rated
wine cellar, late dining. Reservations recommended. Credit Cards: V,
MC, A.

International

Depot $$$ ★ ★ ★

1250 Cabrillo Avenue, ☎ *(310) 787-7501.*
Specialties: Thai-dyed chicken; three-flavor dumplings.
Lunch: 11 a.m.–2:30 p.m., entrees $7–$13.
Dinner: 5:30–10 p.m., entrees $14–$21.

A neighborhood spin-off of Redondo Beach's Chez Melange that's
set in the Old Town Torrance 1912 Red Car electric railway station.
The menu spans the globe, with an emphasis on Asian and Mediterranean dishes. Beer is a specialty here, and over 26 varieties of microbrewed beers are available. Good food all around, and an especially

tempting bar menu. Note the rather eclectic hours: lunch served Monday through Friday; dinner served Tuesday through Sunday. Features: outside dining, own baking, full bar, rated wine cellar, late dining. Reservations recommended. Credit Cards: V, MC, A.

Italian

Fabio $$ ★

23863 Hawthorne Boulevard, ☎ *(310) 373-8187.*
Lunch: 11:30 a.m.–2 p.m., entrees $6–$10.
Dinner: 5:30–10 p.m., entrees $8–$18.

Toscana-style food shines at this neighborhood spot, formerly the Symphonie. Unfortunately, the food is sometimes inconsistent and the service slow. On the other hand, the prices are reasonable and the atmosphere friendly. Don't come expecting to see romance novel coverboy Fabio, though. It may be a disappointment to ardent female fans, but Fabio, the man, has nothing to do with Fabio, the restaurant. Features: own baking, full bar, late dining. Jacket and tie requested. Reservations recommended. Credit Cards: CB, V, MC, DC, A.

Mediterranean

Fino $$ ★★★

24530 Hawthorne Boulevard, ☎ *(310) 373-1952.*
Specialties: lamb shank; grilled escarole; tapas platter.
Dinner: 5–9:30 p.m., entrees $10–$18.

Fino's upscale Mediterranean fare is perfect for garlic-lovers, who will find that the chef uses it generously in almost everything. Italian favorites like osso buco and pastas are well done, and there are enough tapas on the menu to make for satisfying snacking. Don't miss the chef's special family-style dinners on Sunday evenings. The five-course meal costs $18.95 per person, and you are encouraged to bring your own wine (no corkage fee on Sunday nights). Features: outside dining, wine and beer only, rated wine cellar. Jacket requested. Reservations recommended. Credit Cards: V, MC, A.

Breakfast in the South Bay

One of L.A.'s most enduring traditions seems to be having breakfast before spending a day at the beach. Most restaurants are jam-packed by 10 a.m. with lineups until they close. Most folks just kick back and read the paper while they sit in the sun.

Backburner Cafe $

87 14th Street, Hermosa Beach (about 100 yds east of the Strand) ☎ *(310) 372-6973.*
The gals that make the Backburner a local favorite dish out healthy portions, big smiles and plenty of refills. Try the homemade corned beef hash.

C'J's Pantry $

322 South Catalina Avenue, Redondo Beach
☎ *(310) 318-2411 Open 7 a.m. – 3 p.m. daily.*
Healthy specials in a surfer/sports bar motif. Look for the wooden chef they wheel outside.

Breakfast in the South Bay

Eat at Joe's   **$**

400 North Pacific Coast Highway, Redondo Beach
☎ *(310) 376-9570.*
A long way from the beach, but good hearty breakfast served
on summer-camp, get-to-know-your-neighbor benches, but
eternally popular with the surfers and early morning crowd.

Good Stuff   **$**   ★

*1286 The Strand, Hermosa Beach (13th Street and The Strand,
just north of Pier Avenue) Open 7 a.m. to 9 p.m. daily.*
☎ *(310) 374-2334.*
Health food that attracts cyclists, joggers and skaters all the
way from Venice Beach. Once the dayglow-outfitted cyclists
on their $1000 Cinellis show up you can expect a 20–45
minute wait. You have a choice between outside, patio and
inside dining, most with views of the ocean.

Martha's 22nd Street Grill   **$**   ★

23 22nd Street, Hermosa Beach ☎ *(310) 376-7786 (30 yards
east of the Strand)*
You can eat outside if you are lucky enough to get a table.
Great oatmeal, pancakes and egg dishes.

Uncle Bill's Pancake House   **$**

1305 Highland Ave., Manhattan Beach ☎ *(310) 545-5177
(North of the Pier, two blocks up from the beach)*
A popular spot for Manhattanites. Very crowded outside,
even more crowded once you get inside. Just up the hill from
the beach.

Ocean Diner   **$**   ★

959 Aviation Boulevard, Hermosa Beach (just east of P.C.H.)
☎ *(310) 372-3739 6 a.m.–2 p.m. weekdays, 7 a.m. to 3 p.m.
weekends.*
Tiny, crowded morning spot popular with local cops. Fresh
muffins, heaping portions and plenty of coffee. Home of the
"stickiest buns in town" according to the wacky '40s style
advertising and decor.

Polly's on the Pier   **$**

*233 North Harbor Drive (in King Harbor, north of Redondo
Pier, park in the lot)* ☎ *(310) 372-2111 Open 5 a.m.–2 p.m.
daily*
A Fielding Secret Spot that most locals don't even know
about. Polly's caters to insomniacs and fishermen. As you can
imagine, the food will never make the Michelin guide, but
the ambience and ocean setting is worth a breakfast. You can
sit outside.

The Original Pancake House   **$**   ★

*1765 Pacific Coast Highway, Redondo Beach (just east of Riviera
Village), (310)543-9875 Open 7 a.m.–2 p.m.*
A chain, not the real McCoy. This nondescript place serves
up giant made-from-scratch pancakes, crepes and waffles.
Specially blended coffee and fresh squeezed orange juice. Try
the apple pancakes.

LONG BEACH

Long Beach: Things to See and Do

Ports of Call, a major tourist attraction located in San Pedro is only a few minutes from downtown Long Beach.

Long Beach, in addition to its wide, sandy beaches and the *Queen Mary* and her surrounding portside attractions, offers a few rather quirky sightseeing options, including a Foot Museum, the Skinny House and the Gondola Getaway cruises, which are as close as you're going to get to Venice (that's Venice, Italy, not Venice, CA). It also boasts a small museum of art and a children's museum, and the "certified" world's largest mural, "Planet Ocean," which artist Wyland (yes, the same one who did the "Whaling Wall" in Redondo Beach) created to cover the entire 116,000-foot surface of the Long Beach Arena using more than 3000 gallons of paint.

And, oh yeah. Keep your eyes open for the art of the famous Long Beach "Lint Lady," who has been turning lint (yes, lint) into "three-dimensional sculptures conveying social and political messages" for more than 20 years. Her works reportedly include "entire room environments" and a lifesize portrait of John Wayne. Hey! And you thought Long Beach had a shortage of cultural attractions.

And speaking of interesting artistic achievements, don't be fooled by those fancy resort hotels that appear to be rising up out of the sea just off the Long Beach coast. These are merely oil islands in disguise, covered up by a local group anxious to present more aesthetically pleasing vistas than those provided by barren islands studded with politically incorrect oil derricks. (Californians may consume a lot of oil, but they don't like looking at reminders that it exists anywhere off their pristine coast.) The islands are named after astronauts who died in the early U.S. space program: Grissom, White, Freeman and Chaffee.

You can reach all of the Long Beach attractions on the free Runabout Shuttle, operated by Long Beach Transit. Several routes are available, and most shuttles run every six to 15 minutes. Hours vary according to the route chosen, but the *Queen Mary* route (which runs between downtown and the *Queen Mary*) operates from 5:30 a.m. to midnight daily. Information on the historical walking tour of downtown Long Beach, as well as other attractions, is available from the Long Beach Area Convention and Visitors Council, located at One World Trade Center.

Attractions

Museums and Exhibits

Cabrillo Marine Aquarium   ★ ★ ★

3720 Stephen White Drive, San Pedro, 90731, ☎ (310) 548-7562.
Hours open: 12 a.m.–5 p.m.
This excellent small beachside museum has 35 saltwater tanks containing exhibits on local marine life. A shark tank, seashell collection, fossil display, touch tank and multimedia programs are all part of this learning experience. Seasonal whale-watching and tidepool tours can be arranged, and there are many classes offered on marine-related subjects. A great stop for families with kids. Free admission.

Long Beach Firefighters Museum   ★ ★

1445 Peterson Avenue, Long Beach, ☎ (310) 427-0026.
Hours open: 10 a.m.–2 p.m.
This small museum, housed in the city's old (1925) fire station, is dedicated to the city's firefighting history and includes several vintage fire engines and other artifacts, plus early photos of Long Beach. Open only on the second Saturday of the month, or by appointment on Wednesdays. Free admission.

Long Beach Museum of Art   ★ ★ ★

2300 E. Ocean Boulevard, Long Beach, 90803, ☎ (310) 439-2119.
Hours Open: 12 a.m.–5 p.m.
Housed in a 1912 mansion overlooking the ocean, this museum features a permanent collection and changing exhibitions of contemporary and video art. A sculpture garden, coffeehouse and gift store are also located here.

Historical Sites

Long Beach Marine Stadium   ★ ★

5255 Appian Way, Long Beach.
Built in 1932 for the Olympic rowing competition at the Los Angeles Games, this was the first man-made rowing course in the U.S. and the first in the world designed specifically for rowing and boating. Commemorated as a historic site in 1992, it is still used for water-skiing, boating and other events.

Skinny House

708 Gladys Avenue, Long Beach.
Featured in *Ripley's Believe It Or Not* as the nation's narrowest home, this house was built in 1932 by Nelson Rummond on a bet that he could not build a habitable residence on a lot which measured only 10 by 50 feet. Rummond hired unemployed craftsmen to build the compact house, which contains 860 square feet, has three stories, and is built in the Old English Tudor style.

Tours

Ace Aerial Tours ★★★

3333 East Spring Street, #224, Long Beach, 90806, ☎ (800) 595-1544.
View Long Beach or other major Los Angeles sights from above aboard four- to seven-passenger planes, or experience the thrill of barnstorming in a restored 1943 open-cockpit biplane. Tour prices start at $25 per person, and a scenic 35-minute sunset flight along the coast is $75 per couple, including champagne. "Barnstorming" takes place on the first and third Saturdays of the month and is priced at $95 per person for a 30-minute flight.

Catalina Cruises ★★★

320 Golden Shore, Long Beach, 90802, ☎ (800) 538-4554.
Departures to Santa Catalina Island—a two hour trip—twice a day from downtown Long Beach aboard 700-passenger boats. Snacks and beverages are served in an open lounge on board, and glass windows provide expansive views of the sea. One-way cost is $10.50 for adults, $9.50 for children 2-11, $1 for children under 2. Round trip cost is $21.00 for adults, $19 for children 2-11, $2 for children under 2. Whale-watching tours are offered January-March.

Catalina Express ★★

P.O. Box 1391, San Pedro, 90833, ☎ (310) 519-1212.
Leaves from Berth 95, San Pedro.
Ninety-minute service to Catalina Island from San Pedro, Long Beach or Redondo Beach. Faster service aboard new Hydrofoil. Several trips daily.

Discovery Tours ★★

Catalina Island Harbor, Avalon, ☎ (310) 510-2000.
This unique trip to Catalina Island takes visitors on a semi-submersible ship to Catalina's famed Undersea Gardens. Passengers sit in a cabin lined with windows that allow for a nearly 360-degree view under the sea. Prices are $18 for adults and $12 for children for the 40-minute ride.

Gondola Getaway ★★★

5437 Ocean Boulevard, Long Beach, 90803, ☎ (310) 433-9595.
Can't afford that trip to Venice, Italy? Then climb aboard a sleek, wooden gondola and glide, Venice-style, through the romantic canals of Long Beach. Your gondolier provides a basket filled with fresh bread, choice cheeses and mouth-watering salami; you provide the appropriate wine. $55 affords a one-hour cruise for two. Open noon to midnight; reservations required.

Long Beach Carriage Company ★★

2150 Eucalyptus, Long Beach, 90806, ☎ (310) 499-1769.

Take a scenic tour of the California coast in an elegant horse-drawn carriage from this company, based at the *Queen Mary* Seaport. A 30-minute trip for up to four adults is priced at $35.

Queen Mary   ★ ★ ★ ★

Pier J, Long Beach, 90801, ☎ *(310) 435-3511.*
Hours open: 10 a.m.–6 p.m.
Long Beach Freeway (710) south from Los Angeles.

The luxury liner *Queen Mary*, built in 1934, is open for daily tours and will, hopefully, remain so under a new agreement between the city of Long Beach and the Harbor Commission on the Port of Long Beach. On view aboard the *Queen Mary* are the bridge, wheelhouse, engine room, staterooms, dining room, wartime barracks and other areas; a 90-minute guided tour is available for $5. Children 4–11, $4; under 4 free. General admission: $7.

Parks and Gardens

Angel's Gate Park   ★ ★

3601 South Gaffey Street, San Pedro.
The thing to see here is the Korean Friendship Bell, a gift to the people of the U.S. from the people of South Korea in 1976. The 17-ton bell, which is rung three times a year, is purported to be the largest oriental bell in the world.

Long Beach for Kids

The Long Beach Children's Museum is guaranteed to generate lots of hands-on fun, and there are always special programs and workshops going on, especially in summer and around the holidays. Call for a current schedule of events.

Long Beach Children's Museum   ★ ★ ★

445 Long Beach Boulevard, Long Beach, 90802, ☎ *(310) 495-1653.*
Hours pen: 11 a.m.–4 p.m.
In the Long Beach Plaza Mall.

An art kitchen, dress-up section, hospital, MTD bus, puppet theatre, disassembly station and other hands-on exhibits make this small children's museum a hit with the younger set. Special events offered throughout the year include arts and crafts workshops, book fairs and holiday celebrations. A special hands-on arts and crafts activity is offered every Friday afternoon. Children must be accompanied by an adult—and he or she should be prepared to stick like glue to the kid and participate in the fun. Admission for children two–12 is $4.25; children under two are admitted free. General admission: $4.95.

Events

Virtually everyplace that there's a harbor along the L.A. County coast, there are special events associated with it. The harbors are the focal points of many beach cities, and tend to draw a strong tourist following that is sustained by a constant lineup of water-related goings on. These include various festivals, boat shows, music festivals and the ubiquitous Christmas parades of lights, when boats are decked out with a startling array of Christmas lights and decorations and paraded through the harbor. Check with the local tourist office for a complete schedule of events going on while you're in town.

One of the most popular events in Long Beach is its annual Boat Show, which celebrated its 26th anniversary in 1994. The fall show takes place simultaneously at the convention center and the downtown marina, so you can see every sort of water craft you can imagine both on land and in the water. Another top local event is the annual Indy Car circuit Toyota Grand Prix, the nation's biggest race through city streets, which attracts more than 200,000 spectators each spring. If you're in town in late October, the annual Tastes of Sunset Holiday Food & Wine Festival held at the Long Beach Convention Center is great fun, with samples of over 300 specialty foods, wines and microbrewed beers on tap for tasting. Also at the convention center is an annual Country Folk Art Show & Sale, one of the best folk arts and crafts shows in the country.

If you're an experienced diver, call for information on Long Beach's annual Underwater Clean-up, where prizes are awarded to divers who retrieve the most unusual debris from the ocean bottom.

Artist's Market ★★★

2300 East Ocean Boulevard, Long Beach, 90803, *(310) 439-2119.*
This annual juried fine arts and crafts festival takes place in early June at the Long Beach Museum of Art.

Fourth of July Fireworks ★★★

Clark Avenue and Carson Street, Long Beach, 90808, *(310) 420-4018.*
Watch the rockets' red glare at this annual spectacle sponsored by the Long Beach Fire Department.

Long Beach Blues Festival ★★★

1288 North Bellflower Boulevard, Long Beach, 90815, *(310) 985-5566. On the campus of Cal State University Long Beach.*
Weekend blues festival held each September that features various (and usually top-name) blues artists, as well as a bountiful supply of gastronomic delights.

Long Beach Boat Show ★★

Long Beach Convention Center and downtown marina, Long Beach, ☎ *(714) 633-7581.*
This week-long exhibition has been a fixture in Long Beach for more than 25 years, and is a must for boating enthusiasts. All kinds of watercraft are on display, and free boating seminars are conducted daily. The show is held at the Convention Center, but there are also boats on display at the marina so you can see how they operate in the water.

Long Beach Sea Festival

Various locations, Long Beach, ☎ *(310) 421-9431.*
The Long Beach Sea Festival—which celebrates its 63rd anniversary in 1995—takes place the entire month of August at various locations throughout Long Beach. The emphasis is on beach-related activities, and there's something for everyone.

Sports and Recreation

Alfredo's Beach Rentals

Various locations, Long Beach, ☎ *(310) 491-7522.*
From seven locations along the beach, Alfredo's dispenses bikes, skates, boogie boards, boats, rafts, beach chairs and umbrellas—everything you need to enjoy a day at the beach. You have to pay a rental fee, of course.

Go Boats

6201 Bayshore Walk, Long Beach, ☎ *(310) 987-0511.*
Go Boats has everything that floats: *J-24, Cal-20, Cal-14,* and *Laser* sailboats, plus outboard dinghies and canoes. Rental prices vary, but most are between $15 and $40 per hour.

Long Beach Water Sports

730 East 4th Street, Long Beach, ☎ *(310) 432-0187.*
A best bet for kayakers, Long Beach Water Sports has excursions to the harbor estuary, to nearby Laguna Beach and Palos Verdes, and one- and two-day trips to Catalina Island. If you're up to it, they'll even arrange kayaking trips to Hawaii or Mexico! All equipment is included. Beginning and advanced kayaking lessons are also offered, and you learn by doing. Prices generally range from $45 to more than $200.

Skyrider Parasail of Long Beach

Seaport Village/Shoreline Drive, Long Beach, ☎ *(310) 493-4979.*
Have a wild and giddy time on a two-passenger parasail that takes off from a launching pad on the back of a boat and soars 400 feet above the deep blue of the Pacific Ocean shoreline for 10 minutes at a stretch. Souvenir photos of your fantastic flight are included in the general price and gift certificates are available. Admission price is $38 per person.

Toyota Grand Prix of Long Beach

Downtown Long Beach, Long Beach, 90806, ☎ *(310) 436-9953.*
The United States' oldest Formula One street circuit race runs through downtown Long Beach each April and is accompanied by a golf tournament, charity balls and car shows. Some big names in racing are always on hand. Tickets are available at the Grand Prix Ticket Office *(430 East First Street, Long Beach),* or though Ticketmaster outlets.

Long Beach: Music, Dance and Theatre

The beaches are not the cultural center of Los Angeles by any means, yet many of the beach cities have their own performing arts centers and/or several small theatre venues. In addition to those listed below, be sure to contact the ticket offices at local universities (such as Cal State Long Beach) for information on upcoming cultural events.

Music

Concerts in the Grove   ★★★

1250 Bellflower Boulevard, Long Beach, 90840, ☎ *(310) 985-5252.*
July through August, listeners can delight to the melodies of "Concerts in the Grove," performed at the California State University Long Beach Soroptimist House. The series boasts a variety of musical artists, who perform under the stars. Picnic dinners welcome.

Long Beach Opera   ★★★

6372 Pacific Coast Highway, Long Beach, 90803, ☎ *(310) 596-5556.*
This local opera company, directed by Michael Milenski, performs at various L.A. venues.

Long Beach Symphony   ★★★

555 East Ocean Boulevard, #106, Long Beach, ☎ *(310) 436-3203.*

One of the few female symphony orchestra conductors in the nation, Maestro JoAnn Falletta leads the Long Beach Symphony Orchestra, as well as the Virginia Symphony and the Women's Philharmonic of San Francisco.

Dance

L.A. Classica Ballet

1122 E. Wardlow Road, Long Beach, 90810, ☎ (310) 427-5206.
Formerly the Long Beach Ballet, this is Southern California's largest professional resident/touring company. Its December through June season in Long Beach is held at the 3141-seat Terrace Theatre.

Theatre

Long Beach Civic Light Opera

300 East Ocean Boulevard, Long Beach, 90802, ☎ (310) 432-7926.
Performing at the Terrace Theatre at the Long Beach Convention and Entertainment Center, this group celebrates its 46th season in 1995-96.

Long Beach: Nightlife

In Long Beach, forgo the tour of the *Queen Mary* and order a drink from the aft bar while you enjoy the portside ambience.

Birdland West

105 West Broadway, Long Beach, 90802, ☎ (310) 432-2004.
This first-rate jazz club attracts national talent such as Hugh Masekela and Les McCann. An excellent house quintet fills in between headline shows. Tuesday evening is devoted to comedy. Open from 7 p.m.

Hop, The

5201 Clark Avenue, Lakewood, ☎ (310) 630-2229.
Classic rock 'n roll from the '60s to the '80s is featured at The Hop, where live bands perform on Thursday and Friday nights and there's a comedy and hypnotist show on Tuesday nights.

Legends

5236 East Second Street, Long Beach, ☎ (310) 433-5743.
Legends is the ultimate sports bar, and the perfect hangout for the hardcore sports fan. The bar scene is lively, and there are games to watch on eight big-screen TVs.

Lobby Bar

Long Beach Hilton, Long Beach, ☎ (310) 983-3460.
The upscale Lobby Bar is a popular local nightspot—especially between 5 and 7 p.m. Monday through Friday, when it serves complimentary snacks and discounts drinks.

Observation Bar

1126 Queens Highway, Long Beach, ☎ (310) 435-3511.
This art deco lounge aboard the *Queen Mary* is a perfect place to relax, soak up the atmosphere, and look out over the city—or into the eyes of Mr. or Ms. Right. There's live entertainment, too. Open Monday through Thursday, 1-midnight; Friday and Saturday, 12:30 p.m. to 2 a.m.; Sunday, 12:30 p.m. to midnight.

System M Caffe

213-A Pine Avenue, Long Beach, ☎ (310) 435-2525.
Hours Open: 11 a.m.–11 p.m.

Nightly entertainment from jazz to blues to alternative music can be enjoyed at this casual coffee house, where poetry readings also happen periodically. Very hip.

Yankee Doodles

4100 East Ocean Boulevard, Long Beach, ☎ *(310) 439-9777.*
Yankee Doodles has a branch in Long Beach, a branch in Santa Monica, a branch in Calgary (that's Canada, luv) and a branch in Edmonton (also Canada), and it thus proclaims itself "North America's most unique sports and game bar." Well, you'll have to see for yourself if it lives up to its claim, but you'll find plenty to entertain you, including 33 billiards tables, eight games being beamed down by six satellites, darts, shuffleboard, ping pong and foosball accompanied by a lively bar scene and a casual menu of snackables like hot wings, sandwiches and pizza.

Long Beach: Shopping

Long Beach has one of the largest used book stores in the country in the form of **Acres of Books** *(240 Long Beach Boulevard)*, which stocks 750,000 titles. Browsers are always welcome at this family-run store, which has been at the same location for more than 60 years.

For a unique shopping experience, head over to the **PCH Antique Mall** *(3500 E. Pacific Coast Highway)*, where scores of antique vendors sell their wares (including Hollywood memorabilia) under one roof. Other shopping options in Long Beach include **Shoreline Village**, a typical tourist-oriented seaside shopping and amusement center whose shops include **Majestic Counterfeit Jewels** *(425 Shoreline Village Drive)*, just the place for finding something to wear when the family jewels are in the vault; and **The Marketplace** *(where Westminster meets Second on PCH)*, a collection of specialty chops and restaurants set around a lake.

Long Beach: Where to Stay

Long Beach

Hotels and Resorts

Best Western Golden Sails   **$95–$115**   ★★

6285 East Pacific Coast Highway
☎ *(800) 528-1234, (310) 596-1631, FAX: 310-594-0623.*
Single: $95–$105. Double: $105–$115.
This motor hotel built around a courtyard is adjacent to the marina, three miles from the city center. Many rooms have refrigerators, and some have in-room spas. Golfing is free on a nine-hole executive course. Amenities: pool, golf, Jacuzzi, balcony or patio, hair salon, family plan, complimentary airport pickup service. 169 rooms. Credit Cards: CB, V, MC, DC, A.

Holiday Inn Long Beach Airport   **$109–$119**   ★★

2640 Lakewood Boulevard
☎ *(800) 465-4329, (310) 597-4401, FAX: 310-597-0601.*
Single: $109. Double: $119.
Located a half-mile from the Long Beach Airport, this motor inn has refrigerators in some rooms. A courtesy shuttle takes guests to the air-

port, the Convention Center and to nearby attractions such as the *Queen Mary*, Shoreline Village, Disneyland and Knott's Berry Farm. Amenities: pool, golf, exercise room, balcony or patio, family plan, conference facilities, complimentary airport pickup service. 231 rooms. Credit Cards: CB, V, MC, DC, A.

Hotel Queen Mary   **$75–$160**   ★★★

Pier J, Long Beach Harbor
☎ *(800) 437-2934, (310) 435-3511.*
Single: $75–$160. Double: $80–$160.

Guest and public rooms of this famous old ocean liner were redecorated in 1990. Staying on board is truly a unique hotel experience, but not for the claustrophobic, as most staterooms are much smaller than the standard hotel room (but much larger than the typical cruise ship quarters). The decor harks back to the art deco era, and the plethora of rich woods is a real treat. This is a popular tourist attraction; stay elsewhere if you seek solitude. Oh—and just to show you that the *Queen Mary* isn't TOO stuffy—the hotel will arrange for you to spend a night in one of its deluxe staterooms, then jump from its 220-foot bungee tower. In these hard times, you've gotta do what you can to bring in the business. Amenities: exercise room, conference facilities, complimentary airport pickup service. 365 rooms. Credit Cards: CB, V, MC, DC, A.

Howard Johnson Plaza   **$53–$58**   ★★

1133 Atlantic Avenue
☎ *(800) 442-1688, (310) 590-8858, FAX: 310-983-1607.*
Single: $53. Double: $58.

Rooms in this newer motor inn, located in the business district, have refrigerators, and in-room movies are available. The hotel provides 24-hour shuttle service to the Convention Center and to Long Beach Airport. Amenities: pool, golf, Jacuzzi, family plan, conference facilities, complimentary airport pickup service. 135 rooms. Credit Cards: V, MC, DC, A.

Hyatt Regency   **$109–$150**   ★★★

200 South Pine Avenue
☎ *(800) 233-1234, (310) 491-1234, FAX: 310-432-1972.*
Single: $109–$125. Double: $134–$150.

This striking tower hotel is located adjacent to the Convention Center and Long Beach Marina, and much of the facility is surrounded by water. Several good restaurants offer varied fare and the accommodations include cane and wicker chairs, marble tables and combination baths. It may not be as luxurious as the Sheraton, but it's a good value for the price and has a nice, resort-like atmosphere. Amenities: beach location, pool, golf, health club, Jacuzzi, family plan, conference facilities, club floor. 521 rooms. Credit Cards: CB, V, MC, DC, A.

Long Beach Hilton   **$115–$185**   ★★★

Two World Trade Center
☎ *(800) 445-8667, (310) 983-3400, FAX: 310-983-1200.*
Single: $115–$165. Double: $135–$185.

The newer Long Beach Hilton is a business-oriented hotel adjacent to the Greater Los Angeles World Trade Center, offering state-of-the-art business support services and expansive meeting space. Guest rooms feature work desks, two telephones, language line for translations, and dataport plug-in capability. Most rooms have ocean views. Amenities: pool, health club, Jacuzzi, sauna, balcony or patio, family plan, conference facilities, club floor, business services, complimentary airport pickup service. 398 rooms. Credit Cards: V, MC, DC, A.

Marriott Long Beach AP $79–$134   ★★★

4700 Airport Plaza Drive
☎ *(800) 228-9290, (310) 425-5210, FAX: 310-425-2744.*
Single: $79–$134. Double: $79–$134.

Features an attractive rose marble lobby and both an indoor and outdoor pool. Guest rooms are contemporary in style, with two floors designated for nonsmokers. Amenities: pool, golf, exercise room, Jacuzzi, sauna, family plan, conference facilities, club floor, business services, complimentary airport pickup service. 311 rooms. Credit Cards: CB, V, MC, DC, A.

Ramada Inn $59–$119   ★★★

5325 East Pacific Coast Highway
☎ *(800) 272-6232, (310) 597-1341, FAX: 310-597-1341.*
Single: $59–$119. Double: $59–$119.

This recently-renovated motor inn is about a mile from the beach, but it's in a nice location surrounded by tropical gardens and across from a park with tennis courts and a golf course. There are 17 suites in addition to the rooms, and each features a jacuzzi tub. A free shuttle will whisk you around town or to the airport, or you can opt to stay in and eat barbecue at the hotel's country-western saloon, Papas BBQ. Amenities: pool, Jacuzzi, private spas, balcony or patio, family plan, conference facilities, complimentary airport pickup service. 143 rooms. Credit Cards: V, MC, A.

Renaissance Long Beach $95–$155   ★★★

111 East Ocean Boulevard
☎ *(800) 272-6232, (310) 437-5900, FAX: 310-499-2509.*
Single: $95–$155. Double: $95–$155.

The best hotel on the block until the Sheraton opened, this hotel caters to businessmen (the Convention Center is adjacent) and large groups. Suits and ties predominate in the lobby; leisure travelers are certainly welcome but may feel out of place. Fitness options include an outdoor pool and Jacuzzi, a health club and a masseuse on call for guests. Request a westside room for great ocean views. Renovations are scheduled to begin in 1995. Amenities: pool, golf, health club, Jacuzzi, sauna, balcony or patio, family plan, conference facilities, club floor, complimentary airport pickup service. 374 rooms. Credit Cards: CB, V, MC, DC, A.

Residence Inn Long Beach Airport $110–$135   ★★★

4111 East Willow Street
☎ *(800) 331-3131, (310) 595-0909, FAX: 310-988-0587.*
Single: $110–$135. Double: $110–$135.

This Marriott all-suite hotel offers a complimentary continental breakfast and happy hour. Each unit includes a fully equipped kitchen. Recent renovations included replacement of all carpets, furniture and paint in guest rooms, as well as the addition of VCRs. Amenities: pool, Jacuzzi, balcony or patio, family plan, conference facilities, business services, complimentary airport pickup service. 216 rooms. Credit Cards: CB, V, MC, DC, A.

Seaport Marina   **$59–$135**   ★★★

6400 East Pacific Coast Highway
☎ *(800) 434-8451, (310) 434-8451, FAX: 310-598-6028.*
Single: $59–$135. Double: $59–$135.

This hotel has changed both names and hands several times in recent
years. It was once a Hyatt, then the Clarion Edgewater, and now is
independently owned. The good part is that the new owners are spiff-
ing it up considerably, and all guest rooms have been renovated.
Now, they're working on the exterior, which reflects a marine theme
relating to the adjacent marina. With these improvements, this is a
good value. Breakfast and evening cocktails are included in the rate.
Amenities: beach location, pool, Jacuzzi, balcony or patio, family
plan, conference facilities, club floor, complimentary airport pickup
service. 249 rooms. Credit Cards: CB, V, MC, DC, A.

Sheraton Long Beach   **$135–$155**   ★★★

333 East Ocean Boulevard
☎ *(800) 325-3535, (310) 436-3000, FAX: 310-436-9176.*
Single: $135–$155. Double: $135–$155.

Located across the street from the Convention Center, this hotel is
perhaps the best temporary address in town. A palm-lined drive leads
to a light, airy lobby containing both a lounge with a piano bar and a
louder lounge with a DJ. Two eateries serve food and pool-side meal
service is available. Accommodations are more than first class with
thick carpets and light woods. All rooms have TVs hidden in armoires,
minibars and wall-papered combination baths. A complimentary
newspaper is delivered to rooms. Amenities: pool, health club,
Jacuzzi, sauna, balcony or patio, family plan, conference facilities,
business services, complimentary airport pickup service. 460 rooms.
Credit Cards: CB, V, MC, DC, A.

Travelodge Long Beach   **$79–$99**   ★★

700 Queensway Drive
☎ *(800) 255-3050, (310) 435-7676, FAX: 310-437-0866.*
Single: $79–$99. Double: $89–$99.

This oceanfront resort has moorings for 40 guest boats and is within
walking distance of the *Queen Mary*. Some rooms have coffee makers
and refrigerators; most have ocean views. Sports facilities include a
jogging track, volleyball court and tennis courts. Amenities: beach
location, pool, tennis, balcony or patio, family plan, conference facilities, complimentary airport pickup service. 194 rooms. Credit Cards: V,
MC, A.

San Pedro

Hotels and Resorts

Best Western San Pedro   **$95**   ★★★

111 South Gaffey Street
☎ *(800) 528-1234, (310) 514-1414, FAX: 310-831-8262.*
Single: $95. Double: $95.

European ambience dominates this small hotel. Four suites have fireplaces; all rooms have refrigerators. Complimentary continental
breakfast included. Amenities: pool, Jacuzzi, balcony or patio, family
plan, conference facilities. 60 rooms. Credit Cards: V, MC, DC, A.

Best Western Sunrise   **$58–$72**   ★★

525 South Harbor Boulevard

☎ *(800) 528-1234, (310) 548-1080, FAX: 310-519-0380.*
Single: $58–$64. Double: $66–$72.

This motel across from the Los Angeles Maritime Museum offers a complimentary continental breakfast. Free van service to cruise lines. Amenities: pool, Jacuzzi, sauna, family plan, conference facilities. 112 rooms. Credit Cards: V, MC, A.

Doubletree World Port $115–$165   ★★★

2800 Via Cabrillo Marina
☎ *(800) 222-8733, (310) 514-3344, FAX: 310-514-8945.*
Single: $115–$155. Double: $125–$165.

This hotel has much to offer, including views of the harbor, a couple of good restaurants, a lighted tennis court, outdoor heated pool and access to a paved jogging path that runs along the marina. Chocolate chip cookies are offered when you arrive, and there are ample fitness facilities for working them off after you've indulged. Rates include breakfast. Refrigerators and microwaves are available for a small fee. Amenities: pool, tennis, exercise room, Jacuzzi, sauna, hair salon, family plan, conference facilities, complimentary airport pickup service. 226 rooms. Credit Cards: CB, V, MC, DC, A.

Sheraton L.A. Harbor $105–$115   ★★★

601 S. Palos Verdes Street
☎ *(800) 325-3535, (310) 519-8200, FAX: 310-519-8421.*
Single: $105. Double: $115.

Opened in June 1990, this Sheraton offers wonderful harbor views, and is within walking distance of major shipping and cruise lines. Amenities: pool, exercise room, Jacuzzi, sauna, balcony or patio, family plan, conference facilities, club floor, business services. 244 rooms. Credit Cards: CB, V, MC, DC, A.

Seal Beach

Bed and Breakfast

Seal Beach Inn $118–$255   ★★★

212 5th Street
☎ *(800) 443-3292, (310) 493-2416, FAX: 310-799-0483.*
Single: $118–$255. Double: $118–$255.

This small Mediterranean-style inn features individually decorated cottages and villas. Complimentary full breakfast, evening wine, cheese and coffee are offered to guests. Special touches include a private library and a charming garden setting with fountains and a brick courtyard. This is a great place to relax. Amenities: pool, Jacuzzi, balcony or patio, conference facilities. 23 rooms. Credit Cards: CB, V, MC, DC, A.

Hotels and Resorts

Radisson Inn Seal Beach $105–$125   ★★

600 Marina Drive
☎ *(800) 333-3333, (310) 493-7501, FAX: 310-596-3448.*
Single: $105–$110. Double: $115–$125.

Complimentary continental breakfast is included at this hotel located two blocks from the beach. Bicycle rentals are available to guests who want to cruise the nearby bike paths. Amenities: pool, exercise room, Jacuzzi, balcony or patio, family plan, conference facilities. 71 rooms. Credit Cards: V, MC, DC, A.

Long Beach: Where to Eat

The big news in Long Beach is the demise of 555 East, which has been resurrected in the form of Dominick's East Village, an Italian-American restaurant whose reviews have been little more than lukewarm so far.

Long Beach
American

Delius   **$$$**   ★★★★

3550 Long Beach Boulevard, ☎ (310) 426-0694.
Dinner: prix fixe $42.
One seating each evening (7:30 p.m.) for a bargain prix fixe meal that includes very good wines. Don't let the lackluster location fool you: this is an excellent restaurant with a superb menu that changes weekly. Closed: Mon, Sun. Features: own baking, wine and beer only, rated wine cellar. Jacket requested. Reservations required. Credit Cards: V, MC.

Mustard Seed, The   **$$**   ★★★

5624 Atlantic Avenue, ☎ (310) 422-6090.
Lunch: 11:30 a.m.–3 p.m., entrees $6–$13.
Dinner: 5–9 p.m., entrees $9–$20.
The fare is mostly American at this restaurant serving old favorites such as Yankee pot roast as well as trendier dishes with a Mediterranean flair. Reasonable prices make it a local favorite. Closed: Sun. Features: full bar. Reservations recommended. Credit Cards: CB, V, MC, DC.

Shenandoah Cafe   **$$**   ★★

4722 East 2nd Street, ☎ (310) 434-3469.
Specialties: southern-style dinners.
Dinner: 5–10 p.m., entrees $10–$20.
American cooking at its best. The fritters are to die for, and so are the gracious, cozy vibes this little charmer emits. Features: own baking, wine and beer only, late dining. Reservations recommended. Credit Cards: V, MC, A.

French

La Grotte   **$$$**   ★★

300 Ocean Boulevard, ☎ (310) 437-2119.
Specialties: fresh fish; rack of lamb; escargots; crab bisque.
Lunch: 11:30 a.m.–2:30 p.m., entrees $13–$15.
Dinner: 6–10 p.m., entrees $17–$30.
The food isn't cheap here, but La Grotte, in business for more than 20 years at the same location, is solid, offering classic French cuisine and great service. Closed: Sun. Features: outside dining, own baking, full bar, late dining. Jacket requested. Reservations required. Credit Cards: D, CB, V, MC, DC, A.

Italian

Dominick's East Village   **$$$**   ★★

555 East Ocean Boulevard, ☎ (310) 437-0626.
Lunch: from 11:30 a.m., entrees $10–$20.
Dinner: from 5:30 p.m., entrees $10–$25.
Dominick's, on the site of the former 555 East, is the creation of the folks who own the Water Grill and Ocean Avenue Seafood. So far, the food is hit-or-miss, but maybe Dominick's just needs some time to hit

its stride. Best bets are the family-style meals, which range from about
$10 per person at lunch to $19 per person at dinner. The portions are
huge, the service friendly and the ambience pleasant. When the
kitchen gets it together, this will be a great addition to Long Beach.
Lunch served Monday through Friday. Features: own baking, late
dining. Credit Cards: V, MC, DC, A.

L'Opera $$$ ★★★

101 Pine Avenue, ☎ *(310) 491-0066.*
Specialties: vegetarian lasagne; grilled lamb.
Lunch: 11 a.m.–3 p.m., entrees $12–$18.
Dinner: 5–11 p.m., entrees $15–$20.

The pasta is reputed to be as good as any on the West Side, the ambience is exceptional, and the innovative Italian cuisine has everyone
talking. The wine list is a perfect match. Unfortunately, service may
not be up to the rest of the experience, but at least you'll wait comfortably in the palatial surroundings in this former bank building near
the *Queen Mary*. Lunch served Monday through Friday. Features:
own baking, full bar, rated wine cellar, late dining. Reservations
required. Credit Cards: CB, V, MC, DC, A.

Mum's $$$ ★★

144 Pine Avenue, ☎ *(310) 437-7700.*
Lunch: from 11 a.m., entrees $7–$14.
Dinner: to 10 p.m., entrees $17–$22.

Mum's has a fun atmosphere, complete with live jazz and dancing on
the weekends, and the Northern Italian cuisine is pretty good, too. All
of the pasta is homemade, and the menu is just creative enough to be
almost trendy. Best of all, the atmosphere is refreshingly unpretentious. Features: outside dining, own baking, rated wine cellar, late
dining. Reservations recommended. Credit Cards: D, CB, V, MC, DC, A.

Latin American

Cha Cha Cha $$ ★★

762 Pacific Avenue, ☎ *(310) 436-3900.*
Specialties: Jamaican jerk chicken; Cha Cha chicken sandwich.
Lunch: from 11:30 a.m., entrees $6–$15.
Dinner: to 9:30 p.m., entrees $6–$15.

Everything from pizza to soup—all with the characteristic Cha Cha
Cha Caribbean flair—is on the menu at this attractive, tropically
themed restaurant. Fun food and lots of good beers. Features: full
bar. Reservations recommended. Credit Cards: V, MC, A.

Seafood

Simon & Seafort's $$$ ★★

340 Golden Shore Drive, ☎ *(310) 435-2333.*
Specialties: fresh Alaska king salmon; pacific oysters.
Lunch: 11:30 a.m.–2:15 p.m., entrees $8–$13.
Dinner: 5–9 p.m., entrees $12–$30.

A Long Beach favorite, Simon & Seafort's puts an emphasis on seafood, but also offers steak, chops and pasta, as well as a view of the
harbor. Features: splendid view, own baking, full bar. Reservations
recommended. Credit Cards: CB, V, MC, DC, A.

San Pedro

Mediterranean

Papadakis Taverna **$$$** ★★★

301 West Sixth Street, ☎ (310) 548-1186.
Specialties: pastitsio; moussaka; shish kebab.
Dinner: 5–9 p.m., entrees $15–$35.

Selecting your dinner from an eye-popping platter of fresh meats is no easy task, but fans say the lamb chops are always fantastic. The floor show featuring folk-dancing waiters is loads of fun. Features: own baking, wine and beer only, rated wine cellar, late dining, private dining rooms. Jacket requested. Reservations recommended. Credit Cards: V, MC, DC.

ORANGE COUNTY

Say "Orange County" to the average Californian, and he thinks "Disneyland, Disneyland, DISNEYLAND!" (Or, "conservative, conservative, CONSERVATIVE!" More about that later.) Most out-of-staters don't know Disneyland is in Orange County, and they really don't care. They just know it's an "L.A. thing" that they've got to do. Disneyland is arguably the only reason that some people (or hundreds of thousands of people) make a pilgrimage to Southern California each year, and it's one of only two L.A. attractions (the other is, interestingly, Hollywood) that garnered three coveted Michelin stars in the 1994 Michelin Green Guide to California.

The Magic Kingdom has been a prime Orange County tourist attraction since July 17, 1955, when the legendary Mr. Disney, himself, opened the park, which then contained only 18 major attractions. Since then, more than 300 million visitors have passed through the gates, and they come back time after time as the park expands and adds new things to see and do (there are now more than 60 major attractions at Disneyland, with more in the planning stages). The park is celebrating its 40th anniversary in 1995, and special events will be taking place throughout the year to commemorate the milestone.

In many ways, Disneyland is the embodiment of well-scrubbed and squeaky-clean Orange County, which lies outside its borders. Its cast members (everyone—from the costumed Disney characters to the custodial staff—is a "cast member" at Disneyland) are largely drawn from the conservative surrounding community, and 75 percent are fresh-faced college students.

Disney spends a fortune to keep the park immaculate and perfectly groomed (all streets are hosed down and steam-cleaned after closing each night), and it takes a staff of 60 just to care for the landscaping (one million annuals are planted each year throughout the park, and the flower portrait of Mickey at the park's Main Entrance is replanted nine times a year to keep it looking fresh).

More than 50 electricians are on hand to manage the electrical needs of the park, including more than 100,000 light bulbs (all bulbs are changed when they reach 80 percent of their "average life"), and 20,000 gallons of paint keep the place looking spiffy year-round.

While it may not live up to its billing as "the Happiest Place on Earth" to those who have to pay a hefty admission price, stand in huge, snaking lines for over an hour to experience a three-minute thrill ride, eat outrageously expensive (and mostly mediocre) food, and drag around a passel of tired, crabby kids who want to go home and take a nap after the first two hours in the park, Disneyland is still a pretty cool place. (For complete Disneyland information, see "Orange County Theme/Amusement Parks").

Sailing from Newport Beach to Catalina is a fun getaway.

Although most people seem to think that Orange County simply evolved around Disneyland (which is true to some extent), it has actually been in a world of its own since 1889 when it seceded from L.A. County, which lies approximately 28 miles to the north. (The politically correct need no reminding that you must never refer to any part of Orange County as a "suburb" of Los Angeles.)

Now encompassing more than 780 square miles, and home to 2.4 million people, Orange County has its own magazine (*Orange Coast*), its own airport (John Wayne/Orange County), its own world-class performing arts center (the 3000-seat, state-of-the-art Orange County Center for the Performing Arts), and its own duo of professional sports teams (the American Baseball League's California Angels, who play at Anaheim Stadium, and the NHL's Mighty Ducks, who take to the ice at the Arrowhead Pond), any one of which may fly the coop at any moment if a better offer comes along.

It is also known as one of the premiere bastions of conservatism in California, where business (or at least tourism) is booming, population growth is considered a positive thing, median home prices (at $217,000 in 1994) tend to keep undesirables away, family values are held in high esteem, and voters are overwhelmingly Republican. (Cultural diversity is not something you'll hear much about from the Anaheim/Orange County Visitor & Convention Bureau.)

While this profile may be more fiction than fact in some parts of Orange County, especially in the inland sections (a recent drug sweep in Santa Ana netted more than 100 suspects), the perception has always been that Orange County residents are some of Southern California's most Beautiful People: young, rich, sun-bronzed and in fabulous shape.

In fact, a recent study on Orange County singles did much to promote this stereotype by reporting that two-thirds of Orange County's single adults are white and under 40, and that wealth and good looks are the qualities most sought-after by those looking for mates. Of course, if you have the first, getting the second is simple. Plastic surgery is very big business in Orange County.

Adding to Orange County's reputation as an upscale playground—in addition to its amusements parks—are more than 45 golf courses, 15 tennis clubs, 3000 restaurants, 300 miles of walking, hiking, cycling and rollerblading trails, some of the finest surfing beaches in Southern California and more than 46,000 hotel rooms, many of which are on or near the beach. The self-proclaimed "American Riviera" (Santa Barbarans, who always thought they had a lock on that title, might quibble), Orange County includes 42 miles of prime coastal beaches, many of them at the foot of such posh neighborhoods as Laguna or Newport Beach.

All of the above makes Orange County a natural tourist destination, and nearly 40 million visitors flock to the area in any given year.

Unfortunately, some extremely risky financial investments resulted in Orange County defaulting on its loans and having to declare bankruptcy in late 1994, a scenario that will doubtless have a lasting impact on many future projects. While one cynical resident suggested changing the county's name from Orange County to Lemon County, mortified civic leaders struggled to put the dream back together. As this book goes to press, the future of Orange County may have lost quite a bit of its luster.

Orange County: Things to See and Do

When you've tired of amusement parks and need a dose of real culture, Orange County has a lot to offer, scattered among its more kitschy attractions.

Rumor has it that Kevin Costner will be nominated for an Oscar for his newest role at the Movieland Wax Museum.

And speaking of kitschy, the **Movieland Wax Museum** in Buena Park has opened several new exhibits in the last year, including sets featuring Richard Gere in his *Sommersby* role and supermodel Cindy Crawford strutting her stuff as a model. In late 1994, a *Mrs. Doubtfire* exhibit opened, featuring Robin Williams in the popular role of the unusual housekeeper.

For a taste of Southern California beach culture, go to Huntington Beach, home of some of the best waves in California. Sure, there are a lot of excellent surfing beaches in Southern California, but Huntington Beach has carefully cultivated its reputation as the original Surf City, an image carried through with its Surfing Walk of Fame and International Surfing Museum.

The **Surfing Walk of Fame**, which features granite plaques with the image of a surfer on them and the inductee's name engraved at the bottom, was opened at the corner of Main and Pacific Coast Highway in late summer of 1994 as part of the festivities connected with the U.S. Open of Surfing. So far, honored surfers include the legendary "Father of Surfing," Duke Kahanamoku; Robert August, star of the original *Endless Summer* movie; Tom Blake, who invented the surfboard fin (among other things); Mark Richards, a four-time IPA/ASP World Champion from Australia; Bruce Brown, creator of the *Endless Summer* and other surfing films; and Joyce Hoffman, hailed as one of the greatest woman surfers of all time.

The **International Surfing Museum** has all kinds of surfboards and surfing memorabilia, plus, you can watch surfing videos from the museum's library, which contains all of the Bruce Brown films. So, hey, surfer dudes, forget all that Hollywood Walk of Fame stuff and come worship at the way cool shrine of surfdom. After you check out the sights, live the legend—the surf is always up at Surf City.

Surfers may be interested only in "shooting" the Huntington Beach pier, but the structure represents the heart of the city, and has a long history that includes being destroyed by storms and high seas on more than one occasion. The last time the pier was demolished was in 1988 (after a storm rendered it unsafe), but a half million people turned out for the opening of a new, $10.8 million, 1856-foot pier in 1992, with the promise that this time, the structure would last at least 100 years. The pier is the logical focal point for the city's tourism industry, and future plans call for a diner to open at the end of the pier, and a plaza to be built at the pier's entrance.

The **Richard M. Nixon Library and Birthplace** in Yorba Linda, which has gained interest since the late president's death (he is buried here, as is his wife, Patricia), provides an in-depth (if slightly whitewashed) look at Nixon's life and White House years through the eyes of well-trained docents whose protocol dictates, among other things, that they must never speak of President and Mrs. Nixon as "Dick" and "Pat," or argue with visitors about Watergate.

Slated to open on the Nixon library grounds in 1997 is the new Center for Peace and Freedom, to be dedicated to the pursuit of enlightened national interest in foreign policy and "pragmatic idealism" abroad.

The **Crystal Cathedral** *(12141 Chapman Avenue in Garden Grove)*, which is one of the West Coast's most awe-inspiring religious edifices, is of particular interest at Christmas and Easter, when it presents lavish holiday spectacles featuring hundreds of players, live animals and dazzling special effects. (For convenience, you can use your credit card when making a reservation to these big-time pageants, which are arguably a lot more opulent than anything the Lord, himself, ever experienced.)

Parks and Gardens

For a place known best for its amusement parks, Orange County has a lot to offer in terms of tranquil respites from the hustle and bustle. The most splendid is the Bolsa Chica Ecological Reserve, which is a wonderful escape for anyone seeking solace amid the wonders of nature, and more especially a birder's paradise. A 1.5-mile loop trail provides a look at some of the reserve's more than 300 species of avian life (birding is best in winter), as well as plants, a restored wetlands area and a variety of mammals and other animals. Note that dogs (even those on leashes) are not allowed anywhere in the reserve, and that you are admonished to stay on the trail at all times. Bring a pair of binoculars, and pick up a copy of the trail guide before you set out. Guided tours are available on the first Saturday of the month.

Also in Huntington Beach is Central Park, a 350-acre facility that includes nature trails, an equestrian center that features polo matches and horse shows (including the August GTE Directories Everything Pages Summer Classic), a playground, picnicking facilities and the excellent Huntington Beach Library.

You can let your dog run wild at Dog Park on Laguna Canyon Road in Laguna Beach. Everyone does, which means there are occasionally some little doggie disagreements, but mostly all the critters just run around in circles or chase each other. You might not have much fun, but your dog probably will, with two grassy acres for romping. Dog Park etiquette requires that you clean up after your pooch, and bags are thoughtfully provided at the gate.

Theme/Amusement Parks

No matter how many cultural attractions are to be found within its boundaries, Orange County will always be best-known for its amusement parks, especially that proverbial mother-of-all-amusement-parks, **Disneyland**.

Disneyland is not just for kids, by the way. It has rides for the most jaded thrill-seekers, lots of interesting attractions that adults will enjoy, displays of Disney memorabilia, a large selection of shops and restaurants, and some first-rate entertainment. The elaborate parades, filled with colorfully-costumed, bigger-than-life characters from Disney films, and lots of special effects, can be downright amazing (don't miss the Main Street Electrical Parade if it's happening while you're in town, or the astounding "Lion King Celebration," a parade and street show based on the popular animated movie). The park is definitely worth seeing no matter what your age, and you should plan to dedicate at least one full day to the process.

Disneyland: General Information

Some of the worst times to go to the park (in terms of the crowds) are during holiday and summer vacations (when kids are out of school), and on weekends. If you can, take your kids out of school and arrive early on a weekday, or, during the summer, arrive mid-day (when families with little children are starting to leave the park) and plan to stay late. (Note that all major rides and attractions occasionally close for refurbishment, so call ahead to make sure you favorites are open before you go—especially during the "off-season.") Sundays are the best weekend day to visit the park, especially if you get there early. Hours vary seasonally, so call the park's information number (☎ 714 999-4565) to confirm current hours of operation.

Admission to the park varies between about $25 and just over $30. Southern California residents who can show proof of local zip codes often get a substantial discount, and there are also discounted admission prices during the off-season and discounts for children under 12 and senior citizens. A guided tour package is also available, which includes unlimited access to rides and attractions in addition to the tour for $43 for adults, $34.50 for children.

Two- ($55 adults, $44 children) or three-day ($75.00 adults, $60.00 children) passes are the best way to go if you plan to spend more than one day in the Magic Kingdom, and if you visit the park more than four times a year, an annual passport (at about $100) represents significant savings (although it's not valid on holidays such as Thanksgiving, Christmas, New Year's or on holiday weekends). When figuring out your Disneyland budget, don't forget to add parking costs, which are $6 per day (or $25 for an annual parking pass).

Food is extremely expensive inside the park, especially in the sit-down restaurants, but there are a few spots—such as the Terrace in Tomorrowland—where you can get a burger and fries for a reasonable price (Disneyland sells more than four million hamburgers each year, probably because they're among the cheapest food options). You can also bring your own food; near the Parking Lot Tram Shop west of the main gate there are lockers large enough for coolers, and you can retrieve your food later and picnic at one of the tables located there. Or, leave food in your car and take a meal break from the park (be sure to get your hand stamped and retain your ticket for re-admittance) when everyone gets hungry.

It's hard to resist going into all the shops, which are packed with everything from Disney merchandise to "real" clothes and accessories. Most of Disneyland's shops carry goods which relate to the theme of the "land" in which they are located, so you may want to shop accordingly. If you're looking for safari gear, head for Adventureland; Main Street USA has old-time country stores and confections; Frontierland offers dry goods (including a Pendelton shop) and Native American items; Fantasyland has stores full of whimsical music boxes and other Disney-related items. Some of the big emporiums on Main Street have just about anything you can imagine, from cheap souvenirs to T-shirts and sweatshirts to very expensive jewelry, and they are strategically placed to catch your eye on the way out, when your attitude is something like "what the heck, I've just spent a small fortune in this place, so what's another $50 going to matter?" To avoid falling into this trap, set a budget and stick to it.

Your best hope is to limit the kids to a pair of genuine Mickey Mouse ears (embroidered with their names) and the requisite Mickey Mouse helium balloon (which will immediately put your life in danger as it looms ghostlike in your rear-view mirror as you drive, exhausted, down the freeway toward your hotel). Other than that, there's an expensive stuffed animal version of every animated Disney character known to man, and a ton of trinkets, T-shirts and other stuff that will have your kids begging like crazy. Keep a cool head and you'll be able to splurge and buy yourself a Mickey Mouse watch or sweatshirt.

Doing It All In A Day

Even though Disneyland is technically divided into eight themed areas—Adventureland, Fantasyland, Tomorrowland, Frontierland, Main Street USA, New Orleans Square, Bear Country, and the new Toontown—most people go through the "lands" randomly, looking for the rides they most want to go on. Grab a map at the main gate when you come in, then gather the family around and decide if you're going to stick together or split up and meet later at a designated spot. (If you have both teenagers and younger children, the teenagers will definitely be in favor of splitting up, and their tastes will likely run to rides that younger kids—and maybe even you, if you're the queasy type—won't be interested in.) Also, be sure to check times for the day's parades and other special events so that you don't end up stranded halfway to the front of the line at It's a Small World when the kids suddenly decide they'd rather be at the Lion King Celebration. Unless you're an amazingly hang-loose, spur-of-the-moment, take-your-chances sort of person, planning ahead is one of the "bare necessities" at Disneyland.

As far as the rides in the park go, if there are some you just can't imagine missing, it's best to hit them first. You can go back for seconds later if there's time, or devote the rest of the day to attractions of milder interest.

If you're looking for thrills, head for Star Tours, the Matterhorn Bobsleds, Space Mountain, the Big Thunder Mountain Railroad, Splash Mountain or the new Indiana Jones Adventure, which opened in March of 1995. Nearly everyone over the age of 10 who comes to Disneyland is looking for thrills, of course, so these rides are extremely popular, meaning you may have to wait in line for up to an hour before you get to zoom around at warp speed for a few minutes. (One of the most aggravating things about Disneyland is its habit of continuing lines inside its buildings. Just when you think you're "in," you see that the line snakes around inside for another half-hour or so, and all those delightful Disney animated distractions don't always ease the pain of more waiting.)

Veteran Disneyland-goers beat the crowds by arriving at the park when the gate opens, then running (yes, we mean running) to the thrill ride of their choice first, before the rest of the world arrives at the gate. (This also applies if you have little kids that want to ride on Dumbo.) If you're a first time visitor, you may want to ride around the park on the train in order to get your bearings, but if you know your way around, GO FOR IT, or lines will already be long by the time the train returns to the station.

Same with those quaint little horse-drawn trolleys on Main Street. Save them for the end of the day when you're too exhausted to make it from Fantasyland to the front gate with two kids (at least one of which you are carrying), camera gear, stuffed animals, Mickey helium balloons, a couple of hot churros (elongated Mexican fat-and-sugar pastries sold from carts throughout the park) and bags of more pricey souvenirs. By then, you'll be thrilled to hop aboard some handy conveyance that will get you down Main Street without walking. While you've got the energy, though, RUN!

The slightly more faint-of-heart who can still tolerate the dark, noises and a few surprises popping out shouldn't miss Pirates of the Caribbean (which, in some opinions, is the best ride at Disneyland) or The Haunted Mansion, and most of the "theme" rides such as Peter Pan, Snow White (the witch inevitably scares little kids, so caution is advised), and Alice in Wonderland, all of which are "cute" in their own way . (Mr. Toad's Wild Ride in Fantasyland is noisy, but otherwise a big snore.)

If any of the above are too much (watch for the warning signs outside rides that discourage pregnant women, people with bad backs, etc. from going on some rides), be advised that everyone—regardless of the state of their health (or their nerves) will be charmed by the Adventureland Jungle

Cruise (which has been revamped to take you by some of the "jungle" locations featured in the new Indiana Jones ride), the Submarine Voyage, the recently-renovated Storybook Land Canal Boats (which now include a look at the "whole new world" of Aladdin, plus Prince Eric's castle, King Neptune's undersea world and Ursula's grotto from *The Little Mermaid*), the wonderful Fantasyland carousel, just about anything on Main Street USA, the Mad Hatter's Tea Party (if you're subject to motion sickness, you can elect not to spin), and It's a Small World. (Okay, okay. We admit it. Some adults—notably adult males—may experience waves of uncontrollable nausea when exposed to this eternally smiling, singing and dancing collection of colorfully-costumed dolls, but the kids will love it so much they'll insist on going at least four times, so either steel yourself or let grandma take them).

Little kids will love **Mickey's Toontown**, where they can visit Mickey's and Minnie's house, explore the Chip and Dale Tree Slide and Acorn Crawl, climb to their hearts' content in Toon Park (a play area for toddlers), ride Gadget's Go Coaster and Roger Rabbit's Car Toon Spin, or hop aboard the Jolly Trolley for a Toontown tour. (Teenagers, on the other hand, are likely to find this newest themed land basically "lame.")

Parents beware: do everything you can to keep your charming little charges from insisting on a ride on Dumbo, the Flying Elephant. It's one of the slowest-moving lines in the park, and one of the most popular with little kids. The impatient whining of your kids combined with the sniveling of everyone else's is guaranteed to send you over the edge and the thrill of circling around in a plastic elephant for a mercilessly short time (given the time you've invested) only makes things worse. Do yourself a favor and head on over to Toontown instead.

(Note: if, after all you can do, you end up stuck in the Dumbo line with a couple of kids, take along a copy of David Koenig's book, *Mouse Tales: A Behind-the-Ears Look at Disneyland* (1994), a revealing behind-the-scenes look at Disneyland's history. It's filled with anecdotes about the park and its wild, wacky—and sometimes scandalous—goings on over the years. Hint: you're not likely to find the book on sale in the park. Disney image, you know.)

Alas, the Disneyland Skyway, which carried 150 million passengers from one end of Disneyland to the other during its more than 35 years of operation, was closed in the fall of 1994 after being overshadowed by the park's thrill rides. (Not mentioned by Disneyland as part of the decision to close the ride were the several unfortunate Skyway "incidents" that left people stranded in the air or dangling out of the cars—the latter usually as a result of the occupant's own stupidity after ignoring the ride's posted safety rules.)

Disneyland's Future

Walt Disney is reported to have once said that Disneyland would never be completed as long as men still had imagination. True to Walt's words, the park has plans to keep expanding into the next century, and you can bet that gender has little to do with imagination in the '90s.

As noted, Disney's latest creation is the just-opened "**Indiana Jones Adventure**," a $50 million Adventureland thrill ride that is a collaboration between Disney and director George Lucas. After waiting for up to an hour in line (you get to wait inside the "temple," which has all sorts of things to keep you entertained while you wait), guests board 12-passenger, World War II "troop transport" vehicles for an exciting excursion through the ancient ruins of the "Temple of the Forbidden Eye," encountering clouds of smoke, bubbling lava pits, bugs, rodents, snakes, a shaking suspension bridge and a gigantic rolling boulder along the way.

On a wider scale, the Disney Company reportedly has plans to turn Disneyland into a West Coast version of Disney World, with its own Westcot Center, several hotels set amid lush landscaping and a man-made lake, a large shopping area, and a huge amphitheater. The $3 billion concept has drawn criticism from some, and has been on hold while Disney officials consider possible downsizing from the original concept and wrestle with finances.

The other "big name" amusement park in Orange County is Buena Park's **Knott's Berry Farm**, which actually *was* just a berry farm until someone realized the possibilities. You can still sense the "down home" western flavor of the place (and still purchase Knott's famous preserves and eat at Mrs. Knott's Chicken Dinner Restaurant), but the emphasis has definitely changed to accommodate the amusement-park-hungry tourists that flock to L.A., and the park now includes more than 165 attractions.

Like Disneyland (but on a much less ambitious scale), Knott's—which is still owned by the Knott family—has several themed areas, including Ghost Town, Fiesta Village, Roaring '20s, Indian Trails, Wild Water Wilderness and Camp Snoopy (for kids). There are plenty of thrill rides located here, but the park likes to tout its educational slant and the authentic nature of its historical attractions, such as the learning opportunities available at Indian Trails, which is dedicated to the lore, legends, crafts, music and dance of Native American tribes.

The most thrilling of the "thrill" rides at Knott's is the new Jaguar roller coaster that swoops and swerves for four minutes across one-sixth of Knott's total park area, including two 60 ft. drops. Other thrills include the Boomerang roller coaster (you turn upside down six times in less than a minute), Montezooma's Revenge (go 55 miles per hour through two vertical loops), the Parachute Sky Jump (if you have nightmares about falling, better pass on this one), XK-1, where you soar 70 feet above the ground and at least contemplate doing this in an upside-down position, and the Timber Mountain Log Ride, where you float through Timber Mountain in a hollowed-out "log," then take a heart-in-the-throat dive down a 50-foot waterfall. Tame by comparison is the Calico Mine Train, but if you're claustrophobic you might not enjoy being "trapped" underground adjacent to a "working" gold mine.

Knott's offers lots of entertainment options, as well as a variety of special events, many of them centered around holiday themes. One of the park's most popular events with Southern Californians (especially teenagers and college students) is the annual "Halloween Haunt," billed as "the biggest, scariest Halloween party in the world." (Halloween Haunt runs every weekend in October, and sells out every year, so get your tickets when they go on sale at the end of August.) While older kids are getting scared out of their wits at the Halloween Haunt, Camp Snoopy becomes "Camp

Spooky" for kids three–11, and the emphasis is squarely on fun (as opposed to fright).

Knott's Berry Farm is really a pretty fun place, but—fact is—it's just not Disneyland. The park isn't quite as spiffy, the landscaping isn't quite as flawless, the atmosphere isn't quite as magical. If you have the time and money, you might want to hit both theme parks; if you don't, opt for Disneyland.

Half theme park and half restaurant, Medieval Times will be a sure hit with the kids, who get to eat with their hands while watching Medieval displays of jousting, sorcery, falconry and horsemanship. Note that Medieval Times is priced more like an amusement park than a restaurant (up to $35 per person), and that you are shelling out most of the money for the show, not the food. Alcoholic beverages are extra, and so are all the tempting souvenirs (what kid wouldn't want his picture taken with King Arthur?). Be prepared to drop a bundle here.

Orange County for Kids

Of course you're going to take the kids to Disneyland, but Orange County has many other experiences for kids that are more relaxed (and educational) than those afforded by local amusement parks. They'll love the Huntington Beach Library, for example, where a new children's wing opened in January of 1994, making it the largest children's library west of the Mississippi. Here you'll find scads of books and a lot more: a state-of-the-art computer room, a theater, a storytime reading room and a puppet theatre.

Shopping can be fun for kids, too, at the **South Coast Plaza**, where $1 buys a ride on the plaza's huge indoor carousel. (Santa can be found in this general area around Christmas time.) In the Crystal Court section of the mall, the Launch Pad offers more than 30 hands-on scientific exhibits for kids five–12. You can also opt to drag the kids around shopping with you, with stops at the Disney Store, the Sesame Street Store and FAO Schwartz guaranteed to keep them amused.

For a bit of culture, you can't miss with Merlin's Musical Mornings, a Saturday morning series of concerts for kids offered by the Pacific Symphony Orchestra at the Orange County Performing Arts Center October through May. The subject is classical music, but the presentation is all fun, and concerts are short enough that kids don't lose interest.

New since December of 1994 is the Kidseum at the Bowers Museum in Santa Ana. In keeping with the museum's general focus, the 11,000-square-foot center offers numerous hands-on exhibits devoted to teaching children about the history, ceremony and arts of other cultures. Also in Santa Ana, the annual Boo at the Zoo Halloween Festival at the Santa Ana Zoo is guaranteed to be much more of a treat than a trick for kids with its costume parade, animal encounters and trick-or-treat stations.

Events

There's always something going on in Orange County, and not all of it happens within the boundaries of Disneyland. Many of the beach cities have water-related festivals or celebrations (surfers: don't miss Huntington Beach's U.S. Open of Surfing), as well as a summer lineup of special events. The most famous festivals in coastal Orange County are **Laguna Beach's**

Pageant of the Masters and Festival of Arts, a pair of spectacular extravaganzas that draw spectators from around the globe. There's no doubt that the pageant is an amazing thing, but most lump it into the category of Pasadena's Tournament of Roses Parade: you ought to see it at least once in your lifetime; after that, it's not worth the hassle. The annual Sawdust Festival is much more laid-back.

 Farther down the coast, at the **Mission San Juan Capistrano**, you can hang out with everyone else who is perpetuating the myth that the swallows return to the mission from their wintering grounds on the same day each year—March 19. It's a nice little festival, but swallows come and go when they want, and even the locals have to concede that the birds are often early (or late) in making an appearance. The event still gets a lot of media attention on March 19, though.

Sports and Recreation

Orange County is the home of the California Angels and the NHL's Mighty Ducks.

About those Angels. Plagued by a terrible 1994 season that ended abruptly with the baseball strike, owners Jackie and Gene Autry announced plans to sell the club for somewhere around $130 million, with Disney reportedly taking a hard look at acquiring the team. So here's another L.A. team in transition, a fate that has seemingly touched nearly every pro sports club with roots in L.A. in the past several years.

For personal fitness, the sister club to Sports Club/L.A. is located in Irvine (there will soon be three Sports Clubs in the country when the owners of Sports Club/LA and Sports Club/Irvine open a $55 million Reebok Sports Club/NY in New York City). Sports Club has a reputation for being one of the best in L.A., so this is among the most popular places to develop that hard body.

Disneyland has entered into the sports business with an annual Disneyland Marathon, the first of which was run in March of 1995. The 5000-meter event took place in the city of Anaheim, much of it on Disneyland property.

Anaheim Stadium now has its own museum in the Orange County Sports Hall of Fame, which opened in late 1993 on the second floor of the stadium's new wing located near Gate 6. It's open every day and worth a stop if you're in the neighborhood between 10 a.m. and 5 p.m.

Sport fishermen may want to try their luck on the Bolsa Chica Artificial Reef, a structure made out of more than 3500 old Southern California Edison light poles that—along with 5000 tons of concrete rubble—were dumped off Bolsa Chica Beach in an effort to attract sea life—and hence fish—back to local waters. Several artificial reefs have been constructed off the coast in recent years, and fishermen hope that—in 15 years or so, when the reef has had time to mature—Huntington Beach will become one of the premiere fishing destinations in Southern California. In the meantime, fished-out waters are already showing signs of recovering.

Orange County: Music, Dance and Theatre

The Orange County Performing Arts Center in Costa Mesa, the La Mirada Theatre for Performing Arts, the Cerritos Center for the Performing Arts and the Irvine Meadows Amphitheatre are the jewels in the crown of Orange County's performance venues. In addition, Orange County boasts may first-rate music and theatre performance groups that appear in various venues scattered throughout the area.

The city of Garden Grove, for example, is in the process of converting its two-theater Village Green Arts Complex into the new Grove Theatre Center, where a variety of professional productions will be featured in the small, indoor Gem Theatre and in the 550-seat outdoor amphitheatre. The well-respected Fullerton Civic Light Opera appears at the Plummer Auditorium in Fullerton, and the Shakespeare Orange County productions are featured at the Waltmar Theatre on the Chapman University campus in Orange.

While it's not exactly a center for the cultural arts, movie-goers will appreciate Irvine's claim to entertainment fame in the form of its 21-screen, 135,000-square-foot movie theatre complex at the intersection of the Santa Ana and San Diego freeways. Construction began on the project in the fall of 1994, and, when completed, it will be the largest movie theatre complex in the country.

Orange County: Shopping

South Coast Plaza

Orange County has some of the best shopping venues in Southern California, including the exclusive **South Coast Plaza** *(3333 Bristol Street, Costa Mesa)*, where you'll find Barneys New York, Cartier, Chanel, Emporio Armani, Gucci, Polo/Ralph Lauren, Tiffany and Italian men's wear company Ermenegildo Zegna, to name a few of the center's pricey stores. The plaza itself, divided into three shopping areas (South Coast Plaza, South Coast Plaza Village and the Crystal Court), is probably one of the nation's fanciest shopping centers, and is said to be one of the highest-grossing complexes of retail shops in the country. Even the New York Museum of Art has a store here, and you can drop more money than you might care to think about in a very short time. If you don't know how to shop the sales, beef up your checking account before browsing here—it's Orange County's answer to Rodeo Drive. (Those intent on holding on to their cash can stay out of the stores and focus on the plaza's various artworks, which include a 1.6-acre outdoor sculpture "environment" by Isamu Noguchi.)

The **Fashion Island Shopping Center** (*600 Newport Center Drive, Newport Beach*)—which has a lovely setting—is anchored by Robinsons-May, The Broadway and Neiman Marcus, with nearly 200 additional stores within its boundaries. It's not quite as hoity toity as the South Coast Plaza, and has nice touches like a central Atrium Court with a Farmer's Market and a bunch of upscale restaurants, including the ubiquitous California Pizza Kitchen and the Orange County branch of the Hard Rock Cafe.

Other mall options are the **Brea Mall** (*Orange Freeway at Imperial Highway*), whose 175 stores include Nordstrom, The Broadway, Ann Taylor, The Nature Company, Williams Sonoma and the Body Shop; **Main-Place/Santa Ana** (*2800 North Main Street*), featuring Bullock's, Nordstrom, Robinsons-May and nearly 190 other stores, plus a marketplace that showcases international food shops and restaurants; and the **Mall of Orange** (*2298 North Orange Mall*), with 100 stores that include The Broadway, Sears and a variety of restaurants.

Various shopping shuttles will transport you between your hotel and Orange County's best malls, but many of them charge a fee. Among these are the Fashion Island Shopper, the South Coast Plaza Shuttle, and the Main-Place/Santa Ana Shopper Shuttle. Check with your hotel concierge for complete information on these services, or call them direct for fares and schedules. Another option is the Beach Express Shuttle, which operates from 8 a.m. to midnight daily and stops at Disneyland, Planet Hollywood, South Coast Plaza, Triangle Square/Nike Town, Crystal Court, Newport Harbor, Fashion Island and the beaches. One-way fares range from $2 to $7, or you can buy a $20 "hop pass" for unlimited travel throughout the day and night. Reservations are encouraged (☎ *714 434-1140*).

Sports fans won't want to miss the new Nike Town store (*1875 Newport Boulevard*) in Costa Mesa's Triangle Square, a retail store and sports museum featuring a state-of-the-art "media wall," plus statues, photos and archive displays of Nike athletes and sports memorabilia. Touted as a "sports retail theater," the store also has on hand plenty merchandise for you to spend your money on. Also in Triangle Square are a GAP store, a Virgin Records Megastore and other upscale shops and restaurants.

On weekends, the **Orange County Market Place** is open on the Orange County Fair Grounds (*88 Fair Drive, Costa Mesa*) from 7 a.m. to 4 p.m. More than a thousand local merchants and craftsmen display and sell their wares here, with booths containing everything from fresh produce and homemade breads to clothing, crafts and furniture. Great fun for browsing, but arrive early as merchandise gets pretty well picked over by late morning.

Doll City, USA, at *2080 South Harbor Boulevard* in Anaheim, has one of the largest selections of dolls in the world, with more than 4000 individual dolls on hand. You can find everything from trolls to Barbies to highly collectible dolls by recognized artists here, and there's sure to be something for that special doll lover in your life. The store is open daily.

Oh, and just in case you're one of those people with K-Mart taste, Anaheim boasts the nation's first K-Mart superstore, a new concept whereby you can get groceries, buy flowers, rent a video, pick up a prescription, and buy your fabulous K-Mart designer wardrobe, all at the same store. Eureka!

Orange County: Where to Eat

Orange County is loaded with "special occasion" (read: very expensive, elegant and often stuffy) restaurants, many of them associated with fancy hotels, and there's not much to distinguish many of them from the same sort of places in Los Angeles. If you're in the mood for a bit of a change, though, try the cool and sophisticated Gustaf Anders, a Scandinavian restaurant in South Coast Plaza where the cuisine is superb, the service efficient and the wine list first-class. It's one of Orange County's best.

Not to say that "hip" is a concept foreign to Orange County's dining establishments. Drop by Tutto Mare at Newport Fashion Island, Kachina in Laguna Beach, Roxbury South in Santa Ana, Diva in Costa Mesa, or even the original Ruby's Diner on the Balboa Pier for a dash of purely contemporary attitude (and a noise level that's really up there).

ANAHEIM

Anaheim: Things to See and Do

Activities

Museums and Exhibits

Beckman Historical Collection ★★★

241 East Imperial Highway, Suite 370, Fullerton, ☎ (714) 773-6924.
Hours pen: 9 a.m.–3 p.m.
This scientific museum presents a collection of instruments used to explore and discover whether there's life on Mars, among other things. See a DNA synthesizer, and a spectrophotometer that is used for fingerprint analysis. Open Tuesday-Thursday only.

International Printing Museum ★★★

8469 Kass Drive, Buena Park, ☎ (714) 523-2070.
Hours pen: 10 a.m.–5 p.m.
Pre-computer age marvels are preserved here in the form of displays encompassing over 500 years of printing history. Guided tours walk visitors through the intricacies of 150 working antique presses. Students and seniors, $4; children under five free. General admission: $6.50.

Movieland Wax Museum ★★

7711 Beach Boulevard, Buena Park, 90620, ☎ (714) 522-1154.
Hours pen: 9 a.m.–7 p.m.
One block north of Knott's Berry Farm.
Over 240 wax figures of Hollywood stars are shown in re-created movie scenes containing authentic costumes and props. A "Black Box" takes visitors through scenes from horror movies. There's also a movie-themed gift shop, a portrait studio and a restaurant. General admission: $12.95.

Richard Nixon Library ★★★

18001 Yorba Linda Boulevard, Yorba Linda, 92686, ☎ (714) 993-3393.
Hours Open: 10 a.m.–5 p.m.
Tour the birthplace and childhood home of America's 37th president, watch a 28-minute video on Nixon's public and private life and hear the "smoking gun" Watergate tape. On permanent exhibit is "Pat Nixon: Ambassador of Good Will," which includes jewelry and other gifts received by the late first lady during her foreign travels. Admis-

sion for children eight-11 is $1; children seven and under are free; senior admission is $2.95. General admission: $4.95.

Historical Sites

Crystal Cathedral   ★★★

12141 Lewis Street, Garden Grove, 95440, ☎ *(714) 971-4000.*
Hours Open: 9 a.m.–3:30 p.m.
At the intersection of Chapman Avenue and Lewis Street.

This glass church designed by Philip Johnson resembles a four-pointed star. Set on 22 acres, it contains over 10,000 panes of glass and has been recognized as one of the most spectacular religious edifices in the world. Daily tours, plus two spectacular pageants held each year, at Christmas and Easter. Advance reservations are required for pageants. A donation is suggested.

Tours

Fullerton Market   ★★

Wilshire Avenue, Fullerton, ☎ *(714) 738-6545.*
Between Harbor Boulevard and Pomona Avenue.

This outdoor craft and food market is also the venue for classical, jazz and country concerts every second Thursday of the month. The market scene happens every Thursday from 4–9 p.m.

Parks and Gardens

Fullerton Arboretum   ★★★

Associated Road, Fullerton, ☎ *(714) 723-3579.*
Hours pen: 8 a.m.–4:45 p.m.
At Yorba Linda Boulevard.

A 24-acre ecological reserve that is a haven for native birds and plants. While here, visit Dr. George Clark's Heritage House, built in 1894, an example of East Lake Victorian architecture; by appointment only.

Theme/Amusement Parks

Camelot Golfland   ★★

3200 East Carpenter, Anaheim, ☎ *(714) 630-3340.*
Hours pen: 10 a.m.–11 p.m.

Five 18-hole miniature golf courses, ranging from easy to hard, give players a wide variety of challenges. There is a giant arcade with over 350 different games and a pizza parlor too. During the summer, you can get wet on Camelot's own popular water slide, a zig-zagging maze of pipe-shaped runs. Admission for children under 12 is $3.50. General admission: $4.75.

Disneyland   ★★★★★

1313 South Harbor Boulevard, Anaheim, 92803, ☎ *(714) 999-4565.*
Hours pen: 10 a.m.–6 p.m.

Called the Magic Kingdom, this world-famous theme park opened in 1955 and remains one of the most popular attractions in the U.S. It covers 80 landscaped acres where guests are greeted by Mickey Mouse and other Walt Disney characters, then wander the eight main sections—or "lands"—with more than fifty rides to choose from. Themed areas include Tomorrowland, Adventureland, New Orleans Square, Fantasyland, Main Street USA, Frontierland and Critter Country; newer highlights include the kid-oriented Mickey's Toon Town, the "Lion King Celebration," and the brand new Indiana Jones Adventure ride, which opened in March of 1995. The park celebrates its 40-year anniversary in 1995 with many special events. Admission for children three-11, $25; children under three, free; seniors over 60, $27. Two-day passes are $57 for those 12 and over; $44 for children three-11. Southern Californians who have proof of a local zip code often receive a substantial discount; call ahead to find out if it's in effect. Parking costs $6. Extended hours in summer (Memorial Day through early September) and during holidays. General admission: $33.

Knott's Berry Farm's Skyjump and Boomerang rides.

Knott's Berry Farm   ★ ★ ★ ★

8039 Beach Boulevard, Buena Park, 90620, ☎ (714) 220-5200. Hours open: 10 a.m.–6 p.m.

Knott's has always been a sort of wanna-be Disneyland, and while it has some good points, it's just not the Magic Kingdom. Its roots go deep in Orange County, however, and it's trying hard. Formerly a family farm, the theme park is set on 150 acres and includes over 160 rides and attractions, restaurants, shops and live entertainment. Camp Snoopy has rides for small children; thrill rides are available in other areas of the park. Theme areas include Roaring '20s, Wild Water Wilderness, Fiesta Village, Ghost Town, and Mystery Lodge, offering an old storyteller who takes guests on a magical, multisensory journey deep into the Native North American West. The annual "Halloween Haunt," is especially popular with those (mostly teenagers) who enjoy having the hell scared out of them. Admission price for seniors over 60 and children three-11, $18.50; age two and under, free. After 4 p.m., admission for all is $13.95. Summer hours: 9 a.m. to 11 p.m. Sunday through Thursday, 9 a.m. to midnight Friday and Saturdays. Winter weekend hours are 10 a.m. to 10 p.m. Saturdays, and 10 a.m. to 7 p.m. Sundays. Admission is free to the California Marketplace shopping area, which is outside the main gate. General admission: $28.50.

Anaheim for Kids

Atlantis Play Center

9301 Atlantis Way, Garden Grove, ☎ *(714) 892-6015.*
Hours open: 11 a.m.–4 p.m.
Modeled after the legendary lost city of Atlantis, this playground has lots of aquatic-themed toys for kids to play on, including a "sea serpent slide."

Children's Museum of La Habra   ★★★

301 South Euclid Street, La Habra, 90631, ☎ *(310) 905-9793.*
Hours open: 10 a.m.–5 p.m.
If you want to get your kids interactively involved in something informative and fun, this is the place. Permanent exhibits include a preschool playpark, a Kids on Stage theatre, The Science Station, a Dino-Dig for junior paleontologists and a Carousel Room. Buster the Bus lets kids drive or be passengers; Lego City has thousands of pieces for junior builders; The Caboose is a real railcar full of historical exhibits; and a model train village, Bee Observatory, Touch Table and Nature Walk offer more opportunities for learning. Admission for children under two is free. General admission: $4.

Hobby City   ★★

1238 South Beach Boulevard, Fullerton, ☎ *(714) 527-8105.*
Hours open: 10 a.m.–6 p.m.
Hobby City has a Toy Museum, a Cabbage Patch shop and six acres crammed with 24 hobby and craft shops.

Events

Grove Shakespeare Festival

12852 Main Street at Acacia, Garden Grove, 90056, ☎ *(714) 636-7213.*
One block north of Garden Grove Boulevard.
For a magical trip back in time, enjoy an evening of Shakespeare under the stars. Fine theatrical entertainment is patterned after the festivals which took place in Elizabethan England. The festival runs from June through September at the Gem Amphitheatre, which is comprised of two theatres and an art gallery. Call for ticket prices.

International Street Fair

Glassell and Chapman Circle, Orange, ☎ *(714) 538-3581.*
International cuisine, folk dancing, music and over 100 craft booths fill the streets during this three-day fair held in early September.

Sports and Recreation

Anaheim Arena ★★★

2695 East Katella Avenue, Anaheim, 92806, ☎ (714) 704-2700.
Arrowhead Pond, home ice for the Mighty Ducks, is located here,
and the complex is the venue for a wide range of sporting events, from
WWF wrestling to basketball to pro indoor soccer to pro motorcycle
racing.

Anaheim Tennis Center

975 South State College Boulevard, Anaheim, ☎ (714) 991-9090.
There are 12 championship hard surface courts here, all lighted for
night play. A pro is on hand if you need individual instruction, and
there's a ball machine for practicing your returns.

Anaheim Stadium is home to the California Angels.

California Angels

2000 State College Boulevard, Anaheim, 92806, ☎ (714) 625-1123.
American League baseball played April through September at Anaheim Stadium.

Cypress Golf Club

4921 East Katella, Anaheim, ☎ (714) 527-1800.
This public course was designed by Perry Dye, son of legendary Pete
Dye, to harmonize with the environment. Scenic vistas, lakes and
trees are seen throughout the course. Open daily, 6:30 a.m. to 7:30
p.m.

Disneyland Marathon

Disneyland, Anaheim, ☎ (800) 524-9200.
Disney gets into the marathon business with the inaguration of the
Disneyland Marathon and 5K race in March of 1995. The event is
expected to be held annually at the park, where both races finish at
Main Street, U.S.A. $50,000 in prize money was offered for the initial
race, and the festivities included a sports and fitness expo held at the
Disneyland Hotel. Registration forms are available at all Disney Store
locations.

Glacial Garden Ice Arena

1000 East Cerritos Avenue, Anaheim, ☎ (714) 502-9023.
Even though California winters may be balmy, you can ice skate to
your heart's content at Glacial Garden, which is open for public skat-

ing daily, and offers skating lessons, ice hockey and space for birthday parties on its two rinks.

Islands Golf Center

14893 Ball Road, Anaheim, ☎ (714) 635-4653.
This 18-acre aqua practice center and comprehensive golf school is the largest of its kind in the U.S. Lessons are available from PGA and LPGA pros for individuals or groups. Open 7 a.m. to 10 p.m. daily.

La Habra Tennis Courts

351 South Euclid, La Habra, 90631, ☎ (310) 690-5040.
Hours open: 8 a.m.–10 p.m.
There are 12 outdoor courts located here, plus a full line-up of classes, private lessons and services such as racquet restringing and ball machines for rent. The cost for using a court is $1.50 per hour before 5 p.m., $2 per hour after 5 p.m.

Los Alamitos

4961 Katella Avenue, Los Alamitos, ☎ (714) 995-1234.
Live harness racing is held January-April and August-mid-November. Quarterhorse racing takes place May–July and November–January. Thoroughbred racing from other L.A.-area tracks—Santa Anita, Hollywood Park and Del Mar—is simulcast daily. Call for schedules. Open Thursday–Friday 7 p.m. and Saturday–Sunday 6:30 p.m. for races. Early bird wagering 9 a.m.–5 p.m., $3-$4.50. Seniors free on Thursday.

Mighty Ducks

The Pond, Anaheim, ☎ (714) 704-2700.
Okay, so the name sounds too much like a Disney movie to be believed, but Anaheim is very serious about its fledgling hockey team. Time will tell, but most say the Ducks are here to stay. The Mighty Ducks' season runs October–May.

Anaheim: Music, Dance and Theatre

Music

Cerritos Center for the Performing Arts   ★★★★

12700 Center Court Drive, Cerritos, 90701, ☎ (310) 916-8500.
One of the most popular performance venues in Orange County, the $50 million, city-owned Center presents a full schedule of music, dance and theatre events throughout the year. The Pacific Symphony Orchestra performs here most often, sometimes with the Pacific Chorale or in the Center's ballet series.

Concerts in the Park   ★★

401 South Brea Boulevard, Brea, ☎ (714) 990-7735.
From early July to late August, on Wednesday evenings starting at 6 p.m., the sounds of country-western, jazz, bluegrass or pop and soft rock music blanket the Old City Hall Park. Bring your own chair or blanket, relax and enjoy. Free admission.

La Mirada Symphony   ★★★★

14900 La Mirada Boulevard, La Mirada, 90637, ☎ (714) 994-6310.
The La Mirada Symphony has brought classical music to the community for 30 years. Guest soloists have included the concertmasters of both the Los Angeles Philharmonic and New York Philharmonic

Orchestras. Best of all, all performances are absolutely free. Donations requested.

Theatre

Fullerton Civic Light Opera ★★★★
Chapman Avenue & Lemon Street, Fullerton, 92632, *(714) 879-1732.*
At the Plummer Auditorium.
Since opening in 1972, this light opera company has featured more than 75 shows. Both professional and non-equity performers appear in the productions, and many have played the same roles on Broadway or in Los Angeles. An outdoor "theatre on the green" series is featured each summer at the Muckenthaler Estate, *1201 West Malvern Avenue.* Call the box office for show times and ticket prices.

Golden State Children's Theatre ★★★★
14900 La Mirada Boulevard, La Mirada, 90637, ☎ *(714) 994-6310.*
A locally based organization that produces original musicals based on familiar classics, Golden State schedules a Fall-Spring season at La Mirada Playhouse.

Grand Dinner Theatre ★★
1 Hotel Way, Anaheim, ☎ *(714) 991-8846.*
At the Grand Hotel.
Near the main entrance to Disneyland, this Las Vegas-style show-room is the venue for Broadway hit productions.

La Mirada Playhouse ★★★★
14900 La Mirada Boulevard, La Mirada, 90637, ☎ *(714) 994-6310.*
At La Mirada Theatre for Performing Arts.
Under producer Yolanda Robinson, the La Mirada Playhouse has been exposing local talent for 35 years. Its repertoire includes comedies, dramas and mysteries.

La Mirada Theatre for Performing Arts ★★★★★
14900 La Mirada Boulevard, La Mirada, 90637, ☎ *(714) 994-6310.*
This city-owned venue, with a 1264-seat auditorium, opened in 1977 and is a major cultural resource in this region. Artistic directors are Cathy Rigby, former Olympic gymnast and award-winning actress, and Tom McCoy, a Tony Award-nominated producer.

Pair Celebrity Series ★★★★
Chapman Avenue & Lemon Street, Fullerton, 92634, ☎ *(714) 773-3371.*
At the Plummer Auditorium.
This exciting series of theatre, dance and variety shows is presented at the Plummer Auditorium of Cal State Fullerton, which is one of the city's cultural centers.

Vanguard Theatre Ensemble ★★★
699 South State College Boulevard, Fullerton, ☎ *(714) 526-8007.*
This fairly new and well-thought-of theatre company is composed of Cal State Fullerton theatre arts alumni. The ensemble offers six productions per season of theatre in the round, with an emphasis on out-of-the-mainstream productions.

Ticket Agencies

Box Office Ticket Service
2751 East Chapman Avenue, #107, Fullerton, 92631, ☎ *(714) 879-8497.*

The Box Office provides tickets for local and nationwide events, including sports, concerts, theatre and special events.

Anaheim: Nightlife

During football season, the **Lobby Bar** at the Anaheim Hilton and Towers is a hotspot on Monday nights, when everyone hangs around and watches the game while consuming a variety of beverages and snacks. The bar names an "honorary armchair quarterback" for each game, with each winner receiving complimentary drinks and sports-related prizes.

Of course, if you're visiting **Disneyland**, you can sample some of the park's nightlife, but it's pretty tame by most accounts (that Magic Kingdom image, you know).

Club 369
1641 North Placencia, Fullerton, ☎ *(714) 572-1816.*
Club 369 is one of the most happening clubs in Orange County, with Super '70s Disco Night on Tuesdays, $1 Drink Night on Wednesdays, College Night on Thursdays (no cover with school ID), live bands on Fridays and Saturdays, and The Hard Core Hillary Show (featuring punk rock) on Sundays. There's also a dance floor, a full bar and pool tables. Over 21 only.

Cowboy Boogie
1721 South Manchester Avenue, Anaheim, ☎ *(714) 956-1410.*
Yes, cowboys DO boogie here (presumably the boot-scootin' kind), and cowgirls are invited, too. There's live entertainment (shows are at 7 p.m.Tuesday-Saturday, and 4 p.m. on Sunday), free dance lessons, a dancer's showcase on Mondays, and family fun day on Sundays from 12-4:30 p.m. Tuesday and Wednesday, drinks are $1 from 7 p.m. to midnight.

Improv, The
945 East Birch Street, Suite A, Brea, ☎ *(714) 529-7878.*
They say that laughter is the best medicine, and some of the best of the huge new wave of stand-up comedians are always on tap to give you a good dose of merriment at this popular club. Another Orange County branch of the Improv is located at 4255 Campus Drive, in Irvine. Shows at 8:30–10:30 p.m. Cover, $8-$12.

Medieval Times
7662 Beach Boulevard, Buena Park, ☎ *(714) 521-4740.*
Part restaurant, part entertainment extravaganza, Medieval Times offers a four-course Medieval-style feast (which you eat with your hands), accompanied by jousting knights and other colorful pageantry associated with the era. Before the feast, you can wander through the Museum of Torture or the Hall of Banners and Flags. Shows are at 7 p.m. Monday-Thursday; 8 p.m. Friday; 6 p.m. and 8:15 p.m. Saturday; 5 p.m. and 7:30 p.m. Sunday. Cost is $32.95 for adults; $22.95 for children 12 and under. Reservations are advised.

Neon Cactus
1150 West Cerritos Avenue, Cerritos, ☎ *(714) 778-6600.*
In the Disneyland Hotel.
As you might expect from the name, this is a country-western place, but with a few contemporary twists. There's a live band for country

line dancing Wednesday-Sunday from 8 p.m. to 1 a.m., with free
dance lessons between 8 p.m. and 9 p.m. Monday and Tuesday (a DJ
plays music on those days). Sunday is famly night from 6–8 p.m., so
bring the kids and check it out!

Pulse

777 Convention Way, Anaheim, ☎ (714) 750-4321.
This dance club at the Anaheim Hilton and Towers is open on Friday
and Saturday from 8 p.m. to 2 a.m. Drink specials are offered to offset
the $10 cover.

Wild Bill's Extravaganza   ★★★

7600 Beach Boulevard, Buena Park, ☎ (714) 522-6414.
This Wild West show with comedy, Western music, Indian dancing
and knife and rope stunts also comes with a huge, two-hour, four-
course all-you-can-eat Western buffet.

Anaheim: Where to Stay

Anaheim's Pan Pacific Hotel emerged from its $5 million upgrade with
a redesign of its entire property, including guest rooms, meeting facilities,
the lobby, restaurant and pool area. Specially commissioned art was added
throughout. (Note to star-smitten guests: there's a Hollywood Studios
Store in the lobby chock full of merchandise from several major studios.)

New in Anaheim is the Park Inn International, a Tudor-style hotel that
adds a touch of English charm to the area. The hotel has both rooms and
suites, with some suites accommodating up to eight people.

Anaheim

Hotels and Resorts

Best Western Anaheim Inn   **$60–$90**   ★★

1630 South Harbor Boulevard
☎ (800) 854-8175, (714) 774-1050, FAX: 714-776-6305.
Single: $60–$90. Double: $60–$90.
All rooms have refrigerators and some have kitchens. Also available
are several two-bedroom units. Data ports provided for business travelers. Free in-room coffee and shuttle service to Disneyland. Amenities: pool, Jacuzzi, sauna. 88 rooms. Credit Cards: CB, V, MC, DC, A.

Best Western Stovall's   **$55–$155**   ★★

1110 West Katella Avenue
☎ (800) 854-8175, (714) 778-1880, FAX: 714-778-3805.
Single: $55–$155. Double: $55–$155.
A nicely landscaped topiary garden highlights this large Best Western.
The grounds feature two pools plus a wading pool for the kids. Com-
plimentary shuttle to and from Disneyland, two blocks away. Free in-
room coffee. Amenities: pool, Jacuzzi, family plan. 290 rooms. Credit
Cards: CB, V, MC, DC, A.

Candy Cane Inn   **$70–$100**   ★★

1747 South Harbor Boulevard
☎ (800) 345-7057, (714) 774-5284, FAX: 714-772-5462.
Single: $70–$100. Double: $70–$100.
A complimentary shuttle is offered to Disneyland, one block away.
Continental breakfast is included, and each room has a refrigerator.

There's a wading pool for children in the garden courtyard. Amenities: pool, Jacuzzi. 173 rooms. Credit Cards: V, MC, A.

Comfort Park Suites $70–$110   ★★
2141 South Harbor Boulevard
☎ *(800) 526-9444, (714) 971-3553, FAX: 714-971-4609.*
Single: $70–$110. Double: $70–$110.
This all-suite hotel offers refrigerators, microwaves, wet bars, safes and VCRs in each unit, as well as complimentary continental breakfast. Free shuttle service is provided to Disneyland, three blocks away. Amenities: pool, Jacuzzi, private spas, conference facilities. 95 rooms.
Credit Cards: CB, V, MC, DC, A.

Conestoga Hotel $95–$115   ★★
1240 South Walnut Street
☎ *(800) 824-5459, (714) 535-0300, FAX: 714-491-8953.*
Single: $95–$105. Double: $105–$115.
Pleasant hotel with Old West theme located three blocks from Disneyland, with free shuttle provided. Amenities include room service at cafe prices, in-room coffee and daily newspaper. The large pool area has a rock waterfall and very large whirlpool. Suites have wet bars and refrigerators. Amenities: pool, Jacuzzi, family plan, conference facilities. 252 rooms. Credit Cards: V, MC, A.

Crown Sterling Suites $135–$145   ★★★
3100 East Frontera Street
☎ *(800) 433-4600, (714) 632-1221, FAX: 714-632-9963.*
Single: $135. Double: $145.
Formerly Embassy Suites, this all-suite property features wet bars, refrigerators and two TVs in each unit. Complimentary cooked-to-order breakfast, evening cocktail hour and transportation to Disneyland, six miles away. Amenities: pool, Jacuzzi, sauna, conference facilities. 224 rooms. Credit Cards: CB, V, MC, DC, A.

Crystal Suites Hotel $85–$115   ★★★
1752 South Clementine Street
☎ *(800) 992-6484, (714) 535-7773, FAX: 714-776-9073.*
Single: $85–$115. Double: $85–$115.
This new, all-suite hotel is a block and a half from both Disneyland and the Convention Center (free shuttle to each). All units feature a refrigerator, microwave, coffee maker and safe. The heated pool and spa are covered. Amenities: pool, exercise room, Jacuzzi. 130 rooms.
Credit Cards: V, MC, DC, A.

Desert Inn and Suites $49–$159   ★★★
1600 South Harbor Blvd.
☎ *(800) 433-5270, (714) 772-5050, FAX: 714-778-2754.*
Single: $49–$159. Double: $49–$159.
This attractive hotel offers standard guest rooms and suites; all include refrigerators, microwaves and VCRs. The rooftop deck, perfect for sunning, is a great spot to catch the fireworks from Disneyland. Complimentary continental breakfast included. Amenities: pool, Jacuzzi, private spas, conference facilities. 143 rooms. Credit Cards: CB, V, MC, DC, A.

Disneyland Hotel $150–$230   ★★★
1150 West Cerritos Avenue
☎ *(800) 647-7900, (714) 778-6600, FAX: 714-956-6582.*
Single: $150–$230. Double: $150–$230.

A magical kingdom in its own right, this hotel is linked by more than a monorail to Disneyland. A complete entertainment center greets guests after the inevitable long day at the park, and the fun goes on at the hotel's marina with paddle boats for rent, a village of tropical ports and an international marketplace. There are ten championship tennis courts, three pools, Team Mickey's Workout Fitness Center, a video game center and all sorts of entertainment options, restaurants, and bars. Among the eleven eateries is Goofy's Kitchen, a cafe where kids eat with Disney characters; the Monorail Cafe, a '50s-style diner; and Granville's Steak House, for more serious dining. The accommodations vary depending on location, but all are modern and were recently renovated. Guest services include baby sitting referrals, foreign currency exchange, an airline and car rental reservation counter and laundry/dry cleaning service. During the holidays, there are always special events going on and special packages for families. The Disneyland Hotel is a fun alternative to the plethora of motel options in the area, but it can cost you plenty. Those who stay on the concierge level receive a complimentary continental breakfast and evening refreshments. Amenities: pool, tennis, Jacuzzi, balcony or patio, family plan, conference facilities, business services. 1131 rooms. Credit Cards: MC, A.

Grand Hotel $80–$135   ★★

One Hotel Way
☎ *(800) 421-6662, (714) 772-7777, FAX: 714-774-7281.*
Single: $80–$105. Double: $105–$135.
Located just across from the main entrance to Disneyland, with free shuttle service provided, this modern hotel is rather stark, with basic amenities and furnishings. Expansive meeting facilites are highlighted by a dinner theater offering Broadway-style productions. Amenities: pool, exercise room, Jacuzzi, balcony or patio, family plan, conference facilities. 242 rooms. Credit Cards: CB, V, MC, DC, A.

Hilton Hotel & Towers $105–$225   ★★★

777 Convention Way
☎ *(800) 445-8667, (714) 750-4321, FAX: 714-740-4460.*
Single: $105–$205. Double: $125–$225.
Located two blocks from Disneyland, this Hilton caters to both business travelers and tourists. It's one of the largest convention properties in Southern California and accommodates its guests in a modern lobby with a long reception desk and with myriad eateries that include a sushi bar and an Italian seafood room. Accommodations are decorated in soft colors with commercial art on the walls. TVs with movies, individual room thermostats and small combination baths round out the amenities. Disneyland packages are available for those reserving rooms on the VIP floors. Amenities: pool, golf, exercise room, Jacuzzi, sauna, balcony or patio, family plan, conference facilities, club floor. 1576 rooms. Credit Cards: CB, V, MC, DC, A.

Holiday Inn Express $79–$130   ★★

435 West Katella Avenue
☎ *(800) 833-7888, (714) 772-7755, FAX: 714-772-2727.*
Single: $79–$130. Double: $79–$130.
This hotel is located a block from Disneyland and the Convention Center, with free transfers provided to each. All rooms include refrig-

erators and hair dryers; some have microwaves. Complimentary continental breakfast is included. Amenities: pool, exercise room, sauna, private spas, conference facilities. 104 rooms. Credit Cards: CB, V, MC, DC, A.

Holiday Inn Maingate $69–$89   ★★
1850 South Harbor Boulevard
☎ *(800) 465-4329, (714) 750-2801, FAX: 714-971-4754.*
Single: $69–$89. Double: $69–$89.
This comfortably bland hotel offers value, if not excitement, for its reasonable rates. Request a top-story room for a decent view of Disneyland. Free transportation to the park and Knott's Berry Farm, 20 minutes away. Rooms have coffee makers, some have refrigerators. Amenities: pool, sauna, balcony or patio, family plan, conference facilities. 312 rooms. Credit Cards: CB, V, MC, DC, A.

Holiday Inn at the Park $85–$105   ★★★
1221 South Harbor Boulevard
☎ *(800) 545-7275, (714) 758-0900, FAX: 714-533-1804.*
Single: $85–$95. Double: $95–$105.
This inn is located two blocks from Disneyland and near the Anaheim Convention Center. Free shuttles for guests to the Magic Kingdom, Knotts Berry Farm, Medieval Times, the Wax Museum and Anaheim Center. Accommodations are typical Holiday Inn and include TVs, in-room movies and large combination baths. Request a room on the eighth floor, where there are decent views of Disneyland; otherwise you'll be looking out at strawberry fields (or construction when—and if—the proposed Westcot building begins). Amenities: pool, Jacuzzi, conference facilities, complimentary airport pickup service. 256 rooms. Credit Cards: CB, V, MC, DC, A.

Hyatt Regency Alicante $105–$154   ★★★
100 Plaza Alicante
☎ *(800) 972-2929, (714) 971-3000, FAX: 714-740-0465.*
Single: $105–$129. Double: $130–$154.
An architecturally imposing hotel with a 17-story tower joined to a 10-story tower by a glass atrium. There's an Italian restaurant open for dinner, a sixties deli and a cafe and bar in the atrium. Although it's less than a mile from Disneyland, this facility caters to corporate clients. Service could be improved. Amenities: pool, tennis, exercise room, Jacuzzi, balcony or patio, hair salon, conference facilities, business services. 400 rooms. Credit Cards: CB, V, MC, DC, A.

Inn at the Park $125–$170   ★★★
1855 South Harbor Boulevard
☎ *(800) 421-6662, (714) 750-1811, FAX: 714-971-3626.*
Single: $125–$155. Double: $140–$170.
Located adjacent to the Anaheim Convention Center and one block south of Disneyland; request an upper floor in the summertime to view the fireworks from the park. This busy hotel caters mostly to conventioneers; families in town for Disneyland can find more economical rates and similar features elsewhere. Amenities: pool, exercise room, Jacuzzi, balcony or patio, conference facilities. 500 rooms. Credit Cards: V, MC, DC, A.

Jolly Roger Hotel $65–$100   ★★★
640 West Katella Avenue

☎ *(800) 446-1555, (714) 772-7621, FAX: 714-772-2308.*
Single: $65–$98. Double: $70–$100.
This motor inn is located opposite Disneyland (free transfer provided) and adjacent to the Convention Center. It has some nice features for families, including two heated pools, a wading pool for kids and in-room movies. There are some suites available, and some rooms have refrigerators. Amenities: pool, Jacuzzi, balcony or patio, hair salon, family plan. 235 rooms. Credit Cards: CB, V, MC, DC, A.

Marriott Anaheim   **$90–$195**   ★ ★ ★
700 West Convention Way
☎ *(800) 228-9290, (714) 750-8000, FAX: 714-750-9100.*
Single: $90–$175. Double: $95–$195.
This contemporary hotel is situated adjacent to the Anaheim Convention Center and two blocks from Disneyland. It's a good choice for both businessmen and families visiting the area's fun spots. The lobby is lively, the lounge sports its own DJ, and there are two restaurants—one of which is the highly-rated J.W.'s. Rooms include cane and rattan furniture, large closets, TVs with VCRs and combination baths. Unfortunately, views of Disneyland are blocked by the Hilton. Amenities: pool, health club, Jacuzzi, sauna, balcony or patio, conference facilities. 1039 rooms. Credit Cards: CB, V, MC, DC, A.

Pan Pacific Hotel Anaheim   **$105–$175**   ★ ★ ★
1717 South West Street
☎ *(800) 321-8976, (714) 999-0990, FAX: 714-776-5763.*
Single: $105–$175. Double: $105–$175.
Located next to Disneyland and within walking distance of the Anaheim Convention Center, this hotel gives good value for the price. There's an atrium lobby that leads to a sunken lobby bar, a dining room and a Japanese restaurant featuring a sushi and sashimi bar. Accommodations are quite nice, with bentwood armchairs, large closets, TVs with movies and combination baths. Most rooms have a view of Disneyland's parking lot—it may not be panoramic but it beats a brick wall. Amenities: pool, Jacuzzi, balcony or patio, conference facilities. 502 rooms. Credit Cards: CB, V, MC, DC, A.

Peacock Suites Hotel   **$85–$105**   ★ ★
1745 South Anaheim Boulevard
☎ *(800) 522-6410, (714) 535-8255, FAX: 714-535-8914.*
Single: $85–$95. Double: $95–$105.
This new hotel offers suites of two to four rooms. All include microwaves, refrigerators, VCRs, safes and hair dryers. Continental breakfast is complimentary, as is shuttle service to Disneyland and the Convention Center, each two blocks away. Disneyland packages are available. Amenities: pool, exercise room, Jacuzzi, private spas. 140 rooms. Credit Cards: CB, V, MC, DC, A.

Ramada Inn Anaheim   **$59–$79**   ★ ★
1331 East Katella Avenue
☎ *(800) 228-0586, (714) 978-8088, FAX: 714-937-5622.*
Single: $59–$69. Double: $59–$79.
This recently renovated motor inn is a block from Disneyland and the Convention Center (free transfers), and offers complimentary breakfast and in-room coffee. Suites have refrigerators and microwaves. Amenities: pool, Jacuzzi, sauna, conference facilities, complimentary airport pickup service. 240 rooms. Credit Cards: CB, V, MC, DC, A.

Residence Inn $95–$329 ★★★

1700 South Clementine Street
☎ *(800) 331-3131, (714) 533-3555, FAX: 714-535-7626.*
Single: $95–$189. Double: $149–$329.
An all-suites residential-style hotel situated on attractively landscaped grounds. Units have full kitchens and fireplaces, and there are lots of little extras such as a complimentary continental breakfast, morning newspaper, an evening social hour Monday through Thursday, complimentary grocery shopping service and a free shuttle to Disneyland and the convention center. Amenities: pool, Jacuzzi, balcony or patio, conference facilities. 200 rooms. Credit Cards: CB, V, MC, DC, A.

Sheraton Anaheim $79–$145 ★★★

1015 West Ball Road
☎ *(800) 325-3535, (714) 778-1700, FAX: 714-535-3889.*
Single: $79–$145. Double: $100–$145.
A recent renovation has made this hotel—located one mile from Disneyland—a stylish alternative to some of the more expensive properties in the area. The Tudor-style hotel has some of the largest guest rooms in town, nicely decorated in contemporary pale wood furnishings and equipped with coffee makers. Suites are available from $190. Amenities: pool, family plan, conference facilities, complimentary airport pickup service. 491 rooms. Credit Cards: CB, V, MC, DC, A.

Low Cost Lodging

Best Western Stardust $40–$60 ★★

1057 West Ball Road
☎ *(800) 222-3639, (714) 774-7600, FAX: 714-774-3425.*
Single: $40–$60. Double: $40–$60.

A basic motel located three blocks from Disneyland, with free shuttle to and from the park. Some units have Roman tub, wet bar and refrigerator. Amenities: pool, Jacuzzi. 103 rooms. Credit Cards: CB, V, MC, DC, A.

Carriage Inn $45–$65 ★★

2125 South Harbor Boulevard
☎ *(800) 345-2131, (714) 740-1440, FAX: 714-971-5330.*
Single: $45–$65. Double: $45–$65.
This newly remodeled motel offers free shuttle service to Disneyland and the Convention Center, each two blocks away. All rooms have refrigerators and microwaves, and a complimentary continental breakfast is included in the rates. Amenities: pool, tennis, Jacuzzi, private spas. 66 rooms. Credit Cards: CB, V, MC, DC, A.

Castle Inn and Suites $58–$78 ★★

1734 South Harbor Boulevard
☎ *(800) 521-5653, (714) 774-8111, FAX: 714-956-4736.*
Single: $58–$68. Double: $68–$78.
This hotel, located across from Disneyland's main entrance, stands out from the crowd with its castle-like facade. The large rooms feature refrigerators and VCRs, and one third of the accommodations are suites ($88–108). Complimentary morning coffee is included, and there's a wading pool for the kids. Amenities: pool, Jacuzzi, private spas, conference facilities. 197 rooms. Credit Cards: CB, V, MC, DC, A.

Convention Center Inn $48–$68 ★

2017 South Harbor Boulevard
☎ *(800) 521-5628, (714) 740-2500, FAX: 714-750-5676.*

Single: $48–$68. Double: $58–$68.

A motor inn adjacent to the Anaheim Convention Center and half a block from Disneyland (free transportation provided). Complimentary continental breakfast. Parlor suites have refrigerators, some have Jacuzzis. Amenities: pool, Jacuzzi, private spas. 122 rooms. Credit Cards: CB, V, MC, DC, A.

Desert Palm Inn & Suites $59–$69   ★★

631 West Katella Avenue
☎ *(800) 635-5423, (714) 535-1133, FAX: 714-491-7509.*
Single: $59–$69. Double: $59–$69.

This contemporary hotel is located across from the Anaheim Convention Center and one block from Disneyland's south entrance. A recent renovation added a fourth floor and guests are now able to watch Disneyland's spectacular fireworks from a new sundeck. Accommodations include green carpets, armoires hiding TVs, VCRs and minibars. A very good value for the price. Amenities: pool, exercise room, Jacuzzi, sauna, conference facilities. 100 rooms. Credit Cards: CB, V, MC, DC, A.

Hampton Inn $57   ★★

300 East Katella Way
☎ *(800) 426-7866, (714) 772-8713, FAX: 714-778-1235.*
Single: $57. Double: $57.

This motor inn one mile from Disneyland isn't splashy, but it's reasonably priced and offers free transportation to the park. A complimentary continental breakfast is included in the rates. Amenities: pool, conference facilities. 136 rooms. Credit Cards: V, MC, DC, A.

Howard Johnson Lodge $65–$78   ★★

1380 South Harbor Boulevard
☎ *(800) 422-4228, (714) 776-6120, FAX: 714-533-3578.*
Single: $65–$78. Double: $65–$78.

No resort amenities here other than the two pools, and accommodations vary depending on room location and the price you're willing to pay. But it's only one block from Disneyland and the staff is friendly. Amenities: pool, Jacuzzi, balcony or patio, family plan. 318 rooms. Credit Cards: CB, V, MC, DC, A.

Quality Hotel Maingate $65–$95   ★★★

616 Convention Way
☎ *(800) 221-2222, (714) 750-3131, FAX: 714-750-3131.*
Single: $65–$95. Double: $70–$95.

This budget alternative to some of the pricier hotels in the area gives good value for the money. The guest rooms are a bit tired looking, but the central location near Disneyland (two blocks away, free shuttle) and the Convention Center make it popular with both tourists and business travelers. Suites have refrigerators, microwave ovens, and coffee makers. Amenities: pool, conference facilities, business services. 284 rooms. Credit Cards: V, MC, A.

Ramada Maingate $49–$99   ★★

1460 South Harbor Boulevard
☎ *(800) 447-4048, (714) 772-6777, FAX: 714-999-1727.*
Single: $49–$99. Double: $49–$99.

This multistory hotel is located across from Disneyland's main entrance; free shuttle service is provided, but you can walk it in about the same time. The functional but generic guest rooms have coffee makers and refrigerators. There are also suites available in the $110-150 range. Amenities: pool, Jacuzzi, balcony or patio, conference facilities. 465 rooms. Credit Cards: V, MC, A.

Anaheim Hills

Low Cost Lodging

Comfort Suites Hotel   **$55–$80**   ★★

201 North Via Cortez
☎ *(800) 228-5150, (714) 921-1100, FAX: 714-637-8790.*
Single: $55–$70. Double: $60–$80.
This all-suite hotel is located 12 miles from Disneyland. Each unit includes a refrigerator and wall safe; some have Jacuzzis. Continental breakfast included. Amenities: pool, exercise room, Jacuzzi, sauna, conference facilities. 160 rooms. Credit Cards: V, MC, A.

Brea

Hotels and Resorts

Embassy Suites Brea   **$114–$155**   ★★★

900 East Birch Street
☎ *(800) 362-2779, (714) 990-6000, FAX: 714-990-1653.*
Single: $114–$155. Double: $114–$155.
Amenities at this all-suite hotel include complimentary full breakfast and evening cocktails. Public areas are attractively decorated in an Egyptian theme. Each unit has a wet bar, refrigerator and microwave. Amenities: pool, health club, Jacuzzi, balcony or patio, conference facilities, business services. 229 rooms. Credit Cards: V, MC, A.

Buena Park

Hotels and Resorts

Courtyard Buena Park   **$64–$84**   ★★★

7621 Beach Boulevard
☎ *(800) 321-2211, (714) 670-6600, FAX: 714-670-0360.*
Single: $64–$74. Double: $74–$84.
Adjacent to the Wax Museum, one block from Knott's Berry Farm, this Marriott property offers value for the money. Though it primarily attracts business travelers, low weekend rates make it a good spot for tourists visiting the area's attractions. Complimentary in-room coffee. Suites available starting at $94. Amenities: pool, exercise room, Jacuzzi, balcony or patio, conference facilities. 145 rooms. Credit Cards: V, MC, A.

Embassy Suites Buena Park   **$130–$150**   ★★★

7762 Beach Boulevard
☎ *(800) 362-2779, (714) 739-5600, FAX: 714-521-9650.*
Single: $130–$140. Double: $140–$150.
This mission-style all-suite hotel has a peaceful pool area and such niceties as free evening cocktails in the billiards area. All units feature two TVs, coffee makers and makeup mirrors. Complimentary full breakfast and transportation to Disneyland. Amenities: pool, Jacuzzi, conference facilities. 203 rooms. Credit Cards: CB, V, MC, DC, A.

Hampton Inn Buena Park   **$60–$75**   ★★

7828 Orangethorpe Avenue
☎ *(800) 727-7205, (714) 670-7200, FAX: 714-522-3319.*
Single: $60–$70. Double: $65–$75.

Guests receive complimentary continental breakfast and shuttle service to Disneyland (four miles away) and Knott's Berry Farm (a half-mile away). Amenities: pool, Jacuzzi. 184 rooms. Credit Cards: CB, V, MC, DC, A.

Holiday Inn Buena Park $85–$95   ★★★

7000 Beach Boulevard
☎ *(800) 465-4329, (714) 522-7000, FAX: 714-522-3230.*
Single: $85. Double: $95.
This older, well-kept hotel has many newly remodeled, well-furnished guest rooms. Complimentary transportation to Disneyland, Knott's Berry Farm and other local attractions. Rooms include a coffee maker; suites have a parlor and wet bar. Amenities: pool, Jacuzzi, balcony or patio, conference facilities, business services. 246 rooms. Credit Cards: V, MC, A.

Low Cost Lodging

Best Western Buena Park $40–$60   ★★

8580 Stanton Avenue
☎ *(800) 654-2889, (714) 828-5211, FAX: 714-826-3716.*
Single: $40–$55. Double: $45–$60.
Basic, low-cost, almost-no-frills lodging that includes a complimentary continental breakfast and coffee in rooms. Some rooms have refrigerators, microwaves and coffee makers. Amenities: pool. 63 rooms. Credit Cards: CB, V, MC, DC, A.

Buena Park Hotel $64–$85   ★★

7675 Crescent Avenue
☎ *(800) 854-8792, (714) 995-1111, FAX: 714-828-8590.*
Single: $64–$85. Double: $64–$85.
This lively and large hotel lies right at the edge of Knott's Berry Farm, and transfers are available to Disneyland. Some rooms have refrigerators; all guests have privileges at a nearby health club. Lots of conference space makes this a popular spot with business groups. Amenities: pool, health club, Jacuzzi, balcony or patio, family plan, conference facilities, club floor, complimentary airport pickup service. 350 rooms. Credit Cards: CB, V, MC, DC, A.

Fairfield Inn By Marriott $40–$42   ★★

7032 Orangethorpe Avenue
☎ *(800) 228-2800, (714) 523-1488, FAX: 714-523-1488.*
Single: $40. Double: $42.
This economy motor inn is situated a mile from Knott's Berry Farm and seven miles from Disneyland. Comfortable rooms have large work areas; complimentary continental breakfast included. Amenities: pool, conference facilities. 135 rooms. Credit Cards: V, MC, DC, A.

Travelodge $42–$64   ★★

7039 Orangethorpe Avenue
☎ *(800) 854-8299, (714) 521-9220, FAX: 714-521-6706.*
Single: $42–$46. Double: $50–$64.
This older motel a half-mile from Knott's Berry Farm includes a complimentary continental breakfast, and the patio area has gas barbecues. Amenities: pool, Jacuzzi, sauna, conference facilities. 101 rooms. Credit Cards: V, MC, DC, A.

Cerritos

Hotels and Resorts

Sheraton Cerritos Town Center   **$160**   ★★★

12725 Center Court Drive
☎ *(800) 325-3535, (310) 809-1500, FAX: 310-403-2080.*
Single: $160. Double: $160.
Complimentary transportation to Disneyland, Knott's Berry Farm and Long Beach Airport are offered at this contemporary hotel. Rooms have minibars and coffee makers. Amenities for business travelers include data ports and secretarial services, and lovers of the arts will appreciate its location adjacent to the Cerritos Center for the Performing Arts. Amenities: pool, health club, Jacuzzi, sauna, family plan, conference facilities, business services. 203 rooms. Credit Cards: V, MC, A.

Fullerton

Hotels and Resorts

Fullerton Suites   **$90–$125**   ★★

2932 East Nutwood Avenue
☎ *(800) 797-8483, (714) 579-7400, FAX: 714-528-7945.*
Single: $90–$115. Double: $95–$125.
This all-suites hotel offers a complimentary newspaper, continental breakfast, in-room coffee, and weeknight social hour. All suites feature private Jacuzzis and minibars. Amenities: pool, exercise room, sauna, private spas, conference facilities. 96 rooms. Credit Cards: V, MC, A.

Holiday Inn Fullerton   **$85–$100**   ★★

222 West Houston Avenue
☎ *(800) 465-4329, (714) 992-1700, FAX: 714-992-4843.*
Single: $85–$95. Double: $90–$100.
This motor inn is adjacent to a large shopping mall. Free transfers to Disneyland and Knott's Berry Farm, each about three miles away. Rooms have coffee makers. Amenities: pool, exercise room, balcony or patio, family plan, conference facilities. 289 rooms. Credit Cards: V, MC, A.

Marriott Fullerton   **$89–$119**   ★★★

2701 East Nutwood Avenue
☎ *(800) 228-9290, (714) 738-7800, FAX: 714-738-0288.*
Single: $89–$119. Double: $89–$119.
Located at California State University Fullerton, this hotel has extensive conference facilities. Amenities: pool, health club, exercise room, sauna, private spas, club floor. 225 rooms. Credit Cards: V, MC, DC, A.

Low Cost Lodging

Days Inn   **$59–$69**   ★★

1500 South Raymond Avenue
☎ *(800) 329-7466, (714) 635-9000, FAX: 714-520-5831.*
Single: $59. Double: $69.
Formerly Griswold's, this motor hotel offers free transportation to Disneyland and Knott's Berry Farm, each about 10 minutes away. Amenities: pool, exercise room, Jacuzzi, family plan, conference facilities. 250 rooms. Credit Cards: CB, V, MC, DC, A.

Garden Grove

Low Cost Lodging

Best Western Plaza International   **$45–$60**   ★★

7912 Garden Grove Boulevard
☎ *(800) 528-1234, (714) 894-7568, FAX: 714-894-6308.*
Single: $45–$60. Double: $45–$60.
Comfortable motor lodge with complimentary coffee in rooms. Located three miles from Knott's Berry Farm and four miles from Disneyland. Amenities: pool, sauna. 101 rooms. Credit Cards: V, MC, DC, A.

La Mirada

Hotels and Resorts

Holiday Inn Gateway Plaza   **$85–$95**   ★★★

14299 Firestone Boulevard
☎ *(800) 356-6873, (714) 739-8500, FAX: 714-739-4272.*
Single: $85–$95. Double: $85–$95.
This comfortable hotel offers free transportation to Disneyland and Knott's Berry Farm. All rooms have coffee makers; some also have refrigerators. Amenities: pool, exercise room, Jacuzzi, sauna, family plan, conference facilities, complimentary airport pickup service. 300 rooms. Credit Cards: CB, V, MC, DC, A.

Norwalk

Hotels and Resorts

Norwalk Sheraton   **$120–$120**   ★★★

13111 Sycamore Drive
☎ *(800) 325-3535, (310) 863-6666, FAX: 310-868-4486.*
Single: $120. Double: $120.
This suburban hotel located near Disneyland and Knott's Berry Farm (free transfers to both) provides pleasant accommodations but not much pizazz. Rooms have coffee makers and mini bars. Amenities: pool, health club, conference facilities, business services. 175 rooms. Credit Cards: V, MC, DC, A.

Orange

Hotels and Resorts

Doubletree Orange County   **$135–$175**   ★★★

100 The City Drive
☎ *(800) 222-8733, (714) 634-4500, FAX: 714-978-3839.*
Single: $135–$155. Double: $155–$175.
This recently renovated hotel offers complimentary transfers to Disneyland, 10 minutes away. Rooms are comfortable; request one overlooking the Crystal Cathedral for the best view. The concierge floor offers special services. Amenities: pool, tennis, Jacuzzi, conference facilities, club floor, business services, complimentary airport pickup service. 451 rooms. Credit Cards: V, MC, A.

Hilton Suites   **$109–$185**   ★★★

400 North State College
☎ *(800) 445-8667, (714) 938-1111, FAX: 714-938-0930.*
Single: $109–$149. Double: $114–$185.
This 10-story, all-suite hotel is located across from Anaheim Stadium and features an expansive atrium lobby with white marble flooring, wicker furnishings and splashing fountains. Complimentary breakfast

and a cocktail are included in the room rates. Accommodations
include kitchens with microwaves, coffeemakers, two TVs with VCR
and free videos, wet bars and large baths. Popular with businesspeople
and sports fans. Amenities: pool, exercise room, sauna, conference
facilities, complimentary airport pickup service. 230 rooms. Credit
Cards: CB, V, MC, DC, A.

Residence Inn by Marriott $79–$149   ★★★
201 North State College Boulevard
☎ *(800) 331-3131, (714) 978-7700, FAX: 714-978-6257.*
Single: $79–$149. Double: $79–$149.
Each unit in this all-suite hotel includes a fully equipped kitchen, and
some have fireplaces. A complimentary breakfast and dinner buffet are
served daily, and laundry and grocery shopping services are available.
Amenities: pool, tennis, health club, Jacuzzi, balcony or patio, conference facilities, complimentary airport pickup service. 105 rooms.
Credit Cards: V, MC, DC, A.

Washington Suites Hotel $125–$189   ★★★
720 The City Drive South
☎ *(800) 278-4837, (714) 740-2700, FAX: 714-971-1692.*
Single: $125–$189. Double: $125–$189.
This hotel, formerly the Woodfin Suites, offers free transfers to nearby
Disneyland. Each unit has a VCR (free videos), a refrigerator, a microwave and a coffee maker. A complimentary breakfast buffet is served
daily and evening snacks and beverages are available Monday through
Friday. Amenities: pool, Jacuzzi, family plan, conference facilities,
business services. 124 rooms. Credit Cards: CB, V, MC, DC, A.

Anaheim: Where to Eat

Anaheim
American

Cattleman's Wharf $$$ ★★
1160 West Ball Road, ☎ *(714) 535-1622.*
Specialties: prime rib; seafood.
Dinner: 5–10 p.m., entrees $10–$27.
Old American/Continental standby with the standard steak-and-sea-
food format. There are five separate dining areas, each with a different
theme. Sunday brunch is a good value. Features: own baking, Sunday
brunch, full bar, late dining. Jacket requested. Reservations recommended. Credit Cards: V, MC, A.

Foxfire $$$ ★★
5717 E. Santa Ana Canyon Road, ☎ *(714) 974-5400.*
Specialties: seafood; prime rib; steak; pasta.
Lunch: 11:30 a.m.–2 p.m., entrees $10–$13.
Dinner: 5–10 p.m., entrees $10–$55.
Nothing too special here, but the menu of California-style grill food
often satisfies, and there's a good Sunday brunch and early-bird dinners at reasonable prices. Features: Sunday brunch, full bar, late dining. Reservations recommended. Credit Cards: CB, V, MC, DC, A.

J.W.'s $$$ ★★★★
700 West Convention Way, ☎ *(714) 750-8000.*
Specialties: pheasant; veal medallions with lime and ginger.

Dinner: 6–10 p.m., entrees $19–$28.
Associated hotel: Marriott Anaheim.

You might not expect to find a four-star restaurant in a Marriott Hotel, but this is one of the best in Orange County. The dining rooms are rich with plush carpets, antiques, oil paintings on the walls and the classic touch of a single red rose at each table. The only complaint here is that the service can be a bit snooty, but the opulent surroundings and wonderful food compensate. Closed: Sun. Features: own baking, full bar, rated wine cellar, late dining. Jacket requested. Reservations required. Credit Cards: CB, V, MC, DC, A.

Mr. Stox $$$ ★★★

1105 East Katella Avenue, ☎ (714) 634-2994.
Specialties: mesquite broiled seafood; fresh pastas.
Lunch: 11:30 a.m.–2:30 p.m., entrees $8–$15.
Dinner: 5:30–10 p.m., entrees $14–$25.

The American/Continental fare includes seafood, steak, chicken and game, and the wine list is exceptional, as are the homemade desserts. Professional service and reasonable prices make Mr. Stox an Orange County favorite. The restaurant opens earlier for dinner if a corresponding event is going on at the Arrowhead Pond. Features: own baking, full bar, rated wine cellar, late dining, private dining rooms. Jacket requested. Reservations recommended. Credit Cards: CB, V, MC, DC, A.

Italian

Thee White House $$$ ★★★

887 South Anaheim, ☎ (714) 772-1381.
Specialties: veal with porcini mushroom.
Lunch: 11:30 a.m.–2:30 p.m., entrees $7–$15.
Dinner: 5:30–10 p.m., entrees $17–$28.

A great little special-occasion spot, Thee White House is housed in an old Victorian mansion and provides a pleasant diversion from all those trendy restaurants in town. The mostly-Italian menu is enhanced by French and other Mediterranean touches. Lunch served Monday through Friday. Features: full bar, late dining, private dining rooms. Jacket requested. Reservations required. Credit Cards: V, MC, A.

Seafood

Catch, The $$$ ★★

1929 South State College, ☎ (714) 634-1829.
Specialties: fresh fish; prime rib.
Lunch: 11:30 a.m.–2 p.m., entrees $8–$14.
Dinner: 5–9:30 p.m., entrees $11–$24.

Average-to-good American/Continental fare has a loyal local following, but isn't haute cuisine by any means. Lunch served Monday through Friday. Features: outside dining, Sunday brunch, full bar. Reservations recommended. Credit Cards: V, MC, DC, A.

Brea

American

Crocodile Cafe $ ★★

975 East Birch Street, ☎ (714) 529-2233.
Specialties: gourmet pizza; chili; quesadillas.
Lunch: from 11 a.m., entrees $5–$10.
Dinner: to 9:30 p.m., entrees $5–$10.

The wildly eclectic menu features everything from gourmet pizzas to burgers to blue corn tostadas, which means you're bound to find something you like. Busy, crowded and noisy. Features: wine and beer only. Reservations not accepted. Credit Cards: V, MC, A.

French

La Vie En Rose   **$$$**   ★★★

240 South State College Boulevard, ☎ *(714) 529-8333.*
Specialties: rack of lamb.
Lunch: 11:30 a.m.–2:30 p.m., entrees $9–$18.
Dinner: 5:30–10 p.m., entrees $18–$26.
Go to La Vie En Rose and you'll think you're in France. There's a pleasant country French atmosphere in the farmhouse-style decor, and the food is classic French. Although this style of cooking is considered by many to be a little out of date, it's done so wonderfully here that the restaurant has a large following. Desserts here are excellent, and baked fresh daily in the restaurant's bakery. Lunch served Monday through Friday. Closed: Sun. Features: nonsmoking area, late dining, private dining rooms. Jacket requested. Reservations recommended. Credit Cards: D, V, MC, DC, A.

Fullerton

French

Cellar, The   **$$$**   ★★★

305 North Harbor Boulevard, ☎ *(714) 525-5682.*
Specialties: Boneless Loin of Lamb; Breast of Pheasant; Roast Rabbit.
Dinner: 5:30–10 p.m., entrees $18–$27.
This lovely restaurant is built around a wine cellar and its wine list shines with more than 700 selections. The food is as good as the wine, but it's classical French with classically heavy sauces, a cuisine that's currently a bit behind the times. Those willing to splurge for dinner here say the indulgence is worth the calories. Service is friendly and always extremely efficient. Closed: Mon, Sun. Features: own baking, full bar, rated wine cellar, late dining. Jacket requested. Reservations recommended. Credit Cards: D, CB, V, MC, DC, A.

Italian

Mulberry Street   **$$**   ★★

114 West Wilshire, ☎ *(714) 525-1056.*
Lunch: 11:30 a.m.–2:30 p.m., entrees $7–$10.
Dinner: 5–10 p.m., entrees $10–$20.
A cozy hangout where the food is nearly always good, the service friendly and the wine list adequate. Features: full bar, late dining.
Credit Cards: V, MC, A.

La Habra

American

Cat and the Custard Cup   **$$$**   ★★★

800 East Whittier, ☎ *(714) 992-6496.*
Specialties: roasted filet mignon; fresh seafood.
Lunch: 11:30 a.m.–2:30 p.m., entrees $7–$15.
Dinner: 5:30–10 p.m., entrees $15–$23.
An Old-English-inn atmosphere, complete with beamed ceilings and fireplace, seems an odd setting for the surprisingly good American cuisine that turns up here along with some English favorites. The

house may be old and stately, but the food is definitely keeping up with the times. Lunch served Monday through Friday. Features: own baking, full bar, late dining. Jacket requested. Reservations recommended. Credit Cards: CB, V, MC, DC, A.

Orange

Italian

Caffe Piemonte $$$ ★★

1835 East Chapman Avenue, ☎ *(714) 532-3296.*
Lunch: 12 a.m.–1:30 p.m., entrees $8–$23.
Dinner: 5–9 p.m., entrees $8–$23.

This unassuming storefront restaurant draws raves for solid Northern Italian cuisine and warm service. Now that the secret is out, reserve ahead or you'll wait. Lunch served Tuesday through Friday. Closed: Mon. Features: own baking, wine and beer only. Reservations required. Credit Cards: V, MC, A.

SANTA ANA

Santa Ana: Things to See and Do

Activities

Museums and Exhibits

Bowers Museum of Cultural Art ★★★★

2002 North Main Street, Santa Ana, 92706, ☎ *(714) 567-3600.*
Hours open: 10 a.m.–4 p.m.

This excellent museum, which was named one of nine "must see" museums in the U.S., recently reopened after a stunning renovation. Its focus is the cultural arts of many countries, with an emphasis on Africa, the Americas and the Pacific Rim. The exhibits change annually and focus on arts and crafts, folk festivals and regional as well as national cultural arts. There is a fine collection of African masks and American Indian baskets, and on display indefinitely are "Asian Ivories in Cultural Perspective," "Arts of Native America," and "Visions of the Shaman, Songs of the Priest," ancient artifacts from Columbian Mesoamerica. Docent tours Tuesday through Sunday at 1 and 2 p.m. Admission for children, $1.50; $3 for seniors and students. General admission: $4.50.

Discovery Museum of Orange County ★★★

3101 Harvard Street, Santa Ana, ☎ *(714) 540-0404.*
Hours open: 1–5 p.m., Sun. 11 a.m.–3 p.m.

The discoveries to be made at this 11-acre site illustrate what made things tick for early settlers to the area. The H. Clay Kellogg House, a restored Victorian home, is chock full of artifacts, costumes and crafts of the era. There are two other historic buildings as well, and the museum site is a popular place for weddings and children's birthday parties. Children's admission, $1.50; seniors and students, $2. General admission: $2.50.

Irvine Museum ★★★

18881 Von Karman Avenue, Irvine, 92715, ☎ *(714) 476-2565.*
Hours open: 11 a.m.–5 p.m.

This museum features changing exhibits from Joan Irvine Smith's multi-million-dollar collection, which includes over 2000 paintings of California landscapes by known California Impressionists. Most of these works date between 1890 and 1930 and are highly environmental in theme. The museum also sponsors a two-week lecture series on California Impressionists that is repeated several times during the year. Free admission.

Orange County Natural History Museum

La Paz Road, Laguna Niguel, ☎ (714) 831-6625.
Hours open: 11 a.m.–4 p.m.
At Plaza de la Paz Shopping Center.

Peruse a collection of bony, rocky and leafy things at this museum devoted to the geology, archaeology and botany of Orange County. There are also live reptiles, rodents and amphibians. Donation requested.

Tours

Orange County Performing Arts Center Tours

600 Town Center Drive, Costa Mesa, ☎ (714) 556-2122.

If you've attended a performance in the many venues here, tour the facility to see how it all works. Public tours Monday, Wednesday, and Saturday 10 a.m. and 11 a.m. Free admission.

Parks and Gardens

Santa Ana Zoo

Prentice Park, Santa Ana, ☎ (714) 836-4000.
Hours open: 10 a.m.–5 p.m.

This small zoo is home to over 200 animals in exhibits that emphasize South America's native fauna. "Amazon's Edge," a new exhibit that recently opened in conjunction with the zoo's expansion project, features howler monkeys, capybaras, and other South American animals. The new Rain Forest Conservation exhibit houses many tropical animals and shows the effects of rain forest destruction on their habitats. There's also an African aviary, Australian exhibit, children's zoo and a gift shop. Children three-12 are admitted for $1; children under three, free. General admission: $3.

Theme/Amusement Parks

Wild Rivers

8800 Irvine Center Drive, Irvine, 92718, ☎ (714) 768-9453.
Hours open: 11 a.m.–5 p.m.

Water rides attract children of all ages to this 20-acre park adjacent to the Irvine Meadow's Amphitheatre. Popular attractions include "Congo River Rapids," the "Wahtubee" and two wave pools. A children's area has special kid-size slides. The regular season is mid-May to the end of September. Call for Fall/Winter hours. Children's admission, $12.95. General admission: $16.95.

Santa Ana for Kids

Adventure Playground

1 Beech Tree Lane, Irvine, ☎ (714) 786-0854.
At the University Community Park.

Children can build forts, climb, cook and garden at this community park.

Discovery Museum of Orange County   ★★★

3101 West Harvard Street, Santa Ana, 92704, ☎ (714) 540-0404.
Hours open: 1–5 p.m., Sun. 11 a.m.–3 p.m.
At Centennial Park.

Children can relive the days of old as they try churning butter or washing clothes in a washtub. Housed in restored buildings on 11 acres, this museum features arts, crafts and history exhibits. Open Wednesday-Friday. Reduced admission for children. General admission: $2.

Imagination Celebration

Various locations, Costa Mesa, ☎ *(714) 556-2787.*
This annual festival, held in April, is dedicated to bringing art and expression to children. Events include hands-on workshops, demonstrations and live performances by professional artists and student groups.

Kids Karaoke

Golden West St. & Bolsa Avenue, Westminister, ☎ *(714) 898-2550.*
Hours open: 6–8 p.m.
At Westminister Mall.
It's early evening and you know where the kids are—at least on Thursdays, when Westminister Mall hosts Kids Karaoke at the Cafe 405 food court.

Mervyn's Musical Mornings

2151 Michelson Drive, Irvine, 92715, ☎ *(714) 755-5799.*
This special series of Saturday morning concerts, presented by the Pacific Symphony Orchestra, is wonderful fun for the whole family, but is designed especially for kids. Performances take place at the Orange County Performing Arts Center at 10 and 11:30 a.m. Adult admission is $10 per concert; children under 14, $8.

Events

A Taste of Orange County

Irvine Spectrum, Irvine, ☎ *(714) 753-3532.*
At Alton Parkway and Irvine Center Drive.
The best of Orange County restaurants serve up gourmet fare to visitors at A Taste of Orange County, held the last weekend of June. The food is accompanied by music, entertainment and other activities.

Orange County Fair ★★★

88 Fair Drive, Costa Mesa, ☎ *(714) 751-3247.*
Hours open: Noon–midnight.
At the Orange County Fairgrounds.
Each July, the Orange County Fair runs for 17 days, with livestock shows, stage shows, contests, carnival rides, international foods and special exhibits. Highlight events include the rodeo, the gem and mineral show, a flower and garden show, cooking and baking competitions, arts and crafts exhibitions and 4-H projects. Children's admission is $2; under five are free. General admission: $6.

Santa Ana Sports and Recreation

Bicycling

Santa Ana Riverbed Trail, Santa Ana, ☎ *(714) 571-4200.*
At Imperial Highway South and Pacific Coast Highway.
Ride or bike this 29-mile trail that follows the Santa Ana River, passing Anaheim Stadium, Mesa Verde Country Club and ending at Huntington State Beach. It's a relatively safe route through Orange County to the beach, on smooth asphalt eight-12 feet in width. Parks

near the trail provide restrooms and drinking fountains. Open daily
8 a.m.–10 p.m.

Challenge for Children

Bren Events Center, Irvine.
At UC Irvine.
The Byron Scott/Bud Light Challenge for Children is an annual
fundraising event for children's charities featuring Byron Scott and
other NBA stars in a Prostar Charity Basketball Game. Many of the
tickets are distributed to kids, but the game, which in the past has
included Magic Johnson, A. C. Green, James Worthy, Vlade Divac
and Mark Eaton, is open to the public. Usually held in September.

Rancho San Joaquin Golf Course

1 Sandburg Way, Irvine, ☎ *(714) 786-5522.*
This public course has enough variety to challenge most golfers, but
unless it's windy, the course is not overly difficult. Greens fees are $25
Monday-Thursday; $35 Friday; $40 Saturday-Sunday.

Rockreation

1300 Logan Avenue, Costa Mesa, ☎ *(714) 556-7625.*
Want to experience the thrill of rock climbing without driving to the
mountains? Rockreation offers 10,000 square feet of sculpted artificial
rock with a variety of climbing features—indoors! Routes have col-
ored holds that are changed often for a challenge to the regulars.
Beginners must take a safety class. Open Monday-Thursday 11 a.m.–
10 p.m. Friday 11 a.m.–8 p.m. Saturday 9 a.m.–9 p.m.

Santiago Park Bowling Green

Santiago Park, Santa Ana, ☎ *(714) 637-4449.*
Lawn bowling is the rage here, especially for seniors who enjoy this
healthy, enjoyable outdoor exercise.

Tustin Ranch Golf Course

12442 Tustin Ranch Road, Tustin, ☎ *(714) 730-1611.*
This course, designed by Ted Robinson, is among the best-main-
tained public facilities in the state.

Santa Ana: Music, Dance and Theatre

Music

Irvine Meadows Amphitheatre ★★★★

8808 Irvine Center Drive, Laguna Hills, ☎ *(714) 855-4515.*
Famous names highlight the summer calendar at this outdoor amphitheater. Bring a picnic and have dinner on the lawn before the 8 p.m.
performance.

Opera Pacific

9 Executive Circle, Suite 190, Irvine, 92714, ☎ *(714) 474-4488.*
Opera Pacific's season opens in October and showcases several of
opera's most popular works along with a number of world-renowned
artists.

Orange County Performing Arts Center

Costa Mesa, 92626, ☎ *(714) 556-2787.*
At Bristol Street.
The center opened in 1986 and is the main venue for entertainment
in Orange County. Broadway shows, ballet, opera, symphony and

pop concerts are all performed in the center's two theatres. The center is also home to the Pacific Symphony Orchestra, the Orange County Philharmonic Society, the Pacific Chorale and the South Coast Repertory. The popular Broadway series presents contemporary and classical shows featuring top name stars.

Orange County Philharmonic Society

2082 Business Center Drive, Irvine, 92715, ☎ *(714) 553-2422.*
The Society presents a repertoire rich in artistic diversity, with performances at the Orange County Performing Arts Center. Talent featured is always of the highest national and international caliber.

Pacific Symphony Orchestra

2151 Michelson Drive, Irvine, 92715, ☎ *(714) 755-5799.*
The Pacific Symphony offers a Classics series, a Summer Pops series at Irvine Meadows Amphitheatre and a Family series of concerts each season at the Orange County Performing Arts Center.

Theatre

Costa Mesa Civic Playhouse

661 Hamilton Avenue, Costa Mesa, ☎ *(714) 650-5269.*
This local playhouse produces five plays and a Christmas pageant annually.

Irvine Barclay Theatre ★★★

4242 Campus Drive, Irvine, ☎ *(714) 854-4646.*
At U.C. Irvine.
This small, yet elegant, 756-seat theatre, although not directly affiliated with U.C. Irvine, sits on the northern end of the campus and devotes equal time to the college's School of Fine Arts events, conferences and professional performances. The entertainment here is always first-rate, and includes chamber music concerts, recitals, dance, theatre, and a variety of special events.

Saddleback College Cabaret Theatre

28000 Marguerite Parkway, Mission Viejo, ☎ *(714) 582-4646.*
This solidly-supported summer stock theatre program at Saddleback College has maintained commercial and critical success for its repertoire of crowd-pleasing, and ultimately challenging musicals such as *Sweeney Todd.*

Shakespeare Orange County

333 North Glassell Street, Orange, ☎ *(714) 744-7016.*
At the Waltmar Theatre.
Two summer productions and a Christmas extravaganza are presented at this theatre located on the campus of Chapman University.

South Coast Repertory

655 Town Center Drive, Costa Mesa, ☎ *(714) 957-4033.*
This professional resident theatre, founded in 1964, offers a ten-month season—September through June—that includes twelve plays set on two stages at the Orange County Performing Arts Center. The series includes plays by America's finest playwrights, as well as those drawn from classic and modern theatre repertoires.

Way Off Broadway Playhouse

1058 East First Street, #007, Santa Ana, ☎ *(714) 547-8997.*
Like its name says, this theater is from off-Broadway, but not in spirit, as it specializes in original and experimental productions.

Santa Ana: Nightlife

The queen of supper clubs in OC is Santa Ana's **Roxbury South**, where the music changes nightly and crosses the board, from hip-hop to reggae to retro. Dress to be seen—but not in grubbies, or you won't be admitted.

Country Rock Cafe

23822 Mercury Road, Lake Forest, ☎ *(714) 455-1881.*

An upscale country dance club with rock 'n roll thrown in, Country Rock opened in October, 1993 and is a big hit, with hourly dance lessons, live music and a "family day" every Sunday 2 p.m.–7 p.m.

Improv, The

4255 Campus Drive, #138, Irvine, ☎ *(714) 854-5455.*

This outpost of the famous comedy club offers a variety of comedy headliners. Recently appearing here were Bobby Slayton, George Kanter, Jeff Jena and Henry Cho. Call for a list of current performers and showtimes. Another Orange County branch of The Improv is in Brea ☎ *(714) 529-7878.* Shows at 8:30 p.m.–10:30 p.m. Cover $8-$12.

Planet Hollywood

1641 West Sunflower, Santa Ana, 92704, ☎ *(714) 434-7827.*

Another of those hot (and touristy) nightclubs backed by celebrities, this branch of Planet Hollywood is raking in the dough in sophisticated Newport Beach.

Randell's

3 Hutton Centre Drive, Santa Ana, ☎ *(714) 556-7700.*

An eclectic mix keeps this place hopping every night, from Wednesday's "Itzafunkthang" musical theme to owner Randell Young's guitar rhythm and blues performances on Friday nights. Call for current schedule of performers and times. Show times 8 p.m.–midnight nightly.

Roxbury South

2 Hutton Centre, Santa Ana, 92703, ☎ *(714) 662-0880.*

Billed as "Orange County's finest contemporary supper club," Roxbury will provide your dinner, then tempt you to stay into the night with live music and dancing. The two-level mansion features a dining room, live reggae Wednesday night, Retro '70 theme nights Thursday and Rockabilly Blues Dance Club on Friday. There's no cover if you have dinner here, but the dress code—which forbids shorts, sleeveless shirts, tennis shoes, baseball caps and "holey" jeans—is strictly enforced. Call for information on current bands. Open Wednesday-Saturday from 7 p.m.

The Shark Club

841 Baker Street, Costa Mesa, ☎ *(714) 751-0202.*

This hot club combines house, funk, hip-hop and DJ's with billiards and recorded progressive music. There's also a real shark tank with live shark feeding every Thursday at midnight. No cover.

Santa Ana: Where to Stay

Costa Mesa
Hotels and Resorts

Holiday Inn Costa Mesa $75–$75   ★ ★ ★

3131 S. Bristol Street
☎ *(800) 465-4329, (714) 557-3000, FAX: 714-957-8185.*
Single: $75. Double: $75.
Conveniently located to the 405 freeway, this Holiday Inn has a lively lounge with a piano bar and free hors d'oeuvres. The rooms are surprisingly comfortable with combination baths and TVs with movies. The executive wing is plush and can actually compete with the Red Lion across the street. Amenities: pool, exercise room, Jacuzzi, sauna, balcony or patio, family plan, conference facilities, business services, complimentary airport pickup service. 230 rooms. Credit Cards: CB, V, MC, DC, A.

Marriott Suites $69–$99   ★ ★ ★

500 Anton Boulevard
☎ *(800) 228-9290, (714) 957-1100, FAX: 714-966-8495.*
Single: $69–$99. Double: $69–$99.
Convenient to the 405 freeway, located near Metro Center and five miles from the beach. All units have separate living room, two TVs, wet bar and refrigerators. Nice pool area in a park-like setting. Amenities: pool, health club, Jacuzzi, sauna, private spas, balcony or patio, family plan, conference facilities, business services, complimentary airport pickup service. 253 rooms. Credit Cards: CB, V, MC, DC, A.

Red Lion Orange County $79–$172   ★ ★ ★

3050 Bristol Street
☎ *(800) 547-8010, (714) 540-7000, FAX: 714-540-9176.*
Single: $79–$172. Double: $79–$172.
Very good convention hotel with a seven-story lobby atrium and lots of fountains. Courtyard pool and waterfall have adjacent spa, exercise room with sauna and steam room. Tennis and golf privileges. Amenities: pool, exercise room, Jacuzzi, sauna, balcony or patio, hair salon, conference facilities, club floor, business services, complimentary airport pickup service. 484 rooms. Credit Cards: CB, V, MC, DC, A.

Residence Inn $79–$156   ★ ★ ★

881 West Baker Street
☎ *(800) 331-3131, (714) 241-8800, FAX: 714-546-4308.*
Single: $79–$126. Double: $99–$156.
Studio and penthouse suites with full kitchens, most with fireplaces. Complimentary continental breakfast, newspaper and evening beverages Monday through Thursday. Amenities: pool, Jacuzzi, balcony or patio, conference facilities. 144 rooms. Credit Cards: CB, V, MC, DC, A.

Westin South Coast Plaza $99–$169   ★ ★ ★ ★

686 Anton Boulevard
☎ *(800) 228-3000, (714) 540-2500, FAX: 714-662-6695.*
Single: $99–$169. Double: $99–$169.
Recently-renovated hotel known for its friendly staff, individually-decorated rooms and its proximity to the South Coast Plaza shopping center. Lobby features a 20-foot waterfall. There are two restaurants—one is gourmet Italian—and a lounge. Accommodations are

deluxe with light wood furnishings, breakfast tables, new TVs and minibars. Rooms above the 10th floor have ocean views. Amenities: pool, tennis, health club, family plan, conference facilities, business services, complimentary airport pickup service. 392 rooms. Credit Cards: V, MC, A.

Wyndham Garden $79–$79   ★ ★ ★
3350 Avenue of the Arts
☎ *(800) 443-1844, (714) 751-5100, FAX: 714-751-0129.*
Single: $79. Double: $79.

Formerly the Beverly Heritage, this handsome business hotel is one block from South Coast Plaza mall. Lobby highlights include a fireplace and marble floors, and some rooms have coffee makers and refrigerators. The outdoor pool overlooks a park. Request a room facing the lake for the best views. Continental breakfast, and admission to the hotel's cocktail lounge are complimentary. This is an excellent option for the price. Amenities: pool, health club, Jacuzzi, balcony or patio, family plan, conference facilities, business services, complimentary airport pickup service. 238 rooms. Credit Cards: CB, V, MC, DC, A.

Low Cost Lodging

Best Western Newport Mesa $40–$80   ★ ★
2642 Newport Boulevard
☎ *(800) 554-2378, (714) 650-3020, FAX: 714-642-1220.*
Single: $40–$80. Double: $40–$80.

Motor inn located opposite Orange County Fairgrounds, five minutes from Newport Beach. Some of the 11 suites have whirlpools. Complimentary coffee in rooms. Amenities: pool, sauna, private spas, family plan, conference facilities, complimentary airport pickup service. 97 rooms. Credit Cards: CB, V, MC, DC, A.

Country Side Inn and Suites $69–$79   ★ ★ ★
325 Bristol Street
☎ *(800) 322-9992, (714) 549-0300, FAX: 714-662-0828.*
Single: $69–$79. Double: $69–$79.

This inn features a country French atmosphere. There are two heated pools, and some rooms have private Jacuzzis. Guests receive complimentary evening cocktails. Amenities: pool, exercise room, Jacuzzi, balcony or patio, conference facilities, business services, complimentary airport pickup service. 290 rooms. Credit Cards: CB, V, MC, DC, A.

La Quinta Motor Inn $47–$52   ★ ★
1515 South Coast Drive
☎ *(800) 531-5900, (714) 957-5841, FAX: 714-432-7159.*
Single: $47–$52. Double: $47–$52.

This motor inn is five miles from downtown Costa Mesa, eight and a half miles from Disneyland. Soundproofed rooms include a work area, and a complimentary newspaper and morning coffee are offered to guests. Amenities: pool, conference facilities, complimentary airport pickup service. 162 rooms. Credit Cards: V, MC, DC, A.

Irvine

Hotels and Resorts

Atrium Marquis $109–$129   ★ ★
18700 MacArthur Boulevard
☎ *(800) 854-3012, (714) 833-2770, FAX: 714-757-1228.*
Single: $109–$119. Double: $119–$129.

Formerly the Airporter Garden Hotel, this motor inn recently underwent a $5 million renovation. It has spacious rooms, each with a balcony or patio and a coffee maker. In addition to its proximity to the airport, it has decent exercise equipment, a restaurant and bar and a shopping arcade. Suites are furnished with refrigerators and wet bars. Amenities: pool, health club, private spas, balcony or patio, hair salon, conference facilities, complimentary airport pickup service. 215 rooms. Credit Cards: CB, V, MC, DC, A.

Courtyard by Marriott $64–$94 ★★★

2701 Main Street
☎ *(800) 321-2211, (714) 757-1200, FAX: 714-757-1596.*
Single: $64–$94. Double: $64–$94.
This residential-style hotel is located one and a half miles from the John Wayne Airport, five miles from Newport Beach. All rooms have coffee makers. Amenities: pool, exercise room, Jacuzzi, conference facilities, complimentary airport pickup service. 153 rooms. Credit Cards: CB, V, MC, DC, A.

Embassy Suites Irvine $99–$189 ★★★

2120 Main Street
☎ *(800) 362-2779, (714) 553-8332, FAX: 714-261-5301.*
Single: $99–$189. Double: $99–$189.
One-bedroom suites and a few smaller hotel rooms situated around an attractive atrium area. Heated indoor pool. Complimentary full breakfast and afternoon cocktails. Amenities: pool, Jacuzzi, sauna, conference facilities, business services, complimentary airport pickup service. 293 rooms. Credit Cards: V, MC, A.

Holiday Inn Airport $62–$145 ★★★

17941 Von Karman Avenue
☎ *(800) 465-4329, (714) 863-1999, FAX: 714-474-7236.*
Single: $62–$145. Double: $62–$145.
Located in the heart of Orange County's business district in an attractive office park, 10 miles from Disneyland. There's an indoor pool and a modest weight room. Bicycle rentals are available. Amenities: pool, exercise room, Jacuzzi, sauna, conference facilities, club floor, complimentary airport pickup service. 340 rooms. Credit Cards: CB, V, MC, DC, A.

Hyatt Regency Irvine $80–$209 ★★★

17900 Jamboree Boulevard
☎ *(800) 233-1234, (714) 975-1234, FAX: 714-852-1574.*
Single: $80–$184. Double: $80–$209.
Located five minutes away from the Orange County Airport, this hotel caters to conventions, groups, seminars and business travelers. The skylighted lobby has a piano lounge and accommodations are the usual Hyatt standard with blond wood furnishings and TVs with VCRs hidden in armoires. Two-line phones, minibars and combination baths are standard. Ranked restaurant: **Morell's**. Amenities: pool, tennis, health club, Jacuzzi, sauna, balcony or patio, conference facilities, business services, complimentary airport pickup service. 536 rooms. Credit Cards: CB, V, MC, DC, A.

Marriott Irvine $119–$165 ★★★

18000 Von Karman
☎ *(800) 228-9290, (714) 553-0100, FAX: 714-261-7059.*

Single: $119–$165. Double: $119–$165.

A modern highrise geared to large conventions. There's one restaurant featuring seafood and sushi, a sports bar with several TVs tuned to sporting events and a second lounge in the lobby. Floor-to-ceiling windows, traditional dark furnishings and combination baths are about the same in all guest rooms. Best rooms are poolside units. Amenities: pool, tennis, health club, Jacuzzi, balcony or patio, hair salon, family plan, conference facilities, club floor, complimentary airport pickup service. 484 rooms. Credit Cards: CB, V, MC, DC, A.

Radisson Plaza Irvine   **$79–$140**

18800 MacArthur Boulevard
☎ *(800) 333-3333, (714) 833-9999, FAX: 714-833-3317.*
Single: $79–$140. Double: $79–$140.

Located across from the John Wayne Airport, this hotel was recently renovated and offers good value for the price. Accommodations include new carpets, beds and furniture, and a new phone system was installed. Armoires, TVs with movies, and shower massages are other features. Amenities: pool, tennis, exercise room, Jacuzzi, balcony or patio, family plan, conference facilities, business services, complimentary airport pickup service. 289 rooms. Credit Cards: CB, V, MC, DC, A.

Residence Inn Irvine   **$65–$159**   ★★★

10 Morgan Street
☎ *(800) 331-3131, (714) 380-3000, FAX: 714-588-7743.*
Single: $65–$129. Double: $99–$159.

Studio and penthouse suites with living room, fully equipped kitchen and most with fireplaces. Complimentary buffet breakfast daily and evening cocktails and hors d'oeuvres Monday through Friday. Amenities: pool, exercise room, Jacuzzi, balcony or patio, complimentary airport pickup service. 112 rooms. Credit Cards: CB, V, MC, DC, A.

Lake Forest

Hotels and Resorts

Irvine Suites Hotel   **$75–$105**   ★★

23192 Lake Center Drive
☎ *(800) 347-8483, (714) 380-9888, FAX: 714-380-8307.*
Single: $75–$95. Double: $75–$105.

Formerly a Quality Suites, this hotel offers one-bedroom suites that include living rooms, microwaves, refrigerators, VCRs and stereos. Continental breakfast and evening beverages are complimentary. Amenities: pool, exercise room, Jacuzzi, private spas, conference facilities, complimentary airport pickup service. 90 rooms. Credit Cards: CB, V, MC, DC, A.

Santa Ana

Hotels and Resorts

Comfort Suites   **$59–$69**   ★★

2620 Hotel Terrace Drive
☎ *(800) 228-5150, (714) 966-5200, FAX: 714-979-9650.*
Single: $59. Double: $69.

All units include living/working area, oversized bath, mini-bar and microwave. Complimentary breakfast, evening happy hour and daily newspaper. Free parking. Amenities: pool, health club, Jacuzzi, houses, cottages or bungalows, conference facilities, complimentary airport pickup service. 130 rooms. Credit Cards: CB, V, MC, DC, A.

Courtyard by Marriott   **$52–$59**   ★★★

3002 South Harbor Boulevard
☎ *(800) 321-2211, (714) 545-1001, FAX: 714-545-8439.*
Single: $52–$59. Double: $52–$59.
Nicely landscaped courtyard and pool area with indoor whirlpool,
exercise room. All rooms have large work desk and coffee maker.
Suites to $79. Amenities: pool, exercise room, Jacuzzi, balcony or
patio, conference facilities. 145 rooms. Credit Cards: CB, V, MC, DC, A.

Crown Sterling Suites   **$95–$119**   ★★★

1325 East Dyer Road
☎ *(800) 433-4600, (714) 241-3800, FAX: 714-662-1651.*
Single: $95–$119. Double: $95–$119.
Formerly Embassy Suites. All suites have separate bedroom and living
room. Guests receive a complimentary, cooked-to-order breakfast
and attend a nightly reception. Amenities: pool, Jacuzzi, sauna, balcony or patio, family plan, conference facilities, complimentary airport
pickup service. 306 rooms. Credit Cards: CB, V, MC, DC, A.

Doubletree Club   **$115–$125**   ★★★

Seven Hutton Centre Drive
☎ *(800) 528-1234, (714) 751-2400, FAX: 714-662-7935.*
Single: $115. Double: $125.
Set on an attractive location overlooking a three-acre lake, within
walking distance of the Hutton Centre Office Complex. Comfortable
rooms include two phones, mini-bar and coffee maker. Complimentary full breakfast and evening cocktails. Free parking. Amenities:
pool, exercise room, Jacuzzi, conference facilities, business services,
complimentary airport pickup service. 170 rooms. Credit Cards: CB, V,
MC, DC, A.

Quality Suites   **$95–$105**   ★★★

2701 Hotel Terrace Drive
☎ *(800) 221-2222, (714) 957-9200, FAX: 714-641-8936.*
Single: $95. Double: $105.
Two-room suites include two televisions, VCR, microwave, wet bar,
refrigerator and stereo. Complimentary cooked-to-order breakfast,
morning paper, manager's reception and poolside buffet dinner Tuesday through Thursday. Eight miles from Disneyland, five miles from
the beach. Amenities: pool, Jacuzzi, balcony or patio, business services, complimentary airport pickup service. 177 rooms. Credit Cards:
CB, V, MC, DC, A.

Radisson Suites Hotel   **$85–$135**   ★★★

2720 Hotel Terrace Drive
☎ *(800) 333-3333, (714) 556-3838, FAX: 714-241-1008.*
Single: $85–$135. Double: $85–$135.
Complimentary full breakfast and evening manager's reception
included. All suites have microwaves and coffee makers. Located two
miles from John Wayne Airport. Amenities: pool, health club,
Jacuzzi, complimentary airport pickup service. 122 rooms. Credit
Cards: CB, V, MC, DC, A.

Ramada   **$65–$95**   ★★★

2726 South Grand Avenue
☎ *(800) 272-6232, (714) 966-1955, FAX: 714-966-1889.*
Single: $65–$85. Double: $75–$95.

Business-oriented hotel where many rooms have refrigerators and microwaves; some have a private patio. Complimentary full breakfast and morning newspaper. Amenities: pool, exercise room, Jacuzzi, balcony or patio, family plan, conference facilities, complimentary airport pickup service. 183 rooms. Credit Cards: CB, V, MC, DC, A.

Low Cost Lodging

Santa Ana Inn   **$55–$70**   ★★

2600 North Main Street
☎ *(714) 836-5141, FAX: 714-667-8168.*
Single: $55–$60. Double: $60–$70.

Adjacent to Main Place Mall, this motel is located five miles from Disneyland. Complimentary full breakfast and in-room movies are offered to all guests. Amenities: pool, Jacuzzi, conference facilities, complimentary airport pickup service. 122 rooms. Credit Cards: CB, V, MC, DC, A.

Santa Ana: Where to Eat

Costa Mesa

American

Diva   **$$**   ★★★

600 Anton Boulevard, ☎ *(714) 754-0600.*
Lunch: 11:30 a.m.–3 p.m., entrees $5–$10.
Dinner: 5:30–10 p.m., entrees $10–$20.

Another creation by David Wilhelm, Diva is drawing crowds—and for good reason: the cutting-edge New American cuisine is fabulous. Other attractions are live jazz on weekends, an incredibly dramatic decor and a grand selection of cappuccinos and desserts for post-theatre refreshment. It's a natural with the theatre crowd, and they DO crowd the place; it's become THE place to be seen. Features: outside dining, own baking, wine and beer only, late dining. Jacket requested. Reservations recommended. Credit Cards: V, MC, A.

Riviera   **$$$**   ★★

3333 South Bristol Street, ☎ *(714) 540-3840.*
Specialties: pepper steak flambe au cognac; roast leg of lamb.
Lunch: 11:30 a.m.–3 p.m., entrees $7–$30.
Dinner: 5–10:30 p.m., entrees $18–$30.

This little South Coast Plaza restaurant offers fairly consistent American/Continental cuisine with French accents. The four-course pre-theatre menu, served from 5 to 7, is a good buy for $17.50-$22. Closed: Sun. Features: full bar, late dining. Reservations recommended. Credit Cards: CB, V, MC, DC, A.

Wolfgang Puck Cafe   **$$**   ★★★

3333 Bristol Street, ☎ *(714) 546-9653.*
Specialties: Chinois salad; designer pizza.
Lunch: from 11 a.m., entrees $8–$12.
Dinner: to 10 p.m., entrees $8–$12.

This new South Coast Plaza hotspot marks Puck's debut in Orange County, and so far it's a hit. Stars California-style cuisine, including those famous gourmet pizzas, along with good wines and moderate prices. In the Bullock's department store. Features: outside dining, own baking, wine and beer only, rated wine cellar, late dining. Credit Cards: V, MC.

International

Golden Truffle $$$ ★ ★ ★
1767 Newport Boulevard, ☎ *(714) 645-9858.*
Lunch: 11:30 a.m.–2:30 p.m., entrees $8–$13.
Dinner: 5:30–10 p.m., entrees $11–$25.

If you can look past the dreary storefront ambience, you will find lots of things to like about the eclectic cuisine served here. The menu spans the globe, with touches of Asian cuisine here, Pacific Rim cuisine there, Mediterranean cuisine someplace else, and it's almost all extremely good. Closed: Mon, Sun. Features: outside dining, own baking, wine and beer only, rated wine cellar, late dining. Reservations recommended. Credit Cards: V, MC, A.

Italian

Piccola Cucina $$ ★ ★
3333 Bristol Street, ☎ *(714) 556-5844.*
Lunch: from 11:30 a.m., entrees $7–$15.
Dinner: to 9:30 p.m., entrees $8–$15.

South Coast Plaza eatery situated on the third floor, above Barney's. The Northern Italian cuisine often succeeds admirably, but service can falter, and you can usually expect a wait. Great little pizzas and rotisseried meats. Lunch served Monday through Friday. Features: outside dining, Sunday brunch, wine and beer only. Reservations recommended. Credit Cards: V, MC, A.

Scampi $$ ★ ★ ★
1576 Newport Boulevard, ☎ *(714) 645-8560.*
Lunch: 11:30 a.m.–2:30 p.m., entrees $5–$12.
Dinner: 5–10:30 p.m., entrees $8–$19.

Reviews are mixed on the Southern Italian food served here, but you can't go wrong with the pastas, which come in big portions at reasonable prices. The wine list is surprisingly good. Lunch served Monday through Friday. Features: full bar, rated wine cellar, late dining. Reservations recommended. Credit Cards: V, MC, A.

Sfuzzi $$ ★ ★
1870A Harbor Boulevard, ☎ *(714) 548-9500.*
Lunch: from 11:30 a.m., entrees $8–$13.
Dinner: 5:30–11 p.m., entrees $10–$17.

This outpost of the national chain offers the usual trendy menu, service with an attitude and lively bar scene. Stick to the basics—or go for a post-theatre cappuccino and dessert—and you'll probably go away satisfied. A high-energy spot that's great for people-watching. At Triangle Square. Features: outside dining, Sunday brunch, full bar, late dining. Reservations recommended. Credit Cards: V, MC, A.

Seafood

Scott's Seafood Grill $$$ ★ ★ ★
3300 Bristol Street, ☎ *(714) 979-2400.*
Lunch: from 11:30 a.m., entrees $15–$30.
Dinner: to 10 p.m., entrees $15–$30.

Fresh seafood, simply grilled and presented, is the hallmark of this restaurant near the Performing Arts Center. Wine tasting is featured on Wednesday nights. Features: outside dining, Sunday brunch, full bar,

rated wine cellar, late dining. Reservations recommended. Credit Cards:
V, MC, A.

Southwestern

El Torito Grill   **$$**   ★★
633 Anton Boulevard, ☎ *(714) 662-2672.*
Specialties: salsa quemada; tamalitos; mesquite broiled seafood.
Lunch: 11 a.m.–3 p.m., entrees $7–$11.
Dinner: 3–10 p.m., entrees $7–$16.
A noisy, crowded, upscale environment serves as a backdrop for
homemade Mexican, Tex-Mex and Southwestern cuisine, killer mar-
garitas and lots of fun. Features: own baking, Sunday brunch, full bar,
late dining. Reservations recommended. Credit Cards: V, MC, DC, A.

Thai

Bangkok Four   **$$**   ★★★
3333 Bear Street, ☎ *(714) 540-7661.*
Specialties: seafood; garlic chicken.
Lunch: 11 a.m.–3 p.m., entrees $7–$14.
Dinner: 3–10 p.m., entrees $7–$14.
The gracious service gets as many kudos as the food at this pleasant
Thai restaurant located on the third floor of the Crystal Court. Fea-
tures: wine and beer only, late dining. Reservations recommended.
Credit Cards: CB, V, MC, DC, A.

Irvine

American

Gulliver's   **$$$**   ★★
18482 MacArthur Boulevard, ☎ *(714) 833-8411.*
Specialties: prime rib.
Lunch: 11:30 a.m.–2:30 p.m., entrees $7–$18.
Dinner: 6–10 p.m., entrees $15–$25.
English ambience prevails, from the smell of roasting beef to the cos-
tumed waitstaff that constantly banters with the customers. The food
is pricey, but well-prepared and served with flair. Lunch served Mon-
day through Friday. Features: own baking, full bar, late dining. Res-
ervations recommended. Credit Cards: V, MC, A.

French

Chanteclair   **$$$**   ★★★
18912 MacArthur Boulevard, ☎ *(714) 752-8001.*
Lunch: 11:30 a.m.–2:30 p.m., entrees $7–$13.
Dinner: 5–10 p.m., entrees $14–$26.
Lovely country-inn setting includes gardens, fireplaces and French
Provincial decor. Chef Byron Gemmell, arguably one of the best chefs
in Orange County, left the restaurant when it was sold late last year.
There have been a few menu changes since, and a few struggles to
keep the restaurant on an even keel, but you can mostly count on
what comes out of the kitchen at Chanteclair, along with the excellent
service. Lunch served Monday through Friday. Features: outside dining, own baking, Sunday brunch, full bar, rated wine cellar, late dining. Jacket and tie requested. Reservations recommended. Credit Cards:
CB, V, MC, DC, A.

Indian

Clay Oven   **$$**   ★
15435 Jeffrey Road, ☎ *(714) 552-2851.*

Lunch: 11:30 a.m.–2:30 p.m., entrees $7–$9.
Dinner: 5:30–10:30 p.m., entrees $5–$14.

Indian cuisine is served up as spicy as you like it at this Irvine Village Center restaurant. Seafood is especially well done, the desserts are yummy and the lunch buffet (at $6.50) is a real bargain. Features: own baking, wine and beer only, late dining. Credit Cards: V, MC, A.

Italian

Bistango $$$

19100 Von Karman Avenue, ☎ (714) 752-5222.
Lunch: 11:30 a.m.–3 p.m., entrees $8–$14.
Dinner: 5–10 p.m., entrees $13–$20.

Reviews are getting more positive for this Italian/California restaurant near John Wayne Airport. Many dishes on the menu, which changes monthly, succeed admirably, but others sometimes fall short. Service is always professional, and the setting is sophisticated, with fine art on the walls and live jazz in the evenings. Lunch served Monday through Friday. Features: outside dining, full bar, rated wine cellar, late dining. Reservations recommended. Credit Cards: V, MC, A.

Il Fornaio $$

18051 Von Karman Avenue, ☎ (714) 261-1444.
Lunch: from 11:30 a.m., entrees $5–$10.
Dinner: 5:30–11 p.m., entrees $5–$17.

There are a few complaints about uneven cooking and lapses in service, but by and large, Il Fornaio is a winner. Much of its local acclaim revolves around what comes out of its bakery (where breakfast is served): 52 different kinds of hearth-baked, superb preservative-free breads and rolls. A trendy spot. Features: outside dining, own baking, full bar. Reservations recommended. Credit Cards: V, MC, A.

Prego $$

18420 Von Karman Avenue, ☎ (714) 553-1333.
Specialties: oak-fired pizza; house-made pasta.
Lunch: from 11:30 a.m., entrees $7–$19.
Dinner: to 11 p.m., entrees $7–$19.

One of the few complaints about Prego is that its staff has an attitude problem, but the food nearly always lives up to the pretensions (as do the prices). The Northern Italian cuisine is expertly rendered, and the varied menu wins kudos. An Orange County yuppie hangout. Features: outside dining, own baking, full bar, late dining. Reservations recommended. Credit Cards: V, MC, A.

Seafood

McCormick's & Schmick's $$ ★ ★ ★

2000 Main Street, ☎ (714) 756-0505.
Lunch: from 11:30 a.m., entrees $5–$10.
Dinner: to 11 p.m., entrees $10–$20.

Seafood is the star at McCormick's & Schmick's, a chain restaurant that has its origins in the Pacific Northwest. Expect average-to-good renditions of all your favorites, from an international selection of fresh fish to oysters to crab cakes, all served in a San Francisco clublike atmosphere. Features: outside dining, full bar, late dining. Reservations recommended. Credit Cards: V, MC, A.

Santa Ana

Asian

Favori　　　　　　**$**　　　　　　★★

3502 West First Street, ☎ *(714) 531-6838.*
Specialties: catfish.
Lunch: from 11 a.m., entrees $5–$7.
Dinner: to 10 p.m., entrees $7–$10.
French-Vietnamese food is a good bargain here, with prices so afford-
able that you can experiment with a variety of tastes. The atmosphere
is snazzy, and the lights flattering. Features: nonsmoking area, late
dining. Reservations recommended. Credit Cards: V, MC.

Italian

Antoneilo　　　　　　**$$$**　　　　　　★★★★

1611 Sunflower Street, ☎ *(714) 751-7153.*
Specialties: seafood; veal.
Lunch: 11:30 a.m.–2 p.m., entrees $8–$19.
Dinner: 6–10 p.m., entrees $10–$30.

The fare is a bit pricey at this lovely Italian restaurant located across
from the South Coast Plaza, but it's authentic Italian in every way,
from the warm, inviting surroundings to the herbs picked fresh from
the restaurant's own garden. Proprietor Antonio Cagnolo is always on
hand to oversee his dining room and schmooze with guests. Lunch
served Monday through Friday. Closed: Sun. Features: outside din-
ing, own baking, full bar, rated wine cellar, late dining. Jacket
requested. Reservations recommended. Credit Cards: CB, V, MC, DC, A.

Scandinavian

Gustaf Anders　　　　　　**$$$**　　　　　　★★★★

3810 South Plaza Drive, ☎ *(714) 668-1737.*
Specialties: parsley salad; filet with stilton and morel sauce.
Lunch: 11:30 a.m.–2 p.m., entrees $8–$20.
Dinner: 5:30–9:30 p.m., entrees $16–$28.

A past recipient of Orange County's Best Restaurant poll, Gustaf
Anders continues to inspire local diners with its exquisite food and
sublime setting. Here you'll find house-smoked herring, bread freshly
baked in-house, homemade desserts and ice creams and perfect wines.
The Scandinavian cuisine is unique in a world full of trendy Italian restaurants, and you'll go away feeling extremely pampered and well-fed.
Once located in La Jolla, the restaurant relocated to South Coast
Plaza a few years ago. Lunch served Monday through Saturday. Features: outside dining, own baking, Sunday brunch, full bar, rated wine
cellar. Jacket requested. Reservations recommended. Credit Cards: CB,
V, MC, DC, A.

Southwestern

Topaz Cafe　　　　　　**$$**　　　　　　★★★

2002 North Main Street, ☎ *(714) 835-2002.*
Lunch: 11:30 a.m.–3 p.m., entrees $9–$13.
Dinner: 5–8 p.m., entrees $9–$14.
After you've taken in the sights at the Bowers Museum, stop by this
delightful (and dramatically lit) restaurant for lunch or Sunday brunch
(dinner is also served on Thursdays). Both the food and the ambience
sparkle, and desserts are to die for. Closed: Mon. Features: outside

dining, Sunday brunch, no bar. Reservations recommended. Credit
Cards: V, MC, A.

Tustin

American

Mc Charles House   **$$$**   ★★★

335 South C Street, ☎ *(714) 731-4063.*
Lunch: 11:30 a.m.–5 p.m., entrees $7–$15.
Dinner: 5:30–7:30 p.m., entrees $15–$20.

This turn-of-the-century home is a local favorite for traditional Amer-
ican cooking, and especially for afternoon tea, where homemade
cakes, scones and other delicacies are hard to resist. Dinner is served
only on Thursday, Friday and Saturday. Closed: Mon, Sun. Features:
outside dining, own baking, wine and beer only. Reservations recom-
mended. Credit Cards: V, MC, A.

Nieuport 17   **$$$**   ★★

13051 Newport Avenue, ☎ *(714) 731-5130.*
Specialties: prime rib; seafood; steak.
Lunch: 11 a.m.–4 p.m., entrees $8–$14.
Dinner: 4–10 p.m., entrees $18–$35.

A somewhat casual spot for steak and seafood, or for pampering clients in a clublike atmosphere that's a bit dated, but still works. The
bar is also popular for late-night schmoozing. Features: full bar, late
dining. Reservations recommended. Credit Cards: V, MC, A.

Mediterranean

Zov's Bistro   **$$**   ★★★

17440 East 17th Street, ☎ *(714) 838-8855.*
Lunch: 11 a.m.–2:30 p.m., entrees $6–$12.
Dinner: 5–9:30 p.m., entrees $6–$17.

Zov's has a large local following, due as much to the fare coming out
of the new bakery as to its eclectic—and always delicious—Armenian-
inspired cuisine. *Orange Coast* magazine dubbed Zov's sliced grilled
lamb sandwich on a baguette the Best Sandwich in Orange County.
Lunch served Monday through Saturday; dinner served Wednesday
through Saturday only. Located in the Enderle Center. Closed: Sun.
Features: outside dining, own baking, wine and beer only. Reserva-
tions recommended. Credit Cards: V, MC, A.

NEWPORT BEACH

Newport Beach

Newport Beach: Things to See and Do

Activities

Museums and Exhibits

International Surfing Museum ★★★

411 Olive Street, Huntington Beach, ☎ *(714) 960-3483.*
The surf's always up at this memorabilia-filled museum dedicated to
the area's favorite sport. There's a collection of historic longboards,
photos and a video library. Open daily June-September noon–5 p.m.
Closed Monday and Tuesday the rest of the year. Children under six
free. General admission: $2.

Laguna Art Museum ★★★

307 Cliff Drive, Laguna Beach, ☎ *(714) 494-6531.*
Hours open: 11 a.m.–5 p.m.
This museum is one of Orange County's oldest and hippest with several spacious galleries exhibiting works from its permanent collection
focusing on traditional and contemporary paintings and sculpture by
California artists. Additional temporary exhibitions are featured
throughout the year. General admission: $3.

Newport Harbor Art Museum ★★★

850 San Clemente Drive, Newport Beach, 92660, ☎ *(714) 759-1122.*
Hours open: 10 a.m.–5 p.m.
In Newport Center.

Orange County showcase for contemporary art exhibits, paintings, sculpture, photographs, prints, drawings and installations by acknowledged masters of twentieth-century art and by rising young artists of the nineties. Admission for students and seniors is $2; children six-12, free; Tuesday, free to all. General admission: $4.

Surfing Walk of Fame

Main Street and Pacific Coast Highway, Huntington Beach.

If you're more of a surfer dude than a movie fan, forget the Hollywood Walk of Fame and check out the Surfing Walk of Fame, which honors legendary surfers. Since it just opened in August of 1994, there are only six names on the walk (Duke Kahanamoku, Robert August, Tom Blake, Mark Richards, Bruce Brown and Joyce Hoffman), but more will be added each year during the U.S. Open of Surfing. Free admission.

Historical Sites

Mission San Juan Capistrano ★★

31882 Camino Capistrano, San Juan Capistrano, ☎ *(714) 248-2048.*
Hours open: 8:30 a.m.–5 p.m.

The legendary swallows arrive, more or less, around March 19, accompanied by the Fiesta de las Golondrinas (see, under "City Celebrations"), but there's ample reason to visit this historic mission before or after the hoopla surrounding the return of the birds. Founded by Padre Serra in 1776, this is the oldest building in the state. General admission: $4.

Tours

Tall Ship Pilgrim ★★

24200 Dana Point Harbor Drive, Dana Point, ☎ *(714) 496-2274.*

Take a walking tour of the replica of the ship that brought Richard Henry Dana Jr., author of *Two Years Before the Mast*, to Orange County. Children's admission, $1.50. General admission: $3.

Parks and Gardens

Bolsa Chica Ecological Reserve ★★★★

Pacific Coast Highway, Huntington Beach, ☎ *(714) 897-7003.*
Between Warner Avenue and Golden West Street.

Walk the trails at this 530-acre wetland, which is being restored after decades of neglect. Birding enthusiasts have observed some 320 species here, including the Belding's Savannah Sparrow, Brown Pelican and California Least Tern. Open dawn to dusk. Tours first Saturday of the month, 9 and 10:30 a.m.

Crystal Cove State Park ★★★★

8471 Pacific Coast Highway, Laguna Beach, ☎ *(714) 494-3539.*

Sandy beaches, gray whale-watching, historical cottages, fishing and birding are among the myriad things to see and do at this 2791-acre state park which shares boundaries with Corona del Mar. After all the activity, enjoy a date shake at the Crystal Cove Shake Shack at 7408 Pacific Coast Highway. General admission: $6.

Huntington Beach   ★ ★ ★
Coast Highway, Huntington Beach, ☎ *(714) 834-2400.*
This beach and its pier form the mecca of the surf world, the Surf City where surfers coined the famous term, "shooting the pier," but beware of the territorial attitudes of the surfers here. Each September, an annual surfing competition attracts guys and gals who brave the waves around the world, and the city's International Surfing Museum chronicles the history of the sport.

Roger's Gardens   ★ ★ ★
2301 San Joaquin Hills Road, Newport Beach, ☎ *(714) 640-5800.*
Hours open: 9 a.m.–6 p.m.
Visit this beautiful seven-acre nursery with a year-round garden festival that makes green thumbs out of brown ones. Many exhibits, shows and contests are held in the Gardens' outdoor amphitheatre. Winter hours 9 a.m.–5 p.m.

Upper Newport Bay Ecological Reserve   ★ ★ ★
Between Jamboree Road and PCH, Newport Beach, ☎ *(714) 640-6746.*
Whether your interest is hiking, birding, cycling, boating, fishing or just sitting back and contemplating nature, you'll enjoy this stunning 1000-acre coastal preserve, also called Back Bay, which was purchased by the State of California in 1975 in order to preserve its critical habitat. There are guided nature tours, designated hiking, biking and horse trails, and various nature programs throughout the year. Dawn and dusk are best hours to visit. Kayak tours are offered on Sundays at 10 a.m., and guided tours are conducted on the first and third Saturdays of each month at 9 a.m. Call for reservations. **The Friends of Newport Bay** ☎ *(714) 646-8009)* provides more information on the preserve's tours and other activities.

Balboa Island

Theme/Amusement Parks

Balboa Fun Zone   ★ ★ ★
600 East Bay Avenue, Newport Beach, ☎ *(714) 675-9152.*
Next to Balboa Pavilion.
Newport-Balboa's version of Coney Island is an old-fashioned family fun attraction with a Ferris wheel, restored merry-go-round, shops, arcades, boat tours and restaurants.

Events

Baroque Music Festival ★★
Sherman Library and Gardens, Corona del Mar, ☎ *(714) 760-7887.*
This music festival is held annually in June and features works by renowned and less-than-renowned Baroque composers. Call for exact dates, times and ticket prices.

Christmas Boat Parade of Lights ★★
Newport Harbor, Newport Beach, ☎ *(714) 729-4400.*
Watch and enjoy more than 200 colorfully decorated boats as they parade through Newport Harbor. Many vantage points are available along the route, but it still gets very crowded.

Concours d'Elegance ★★★
Cental Park, Huntington Beach, ☎ *(714) 960-8836.*
Every June, the Concours d'Elegance features more than 200 classic cars from Europe and the U.S. In addition to the classics, vintage racers, exotic autos and special creations spice up the show. Add food, music and live entertainment, and you have an automobile buff's fantasy.

Dana Point Festival of the Whales ★★
Dana Point Harbor, Dana Point, ☎ *(714) 496-1094.*
This annual winter festival celebrates the migration of the California gray whale with two weeks of entertainment, an art show, a street fair and live entertainment in the Harbor area, at Doheny Beach and at the **Orange County Marine Institute**, *24200 Dana Point Drive.* Usually held from mid-February to early March, weekends only.

Festival of Arts ★★★★
650 Laguna Canyon Road, Newport Beach, 92651, ☎ *(714) 494-1145.*
Hours open: 10 a.m.–11:30 p.m.
At Irvine Bowl Park.

The Festival of Arts is an annual event which began in 1932 and is held in spacious park-like grounds on which 160 artists and craftspersons display their original works in a juried show. Paintings, sculpture, woodcrafted items, jewelry, etched glass, weavings and even furniture are displayed, and there are also performances by various musical groups. Truly an art aficionado's paradise, the festival takes place in July and August. Shuttle buses take festival-goers from lots in Laguna Canyon or downtown to the festival site. The popular "Pageant of the Masters" is held at the bowl as part of the festival. General admission: $3.

Fiesta de las Golondrinas ★★
Various locations, San Juan Capistrano, ☎ *(714) 493-5911.*
The annual migration of the swallows back to the Capistrano mission is celebrated each year in March and April. There is a Swallows Day Parade, a golf tournament, a community fair, a 10K run and 3K walk and various other contests. The swallows supposedly make their appearance on March 19, but even the experts concede that it's "give or take a few days." Unfortunately for local tourism, the swallows' nests were pretty much all knocked down while earthquake repairs were being made, and nearby development has also made the area less hospitable. But not to worry; if the swallows don't show up on time, there are plenty of pigeons to feed.

Huntington Harbour Cruise of Lights ★★★

Huntington Harbour, Huntington Beach, ☎ *(714) 840-7542.*
Among all of the Christmastime "parade of lights" celebrations in
Southern California harbors, this one stands out. You board a boat
and cruise up and down the channels of Huntington Harbour,
observing decorated waterfront homes and boats that include thousands of lights, artwork, and animated figures. The celebration lasts
ten days, and tickets (prices vary, but all are under $10.00) may be
purchased by phone, or by writing the Huntington Harbour Philharmonic Committee at *16897 Algonquin Street, Suite I, Huntington
Beach, CA 92649.*

Mission Rancho Days ★★★

31822 Camino Capistrano, San Juan Capistrano, ☎ *(714) 248-2048.*
Join in the Western festivities as the Mission celebrates the "Rancho
Era." Food, entertainment, lawmen, desperados and western exhibits
are all part of this summer event, held in late August.

Newport Seafest ★★

Various locations, Newport Beach, ☎ *(714) 729-4400.*
Every September, this 10-day celebration includes a kite-flying festival, a pier swim and a boat show. Visitors can try small portions of a
variety of specialties from local restaurants at The Taste of Newport
food-sampling event.

Orange County Blues Festival ★★★

12174 Euclid Street, Dana Point, ☎ *(800) 786-8774.*
In Heritage Park.
This event, held each September, is a three-day tribute to the blues
with performances by nationally known artists such as Etta James,
Randell Young and the Actuals, Johnny Clyde Copeland, and Rod
Piazza and the Mighty Flyers. A fine-arts fair and gourmet foods and
wine are also part of the celebration.

Pageant of the Masters ★★★★

650 Laguna Canyon Road, Laguna Beach, 92651, ☎ *(800) 487-3378.*
At Irvine Bowl Park.
Here is performance art at its best! Live models re-create great works
of art accompanied by a full orchestra. Performances are given in the
beautiful Irvine Bowl beneath the stars at 8:30 p.m. during the Festival of the Arts. The Bowl seats 2500. The Pageant began in 1933 and
is an annual attraction for tourists from around the world. Ticket
prices range from $9 to $38, and reserved seating is required.

Sand Castle and Sand Sculpture Contest ★★★

Corona del Mar State Beach, Corona del Mar, ☎ *(714) 729-4400.*
Between Ocean Blvd. and Iris Avenue.
Adults and children as well as amateurs and professionals create dazzling displays in the sand during this unusual, annual contest held in
September.

Sawdust Festival ★★★★

935 Laguna Canyon, Laguna Beach, 92657, ☎ *(714) 494-3030.*
Hours Open: 10 a.m.–10 p.m.
Set in scenic Laguna Canyon just northeast of the blue Pacific, this
original arts-and-crafts fair features artists and artisans, unique art,
entertainment and rustic embellishments. Reduced admission prices
for seniors; children under 12 are free. General admission: $5.

Tallships Festival

35502 Dana Point Harbor Drive, Dana Point, ☎ *(714) 496-2274.*

Celebrate the return of the Tallship *Pilgrim* from her annual summer cruise at this festival held each September. There are maritime exhibits and activities for the entire family, including ship tours, arts and crafts and square-rigged-sailing skill demonstrations.

Sports and Recreation

Bicycling

Huntington Beach Bike Trail, Huntington Beach, ☎ *(714) 834-2400.*
Between Warner Avenue and Brookhurst Street.

This eight-mile bike trail is separated from car traffic. At the south end of Bolsa Chica State Beach, the trail climbs a bluff but soon drops, winding down under the Huntington Beach Pier. Crowded on weekends. Open dawn to dusk.

Davey's Locker Sport Fishing

40 Main Street, Balboa Island, ☎ *(714) 673-1434.*
At Balboa Pavilion.

Davey's Locker offers year-round sportfishing trips and supplies. Half-day trips are available.

Monarch Beach Golf Links

23841 Stonehill Drive, Dana Point, ☎ *(714) 240-8247.*

This seaside public golf course at Laguna Niguel is somewhat short—6224 yards from the blue tees—but it has some exceptional holes, including the par-four 12th, which actually abuts the beach. Weekday fees are $75; weekends, $100.

Newport Beach Golf Course

3100 Irvine Avenue, Newport Beach, ☎ *(714) 852-8681.*

An 18-hole, par-59 lighted course plus driving range, restaurant and pro shop. Green fees $11 Monday-Friday; $16 Saturday-Sunday. Carts included.

Pelican Hill

22653 Pelican Hill Road, Newport Beach, ☎ *(714) 760-0707.*

This 18-hole, par-70 championship course designed by Tom Fazio is a local favorite, as much for its breathtaking ocean views as for its challenging layout. Putting and chipping greens and a practice range are also here. Reserve a tee time up to a week ahead. Green fees are hefty (over $100), especially on weekends. Carts included.

Windsurfing Pacifica

Dana Point Harbor Drive, Dana Point, ☎ *(714) 363-9463.*
Dana Point at Dana Point Harbor Drive.

Windsurfing Pacifica specializes in a beginner's basic certification class covering rigging, sailing and theory. By appointment only. Cost is $80.

Laguna Beach is a famous art center and weekend retreat.

Newport Beach: Music, Dance and Theatre

Theatre

Huntington Beach Playhouse ★★★

7111 Talbert Avenue, Huntington Beach, ☎ *(714) 375-0696.*
Annual stage offerings include dramas, comedies, a Shakespearean play and a musical presented at the Huntington Beach Public Library and Amphitheatre.

Laguna Playhouse ★★★

606 Laguna Canyon Road, Laguna Beach, 92651, ☎ *(714) 497-9244.*
The venerable playhouse, founded in 1920, has been providing top-notch theatre to Orange County residents longer than any other company in the area. The Playhouse's Moulton Theater has excellent sight-lines and acoustics and provides a performance of each play for the hearing-impaired. Its season runs September-June.

Newport Theatre Arts Center ★★

2501 Cliff Drive, Newport Beach, ☎ *(714) 631-0288.*
A cozy community theatre overlooking the harbor, where the view at intermission can be as enjoyable as the play.

Newport Beach: Nightlife

There's a **Hard Rock Cafe** in Newport Beach that you'll probably want to see if you're a tourist (you can add to your HRC T-shirt collection for a small fortune), but it's not really a local hangout. The place has all the requisite Hollywood memorabilia hanging on the walls, and the food is merely average and way over-priced.

Hard Rock Cafe

451 Newport Center Drive, Newport Beach, 92660, ☎ *(714) 640-8844.*
Hours open: 11:30 a.m.–12 p.m.
A giant neon Fender stratocaster guitar marks the entrance to the newest Hard Rock Cafe, located on Fashion Island. This one has a '59 Cadillac suspended over the bar, Prince's "Purple Rain" suit, some Elton John sunglasses and a surf and rock decor. The party atmo-

sphere is the thing here, but you can also get burgers, fries, milkshakes, salads, grilled fish or chicken wings. Don't forget to check out the famous Hard Rock Cafe logo T-shirts.

Newport Landing

503 East Edgewater Avenue, Balboa Peninsula, ☎ *(714) 675-2373.*
A variety of entertainment is featured in this lounge and oyster bar located at the ferry landing. Calypso music happens on Sundays, there's karaoke on Sunday and Monday nights and rock and blues on Saturdays.

White House

340 South Coast Highway, Laguna Beach, ☎ *(714) 494-8088.*
Michael Jordan has been sighted at this venerable nightlife institution that has been around since 1918, when it was "the Waldorf Astoria Restaurant." Dinner is served beginning at 5 p.m., and you should plan to get here early. Reggae Monday and Tuesday. Live music, 9:30 p.m.–1:30 a.m.

Newport Beach: Where to Stay

Many of Orange County's most distinguished hotels have just finished or are in the process of completing expensive makeovers. The Newport Beach Marriott Hotel and Tennis Club completed a $3 million renovation in 1994 that upgraded all guest rooms and revamped the California Ballroom, concierge levels and the pool and atrium levels. Also added was a voice mail system for guests and an upscale health club.

The Waterfront Hilton in Huntington Beach has added a 20,000-square-foot pavilion adjacent to the property, which will provide additional space for meetings and trade shows.

At some hotels, of course, you can always expect the best. Such is the case with the stunning Four Seasons Newport Beach and the Ritz Carlton Laguna Nigel, arguably two of the best hotels in California.

Dana Point

Bed and Breakfast

Blue Lantern Inn   **$135–$350**   ★★★

34343 Street of Blue Lantern
☎ *(800) 950-1236, (714) 661-1304, FAX: 714-496-1483.*
Single: $135–$350. Double: $135–$350.

Located on a bluff overlooking Dana Point Harbor, all the beautifully decorated rooms here have coastal views, refrigerators stocked with complimentary beverages, fireplaces and tubs with Jacuzzi jets. A full buffet breakfast and hors d'oeuvres are included in the price at this elegant, New England-style hotel. Amenities: beach location, exercise room, Jacuzzi. 29 rooms. Credit Cards: V, MC, A.

Hotels and Resorts

Dana Point Hilton Inn   **$85–$95**   ★★★

34402 Pacific Coast Highway
☎ *(800) 445-8667, (714) 661-1100, FAX: 714-489-0628.*
Single: $85–$95. Double: $85–$95.

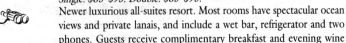

Newer luxurious all-suites resort. Most rooms have spectacular ocean views and private lanais, and include a wet bar, refrigerator and two phones. Guests receive complimentary breakfast and evening wine tasting; championship golf, sailing, tennis and deep-sea fishing are conveniently located nearby. A great vacation destination, as many activities are family-oriented, with special goings-on for kids. Amenities: pool, exercise room, Jacuzzi, sauna, private spas, balcony or patio, family plan, conference facilities, business services. 200 rooms. Credit Cards: V, MC, DC.

Dana Point Resort   **$129–$294**   ★★★
25135 Park Lantern
☎ *(800) 533-9748, (714) 661-5000, FAX: 714-661-5358.*
Single: $129–$294. Double: $129–$294.
Bluff-top, New England style resort overlooking the Pacific Ocean and yacht harbor, and surrounded by forty-two acres of luxurious grounds. Recreational facilities include two heated swimming pools, croquet, volleyball and basketball courts, jogging trails and bicycle paths. All the rooms have private terraces and whale-watching packages are available in season. During the summer, the cheapest rates start at over $200, making this a a great deal for a WINTER getaway. Amenities: pool, golf, tennis, sailing, health club, Jacuzzi, sauna, private spas, balcony or patio, conference facilities, club floor. 341 rooms. Credit Cards: CB, V, MC, DC, A.

Fountain Valley

Hotels and Resorts

Residence Inn by Marriott   **$72–$154**   ★★
9930 Slater Avenue
☎ *(800) 331-3131, (714) 965-8000, FAX: 714-962-3439.*
Single: $72–$132. Double: $85–$154.
This all-suite hotel, seven miles south of Newport Beach, offers fully equipped kitchens, a complimentary continental breakfast and evening hospitality hour. Some rooms have fireplaces. Amenities: pool, Jacuzzi, family plan, conference facilities, business services, complimentary airport pickup service. 80 rooms. Credit Cards: CB, V, MC, DC, A.

Low Cost Lodging

Courtyard Fountain Valley   **$57–$67**   ★★
9950 Slater Avenue
☎ *(800) 321-2211, (714) 968-5775, FAX: 714-968-0112.*
Single: $57–$67. Double: $57–$67.
This residential-style hotel is located seven miles south of Newport Beach. Rooms have fully equipped kitchens, some with fireplaces. Complimentary continental breakfast and evening hospitality hour. Amenities: pool, exercise room, Jacuzzi, conference facilities. 150 rooms. Credit Cards: CB, V, MC, DC, A.

Huntington Beach

Hotels and Resorts

Holiday Inn   **$89–$89**   ★★★
7667 Center Avenue
☎ *(800) 465-4329, (714) 891-0123, FAX: 714-895-4591.*
Single: $89. Double: $89.
Located five miles from downtown, close to the business and financial districts, and adjacent to the Huntington Beach Mall and Old World Village, this hotel offers complete business services, an indoor pool

and spa and complimentary in-room coffee. Amenities: pool, exercise room, Jacuzzi, sauna, conference facilities, complimentary airport pickup service. 224 rooms. Credit Cards: V, MC, A.

| **Waterfront Hilton** | **$120–$240** | ★★★ |

21100 Pacific Coast Highway
☎ *(800) 822-7873, (714) 960-7873, FAX: 714-960-3791.*
Single: $120–$205. Double: $210–$240.

Newer hotel that offers complimentary breakfast, a multilingual staff, nine lighted tennis courts, full-sized and lap pools, shops and restaurants. Golfers have privileges nearby. Each room at this Italian villa-style hotel has its own lanai that looks out over the ocean. Amenities: beach location, pool, golf, tennis, health club, Jacuzzi, sauna, balcony or patio, conference facilities, club floor, business services. 300 rooms. Credit Cards: CB, V, MC, DC, A.

Laguna Beach

Bed and Breakfast

| **Carriage House** | **$95–$150** | ★★ |

1322 Catalina Street
☎ *(714) 494-8945.*
Single: $95–$150. Double: $95–$150.

This charming bed and breakfast inn has one- and two-bedroom suites, and all but one unit has a kitchen. A nice change from the big tourist hotels. Amenities: balcony or patio. Six rooms. Credit Cards: Not Accepted.

Hotels and Resorts

| **Best Western Laguna Reef** | **$75–$100** | ★★★ |

30806 Coast Highway
☎ *(800) 922-9905, (714) 499-2227, FAX: 714-499-5575.*
Single: $75–$100. Double: $75–$100.

Fairly unremarkable motel in a garden setting. A complimentary continental breakfast is included in the rates, and more than a dozen rooms have kitchens. Amenities: pool, Jacuzzi, sauna, conference facilities. 43 rooms. Credit Cards: V, MC, DC, A.

| **Surf and Sand** | **$160–$700** | ★★★ |

1555 South Coast Highway
☎ *(800) 524-8621, (714) 497-4477, FAX: 714-494-2897.*
Single: $160–$700. Double: $160–$700.

Special "Pageant of the Masters" packages are available during July and August at this hotel, which is notable for its beach location and posh, artsy crowd (who can presumably afford some of its posh, artsy prices). Most rooms have an ocean view, and some have fireplaces. Suites are also available. Ranked restaurant: **Splashes**; **The Towers**. Amenities: beach location, pool, houses, cottages or bungalows, balcony or patio, hair salon, conference facilities. 157 rooms. Credit Cards: CB, V, MC, DC, A.

Inns

| **Aliso Creek Inn** | **$78–$189** | ★★★ |

31106 South Coast Highway
☎ *(800) 223-3309, (714) 499-2271, FAX: 714-499-4601.*
Single: $78–$189. Double: $78–$189.

This recently renovated hideaway is popular with golfers who play on its nine-hole course; the beach is a quarter-mile stroll. The tranquil setting surrounded by steep canyons is a nice respite from the area's busy beach activity, and every room has a kitchen with a coffeemaker. Amenities: pool, golf, Jacuzzi, private spas, houses, cottages or bungalows, balcony or patio, family plan, conference facilities, business services. 62 rooms. Credit Cards: V, MC, A.

Inn at Laguna Beach $105–$305 ★★★

211 North Pacific Coast Highway
☎ *(800) 544-4479, (714) 497-9722, FAX: 714-497-9972.*
Single: $105–$305. Double: $105–$305.
Recently renovated blufftop inn overlooking the Pacific. There's a rooftop lounge and sundeck, and many rooms have an ocean view. Guests receive a complimentary continental breakfast, and can walk to nearby shops and art galleries. Amenities: beach location, pool, conference facilities. 70 rooms. Credit Cards: CB, V, MC, DC, A.

Laguna Hills

Hotels and Resorts

Courtyard by Marriott $59–$74 ★★★

23175 Avenida de la Carlota
☎ *(800) 321-2211, (714) 859-5500, FAX: 714-454-2158.*
Single: $59–$74. Double: $59–$74.
This residential-style hotel is located seven miles from Newport Beach. Rooms include large work desks and coffee makers. Amenities: pool, Jacuzzi, balcony or patio, conference facilities. 148 rooms.
Credit Cards: CB, V, MC, DC, A.

Holiday Inn Laguna Beach $75–$105 ★★★

25205 La Paz Road
☎ *(800) 465-4329, (714) 586-5000, FAX: 714-581-7410.*
Single: $75–$95. Double: $80–$105.
This motor inn has a nice pool area dotted with tall palm trees. Area transportation is provided within a 10-mile radius. Amenities: pool, conference facilities, complimentary airport pickup service. 148 rooms. Credit Cards: CB, V, MC, DC, A.

Laguna Niguel

Hotels and Resorts

Ritz-Carlton $215–$435 ★★★★★

One Ritz Carlton Drive
☎ *(800) 241-3333, (714) 240-2000, FAX: 714-240-0829.*
Single: $215–$435. Double: $215–$435.
The manager of this Mediterranean villa-style resort has declared it the flagship hotel in the Ritz-Carlton chain, and there is plenty here to back up his claim. The rooms feature 18th- and 19th-century furnishings, art and carpets, and the service is legendary (Hollywood bigwig Stephen Spielberg reportedly didn't like his mattress, so a new one was promptly provided. Of course, if you're not Stephen Spielberg, you may have to go with what you've got). Amenities include a golf course designed by Robert Trent Jones, a jogging trail, volleyball courts, a plethora of water-related activities on the beach (lessons in surfing and windsurfing are available) and one of the best ocean views in America. Not everyone comes here to have fun, though. The late Richard Nixon reportedly checked into the $3000-a-day presidential suite to write his book. Ranked restaurant: **Ritz Carlton Dining Room**.

Amenities: beach location, pool, golf, tennis, health club, Jacuzzi, private spas, balcony or patio, hair salon, family plan, conference facilities, complimentary airport pickup service. 393 rooms. Credit Cards: CB, V, MC, DC, A.

Newport Beach

Bed and Breakfast

Doryman's Ocean Front Inn $135–$275   ★★★

2102 West Ocean Front
☎ *(800) 634-3303, (714) 675-7300.*
Single: $135–$275. Double: $135–$275.

This small inn near the pier and dory landing is Newport's only harborfront hotel. A continental breakfast is served in a Victorian parlor and there's a roof top terrace—a great place to take in the view. Guest rooms include fireplaces, marble and skylighted baths, antique furnishings and impressionist paintings. Only six of the 10 rooms have water views. Amenities: Jacuzzi, private spas, conference facilities. 10 rooms. Credit Cards: CB, V, MC, DC, A.

Little Inn on the Bay $100–$200   ★★

617 Lido Park Drive
☎ *(800) 438-4466, (714) 673-8800, FAX: 714-673-8800.*
Single: $100–$200. Double: $100–$200.

Bicycles for exploring the waterfront are available to guests at this New England-style hotel on the bay. Breakfast, afternoon wine and bedtime milk and cookies are also on the house, and there's a small Jacuzzi for relaxing. Amenities: beach location, sailing, Jacuzzi, conference facilities. 30 rooms. Credit Cards: CB, V, MC, DC, A.

Portofino Beach Hotel $100–$235   ★★★

2306 West Oceanfront
☎ *(714) 673-7030, FAX: 714-723-4370.*
Single: $100–$235. Double: $100–$235.

Old World charm emanates from this small beachfront hotel decorated with Victorian furniture and antiques. Most rooms have views of the ocean and marina, and bicycles are provided for guests who want to tour the area on wheels. Complimentary breakfast is provided. Amenities: beach location, Jacuzzi, balcony or patio, conference facilities, business services. 15 rooms. Credit Cards: CB, V, MC, DC, A.

Hotels and Resorts

Four Seasons Newport Beach $245–$355   ★★★★★

690 Newport Center Drive
☎ *(800) 332-3442, (714) 759-0808, FAX: 714-759-0568.*
Single: $245–$355. Double: $245–$355.

Beautiful highrise hotel overlooking Newport Harbor (all rooms have an ocean view) and situated in the Newport Center/Fashion Island complex, constructed in 1986. Accommodations are decorated in California pastels (half have balconies), and the friendly and efficient staff aims to please. Amenities include bicycles for exploring the area and advanced booking at the Pelican Hill Golf Club, whose Ocean Course was ranked as the "best new resort golf course in America" by *Golf Digest*. One of THE best hotels in Orange County, but tourists may prefer accommodations closer to the beach. Ranked restaurant: **Pavilion**. Amenities: pool, tennis, health club, Jacuzzi, sauna, balcony or patio, conference facilities, business services, complimentary airport pickup service. 285 rooms. Credit Cards: V, MC, A.

Hyatt Newporter $140–$190   ★ ★ ★
1107 Jamboree Road
☎ *(800) 233-1234, (714) 729-1234, FAX: 714-644-1552.*
Single: $140–$170. Double: $155–$190.
A 26-acre resort overlooking Newport's Back Bay. Brick terraces, landscaped walkways and a jogging path give a feeling of roominess to this old hotel that is synonymous with Newport Beach. Accommodations have rattan seating, antique-style tables, king or double beds, TVs, minibars and combination baths. There's also a nine-hole, par-three golf course and tennis courts. Amenities: pool, golf, tennis, health club, Jacuzzi, sauna, private spas, houses, cottages or bungalows, balcony or patio, hair salon, conference facilities, business services, complimentary airport pickup service. 410 rooms. Credit Cards: CB, V, MC, DC, A.

Marriott Hotel & Tennis Club $95–$175   ★ ★ ★
900 Newport Center Drive
☎ *(800) 228-9290, (714) 640-4000, FAX: 714-640-5055.*
Single: $95–$175. Double: $95–$175.
This large convention and resort hotel recently completed an extensive renovation. Amenities include eight lighted tennis courts, golf privileges nearby, a concierge level and access to the Fashion Island shopping center across the street. This property was designed to provide ocean views in about 90 percent of the tower rooms; if you get a room without one, take the elevator to the 16th-floor lounge, where the view is stunning. Because of the size of this resort, bring your walking shoes; long walks are sometimes necessary. Amenities: pool, tennis, health club, Jacuzzi, sauna, balcony or patio, hair salon, family plan, conference facilities, club floor, business services, complimentary airport pickup service. 586 rooms. Credit Cards: CB, V, MC, DC, A.

Marriott Suites Newport $109–$109   ★ ★ ★
500 Bayview Circle
☎ *(800) 228-9290, (714) 854-4500, FAX: 714-854-3937.*
Single: $109. Double: $109.
All units include wet bar, refrigerator and two TVs, and some rooms have refrigerators and views of the bay. Pleasant but standard accommodations, located 20 minutes from Disneyland. Amenities: pool, health club, Jacuzzi, sauna, balcony or patio, family plan, conference facilities, business services, complimentary airport pickup service. 250 rooms. Credit Cards: V, MC, DC, A.

Sheraton Newport Beach $115–$165   ★ ★ ★
4545 MacArthur Boulevard
☎ *(800) 325-3535, (714) 833-0570, FAX: 714-833-0570.*
Single: $115–$145. Double: $130–$165.
Resort-style hotel set in office-park surroundings but livelier than other corporate hotels in the area. Guest rooms in the older tower are decorated in a light, beachy decor. Rooms in the newer tower are more traditional. All rooms have dressing areas, sliding glass doors opening onto balconies and wicker armchairs. Beware of the lack of thermostats in rooms in the older tower. A full buffet breakfast and an afternoon cocktail are included in the room rate. Amenities: pool,

tennis, health club, Jacuzzi, balcony or patio, conference facilities, business services, complimentary airport pickup service. 338 rooms. Credit Cards: V, MC, DC, A.

Sutton Place $155–$215   ★★★★

4500 MacArthur Boulevard
☎ *(800) 243-4141, (714) 476-2001, FAX: 714-476-0153.*
Single: $155–$195. Double: $175–$215.

Formerly Le Meridien (the sales office swears that "nothing has changed but the name"), this is a hotel of European elegance. It boasts distinctive architecture, an expansive entry set amid flower beds and bordered by shallow pools, a lobby with elegant furnishings and European art. The accommodations are equally beautiful, with fabric wallpaper, plants, louvered closets, minibars and combination baths. The staff is about as good as can be found, and room service is around the clock. The atrium lobby is especially striking. Ranked restaurant: **Antoine**. Amenities: pool, tennis, health club, Jacuzzi, sauna, balcony or patio, family plan, conference facilities, business services, complimentary airport pickup service. 435 rooms. Credit Cards: V, MC, A.

Sunset Beach

Inns

Harbour Inn $69–$109   ★★

16912 Pacific Coast Highway
☎ *(310) 592-4770, FAX: 310-592-3547.*
Single: $69–$109. Double: $69–$109.

This two-story inn overlooks Huntington Harbor and is a block from the beach. All rooms have minibars; some have kitchens and views of the ocean or harbor. A big plus is an extensive continental breakfast that includes more than 40 items to choose from. Amenities: conference facilities. 24 rooms. Credit Cards: CB, V, MC, DC, A.

Newport Beach: Where to Eat

Corona del Mar

American

Five Crowns $$$ ★★★★

3801 East Coast Highway, ☎ *(714) 760-0331.*
Specialties: prime rib.
Dinner: 5–10 p.m., entrees $15–$27.

English pub decor and hefty portions of prime rib are the trademarks of this Orange County institution. Built to resemble Ye Old Bell, one of England's oldest inns, the restaurant is as interesting for its atmosphere as it is for its food. Another plus is the very fine wine list, one of the best in Orange County. Features: outside dining, own baking, Sunday brunch, full bar, rated wine cellar, late dining, private dining rooms. Jacket requested. Reservations recommended. Credit Cards: D, CB, V, MC, DC, A.

Trees $$ ★★★

440 Heliotrope Avenue, ☎ *(714) 673-0910.*
Specialties: Maryland crabcakes; meatloaf; spring rolls; potstickers.
Dinner: 5:30 p.m.–midnight, entrees $10–$20.

Dining here is relatively inexpensive and the ambience is slightly formal, which makes it a nice place to go for a special occasion without spending a fortune. The food is a sort of mix of American, California and Asian cuisine that doesn't always succeed, but when it does it's very good. Features: own baking, full bar, late dining. Reservations recommended. Credit Cards: V, MC, A.

Indian

Mayur $$$

2931 East Pacific Coast Highway, ☎ *(714) 675-6622.*
Lunch: 11 a.m.–2:30 p.m., entrees $10–$14.
Dinner: 5–10 p.m., entrees $11–$21.

One of the area's best-kept secrets, Mayur may well be the highest-quality Indian restaurant in Orange County. Features: own baking, Sunday brunch, late dining. Credit Cards: V, MC, A.

Seafood

Oysters $$$

2515 East Coast Highway, ☎ *(714) 675-7411.*
Dinner: 5–10 p.m., entrees $11–$22.

It's all in the name here, with oysters—as well as other seafood—topping the menu, along with fresh, home-grown vegetables and Santa Ynez Valley wines. Everything is simple and very satisfying. Features: own baking, full bar, rated wine cellar, late dining. Reservations recommended. Credit Cards: V, MC, A.

Huntington Beach

Italian

Baci $$ ★★★

18748 Beach Boulevard, ☎ *(714) 965-1194.*
Lunch: 11:30 a.m.–2 p.m., entrees $7–$12.
Dinner: 5–10 p.m., entrees $10–$19.

There's a decided lack of ambience at this neighborhood spot, but the food—which hails from several regions of Italy—is almost always delicious and the service is first-rate. Closed: Mon. Features: wine and beer only, late dining. Credit Cards: V, MC, A.

Niccole's $$ ★★★

520 Main Street, ☎ *(714) 960-8091.*
Dinner: 5–10 p.m., entrees $8–$20.

Niccole's is an upscale little restaurant with floor-to-ceiling windows and soft lighting at night that offers sometimes unique Italian food at reasonable prices. Wednesdays from 6-8 p.m. are perfect for wine lovers; if you buy a glass of wine, the buffet dinner is complimentary. Every night has something nice to offer, though, and the service is excellent. Features: own baking, full bar, rated wine cellar, late dining, private dining rooms. Reservations recommended. Credit Cards: V, MC, DC, A.

Laguna Beach

American

Cafe Zinc $ ★★★

350 Ocean Avenue, ☎ *(714) 494-6302.*
Specialties: soups.
Lunch: 11:15 a.m.–5 p.m., entrees $5–$7.

This little sidewalk cafe serves breakfast and lunch only and offers healthful alternatives such as veggie sandwiches along with terrific pastries and muffins and oh-so-trendy cappuccinos. A great spot for snacking and hanging out, always crowded on weekends. Features: outside dining, own baking. Credit Cards: Not Accepted.

Cedar Creek Inn   **$$$**   ★★

834 Forest Avenue, ☎ *(714) 497-8696.*
Specialties: seafood; salads; sandwiches; oyster bar.
Lunch: from 11 a.m., entrees $5–$10.
Dinner: to 11:30 p.m., entrees $13–$23.

You'll seldom be disappointed at Cedar Creek Inn, which has been turning out solid American cuisine in a pleasant, rustic cabin atmosphere for years. There's both an oyster bar and a piano bar, and the prices are reasonable. Features: own baking, Sunday brunch, full bar, late dining. Reservations recommended. Credit Cards: V, MC, A.

Chinese

Five Feet   **$$$**   ★★★

328 Glenneyre Street, ☎ *(714) 497-4955.*
Specialties: hot and spicy catfish.
Dinner: 5–10 p.m., entrees $14–$26.

Chef/owner Michael Kang turns out an interesting array of nouvelle Chinese dishes that are mostly dazzling. Some think the cutting edge has gotten blunt over the years, but Five Feet remains a solid choice for adventurous Asian fare. Lunch served on Fridays only. Features: full bar, rated wine cellar, late dining. Reservations recommended. Credit Cards: CB, V, MC, DC, A.

French

Towers, The   **$$$**   ★★★

1555 South Coast Highway, ☎ *(714) 497-4477.*
Specialties: rack of lamb; fresh fish; stuffed boneless chicken breast.
Dinner: 5:30–9:30 p.m., entrees $16–$30.
Associated hotel: Surf and Sand.

You won't find a more beautiful dining room—or view—in Orange County, and the food, mostly French but with other Mediterranean touches, is often very good, but doesn't always live up to the surroundings (or the price). Features: splendid view, Sunday brunch, full bar, rated wine cellar. Jacket requested. Reservations recommended. Credit Cards: CB, V, MC, DC, A.

Indian

Bombay Duck   **$$**   ★★

229 Ocean Avenue, ☎ *(714) 497-7307.*
Lunch: 11 a.m.–3 p.m., entrees $7–$10.
Dinner: 5–11 p.m., entrees $8–$14.

Eclectic is certainly the word to describe this sophisticated bistro, a favorite with the yuppie crowd that serves up Indian dishes with more than a touch of California influence. There's even espresso! Features: outside dining, own baking, Sunday brunch, wine and beer only, late dining. Reservations recommended. Credit Cards: CB, V, MC, DC, A.

Natraj   **$$**   ★★

998B South Coast Highway, ☎ *(714) 497-9197.*
Lunch: 11 a.m.–2:30 p.m., entrees $6–$15.
Dinner: 5–10 p.m., entrees $8–$15.

A good lunch buffet ($5.95 for all you can eat) and warm service complement the mild Indian cuisine here, which varies from good to excellent. Other locations in Laguna Hills and Long Beach. Features: wine and beer only, late dining. Credit Cards: V, MC, A.

Italian

Rumari $$ ★★

1826 South Coast Highway, ☎ (714) 494-0400.
Specialties: black linguini pasta baked with seafood.
Dinner: 5:30–9:30 p.m., entrees $8–$22.

Pleasant, family-owned restaurant where personal touches show in both the food—a combination of northern and southern Italian specialties—and the ambience. Closed: Mon. Features: outside dining, own baking, full bar. Reservations recommended. Credit Cards: CB, V, MC, DC, A.

Sorrento Grill $$ ★★★

370 Glenneyre Street, ☎ (714) 494-8686.
Lunch: 11:30 a.m.–2 p.m., entrees $6–$7.
Dinner: 6–10 p.m., entrees $10–$18.

Sorrento Grill has a solid following of locals, who laud the simple but contemporary Italian fare. It's a bit pretentious, but the excellent seafood and salads compensate. Nearly everything is homemade, including the bread, which will fill you up before you get your meal if you're not careful. Free-range chicken and produce from the Chino Ranch are part of the commitment to fresh regional ingredients. Drawbacks are a crowded dining room and high noise level. Lunch served Wednesday through Saturday. Features: own baking, full bar, late dining. Reservations recommended. Credit Cards: V, MC, A.

Mediterranean

Splashes $$$ ★★★

1555 South Coast Highway, ☎ (714) 497-4477.
Lunch: 11:30 a.m.–4:30 p.m., entrees $1.
Dinner: 5–10 p.m., entrees $14–$22.
Associated hotel: Surf and Sand.

The ambience is lovely, the view fabulous (Splashes almost literally gets splashed by the blue Pacific, especially at high tide), and the Mediterranean-inspired food nearly always lives up to the surroundings. Fresh seafood and grilled meats are the best bets on any occasion, but the menu, overseen by chef William Happy, changes every day and may include such Mediterranean specialties as paella, osso buco or risotto. Individual pizzas are also good. Although service has been shaky in the past, Splashes seems to have hit its stride on all counts. Features: splendid view, outside dining, own baking, Sunday brunch, full bar, rated wine cellar, late dining. Reservations recommended. Credit Cards: CB, V, MC, DC, A.

Mexican

Las Brisas De Laguna $$$ ★★★

361 Cliff Drive, ☎ (714) 497-5434.
Specialties: salmon a la parilla; camarones tampiquenos la asada.
Lunch: 11 a.m.–3:30 p.m., entrees $7–$12.
Dinner: 5–10 p.m., entrees $12–$22.

The scene is the thing at Las Brisas, where a yuppy crowd gathers to sip margaritas and down intriguing appetizers while gazing out over the California coast. Opinions of the food range from "so-so" to fabulous. Try the Sunday brunch for the best taste of what Las Brisas has to offer. Breakfast and lunch served Monday through Saturday. Features: splendid view, outside dining, own baking, Sunday brunch, full bar. Reservations recommended. Credit Cards: D, CB, V, MC, DC, A.

Southwestern

Kachina $$$ ★★★

222 Forest Avenue, ☎ (714) 497-5546.
Specialties: mesquite-smoked duckling; swordfish in desert sunset sauce.
Dinner: 5:30–9 p.m., entrees $12–$19.

David Wilhelm's tiny restaurant offers such splendid and creative cuisine that it's always packed with the faithful, so you'd better make a reservation or you may be disappointed. The decibel level is high, but fabulous food compensates. Lunch is served only on Saturday. Features: outside dining, own baking, Sunday brunch, wine and beer only. Reservations recommended. Credit Cards: V, MC, A.

Laguna Niguel

Chinese

China Moon $$ ★★

30001 Town Center Drive, ☎ (714) 249-6868.
Lunch: 11 a.m.–3 p.m., entrees $5–$8.
Dinner: 4:30–10 p.m., entrees $8–$15.

The menu is as diverse as the ingredients used to prepare a plethora of imaginative dishes. Whether you order the tried and true or opt for the exotic, you'll come away satisfied. Features: wine and beer only, late dining. Credit Cards: V, MC, A.

French

Ritz-Carlton Dining Room $$$ ★★★★

33533 Shoreline Drive, ☎ (714) 240-2000.
Specialties: Maine lobster; escargot souffle.
Dinner: 6–9:30 p.m., prix fixe $39–$70.
Associated hotel: Ritz-Carlton.

A breathtaking view of the Pacific, an elegant, antique-filled dining room, a winning wine list, excellent service and use of fresh, regional ingredients are the hallmarks at this signature restaurant of the gorgeous Ritz-Carlton Hotel. You'll spend like royalty, but you'll be treated like it as well. What your dinner costs depends on the number of courses you select, and you have a choice of from two to seven courses, with a price range of $39 (two courses) to $70 (seven courses). Less costly fare is available at the Cafe. Closed: Mon, Sun. Features: own baking, full bar, rated wine cellar. Jacket and tie requested. Reservations required. Credit Cards: CB, V, MC, DC, A.

Newport Beach

African

Marrakesh $$$ ★★

1100 West Coast Highway, ☎ (714) 645-8384.
Specialties: couscous; lamb; rabbit; quail.
Dinner: 5–11 p.m., prix fixe $18–$22.

One of the nicest of the Marrakesh restaurants, this one has the same format as the rest: you sit on pillows, eat the regional dishes of Morocco with your fingers, and watch belly dancers perform. Features: full bar, late dining, private dining rooms. Reservations recommended. Credit Cards: V, MC, DC, A.

American

Arches, The $$$ ★★★
3334 West Coast Highway, ☎ *(714) 645-7077.*
Specialties: veal saltimbocca; stuffed rainbow trout; steak diane.
Lunch: 11:30 a.m.–3 p.m., entrees $10–$12.
Dinner: 4:30 p.m.–1 a.m., entrees $17–$50.
The Arches is the oldest restaurant in Newport Beach (it opened in 1922), and it is still a local favorite. Plush booths, friendly service, good mixed drinks and reliable American/Continental cooking draw an upscale crowd. Features: Sunday brunch, rated wine cellar, late dining. Jacket requested. Reservations recommended. Credit Cards: CB, V, MC, A.

Bistro 201 $$ ★★★
333 West Pacific Coast Highway, ☎ *(714) 631-1551.*
Specialties: rack of lamb; duck with sun-dried sour cherries.
Lunch: 11:30 a.m.–3 p.m., entrees $8–$15.
Dinner: 5:30–10 p.m., entrees $9–$18.
Presentation is as lovely as the food at Bistro 201, which recently relocated to Newport Beach from its original home in Irvine. Ask about the monthly international bistro theme dinners, which bring the cuisine of different countries to the menu along with the regular specialties. No matter what catches your eye, you can count on everything on the eclectic menu being well-prepared. Closed: Sun. Features: outside dining, own baking, full bar, rated wine cellar, late dining. Reservations recommended. Credit Cards: V, MC, A.

Daily Grill $$ ★★
957 Newport Center Drive, ☎ *(714) 644-2223.*
Specialties: steak; meat loaf with mashed potatoes; chicken pot pie.
Lunch: from 11:30 a.m., entrees $6–$10.
Dinner: to 11 p.m., entrees $8–$15.
The Newport Beach outpost of the Daily Grill chain, this casual spot turns out American comfort food at prices nearly everyone can afford. Features: Sunday brunch, full bar, late dining. Credit Cards: V, MC, A.

Ritz, The $$$ ★★★★
880 Newport Center Drive, ☎ *(714) 720-1800.*
Specialties: rack of lamb; roast duck; baby abalone; steamed mussels.
Lunch: 11:30 a.m.–3 p.m., entrees $9–$16.
Dinner: 6–10 p.m., entrees $18–$30.
This excellent restaurant located in the Fashion Island complex offers classic American/Continental cuisine turned out by chef Hans Prager, formerly of Scandia. An elegant, clubby atmosphere, service that consistently tops the list in nationwide polls and Prager's uncompromising dedication to quality make this one of the best restaurants in the city. Valet parking only. Lunch served Monday through Friday. Features: full bar, rated wine cellar, late dining, private dining rooms. Jacket requested. Reservations recommended. Credit Cards: V, MC, DC, A.

Ruby's $ ★★
1 Balboa Pier, ☎ *(714) 675-7829.*
Specialties: burgers; malts; onion rings; fries.
Lunch: from 11:30 a.m., entrees $3–$7.

Dinner: to 9 p.m., entrees $3–$7.

Ruby's is the quintessential American diner, serving up all your old favorites with a dash of sass. Lots of fun—and lots of noise. This Balboa Pier restaurant is the original and a favorite with locals, but there are Ruby's at many other Orange County/L.A. locations. Breakfast served from 7 a.m. Features: splendid view, wine and beer only. Credit Cards: V, MC, A.

Chinese

China Palace   **$$**   ★★★

2899 West Coast Highway, ☎ *(714) 631-8031.*
Lunch: 11:30 a.m.–3 p.m., entrees $5–$10.
Dinner: 5–10 p.m., entrees $10–$15.

Named the county's Best Chinese Restaurant in the March, 1994 issue of *Orange Coast* magazine, China Palace offers well-prepared Mandarin and Szechuan dishes in a sophisticated dining room. The lunch special, at $6, is especially popular. A local favorite. Features: wine and beer only, late dining. Reservations recommended. Credit Cards: V, A.

French

Antoine   **$$$**   ★★★★

4500 MacArthur Boulevard, ☎ *(714) 476-2001.*
Dinner: 6–9:30 p.m., entrees $25–$35.
Associated hotel: Sutton Place.

Formal French restaurant serving exceptional food, with an emphasis on fresh regional products. The decor is just as outstanding as the cuisine, and features silk wallcoverings, gilded mirrors, crisp linens and sparkling place settings. Both the service and the wine list follow suit, contributing to an opulent dining experience that is hard to beat in Orange County—or even in all of L.A. Closed: Mon, Sun. Features: own baking, rated wine cellar. Jacket requested. Reservations required. Credit Cards: V, MC, DC, A.

Pascal   **$$$**   ★★★★

1000 North Bristol Street, ☎ *(714) 752-0107.*
Specialties: sea bass with thyme crust.
Lunch: 11:30 a.m.–2:30 p.m., entrees $10–$14.
Dinner: 6–9:30 p.m., entrees $17–$23.

The best French restaurant in Orange County, Pascal is touted as the place that finally put Orange County on the culinary map. Chef/owner Pascal Olhat has poured heart and soul into his restaurant, and it shows in every detail, from the carefully rendered Provencal-style food to the warm service to the pleasant, flower-filled dining room. If you can't afford the restaurant, you can opt for takeout from the shop next door. Closed: Sun. Features: outside dining, own baking, rated wine cellar. Reservations recommended. Credit Cards: V, MC, DC, A.

Indian

Royal Khyber   **$$**   ★★★

1000 Bristol Street North, ☎ *(714) 752-5200.*
Specialties: tandoori and moghlai dishes.
Lunch: 11:30 a.m.–2:30 p.m., entrees $8–$10.
Dinner: 5:30–10 p.m., entrees $10–$20.

Critics differ on the merits of this Indian restaurant, but reasonable prices and authentic dishes that are nearly always well-prepared and presented have a loyal following. Sunday brunch is a treat. Features: own baking, Sunday brunch, full bar, late dining. Jacket requested. Reservations recommended. Credit Cards: CB, V, MC, DC, A.

Italian

Sapori $$ ★★★

1080 Bayside Drive, *(714) 644-4220.*
Specialties: homemade pasta.
Lunch: 11:30 a.m.–3 p.m., entrees $7–$15.
Dinner: 3–10 p.m., entrees $9–$20.
Depending upon whom you ask, this busy trattoria is either the best thing since garlic bread or woefully lacking. Most agree the patio is the best place to be seated and that the service could be better. Judge for yourself. Lunch served Monday through Friday. Features: outside dining, own baking, full bar, rated wine cellar, late dining. Reservations recommended. Credit Cards: D, CB, V, MC, DC, A.

Tutto Mare $$$ ★★★

545 Newport Center Drive, *(714) 640-6333.*
Specialties: whole Dover sole.
Lunch: 11:30 a.m.–5 p.m., entrees $9–$24.
Dinner: 5–11 p.m., entrees $9–$24.
Good Italian food served in an upscale dining room at Newport Fashion Island has a strong local following. The scene is just as hot as the food, and Tutto Mare is definitely one of THE places to be seen in Orange County. The hot bar scene attracts affluent yuppies. Features: outside dining, own baking, Sunday brunch, full bar, rated wine cellar, late dining. Reservations required. Credit Cards: CB, V, MC, DC, A.

Villa Nova $$ ★★

3131 West Coast Highway, *(714) 642-7880.*
Specialties: mozzarella appetizer; piatto Villa Nova.
Dinner: 5–11 p.m., entrees $10–$20.
A nice view of the harbor serves as a backdrop for homemade Italian cooking that emphasizes the regions of central and northern Italy. Especially friendly service is also a plus. A recent renovation has drawn kudos for improving the view (and access for boaters). If you haven't been here in awhile, it's time to try Villa Nova again. Lunch served only on Sunday. Features: splendid view, full bar, rated wine cellar, late dining. Reservations recommended. Credit Cards: D, CB, V, MC, DC, A.

What's Cooking $$ ★★★

2632 San Miguel, *(714) 644-1820.*
Lunch: 11:30 a.m.–2:30 p.m., entrees $5–$9.
Dinner: 5–9:30 p.m., entrees $6–$15.
"What's cooking" is a first-rate menu of Northern Italian cuisine lovingly prepared by chef/owner Lucy Luhan, who adds wonderful touches like homemade olive oil and pastas. Features: outside dining, own baking, full bar. Reservations recommended. Credit Cards: V, MC, A.

Japanese

Kitayama $$ ★★★★

101 Bay View Place,   *(714) 725-0777.*
Specialties: omakase kaiseki.
Lunch: 11:15 a.m.–2 p.m., entrees $8–$15.
Dinner: 6–10 p.m., entrees $9–$21.

Everything is pretty pricey here, but the beautiful and serene dining rooms, the first-rate sushi, and the quality service provided by kimono-clad waitresses are worth it. One of the area's best Japanese restaurants. Go for lunch for the best prices. Lunch served Monday through Friday. Features: full bar, private dining rooms. Jacket requested. Reservations recommended. Credit Cards: CB, V, MC, DC, A.

Nouvelle

Pavilion $$$

690 Newport Center Drive, ☎ (714) 759-0808.
Specialties: thin potato crepe with beluga caviar; lobster strudel.
Lunch: 11 a.m.–2:30 p.m., entrees $10–$14.
Dinner: 6–10 p.m., entrees $20–$27.
Associated hotel: Four Seasons Newport Beach.
Excellent "power" breakfasts, a memorable brunch buffet, and good nouvelle-Frenchish cuisine star at this expensive "special-occasion" restaurant that is quintessentially Southern Californian, from its light, pastel decor to the contemporary touches that show up in the food. Dress up and come for a special occasion. Valet parking only. Features: outside dining, own baking, Sunday brunch, late dining. Jacket requested. Reservations required. Credit Cards: CB, V, MC, DC, A.

Seafood

21 Oceanfront $$$

2100 West Ocean Front, ☎ (714) 675-2566.
Specialties: abalone; live Maine lobster.
Dinner: 5:30–10 p.m., entrees $19–$49.

The site of the old Rex restaurant now houses this excellent seafood place with a wonderful ocean view. It's a romantic hideaway with prices that are up there, but everything is almost always good enough to justify the cost. Orange County yuppies hang out at the upscale bar. Features: own baking, rated wine cellar, late dining. Jacket requested. Reservations recommended. Credit Cards: CB, V, MC, A.

Cannery, The $$$

3010 Lafayette Avenue, ☎ (714) 675-5777.
Specialties: abalone; prime rib.
Lunch: 11:30 a.m.–3 p.m., entrees $6–$16.
Dinner: 5–10 p.m., entrees $16–$32.
A historic old cannery houses this pleasant restaurant, which looks out over the harbor. The mostly seafood menu features a fresh catch of the day and other concoctions that can be quite good. Weekend brunch cruises are offered at 10 a.m. and 1:30 p.m. Reserve ahead for cruises. Features: outside dining, Sunday brunch, late dining. Reservations recommended. Credit Cards: V, MC, DC, A.

Southwestern

El Torito Grill $$

951 Newport Center Drive, ☎ (714) 640-2875.
Specialties: mesquite-grilled dishes; tamalitos; soft tacos.
Lunch: from 11 a.m., entrees $7–$11.
Dinner: to 10 p.m., entrees $7–$15.
Splashy, noisy and fun, this outpost of the upscale chain serves the signature mix of Mexican, Tex-Mex and Southwestern cuisine. Features: own baking, Sunday brunch, full bar, late dining. Reservations recommended. Credit Cards: V, MC, DC, A.

San Clemente
French
Etienne's **$$$** ★★
215 South El Camino Real, ☎ *(714) 492-7263.*
Specialties: Dover sole; rack of lamb; filet capella.
Dinner: 6–10 p.m., prix fixe $25–$30.
A small, family-owned restaurant that never fails to please with warm service and good food from a varied menu. It's wonderfully relaxing and unpretentious here, a true respite from some of the area's trendier spots. The three-course prix fixe menu (including wine) is served Monday through Thursday. Friday and Saturday, the menu is à la carte. Closed: Sun. Features: splendid view, outside dining, own baking, full bar, late dining. Jacket requested. Reservations recommended. Credit Cards: CB, V, MC, DC, A.

German
Swiss Chalet **$$** ★★
216 North El Camino Real, ☎ *(714) 492-7931.*
Specialties: wienerschnitzel; bratwurst.
Dinner: 5–8:30 p.m., entrees $9–$15.
The place to go for authentic German and Swiss cuisine, hearty and loaded with all that delicious fat that Americans now seem to avoid like the plague. If you've fallen off the healthful eating bandwagon, this is worth splurging for. Closed: Mon, Sun. Features: own baking, wine and beer only. Reservations recommended. Credit Cards: V, MC.

San Juan Capistrano
French
L'Hirondelle **$$** ★★★
31631 Camino Capistrano, ☎ *(714) 661-0425.*
Specialties: cherry duck; rabbit.
Dinner: 5–10 p.m., entrees $10–$19.
An antique-studded dining room is the backdrop for both French and Belgian cooking at this pleasant little restaurant. Lunch is served on Friday and Saturday only, from 11:30 a.m. to 2 p.m. Closed: Mon. Features: own baking, Sunday brunch, wine and beer only, late dining. Jacket requested. Reservations required. Credit Cards: V, MC, A.

DAY TRIPS AND GETTING AWAY FROM L.A.

Best Day Trips

There is little to recommend just cruising through L.A. Try to combine one of these day trips into your L.A. Agenda.

The Anza Borrego park can be explored via its hundreds of trails.

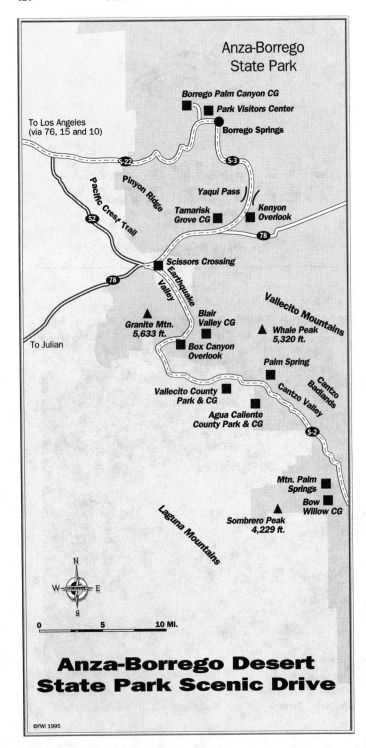

Anza-Borrego Desert State Park Scenic Drive

©FWI 1995

Anza Borrego Desert ★★

☎ *(619) 767-5311*

A 6000-acre park that at first glance looks as though it had an atomic bomb dropped on it. Those who come expecting giant saguaros or Monument Valley will be disappointed, but if you take the time to look closely, you'll come to appreciate the gentle rhythms of the desert. The visitor in a hurry should stop at the interpretive center in Borrego Springs, then blast around the shimmering blacktop in search of scenery. Those with more time (and in better shape) can explore the more than 700 miles of hiking trails in search of waterfalls and oases, badlands, babbling streams and dramatic canyons. If you have a four-wheel-drive vehicle, take the dirt roads to the more remote regions of the park. There is even an arduous back door into Terwilliger to the north, along Coyote Canyon. One of the park's major attractions is the 600 species of wildflowers that bloom each year in February and March. Then, the winter rains unlock the desert's colorful secrets and a canvas of yellows, reds, pinks and blues extends over the landscape. If you want to stay overnight, the Casa del Zorro is a famous—albeit expensive—choice for lodging. Other accommodations can be arranged by calling ☎ *(619) 767-5555*. 370 miles round trip.

Catalina has Southern California's best fishing and diving.

Catalina Island

☎ *(310) 510-2500*

Twenty-six (or twenty-two, depending on whom you ask) miles across the open ocean from L.A. lies the 76-square-mile island of Santa Catalina and its principal town of Avalon. The Wrigley family (of chewing gum fame) owned most of the island until the early 1970s, when it was turned into a conservancy. Access to Catalina Island is by boat (approximately two hours from San Pedro or Long Beach), or by plane or helicopter (much faster, but also more expensive). Once you get there, you can rent a bike and tour the island, take an excursion aboard a glass-bottomed boat (an island specialty), visit some wild buffalo (they were left behind after Cecil B. deMille filmed *The Vanishing American* on the island in 1924), see the famous Avalon Casino (once a popular dance hall), or take the 66-mile guided tour that includes the more pastoral side of the island. Diving and fishing trips are also available, but should be booked out of San Pedro or Long Beach before departing. Overnight guests should consider one of Catalina's charming bed and breakfast establishments, which run the gamut in price from reasonable to exceedingly expensive. Note that the island can be extremely crowded on weekends—especially in summer.

Catalina Island: Where to Stay
Bed and Breakfast

Inn on Mount Ada   **$320–$590**   ★★★★

398 Wrigley Road
☎ *(310) 510-2030, FAX: 310-510-2237.*
Single: $320–$590. Double: $320–$590.

A lovely old Georgian home, formerly the Wrigley Estate, furnished with antiques and offering splendid views of the ocean and mountains. All rooms are nonsmoking. Children over 14 only. Rates include breakfast, plush robes and golf carts for island sightseeing. Book early; this popular place often sells out, despite its astronomical rates. Amenities: balcony or patio. 6 rooms. Credit Cards: V, MC, A.

Inns

Hotel Metropole   **$89–$295**   ★★★

205 Crescent Avenue
☎ *(800) 541-8528, (310) 510-1884, FAX: 310-510-2534.*
Single: $89–$295. Double: $89–$295.

The atmosphere at this elegant little hotel is reminiscent of New Orleans' French Quarter, and the colorful lobby nicely assaults the senses. Accommodations include fireplaces, ocean views, spas and private balconies. A rooftop sundeck is especially appealing. There are limited meeting facilities, but it's a very nice alternative to large, business-oriented hotels. Amenities: Jacuzzi, private spas, balcony or patio, hair salon, family plan, conference facilities. 47 rooms. Credit Cards: V, MC, A.

Hotel St. Lauren   **$55–$260**   ★★

231 Beacon
☎ *(800) 298-8308, (310) 510-2299, FAX: 310-510-1369.*
Single: $55–$260. Double: $55–$260.

This Victorian-style mansion on a hilltop has charming rooms furnished with rosewood furniture, and some suites with an ocean view. Complimentary continental breakfast is included, and the rooftop patio is especially inviting. Amenities: private spas, balcony or patio, conference facilities, business services. 42 rooms. Credit Cards: V, MC.

Vista del Mar   **$65–$275**   ★★★

417 Crescent Avenue
☎ *(310) 510-1452, FAX: 310-510-2917.*
Single: $65–$275. Double: $65–$275.

This small hotel with a Mediterranean flair, atrium courtyard and fireplaces in all rooms overlooks Avalon Bay. All rooms contain wet bars, refrigerators and fireplaces, and suites have ocean views and private spas. A complimentary breakfast is offered to all guests. No smoking allowed. Amenities: beach location, private spas, balcony or patio, conference facilities. 15 rooms. Credit Cards: V, MC, A.

The high desert is a center for rock climbing and winter hiking.

Joshua Tree   ★ ★ ★

Visitors Center ☎ *(619) 367-7511*

A sparse setting marks the home of the Joshua tree, a large (growing up to 40 feet tall) member of the yucca family that can only be found in the high desert at an elevation above 3000 feet. If you're looking for a Palm Springs-like experience, you won't find it here. Winters are cold, and there isn't a luxury resort to be found. But Joshua Tree is a haven for rock climbers, and a combination of dirt and paved roads allows you to see a wide variety of desert life and geological formations. The park is open year-round; try to go in the spring and summer, when the wildflowers are in bloom. About 280 miles round trip.

Apples are the new mother lode of historic Julian.

Julian

☎ *(619) 765-1857*

This ramshackle collection of wooden houses in San Diego County was once a mining town, and is now an amiable tourist trap. It was here that gold was discovered in 1870 and there are still cagey folks working mines in the mountains outside of town. At 4200 feet above sea level, Julian is a perfect stop for frolicking in the winter snow,

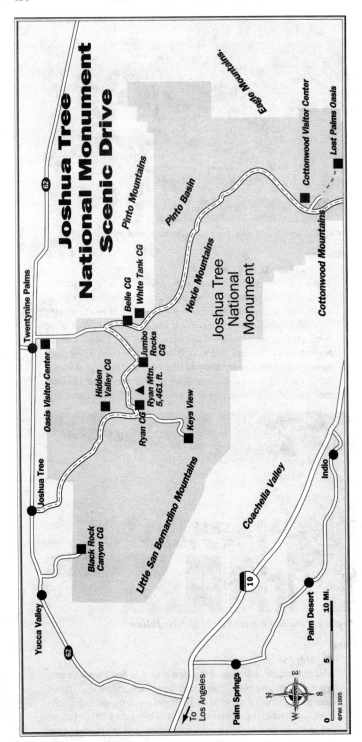

shopping for antiques, or buying apples (the area's largest crop). If you don't have time for lunch, have a piece of apple pie or try some cider, both made from locally-grown apples. Even if you don't like apples, the smell of pine trees and the terrific views will make your trip worthwhile. All roads in or out of town are quite scenic, and you should leave some time for wandering into the Anza Borrego Desert to the east, or through the lush agricultural regions to the west. 290 miles round trip.

La Jolla   ★ ★
☎ *(619) 454-1444*

The Beverly Hills of San Diego is blessed with beautiful carved sandstone coves and crystal clear waters that are perfect for snorkeling or diving. If you're not into underwater sports, the shopping's terrific here, and there are many excellent restaurants overlooking the sea. Don't miss the **Stephen Birch Aquarium** *(☎ 619-535-3474)*, an oceanography museum that showcases tide pools, fish and other ocean-going flora and fauna. 200 miles round trip.

Ojai brings back the L.A. of the 1920's.

Ojai   ★
☎ *(805) 646-8126*

A new bohemian mecca, Ojai is populated by artists, retired movie stars and lots of other people who just want to be alone. It's also a favorite getaway for L.A. movie industry types who need a respite from the hustle and bustle of The Biz. There is a variety of music and arts festivals held here, the golf course is excellent, and the drive up is spectacular when the wildflowers and orange blossoms bloom in April and May. 160 miles round trip.

Palm Springs is a golfer's paradise.

Palm Springs

☎ *(619) 770-9000*

Punks and polyester used to make for an odd mix in this famous desert town, but today Palm Springs is a favorite winter weekend getaway for smog- and crowd-weary Angelenos. Over two million people spend at least one night in Palm Springs every year, with the more discriminating (and rich) choosing the famous resorts at La Quinta and Indian Wells. The tennis-and-golf set (there are more than 80 golf courses in the Coachella Valley and scads more tennis courts) is supplemented by college students on Spring Break, who generally like the cheapest accommodations and the self-made party atmosphere of downtown (avoid this area like the plague when Spring Break is happening). For nature lovers, a stop at the **Living Desert Botanical Garden and Zoo** (☎ *619-346-5694*) gives a glimpse of what natural wonders surround the city. If you want to get above the landscape (and aren't afraid of heights), opt for a 14-minute trip up the Palms Springs Aerial Tramway, which heads up the mountain to an elevation of 8516 feet. Palm Springs' hotels and condos are nearly always full during the winter, so make sure you have a reservation before departing. Summer is the time for lodging values, but it's so hot you may want to pass. Don't overlook some of the side trips from Palm Springs, such as a visit to Joshua Tree. About 210 miles round trip.

Santa Barbara County Courthouse

Santa Barbara ★★★
☎ *(805) 966-9222*

The most Mediterranean and pristine of any California seaside town, Santa Barbara is populated by a mix of artists, retirees, yuppies, movie stars and college students who attend the University of California's Santa Barbara campus. The Spanish Colonial architectural theme (the county courthouse, built in 1929, is a stunning example) gives a harmonious feel to the city and invites exploration in and of itself. You can also opt to cruise State Street (the tourist-oriented wharf is at the south end), visit the Queen of the Missions, or take the long, winding road up behind the city and into the Santa Ynez Mountains for breathtaking views. Several wineries are also located in northern Santa Barbara County, and are inviting stops for picnicking or wine tasting. 200 miles round trip.

Balboa Park in San Diego

San Diego   ★★★★

☎ *(619) 236-1212*

A good two hour scenic drive down Interstate 5 will put you in the middle of one of California's most beautiful cities. The old downtown area is currently undergoing a revitalization, but, overall, San Diego delivers good value and lots to do for the tourist. Tops are the San Diego Zoo, Sea World, Balboa Park, Old Town (margaritas, chips and salsa are a must at any one of the bustling restaurants here), and Horton Plaza, a mall that's a wacky mix of Old and New World architecture and ambience. The buildings in Balboa Park, a 1200-acre site used for the 1915 and 1935 World Fairs, include fantasy Moorish, art deco, baroque, and Rococo architectural styles. They were built for temporary use in conjunction with the fairs, but proved so popular that most have been rebuilt or restored. Don't miss the Hotel del Coronado on Coronado Island for a look back at Victorian-era California tourism. The hotel only took 11 months to build in 1888 and immediately attracted the "creme de la creme" of society (it's rumored that Edward, Prince of Wales, met Wallis Simpson here). More recently, "the Del" was featured in the Billy Wilder hit, *Some Like it Hot*. 250 miles round trip.

Tijuana

☎ *(800) 522-1516*

Unlike the colorful, Disneyesque replicas of Mexico you'll find in several parts of California, this is definitely the real thing—and definitely the third world. The line waiting to cross the border can be long and sweltering (you'll need Mexican car insurance—available at the border—to cross, and American I.D. to get back), and most of the stories you've heard about Tijuana are true, so be careful. Once you get there, you'll be assailed by tourist-oriented vendors hawking piñatas, baskets, clothing, food and other cheap merchandise. If you want to see the real Mexico, head farther south to the Baja Peninsula, or east into the quiet mountain town of Tecate. 275 miles round trip.

Baja California   ★★★

☎ *(619) 231-8414*

It is hard to imagine that there could be so many wide-open spaces next to some of North America's most populated cities, but Baja offers a definite escape from the madding crowds. Once you leave Ensenada behind (about 70 miles south of the border), you are in a land that probably replicates California 200 years ago. A sturdy, well-maintained vehicle (preferably four-wheel drive, especially if you want to stray off the main highway) is required, and it helps to have at least a rudimentary knowledge of Spanish. Other than that, time is all you need to explore this dramatic desert region and its forests of giant cardon cactus, massive boulders and endless vistas. Activities available here include seeing California gray whales up close in Scammons Lagoon (late January to early March), off-roading and some of the best deep-sea fishing in America. The very tip of Cabo San Lucas is a popular resort area complete with upscale lodging. You'll find Baja more laid-back, less populated and safer than much of the rest of Mexico. The best time to visit is December through March. The 1069-mile Trans-Peninsula Highway is paved, and there are hotels at well-spaced intervals. If you want to keep going, there are ferries to the Mexican mainland.

Big Bear ★

☎ *(714) 866-5877*

Big Bear is the quickest way to escape the heat and smog of L.A. Unfortunately, however, you won't escape the crowds. The Big Bear and Lake Arrowhead areas are one big traffic jam on summer weekends. The elevation here goes up to 8600 feet, giving it snow cover in the winter and cool temperatures in the summer. The Rim of the World Highway is worth a drive (but do it on a weekday). 200 miles round trip.

Fielding's Choice: Getaways

Ready for a getaway from L.A.? These are some nearby (two hours or less by car) options guaranteed to deliver some peaceful (and romantic) R & R:

The Inn on Summer Hill (☎ 800 999-8999). *This charming, New England style inn is perched on a hill in Summerland, just this side of Santa Barbara. Enjoy a garden setting and minisuites with fireplaces, ocean views and canopied beds.*

Ojai Valley Inn (☎ 800 422-6524). *Cottages nestled among the oak trees, an excellent 18-hole golf course and prime tennis facilities are among the offerings at this 1920s resort hotel in Ojai that was completely refurbished in 1988. The grounds include some 200 acres, with a wide variety of outdoor recreational opportunities available. Or, if you prefer, stick close to the lodge and wrap yourself in a cozy afternoon tea.*

The Inn on Mt. Ada (☎ 310 510-2030). *This fabulous, six-room, Georgian-colonial inn set on Catalina Island used to be the home of chewing gum magnate William Wrigley, Jr. Now, it is an exclusive (and expensive) getaway spot where you can curl up in front of the fireplace, or watch the sea from your room. Meals are included. Nonsmokers only.*

Fielding's Choice: Getaways

The Ritz-Carlton Rancho Mirage (☎ 800 241-3333). *Okay, so this costs a small fortune; you DESERVE it, don't you?! One of the ritziest accommodations in the Palm Springs area, this tony resort promises as much pampering as you can pay for. Golf, tennis, lawn games, health club, Jacuzzi, sauna, lush gardens and a view of the desert that will make you forget you just spent two hours fighting L.A. traffic.*

Way Out of Town

Death Valley   ★★

☎ *(619) 786-2331*

Hot, hot, HOT is the watchword here, where the low-lying areas of the park average 116 degrees in July! In the winter, however, temperatures drop to around 85 degrees, and the 3.3-acre national park becomes a weekend getaway for the adventurous and/or well-heeled. **The Furnace Creek Inn** ☎ *(619) 786-2361* is where the bucks-up group stays, while regular folks end up at the nearby **Furnace Creek Ranch** ☎ *(619) 786-2345.* (Birders, who flock here in late May to catch the spring migration, usually just camp out.) The park is a geologist's delight with its tortured rock formations, salt pans and 700-foot sand dunes. Elevations go from 282 feet below sea level to 11,049 feet above, making for an interesting variety of landscapes. If you can't find enough to interest you in the park, there are another 1.3 million acres to explore adjacent. 650 miles round trip.

Mammoth   ★★★

Nancy Upham, ☎ *(619) 873-2400*
Ski Lodge, ☎ *(619) 934-2571*
Tourism Bureau, ☎ *(619) 934-2712*

Mammoth is one of the most popular ski resorts in California for serious skiers. A caravan of sport vehicles blasts up Highway 395 every Friday night in winter, and back down on Sunday, with the police sitting like duck hunters waiting to pick off speed demons. It may seem a bit obsessive to drive more than 300 miles to ski for a day and a half, but Mammoth has rewards equal to the six-hour trip. One of the state's most beautiful ski areas, long-dormant volcano features a natural amphitheater surrounded by snow-capped peaks, lakes and alpine forest. Along with scenery that rivals anything you'll find in Switzerland, downhill and cross-country skiing are superb. 640 miles round trip.

Lake Tahoe

☎ *(916) 541-5255*

Lake Tahoe has all the makings of the next Las Vegas—only it's a lot less, well, grungy—and it's high in the mountains, which means the weather is lovely in summer. In addition to gambling, it offers paddle boat rides on the lake, great scenery, camping, skiing, horseback riding, hiking and lots of other outdoor activities. Although it's technically in Nevada, the lake actually sits right on the California border (make sure you're on the Nevada side if you want to gamble). Can be crowded on weekends. Lots of timeshare condos here. 1000 miles round trip.

Neptune Pool at Hearst Castle

Hearst Castle ★★★★
☎ *(805) 927-2093*

It's a pity that Hearst Castle isn't in Los Angeles, because it was definitely built on the same principle as some of L.A.'s showier estates. Only this 127-acre "castle" built by William Randolph Hearst beginning in 1919 takes the word "showy" to new heights. A state park since 1957, Hearst Castle is one of the most opulent homes in the world. The 65,000-square-foot main house has 115 rooms, once had its own zoo and served as a showcase for Hearst's art collection. This and the other buildings are filled with priceless antiquities (some rooms were brought in their entirety from Europe) and art, gorgeous pools, and other facilities for entertaining Hearst's mostly-famous guests. The only way you can see the estate is by taking one of the four tours (about an hour and 45 minutes each), which are somewhat disappointing because you are rushed through in a group, don't have time to browse, and get in big trouble if you touch anything or step off the carpet. Still, if you want to see where the rich and famous frolicked (although guides will tell you that all "frolicking" at the famous estate was in good taste), don't miss this. Reservations are required. Pick a tour with a good general overview, or do the whole nine yards.

Las Vegas

☎ *(702) 933-9321*

If you think L.A. is superficial, tacky and tawdry, then you obviously haven't been to Las Vegas. This tiny gambling town known for its casinos, cheap food and flashy entertainment, has lately begun promoting itself as a family vacation destination. In fact, Bugsy Siegal wouldn't even recognize the pyramids, laser light shows, nonstop circus atmosphere and fantasy palaces that now rule the famous Strip. Nearly every hotel offers special values on rooms, discounts on shows and sometimes free drinks or gaming chips. Check with your travel agent for the best deals. 700 miles round trip.

Grand Canyon ★★★★★

☎ *(602) 638-7888*

Europeans always like to include an excursion to the Grand Canyon in every trip to Southern California. Although they probably don't realize that it's a good five-hour drive beyond Las Vegas to Arizona, the view is worth the trip. A visit to the park—which contains more than one million acres—is not complete without a peek over the rim, followed by some time spent in stunning Monument Valley. On a clear day, visibility extends to 200 miles, but smog has reduced the view to less than 20 on days when the air quality is poor. To see it all from the air, you can opt for an aerial sightseeing tour, but be aware that the safety record of some of these companies isn't the best. About 1200 miles round trip.

The perfect antidote to Southern California is a trip to cool and foggy San Francisco.

San Francisco

☎ *(415) 391-2000*

The City by the Bay is an excellent add-on to your L.A. trip, especially if you're interested in seeing why northern California has threatened to secede from the state. San Francisco probably has less in common with L.A. than even New York or Miami, with its very "left coast" state of mind quite apparent in its "love, peace and granola" mentality combined with a sound disdain for "El Lay." There's a definite difference in style between San Francisco's ("Frisco" is a word that's definitely passé) history, scale, charm and grace and L.A.'s energy, brashness and sprawling awkwardness, but you're bound to find something you like at both ends of the coast highway. San Francisco has wonderful museums, cultural arts and lots of damp, foggy days and the California wine country is just over the hill. Plan to drive up the coast with stops in San Simeon (Hearst Castle), Big Sur, Carmel and Monterey (spend a couple of days to see everything), or opt for a day long train trip or speedier travel by air. About 1200 miles round trip.

Bridal Veil Falls in Yosemite

Yosemite National Park   ★ ★ ★ ★ ★

Although this place has lost much of its appeal because of the crowds, it's still the most dramatic park in California. More than three million people visit Yosemite annually, creating huge traffic jams on weekends and filling the air with the unwelcome sounds of ghetto blasters, dogs, kids on bikes and the general hubbub of too many people jammed into a small space. Come on an off-day, though, and you will see deer in the meadow, stand in awe of the second-highest waterfall in the world and imagine you're Ansel Adams as you photograph Half Dome. More that 800 miles of trails allow you to experience this High Sierra wonderland, and get you away from the main roads. Campgrounds and outlying hotels are packed in summer, so reserve well ahead. Inside the park, you can rent a bike or take the shuttle. 600 miles round trip.

The biggest sequoias in the park are named after Civil War generals.

Sequoia/Kings Canyon   ★ ★ ★

☎ *(209) 565-3134*

Big trees and steep cliffs sum up these two spots, where hiking is the preferred method of transportation and there are more than 850,000 acres to explore. If you're not into hiking, you can still check out the trees, which are some of the oldest (more than 2500 years old), tallest (up to 267 feet), and largest (with enough lumber to make a 12-inch-wide walkway 119 miles long) in the world. 450 miles round trip.

Diving in Southern California

With year-round warm weather and picturesque beaches, it doesn't take a genius to figure out that Southern California offers excellent scuba diving. Although the water may not be as crystal clear or warm as that in the Caribbean, sea life is abundant and unique.

There are numerous dive shops throughout the area; just open the Yellow Pages to the section labeled "Divers." The majority of Southern California dive shops not only offer scuba equipment for both purchase and rental, they have day and night boat trips to a number of locations. Refer to the end of this section for our favorite shops.

A full scuba setup—which includes mask, fins, tank, buoyancy compensator, regulator and wet suit—will run you about $50 per day. Tank refills are about $5. Please keep in mind that you will be required to show your certification card (PADI and NAUI are preferred). For those who have never taken the plunge, or haven't in a singnificant while, there are lessons and refresher courses offered at most facilities.

Top Southern California Dive Spots

San Nicolas Island

About 56 miles of the coast of Los Angeles
San Nicolas Island is a favorite place for lobster divers. Boats from the mainland usually depart in October and November when lobster season begins. Even if you're not interested in catching lobster, the waters around San Nicolas are clear (usually 80- to 100-feet visibility) and the game is large. You'll see more larger fish here than any other dive spot in Southern California.

Santa Barbara Island

About 40 miles of the coast of Santa Barbara
The reason Santa Barbara Island is so popular for divers is the sea lions. On most days, you'll see more sea lions than you can count. What's more, they are not afraid of humans. They'll actually play with you. Summer is the best time to go. Visibility is good, but the water can be quite cold. Many of the area's dive shops offer monthly boat trips.

Catalina Island

26 miles off the coast of Los Angeles
The waters around Catalina are filled with sea life—including sharks in some areas! Visbility can be as much as 100 feet, but usually it is more like 50. Because Catalina Island is so close by, it is easily the most popular dive spot in Southern California. You can sign up for a boat trip from virtually any dive shop in the area. A full-day trip, which begins at San Pedro Harbor, runs anywhere from $40 to $75. These trips are all boat dives and you'll probably not set foot on the island itself.

San Clemente Island

About 40 miles of the coast of Los Angeles
San Clemente Island is a Navy-controlled island, which, during the summer becomes one of Southern California's favorite dive spots. San Clemente is one of the few places in the area that offers wreck diving. The best time to go is in July when the water is warmest and the visibility best. Sign up at various dive shops around California.

Palos Verdes Peninsula

On the coast north of San Pedro
Palos Verdes is accessible by land and by boat. If you would like to drive to your dive spot, the best place to go is Malaga Cove, off Palos Verdes Drive West and Paseo del Mar), but we recommend you go by boat. American Diving offers a half-day boat trip to the best dive spots off Palos Verdes that are inaccessible by land. These are well worth your time and money because the visibility is good and marine life plentiful. Lots of kelp to dive through.

Laguna Beach

In Orange County, south of Newport Beach

This is the best place in the area for a beach dive. Entry is easy, just walk in. You'll be smart to go early in the morning when the water is clearest. Marine life is abundant and there's a good dive shop nearby, Laguna Sea Sport.

Redondo Beach

Below the Palos Verdes Peninsula, south of the airport

In Los Angeles County, the best place for a beach dive is Redondo Beach. A few hundred yards out there is a shelf that dramatically drops from 60 feet to who knows? You can reach depths up to 200 feet, if you choose. I prefer to dive at night here because of the variety of nocturnal life from octopus to squid. I recommend stopping at about 80 feet because the water can get very cold and decompression stops may force you to stay under longer than you may want.

Favorite Dive Shops

American Diving

1901 Pacific Coast Highway
Lomita, California
☎ *(310) 326-6663*

Aquatic Center

4537 West Pacific Coast Highway
Newport Beach, California
☎ *(714) 650-5783*

Laguna Sea Sport

925 North Pacific Coast Highway
Laguna Beach, California
☎ *(714) 494-6965*

Sea 'd Sea

1911 South Catalina Avenue
Redondo Beach, California
☎ *(310) 373-6355*

Skiing in Southern California

You're on a sunny beach soaking up a tan. Hop into your car, drive three hours and you could be in the middle of a snow-covered mountain. That's what makes Southern California so special. If you're in Los Angeles anytime between Thanksgiving and Easter, and your schedule allows you a few extra days, head for the mountains where you can enjoy the excitement and challenge of skiing or snowboarding.

Even if you've never tried skiing, each resort offers a ski school for a small fee (sometimes additional, about $20 to $40). Often you may be able to obtain beginner's packages that include lift ticket, lessons, skis, boots and poles for just a bit more than the normal lift ticket price. An advantage for beginners is the head-of-the-line privileges (meaning no waiting in lift lines) often afforded ski school groups.

There are plenty of places to rent skis, including at the resorts themselves. Your best bet however, is at local area ski shops down the mountain. Some sporting goods shops rent skis, boots and poles as a package for as little as $36 for a three-day ski outing. Prices vary with shops and equipment. Serious racing skis will cost somewhat more. Up the hill, you're on their turf and the prices show it.

Top Southern California Ski Resorts

Snow Summit

San Bernardino National Forest, off Highway 18
☎ *(909) 866-5766*
Snow Report: ☎ *(310) 390-1498, 24-hr.*
Adult: $41, Children: $21

With 31 major runs and limited number of ticket sales, you would think that this resort would not be too congested. Wrong. Because Snow Summit offers a good variety of runs—from beginner to expert—and the snow is always in good condition, it is the most popular ski resort in Southern California.

Mountain High

Wrightwood, off the 138 Highway
Snow Report: ☎ *(310) 578-6911, 24 hr.*
Adult: $45, Children: $35

This is one of the closest ski resorts from Los Angeles County. About an hour and a half from L.A., Mtn. High features 11 chair lifts and one of the largest snow-making systems in the world, covering 90 percent of the mountain. Therefore, even if the weather is warm, there is usually a lot of snow.

Bear Mountain

San Bernardino National Forest, off Highway 18.
Snow Report: ☎ *(213) 683-8100, 24-hr.*
Adult: $38, Children: $21

This resort sits above Snow Summit, about a half hour to an hour drive up Highway 18. It's not as nice as Summit, but it does offer good skiing, featuring 11 lifts and a number of challenging runs. Because of its higher elevation, the snow can be quite icy on cold days, so wear some padding if you're prone to falling.

Snow Valley

San Bernardino National Forest, off Highway 18.
☎ *(909) 867-2751*
Snow Report: ☎ *(800) 680-SNOW, 24-hr.*
Adult: $35, Children: $21

This resort, which is on the way to Snow Summit, is a perfect place for first-timers because of the expansive beginner runs. However, because it sits at a lower elevation than most resorts, snow is sometimes scarce. Be sure to check the 24-hour snow report before you go.

INSIDER TIP

If your schedule allows it, head for Mammoth Mountain. It is about a six- to seven-hour drive, but the quality of snow and the number of lifts and runs are astounding. Make reservations early for lodgings because, despite its distance, it's extremely popular during the holidays. Mammoth Mountain is located of Interstate 395 in Mammoth Lakes, California. Call ☎ *(800) 367-6572 for more info.*

FIELDING'S
PICKS FOR...

Hotels with the Best Ambience

Rank	Hotel	Phone	Price
1	**Ritz-Carlton Huntington** *1401 South Oak Knoll Avenue* *Pasadena*	☎ (818) 568-3900	$165–$265
2	**Four Seasons Newport Beach** *690 Newport Center Drive* *Newport Beach*	☎ (714) 759-0808	$245–$355
3	**Bel Air Hotel** *701 Stone Canyon Road* *Bel Air*	☎ (310) 472-1211	$285–$435
4	**Regent Beverly Wilshire** *9500 Wilshire Boulevard* *Beverly Hills*	☎ (310) 275-5200	$260–$4000
5	**Four Seasons** *300 South Doheny Drive* *Beverly Hills*	☎ (310) 273-2222	$295–$510
6	**Ritz-Carlton Marina del Rey** *4375 Admiralty Way* *Marina del Rey*	☎ (310) 823-1700	$225–$525
7	**Shutters on the Beach** *1 Pico Boulevard* *Santa Monica*	☎ (310) 458-0030	$260–$1900
8	**Loews Santa Monica Hotel** *1700 Ocean Avenue* *Santa Monica*	☎ (310) 458-6700	$200–$355
9	**Wyndham Checkers Hotel** *535 South Grand Avenue* *Los Angeles Downtown*	☎ (213) 624-0000	$209–$229
10	**Wyndham Bel Age** *1020 North San Vicente Blvd.* *West Hollywood*	☎ (310) 854-1111	$250–$500

The Best Hotels for Honeymooning

Rank	Hotel	Phone	Price
1	**Ritz-Carlton Huntington** *1401 South Oak Knoll Avenue* *Pasadena*	☎ (818) 568-3900	$165–$265
2	**Bel Air Hotel** *701 Stone Canyon Road* *Bel Air*	☎ (310) 472-1211	$285–$435
3	**Malibu Country Inn** *6506 Westward Beach Road* *Malibu*	☎ (310) 457-9622	$95–$155
4	**Malibu Beach Inn** *22878 Pacific Coast Highway* *Malibu*	☎ (310) 456-6444	$130–$275
5	**Shutters on the Beach** *1 Pico Boulevard* *Santa Monica*	☎ (310) 458-0030	$260–$1900
6	**Sunset Marquis Hotel** *1200 North Alta Loma Road* *West Hollywood*	☎ (310) 657-1333	$215–$275
7	**Wyndham Bel Age** *1020 North San Vicente Blvd.* *West Hollywood*	☎ (310) 854-1111	$250–$500
8	**Hotel Metropole** *205 Crescent Avenue* *Catalina Island*	☎ (310) 510-1884	$89–$295
9	**Chateau Marmont** *8221 Sunset Boulevard* *Hollywood*	☎ (213) 656-1010	$170–$1200

The Most Relaxing Hotels

Rank	Hotel	Phone	Price
1	**Four Seasons Newport Beach** *690 Newport Center Drive* *Newport Beach*	☎ (714) 759-0808	$245–$355
2	**Shutters on the Beach** *1 Pico Boulevard* *Santa Monica*	☎ (310) 458-0030	$260–$1900
3	**Loews Santa Monica Hotel** *1700 Ocean Avenue* *Santa Monica*	☎ (310) 458-6700	$200–$355

The Most Relaxing Hotels

Rank	Hotel	Phone	Price
4	**Wyndham Checkers Hotel** *535 South Grand Avenue* *Los Angeles Downtown*	☎ (213) 624-0000	$209–$229
5	**Sunset Marquis Hotel** *1200 North Alta Loma Road* *West Hollywood*	☎ (310) 657-1333	$215–$275
6	**Wyndham Bel Age** *1020 North San Vicente Blvd.* *West Hollywood*	☎ (310) 854-1111	$250–$500
7	**Seal Beach Inn** *212 5th Street* *Seal Beach*	☎ (310) 493-2416	$118–$255

The Most Romantic Hotels

Rank	Hotel	Phone	Price
1	**Ritz-Carlton Huntington** *1401 South Oak Knoll Avenue* *Pasadena*	☎ (818) 568-3900	$165–$265
2	**Malibu Country Inn** *6506 Westward Beach Road* *Malibu*	☎ (310) 457-9622	$95–$155
3	**Malibu Beach Inn** *22878 Pacific Coast Highway* *Malibu*	☎ (310) 456-6444	$130–$275
4	**Shutters on the Beach** *1 Pico Boulevard* *Santa Monica*	☎ (310) 458-0030	$260–$1900
5	**Wyndham Checkers Hotel** *535 South Grand Avenue* *Los Angeles Downtown*	☎ (213) 624-0000	$209–$229
6	**Sunset Marquis Hotel** *1200 North Alta Loma Road* *West Hollywood*	☎ (310) 657-1333	$215–$275
7	**Wyndham Bel Age** *1020 North San Vicente Blvd.* *West Hollywood*	☎ (310) 854-1111	$250–$500
8	**Regent Beverly Wilshire** *9500 Wilshire Boulevard* *Beverly Hills*	☎ (310) 275-5200	$260–$4000
9	**Hotel Metropole** *205 Crescent Avenue* *Catalina Island*	☎ (310) 510-1884	$89–$295
10	**Chateau Marmont** *8221 Sunset Boulevard* *Hollywood*	☎ (213) 656-1010	$170–$1200

The Most Scenic Hotels			
Rank	Hotel	Phone	Price
1	**Ritz-Carlton Huntington** *1401 South Oak Knoll Avenue* *Pasadena*	☎ (818) 568-3900	$165–$265
2	**Four Seasons Newport Beach** *690 Newport Center Drive* *Newport Beach*	☎ (714) 759-0808	$245–$355
3	**Malibu Country Inn** *6506 Westward Beach Road* *Malibu*	☎ (310) 457-9622	$95–$155
4	**Malibu Beach Inn** *22878 Pacific Coast Highway* *Malibu*	☎ (310) 456-6444	$130–$275
5	**Shutters on the Beach** *1 Pico Boulevard* *Santa Monica*	☎ (310) 458-0030	$260–$1900
6	**Loews Santa Monica Hotel** *1700 Ocean Avenue* *Santa Monica*	☎ (310) 458-6700	$200–$355
7	**Wyndham Bel Age** *1020 North San Vicente Blvd.* *West Hollywood*	☎ (310) 854-1111	$250–$500
8	**Hotel Metropole** *205 Crescent Avenue* *Catalina Island*	☎ (310) 510-1884	$89–$295

Restaurants with the Best Ambience			
Rank	Restaurant	Phone	Price
1	**Maison Magnolia** *2903 South Hoover Street* *Los Angeles*	☎ (213) 746-1314	$50
2	**Saddle Peak Lodge** *419 Cold Canyon Road* *Calabasas*	☎ (818) 222-3888	$18–$30
3	**Antoine** *4500 MacArthur Blvd.* *Newport Beach*	☎ (714) 476-2001	$25–$35
4	**Bel Air Hotel Dining Room** *701 Stone Canyon Road* *Bel Air*	☎ (310) 472-1211	$25–$35

Restaurants with the Best Ambience

Rank	Restaurant	Phone	Price
5	**Ritz-Carlton Dining Room** *33533 Shoreline Drive* *Laguna Niguel*	☎ (714) 240-2000	$39–$70
6	**L'Orangerie** *903 North La Cienega* *West Hollywood*	☎ (310) 652-9770	$27–$35
7	**Diaghilev** *1020 North San Vicente* *West Hollywood*	☎ (310) 854-1111	$15–$34
8	**Dining Room, The** *9500 Wilshire Boulevard* *Beverly Hills*	☎ (310) 274-8179	$15–$30
9	**Cellar, The** *305 North Harbor* *Fullerton*	☎ (714) 525-5682	$18–$27
10	**J.W.'s** *700 West Convention Way* *Anaheim*	☎ (714) 750-8000	$19–$28

Highest Rated Cuisine

Rank	Restaurant	Phone	Price
1	**Chinois on Main** *2709 Main Street* *Santa Monica*	☎ (310) 392-9025	$21–$30
2	**Gustaf Anders** *3810 South Plaza Drive* *Santa Ana*	☎ (714) 668-1737	$16–$28
3	**Valentino** *3115 Pico Boulevard* *Santa Monica*	☎ (310) 829-4313	$20–$24
4	**Diaghilev** *1020 North San Vicente* *West Hollywood*	☎ (310) 854-1111	$15–$34
5	**Patina** *5955 Melrose Avenue* *Hollywood*	☎ (213) 467-1108	$22–$26
6	**Pangaea** *465 La Cienega Blvd.* *Beverly Hills*	☎ (310) 246-2100	$7–$29
7	**Nouveau Cafe Blanc** *9777 Little Santa Monica Blvd.* *Beverly Hills*	☎ (310) 888-0108	$32–$38
8	**La Cachette** *10506 Little Santa Monica Blvd.* *Century City*	☎ (310) 470-4992	$12–$20

Highest Rated Cuisine

Rank	Restaurant	Phone	Price
9	**Abiquiu** *1413 Fifth Street* *Santa Monica*	☎ (310) 395-8611	$12–$18
10	**Antoine** *4500 MacArthur Blvd.* *Newport Beach*	☎ (714) 476-2001	$25–$35

The Most Romantic Restaurants

Rank	Restaurant	Phone	Price
1	**Maison Magnolia** *2903 South Hoover Street* *Los Angeles*	☎ (213) 746-1314	$50
2	**Saddle Peak Lodge** *419 Cold Canyon Road* *Calabasas*	☎ (818) 222-3888	$18–$30
3	**Bernard's** *506 South Grand Avenue* *Los Angeles*	☎ (213) 612-1580	$30–$45
4	**Bel Air Hotel Dining Room** *701 Stone Canyon Road* *Bel Air*	☎ (310) 472-1211	$25–$35
5	**L'Orangerie** *903 North La Cienega* *West Hollywood*	☎ (310) 652-9770	$27–$35
6	**Diaghilev** *1020 North San Vicente* *West Hollywood*	☎ (310) 854-1111	$15–$34
7	**Antoine** *4500 MacArthur Blvd.* *Newport Beach*	☎ (714) 476-2001	$25–$35
8	**One Pico** *1 Pico Blvd.* *Santa Monica*	☎ (310) 587-1717	$13–$20
9	**Camelions** *246 26th Street* *Santa Monica*	☎ (310) 395-0746	$15–$21
10	**L'Opera** *101 Pine Avenue* *Long Beach*	☎ (310) 491-0066	$15–$20

The Most Scenic Restaurants

Rank	Restaurant	Phone	Price
1	**Saddle Peak Lodge** *419 Cold Canyon Road* *Calabasas*	☎ (818) 222-3888	$18–$30
2	**One Pico** *1 Pico Blvd.* *Santa Monica*	☎ (310) 587-1717	$13–$20
3	**Bel Air Hotel Dining Room** *701 Stone Canyon Road* *Bel Air*	☎ (310) 472-1211	$25–$35
4	**Pedals** *One Pico* *Santa Monica*	☎ (310) 587-1707	$10–$20
5	**Ocean Avenue Seafood** *1401 Ocean Avenue* *Santa Monica*	☎ (310) 394-5669	$18–$20
6	**Ritz-Carlton Dining Room** *4375 Admiralty Way* *Marina del Rey*	☎ (310) 823-1700	$21–$28
7	**Geoffrey's** *27400 Pacific Coast* *Malibu*	☎ (310) 457-1519	$12–$28
8	**Ritz-Carlton Dining Room** *33533 Shoreline Drive* *Laguna Niguel*	☎ (714) 240-2000	$39–$70
9	**Towers, The** *1555 South Coast Highway* *Laguna Beach*	☎ (714) 497-4477	$16–$30
10	**Yamashiro** *1999 North Sycamore* *Hollywood*	☎ (213) 466-5125	$16–$30

SEATING PLANS

Location	Phone
Anaheim Stadium	(714) 254-3000
Coliseum, LA Memorial	(213) 747-7111
Dodger Stadium	(213) 224-1400
Dorothy Chandler Pavilion	(213) 972-7300
Forum, the	(310) 673-1300
Greek Theater	(213) 665-1927
Hollywood Bowl	(213) 850-2000
Jack Murphy Stadium	(619) 525-8282
Mark Taper Forum	(213) 466-1767
Pantages Theater	(213) 468-1770
Pauley Pavilion	(310) 825-2101
Rose Bowl	(818) 577-3106
Royce Hall UCLA	(310) 825-2101
Santa Monica Civic	(310) 393-9961
Shrine Auditorium	(213) 749-5123
Shubert Theater	(310) 201-1500, (800) 233-3123
Sports Arena, LA Memorial	(213) 748-6131
Universal Amphitheatre	(818) 980-9421
Westwood Playhouse	(310) 208-5454
Wilshire Theater	(213) 468-1700

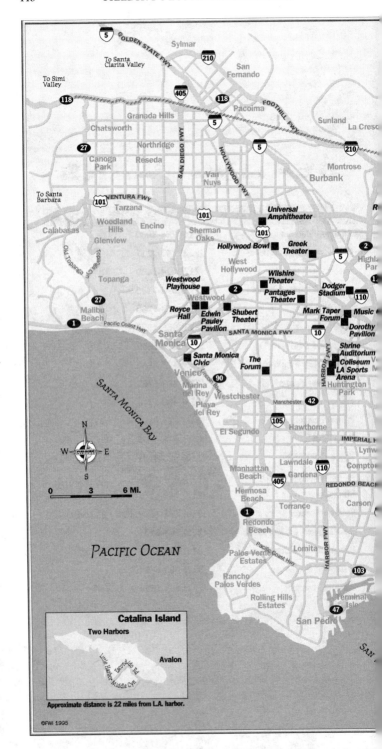

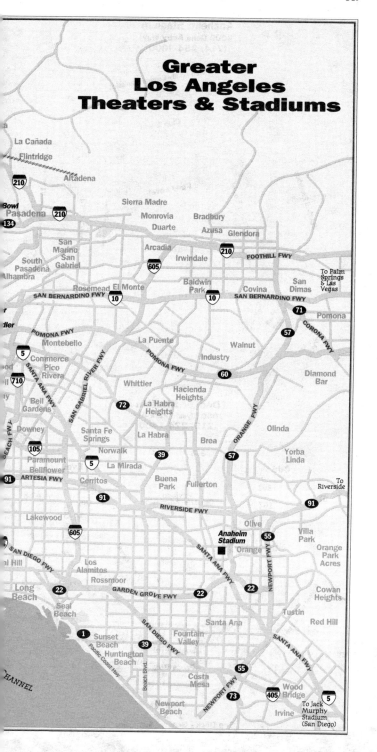

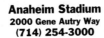

Anaheim Stadium
2000 Gene Autry Way
(714) 254-3000

Dodger Stadium
1000 Elysian Park Ave
(213) 224-1400

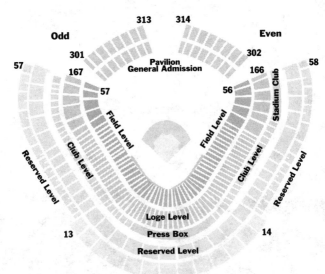

Los Angeles Memorial Coliseum
3911 S. Figueroa St.
(213) 747-7111

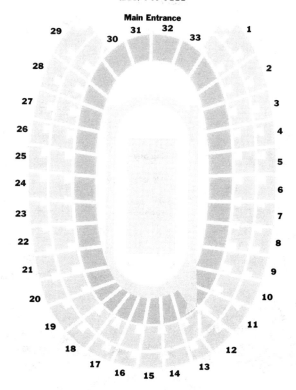

Main Entrance

29   31   32   33   1
30

28   2

27   3

26   4

25   5

24   6

23   7

22   8

21   9

20   10

19   11

18   12

17   16   15   14   13

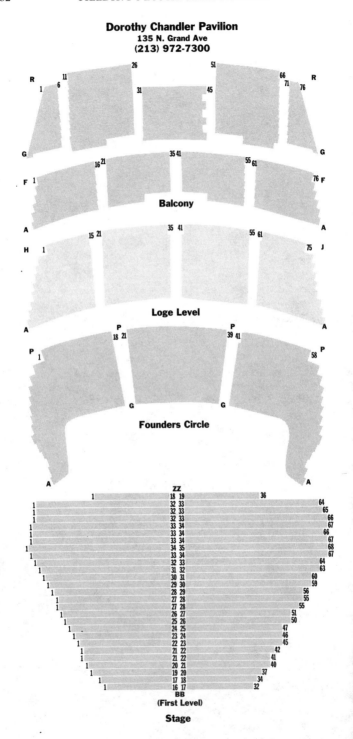

Dorothy Chandler Pavilion
135 N. Grand Ave
(213) 972-7300

The Forum
3900 Manchester Blvd.
(310) 673-1300

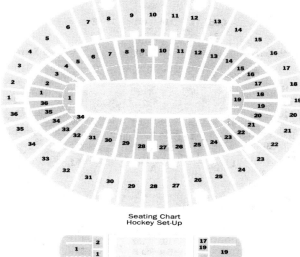

Seating Chart
Hockey Set-Up

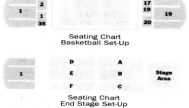

Seating Chart
Basketball Set-Up

Seating Chart
End Stage Set-Up

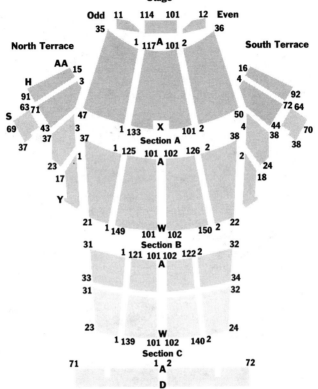

Greek Theater
2700 N. Vermont Ave
(213) 665-1927

Stage

Odd   11   114   101   12   Even
35   36

North Terrace   1 117 A 101 2   South Terrace

AA 15   16
H   3   4
91   92
63 71   72 64
S   47   50
69   43 3   X   4   70
37 37   37   1 133   101 2   38   38
37   1 125   101 102   126 2   44 38
1   A   2
23   24
17   18
Y

21   1 149   101 W 102   150 2   22
31   Section B   32
1 121 101 102 122 2
A
33   34
31   32

23   24
1 139   101 W 102   140 2
Section C
71   1 A 2   72
D
Benches

Hollywood Bowl
2301 N. Highland Avenue
(213) 850-2000

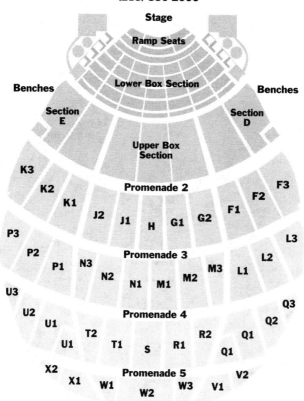

Stage

Ramp Seats

Lower Box Section

Benches

Section E

Upper Box Section

Section D

Benches

K3

K2

K1

J2

J1

H

G1

G2

F1

F2

F3

Promenade 2

P3

P2

P1

N3

N2

N1

M1

M2

M3

L1

L2

L3

Promenade 3

U3

U2

U1

T2

U1

T1

S

R1

R2

Q1

Q1

Q2

Q3

Promenade 4

X2

X1

W1

W2

W3

V1

V2

Promenade 5

Jack Murphy Stadium
9449 Friars Road, San Diego
(619) 525-8282

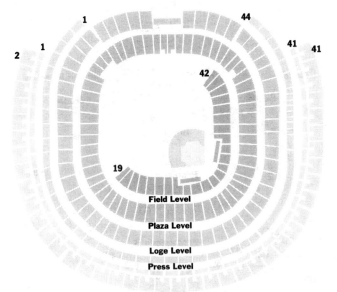

Field Level

Plaza Level

Loge Level

Press Level

View Section - General Admission

Mark Taper Forum
135 N. Grand Ave
(213) 466-1767

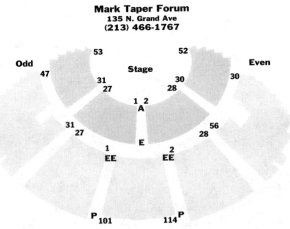

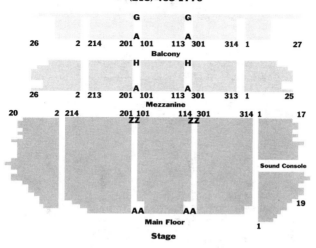

Pantages Theatre
6233 Hollywood Blvd.
(213) 468-1770

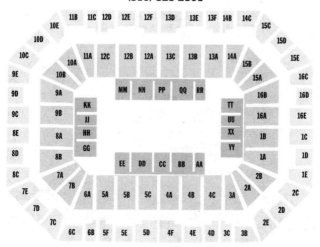

Edwin Pauley Pavilion
Circle Drive West and Gayley Ave.
(310) 825-2101

Rose Bowl
1001 Rose Bowl Drive
(818) 577-3106

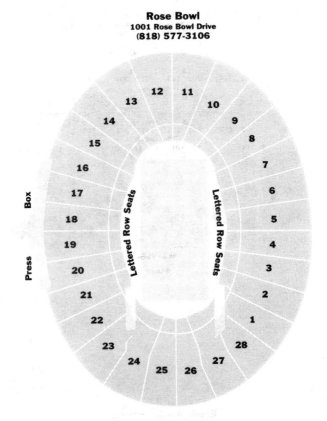

Royce Hall UCLA
Between Circle Drive North and Circle Drive East
(310) 825-2101

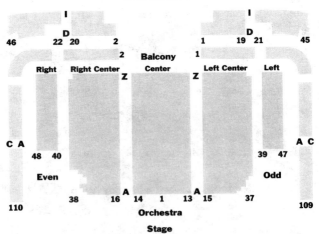

Santa Monica Civic
1855 Main St.
(310) 393-9961

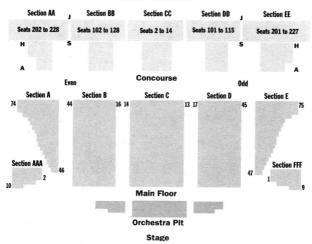

Shrine Auditorium
655 W. Jefferson Blvd.
(213) 749-5123

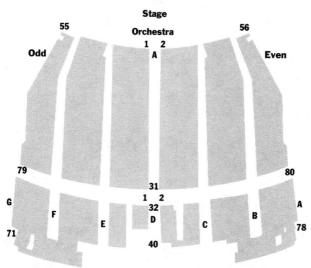

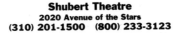

Shubert Theatre
2020 Avenue of the Stars
(310) 201-1500   (800) 233-3123

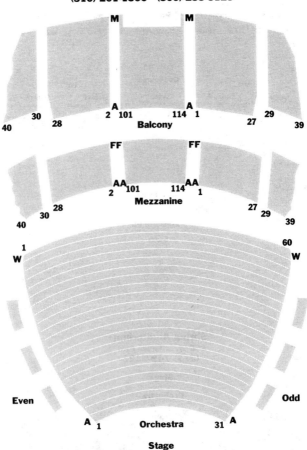

Los Angeles Sports Arena
3939 S. Figueroa St.
(213) 748-6131

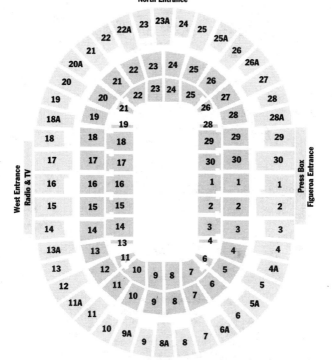

Universal Amphitheatre
100 Universal City Plaza
(818) 980-9421

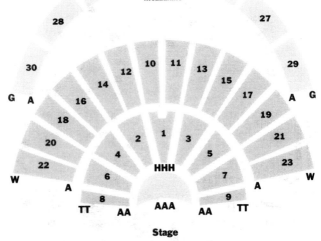

Wilshire Theatre
8440 Wilshire Blvd.
(213) 468-1700

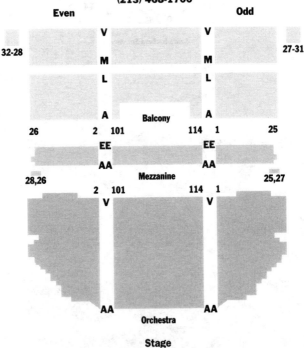

Westwood Playhouse
10886 Le Conte Ave
(310) 208-5454

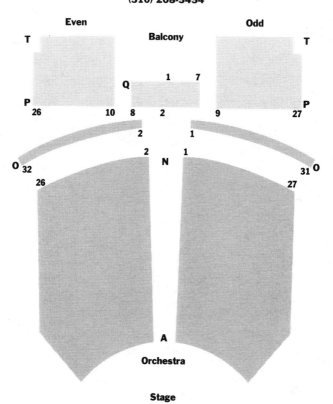

LIST OF ATTRACTIONS

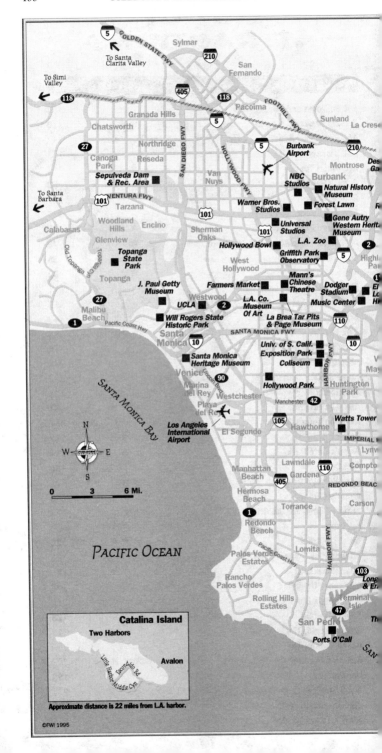

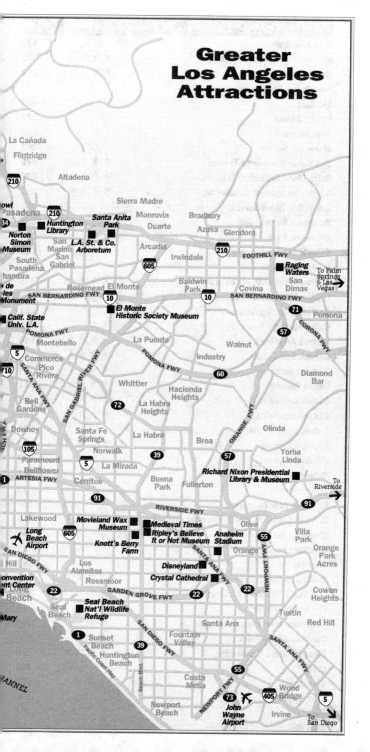

Attraction	Rating	Pg.
Club Shelter		240
Coconut Teaszer		151
Coleman Chamber Music Association	★★★★	239
Colony Studio Theatre	★★	82
Comedy and Magic Club		306
Comedy Store		151
Concerts in the Grove	★★★	326
Concerts in the Park	★★	358
Concours d'Elegance	★★★	398
Cornerstone Theater Company	★★★	282
Costa Mesa Civic Playhouse	★★	381
Country Rock Cafe		382
Country Star Hollywood		213
Cowboy Boogie		360
Cowboy Palace Saloon		49
Crush Bar		84
Crystal Cathedral	★★★	354
Crystal Cove State Park	★★★★	396
Culver City Ice Arena		183
Cypress Golf Club		357
Da Camera Society	★★★	184
Dana Point Festival of the Whales	★★	398
Dance at the Fountain	★★	147
Davey's Locker Sport Fishing		400
David B. Gamble House	★★★★	234
Death Valley	★★	430
Derby, The		85
Descanso Gardens	★★★	235
Discovery Museum of Orange County	★★★	377
Discovery Museum of Orange County	★★★	378
Discovery Tours	★★	323
Disneyland Marathon		357
Disneyland	★★★★★	354
Domenico's		241
Doo Dah Parade	★★★	237
Doolittle Theatre	★★	147
Downtown Lives!	★★★	76
East-West Players	★★★	83
Eaton Canyon County Park & Nature Center	★★	236
Eaton Canyon		237
El Alisal		234
El Pueblo de Los Angeles Park	★★★	71
Endless Summer Sportsbar		283
Epicentre		85
Farmer's Market	★★★	72
Festival of Arts	★★★★	398
Fiesta de las Golondrinas	★★	398

Attraction	Rating	Pg.
Fisher Art Gallery	★★★	68
Forum Boxing		78
Fountain Theatre	★★	147
Fourth of July Fireworks	★★★	325
Fowler Museum of Cultural History	★★★	182
Fred Hayman		45
Front Row Center Tickets		184
Fullerton Arboretum	★★★	354
Fullerton Civic Light Opera	★★★★	359
Fullerton Market	★★	354
Gardenia		151
Garlic Festival	★★★	183
Gate, The		85
Gene Autry Western Heritage Museum	★★★★	138
Gene Autry Western Museum		50
George C. Page Museum	★★★★	69
Glacial Garden Ice Arena		357
Glam Slam		85
Glendale Symphony Orchestra	★★★	239
Go Boats		326
Gold's Gym		281
Golden State Children's Theatre	★★★★	359
Gondola Getaway	★★★	323
Gotham Hall		283
Grand Avenue Bar		85
Grand Canyon	★★★★★	432
Grand Dinner Theatre	★★	359
Grand Hope Park	★★	73
Grave Line Tours	★★★★	141
Greater Los Angeles Auto Show	★★★	76
Greek Theater	★★★	147
Griffith Observatory	★★★	139
Griffith Park	★★★	142
Groundling Theatre	★★★	148
Grove Shakespeare Festival	★★★	356
Halloween Carnaval		144
Hard Rock Cafe		401
Harding Golf Course		145
Harvelle's	★★	283
Harvest Festival	★★	77
Hearst Castle	★★★★	431
Heli USA		278
Heritage Square	★★★	234
Historic Adamson House		278
Hobby City	★★	356
Holiday Spa Health Club		79
Hollyhock House	★★★	139

Attraction	Rating	Pg.
Kidspace Museum	★★★★	236
Knightsbridge Theatre	★★	240
Knott's Berry Farm	★★★★	355
L.A. Classic Jazz Festival	★★★★	81
L.A. Classica Ballet	★★★	327
L.A. County Museum of Art		86
La Habra Tennis Courts		358
La Jolla	★★	425
La Mirada Playhouse	★★★★	359
La Mirada Symphony	★★★★	358
La Mirada Theatre for Performing Arts	★★★★★	359
Laguna Art Museum	★★★	395
Laguna Beach		436
Laguna Playhouse	★★★	401
Laguna Sea Sport		436
Lake Tahoe		430
Las Vegas	★★	432
Laugh Factory		151
Legends of Hollywood Jazz Club		213
Legends		327
Lewitzky Dance Company	★★★	82
Lighthouse Cafe		306
Lobby Bar		327
Lobby Court Bar		185
Long Beach Blues Festival	★★★	325
Long Beach Boat Show	★★	325
Long Beach Carriage Company	★★	323
Long Beach Children's Museum	★★★	324
Long Beach Civic Light Opera	★★★	327
Long Beach Firefighters Museum	★★	322
Long Beach Marine Stadium	★★	322
Long Beach Museum of Art	★★★	322
Long Beach Opera	★★★	326
Long Beach Sea Festival		325
Long Beach Symphony	★★★	326
Long Beach Water Sports		326
Longhorn Saloon		49
Los Alamitos		358
Los Angeles Bach Festival	★★★	81
Los Angeles Baroque Orchestra	★★★	281
Los Angeles Central Library	★★★	71
Los Angeles Chamber Orchestra	★★★	81
Los Angeles Children's Museum	★★★★	75
Los Angeles City Hall	★★	72
Los Angeles Clippers		79
Los Angeles Conservancy		51
Los Angeles Conservancy	★★★	72

Attraction	Rating	Pg.
Newport Harbor Art Museum	★★★	396
Newport Landing		402
Newport Seafest	★★	399
Newport Theatre Arts Center	★★	401
Nisei Week Festival	★★★	77
Nissan Open Golf Tournament		281
Norton Simon Museum of Art	★★★★	233
Nucleus		152
Observation Bar		327
Odyssey Theatre	★★★	148
Odyssey Theatre	★★★	183
Off the Wall		46
Ojai	★	425
Old Pasadena Tour	★★	235
Open House at the Hollywood Bowl	★★★	143
Opera Pacific	★★★	380
Orange County Blues Festival	★★★	399
Orange County Fair	★★★	379
Orange County Natural History Museum	★★★	378
Orange County Performing Arts Center Tours	★★★	378
Orange County Performing Arts Center	★★★	380
Orange County Philharmonic Society	★★★★	381
Oskar J's Sightseeing Tours	★★	209
Outdoor Courts at California Plaza	★★★	82
Pacific Asia Museum	★★★	233
Pacific Stock Exchange	★★★	73
Pacific Symphony Orchestra	★★★	381
Pageant of the Masters	★★★★	399
Pair Celebrity Series	★★★★	359
Palace, The		152
Palm Springs		426
Palomino, The		213
Palos Verdes Peninsula		435
Pantages Theatre	★★★★	148
Paramount Ranch		278
Paramount Tickets		148
Pasadena Civic Auditorium	★★★	240
Pasadena Historical Museum	★★	233
Pasadena Ice Skating Center		238
Pasadena Jazz Festival	★★★	239
Pasadena Playhouse	★★★	235
Pasadena Pops	★★★	236
Pasadena Symphony Orchestra	★★★	239
Pelican Hill		400
Petersen Automotive Museum	★★★★	70
Planet Hollywood		382
Playboy Jazz Festival	★★★★	147

Attraction	Rating	Pg.
Shakespeare Orange County	★★★	381
Shark Club		86
Shubert Theatre	★★	184
Simon Rodia Watts Towers	★★★	72
Six Flags Hurricane Harbor	★★★★	209
Six Flags Magic Mountain	★★★★	209
Ski Dazzle	★★★	80
Skinny House		323
Skirball Museum	★★	182
Skyrider Parasail of Long Beach		326
Snow Summit		437
Snow Valley		437
Solstice Canyon Park	★★★	279
South Coast Repertory	★★★	381
Southern California Boat Show	★★	77
Southern California Ticket Service		240
Southwest Museum	★★★	234
Sports Club L.A.		184
St. Germain Cafe		152
St. Mark's		284
Sunset Sail Charter Company	★★★	279
Surfing Walk of Fame		396
Surfrider Beach		281
System M Caffe		327
Tall Ship Pilgrim	★★	396
Tallships Festival	★★★	400
Tatou		112
The Comedy & Magic Club		44
The Crush Bar		49
The Farm	★★	210
The Improvisation		86
The Merchant of Tennis		80
The Milky Way Restaurant		46
The Normandie Casino		50
The Palace		49
The Palms		49
The Salton Trough		45
The Shark Club		382
The Strand		307
The Tennis Place		80
Theatre 40	★★★	111
Theatre Arts Festival for Youth	★★★★	210
Theatre/Theater	★★	148
Thousand Oaks Civic Arts Plaza	★★★★	211
Ticket Time		185
Ticketmaster		83
Ticketron/Teletron		83

LIST OF HOTELS

Hotel	Price	Rating	Pg.
Airport Hilton and Towers	$99–$184	★★★	307
Airport Marina	$69–$109	★★	308
Aliso Creek Inn	$78–$189	★★★	404
Argyle, The	$170–$1200	★★★★	158
Atrium Marquis	$109–$129	★★	384
Barnabey's	$98–$159	★★★	312
Bel Air Hotel	$285–$435	★★★★★	187
Best Western Airtel Plaza	$119–$129	★★★	218
Best Western Alhambra Inn	$55–$100	★★	242
Best Western Anaheim Inn	$60–$90	★★	361
Best Western Buena Park	$40–$60	★★	369
Best Western Canoga Park	$49–$54	★★	216
Best Western Colorado Inn	$50–$55	★★	245
Best Western Galleria Inn	$55–$70	★★★	312
Best Western Golden Key	$81–$86	★★	243
Best Western Golden Sails	$95–$115	★★	328
Best Western Hollywood Plaza	$70–$90	★★	157
Best Western Jamaica Bay	$105–$145	★★★	286
Best Western Laguna Reef	$75–$100	★★★	404
Best Western Mayfair	$80–$130	★★	88
Best Western Mikado	$70–$90	★★	216
Best Western Newport Mesa	$40–$80	★★	384
Best Western Plaza International	$45–$60	★★	371
Best Western Redondo Beach	$85–$100	★★★	312
Best Western Royal Palace	$64–$70	★★	308
Best Western Royale	$50–$55	★★	245
Best Western San Pedro	$95	★★★	331
Best Western Stardust	$40–$60	★★	366
Best Western Stovall's	$55–$155	★★	361
Best Western Sunrise	$58–$72	★★	331
Best Western Sunrise	$80–$110	★★	313
Best Western Sunset Plaza	$72–$190	★★★	158
Beverly Hills Ritz	$105–$295	★★★	188
Beverly Hilton	$170–$220	★★★	114
Beverly Plaza	$139–$179	★★★	114
Beverly Prescott Hotel	$185	★★★	115
Beverly Rodeo	$145–$185	★★	115
Biltmore	$185–$275	★★★★	88
Blue Lantern Inn	$135–$350	★★★	402
Buena Park Hotel	$64–$85	★★	369
Burbank Airport Hilton	$109–$159	★★★	215
Candy Cane Inn	$70–$100	★★	361

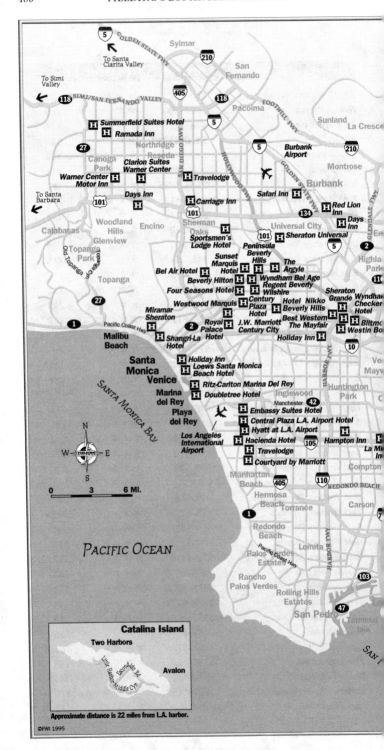

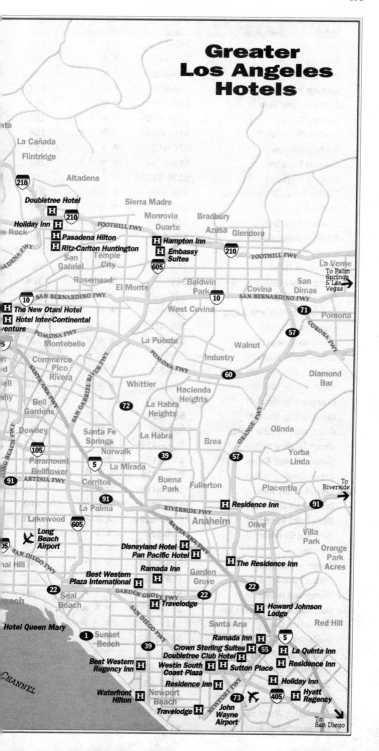

Greater Los Angeles Hotels

La Cañada
Flintridge

Altadena

Sierra Madre

Monrovia   Bradbury

Duarte   Azusa   Glendora

Doubletree Hotel

Holiday Inn

Pasadena Hilton

Ritz-Carlton Huntington

FOOTHILL FWY

Hampton Inn

Embassy Suites

FOOTHILL FWY

La Verne
To Palm
Springs
& Las
Vegas

San
Gabriel

Temple
City

Rosemead   El Monte

Baldwin
Park

Covina   San
Dimas

Pomona

SAN BERNARDINO FWY

West Covina

SAN BERNARDINO FWY

The New Otani Hotel

Hotel Inter-Continental

enture

POMONA FWY

Montebello

Commerce
Pico
Rivera

Bell
Gardens

Downey

Paramount
Bellflower

Lakewood

Whittier

Santa Fe
Springs

Norwalk

Cerritos

La Palma

Long
Beach
Airport

La Puente

Industry

Hacienda
Heights

La Habra
Heights

La Habra

Buena
Park

POMONA FWY

Walnut

Brea

Fullerton

Olinda

Yorba
Linda

Placentia

71

57

CORONA FWY

Diamond
Bar

ORANGE FWY

RIVERSIDE FWY

ARTESIA FWY

La Mirada

Residence Inn

To
Riverside

Anaheim   Olive

Villa
Park

Orange
Park
Acres

Seal
Beach

Disneyland Hotel
Pan Pacific Hotel

Ramada Inn

**Best Western
Plaza International**

GARDEN GROVE FWY

Garden
Grove

The Residence Inn

Travelodge

**Howard Johnson
Lodge**

Hotel Queen Mary

Sunset
Beach

**Best Western
Regency Inn**

**Waterfront
Hilton**

Travelodge

Santa Ana

Ramada Inn

Crown Sterling Suites
Doubletree Club Hotel

**Westin South
Coast Plaza**

Residence Inn

Newport
Beach

John
Wayne
Airport

Red Hill

La Quinta Inn

Residence Inn

Sutton Place

Holiday Inn

**Hyatt
Regency**

To
San Diego

Hotel	Price	Rating	Pg.
Carlyle Inn	$95–$105	★★★	117
Carriage House	$95–$150	★★	404
Carriage Inn	$45–$65	★★	366
Carriage Inn	$80–$99	★★★	217
Castle Inn and Suites	$58–$78	★★	366
Century City Inn	$104–$165	★★★	189
Century Plaza Hotel	$165–$245	★★★★	188
Century Wilshire	$70–$90	★★	189
Channel Road Inn	$95–$200	★★★	287
Chateau Marmont	$170–$1200	★★	157
Clarion Suites Warner Center	$59–$99	★★★	216
Comfort Inn	$51–$56	★★	245
Comfort Park Suites	$70–$110	★★	362
Comfort Suites Hotel	$55–$80	★★	368
Comfort Suites	$59–$69	★★	386
Conestoga Hotel	$95–$115	★★	362
Continental Plaza LAX	$65	★★	308
Convention Center Inn	$48–$68	★	366
Country Side Inn and Suites	$69–$79	★★★	384
Courtyard Airport	$69–$102	★★★	311
Courtyard Buena Park	$64–$84	★★★	368
Courtyard by Marriott	$119	★★★	188
Courtyard by Marriott	$52–$59	★★★	387
Courtyard by Marriott	$59–$72	★★★	314
Courtyard by Marriott	$59–$74	★★★	405
Courtyard by Marriott	$64–$94	★★★	385
Courtyard Fountain Valley	$57–$67	★★	403
Crown Sterling Suites	$135–$145	★★★	362
Crown Sterling Suites	$89–$150	★★★	311
Crown Sterling Suites	$95–$119	★★★	387
Crystal Suites Hotel	$85–$115	★★★	362
Dana Point Hilton Inn	$85–$95	★★★	402
Dana Point Resort	$129–$294	★★★	403
Days Inn Glendale	$64–$74	★★	243
Days Inn	$59–$69	★★	370
Desert Inn and Suites	$49–$159	★★★	362
Desert Palm Inn & Suites	$59–$69	★★	367
Disneyland Hotel	$150–$230	★★★	362
Doryman's Ocean Front Inn	$135–$275	★★★	406
Doubletree Club	$115–$125	★★★	387
Doubletree Club	$69–$112	★★	311
Doubletree L.A. Airport	$79–$154	★★★	308
Doubletree Marina del Rey	$135–$145	★★★	286
Doubletree Orange County	$135–$175	★★★	371
Doubletree Pasadena	$99–$205	★★★	244
Doubletree World Port	$115–$165	★★★	332
Embassy Suites Brea	$114–$155	★★★	368

Hotel	Price	Rating	Pg.
Embassy Suites Buena Park	$130–$150	★★★	368
Embassy Suites Irvine	$99–$189	★★★	385
Embassy Suites LAX	$230	★★★	309
Embassy Suites	$109–$170	★★★	242
Fairfield Inn By Marriott	$40–$42	★★	369
Four Seasons Newport Beach	$245–$355	★★★★★	406
Four Seasons	$295–$510	★★★★★	115
Fullerton Suites	$90–$125	★★	370
Grand Hotel	$80–$135	★★	363
Guest Quarters Suites	$170–$210	★★★	288
Hacienda	$40–$76	★★	311
Hampton Inn Buena Park	$60–$75	★★	368
Hampton Inn	$57	★★	367
Hampton Inn	$60–$78	★★	243
Harbour Inn	$69–$109	★★	408
Hilgard House	$99–$109	★★	190
Hilton and Towers	$125–$175	★★★	217
Hilton Hotel & Towers	$105–$225	★★★	363
Hilton Suites	$109–$185	★★★	371
Holiday Inn Airport	$62–$145	★★★	385
Holiday Inn at the Park	$85–$105	★★★	364
Holiday Inn Bayview Plaza	$110–$150	★★★	288
Holiday Inn Beverly Garland	$85–$115	★★	216
Holiday Inn Brentwood/Bel Air	$99–$129	★★	187
Holiday Inn Buena Park	$85–$95	★★★	369
Holiday Inn City Center	$105–$140	★★★	89
Holiday Inn Costa Mesa	$75–$75	★★★	383
Holiday Inn Crowne Plaza	$135–$180	★★★	313
Holiday Inn Crowne Plaza	$79–$109	★★★	309
Holiday Inn Express	$79–$130	★★	363
Holiday Inn Fullerton	$85–$100	★★	370
Holiday Inn Gateway Plaza	$85–$95	★★★	371
Holiday Inn Harbor Gateway	$91	★★★	314
Holiday Inn Hollywood	$80–$125	★★★	157
Holiday Inn Laguna Beach	$75–$105	★★★	405
Holiday Inn LAX	$100–$119	★★	309
Holiday Inn Long Beach Airport	$109–$119	★★	328
Holiday Inn Maingate	$69–$89	★★	364
Holiday Inn Marina	$79–$99	★★	286
Holiday Inn Monrovia	$82–$82	★★★	243
Holiday Inn Pasadena	$92–$104	★★★	244
Holiday Inn Torrance	$95–$105	★★	314
Holiday Inn Westwood Plaza	$120	★★	189
Holiday Inn Woodland Hills	$94–$109	★★	218
Holiday Inn	$105–$165	★★	288
Holiday Inn	$89–$89	★★★	403
Holiday Inn	$99	★★	215

Hotel	Price	Rating	Pg.
Hotel Del Capri	$90–$105	★★	189
Hotel Inter-Continental	$160–$200	★★★★	89
Hotel Metropole	$89–$295	★★★	422
Hotel Nikko Beverly Hills	$250–$450	★★★★	115
Hotel Queen Mary	$75–$160	★★★	329
Hotel St. Lauren	$55–$260	★★	422
Howard Johnson Lodge	$65–$78	★★	367
Howard Johnson Plaza	$53–$58	★★	329
Hyatt Airport	$89–$109	★★	309
Hyatt Newporter	$140–$190	★★★	407
Hyatt on Sunset	$135–$185	★★★	158
Hyatt Regency Alicante	$105–$154	★★★	364
Hyatt Regency Irvine	$80–$209	★★★	385
Hyatt Regency	$100–$200	★★★	89
Hyatt Regency	$109–$150	★★★	329
Inn at Laguna Beach	$105–$305	★★★	405
Inn at the Park	$125–$170	★★★	364
Inn on Mount Ada	$320–$590	★★★★	422
Irvine Suites Hotel	$75–$105	★★	386
J.W. Marriott Century City	$205–$225	★★★★	188
Jolly Roger Hotel	$65–$100	★★★	364
L.A. Renaissance Hotel	$79–$120	★★★	309
La Quinta Motor Inn	$47–$52	★★	384
Le Montrose de Gran Luxe	$145–$350	★★★	159
Le Parc	$170–$230	★★★	159
Le Reve	$115–$175	★★★	159
Little Inn on the Bay	$100–$200	★★	406
Loews Santa Monica Hotel	$200–$355	★★★★	288
Long Beach Hilton	$115–$185	★★★	329
Malibu Beach Inn	$130–$275	★★★	286
Malibu Country Inn	$95–$155	★★	285
Marina del Rey Hotel	$130–$215	★★★	287
Marina International	$115–$295	★★★	286
Marriott Airport	$150–$160	★★★	310
Marriott Anaheim	$90–$195	★★★	365
Marriott Courtyard	$49–$69	★★★	314
Marriott Fullerton	$89–$119	★★★	370
Marriott Hotel & Tennis Club	$95–$175	★★★	407
Marriott Irvine	$119–$165	★★★	385
Marriott Long Beach AP	$79–$134	★★★	330
Marriott Marina del Rey	$99	★★★	287
Marriott Suites Newport	$109–$109	★★★	407
Marriott Suites	$69–$99	★★★	383
Marriott Torrance	$130–$170	★★★	314
Marriott Warner Center	$125–$175	★★★	218
Metro Plaza Hotel	$60–$75	★★	89
Miramar Sheraton	$205–$800	★★★	288

Hotel	Price	Rating	Pg.
Miyako Inn	$89–$99	★★	90
Mondrian	$125–$250	★★★	159
New Otani Hotel & Garden	$155–$230	★★★	90
Norwalk Sheraton	$120–$120	★★★	371
Omni Los Angeles	$130–$150	★★★	90
Pacific Shore	$110–$140	★★	289
Palos Verdes Inn	$80–$115	★★	313
Pan Pacific Hotel Anaheim	$105–$175	★★★	365
Park Sunset	$80–$160	★★	160
Pasadena Hilton	$94–$139	★★★	244
Peacock Suites Hotel	$85–$105	★★	365
Peninsula Beverly Hills	$300–$330	★★★★★	116
Portofino Beach Hotel	$100–$235	★★★	406
Portofino Inn	$135–$193	★★★	313
Quality Hotel Airport	$69–$89	★★	310
Quality Hotel Maingate	$65–$95	★★★	367
Quality Inn Alhambra	$60–$68	★★	242
Quality Suites	$95–$105	★★★	387
Radisson Bel-Air Summit	$150	★★★	187
Radisson Beverly Pavilion	$155–$200	★★★	116
Radisson Hollywood Roosevelt	$80–$110	★★★	157
Radisson Huntley Hotel	$115–$125	★★★	289
Radisson Inn Seal Beach	$105–$125	★★	332
Radisson Plaza Irvine	$79–$140	★★★	386
Radisson Plaza	$79–$119	★★★	312
Radisson Suites Hotel	$85–$135	★★★	387
Radisson Valley Center	$125–$160	★★	217
Radisson Wilshire Plaza	$110–$140	★★	90
Ramada Airport North	$70–$90	★★	285
Ramada Beverly Hills	$110–$145	★★★	116
Ramada Inn Anaheim	$59–$79	★★	365
Ramada Inn Burbank AP	$85–$105	★★	216
Ramada Inn	$59–$119	★★★	330
Ramada Maingate	$49–$99	★★	367
Ramada West Hollywood	$90–$115	★★★	160
Ramada	$65–$95	★★★	387
Red Lion Airport	$80–$115	★★★	285
Red Lion Hotel	$159–$174	★★★	243
Red Lion Orange County	$79–$172	★★★	383
Regent Beverly Wilshire	$260–$4000	★★★★	117
Renaissance Long Beach	$95–$155	★★★	330
Residence Inn by Marriott	$72–$154	★★	403
Residence Inn by Marriott	$79–$149	★★★	372
Residence Inn By Marriott	$85–$145	★★★	242
Residence Inn by Marriott	$89–$124	★★	315
Residence Inn Irvine	$65–$159	★★★	386
Residence Inn Long Beach Airport	$110–$135	★★★	330

Hotel	Price	Rating	Pg.
Residence Inn Manhattan	$149–$185	★★	312
Residence Inn	$79–$156	★★★	383
Residence Inn	$95–$329	★★★	366
Ritz-Carlton Huntington	$165–$265	★★★★	245
Ritz-Carlton Marina del Rey	$225–$525	★★★★★	287
Ritz-Carlton	$215–$435	★★★★★	405
Royal Palace Westwood	$60–$96	★★	189
Santa Ana Inn	$55–$70	★★	388
Seal Beach Inn	$118–$255	★★★	332
Seaport Marina	$59–$135	★★★	331
Shangri-La	$110–$160	★★★	289
Sheraton Anaheim	$79–$145	★★★	366
Sheraton Cerritos Town Center	$160	★★★	370
Sheraton Grande	$180–$450	★★★★	90
Sheraton L.A. Airport	$140–$140	★★★	310
Sheraton L.A. Harbor	$105–$115	★★★	332
Sheraton Long Beach	$135–$155	★★★	331
Sheraton Newport Beach	$115–$165	★★★	407
Sheraton Universal	$160–$245	★★	218
Shutters on the Beach	$260–$1900	★★★★	289
Sofitel Los Angeles	$195–$450	★★★	117
Sportsmen's Lodge	$105–$125	★★★	217
Summerfield Suites El Segundo	$150–$190	★★★	311
Summerfield Suites	$100–$180	★★★	160
Summerfield Suites	$95–$130	★★	315
Sunset Marquis Hotel	$215–$275	★★★★	161
Surf and Sand	$160–$700	★★★	404
Sutton Place	$155–$215	★★★★	408
Travelodge LAX	$70–$80	★★★	310
Travelodge Long Beach	$79–$99	★★	331
Travelodge	$42–$64	★★	369
Vista del Mar	$65–$275	★★★	422
Warner Center Hilton	$119–$129	★★★	219
Washington Suites Hotel	$125–$189	★★★	372
Waterfront Hilton	$120–$240	★★★	404
Westin Bonaventure	$157–$175	★★★	91
Westin South Coast Plaza	$99–$169	★★★★	383
Westwood Marquis	$220–$475	★★★★	190
Wyndham Bel Age	$250–$500	★★★★	161
Wyndham Checkers Hotel	$209–$229	★★★★	91
Wyndham Garden	$65–$105	★★	244
Wyndham Garden	$79–$79	★★★	384

LIST OF
RESTAURANTS

Restaurant	Price	Rating	Pg.
21 Oceanfront	$$$	★★★	416
72 Market Street	$$$	★★★	301
A Thousand Cranes	$$$	★★★	97
Abiquiu	$$	★★★★	301
Adriano's Ristorante	$$$	★★★	192
Akbar	$	★★	220
Al Amir	$$	★★★★	98
Alto Palato	$$$	★★★	172
Antoine	$$$	★★★★	414
Antonello	$$$	★★★★	392
Antonio's	$$	★★	167
Arches, The	$$$	★★★	413
Arnie Morton's of Chicago	$$$	★★★	195
Art's Delicatessen	$$	★★	222
Atlas	$$$	★★★	98
Authentic Cafe	$$	★★★	166
Baci	$$	★★★	409
Backburner Cafe	$		318
Bambu	$$$	★★★	290
Bangkok Four	$$	★★★	390
Barefoot	$$	★★★	197
Barney Greengrass	$$$	★★★	118
Barsac Brasserie	$$	★★★	221
Basix Cafe	$$$	★★★	168
Beau Rivage	$$$	★★★	291
Beckham Place	$$$	★★	247
Bel Air Hotel Dining Room	$$$	★★★★	192
Belvedere	$$$	★★★★	118
Bernard's	$$$	★★★★	92
Bistango	$$$	★★★	391
Bistro 201	$$	★★★	413
Bistro 45	$$$	★★★	250
Bistro Garden Coldwater	$$$	★★★	223
Bistro Garden	$$$	★★★	118
Bo Kaos	$$$	★★	124
Bob's Big Boy	$		212
Bombay Duck	$$	★★	410
Bombay Palace	$$	★★★	123
Border Grill	$$	★★	300
C'J's Pantry	$		318
Ca' del Sole	$$	★★★	221
Ca'Brea	$$$	★★★	95

Restaurant	Price	Rating	Pg.
Cafe Athens	$$$	★★	299
Cafe del Rey	$$$	★★★	292
Cafe La Boheme	$$$	★★★	172
Cafe Pierre	$$	★★	316
Cafe Zinc	$	★★★	409
Caffe Piemonte	$$$	★★	375
Caioti	$$	★★	166
Califia	$$$	★★★	316
California Pizza Kitchen	$$	★★	124
Camelions	$$$	★★★	296
Campanile	$$$	★★★	93
Cannery, The	$$$	★★★	416
Capri	$$	★★★	303
Cardini	$$$	★★★	96
Carrots	$$$	★★★	293
Cat and the Custard Cup	$$$	★★★	374
Catch, The	$$$	★★	373
Cattleman's Wharf	$$$	★★	372
Cava	$$$	★★★	128
Cedar Creek Inn	$$$	★★	410
Cellar, The	$$$	★★★	374
Cent' Anni	$$$	★★★★	124
Cha Cha Cha	$$	★★	334
Cha Cha Cha	$$	★★★	101
Cha Cha Cha	$$$	★★	221
Chalet de France	$$$	★★	317
Chan Dara	$	★★	167
Chanteclair	$$$	★★★	390
Chaya Brasserie	$$$	★★★	173
Chaya Venice	$$$	★★★	303
Checkers	$$$	★★★★	93
Chez Helene	$$$	★★★	122
Chez Melange	$$	★★★	317
Chez Sateau	$$	★★★	246
Chi Dynasty	$$	★★★	100
Chianti & Chianti Cucina	$$$	★★★	166
China Moon	$$	★★	412
China Palace	$$	★★★	414
Chinois on Main	$$$	★★★★★	296
Chronicle, The	$$$	★★★	248
Cicada	$$$	★★★	173
Cinnabar	$$	★★★	247
Citrus	$$$	★★★★★	163
Clay Oven	$$		390
Clearwater Cafe	$$$	★★	248
Clinton Street	$$	★★★	168
Critixx	$$	★★	252

Restaurant	Price	Rating	Pg.
Crocodile Cafe	$	★★	246
Crocodile Cafe	$	★★	293
Crocodile Cafe	$	★★	373
Cutters	$$	★★	299
Da Pasquale	$$	★★	124
Da Vinci Ristorante	$$$	★★	125
Daily Grill	$$	★★	193
Daily Grill	$$	★★	413
Dan Tana's	$$$	★★	172
Dar Maghreb	$$$	★★	163
David Slay's La Veranda	$$$	★★★	119
DC-3	$$	★★	293
Delius	$$$	★★★★	333
Depot	$$$	★★★	317
Derby, The	$$$	★★	246
Descanso	$$	★★★	315
Diaghilev	$$$	★★★★★	174
Dining Room, The	$$$	★★★★	119
Diva	$$	★★★	388
Dive!	$$	★	194
Dominick's East Village	$$$	★★	333
Drago	$$$	★★★	297
Dragon Regency	$$$	★★	102
Drai's	$$$	★★★	171
Dynasty Room	$$$	★★★★	196
Eat at Joe's	$		319
Eclipse	$$$	★★★	173
El Torito Grill	$$	★★	390
El Torito Grill	$$	★★	416
El Torito Grill	$$	★★★	128
Emilio's	$$$	★★★	166
Emporio Armani Express	$$$	★★★	125
Empress Pavilion	$$	★★★	94
Engine Company No. 28	$$	★★★	93
Epicentre	$$	★★	93
Etienne's	$$$	★★	417
Fabio	$$	★	318
Fama	$$	★★★	299
Far Niente	$$	★★	247
Farfalla	$$	★★	96
Favori	$	★★	392
Fenix	$$$	★★★	168
Fino	$$	★★★	318
Fish House	$$	★★★	128
Five Crowns	$$$	★★★★	408
Five Feet	$$$	★★★	410
Four Oaks Restaurant	$$$	★★★	192

Restaurant	Price	Rating	Pg.
Foxfire	$$$	★★	372
Fung Lum	$$	★★	225
Garden Grill	$$$	★★★	97
Gardens	$$$	★★★	122
Gaylord India Restaurant	$$	★★★	123
Geoffrey's	$$$	★★★	291
Georgia	$$$	★★★	164
Gilliland's	$$	★★★	293
Ginza Sushi Ko	$$$	★★★★	126
Giorgio	$$$	★★	298
Gladstone's 4 Fish	$$$	★★	292
Golden Truffle	$$$	★★★	389
Good Stuff	$	★	319
Gordon Biersch Brewery	$$	★★	248
Granita	$$$	★★★★	291
Gratis	$	★★	193
Grill Lyon	$$$	★★	95
Grill, The	$$$	★★★	119
Gulliver's	$$$	★★	390
Gustaf Anders	$$$	★★★★	392
Harbor Village	$$	★★★	102
Harry's Bar & American Grill	$$	★★★	195
Hollywood Canteen	$$	★★	164
House of Blues	$$	★★	168
Il Cielo	$$$	★★★	125
Il Fornaio	$$	★★	252
Il Fornaio	$$	★★	391
Il Mito	$$	★★★	223
Il Moro	$$	★★★	197
Ivy at the Shore	$$$	★★★	294
Ivy	$$$	★★★	169
J.W.'s	$$$	★★★★	372
Jackson's	$$$	★★★	169
Jade West	$$	★★	194
Jimmy's	$$$	★★★★	123
Joe's	$$	★★★	302
Jones	$$$	★★	174
Kachina Grill	$$	★★	100
Kachina	$$$	★★★	412
Katsu 3rd	$$	★★★	98
Katsu	$$	★★★	101
Kitayama	$$	★★★★	415
Kix	$$	★★	246
Knoll's Black Forest Inn	$$$	★★★	297
L.A. Farm	$$	★★★	294
L'Hirondelle	$$	★★★	417
L'Opera	$$$	★★★	334

Restaurant	Price	Rating	Pg.
L'Orangerie	$$$	★★★★	171
La Bruschetta	$$$	★★★	197
La Cachette	$$$	★★★★	195
La Dolce Vita	$$$	★★	125
La Grotte	$$$	★★	333
La Loggia	$$	★★★	224
La Parisienne	$$$	★★★	247
La Pergola	$$	★★	222
La Rive Gauche	$$$	★★★	316
La Scala	$$$	★★★	125
La Vie En Rose	$$$	★★★	374
Lake Spring	$$	★★	102
Las Brisas De Laguna	$$$	★★★	411
Lawry's The Prime Rib	$$$	★★★	119
Le Chardonnay	$$$	★★★★	174
Le Dome	$$$	★★★	171
Le Petit Bistro	$$	★★★	171
Le Sanglier	$$$	★★	225
Les Arts	$$$	★★★	250
Lincoln Bay Cafe	$$$	★★	294
Locanda Veneta	$$$	★★★★	96
Louise's Trattoria	$	★★	101
Lula	$	★★	300
Lunaria	$$$	★★★	196
Madame Wu's Garden	$$	★★	296
Madeo	$$$	★★★	172
Maison Magnolia	$$$	★★★★	95
Mandalay	$$	★★	165
Maple Drive Restaurant	$$$	★★★	120
Marino	$$	★★★	167
Marquis West	$$$	★★	298
Marrakesh	$$$	★★	412
Marrakesh	$$$	★★★	222
Martha's 22nd Street Grill	$	★	319
Matsuhisa	$$$	★★★★★	127
Matteo's	$$$	★★★	197
Mayur	$$$	★★★	409
Mc Charles House	$$$	★★★	393
McCormick's & Schmick's	$$	★★★	252
McCormick's & Schmick's	$$	★★★	391
McCormick's & Schmick's	$$	★★★	99
Mezzaluna	$$	★★	193
Mi Piace	$$	★★	252
Michael's	$$$	★★★★	300
Mishima	$	★★	198
Misto Caffe	$$	★★★	317
Mistral	$$$	★★	221

Restaurant	Price	Rating	Pg.
Miyako	$$	★★	252
Mon Grenier	$$$	★★	220
Mon Kee	$$	★★★	94
Monty's	$$$	★★★	226
Morton's	$$$	★★★	169
Mr. Chow	$$$	★★	122
Mr. Stox	$$$	★★★	373
Mulberry Street	$$	★★	374
Mum's	$$$	★★	334
Muse	$$	★★★	93
Musso & Frank Grill	$$$	★★	164
Mustard Seed, The	$$	★★★	333
Natraj	$$	★★	410
Niccole's	$$	★★★	409
Nicola	$$$	★★★	94
Nieuport 17	$$$	★★	393
North Beach Bar & Grill	$$	★★★	302
Nouveau Cafe Blanc	$$$	★★★	123
O'toto	$	★★	98
Ocean Avenue Seafood	$$$	★★★	301
Ocean Diner	$	★	319
Ocean Star	$$	★★★	101
One Pico	$$$	★★★	294
Orleans Restaurant	$$	★★★	196
Orso	$$	★★★	96
Osteria Romana Orsini	$$	★★★	197
Oysters	$$$	★★	409
Pacific Dining Car	$$$	★★★	295
Palm, The	$$$	★★★	170
Panda Inn	$$$	★★	249
Pane e Vino	$$	★★★	96
Pangaea	$$$	★★★	121
Papadakis Taverna	$$$	★★★	335
Papashon	$$$	★★	251
Parkway Grill	$$$	★★★★	248
Pascal	$$$	★★★★	414
Patina	$$$	★★★★★	165
Patinette at MOCA	$$	★★	99
Pavilion	$$$	★★	94
Pavilion	$$$	★★★★	416
Pedals	$$	★★★	295
Peppone	$$$	★★★	193
Piazza Rodeo	$$	★★	126
Piccola Cucina	$$	★★	389
Piero's Seafood House	$$$	★★	219
Pink's Famous Chili Dogs	$	★★	164
Pinot	$$$	★★★	223

Restaurant	Price	Rating	Pg.
Planet Earth	$$	★★	297
Players, The	$$	★★★	122
Polly's on the Pier	$		319
Posto	$$$	★★★	222
Prego	$$	★★★	126
Prego	$$	★★★	391
Primi	$$	★★★	197
Raymond, The	$$$	★★★★	249
Rebecca's	$$$	★★★	303
Reed's	$$$	★★★	316
Remi	$$$	★★★★	298
Rex II Ristorante	$$$	★★★★	97
Ritz, The	$$$	★★★★	413
Ritz-Carlton Dining Room	$$$	★★★★	292
Ritz-Carlton Dining Room	$$$	★★★★	412
Ritz-Carlton Grill	$$$	★★★★	249
Riva	$$$	★★★	295
Riviera	$$$	★★	388
RJ's The Rib Joint	$$$	★★	120
Rockenwagner	$$$	★★★	300
Roxxi	$$$	★★★	249
Royal Khyber	$$	★★★	414
Rubin's Red Hot	$		221
Ruby's	$	★★	413
Rumari	$$	★★	411
Rustica	$$$	★★★	127
Ruth's Chris Steak House	$$$	★★★	120
Saddle Peak Lodge	$$$	★★★★	220
Sapori	$$	★★★	415
Scampi	$$	★★★	389
Scarlatti	$$	★★	97
Schatzi on Main	$$$	★★	295
Scott's Seafood Grill	$$$	★★★	389
Sfuzzi	$$	★★	389
Shenandoah Cafe	$$	★★	333
Shiro	$$$	★★★	253
Simon & Seafort's	$$$	★★	334
Sofi	$$	★★★	99
Sonora Cafe	$$$	★★★	100
Sorrento Grill	$$	★★★	411
Spago	$$$	★★★★	170
Splashes	$$$	★★★	411
Sushi Nozawa	$	★★★	224
Swiss Chalet	$$	★★	417
Sylvio	$$	★★★	127
T. J. Peppercorn's	$$$	★★	195
Talesai	$$	★★★	174

Restaurant	Price	Rating	Pg.
Talesai	$$	★★★	224
Tam-O-Shanter Inn	$$$	★★	165
Tatou	$$$	★★★	120
Terrazza Toscana	$$	★★★	220
Teru Sushi	$$	★★★	224
The Original Pancake House	$	★	319
Thee White House	$$$	★★★	373
Thunder Roadhouse	$$	★★	170
Topaz Cafe	$$	★★★	392
Toscana	$$$	★★★	194
Tower, The	$$$	★★★	95
Towers, The	$$$	★★★	410
Tra Di Noi	$$	★★	292
Trader Vic's	$$$	★★★	127
Trees	$$	★★★	408
Tribeca	$$	★★★	121
Trilussa	$$	★★	126
Tutto Mare	$$$	★★★	415
Twin Palms	$$	★★★	251
Typhoon	$$	★★	296
Uncle Bill's Pancake House	$		319
Uzbekistan	$$	★★★	167
Val's	$$$	★★★	225
Valentino	$$$	★★★★	298
Vida	$$$	★★★	100
Villa Nova	$$	★★	415
Warszawa	$$	★★★	296
Water Grill	$$$	★★★★	99
West Beach Cafe	$$$	★★★	302
What's Cooking	$$	★★★	415
Wine Bistro	$$	★★	223
Wolfgang Puck Cafe	$$	★★	225
Wolfgang Puck Cafe	$$	★★	299
Wolfgang Puck Cafe	$$	★★★	388
Woo Lae Oak	$$	★★★	121
Xiomara	$$$	★★★	251
Yamashiro	$$$	★★	167
Yujean Kang's	$$	★★★	250
Zenzero	$$$	★★★	297
Ziggy G's	$$$		170
Zov's Bistro	$$	★★★	393

INDEX

A

T

Favorite People, Places & Experiences

ADDRESS:	NOTES:

Name

Address

Telephone

Name

Address

Telephone

Name

Address

Telephone

Name

Address

Telephone

Name

Address

Telephone

Name

Address

Telephone

Name

Address

Telephone

Favorite People, Places & Experiences

ADDRESS:	NOTES:

Name

Address

Telephone

Name

Address

Telephone

Name

Address

Telephone

Name

Address

Telephone

Name

Address

Telephone

Name

Address

Telephone

Name

Address

Telephone

Favorite People, Places & Experiences

ADDRESS:	NOTES:

Name

Address

Telephone

Name

Address

Telephone

Name

Address

Telephone

Name

Address

Telephone

Name

Address

Telephone

Name

Address

Telephone

Name

Address

Telephone

Favorite People, Places & Experiences

ADDRESS:	NOTES:

Name

Address

Telephone

Name

Address

Telephone

Name

Address

Telephone

Name

Address

Telephone

Name

Address

Telephone

Name

Address

Telephone

Name

Address

Telephone

Favorite People, Places
& Experiences

ADDRESS:	NOTES:

Name

Address

Telephone

Name

Address

Telephone

Name

Address

Telephone

Name

Address

Telephone

Name

Address

Telephone

Name

Address

Telephone

Name

Address

Telephone

Favorite People, Places
& Experiences

ADDRESS:	NOTES:

Name

Address

Telephone

Name

Address

Telephone

Name

Address

Telephone

Name

Address

Telephone

Name

Address

Telephone

Name

Address

Telephone

Name

Address

Telephone

Favorite People, Places & Experiences

ADDRESS:	NOTES:

Name

Address

Telephone

Name

Address

Telephone

Name

Address

Telephone

Name

Address

Telephone

Name

Address

Telephone

Name

Address

Telephone

Name

Address

Telephone

Favorite People, Places & Experiences

ADDRESS:	NOTES:

Name

Address

Telephone

Name

Address

Telephone

Name

Address

Telephone

Name

Address

Telephone

Name

Address

Telephone

Name

Address

Telephone

Name

Address

Telephone